THE EUROPEAN SUN

THE EUROPEAN SUN

Proceedings of the Seventh International Conference on
Medieval and Renaissance Scottish Language and Literature

University of Strathclyde
1993

Edited by
Graham Caie, Roderick J. Lyall, Sally Mapstone
and Kenneth Simpson

TUCKWELL PRESS

First published in Great Britain in 2001 by
Tuckwell Press
The Mill House
Phantassie
East Linton
East Lothian EH40 3DG
Scotland

Copyright © The contributors, 2001

ISBN 1 898410 97 6

Our thanks go to the Carnegie Trust for the Universities of Scotland, the University of Glasgow, and the University of Strathclyde for their financial assistance in the production of this volume.

British Library Cataloguing in Publication Data

A catalogue record for this book is available
on request from the British Library

Typeset by Hewer Text Ltd, Edinburgh
Printed and bound by Bell and Bain Ltd, Glasgow

Contents

	Introduction RODERICK J. LYALL	ix
1	Henryson and the Art of Precise Allegorical Argument R.D.S. JACK	1
2	Duns Scotus on Intellect and Will ALEXANDER BROADIE	12
3	Scotland on the European Storytelling Map SHEILA DOUGLAS	24
4	The Song of the Cherubim JOHN PURSER	30
5	Scottish Poetry of the Reign of Mary Stewart A.A. MACDONALD	44
6	Soldiers and Divines: Scottish-Danish Relations, 1589–1707 THOMAS RIIS	62
7	The Foundations of Cosmopolitan Culture: Scottish Involvement Abroad before the American Colonisation NED C. LANDSMAN	70
8	The Experience of Being a Bilingual Writer IAIN CRICHTON SMITH	80
9	The Legacy of the Makars EDWIN MORGAN	91
10	Gilbert Hay and the Problem of Sources: The Case of the *Buke of the Ordre of Knychthede* JONATHAN A. GLENN	106
11	French Connections? From the *Grands Rhétoriqueurs* to Clément Marot PRISCILLA BAWCUTT	119
12	The Scots, the French, and the English: an Arthurian Episode SALLY MAPSTONE	129
13	A Story of One Faith and Blood – *Orkneyinga saga* and the Poetics of Historical Continuity BERTHOLD SCHOENE-HARWOOD	145
14	The Literary Culture of the Early Scottish Court BENJAMIN HUDSON	156
15	Turning Law into Literature: The Influence of the *Ars Notaria* on Fifteenth-Century Scottish Literature R.L. KINDRICK	166

16	Who Knows if all that Critics Wrote was True? Some thoughts on Robert Henryson's 'biography' ROSEMARY GREENTREE	181
17	William Dunbar's Rhetoric of Power JOANNE S. NORMAN	191
18	Narrative Subjectivity and Narrative Distancing in James I of Scotland's *Kingis Quair* MAURY MCCRILLIS III	202
19	The European Tragedy of Cresseid: The Scottish Response ANNE M. MCKIM	211
20	Cresseid as the Other R.D. DREXLER	221
21	Robert Henryson, Pico della Mirandola, and Late Fifteenth-Century Heroic Humanism STEVEN R. MCKENNA	232
22	Robert Henryson on Man and the *Thing Present* MATTHEW P. MCDIARMID	242
23	Lions Without Villainy: Moralisations in a Heraldic Bestiary L.A.J.R. HOUWEN	249
24	*The Freiris of Berwik* and the Fabliau Tradition R. JAMES GOLDSTEIN	267
25	Re-evaluating the case for a Scottish *Eger and Grime* DEANNA DELMAR EVANS	276
26	*The Thewis of Gudwomen*: Middle Scots Moral Advice with European Connections? KATHRYN SALDANHA	288
27	'Chrystis Kirk on the Grene': Dialoguic Satire in Fifteenth-Century Scotland C.MARIE HARKER	300
28	Scottish Historiographical Writing: The Evolution of Tradition K.D. FARROW	309
29	Some Scottish Humanists' Views on the Highlanders ULRIKE MORÉT	323
30	Lyndsay and Europe: Politics, Patronage, Printing J.HADLEY WILLIAMS	333
31	Scots/English Interaction in *The Complaynt of Scotland?* M. NIEVES RODRÍGUEZ LEDESMA	347
32	Traditions of Myth and Fabliau in 'The Cupar Banns' EVELYN S. NEWLYN	355
33	Alexander Allan (Alesius) and the Development of a Protestant Aesthetics RODERICK J. LYALL	368

34	Scots Words and their Glosses in the Kailyard Novels CLAUSDIRK POLLNER	381
35	Memoirs of a European Scotland ALAN MACGILLIVRAY	388
36	Teaching Older Scots . . . as a Foreign Language? JOHN CORBETT	399
37	Teaching Henryson in Senior School MORNA R. FLEMING	412
38	The Bannatyne Manuscript Lyrics: Literary Convention and Authorial Voice THEO VAN HEIJNSBERGEN	423
39	Enargeia in *The Cherrie and the Slae* CHARLES CALDER	445
40	'Counterfeiting God': James VI (I) and the Politics of *Dæmonologie* DANIEL FISCHLIN	452
41	Sir William Alexander: The Failure of Tragedy and the Tragedy of Failure T. HOWARD-HILL	475
42	Who was Laurence Fletcher? D. ANGUS	487
43	Drummond of Hawthornden and Poetic Translation J.D. MCCLURE	494
44	The Poetic Voices of Robert Ayton DAVID W. ATKINSON	507
45	What William Lithgow was Doing Abroad: *The Rare Adventures and Painfull Peregrinations* DAVID REID	520
46	Mistress and Mother as Political Abstraction: The Apostrophic Poetry of James Graham, Marquis of Montrose, and William Lithgow EDWARD J. COWAN	534

Introduction

> .... Pause stranger at this small town's edge –
> The European sun knew these streets . . .
>
> George Bruce, 'A gateway to the sea'

If George Bruce's fine poem describes St Andrews rather than Glasgow, and if the latter is no longer a 'small town', the image which provides the title for this volume nevertheless captures very well the spirit which infused the 1993 International Conference on Scottish Language and Literature (Medieval and Renaissance), the seventh of its kind, the proceedings of which are published here. Jointly organised by the Universities of Strathclyde and Glasgow, the conference had as its central focus the cultural relations between Scotland and its European neighbours, a fitting theme in a city which had recently been honoured with the title 'European City of Culture'. If the sun did not always shine in a literal sense, an awareness of the close historical links between Scotland and the rest of Europe, including England, remained at the centre of the participants' concerns, and the high quality of many of the papers will, the editors hope, be apparent to the reader of this volume.

Since the inception of the series at Edinburgh in 1975, these international conferences have brought together scholars from all over the world to present the results of their research and to debate key questions in the literary and linguistic history of Scotland. They have been marked by a breadth of subject matter, from Celtic Scotland to (by a liberal interpretation of their remit) the influence of Older Scots literature after the Union, and by a wide diversity of methodological approaches. Some trends are clear, and are reflected in this volume: a steady broadening of the canon, for example, is evident, and whereas the first meetings in the series placed a heavy emphasis on the best-known medieval poets, especially Henryson and Dunbar, more and more attention has been given over the years to the work of their predecessors, contemporaries and successors. This is linked to a greater recognition of the importance of the later sixteenth and earlier seventeenth centuries in the history of Scottish literature, a tendency evidenced here by a number of important papers on writers of this period.

The period during which the Medieval and Renaissance Scottish Conference has established itself as a regular triennial event has seen many important changes in the disciplines with which it is mainly concerned. The emergence of new kinds of historicist approach in literary studies, for example, has had a demonstrable effect on a field in which historicism of various kinds has always been central; and the interaction of such ways of reading with more traditional philological methods often produces valuable insights during both the formal sessions and the more social parts of the programme. The Strathclyde/Glasgow conference was no exception in this respect: whether during the memorable visit to Paisley Abbey (where a carving of the vision of St Mirren reinforced the image of an inspiring sun which underlies our title), or on the excursion to Doune and Inchmahome, or at dinner in the astonishing Neo-Gothic splendour of Glasgow University's Bute Hall, scholars from very different backgrounds and academic traditions found the opportunity to continue the discussion of fine points of editorial practice, the intricacies of Older Scots phonology or syntax, or the hermeneutic difficulties of Hay or Drummond. And as always with these conferences, the organisers were delighted to note the ease with which new participants, including postgraduate students at the outset of their career, were assimilated into a community of established scholars.

For a variety of reasons, the organisers of the 1993 conference were unable to ensure that, as had become traditional, the proceedings appeared during the interval between that meeting and the next, held at Oxford in 1996. It was, indeed, impossible for it to appear before the 1999 St Andrews conference. This is, naturally, a matter for great regret; and we wish to thank the many contributors for their forbearance while their papers have remained 'forthcoming'. We hope that the eventual product is worth the wait, and we are confident that *The European Sun* will make as substantial a contribution to the deveolopment of the study of medieval and Renaissance Scotland as its predecessors.

Roderick J. Lyall

R. D. S. JACK

1.   *Henryson and the Art of Precise Allegorical Argument*

It is nice to be asked to give a keynote address. It is even nicer to be asked to give it in a Town and Gown context. For me personally, it is nicest of all to be asked to do so through a return to my alma mater. It is less nice to have to write it; not only for the obvious reasons but because it seems at first sight impossible to meet the implied requirements nicely in another sense – that is exactly, with precision. To open interestingly, yet harmoniously; to hold the attention of all without alienating any is a weighty remit.

To hit an effective key-note for a large body of colleagues, you have first to resolve a *Catch 22* situation. If you say something which you believe is new and exciting, many of that audience will still find the old vision preferable. For them, you will have hit a discordant note. Instead, resort to truisms and you will no doubt carry everyone with you. They will unanimously agree that everyone's valuable time has been well and truly wasted. Here, you will have opened proceedings on a flat note. To hit a minor key for Town as well as Gown intensifies the dilemma. Is your topic to be related to the Conference theme within the discipline or from that discipline outwards to a world gasping to hear the latest word from the Ivory Tower? Whichever tune you select, for one group you may be playing in the wrong key.

Let me be more specific. I have been given a Conference theme – 'Scotland and its connections with Europe' – to be related to a given body of work – 'Early Scottish Literature.' The result has to be directed towards an audience, if not of infinite variety, of more than enough contradictions in individuality to be going on with. In addition, my broad title – Henryson and Allegory – appears to ignore Town in its 'literariness' and address Gown through a topic, whose relevance to Europe is obscure.

In fact, the modes of argument favoured in the Middle Ages and well exemplified by Maister Henrysoun, rescue me from the apparent dilemma. An old and different perspective finds harmony in comprehensiveness, where the modern mind sees discordance in opposition. An older disciplinary definition of imaginative literature's function and proper referential focus provides exactness in theory for precision in practice.

In a fourteenth- or fifteenth-century University, I should at this point be expected to do at least four things: define, within the theme, my chosen thematic focus or Sententia; explain why I chose it; outline my proposed means of developing it; precisely state my own perspective. In doing this, I shall try primarily to persuade representatives of town and industry that medieval modes of thought may still be of value to them.

The set theme, 'Scotland and its connections with Europe', I have interpreted as the need for accurate inter-national communication across geographic and linguistic boundaries. If this really were the Middle Ages, of course, the linguistic boundary would scarcely exist. Irrespective of country of origin, contributors would discuss in the shared Latin tongue, subtlest of all verbal media. Whatever advantages the growth of different vernaculars had — and these are of course many — the loss of Latin's comprehending power and the shared spirit of enquiry it engendered increased not only the potential for linguistic misunderstanding, it also narrowed and nationalised strategies of discussion.

Within this broad theme, I will use the 'Prolog' of Henryson's *Morall Fabillis*, to question the assumption shared by Derrida and most of my undergraduates, that the Medieval period is logocentric — that is, oriented towards a mimetic centre. On this view, its literature is held rigidly to imitate Christian dogma and the Wall of Allegory is used as an example of how texts are related to an immutable category of meaning. Henryson's nine stanzas, I would contend, challenge each and every one of these generalisations.

Why do I consider 'Precision through Perspective' an apposite and important theme? I think, today, we could learn from Henryson and Scholastic thought. Our own modes of argument, in Ivory Tower and beyond, seem to me on the one hand less open and on the other less self-conscious. We are all, of course, by 'lawe of kynde,' more certain about our own perspective and therefore what others ought to think, than where they come from and what they are trying to say to us. Medieval thought in spirit and method started from an acceptance of these subjective tendencies and sought to counteract them in humility, through careful techniques of argument. The modesty topos of the medieval writer, then, is not only a rhetorical convention, it emerges from a genuine humility before God and Minerva.

Referentially each discipline's limitations were as rigorously defined in quiddity as were its unique strengths. The methods of argument within that discipline's delimited focus began by not assuming agreement but rather by arguing on both sides of the question. When Henryson, in 'The Cock and the Fox' writes 'Now worthie folk suppose this be ane fabill,'[1] rather than 'Listen, less enlightened people, and I'll tell you,' he follows both spirit and method.

Twentieth-century thought is less aware of the problem; is often imprecise; and, where it does embody personal perspective, may employ it to exclude and hector rather than include and persuade. I give two examples of the tendency. The first is for 'Gown' and the second for 'Town'.

Within our discipline, the worst examples come from over-dogmatic 'ism' theorists. Let us suppose we had a group of Pinkpiggist critics, devoutly anxious to prove literature's support for Pinkpiggist theories. A poor Pinkpiggist critic is tempted by the clarity in simplification of his starting-point to look at texts with

---

1 References follow *Robert Henryson: The Poems*, ed. Denton Fox, (Oxford, 1987.) Since I gave this talk a fine discussion of Henryson's dialectical training and its effect on his verse has appeared: Robert L. Kindrick, *Henryson and the Medieval Arts of Rhetoric* (New York and London, 1993).

two extremely dubious assumptions in mind: that any author can be read as if he wrote as our contemporary; that if an author is not overtly dealing with pink pigs, he ought to be and will be assessed accordingly. For geniuses, the code changes a bit to versions of the following argument – Shakespeare was a great liberal thinker, so if he doesn't appear to support Pinkpiggism on the surface, we must unearth from his images and from what he doesn't say, the powerful case for pink pigs he must *a priori* be advancing.

In the outside world, the dialectical tendency to combativeness in imprecise certainty is conveniently enacted in TV recordings from the British House of Commons, where 'Isms' face each other across the floor. The unexamined assumption behind debate is that either Conservatism or Socialism has exclusively and at all referential levels of any question the exclusive truth. 'This and not that, in all instances' controls the supposed quest for truth. The nature of political dialectic is necessarily delimited but there is a boundary, beyond which manipulation of evidence and perversion of counter-evidence become designed to preserve an 'ism's' purity at the expense of precision and objectivity. Listen to Members of Parliament claiming any election result, loss or victory, as proof of their own party's superiority. Listen to a politician claiming from an absolute slogan, that his viewpoint is one 'which all right-thinking people hold.' The dialectics of the Middle Ages defended it from this type of sophistry.

How do I propose to progress? Those of you who have noted my topical repetitions, without variation – 'Precision through Perspective' – will know in advance that I intend to enact that dialectical approach as well as explain it. Already, I have used and will continue to use the happy coincidence that I am 'talking' to use memorial devices – alliteration as well as re-iteration: 'Precision through Perspective' rather than, say, 'Exactness through defined approach.'

The modes of aurality and the devices of memory dominate for imaginative fiction in the Middle Ages, when few texts were available and an oratorical tradition of reading aloud pertained. In the opening stanza of the 'Prolog,' Henryson writes, 'Thair polite termes of sweit rhetorel Richt plesand ar unto the eir of man.' In 'The Trial of the Fox,' he presents his own Sententia in interim fashion so that individuals may later refine it memorially, 'Sad sentence men may seik, and efter fyne.'

As it happens, my own medium this evening is also oratorical. Following Medieval advice for preachers, I have tried to use humour to draw you on to my bridge or pulpit, 'In ernistfull thochtis and in studying, with sad materis sum merines to ming.' I have used images and examples from commonly shared experience in the spirit of my medieval authorities. It is modern criticism with its distrust of anything but seriousness and polysyllables which is unrelievedly erudite. The much maligned Scholastics often used simple analogies and humour to transmit their meaning effectively. Henryson's 'Prolog' is structured on a series of accessible images – earth, nut, music. Similes and analogies abound, apposite to the branch of persuasive rhetoric, quidditatively given over to the faculty of Imagination within the referential field of practical ethics. Perspective is precisely defined in relation to function.

That medieval fiction saw even its most sublime texts as having a useful, individual and practical function, implying specific hermeneutic re-translation for each new text and audience is confirmed over and over again by writers within the commentating tradition. Peter Abelard, when he advises those, 'who wish to speak with a view to teaching,' tells them they 'must vary their language according to the different conditions of those to whom they are speaking.' Dante, when advising Can Grande on how to approach the *Divine Comedy*, states, 'The branch of philosophy to which the work is subject, in the whole as in the part, is that of morality or ethics; inasmuch as the whole as the part was conceived, not only for speculation but with a practical object.'[2] Henryson shares these effective and affective principles. He sums them up briefly in 'The Fox and the Wolf,' when he explains that he has used concrete examples, so that he may exhort the mass of people to better living practices.[3]

'Lordingis, quha likis for till her, The mater now begynnys her.'[4] How can precise study of the 'Prolog' persuade those who believe Medieval literature is closed and dogmatic to re-consider? I shall first argue that this error derives from misunderstanding of one major category of literary thought, the Wall of Allegory. The Scottish poets Henryson, Douglas and Dunbar are known as the 'makars' because writers were then seen as skilled craftsmen, building with words. It naturally follows that construction metaphors are used to describe the verse-structures they produce. Geoffrey of Vinsauf consistently uses building analogies. Hugh of St Victor relates the art of Allegory specifically to that of the stonemason who, as the building rises, 'asks for other stones . . . and if by chance he finds some that do not fit with the fixed course he has laid, he takes his file and smooths off the protruding parts.'[5]

As a focus for this, the negative or corrective argument, I shall use the opening four stanzas of the 'Prolog' and Henryson's employment of the key word 'fe(i)nyeit' in its different Middle Scots senses of 'hidden,' 'deceitful' and 'invented.' I shall then introduce another category of meaning – the Causal Line to present the positive case. Here, my focus will be on 'Prolog,' stanzas 5–8 and 'fe(i)nyeit' in its senses of 'forged' and 'contrived.' My intention is to work towards a conclusion, which will demonstrate how far and how subtly Medieval 'Precision through Perspective' draws us away from the assumption that literature, in this period, is a closed book.

Far from denying that he is writing allegorically, the narrator openly announces that his fables contain feigned or 'hidden' messages. His story will also sign – 'be figure of ane uther thing' (stanza 1). Underneath its soil lies 'ane morall sweit sentence' (stanza 2). Just as one breaks open the shell of a nut in order to

---

2 The citations are taken from *Medieval Literary Theory and Criticism c1100–c1375, the commentary – tradition* ed. A.J. Minnis and A.B. Scott (Oxford, 1988). Peter Abelard, 'Prologue to the *Sic et non*,' p. 87; Dante, *Epistle to Can Grande*, Section 16, p. 462.
3 See especially lines 777 and 779 with its combined interest in influencing effectively and widely. His tale '*Exempill is* exhortant folk to mend,' 'For *mony* gois now to confessioun, Can not repent . . .'
4 With apologies to John Barbour, *Bruce*, Book 1, lines 445–6.
5 Hugh of St Victor, *Didascalicon*, Book VI, Chapter 4.

taste the kernel inside, so the poet writes pleasurably in order that his readers may profit from the allegorical meaning concealed within (stanza 3). This is absolutely consistent with the Wall model as set out below. The superior courses of tropology, allegory and anagogy rise pedagogically from the foundations of the fable and are its justification:

Sententia:	ANAGOGY	Criteria:	Ontological, Mystical
	ALLEGORY		Spiritual, Christian
	TROPOLOGY		Philosophical, Ethical
Sensus:	'FABLE'/'HISTORY'		Rhetorical, Dialectical
Littera:	WORDS		Grammatical, Linguistic

But Henryson also sounds out two major warnings to those who would suggest that this confirms his desire to 'wall' them in to his own views, political moral and divine. First, as a Christian whose theology emphasised individual, unique relationships with the Creator,[6] he defines the way towards these truths as dependent on personal interpretation. He uses his symbols ('be figure') for 'the . . . O man' (stanza 1). The 'morall sweit sentence' is for 'mannis sustenence' (stanza 2) and to 'blyth the spreit' (stanza 3). Each of us, as a unique reader, has to labour diligently on the hard soil of the text, because profit in Henryson's 'subtell dyte of poetry' (stanza 2) as in Dante's 'versi strani'[7] is reserved for those who can 'weill apply' them and make them his or her own.

The Wall of Allegory is not used by Medieval writers to describe what they are imitating. It does not represent either a hierarchically arranged outside world or a series of vertically graded truths, although these were generally accepted tenets at the time and a pattern conforming to accepted modes of thinking is always pedagogically advisable. The Allegoric Wall arranges, within a memorable pattern, for the benefit of author and reader alike, the maximal range of senses available for any and all imaginatively conceived texts. To change metaphors, it is an aesthetic sieve, designed so that any one text, necessarily delimited by its own specific words and story line, may helpfully be passed through its refining net.

The other major misunderstanding may be introduced anecdotally. I was taught that Chaucer was the first author who truly freed vernacular English literature from this (non-existent) dogmatism as represented by the Wall. Virginia Woolf's judgment that, in *The Canterbury Tales*, he 'fixed his eyes on the road before him, not upon the world to come,'[8] were trotted out in a tone which silently added 'And thank goodness for that.' This compounds misunder-

---

6 Etienne Gilson, *The Spirit of Mediaeval Philosophy* (New York, 1940). See Chapter 10, 'Christian Personalism.'
7 Dante, *Divina Commedia*, 'Inferno,' Canto 9 lines 62–63. 'Mirate la dottrina che s'asconde Sotto 'l velame de li versi strani.' (Pay attention to the teaching hidden beneath the veil of the strange lines.)
8 Virginia Woolf, *The Common Reader* (London, 1925) cited in *Geoffrey Chaucer*, ed. John Burrow (Harmondsworth, 1969) p. 125.

standing. Having falsely identified the Wall of Allegory with imitation of the world, the critic now deems the object of that (non-existent) mimetic intention to be false by drawing in an unsubstantiated aesthetic judgment. The poet *should* imitate the actual and not the ideological.

Henryson does not deny that his fables are 'fenyeit' in this sense. Indeed it is their 'deceitful' nature with which he begins. His feigned (=deceitful) tales are not 'al grunded upon truth' (stanza 1). This is self-evident. Animals do not talk. He does not (unsurprisingly) defend his use of the allegorical method in mimetic or naturalist terms for he was not thinking primarily in these ways. Instead, he justifies his work through the beneficial ethical effects it may have on some readers. The task he has set himself in these feigned (=invented) fables is to set up a rhetoric of pleasure to reprove bad behaviour (stanza 1). The means of achieving persuasively this ethical end are enacted in the following three stanzas. Particular images (e.g. earth, nut) and analogies (e.g. as an ever taught bow string is to the bow so the ever studious mind is to man's spiritual wellbeing) are related to practical ethical teaching (e.g. the wisdom of mixing pleasure with study). They are always imaginatively posited and referred to individual experience. This is exactly in accordance with Aristotle's quidditative definition of Literature's persuasive openness within the realm of imagined possibility as stated in *The Poetics* and in *The Rhetoric*.[9] It also confirms Dante's account of the Imagination as Literature's definitive soul-faculty in the *Divine Comedy*.[10]

Henryson's 'Prolog,' then, moves us from modern dualistic, antithetical reasoning to a characteristically Medieval trinal dialectics in potentiality and interrelationship, fitting for Christian literature's position: facing the Trinity from within the Trivium. Literature does not imitate ideas; it uses particulars in relation to ideas as signs, pushing towards understanding of an impenetrable mystery. True, that mystery will resolve all but not in literature or in life; in another state, beyond words and time. Mimetic models in the Middle Ages are dynamic and inter-related on the model of Nature. The Wall is discrete and layered *precisely because it is not an image of what the text represents or of how it works* – only a general map of the fullest possible range of meaning within which the author may helpfully sign and the reader studiously follow.

If this is doubted, then a glance at Dante's language in the 'Epistle to Can Grande' or Henryson's *Morall Fabillis* will reassure. Never does a Moral state that the story seeks to convey an absolute truth. The language is always contingent, conditional and personalised. 'This selie scheip *may present;*' 'this wolf I *likkin to;*' 'Sad sentence *men may seik,*' 'My brother . . . be this fabill thow *may persave and se.*'[11] Such are the particular suggested paths of persuasion offered by these particular 'lying', 'invented' fables and their 'hidden' 'sentences'. Their 'end' lies in the hope that some men and women may be moved by their images to lead better lives.

Any modern assumption that Medieval literature seeks to impose outmoded

---

9 Aristotle, *Poetics*, Chapter 9; *Rhetoric*, I/1; I/2.
10 See Dante, *Divina Commedia*, 'Purgatorio' Canto XVII, 13ff.
11 My italics. 'The Sheep and the Dog,' 1258; 'The Fox, the Wolf and the Husbandman,' 2427; 'The Trial of the Fox,' 1100; 'The Paddock and the Mouse,' 2911 and throughout the *Fabillis*.

ideas or outmoded actuality is, therefore, fundamentally flawed. It is at odds with that period's philosophical and literary refusal to permit any 'Art of Words' to do more than suggest possible interrelationships for individual contemplation. This persuasive view of Literature's function in affective effectiveness was mirrored in another category. The Causal Line, set out below, may be regarded as the Medieval guide to Practical Criticism. I shall use it as the centre for my positive case now that misleading views of the Allegoric Wall have been dismissed. As promised, I shall do so by introducing two other meanings of the word 'fenyeit.' My focus moves forward to stanzas 5–8.

AUTHOR — TEXT — MOVING AN AUDIENCE
(Efficient Cause) (Material/Formal Causes) (Final Cause)

Four different 'precise perspectives' are set out in this line. A reader or listener taught to analyse along it, will expect Henryson, especially in a 'Prolog,' to explain his attitudes to authorship (causa efficiens); the craft of words (causa materialis); the art of 'making' or structuring (causa formalis) and the end in persuasion (causa finalis). Does he do this? If so, how do the defined perspectives bear on our own topic – the openness and non-dogmatism of most Medieval literature and literary theory?[12]

The *Dictionary of the Older Scottish Tongue* lists 'forged' as another possible meaning for 'fenyeit.' Henryson, in stanza 5, admits that his poems are unworthy imitations in two senses. They are 'translations' from Aesop and have originated, 'Nocht of my self,' but at the request and under the precept of a Lord, who does not need to be named. One must not take such statements at face value because this is a modesty topos with all the rhetorical exaggeration and self-contradiction permitted by that Figure of Thought. In fact, Henryson will not simply translate Aesop or any of his sources. The 'lord' in whose mind these poems originate may be a real patron or simply a rhetorical flourish.

Nonetheless, Medieval authors, seeing themselves as 'efficient' (that is – 'caused') causes of their own work, readily accepted authorities greater than their own *because* they saw themselves humbly. Their aesthetics made them word-artisans. Their metaphysics placed them as shadow-signs of the first cause using an inadequate signing system (words) within a referential mystery.[13] Seen from this precise perspective, the phrase, 'Of quhome the name it neidis not record' becomes a series of particularly ambiguous strokes of the pen or sounds in the air. They suggest at once, that the exact identity of the 'first cause' of Henryson's tales is 'unimportant' (human; rhetorical) and that its identity is 'so obvious that I need not name it' (God; metaphysical).

---

12 Consider, for example, the Medieval theatre's audience-involvement strategies and anticipation of Theatre in the Round or the involvement topoi of opening and non-closure (re-opening) in Medieval poetry.
13 See A.J. Minnis, *The Mediaeval Theory of Authorship* (Philadelphia, 1984) for a full discussion of the grades of authorship under God.

The opening stanza of the 'Prolog' with its reference to 'misleving' reminds us of the Fall, which is the Christian grounding for this perspectival pessimism. An author may have greater gifts of vision than most other humans but it remains 'plain that self-existence can be the attribute of one being only'[14] and so even he must be, in any absolute sense, ontologically blind. Henryson develops these ideas in 'The Preaching of the Swallow.' In what is essentially a second 'Prolog' at the start of that tale, the narrator describes the mysteries 'signed' in Nature, confirming both God's status as original mysterious Author of all and our incapacity to read His book because of our blindness in corruption:

> The hie prudence and wirking mervelous,
> The profound wit off God omnipotent,
> Is sa perfyte and sa ingenious,
> Excellent far all mannis jugement . . . (1622–5)

> We may not cleirlie understand nor se
> God as he is, nor thingis celestiall;
> Our mirk and deidlie corps materiale
> Blindis the spirituall operatioun,
> Lyke as ane man wer bundin in presoun. (1631–5)

If the author is himself 'feigned,' a mere 'forged impression' of the original cause, he also works with a 'material cause' – words – which may pretend to represent nature but in fact constitute an inadequate signing system at one remove from the actual and another from the idea. This was the conventional wisdom of Medieval Aesthetics. Once more, it was re-interpreted and intensified through Biblical myths. Originally, God did not need to speak to Adam. Verbal communication was an effect of the Fall. Further human disobedience brought Babel. Seventy-two languages were introduced to divide men further.

Thus, Henryson's comment that accurate representation must elude him because 'In hamelie language and in termes rude/Me neidis wryte' (stanza 6) is again a conventional topos, which nonetheless heightens a genuine belief. Deconstructionists reach the same conclusion with regard to the fallen word, ultimately capable only of signing itself. Rather like Gawain at the end of Fitt IV of *Gawain and the Green Knight*, however, they set that failure in perfectionist pessimism against the criteria of absolutism. This results in arguments focused on the gaps in the liguistic pentangle, which tend to equate the goals of imaginative art with those of rationalist philosophy. Henryson follows the Augustinean line and so, to pursue the analogy, provides the gentle laughter of the pragmatic Court of Arthur. Like most Medieval thinkers he has a 'precise perspective,' focussed on three 'nice' distinctions.

> (1) The fact that all languages cannot imitate perfectly does not prevent the imperfect verbal sign system from working tolerably well as a vehicle for

---

14 Dante, 'Epistle to Can Grande,' Section 21.

human communication. Those who can understand a language will interpret its codes more effectively than those who cannot. Those who study their chosen language(s) carefully will interpret better than those who do not.
(2) The lack of the ideal Universal Language, key to all philosophy, does not prevent some languages from transmitting with greater subtlety than others.
(3) A Trivial discipline deals with interrelationships while working persuasively. Its defined purpose is the imaginative opening out of ideas rather than rational or philosophical closure.

In such a context, individual reinterpretation of the signs in their 'rudeness' becomes part of the positive definition of the discipline. Henryson's 'Prolog' introduces the necessarily fallen word in this pragmatic, comparative manner. In stanza 1 he places his hope in 'Thair polite termes of sweit rhetore.' In stanza 5 he laments the impotence of his own 'hamelie' and 'rude' vernacular against the greater range of Latin.

Stanza 6, with its modesty topos, leads into the last sense of 'fenyeit' as 'contrived' or 'fabricated,' while giving authorial guidance on the last two stages on the Causal Line. It does so by indicating what is *not* feigned. Medieval Art very seldom seeks to pass itself off as life. Very seldom, indeed, does a Medieval author consider the shadows of life's journey important enough to warrant such attention in and for themselves. Therefore, while a Medieval writer may start from and include imitation of the actual, he is expected to do more challenging things. He should use the actual to exemplify the possible and the conceptual. He should announce his artistry through 'artificial' orderings, designed to mirror that theme or facilitate its persuasive effectiveness. Geoffrey of Vinsauf in the *Poetria Nuova* argues this case, starting from the premise that following 'the smooth road of Nature' is the least of the artist's goals because it is the most simply achieved.[15]

Rhetorically, the modest references to authorship in this stanza announce Henryson's own claims to be a 'makar'. He does not ask us to suspend disbelief but to accept that this game or 'sport' (stanza 3) has its own rules. The modesty topos, as employed in stanza 6, announces lack of artistry in a particularly ornate and well-crafted stanza. Henryson, therefore, conveys on the surface level one message, which is directly contradicted by the inner sentence available to those who have worked hard at 'the subtell dyte' of his poetry.

In stanzas 7 and 8, he explains how his 'fenyeit fabillis' as 'contrived' structures (causa formalis) are related to the end of persuasion (causa finalis) as defined by Dante – the moving of individual listeners/readers from one state of mind to another.[16] His case reminds us of the interrelated picture of the world which

---

15 Geoffrey of Vinsauf, *Poetria Nova*, translated by Margaret F. Nims (Toronto, 1967) 87–202 (pp. 18–23).
16 Dante, 'Epistle to Can Grande,' Section 15. 'It may be stated briefly that the aim of the whole and of the part is to remove those living in this life from a state of misery and to bring them to a state of happiness.'

encouraged Medieval thought in its relativity and contingency. God may have ordered creatures hierarchically but the lowest level of each kind overlaps with the highest of the kind beneath it. Man is unique in also having the 'shadow' form of God. It is, therefore, wholly appropriate to use the dialectical mode of argument referred to as 'varius sis sed tamen idem' because it mirrors the similarity in difference of man and animals.

In stanza 7 of his 'Prolog,' Henryson states that he has chosen animals because they are close to man, sharing the animal soul in 'operatioun;' a claim he will repeat, especially in 'Chauntecleir and the Fox'. When he goes on to posit similarity in 'conditioun,' he is in the realm of invention for man's soul has an additional element – reason – which, actually, makes that 'conditioun' different. But the categories are not discrete – the appetitive soul is shared and in certain situations human and animal needs may coincide.

'The 'Tale of the Cok and the Jasp,' which opens the collection, illustrates this strategy very clearly. The story of the starving bird raises the question of rejecting a jewel in the case of starvation, a 'conditioun' shared by man and animal with a shared implication in sensible 'operatioun.' It would be silly for either man or beast to scorn luxuries when necessities are the thing. Henryson, then, imaginatively changes the premises in the Moral to highlight a case where reason makes man's problem different. 'Let us suppose the jewel represent knowledge and then re-run the case.' This is the subtle challenge to the reader. The drama of dialectical subversion involves the intellects of an audience, who are constantly being asked to review their understanding of an apparently simple text.[17]

My own talking is over. For an evening keynote address, that first tale of the cock and the jewel is a good and salutary ending. It reminds the preacher not to over-polish his own jewel of science when people are ready to eat. For Town, I note, that it also urges clerks not to escape the duties of government. There is something of an irony across the ages here. Modern 'clerkis of humanitie' are very seldom wanted in government. Our additional concern with matters other than the material and the worldly in an age committed to the common denominator of the animal soul gives to 'academic' the sense of irrelevent. It permits salesmen, on imprecise analogic models of thought drawn from their craft, to dictate to educationists in theirs as if our 'operaciouns' were identical and our student-products so many clocks or black puddings. Maister Robert Henrysoun lived in another age, where the comforts of the animal soul were less well cared for but the qualities of the rational soul more highly regarded. He would have been a troublesome member of any of to-day's education committees because he would not have allowed conclusions to be reached until the most precise ground for argument had been established.

To Gown, I briefly recapitulate the three ways in which his 'Prolog' provides a powerful defence of Medieval literature against assumptions that it seeks to

---

17 In most 'league tables' of Allegory, Fable occupied a low position because, conventionally, it used a simple case and then provided an answer without involving either great authorial or audience involvement. Modally, Henryson is 'upsetting' as well.

imitate dogma within a closed Christian world vision. (1) By showing that the major model on which such arguments are based – the Wall of Allegory – is not prescriptively formulated. It is an aesthetic pattern, which organises into conveniently memorable form the maximal range of possible senses persuasively available for individual interpretation. The simple banded pattern describes the specific concerns (moral, ontological etc) of those other disciplines into whose hermeneutic criteria a trivially contingent discipline must inevitably open out. (2) The statement, 'Henryson's Prolog imitates God as Word-centre', when retranslated along the Causal line comes out as – 'Henryson as shadow author hopes that his own failed vision, expressed through failed signs may persuade some of his infinitely diverse and fallen readers to reinterpret his blindness in terms of their own in such a way that they may lead better lives and so finally come, in death, to understand a mystery obliquely signed in Nature by a providence beyond time'. (3) As befits a word-craftsman or 'maker', Henryson wittily uses at least five different senses of 'feigned' – hidden, deceitful, invented, forged and contrived – as a control for the intricacies of his argument.

ALEXANDER BROADIE

2.   *Duns Scotus on Intellect and Will*

The recent beatification of John Duns Scotus[1], the greatest philosopher that Scotland has produced, was not due simply to the quality of his philosophy. Nevertheless, the philosophy was an essential part of the man beatified. He is indeed the first Scottish philosopher to have risen so high in the estimation of the universal church. The second greatest philosopher from the Scottish Borders, David Hume, is unlikely to follow Scotus so far up the same ecclesiastical ladder.

I say that Scotus was the greatest Scottish philosopher. Yet many have regarded him as merely a notable representative of the logic-chopping schoolmen, a dessicated peddler of soulless wares. Yet this same man inspired Gerard Manley Hopkins, a free-flying spirit if ever there was one, who found in Scotus a companion spirit, rejoiced in his ideas, and celebrated him.

> Yet ah! this air I gather and release
> He lived on; these weeds and waters, these walls are what
> He haunted who of all men most sways my spirits to peace.[2]

What was it that made Scotus the object of the intense intellectual passion of no less than Hopkins? Part of the answer is that that same intensity of intellectual passion was in Scotus also, a philosopher who placed the concept of love at the centre of his system and who wrote with energy and fire when love was the reality he was dealing with – as it often was, for it is basic to his metaphysics and his philosophy of mind, and especially his ethics. In focusing thus upon love Scotus reveals himself as a true Franciscan; his Franciscan background was of central importance in the development of his philosophy.

Here I shall attend to the philosophical context of his doctrine of love. That context is his teaching on the will, for he holds that the will is the psychological faculty within which love is located. In particular I shall attend to his doctrine that will has primacy over intellect. What he says on the matter is of lasting value, dealing, as it does, in an innovative way with a topic of perennial interest.[3]

---

1 Very little is known about his life. For many of the sparse details see C.Balic, 'The life and works of John Duns Scotus', in J.K.Ryan and B.M.Bonansea (eds.), *John Duns Scotus 1265–1965*, Catholic University of America (1965). See also entry under 'Scotus' by A. T. Wolters in P.Edwards, *Encyclopedia of Philosophy*, vol. 4.
2 Gerard Manley Hopkins, *Duns Scotus's Oxford*, lines 9–11.
3 For an invaluable selection of Scotus's writings on the topics I shall be dealing with see *Duns Scotus on the Will and Morality*, Selected and translated with an Introduction by Allan B. Wolter, O.F.M., (Washington D.C. 1986). For a valuable extended discussion 'Duns Scotus's voluntarism', see B.M.Bonansea in J.K.Ryan and B.M.Bonansea (eds.), *op.cit.* fn.1.

The doctrine of the primacy of the will is of major significance in relation to the history of western philosophy because of the link between that doctrine and the dispute between nominalists and realists, the central dispute within the universities of the Middle Ages. There are two broad categories of philosophers, voluntarists and intellectualists; voluntarists accept the doctrine of the primacy of the will, and intellectualists accept its chief rival, the doctrine of the primacy of the intellect. Consider for example the question of the mode of existence of values. The fact that there are values prompts enquiry into the way they exist. A theistic voluntarist focuses upon the role of the will in dealing with this question. He holds that whether a mode of action is good or not depends upon God's will. On this account God is not constrained to command particular kinds of acts because he sees them to be good, but on the contrary his commanding them is itself what makes such acts good. Their goodness exists by divine fiat. A modern secular version of this position holds that it is we human beings who create our values by an act of choice rather than merely finding ourselves confronted by our values, as if they had a totally distinct reality, existing independently of our will, and constraining us from the outside. Thus voluntarists tend to be nominalist about values. On the other hand a value realist holds that values have a relatively independent existence in the sense that the value possessed by a thing is not a matter subject to our choice. Nevertheless the value realist does hold that values are possible objects of the intellect even though not of the will. Hence value realists are intellectualists and not voluntarists as regards their teaching on the mode of existence of values.

The situation is the same as regards the problem of the mode of existence of universals, the common natures possessed by members of a given species in virtue of which they are members of their species. The voluntarist holds that universals are not things whose existence owes nothing to us. He holds instead that they are mental entities, the concepts formed in and by our intellect enabling us to classify the contents of our world. Otherwise stated, universals are principles of classification. We do of course in many cases adopt such principles by an act of will. And they are not the less universal for being objects of will. As objects of that kind they certainly do not have an existence independently of us human beings. That is, the voluntarist tends to be nominalist on the subject of universals. On the other hand the realist holds that universals have a relatively independent existence, being able to get along without our mental acts. Existing in that way, universals are indeed possible objects of the intellect, though not objects of our will. Hence the realist is intellectualist about universals: he is not voluntarist about them.

In brief, the debate between voluntarists and intellectualists, between those who assign primacy to the will and those who assign it to the intellect, comes very close at times to being the debate between nominalists and realists, and that latter debate has characterised the western philosophical enterprise since earliest times. On that basis we are entitled to conclude that the dispute between voluntarists and intellectuals is of the first importance in the history of philosophy. It is easy to attach names to the dispute. As far as reputation goes, the great intellectualist is St Thomas Aquinas, and the great voluntarist is John Duns Scotus. Later I shall argue against this way of personalising the dispute, for it is easy, rather too easy, to exaggerate the philosophical distance between these two great thinkers.

There is a spectrum here, with extreme positions and intermediate ones. As a matter of conceptual fact, and also of historical, voluntarism shades into intellectualism. It is at this point that my reservations about the personalisation of the dispute start to take shape, for Duns Scotus, *Doctor Subtilis* to subsequent generations of scholastic writers, inhabits a rather shady part of the spectrum, that is, a part in which the two categories apply to him in almost equal measure. Scotus is undoubtedly a voluntarist of sorts, but let us determine precisely what sort; as will emerge later in this paper, he was no extremist. I am sure that the usual modern account of his voluntarism fails to take due cognisance of some of his key pronouncements, and in consequence greatly underestimates the role he ascribes to the intellect in the guidance of the will.

This point derives particular significance from the fact that Scotus is thought by some to be the leading exponent of voluntarist philosophy,[4] and also to be a realist at least in respect of his teaching on universals. But how can he be a realist on that central topic given that voluntarism is so closely allied to nominalism? The first step to resolving this difficulty is to recognise slogans for what they are. Voluntarism, realism, and so on are very crude categories, each allowing room for systems of great variety and differing from each other in ways both gross and subtle. It is necessary to get inside Scotus's system, and to see in detail to what extent he deserves the title 'voluntarist' and to see indeed what the term means as applied to his ideas. Without some knowledge of the details we cannot understand his doctrine that the will has primacy over intellect. More of that later.

More immediately, discussion of whether it is the will or the intellect that has primacy presupposes that the two faculties are sufficiently distinct for either to have primacy over the other. Yet that presupposition is not free of difficulty. Two positions need to be considered here, and the positions figure significantly in Scotus's philosophy since he constructs his own doctrine explicitly in opposition to those two others.[5]

Henry of Ghent is interpreted by Scotus as having identified the will and the intellect with each other and both with the soul. The pressure to make such an identification stems chiefly from the metaphysical intuition that the soul has a

---

4 Another contender for this title is Immanuel Kant. For his contribution to the debate see especially *Critique of Practical Reason*, Pt.1, Bk.2, Ch.3, Sect.3, and L.W. Beck, *A Commentary on Kant's Critique of Practical Reason* (1960), pp. 249–50.

5 A key text is Ox.II.d.16, quaestio unica; Wadding ed. vol.XIII, pp.23a–59b. Scotus there discusses a number of opposed positions including those of Henry of Ghent and Aquinas. Scotus represents Aquinas's position thus (*ibid*. pp 24a–b): 'Intellectus et voluntas sunt duae potentiae realiter distinctae inter se, et ab essentia animae (de memoria modo non loquor); passiones enim animae sunt illae duae potentiae et proprietates, et accidentia fluentia ab ipsa; accidens autem realiter differt a substantia.' (Cf. Aquinas *Summa Theologiae* Pt.1, q.77). Scotus represents Henry's position thus (*ibid*. 35b–36a): 'Alii dicunt quod potentiae animae sunt idem essentiae animae, distinctae tamen inter se realitate relativa, ita quod potentia animae non dicit nisi esse cum respectu coassumpto . . . quod anima secundum se comparatur ad diversos actus, sunt in anima diversi respectus qui dicuntur diversae potentiae, et per huiusmodi diversos respectus determinatur ad diversos actus.'

special unity, one so great that it is impossible for any part of it to be really distinct from any other. On this basis it should be held that the soul acts in different ways – it wills and it understands – but it is a single principle of action, the soul, which performs those distinct acts. On this view it is no mistake to suppose that the acts of willing and understanding are different; the mistake is to take the further step of referring these different sorts of act to different principles of action within the soul – as if the soul had a multiplicity of parts, when in reality it is an indivisible unity.

In contrast with Henry of Ghent's position is that of St Thomas Aquinas. As Scotus reads Aquinas the latter holds that intellect and will have a different kind of being from the soul, for the soul is the substance of which will and intellect are accidents. And will and intellect are also distinct from each other, being different accidents of the soul.

It is plain that Scotus sees merit in each of these mutually opposed positions. For Henry of Ghent takes due notice of the fact that the soul and its faculties form an unbreakable unity, and Aquinas is responsive to the fact that acts as different as willing and understanding must be referred to metaphysically distinct principles of action.

Scotus responds to the merit in each of these mutually incompatible positions by seeking a compromise between them. The compromise comes in the form of the deployment of one of his most characteristic concepts, that of the formal distinction, or more precisely the formal objective distinction (*distinctio formalis a parte rei*).[6] Scotus holds that in the human soul will and intellect are held together in an absolutely unbreakable bond, absolute in the sense that not even God could annihilate one while preserving the other. In that sense they are not really distinct; that is, will and intellect are not distinct beings. Nevertheless they are not indistinguishable, for it is possible for each to act independently of the other. More especially it is a matter of common experience that our will can say no to whatever proposal the intellect may commend to it. Yet if will and intellect are, in the sense just outlined, not really different, how are we to speak of the difference between them? The word Scotus uses is 'formality'. Will and intellect are different *formalities* of the soul. Such a difference falls between a mere difference of reason on the one hand, and a difference of reality on the other.

This distinction is extraordinarily difficult to grasp and is a main reason for Scotus's honorific title of *Doctor Subtilis*. In making sense of it we should hold on to the context of its formulation. It is not a distinction plucked randomly out of the air, but is instead forced upon Scotus by the need to find a compromise position between the unacceptable and mutually incompatible positions of Henry of Ghent and St Thomas Aquinas. Since the distinction between will and intellect is

---

6 Scotus's position is stated unambiguously at *ibid.* pp.43b–44a: 'Sic ergo possumus accipere de intellectu et voluntate, quae non sunt partes essentiales animae, sed sunt unitive contenta in anima quasi passiones eius, propter quas anima est operativa, non quod sint essentia eius formaliter, sed sunt formaliter distinctae, idem tamen identice et unitivem ut in *Primo Libro* probatum est de attributis divinis.'

formal but is all the same grounded in reality, Scotus can maintain both that the soul is an unbreakable unity and that the very different sorts of act, of the will on the one hand and the intellect on the other, must be referred to different principles of action.

A further distinction, one which I think is more readily grasped, must here be made, that between two sorts of will.[7] We need to be clear about these two sorts, for when Scotus ascribes primacy to will over intellect, it is just one of these sorts of will that he has in mind. There are certain imperatives with which we seem by our very nature to be confronted. Most fundamentally the organism demands its continued existence. We can of course decide to reject the demand, but if we do then we do not silence that natural voice within us; instead we overrule it. The organism wills one thing, and we will to the contrary, and on such an occasion the organism might lose. But there are many other things also that we will by our nature. All these things can be grouped under the heading of 'perfection', the perfection of the natural organism. I am speaking here of its flourishing or well-functioning. The principle in us by virtue of which we have a natural tendency or bias or inclination to our perfection is in a sense a principle of passivity. For when, if ever, we give nature its head and follow through such tendencies we are living according to nature and nature's laws; we are responding passively to nature as it is articulated in us.

But there is within us another principle, this time an active one, which is also termed 'will'. This latter principle is exercised when we do not passively sit back and let nature take its course, but instead we interfere with the orderly working out of nature. We stand against nature and either will contrarily to it, or we will consistently with it but not in virtue of being compelled by nature. That there is such a principle in us is evidenced by the fact that a person can overcome his natural fear of death, and will his death. The fear remains, that voice of nature within us, willing the organism to do whatever is necessary to ensure its survival. And yet we can take a stand against our nature by saying no to its demand. The will by which we reject life and instead go voluntarily towards death, is clearly a different principle of action within us from the natural principle by which we will to live. If the latter sort of will should be called 'natural will' what should the former sort be called? Scotus says that it is a 'free will'. There are two reasons, one negative, the other positive, for calling it free. The first is plain, namely, that the will is *free from nature* in this sense at least, that the will is not determined to act by any act of nature. To say that an act of will is determined by natural law is precisely to say that the act is unfree.

That however, as just stated, is to characterise free will negatively; we are saying what it is free from. But Scotus is equally interested in the positive characterisation of such a will, and in developing the positive side of his story Scotus employs a distinction between rational and irrational powers.[8] He takes

---

7 Wolter, *Ibid.* pp. 180–3.
8 For Scotus on rational and irrational powers see Wolter, *Duns Scotus on the Will and Morality*, pp. 144–73. Wolter's text is a revised version of Scotus *Opera Omnia*, ed. Wadding, vol. VII, pp. 606–17.

the distinction from Aristotle,[9] but what he makes of it is more than, and perhaps entirely other than, anything intended by Aristotle. Be that historical speculation as it may, in Scotus's hands the distinction becomes that between a power which can produce opposite effects, this being a rational power, and that which can produce only one effect, this being irrational. For example, our free will is rational since in one and the same circumstance we can will to walk and equally will to run. A fire, on the other hand, is not a rational power, since it heats the object that is adjacent to it, and it can do nothing about that. That is its nature, and it is constrained entirely by nature's laws.

The formulation of this distinction perhaps needs to be tightened up, as Scotus was well aware. To say that the free will, a rational power, can produce opposite effects is not to imply that it can produce them simultaneously. Such an act would be impossible. It is to say instead that at the moment it produces one effect, it could equally, and in the very same circumstance, have produced another instead.

Likewise it might be argued that if the free will is equally able, from within its own resources, to produce opposite effects, then which of the opposites it produces is not explained simply in terms of the power of the will; the fact that that particular effect rather than any other was produced must therefore be explained by reference to some further power, for example, desire. And if it must be explained in some such way then the free will is, after all, not equally able to produce each of the opposite effects. Indeed by itself it apparently cannot produce either of them. The reply to this criticism of the claim that the free will *qua* rational power can produce opposite effects is that the criticism is based upon a misunderstanding of the nature of the free will. What makes it free is precisely that without any further determination, and in particular without input from any further psychological power, the will is able to determine, from within its own resources, which of the various possible effects equally within its power it should will into actuality.

One further problem should be mentioned here. If a will is truly free then it must, as we have seen, be able to will opposites. The will can certainly will good *qua* good, and hence it should be able to will the opposite to that, namely, evil *qua* evil. But surely it cannot do that. Surely whenever a person wills evil it is for the sake of a greater good, or it is evil perceived by the agent as good. Hence the will is determined to will what it perceives to be good, say, happiness. In that case it is determined to a single effect, and in that case it is, after all, not free. Scotus's reply to this difficulty is to concede the premises but to resist the conclusion that the will is determined to a single effect and therefore is not free. In effect his reply is that faced with a good, say happiness, the will can will it, or nill it, or simply refuse to choose. It is true that it cannot respond by willing misery, an evil, for its own sake. But it still has an alternative available to it, namely the alternative of doing nothing. And since the will faced with the possibility of happiness can refrain

---

9 Aristotle, *Metaphysics* IX, 1046 b 1–4: 'It is clear that some potencies will be nonrational but others will be with reason. Hence all the arts or productive sciences are potencies'.

from willing happiness, it is not determined to a single effect. Consequently the argument under consideration does not prove that the will is not free.[10]

It is interesting to compare Scotus's account of will with the metaphysical concept of matter. Will and matter have something in common, namely, their indeterminacy. Matter is indeterminate since it is able to receive any one of an indefinite number of forms, for whatever the form by which matter is informed it can come to be informed by something else. Thus it is not determined, merely in virtue of anything within its own nature, to receive just the form it does rather than another. And free will also is indeterminate, for it is indeterminate in respect of what it will do; it can equally will to produce any one of an indefinite number of effects.

Yet the contrast between matter and free will is stark. Matter is a principle of passivity or receptivity. It receives forms; and those forms, by giving form to the matter, are active in relation to the matter. On the other hand free will is a principle of activity, and perhaps in the whole universe it is the paradigm of an active principle. Though indeterminate, its indeterminacy is due to what Scotus terms its 'superabundant sufficiency', as if the will has more being than it needs for itself, and therefore can afford to give some of its being to other things. Of course, the will is not in any way diminished when it gives. It is of the nature of its superabundant sufficiency that however much of its being it gives by willing, it remains superabundant in its own being. Hence though both principles, will and matter, are indeterminate, they are so for opposite reasons; one because it is a principle of activity, and the other because it is a principle of passivity.

I shall turn now to the question of the relation between between free will and intellect. Earlier I spoke about the formal distinction between those two faculties, a distinction which, though not between different beings, is more than merely a distinction of reason and therefore permits room for the question of which of the two faculties, will or intellect, has primacy. In attending to the relation between these formally distinct things, let us start by considering two positions which are the opposite termini on a spectrum. One position is extreme voluntarism and the other extreme intellectualism.

The intellectualist position first. According to it the will by itself is blind, and requires a judgment of the intellect if an act of will is to occur. Thus intellect presents will with an object, a plan of action, and the will wills that plan into reality. A corollary of the doctrine that the will is blind is precisely that it can do nothing by itself, and requires direction from the intellect if it is to act. This is not to say that the will plays no role in action. It is to say instead that the cause of an act, the reason why we go in one direction rather than in another, and why we go anywhere rather than nowhere, is that will has been directed by the intellect. It is

10 See Wolter, *Ibid.* pp. 144–5, 192–5, esp. pp. 194–5: 'Hence, when [will] is shown happiness, it can refrain from acting at all. In regard to any object, then, the will is able not to will it or nill it, and can suspend itself from eliciting any act in particular with regard to this or that. And this is something anyone can experience in himself when someone proffers some good. Even if it is presented as something to be considered and willed, one can turn away from it and not elicit any act in its regard.'

easy to construct a concept of freedom which is compatible with this version of events. Thus to say that an act is freely performed is to say that the will wills it under the direction of the intellect. The will itself is free and the cause of the freely willed act is the intellect's directive.

It is not entirely fanciful to suppose that some philosophers have held this position. Thomas Aquinas speaks in terms very similar to the ones I have just employed. For example, he tells us that so far as what is at issue is the subject of freedom, that is, what has freedom as an attribute, then the root of freedom is the will, but so far as what is at issue is the cause of freedom, then the root of freedom is reason.[11] On Scotus's interpretation of this position, it is saying that the free activity of the will is fully accounted for by events on the side of the intellect, and in Scotus's view this cannot be correct for it involves a misappropriation of the term 'freedom'. In effect what is being called 'freedom' is determinism under another name. To be precise it is determinism by the intellect. But intellectual determinism is not the less determinism for being of the intellectual variety. In brief, how can the will be free if it is bound to do whatever it is told to by the intellect? It is not even vicariously free, owing such freedom as it has to being under the direction of a free faculty, for no-one supposes the faculty of intellect itself to be free. If freedom is to be located anywhere it must be in the will. I am not saying that Aquinas is committed to the version of intellectualism just outlined, though there is no doubt that he leaves himself open to being understood in the way Scotus understands him, and according to that understanding of the matter one might almost speak of the will as having been totally appropriated by the intellect. The will has been fully intellectualised, being left with nothing to do beyond what it is told.

However if the doctrine at the intellectualist extremity of the spectrum is unacceptable, then the doctrine at the opposite, the voluntarist, extremity seems no less so. For extreme voluntarism declares that the will acts without regard to the deliverances of reason. This anti-intellectualism is no more acceptable than its extreme opposite, for it is contrary to experience. We observe as a matter of course that people do act in ways sanctioned by reason, at any rate sanctioned by their reason. And their acting in a rational way is not reckoned as evidence of un-freedom. In particular it is not regarded as evidence of intellectual determinism.

Clearly what is required is a position between the two extremes. And Scotus, though he has a reputation as a voluntarist, is the very voice of moderation on this matter. That he is committed to a compromise position is already implied in his metaphysical doctrine of the formal distinction between will and intellect, according to which the two faculties are not distinct realities in the soul but on the contrary have an irrefragable unity of being. In that sense, the will and the intellect are the same, that is, the same reality. Since not even God can separate them in reality, Scotus leaves himself no room to argue that the will can act as if the intellect does not exist.

Closely related to this doctrine, and related to it in a variety of ways, is the

---

11 *Summa Theologiae* 1a2ae, 17, 1 ad 2.

further doctrine that nothing is willed that is not previously known – *Nihil volitum quin praecognitum*. Willing is an intentional act; we cannot will without willing something. There is thus in the mind of the willer a concept of what is willed, a plan of action, something formed by an act of intellect, that is to be put into effect by means of an act of will. Considered in the light of this doctrine, it has to be concluded that to will blindly is not to will at all; and this is an important insight, if extreme voluntarism turns out to be in effect the doctrine that willing is a blind act. For in that case extreme voluntarism would imply that it is impossible for the will to act. Scotus is explicit on the closeness of willing and understanding. Speaking about the necessary relation between the acts of willing and understanding, he writes: 'On account of that necessary relation an act of will cannot be caused by the faculty of will unless an act of understanding has already been caused by the intellect.'[12]

That an act of will cannot occur without a prior exercise of the intellect, and cannot occur without due account being taken by the will of the content of the intellectual act, does not however imply that the act of will is fully determined by that prior intellectual act. There are degrees of influence that fall short of full determination, and it is such a limited influence that is at issue in this context. Scotus's phrase is *pondus et inclinatio*.[13] The deliverances of the intellect carry weight with the will and incline it; but not more than that. No such deliverance can carry such weight that the will finds it irresistible. When the weight is irresistible the will is simply not engaged at all, because for the will to be engaged is for it to act as will, and an act of will is a free act. In this context to speak of the will as free is to say that it has the power to produce opposite effects. Thus whatever it does now it could in these very same circumstances have done otherwise.

I am not concerned here to argue for the claim that we do have the power to produce opposite effects. I merely say that if we do not then, at least on Scotus's view of the matter, we are not free agents. In particular an extreme intellectualist account of free will, according to which the free will's acts are fully determined by the deliverances of the intellect, would not be, on Scotus's reckoning, an account of *free* will at all. Consequently, if we have a free will we must be able to stand sufficiently far back from any directive of our intellect to be able to reject it. Even if we do not reject it, and would be judged crazy if we did, the possibility of rejecting it remains open to us, right up to the moment we act. And even when performing the act thus sanctioned by the intellect the possibility of curtailing the act, however crazy it would be to do so, remains open to us. That a particular possibility in our power is a crazy one for us to actualise, is no doubt going to be

12 '... volitio est effectus posterior intellectione naturaliter, et intellectio phantasmate vel phantasiatione, et propter illum ordinem necessarium, non potest causari volitio a voluntate, nisi prius causetur ab intellectu intellectio.' [Ox.,II, d.25, q.un., n.19; Wadding ed., vol. XIII, p.212b].
13 *Collationes* XVI, n.3; Wadding ed., vol. V, p.209b. Scotus first uses the phrase in the course of an argument to the effect that the will is necessitated: 'Impressio facta ab objecto in voluntate est pondus, et inclinatio; sed omne pondus inclinans necessitat inclinatum suum, nisi inclinatum renitatur, sed non renitatur, nisi per actum, etc.' But *ibid.* 210b he rejects the argument: 'sed impressum in voluntate est tantum inclinans, ideo voluntas nunquam necessitatur ab obiecto.'

our reason or part of our reason for not actualising it. But that is not to say that we *cannot* actualise it; it is simply the reason why we *will* not. That is what it is for the intellect to have *pondus et inclinatio* in its relation to the will. As just noted, to say it is impossible for us to reject the judgment of the intellect is precisely to deny our freedom.

We might however wonder whether the judgment of the intellect really can carry weight with the will if the will does not itself include an intellectual component. For surely weighing up the judgment of the intellect is itself an intellectual act, and hence if the will can perform such an act is it not itself an intellectual faculty? But if will and intellect are one then has the will not thereby been intellectualised? And in that case since the intellect is not free neither is the will. That is, to attribute properties of the intellect to the will is to imply intellectual determinism. On the other hand, if the will does not have an intellectual component then why should the judgments of the intellect make any difference to it? And if its judgments make no difference then surely our freely willed acts would be random. But, as noted earlier, experience teaches us very plainly that our acts, especially those we regard as free, do not appear to be random. And in all his philosophising Scotus never loses sight of the deliverances of experience.

These are difficult questions, and ones I think that Scotus has in mind when he applies his concept of the formal objective distinction to his account of the relation between will and intellect. He teaches that the will and the intellect are in one respect the same and in another distinct. The soul and its faculties are really one. Hence will and intellect are really one, in the sense that not even by God's absolute power can they become realities distinct from each other. The will cannot in reality ever distance itself sufficiently from the intellect to be able to ignore its judgments. Yet those two faculties are not in all respects identical – they are after all two faculties, not one. As we have seen, the kind of distinction here in question is termed by Scotus 'formal'. Will and intellect are distinct *formalities* in the soul, and this distinction between them is sufficient to allow the will freedom of manoeuvre.

In a word, the real identity of the two faculties prevents our free acts from being random, and the formal distinctness of the faculties ensures that our free acts are not wholly determined by the intellect. The will determines itself, though always in the light of a judgment of the intellect. To adapt a common phrase: 'The intellect proposes but the will disposes'. The last word lies with the will, and the will is no slave of the intellect, even though it is sometimes driven very hard by it. That the words of the intellect can never simply be ignored is plainly acknowledged by Scotus when he writes: 'It is difficult for the will not to be inclined towards the final judgment of practical reason, but it is not impossible'.[14] This is voluntarism only in so far as it acknowledges that the will is a self-determining

---

14 'Difficile est voluntatem non inclinari ad id, quod est dictatum a ratione practica ultimatim, non tamen est impossibile.' *Rep. Par* . . II, d.39, q.2, n.5; Wadding ed., vol.XXIII, p.205a. Scotus is here contrasting free will with practical reason. The passage just quoted is preceded by the assertion: 'intellectus practicus est, qui necessario assentit agibilibus, voluntas autem libere.'

faculty, but anyone who believes in a free will is, in that sense and to that extent, a voluntarist. However, Scotus's position is far from the extreme voluntarism which denies that the intellect plays any role in shaping our volitions. Indeed it could hardly play a greater role compatible with the avoidance of intellectual determinism.

Earlier I spoke about the close relation between voluntarism and nominalism on the one hand and between intellectualism and realism on the other, and wondered how Scotus could be a voluntarist and a realist at the same time. We are now half-way to an answer, namely, that his voluntarism is of the most moderate sort, so moderate that an equally moderate intellectualist would be close enough to him to be able to shake his hand. I hope to argue elsewhere that Scotus's realism is as moderate as his voluntarism, and that a sufficiently moderate nominalist would also be close enough to shake his hand.

Yet if Scotus is as much a centrist as I have been arguing, how can he ascribe primacy to the will over the intellect? Should he not be giving them equal weight? The answer is no. And an important part of the reason for this answer lies outside philosophy, and inside theology, in particular in the kind of theology we associate especially with Franciscans. It is typical of Franciscans to subscribe to the doctrine of the primacy of love. Love is superior to knowledge and, especially, love of God is superior to knowledge of him. This has immediate implications for the primacy of the will, since love is located in the will and not in the intellect. If the highest act of which we are capable is an act of will and not of intellect then will has primacy over intellect.

Yet this matter is not plain sailing. Let us return to the principle 'Nihil volitum quin praecognitum.' The will cannot do anything except in the light of a prior act of intellect. The intellect on the other hand can certainly act without a prior act of the will. It follows that the two faculties are not after all on a par, for will is dependent upon intellect, and intellect is not dependent upon will. But what is dependent cannot have primacy over what it depends on. Therefore will cannot have primacy over intellect. Scotus mentions this argument but is not impressed with it. The question at issue is whether what is dependent can have primacy over that upon which it depends.

Scotus offers as a counter example the relation between means and ends.[15] The end is dependent upon the means. If we cannot employ the means then their end will not be achieved. Yet it is plain that even though the end is dependent for its existence upon the means, it is the end, rather than the means, that has primacy. Hence the fact that something is dependent does not imply that it does not have primacy over what it is dependent on.

Of course Scotus is leaving it to us to recognise that even if in one respect the end depends upon the means, in other respects the dependency relation goes in the opposite direction. First there is a dependency of existence. For if the means were adopted only in order to produce the end aimed at, then the means would not exist if it were not for the end. In that sense the existence of the means depends

---

15 *Oxon.*, IV, d.49, q. ex lat., n.189; Wadding ed., vol.XXI, p.155.

upon the existence of the end, and not vice versa. Secondly there is a dependency of value. For the value of the means depends upon the value of the end – something in which we find no value becomes vested by us with value when we see in the thing the possibility of using it as a means to an end that we seek to realise.

It is really the primacy of value that Scotus is speaking about when he discusses the primacy of the will over the intellect. Here we must focus upon the Franciscan idea that love of God has greater value than has knowledge of him. To put Scotus's position starkly: if it were possible, which it is not, to love God without knowing him and to know God without loving him, we should love him. Yet love is located in the will as knowledge is located in the intellect. On that basis, the conclusion Scotus draws, that will has primacy, is irresistible. To deprive Scotus of that conclusion would be to undermine his theology and to strip him of his Franciscan inheritance, without which he would be unrecognisable. His life was dedicated to the systematic investigation of the primacy of love, and he pursued the investigation with intellectual passion. That John Duns Scotus was the intellectual hero of no less than Gerard Manley Hopkins is entirely fitting.

SHEILA DOUGLAS

3. *Scotland on the European Storytelling Map*

The European storytelling map is of course part of a world map and I'm sure if there's life on other planets it would extend to them as well. Storytelling is the oldest and most universal art form and for any country to deny or forget that it has a story tradition is for it to deny or forget that it has cultural roots. But like other parts of folk culture nowadays even when its existence is admitted, it is usually regarded as belonging to the past and if not moribund at least on its deathbed. The great upsurge of interest in folk song – and our song tradition is also narrative – that took place in the Sixties has passed almost unnoted by the commercial and the academic world but as in ages past, its impetus is still felt. Storytelling is also going on – and I am involved in that, as I have been with folk song – and if you wonder what that has to do with medieval and Renaissance Scottish culture I would say – everything. The most spectacular of the stories are those great wonder tales that seem to be enacted against a medieval landscape of strong castles and great forests, high mountains and silvery streams, humble cottages, country villages, fairs and markets. When you come to study the stories you find this is a psychological rather than a geographical landscape, but it could be based on a folk memory of medieval times when oral tradition prevailed. The characters of these stories also seem to hark back to a medieval social order with kings and queens, magicians and ogres, old wise men and women, poor woodcutters, shepherds and fishermen, reflecting a society where there is a great gulf between rich and poor, noble and plebeian. Violence is rife and magic is needed to overcome threats and difficulties.

It was in 1973 that I first became aware of the European storytelling map and the fact that Scotland was a part of it. I had known before in theory that storytelling was an international, indeed a universal human art form, but I had not made any systematic study of this or experienced any illustration of it. What started me off was something almost accidental and nothing to do with discovering old manuscripts or literary evidence, but directly resulting from the Folk Revival. I was organising a folk festival in Perth as part of the third Perth Festival of the Arts and I decided to have a workshop on storytelling as part of it. This was something new to Scottish folk festivals but something that seemed to me to be part of folk tradition. Several storytellers came along, including the Stewarts of Blair, Willie MacPhee and Stanley Robertson, all renowned storytellers and all friends of mine. Most importantly the workshop was attended by Dr Hamish Henderson, of the School of Scottish Studies, the leading figure in the collecting and study of Scottish tradition. It was he, who as far as I was concerned, opened the magic door for me, revealing a whole new world. With the lightness of touch that only he can bring to academic discourse, he sketched in the background and context of all the story versions we listened to and as a result there took shape before me a European network of story tradition that even the storytellers present were unaware was international. My eyes were opened then and have never closed since I became aware that what we were listening to was not just Scottish, not just a local phenomenon, but something that was shared other countries of Europe and even the world. I resolved then to acquire more knowledge of this, not just for enjoyment but for the insight I was sure it could give into the human condition.

This experience had far-reaching results. First of all, because I wished to encourage storytelling as a grass-roots activity, it meant that, as part of the Traditional Music and Song Association's Festival at Kinross in 1974, the Douglas Cup for Storytelling was awarded, and is still being awarded at the TMSA's Kirriemuir Festival. Other cups were thereafter donated at TMSA Festivals, the Stewart Cup at Keith, the Hamish Henderson Cup at Auchtermuchty and the Calum MacLean Memorial Quaich at Edinburgh. A Young Storyteller Cup was also given by me to Kirriemuir Festival. Each festival also holds a storytelling workshop or session, and I have hosted the one at the TMSA Festival at Auchtermuchty, but as yet the TMSA has not run much in the way of storytelling events throughout the year, which is the best way to promote interest in the competitions and in storytelling generally.

More recently the Scottish Storytelling Festival run by Dr Donald Smith of the Netherbow Arts Centre in Edinburgh has led to the founding of the Scottish Storytelling Centre, with the Guid Crack Company of Storytellers, which includes Stanley Robertson, Willie MacPhee, Sheila Stewart, Duncan Williamson and others, including myself – I have always maintained the importance of actually doing what I presume to talk about to others – and a monthly storytelling club as well as tours and visits to schools and community groups in other parts of the country. This year, for example, our storytellers are going to be active in Skye, in Angus, in Cunninghame District in Ayrshire and in Glasgow as part of the Tryst Festival. As a result, storytelling is enjoying quite a revival. This is all in the present day, but from the experience I have had I think it can give us a better understanding of times when people made their own entertainment, when songs and stories, orally composed and transmitted, abounded in a multiplicity of versions and oral tradition influenced literary tradition, as it has always done in Scotland. This was also a time when stories had several different functions in people's lives, apart from their entertainment value. They were used to reinforce family and social ties, maintain beliefs, attitudes and values and deal therapeutically with emotional problems caused by fear, deprivation or hatred.

Another result of my experience in 1973 was that when I came to do a postgraduate project at Stirling University in 1979 under Dr David Buchan, I chose to do it on the story traditions of Perthshire, as exemplified in the stories of the Stewarts of Blairgowrie and their cousin Willie MacPhee. This led to a large number of field recordings most of which were published later by Aberdeen University Press under the title of The King o the Black Art which is the story I shall talk about first. It was while doing this project that I really explored the

European tradition, finding parallel versions for my informants wonder tales. In the course of this work, I learned the differences between oral and literary versions of stories and how different story versions can reflect the culture to which they belong. I also became aware of the common human concerns that underlay all the different tale types and how the same motifs could crop up in stories from countries as far apart as Scotland and Russia, Norway and Italy. It surprised and irritated me to find that Celtic storytelling tradition in Britain is represented in some collections only by Irish stories, but on reflection I understood the reason for this being that there is very little of Scottish story tradition on record in print as it has been carried on by oral tradition up to the present day, whereas Irish story tradition was recorded in manuscript from earliest times by monks and scholars. Also the Irish have not had the same problems with their language and culture as Scotland has through English domination and political suppression.

To illustrate how Scotland relates to Europe in matters of story tradition, I would like to refer to The King o the Black Art, which is a Scottish example of a story that is found in almost every country of Europe. In the Aarne Thompson tale type index, called Types of the Folktale, it is No. 325, called The Magician and his Pupil. The well-known story of the Sorcerer's Apprentice is another example. The common features of the many international versions are as follows:

(1) A poor boy becomes the pupil or apprentice of a great magician.
(2) When the boy's father tries to get him back he has to be able to pick his boy out of a number of apprentices transformed into animals or birds.
(3) When the magician pursues him there is a contest of magic taking the form of dealing at a fair.
(4) The magician recaptures the boy who escapes and after a transformation chase through the four elements, overcomes the magician.

The story is not about the fight between good and evil so I take it to be pre-Christian and it seems to me to be about survival. Like most of the international wonder tales, it is something much more than a children's fairytale, although it can be enjoyed on that level too. It has however much deeper symbolic meanings and shows very clearly that stories had important psychological functions in ancient times.

The Scottish versions of the story which I collected from the Stewarts, who were Highland travelling people, not only reflect their lifestyle but also feature old clan customs and values and reinforces the idea that our travelling people are indigenous and aboriginal. First of all, in The King o the Black Art, the magician comes seeking an apprentice, and takes away the boy who is a foundling, reared by a fisherman and his wife. This fostering of a likely lad of mysterious origin is found often in Celtic culture, in the tales of Finn McCuil and Cuchulain and others. Not surprisingly I found that in the Gaelic versions of the story I was able to find, in Ian Og an Ile's Tales of the West Highlands gathered in the middle of the last century, the same thing happens: the magician meets the father and asks for the boy, in Fichaire Gobha or Fichaire the Smith and Gille a'Bhuidseir or the Wizard's Boy. It is interesting to note that in the first of these Gaelic versions, the magician is also a smith. Scottish travelling people, traditionally itinerant metal workers, were also in the past thought to have magic powers. As my storytellers' ancestors were Gaelic-speaking, one would expect their story versions to be close to the Gaelic versions, as these are. The Gaelic versions were from Ian Og an Ile's Popular Tales of the West Highlands and while obtained from oral sources, they were taken down from dictation or from memory, which renders them stilted in many cases, and being read in translation just compounds the fault. This would, of course, present no difficulty to an oral storyteller, who would use the outline as a basis for his way of the story. Willie MacPhee does this all the time. Unable to read and write, he holds the structure and outline of the story in his head, like a skeleton, and fleshes it out it differently each time he tells it, suiting the version to the audience, the time available and the ambience. This system of constants and variables is common in folktale tradition.

When I looked at the European versions, for example, in the French of Perrault, the German of the Brothers Grimm, the Italian Popular Tales of T.F.Crane the Russian of Afanassiev and Webb Dasent's Popular Tales of the Norse, I had the same difficulty. As collectors in the past had not the benefit of the tape recorder and as they were also mostly literary men, most of the European versions were very literary in character, with more lengthy description, less dialogue and a more pretentious style than the lively, atmospheric, orally structured versions I had recorded. I also found an important difference between them and the Scottish and Gaelic versions: in the French version, for example, the father takes his son to the magician and asks him to take him on as an apprentice. This is found also in all the other European versions. But all of them, from Scotland and elsewhere, featured the dealing at the fairs and the transformation chase ending in the death of the magician.

Another story which had significant differences between the Scots and Gaelic and the other European versions is The Three Dogs, as my storytellers called it. In Gaelic it is Tri Coin an Srang Uaine or The Three Hounds with the Green Strings. In these versions a boy is sent three times by his mother or his sister to sell a cow at the market and three times he meets a stranger on the road who sells him a magical dog. His mother or sister is furious but the dogs are actually more use than money because they can hunt and kill game and keep the household pot boiling and they also save his life. The mother or sister drives the boy away (in the case of the sister after having killed him and he is brought back to life by the dogs) and he eventually gains a bride and an estate but forgets about his dogs. When he finds they are missing he goes to look for them and traces them by their hearts, liver and lungs spewed out on the ground. When he is reunited with them and restores them to life, they turn into his three long-lost brothers. This motif of restoring life by means of vital organs is common in folklore. That is the complete story as I collected it and as it appears in Ian Og an Ile's collection, but in European tales it is the first part of a longer story called the Dragonslayer, as it appears in the Aarne Thompson index No. 303, in which the boy goes on to fight and slay a dragon and win a princess. The Scots and Gaelic versions seem to be more concerned with Celtic love of nature and the importance of learning to live in the natural world. The three dogs are called in the Stewart version Swift,

Know-all and Able, and in the Gaelic version Luath, Fios and Trom, which seem to suggest the qualities needed for the life of the hunter-gatherer. The dogs kill but it is to provide food and not out of hate or blood-lust. It may be that the Dragonslayer story got grafted on to the one about the three dogs at a later stage. In Celtic tradition this certainly did happen and I have even witnessed it myself among the storytellers I have dealt with.

Another story found all over Europe is called in the Aarne-Thompson index No. 503 The Gifts of the Little People. The Stewarts' version is called The Humph at the Heid o the Glen and the Humph at the Fit o the Glen, and like the European versions is about two hunchbacks. They hear the fairies sing in the wood and try to add to their song. The first one succeeds because he is the good one and is doing it from generosity. He is rewarded by being granted a wish and wishes his hump away. The second one is the bad one and he can't sing but wants to get a reward too, but his efforts are not appreciated by the fairies who punish him by giving him the other lad's hump as well as his won. In Willie MacPhee's version of this he is granted a wish but wishes for two of everything. A feature of this story, which is a cante-fable; is the song sung by the fairies. In every European version including the Scots and Gaelic ones, the song mentions the days of the week. In the Stewart version it goes:

> Saturday, Sunday, Monday,
> Saturday, Sunday, Monday

and the first hunchback adds 'Tuesday!' Then the second one adds, 'Wednesday!' which is clumsy and sung off-key. In the Gaelic version it is 'Di-luan, Di-mairt' with the same addition, the Italian 'Due Fratelli Gobbi' goes, 'Sabato, Domenica', and Lunedi is added, them Martedi. In Spain it is 'Lunes y Martes y Miercoles tres' and there is added, 'Jueves y Viernes y Sabado seis,' then the second hunchback sings, 'Y Domingo, siete.' This last phrase has become a byword in Spanish for anything done inappropriately. In having this story in Scots tradition, we seem to be very much a part of Europe.

More than twenty of my informants stories appeared in the Aarne-Thompson index including, in addition to those already mentioned, and with varying titles, The Water of Life, The King of the Liars, Friday Saturday (which is The Twins or Blood Brothers), The Speaking Bird of Paradise, The Three Feathers (which is the Frog Princess), The King's Questions, The Enchanted Pot, The Nine Stall Stable, Christ and the Smith, Aipplie and Orangie (My Mother Killed Me, My Father Ate Me), The Little Tailor (The Boy Who Wanted to know What Fear Was), Johnny Pay Me For my Story (which includes The Man Who Could Fly like Bird and Swim like a Fish, the Four Skilful Brothers and The Giant Whose Heart was in an Egg).

It does tend to be the wonder tales that are international with the format of the unlikely hero attempting an impossible task or going on a seemingly hopeless quest to overcome some arbitrary authority figure by means of ancestral wisdom in the guise of a wise old man or woman, helped by talking birds or animals, often grateful for something done for them by the hero, and magic objects. I found the symbolism of Jungian psychology very relevant to these stories, which could then be interpreted in terms of the development of the unindividuated self to full potential, and the stories could consequently be seen as templates for personal development. This also seems to me in keeping with the humanism of the Renaissance period, which sees man as the noblest of created beings, capable of the greatest feats of skill. The travellers who have kept these tales alive in Scotland don't know anything about Jung or the Renaissance but they have very true psychological intuitions and seem to understand Renaissance thinking, for they say, 'These stories were our education.'

Supernatural tales tend to be localised and are often told as personal experience or the experience of a member of the family or a close friend, but this can be simply a storytelling device to add impact. Every country has its own supernatural beings and creatures, some benevolent and some malevolent. But allowing for different local settings and for different kinds of fairies, ghosts, witches and ogres, there are plenty of similarities between supernatural tales all over Europe. Revenants, haunted places and prophetic figures abound, enchantments are laid on with spells and broken often by acts of violence (the cutting off of the head of a monster) or by acts demanding the overcoming of revulsion (like kissing a frog). Inner fears are externalised in the form of monsters, giants and other terrifying creatures.

One of the most extraordinary stories I recorded was called Jack and the Seven Enchanted Islands. After I recorded it from John Stewart, the greatest of the Stewart storytellers, I was reading about Irish immram or voyage tales and I discovered that the Jack story was a version of an ancient Irish immram called the Voyage of Maelduin, first written down by an Irish monk in the 8th century and in oral tradition for goodness knows how long before. It involves a quest for vengeance against probably Viking invaders who killed Jack's or Maelduin's father. A druid advises him on how to make a boat out of hides, how many men to take with him and which direction to sail in. On their way they land on a series of islands and have strange adventures. One of the islands is the Island of Women, to which they are drawn back by a golden thread when they try to sail away and one of them has to cut off his hand to break free; another has a monster who drives them away; another is a paradise-like place with a huge bird that brings healing fruit on a branch; another has a beautiful princess with whom Jack falls in love but who vanishes. There are many clear echoes of classical Greek tradition in the story, which John Stewart's father got from a Donegal storyteller called Mosie Wray. The interesting thing about the ending of the story is that it differs from the version written down by the monk, who makes Maelduin forgive his enemies, in that Jack meets and fights with his enemies and all are killed except him. Then the great bird comes and takes him back to the island, heals his wounds with the magic fruit and reunites him with the princess he fell in love with. This sounds to me like the sort of ending the story would have had before it was christianised. To have a twentieth-century Scottish storyteller re-telling this ancient story with its classical motifs seems to me to put Scotland very firmly on the European storytelling map.

JOHN PURSER

4. *The Song of the Cherubim*

I could have chosen many topics proper to this event. The wonderful music and words of Tobias Hume – now proven to be a Scot, recognised as such when he turned up begging for favours from Queen Anne in 1606, but with impeccable European credentials as a mercenary. The longed-for emergence of the superb keyboard music of William Kinloch, composed probably in the late sixteenth century, with its continental and English connections and the political significance of his Battle of Pavie in the court of James VI are but two examples. Instead I am whizzing through a few highlights of sacred music in mediaeval and renaissance Scotland.

The relationship between literature and music, so intimate in the past that composer and wordsmith were often one and the same person, is as intimate today only in the world of popular and traditional music and, as such, tends to be associated primarily with an oral rather than a written culture.

We all know that in medieval and renaissance times, that intimacy was just as evident in the written culture. I know Henryson claimed he could not sing a note, but Alexander Scott and, indeed James I are counter-examples. If we could find the lost compositions of James I we would have treasure indeed to fill the vast gaps in our sources for medieval music in Scotland. By the way, I am grateful to the conference for retaining those useful terms, medieval and renaissance, having been recently taken to task by an Oxford don for using them in my book on Scotland's Music. I was tempted to write to him that one can only recognise perspective if one does not insist on squinting.

My title is The Song of the Cherubim and it is inspired by two particular pieces of Scottish music and their texts and contexts; both in Latin, one medieval, the other renaissance. One for solo voice, the other for a choir singing in ten parts. One anonymous, the other by Robert Carver. Europe will feature as that is part of the conference theme; and I intend to fulfil the promise of Professor Jack's keynote address by displaying the post-medieval hierarchy of the musical stave while extracting us from the vile darkness and error of original sin in which it seemed to me the professor was positively wallowing. But I am going to start very much earlier with a quotation from the eleventh century Fis Adamnan – Adamnan of Iona's vision – adapted from a translation from Gaelic by my great-great-uncle, Whitley Stokes. Irish or Scottish? I don't care. It belongs to both of us. Here it is.

'Three matchless birds on the chair before the King, and their minds set on their Creator through all time; that is their part. The eight hours of prayer, these they celebrate by praising and acclaiming the Lord, with chanting of Archangels joining in harmony. The birds and the Archangels lead the song, and all Heaven's family, both saints and holy virgins, answer in antiphony.'

It is natural to think of the birds singing in heaven – it is precisely what they do – and only a small flight of imagination is required to raise them high enough to join the Seraphim and Cherubim. So much for hierarchy in Celtic Christianity in which the birds lead one to eternal joy – the story of the little bird is the classic example. As for their motivation, I see no reason for supposing that swollen gonads and pure joy are mutually exclusive. Au contraire. If the dove of the Holy Spirit can brood over the creation, there must have been swollen gonads in heaven too, and no doubt the 'Three matchless birds' of the Holy Trinity sang us into existence, full of the joy and high hopes that are the lot of uninstructed parenthood.

So, how have we, their Scottish musical children, behaved?

Not badly, I believe. We have done our best over the centuries to keep the resonance of our song in tune with nature as the uncorrupted link between humanity and heaven; and we have, on occasion, attempted to evoke the heavenly chorus as a reminder that our earthly music is but a faint pre-echo of the song of the birds and the Archangels and all Heaven's family.

In Scotland the study of bird-song goes deep, for the Gaelic version of Nennius reports that the Picts were reputed to have brought to Ireland 'every spell, charm, sneeze and augury by the voices of the birds, and every omen.' and the Scots and the Irish share the music of the pre-Christian lament with the birds. This music will have been heard often and often at funeral after funeral, through the centuries of Scottish language and literature which it is the business of this conference to study. It survived in the tradition in both countries as the Pi-li-li-liu. That is the text. Pi-li-li-liu, followed by the name of the deceased – in this case Eoghan. Pi-li-li-liu. Nothing is beneath attention. It was a close study of that text that finally led me to an understanding of its profound symbolism. It was surely the song of a bird (a guess later backed by oral tradition). And finally I identified it – the redshank, whose habitat is between land and ocean, life and death; whose cry is fit symbol for the transition of the soul from one element to another, from time to eternity. In that tricky transition, the guide whose voice leads us, is an experienced traveller.

On this recording you will hear the calls of the redshanks and the sound of waves. The link between the birdcall and the human call is obvious. But listen too to the shape of the sound of the waves and the shape of the whole phrases of the keening – the lament – and you will understand why, long ago in the twelfth century, this poem was penned in Gaelic:

> I long to be in the heart of an island,
> on a rocky peak, to look out often upon the smooth
>   surface of the sea.
>
> To see the great waves on glittering
> ocean ceaselessly chanting music to
>   their Father.

To watch without melancholy its smooth,
bright-boardered strand, to hear the cry of
wondrous birds – what pleasing sound!

To hear the murmur of little waves
against the rocks, to listen to the
sea-sound, like keening by a graveyard.

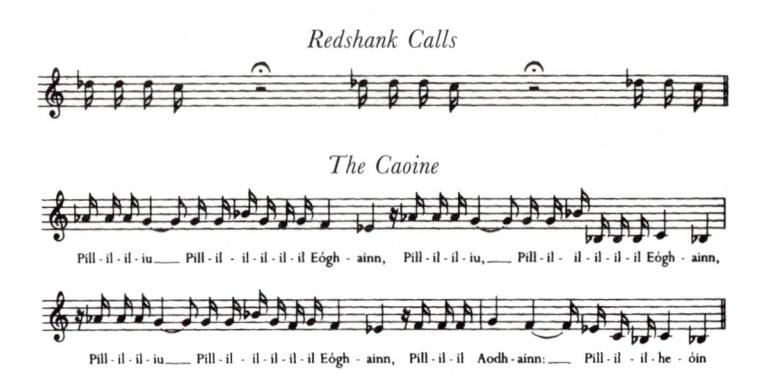

Redshank Calls

The Caoine

Pill - il - il - iu___ Pill - il - il - il - il - il Eógh - ainn, Pill - il - il - iu,___ Pill - il - il - il - il - il Eógh - ainn,

Pill - il - il - iu___ Pill - il - il - il - il - il Eógh - ainn, Pill - il - il Aodh - ainn:___ Pill - il - il - he - óin

Well, an unlikely text has yielded an image of profound beauty. Not yet the song of the Cherubim, but, now that we are dead, we are on our way. So the birds are the link. Uncorrupted. But what of the voices we ourselves are endowed with? We too, might we not also have natural gifts that link us to heaven?

Here I make a plea to all you sophisticates. Never discount your sources as mere fancy, foolish hagiography. Read such texts as attempts to fill out the effects of experiences that may well have been genuine, and repeated from life to life and miraculous account to miraculous account because they actually occurred, and occurred more than once. Take this account of St Columba, written by St Adomnan in the late seventh century. Adomnan knew people who had known Columba and his account, miracles and all, deserves the closest attention. This story refers to a fortress near Inverness belonging to the Pictish King Brude whom Columba had converted to Christianity, to the dismay of the Druids:

> When the saint himself was chanting the evening hymns with a few of the brethren, as usual, outside the king's fortifications, some Druids, coming near to them, did all they could to prevent God's praises being sung in the midst of a pagan nation. On seeing this, the saint began to sing the 44th psalm, and at the same moment so wonderfully loud, like pealing thunder, did his voice become, that king and people were struck with terror and amazement.

'What is stranger still,' writes Adomnan of other occasions, 'to those with him in the church his voice did not sound louder than that of others; and yet at the same time persons more than a mile away heard it so distinctly that they could mark each syllable.'

A ninth-century text states that Columba had a carrying voice heard at 1500 paces and that it was like a melodious lion. Mere fancy, one might say. But listen. One voice only can sing Kyrie Eleison, in a way that might well frighten a credulous audience. The sound is indeed like a melodious lion. Adomnan admits Columba rarely performed his vocal feats, and only when he was inspired. I am not saying what you have just heard or are about to hear was what Columba actually did. I'm sure he did much better. But what if Adamnan had written that Columba sang with two voices simultaneously, one so high that it sounded as though it was the call of the Cherubim from heaven itself? Rubbish, I would have said. Impossible. This is Adamnan endowing his hero-saint with heavenly, not earthly powers. The song of the Cherubim, maybe, but not the voice of man. Well listen again. Everything you can hear on the recording (Part 1 on *The Harmonic Choir* Ocora C 558607) is produced by one human voice, untreated electronically in any way. Just one human voice. Even the most extravagant hagiography would be hard put to it to find words to explain this sound. But it is real. It was and is a widespread technique in religious worship in the middle and far east, and was probably used in mediaeval churches. Indeed really good chanting naturally produces it and, in the case of the deep sounds you first heard, some Tibetan monks lose the power of speech by over-use of the technique. They dedicate their voices to God.

All this by way of introduction. To give you an idea of the vocal threads that may be drawn between earth and heaven without using any text, but, I trust, giving greater meaning and credence to texts that might be treated with indulgence rather than respect.

Now for Latin. 'The subtlest of all known media' claimed Professor Jack. Well tiddlywinks to that. Music is the subtlest, Latin lucky to claim an occasional influence on the Gaelic. St Columba. The dove. His languages. The languages of nature, of Gaelic, of Celtic Latin. St Kentigern and the miracle of the bird. His languages. The languages of nature, of Welsh (alright British, if you must), of Latin. For both of these saints we have music and poetry which still remains basically unstudied, although it is from at least as early as the thirteenth century and some of it may be very much older. This is all the sadder because these are in fact some of the very oldest literary manifestations to be found in any Scottish manuscripts, and the poetry and ornate prose they contain is fascinating not just for its linguistic interest, but for its artistic beauty both in sound and sense. Celtic Latinists, we need you. What is also of peculiar importance to these texts is that we have music for them. Music which can give a clue to stress, rhyme, metre, emphasis, meaning and symbolism. There should be nests of scholars working on them. Here is a chant for St Columba's feast day. It is full of elaborate assonance and rhyme, within a syllabic structure which is reflected in musical rhymes and assonances:

> O mira regis Christi
> clementia nam tota
> refulget ecclesia

signis et preludiis
Columbe mirabilibus
certat plebs magnivoca
felici memoria
patris pii precibus

Gloria Patri et Filio
et Spiritui sancto.

O Mira Regis

'O wondrous clemency of Christ the King! The whole church gleams with the signs and wondrous portents of Columba. The people vie with full voices in blessed remembrance and prayers to the devoted father.'

Not perhaps the Cherubim, but imagine this sung at vespers at the vigil on the eve of June the 9th on Inchcolm, the twenty lighted candles at the high altar, the people singing with full voices in blessed remembrance, the sweet tones of the clarsach accompanying the chant (as we know was common practice among Celtic monks), and one feels a little closer to the company of angels.

It is important to recollect that this material may even have been in use in the late fifteenth century and actively encouraged, as suggested by the following quotation from the licence granted to Chepman and Millar for the first printing press in Scotland:

> And als it is divisit and thocht expedient be us and our counsall that in tyme cuming mess bukis, manualis, matyne bukis and portuus bukis efter our awin Scottis use and with legendis of Scottis sanctis as is now gaderit and ekit be ane reverend fader in God and our traist counsalour Williame, bischop of Abirdene, and utheris, be usit generaly within al our realme als sone as the sammyn may be imprentit and providit; and that na maner of sic bukis of Salusbery use be brocht to be sauld within our realme in tym cuming . . . under pane of escheting of the bukis and punising of thair persons, bringaris thairof within our realme in contrar this our statut, with al rigour as efferis.

Like St Columba, St Kentigern was also widely venerated. He is buried underneath Glasgow Cathedral in one of the finest crypts in Europe. A forest of stone surrounding him, sacred, almost as dark and Druidic as the encounter he was supposed to have had with Merlin. The Sprouston Breviary contains a complete set of services for Kentigern. I had to teach myself neumes to transcribe the music. The texts were long ago transcribed by A.P. Forbes, but they remain untranslated and scarcely analysed. The poetry has certainly not been analysed as such and I was not helped by one scholar saying the prosa was in Leonines and the other saying it was in Victorines – two mutually exclusive forms, I discovered when I tracked them down. One of these two then said that a hepto-octo-syllabic set-up smacked of a post-twelfth-century style, though the Bangor Antiphonary of the seventh century is full of hepto and octosyllabic poetry – it was almost the norm. The music for the prosa, by the way, was a popular tune. You would have heard it sung for St David in Wales and for St Thorlak in Iceland, among others, no doubt.

Two further manuscripts containing musical offices for St Kentigern have been lost in this century. One by the Bolandistes Library, the other by a dealer in London. All I can say is, thank God I got to this one before somebody nicked it from the NLS. Here is one of St Kentigern's miracles in thirteenth-century song. It is the miracle of the fish and the ring in which the Queen of Cadzow's husband, finding a ring he gave her on the finger of another man, removes it when the man is asleep, throws it into the Clyde and then demands it of his wife, most uncivilly. Finding she cannot oblige, but protesting her innocence, she goes to St Kentigern, who promptly goes fishing and catches a salmon with the Queen's ring in its

36   *The European Sun*

mouth. It is duly returned and the King chooses to accept the return as token of his wife's innocence.

The chant likens this miracle to the story of Peter finding the coin in the fish's mouth in Galilee. It is a subtle way of side-stepping the moral dilemma posed by the Queen's questionable behaviour. After all, how come another man was wearing it? To whom should it be returned? To the King who first gave it, to the Queen who apparently passed it on, to the knight who was wearing it?

To whom does it belong? asks Peter of Christ with respect to his coin. Whose image is upon it, asks Christ? Caesar's, says Peter. Render unto Caesar that which is Caesar's says Christ. And so in like manner the ring is returned to its rightful owner, she who claims it as her own; image of her unbroken fidelity.

Notice how the chant rises to its highest point at the mention of Kentigern, and listen to the beautiful melismas which coil around the vowels like the water round the fish in the shallows of the Clyde. This is a responsory for the third nocturn of Matins – St Mungo's Matins, mentioned by Lindsay in the *Papingo* as still being sung in the 1530s.

Jubente Petrus/Gens Cambrina
Responsory/Sequence from the Office for St. Kentigern.
Transcribed by John Purser © 1992

Sprouston Breviary fols 38^r–38^v (MS Edinburgh, NLS, Adv. 18.2.13B)

The Song of the Cherubim 37

Sic Ken-te-ger——ni me—ri-to
re-gi-ne pi——scis ba——i—u-lo
de sta——gno au-rum at——tu—lit
quo
ve-lut in-sons da-ru—it.

Verse

Re—gi—nam rex sup—pli-ci——o
mor-tis pro ad-ul-te-ri-o
Tor—que—bat sed re-dem-pti—o,
mi-ran-da fit in an-u-lo.

38 *The European Sun*

Resp.
Quo
ve—lut in—sons cla-ru——it.

Gloria
Glo—ri—a Pa—tri et fil—li—o
et Spi-ri-tu——i San——cto.

Resp.
Quo
ve—lut in—sons cla-ru——it.

Well, no Cherubim there, but a saint reaching out towards heavenly justice, by a symbolic as well as miraculous sympathetic relationship with nature.

About half a century before that chant was written down, the great St Andrews manuscript was compiled, containing some of the works from the period of Leonin and Perotin to which Professor Jack referred. However, at the ends of the fascicles of this manuscript and in the whole of fascicle 11, the scribes added material which is without Parisian concordances but which shows traits broadly known as 'insular' – a disgraceful term which buries Scotland and Wales and Ireland under England in the hope that they will Go Away.

Well, we won't. Listen now to this. This is indeed the voice of the Cherubim, because it says it is. It is virtuosic, extravagant, it is almost certainly Scottish, and on this recording has been used to supplement a reconstruction of a Notre Dame easter mass because they either didn't have such exciting music in Paris, or it has not survived. It is a Sanctus trope, describing the melody of heaven, the song of the Cherubim, resonating in the church. It is as near as a trained voice can get to the extended song of a bird.

Nothing, however, is above criticism. It is possibly this sort of singing that Ailred of Rievaulx complained about in his book *The Mirror of Charity*, which he wrote in 1142. Ailred came from Yorkshire but his formative years were spent in the south of Scotland attached to the court of King David I for whom he worked for about ten years, so he had ample opportunity to hear what was being sung in Scotland and northern England:

For what end is this contraction and dilation of the voice? We hear monks doing all sorts of ridiculous things, plaguing us with womanish falsettos, spavined bleating and tremolos. I myself have seen monks with open mouths, not so much singing, as doing ludicrous feats of breathing, so that they looked as if they were in their last agony or lost in rapture. Their lips are contracted, their eyes roll, their shoulders are shaken upwards and downwards, their fingers move and dance to every note. And this ridiculous behaviour is called religion for they think they are giving God a greater honour than if they sang without all this fuss.

Well, that is the extravagant sound of solo chanting such as you would have heard in St Andrews in the mid-thirteenth century – but what of counterpoint – the art of singing more than one tune at a time and which was only just developing? Imagine yourself one of the countless European pilgrims to St Andrews. Perhaps you have never heard two-part singing if you come from the provinces. You enter the cathedral to attend mass. An introductory church drama is performed – a *visitatio sepulchri*, sinuous lovely single lines searching out the architecture of one of the great buildings of Europe. But now the mass proper begins. The old familiar Greek words, so perfectly designed for singing, just nothing but vowels and vowels and vowels, Kyrie eleison, Christe eleison, kyrie eleison – but magically, incredibly, the line divides into two. The effect is ethereal, an exquisite blend of decoration and simplicity as text and chant are troped. This music comes from the eleventh fascicle of the St Andrews Music Book. It is again almost certainly Scottish, though clearly based on the Parisian tradition. Hierarchy? Well, yes and no. The parts cross and recross although the cantus firmus is mostly the lower of the two. But the text for both is a trope.

The idea that men and angels could converse in music is primarily associated with the shepherds in the Christmas story. Bach symbolises the two in the Christmas oratorio, the shepherds playing pipes.

In Scotland it was illustrated with delightful naïveté in the Christmas medley All Sons Of Adam:

> All sons of Adam rise up with me,
> Go love the blissed Trinitie.
> Sing we now-ell, nowell, nowell,
> Cry Kyrie with Hosanna,
> Sing Sabaoth, sing Alleluja,
> Now save us all Emanuel.

Now the music changes because Gabriel is going to speak. The first statement 'Then spak archangel Gabriel' is straightforward, but when Gabriel himself 'said Ave mary mild, the Lord of Lords is with thee, now sall thou go with child, Ecce ancilla Domini.' Then the part writing becomes more strictly and obviously imitative. More like church. Mary's reply takes up this style for 'Then said the virgin young, As thou hes said so mot it be.' But as soon as her own thought enters, 'Welcom be heavin's king'; the music is simplified and leads into a lovely passage which is probably the earliest known version of 'I saw three ships'. The picture is a musical one:

> Then cam a ship fair sailland then,
> St Michael was the stiersman, Sanct John sat in the horn.
> Our Lord harpit, our Lady sang,
> And all the bells of heav'n they rang
> On Christsonday at morn.

Now the angels join in and the music changes again. They sing in Latin, of course, and they use an improvisatory but well-established technique of part-singing known as faburdon in which the main voice is parallelled by the others. In this instance the example is of faburdon of the first kind as explained in the later Scottish Anonymous treatise of the 1580s. Then the sons of Adam round it all off joyously 'with honor and perpetual jo'. The whole thing operates at at least three different levels of register for mankind and Mary, for the Archangel, and for the Angels all and sum.

But this, though delicious and charming, is not the sophisticated concept of hierarchical dialogue which Professor Jack spoke of when he used the image of the musical stave. For that we have to go to Robert Carver's ten-part mass.

The darkness of the fall of man. Human speech a mere Babel. All words but shadows of that which they signify? The hierarchy established with God, angels, mankind, animals and plants in that order. Remember the birds? So close to God all you have to do is follow the song of a little bird as the old monk in the Celtic folk tale did, and he passed beyond time into an eternity of joy. When he recollected himself and returned to the monastery orchard, it had been cut down and he was no longer recognised. Hundreds of years had passed in the song of that bird.

The medieval mind no doubt had its schemes and its orders of rhetoric and argument. But music and poetry and story skip across these boundaries even while honouring them – as you shall hear.

When God set up the hierarchy of heaven there were ten orders within it:

> Seraphim, Cherubim, Thrones in the first circle.
> Dominions, Virtues and Powers in the second circle.
> Principalities, Archangels and Angels in the third circle.

That makes nine. The tenth order was the order of Satan, The Fallen angels. Mankind was created in the fond parental hope that we would make up for the failure of Heaven's first parturition which was to create hell. One hell of a responsibility, one might, with justice, protest.

This is not just speculation. It was part and parcel of religious observance. In the Chapel Royal at Stirling, dedicated to St Michael and the Virgin, the devil was under direct assault. St Michael as the warrior archangel, the dragon-slayer: the Virgin as the mother of Christ whose heel would bruise Satan's head. Not far away a few miles down the river Forth, was built the Great Michael, launched on the 10th October 1511. She was Europe's biggest warship. She was probably intended to lead a crusade against the Turks – the devil incarnate. One is tempted to suggest that the launch was eleven days late, St Michael's day being the 29th September. Perhaps weather, or the usual delays in such projects, were the cause. James Reid-Baxter has suggested fascinating connections with the Burgundian court and the order of the golden fleece. But it appears to have been earlier, in 1506, that Carver's ten part mass was completed. The music is based on a cantus firmus drawn from a Magnificat Antiphon with these words: 'Dum sacrum mysterium cerneret Johannes, Archangelus Michael tuba cecinit.' 'While John beheld the sacred mystery, Michael the Archangel sounded the trumpet.' And it goes on: 'Forgive oh Lord, our God Thou who openest the Book and loosest the seals thereof.'

This is apocalyptic stuff, but why not nine parts like Wylkynson's Salve Regina in the Eton Choirbook almost certainly known to Carver, and in which each voice part was given the name of one of the orders of angels? Because, in Carver's work, mankind has a place too. The sequence for St Michael's day enumerates the nine orders of angels and then continues 'The angels are the work of Thy primeval hand, we the latest in Thine image fashioned.'

What we have in this great work, then, is not just the heavenly chorus itself, but mankind joining in it. Not a dialogue between shepherds and angels, each holding their proper musical stations, but a hierarchy in which mankind has a potential place and to which he may aspire.

In the *Qui sedes* – who sittest on the right hand of the Father – we have a vision (we have no single word for a hearing experience, one of the greatest single omissions in the English language), so it is a vision in sound of the heavenly chorus, the great waves of sound beating on the ear drums like vast wingbeats.

The technicalities of this music are fascinating. The alternating chords a tone apart are a particular device of Carver's, some suggest related to the Scottish love of the double tonic in traditional music. It is plausible. The curious mixture of major and minor versions of the same chord, because Carver in fact operates on a hexachordal system which allows him to exploit that bitter-sweet contrast. The passing dissonances within the vast throbbing texture. The monumental effect of parallel intervals. These devices may all be part of a technique known to us from Gavin Douglas as Cant Organe. Douglas alone uses the term, and this suggests it may be peculiar to Scotland, and it has been suggested that it describes an improvisatory technique in which voices move freely from one chord to another, oscillating and ornamenting.

This work is connected to others of Carver's. To the Mass *L'Homme Armé* by its warlike subject matter. To the six-part Mass through musical links and possibly links with the launch of the *Great Michael*, to his great 19-part motet, *O Bone Jesu*, by direct quotation.

In part of the *Agnus Dei*, James Ross has suggested that if the voice parts do correspond to the hierarchy of angels in detail as well as in general, then we are about to hear the Seraphim and Cherubim as they float on the soprano voices above the altos of Thrones and Dominions.

Now compare it with a passage from Carver's *O Bone Jesu* in 19 parts. The same music is quoted. The Seraphim and Cherubim above the Thrones and Dominions, leading to the final part of the prayer on these words:

> O dulcis Jesu, recognosce quod tuum est, et absterge quod alienum est.
> O amantissime Jesu, O desideratissime Jesu, O mitissime Jesu,
> O Jesu admitte me intrare regnum tuum, dulcis Jesu.

Why the quotation from the ten-part mass? Because, surely, this is a personal request on behalf of James the Fourth, already occupying the earthly parallel of Thrones and Dominions, to enter truly into that community of heaven. Isobel Woods has suggested that this composition was commissioned by the King as part of his elaborate penance for his involvement in his father's death. A king who dethroned his own monarch, his own father. Seeking expiation. The iron links around his waist. The intended crusade:

>Admitte me intrare regnum tuum.
>Permit me to enter *thy* kingdom.

What ironies lie there for the young king. If the sound of ten parts, humans joining the angels was already stupendous, what is one to say of this immense nineteen-part texture – the maximum the Chapel Royal choir could achieve with their sixteen men and six boys, two each to the three top parts? Or is it a deep numerical allegory, not just the nine choirs of angels, but the ninth hour, the hour of crucifixion: not just the ten choirs when mankind is included, but the Roman ten – the X for Christus in Greek, the X for the cross of St Andrew? These two combined? Who is to say?

One thing is certain. In this monumental work the name of Jesu is reiterated over and over, and every time in the score, Carver places above it a Corona – the Latin name for a musical pause – a crown. And before that crown the music pauses to allow the congregation to genuflect at the Holy Name.

NOTE The music referred to can be heard on the following recordings:

Scotland's Music double CD or cassette or vinyl, Linn Records CKD, CKC, CKH 008:
 The Pi-li-li-liu
2 *Chants for St Columba* from the Inchcolm Antiphoner, similar to *O Mira Regis*
Jubente Petrus from the Sprouston Breviary
Sanctus Ierarchia from the St Andrews Music Book
Kyrie Virginum Amator from the St Andrews Music Book
O Bone Jesu by Carver
O Mira Regis can be heard on *Columba Most Holy of Saints* CD, CD GAU 129 (ASV Gaudeamus label)
All Sons of Adam can be heard on *A History of Scottish Music 1 The King's Music*, Scottish Records SRSS 1
The Ten Part Mass by Carver is on *Scottish Renaissance Polyphony* 1 Gaudeamus CD GAU 124

A.A. MACDONALD

5.   *Scottish Poetry of the Reign of Mary Stewart*

The return to Scotland

There was in sixteenth-century Scotland a custom, whereby court poets had the opportunity, or were expected, formally to address their respective sovereigns at New Year. Within the terms of the literary subgenre to which this custom gave rise, it was normal for the poet to combine seasonal salutations with words of praise, before discreetly shifting the focus towards his own situation. As was only fitting, the king would be assured in advance of the poet's gratitude for any favours received. Prince-pleasing was the name of the game, but the game involved an element of reciprocity, and implied shared assumptions regarding the roles of both monarch and poet. In terms of this special kind of discourse, personal-sounding address was in reality just as much the vehicle for public utterance, and both poet and king, together with the indispensable onlookers, became party to a court ritual. This ensured not only that literary talent would have an occasion on which to be rewarded, but also that the poet would confer a favour on the king, by giving the latter an opportunity to display his magnificence and liberality. Thus, Renaissance sovereigns had at least one thing in common with their early Germanic forebears: namely, that they were appreciated not only for what they possessed, but also for what they gave away. In a well-functioning court, the sovereign and the poets around him would thus be inescapably linked in a close, quasi-conspiratorial relationship, and this, accordingly, is precisely what one finds in the New Year poems of William Dunbar and William Stewart.[1]

During the period of Mary Queen of Scots, however, this feature of Scottish culture, like so many others, was to undergo modification. The first New Year poem which Mary received in her own country was that of Alexander Scott, and dates from January 1562. Scott's poem departs from the conventions of the New Year poem in terms both of form and content. Normally such poems are composed to be delivered orally, in the chamber of the sovereign, and the implied circumstances of presentation will be familiar and intimate: William Stewart, on just such an occasion, mentions how Mary's father, James V, slid two shillings into the poet's hand.[2] At the very outset of Scott's poem, by contrast, one

---

1 On Dunbar see: Priscilla Bawcutt, *Dunbar the Makar* (Oxford, 1992), pp. 78–130. On William Stewart see: A.A. MacDonald, 'William Stewart and the Court Poetry of the Reign of James V', in *Stewart Style 1513–1542: Essays on the Court of James V*, ed. Janet Hadley Williams (East Linton, 1996), pp. 179–200.
2 *The Bannatyne Manuscript*, ed. W. Tod Ritchie, STS, 4 vols. (Edinburgh and London, 1928–34), II, 254–55.

is at once aware that such closeness is impossible; in this later work the discourse belongs rather to another genre – that of the poem of welcome:

> Welcum, illustrat ladye and our quene:
> welcum oure lyone with the floure delyce:
> welcum, oure thrissill with the Lorane grene:
> welcum, oure rubent rois upoun the ryce:
> welcum, oure jem and joyfull genetryce:
> welcum, oure beill of Albion to beir:
> welcum, oure plesand princes maist of price:
> God gif thee grace aganis this guid New Yeir!³ (1–8)

This was Mary's first New Year in Scotland as an adult, reigning monarch, and the occasion provided the first chance for the poet to ingratiate himself; intimacy of the traditional type is therefore scarcely to be expected. At the end of the poem we find further generic innovations. In the Bannatyne Manuscript, in which the unique text of the poem is preserved, the rubrics 'Lenvoy' and 'Lectori' are found, before the penultimate and final stanzas respectively:

> Lenvoy
> Prudent, maist gent, tak tent and prent the wordis
> intill this bill with will thame still to face
> quhilkis ar nocht skar to bar on far fra bawrdis
> bot leale but feale may haell avaell thy grace.
> Sen, lo, thou scho this to now do hes place,
> resaif, swaif and haif ingraif it heir
> this now for prow that thou sweit dow may brace
> lang space with grace, solace and peace this yeir.
>
> Lectori
> Fresch fulgent flurist fragrant flour formois,
> lantern to lufe, of ladeis lamp and lot,
> cherie maist chaist, cheif charbucle and chois,
> smaill sweit smaragde smelling but smit of smot,
> noblest natour, nurice to nurtour, not
> this dull indite, dulce double dasy deir,
> send be thy sempill servand Sanderris Scott,
> greiting grit God to grant thy grace gude yeir. (209–24)

Such features as these are clearly intrusions from the genre of courtly verse-epistle. Scott's poem, one observes, is a 'bill' (210) – a word typically used in this sort of poetry for correspondence between lovers; Scott even signs with his own name, and declares that he has sent the poem (223), like an open letter, to the

---

3 Text quoted from: *A Choice of Scottish Verse 1470–1570*, ed. John and Winifred MacQueen (1972), pp. 179–87.

Queen. Scott's most extended composition is notable, therefore, for its adroit manipulation of at least three different genres: the New Year poem, the welcome poem, and the verse-epistle.

The most striking departure from the conventions of the New Year genre, however, is to be seen in the contents of this poem. Whereas in the expression of good wishes New Year poems do not usually transcend the routine sentiments, Scott's poem departs entirely from this pattern to provide a serious discussion of the moral and political evils of the times. Scott reviews the failures of the Catholics – both the personal peccadilloes of the prelates and the defatigations of a jejune observance – before proceeding to denounce the sanctimoniousness and rapacity of the Protestants. With this as its principal topic, the poem reveals itself to be a general satire, and, on account of the exhortations to the Queen, it might even be classed among other works of the *speculum principis* sort.[4]

If Scott's poem was indeed spoken directly to the sovereign on New Year's day itself or soon after, it would surely have had a sobering influence on the customary festivities of the court, and, in directing collective attention away from the normal hilarity and towards the political situation, Scott's poem would have marked a striking departure from precedent. This very fact might prompt one to wonder whether Scott's poem was indeed delivered in the traditional and public manner. In view of the exceptional length of this work, as compared with other New Year poems, and also of the notable epistolary features, it seems not impossible that Scott's poem was composed as a kind of tract for the times, one perhaps designed to be read rather than to be heard, and to be read (eventually, if not immediately) by many more persons than those who normally comprised the court circle.[5]

The circumstances of January 1562 were rather unusual. Mary had only been back in Scotland since August. She had recently made an extraordinary royal entry into her capital city, during which she had been given not only the expected honorific compliments but also some blunt and unpalatable lessons in how to govern both country and church. Not long after this event she had succeeded in having the Reform-minded Town Council replaced with another which would be more pliant to her will.[6] After this initial whirl of activity, Mary may have appreciated the opportunity to relax somewhat in the company of friends. She found these friends in the house of George, 5th Lord Seton, where she stayed for five days at the beginning of the month of January.[7] In going to Seton, Mary

---

4 For a discussion of this topic see: Sally Mapstone, *The Wisdom of Princes* (Oxford, forthcoming).
5 It would not at all be surprising to learn that this poem, on account of its topicality and royal interest, had been printed. A comparable example of this sort of public welcome poem would be Dunbar's salutation to Bernard Stewart (1508), printed by Chepman and Myllar: *The Poems of William Dunbar*, ed. Priscilla Bawcutt, 2 vols. (Glasgow, 1998), I 177–79.
6 A.A. MacDonald, 'Mary Stewart's Entry to Edinburgh: an Ambiguous Triumph', *Innes Review*, 42 (1991), 101–10; Peter Davidson, 'The entry of Mary Stewart into Edinburgh, 1561, and other ambiguities', *Renaissance Studies*, 9 (1995), 416–25; A.R. MacDonald, 'The Triumph of Protestantism: The Burgh Council of Edinburgh and the Entry of Mary Queen of Scots, 2 September 1561', *Innes Review* 48 (1997), 73–82; Gordon Kipling, *Enter the King: Theatre, Liturgy, and Ritual in the Medieval Civic Triumph* (Oxford, 1998), pp. 352–56.
7 Edward M. Furgol, 'The Scottish Itinerary of Mary Queen of Scots, 1542–8 and 1561–8', *PSAS*, 117 (1987), 219–31 and microfiche.

could be said to be making a political statement: she was forsaking her own palace, and associating with some of the most conspicuously royalist and Catholic of her subjects. Whether or not Alexander Scott was present at the grand house-party, his poem owes its *raison d'être* to this moment in the career of the Queen: if Scott was included, he would have been expected to address his sovereign in the usual manner; if he was excluded from Seton, the poem would still have a validity as a more general New Year salutation.

Scott's work, however, is not the first poem from Mary's reign to take the situation of the New Year for its starting-point. Sir Richard Maitland of Lethington composed three such specimens. *Eternall God, tak away thy scurge*, is explicitly said to date from New Year's mass 1559 (i.e. 1560).[8] For its part the carol, *I can not sing for þe vexatioun*, refers to the conflict between the French troops and the forces of the Congregation, and may perhaps be assigned to 1559.[9] A third poem, *O hie eternall God of micht*, invokes the name of Mary near the opening, before expressing the hope that the Queen-Regent will punish by law oppressors of the innocent.[10] To some extent, these three poems evince the frustration of a poet who, by reason of the absence of the sovereign from her own country, was prevented from penning more traditional poems of seasonal greetings. Sir Richard was, of course, an instinctive royalist and an ardent francophile. In 1558 he wrote a poem congratulating King Henry II on the recapture of Calais from the English, and ended by hoping that Henry's achievement would spur on the Scots to mend their frontiers by retaking Berwick from the common enemy.[11] In the following year he expressed his delight in the contract of marriage between Mary and the Dauphin, Francois, and Maitland thanked Mary of Guise for her efforts in coupling the two kingdoms together in one chain. The *portée* of the following remarks must have been clear to all:

> Scottis and Frenche now leif in vnitie,
> As ȝe war brether borne in ane countrie,
> Without all maner of suspitioun,
> Ilk ane to other keip trew fraternitie.
> Defend ane other bayth be land and sie,
> And, gif onye of euill conditioun
> Betuixt ȝow twa wald mak seditioun,
> Scottis or Frenche, quhat man that euer he be,
> With all rigour put him to punitioun.[12] (64–72)

---

8 *The Maitland Quarto Manuscript*, ed. W.A. Craigie, STS (Edinburgh and London, 1920), pp. 23–25.
9 *Ibid.*, pp. 26–27.
10 *Ibid.*, pp. 10–14.
11 *Ibid.*, pp. 30–32. On Maitland see: Maurice Lee Jr., 'Sir Richard Maitland of Lethington: A Christian Laird in the Age of Reformation', in *Action and Conviction in Early Modern Europe*, ed. T.K. Rabb and J.E. Seigel (Princeton, 1969), pp. 117–32; A.A. MacDonald, 'The Poetry of Sir Richard Maitland of Lethington', *Transactions of the East Lothian Antiquarian and Field Naturalists' Society*, 13 (1972), 7–19.
12 *Maitland Quarto*, ed. Craigie, pp. 19–23.

One of Maitland's most enthusiastic poems is *Excellent princes, potent and preclair*, written to welcome Mary 'hame to [her] native people *and* countrie'.[13] In this work we find the characteristic Maitland themes: lament for the troubles of the times, royalist fervour, and a somewhat naive expectation that Mary will be able to sort out the current political conflicts. Like Alexander Scott in his poem of welcome, Maitland is prolific in his advice to the Queen, and he too ends his poem with a flourish: 'Viue Marie, trenoble royne d'Escoss!' Since the family of Sir Richard Maitland was related by marriage to that of the Setons (of which, indeed, he wrote a history[14]), it is highly likely that Maitland would have been present at the memorable New Year party of January 1562.

The works of Scott and Maitland reveal how certain poets in Scotland regarded Mary Queen of Scots at the outset of her reign. The rejoicing at the return of a Stewart sovereign to her native land was apparently sincere, and the expectations were high. Mary, even before she had set foot on the quayside at Leith, had become a symbol of national pride: she was also expected to raise the morale of the nation, bind up the wounds of civil war, and restore the customs of the good old days. Unfortunately, Maitland – a conservative-minded judge and minor landowner – and Scott – a musician at the privileged institution of the Chapel Royal – could not really hope to speak for the entire nation. Although such poets might nostalgically evoke the court customs of the reigns of Mary's father and grandfather, it would take more than a display of rhetoric to make Mary play the part prescribed for her.

Poetry and the court

It is perhaps useful to contrast the inception of Mary's personal reign with that of her father. In the case of James V there was a regency of fifteen years; in that of Mary one of nineteen. James, once he had freed himself from the trammels of the Douglases, was able to slip without much difficulty into the role of Scottish monarch. With Mary it was otherwise: in Paris she had been used to a sophisticated court, and her horizons were truly European. James succeeded to the throne of a country still unaffected by religious schism, whereas Mary had to cope with doctrinal controversy. James could use his father as a political model to emulate; if Mary, however, were to do likewise, she would be likely to alienate a sizeable number of her subjects. In the case of James V, royalist and religious sentiment formed an organic whole; in that of Mary there was a dichotomy, and each component was susceptible of more than one interpretation. In Mary's Scottish court, unlike that of her father, there were both Protestant and Catholic magnates, and her officials (such as the royal secretary, William Maitland of Lethington, son of Sir Richard) had to be realistic and flexible enough to work

---

13 *Ibid.*, pp. 27–30.
14 Sir Richard Maitland of Lethington, *The History of the House of Seytoun to the year MDLIX*, ed. John Fullarton, Maitland Club (Glasgow, 1829). Maitland's wife was probably a sister of William Cranston, provost of Seton in 1549: John Durkan, 'Foundation of the Collegiate Church of Seton', *Innes Review*, 13 (1962), 71–76 (71).

with people of either persuasion. In the city of Edinburgh the merchants, burgesses and tradesmen were all riven by religious disputes. Reformed clergymen might have taken over control of the kirk of St Giles, but the Catholic archbishop of St Andrews, in whose diocese the capital was situated, had not relinquished ecclesiastical jurisdiction over the city. Faced with these complexities and dissensions in a strange country, it is small wonder that at the first opportunity Mary betook herself to Seton, there to be among friends whose sympathy with the Queen's religious and political views could be taken for granted.

In view of the flurry of verses which were prompted by the Queen's return to Scotland, it is perhaps surprising that there is not more poetry that can be precisely connected with the events of Mary's actual reign. But one must not overlook the poem of Sir Thomas Craig, published in 1565 to celebrate the Queen's second marriage: *Henrici Illustrissimi Ducis Albaniae Comitis Rossiae etc. et Mariae Serenissimae Scotorum Reginae Epithalamium*.[15] The publication of this poem in the learned, international language probably stemmed from more than one consideration, among which one might propose: the exigencies of the epithalamium genre and the stylistic exhibitionism of the Neolatin poet; the ceremonial dignity of the occasion; the political significance of the event itself. Henry Stewart, Lord Darnley, was the elder son of Matthew, 4th Earl of Lennox, and of Margaret Douglas. The latter was the daughter of Margaret Tudor by her second husband, Archibald Douglas, 6th Earl of Angus. Through this marriage Mary was strengthening her claim on the throne of England, based now on a double and legitimate descent from the daughter of Henry VII. All parties in Scotland could rejoice at this marriage: while Catholics might look to the reclaiming of England through Mary, Protestants might expect the protection of their Reformation through Darnley. By virtue of her second marriage Mary might be thought to be prolonging the policy of religious equipoise which she had initiated soon after returning to her kingdom.

Although there is little poetry in the years 1562–7 which stems directly from particular events, there is much that can be said about the factors bearing upon literary culture during this period. The Bannatyne Manuscript preserves a poem, *Be gouernour baith guid and gratious*, by one Henry Stewart, who may be Darnley:

> Be to rebellis strong as lyoun eik;
> Be ferce to follow þame *quhair* evir thai found;
> Be to thy liege men bayth soft and meik;
> Be þair succour and help þame haill and sound;
> Be-knaw thy cure and caus quhy thow was cround;
> Be besye evir that iustice be nocht smord;
> Be blyith in hart, þir wordis oft expound;
> Be bowsum ay to knaw thy God and Lord.[16] (33–40)

15 STC 5970.
16 *Bannaytne MS*, ed. Ritchie, II, 227–28.

50   *The European Sun*

One notices the use, in these lines, of the well-worn reference to the lion, king of beasts, who spares and protects those who accept his authority.[17] The political, moral and religious sentiments voiced in the poem are of a superlatively platitudinous sort, suggestive of mechanical composition. One notes that the work which precedes the Darnley poem in the manuscript deals in an identical manner (including the omnipresent anaphora of 'be' at the beginning of each line) with the Seven Deadly Sins.[18]

If Bannatyne's attribution of another poem to 'King Hary Stewart' is correct, the work in question must date from between 29 July 1565 (the date of Darnley's marriage to Mary) and 10 February 1567 (the date of his murder). Since this poem is a song of love, and since it did not take long for Mary and Darnley to become estranged, one may incline towards the earlier of the two *termini*. The following may serve as a sample:

> Schaw, schedull, to that sueit
> My pairt so permanent,
> That no mirth quhill we meit
> Sall caus me be content;
> Bot still my hairt lament
> In sorrowfull siching soir;
> Till tyme scho be present,
> Fairweill, I say no moir.[19] (33–40)

As a poem this specimen is no worse that many others which merely reshuffle the cards in an endless game of literary patience. Every thought, and almost every turn of phrase, is derivative; even the final punch-line can be paralleled from love-lyrics, among them Alexander Scott's 'Lament for the Master of Erskine'.[20] If Darnley really was the author of these two poems, it is small wonder that Mary tired of him.

The great poet of the decade was Alexander Scott. His skill at love-lyric has been widely praised, and it seems only natural to seek a connection between his production and the existence of a glittering court circle under Mary. Scott wrote not only many fine poems on the traditional pleasures of courtly love, but also some fascinating lyrics which subvert the normal erotic conventions. The 'Slicht remeid of luve' is one such poem:

> Bot, wald ӡe rewill ӡow, keip this regiment:
> Be subteill, screit, sobir in thair sicht,
> Facound of wordis, bot feckill of intent,
> And nevir lat ӡour mowth and mynd go richt;

---

17 This was familiar from bestiaries and is reflected in the line, 'Parcere prostratis scit nobilis ira leonis', quoted by both Henryson and Dunbar: see Bawcutt, *Dunbar the Makar*, p. 99.
18 *Bannatyne MS*, ed. Ritchie, II, 224–6.
19 *Ibid.*, III, 338–9.
20 *Ibid.*, III, 344–5.

> Swey as thay swey, be blyth quhen thay ar licht,
> And preis ȝow ay in presens to repair;
> Forvey no tyme, be reddy day and nicht
> Vpoun ȝour kneis to serve thame soletare.²¹ (9–16)

If there is a religion of courtly love, them these lines are heretical; they contrast absolutely with Shakespeare's definition (Sonnet 116): 'Love is not love/Which alters when it alteration finds,/Or bends with the remover to remove'. In other poems, Scott can be even blunter:

> Sum monebrunt madynis myld,
> At nonetyd of the nicht,
> Ar chappit vp with chyld
> But coile or candill licht;
> Sua sum said maidis hes slicht
> To play and tak no pane,
> Syne chift thair seid fra sicht:
> I sall not said agane.²² (65–72)

It should be noted that these poems are grouped by Bannatyne in his section of comic poems. This seems to be an indication that the taste of the contemporary élite could happily accommodate not only idealistic emotion, but also realistic exuberance. Since this was true at the court of James IV, as the poetry of Dunbar demonstrates, one cannot be surprised to discover that the same gamut of aesthetic response is also to be encountered at the court of Mary.

It was formerly critical orthodoxy to view the wide stylistic and thematic variety within the *oeuvre* of Alexander Scott as a reflection of the poet's development from a personality interested in love-lyrics to one more inclined towards morality and religion.²³ More recently, however, the biographical assumption inherent in such a hypothesis has been challenged, and the position of Scott's poetry within a particular, historically conditioned discourse has been singled out for attention.²⁴ To some extent earlier attitudes to Scott have been influenced by the celebrated critical categories of the Bannatyne Manuscript, in which the poet's works are contained. As a result, Bannatyne's quadruple division of love poems into 'songs of love', 'contempts of love and evil women', 'contempts of evil, false, vicious men' and 'ballatis detesting of love and lechery' have been applied

---

21 *Ibid.*, II, 325–26.
22 *Ibid.*, II, 339–42.
23 For example: *Ballattis of Luve*, ed. John MacQueen (Edinburgh, 1970), p.xlvi.
24 See Denton Fox's review of MacQueen's *Ballattis of Luve*: *NQ*, New Series 19 (1972), 32–36; Theo van Heijnsbergen, 'The Love Lyrics of Alexander Scott', *SSL*, 26 (1991), 366–79 (376); *idem*, 'The Sixteenth-Century Scottish Love Lyric', in *Sacred and Profane: Secular and Devotional Interplay in Early Modern British Literature*, ed. Helen Wilcox, Richard Todd and Alasdair MacDonald (Amsterdam, 1996), pp. 45–61; A.A. MacDonald, 'Early Modern Scottish Literature and the Parameters of Culture', in *The Rose and the Thistle: Essays on the Culture of late Medieval and Renaissance Scotland*, ed. Sally Mapstone and Juliette Wood (East Linton, 1998), pp. 77–100 (79–80).

to Scott as if they had some relevance to the *development*, as distinct from the *range*, of Scott's achievement. A teleological reading of Bannatyne's categories within this one section of the manuscript, however, is as unsafe as one based upon the five main categories of the manuscript as a whole. George Bannatyne, as it happens, begins his anthology with the religious and moral verse, and progresses through comic and erotic poems to reach the fables. If the sequence of critical classifications in one section of the manuscript is held to match the development of Alexander Scott, this ought logically to apply also to the whole of the collection. However, the overall disposition of the material in the Bannatyne Manuscript clearly militates against the artistic and personal development proposed for Scott – at least in as much as this might imply a simplistic shift from youthful amorousness to mature high seriousness.[25] In fact, it has been demonstrated that the critical categories used by Bannatyne have much more to do with the contemporary political and cultural situation than with a concern with the development of any poet whatsoever.[26]

Poetry and publishing

Such considerations impel one to examine the conditions within which the poetry of Mary's reign was constrained to exist. One significant factor, for example, is that in the decade of the 1560s Scotland for the first time had more than one printer at work. Robert Lekpreuik began with a *Confession of Faith* in 1561, and he continued as the printer most associated with the Protestant Church and its supporters. John Scot, for his part, had already been active in the time of Mary of Guise, and printed such distinctively Catholic works as the *In dominicam orationem pia meditatio* of Patrick Cockburn (1555), the *Compendius Tractiue* of Quintin Kennedy (1558), together with the *Catechisme* (1552) and the *Godlie Exhortatioun* (1559) of Archbishop Hamilton. Scot's printing activities were characterised more by professionalism than conviction, and he subsequently competed with Lekpreuik in also publishing the *Confessioun of Faith* (1561); at the same time, seeing no reason to desert his regular customers, Scot printed in 1562 two works by the Catholic controversialist, Ninian Winzet. This so displeased the burgh authorities that Scot was imprisoned and his equipment confiscated.[27]

In the same decade one can speak not only of printers, but also of publishers.

---

25 See, for example, the opinions of the poet's modern editor and namesake: *The Poems of Alexander Scott*, ed. Alexander Scott (Edinburgh, 1952), p.9. For the idea that Bannatyne's sequence of categories is philosophically meaningful see: Joan Hughes and W. S. Ramson, *Poetry of the Stewart Court* (Canberra, 1982).

26 A.A. MacDonald, 'The Bannatyne Manuscript – A Marian Anthology', *Innes Review*, 37 (1986), 36–47; idem, 'The printed book that never was: George Bannatyne's poetic anthology (1568)', in *Boeken in de late Middeleeuwen*, ed. Jos M.M. Hermans and Klaas van der Hoek (Groningen, 1994), pp. 101–10.

27 For the details of the editions mentioned in this, and following paragraphs see: Robert Dickson and J.P. Edmond, *Annals of Scottish Printing* (Cambridge, 1890; reprint Amsterdam, 1975), *passim; A List of Books Printed in Scotland before 1700*, ed. H.G. Aldis, revised edition (Edinburgh, 1970). See also: W.T. Dobson, *History of the Bassandyne Bible* (Edinburgh, 1887); Michael Lynch, *Edinburgh and the Reformation* (Edinburgh, 1981), p.316.

Whereas Lekpreuik worked for the Protestant Church and its supporters, and printed for them works of Protestant theology (Beza, Knox, Calvin), works of Protestant controversy, works of religious practice (confessions of faith, psalm books, forms of prayer, in both Scots and Gaelic), he was also the printer of such official works as the *Actis* of Scotland (in 1566 given their first updating since the days of James V). Moreover, it was from the press of Lekpreuik that there poured the flood of satirical verse that ensued upon the deposition of Mary in 1567. Two other publishers, however, began to be active in the 1560s. Thomas Bassandyne financed the printing of the *Gude and Godlie Ballatis* in 1565, using John Scot as printer. This book was reissued, in expanded form and with many changes, in 1567, and in the same year Scot may have printed an edition of the Sternhold and Hopkins *Psalms* (only the title-page survives). Thereafter Bassandyne lay low for a few years, only to emerge again after the Civil War (his *magnum opus* was the publication, with Alexander Arbuthnet, of the Geneva Bible, in 1576 and '79). The last year of Mary's presence in Scotland, moreover, saw the *début* of Henry Charteris as publisher, with the edition of Lindsay's *Warkis*, printed by John Scot.

The large issues which determined the course of the literary scene during Mary's reign had a direct bearing upon the activities of these two printers and three publishers. While all of them doubtless shared a keen mercantile instinct, there are differences of emphasis in their productions, and the latter have implications for the world of letters. The poetry published by Lekpreuik during Mary's reign consisted of: *The Meroure of an Chr[i]stiane* (1561) of Robert Norvell, a poet who was an enthusiastic Protestant and favourite of John Knox; the *Psalms* of Sternhold and Hopkins (1564, 1565); the *Epithalamium* of Sir Thomas Craig (1565), mentioned earlier; the *Cento ex Virgilio* of Lelio Capilupi (1565), a work which may have had a pedagogical function, but which was in any case full of anticlerical satire;[28] and, at the end of the reign, sundry satirical ballads, by Sempill and others. Bassandyne had perhaps a more developed literary sense than Lekpreuik, but in putting out the *Gude and Godlie Ballatis* he was certainly playing safe from the religious point of view. The same may be said for Charteris, publisher of the *Warkis* of Lindsay in 1568, since this author could be claimed retrospectively as the prophet of Protestantism. Through one of life's little ironies, the printer of this book was none other than John Scot, the man who had printed Lindsay's *Dialog betuix Experience and ane Courteour* in 1554, when Lindsay, despite his obviously reformist inclinations, still counted officially as a Catholic. This detail might remind one that the Reformation in Scotland may be seen not only as a heroic struggle between the forces of darkness and light but also as a matter of social manoeuvring and mundane circumstance, exploited for commercial advantage.

An interesting illustration of the competition between the publishers may be given from the collections of psalms which were available to the virtuous in the

---

28 As the title further declared, this work was concerned 'de vita monachorum'; a later edition, entitled *Cento Vergilianus, de vita monachorum, quos vulgò fratres appellant*, appeared at Rome in 1575. Each line of the *cento* was composed of two half-lines, normally from the *Aeneid*, but occasionally from the *Eclogues* or the *Georgics*. See: V. Carpino, *Un poemetto contro i monaci di L. Capilupi* (Girgenti, 1904).

first years of the Reformation. Lekpreuik, as already mentioned, printed the English versifications, by Sternhold and Hopkins, with the official approval of the Protestant Church. The corollary hereof, one presumes, was that no-one else was allowed to print these psalms. The psalms in the Bassandyne-Scot *Gude and Godlie Ballatis* would therefore have to be different. Some of them, perhaps, had been in circulation in Scotland as early as 1546, since John Knox reports that lines from Psalm 50 were sung on the eve of the arrest of George Wishart.[29] (Knox's account was written after the publication of the 1565 edition of the *Gude and Godlie Ballatis*, however, and he may simply have quoted from this conveniently available print.) Many of these Scottish psalm translations are based on Continental models, yet they have a force of their own, in which the Scottish element sporadically shines through. Some lines of Psalm 124 may serve to bring this out. In the Authorized Version, which I quote for the sake of familiarity, these run:

(3) Then they had swallowed us up quick, when their wrath was kindled against us.
(4) Then the waters had overwhelmed us, the stream had gone over our soul;
(5) Then the proud waters had gone over our soul.

In the *Gude and Godlie Ballatis* we find the following:

> For lyke the welterand wallis brym,
> Thay had ouerquhelmit vs with mycht
> Lyke burnis that in spait fast rin,
> Thay had ouerthrawin vs with slycht.
> The burland stremis of thair pryde,
> Had peirsit vs throw bak and syde,
> And reft fra vs our lyfe full rycht.[30]

Such a version distinguishes itself immediately from that of William Whittingham, added to the collection of Sternhold and Hopkins:

> Now long ago they had devourde vs all,
> And swallowde quicke, for ought that we coulde deme:
> Suche was their rage, as we might wel esteme,
> And as the floods with mightie force do fall,
> So had they now our lyfe euen brought to thrall.
>
> The raging streames, moste proude in roaring noyce,
> Had long ago ouerwhelmde vs in the depe: . . .[31]

---

29 *Works of John Knox*, ed. David Laing, Bannatyne Club, 6 vols. (Edinburgh, 1846–64), I, 139.
30 *The Gude and Godlie Ballatis*, ed. A.F. Mitchell, STS (Edinburgh and London, 1897), p.111.
31 Text quoted from *Forme of Prayers* (Edinburgh: Lekpreuik, 1565).

The superior expression of the *Gude and Godlie Ballatis* in this instance is surely self-evident. Nevertheless, the Church in Scotland never gave its official approval to this version, and only the Sternhold and Hopkins psalms were licensed for use in worship. As it happens, in the 1565 edition of the *Gude and Godlie Ballatis*, which was rediscovered as recently as 1978, we find two specimens of Sternhold and Hopkins psalms.[32] Since these are absent from the 1567 edition, one may surmise that the Church censor, acting in the interest of the Church's printer, Lekpreuik, objected to Bassandyne's unauthorised use of such privileged material.

A clear indicator of Protestant poetic taste in the reign of Mary is furnished by Robert Norvell's *Meroure of an Christiane*. This volume consists of three parts, of which the first two are long poems on the topics of sin and redemption, and the sufferings of the prophets and martyrs. The third part, entitled 'Godlie Ballades', is a concise anthology of the type common in Protestant *enchiridia*: here we find the Lord's Prayer, the Creed, the Decalogue, Graces before and after dinner, with miscellaneous religious poems, including a psalm.[33] Norvell, formerly a soldier serving with the Scots Guard in France, is far from being a great poet; he has not undeservedly been called a 'tedious rimester',[34] and, indeed, his writings show that the sword can sometimes be mightier than the pen. Norvell, moreover, is not altogether original, and the majority of his 'godlie ballades' are actually translations of poems by Clément Marot. The latter had good Protestant credentials, and was a writer approved of at the French court. In his choice of Marot as a model, Norvell may have sought to demonstrate that Protestantism was not absolutely incompatible with courtliness, and that some good, at least, could come out of France.

The Bannatyne Manuscript and its literary context

Norvell's *Meroure* was chronologically the first collection of Scottish verse published during the reign of Mary; the others – if we discount the Sternhold and Hopkins psalms included with the various printings of the *Forme of Prayers* – were the Bassandyne-Scot *Gude and Godlie Ballatis* and the Charteris-Scot *Warkis* of Lindsay. Another great anthology, however, was compiled in the same period, though it was not to reach print until modern times. This was, of course, the Bannatyne Manuscript, on which the last word has not been said, despite the not inconsiderable attention paid to the manuscript in the last few years.[35] It was

---

32 Bernhard Fabian, 'An Eighteenth-Century Research Collection: English Books at Göttingen University Library', *The Library*, 83 (1979), 224.
33 See: A.A. MacDonald, The Middle Scots Religious Lyrics, Ph.D. diss., University of Edinburgh, 1978, pp.399–408 (402).
34 William Beattie, 'Some early Scottish books', in *The Scottish Tradition*, ed. G.W.S. Barrow (Edinburgh, 1974), pp. 107–20 (120).
35 See note 26, above; Theo van Heijnsbergen, 'The Interaction between Literature and History in Queen Mary's Edinburgh: the Bannatyne Manuscript and its Prosopographical Context', in *The Renaissance in Scotland*, ed. A.A. MacDonald, Michael Lynch and Ian B. Cowan (Leiden, 1994), pp. 183–225.

argued long ago, and has been again recently, that this collection was compiled with a view to being printed. If this hypothesis is to convince, it is necessary to construct a scenario which would render such a publication a likely event.

If George Bannatyne did indeed intend to try to publish his collection, such an enterprise would have to accord with the cultural trends of the time, and it would also have to be explicable in terms of financial and technical considerations. Now, the contemporary interest in assembling anthologies has already been established. It is true that Norvell's *Meroure* and the *Gude and Godlie Ballatis* by virtue of their subject-matter have an obvious relevance in a time of Reformation, and the poems of Lindsay, for their part, evince a reformist spirit as to religion. Yet the Bannatyne Manuscript, in its final form (of 1568), also lays considerable emphasis on religion and morality, and the scribe has been shown to be greatly concerned over doctrinal rectitude.[36] The 1568 print of Lindsay's *Warkis*, again, shows that there was a contemporary market for the classics of courtly literature from the time of James V. Bannatyne's anthology might thus be said to combine and to cater for both of these interests, religious and patriotic. The sections of comic and love poems would not have been unacceptable in 1568. Comic poems have a perennial attraction, and in any case much of the humour of the poems here gathered by Bannatyne turns on the ways of the pre-Reformation Church. It is significant that Bannatyne eventually decided to incorporate interludes drawn from Lindsay's *Satyre of the Thrie Estaitis*: this editorial decision imparted a political colouring to the manuscript and greatly swelled the dimensions of the central section. Any residual material which might have seemed doctrinally objectionable to the Protestant party would thus effectively be neutralised and rendered harmless through its location within a comic context. That the recreational element within Scottish culture was nonetheless felt to be important may be seen from the best-known work of Sir Richard Maitland of Lethington, which is a lament at the loss of the pleasures of earlier days:

> Quhair is the blyithnes that hes beine,
> Baith in burgh and landwart sene,
> Amang lordis and ladyis schene,
> Daunsing, singing, game and play?
> Bot now I wait not quhat thay meine,
> All merines is worne away.[37] (1–6)

As for Bannatyne's selection of love poems, these, as has already been mentioned, have four subdivisions; the latter, in their progressive seriousness of purpose, indicate the ways in which such poems might be approached in a godly age. Thus one concludes that Bannatyne had reason to believe that the poems in his collection in its final form would find eager readers in 1568.

---

36 A.A. MacDonald. 'Poetry, Politics, and Reformation Censorship in Sixteenth-Century Scotland', *English Studies*, 64 (1983), 410–21.
37 *Maitland Quarto MS*, ed. Craigie, pp.15–19.

However, Bannatyne's collection was not initially assembled with an eye to the taste of 1568. The first section to be assembled was actually that of the love poems; these were collected in 1565 – the year of the Queen's marriage and of Craig's *Epithalamium*. It is thus possible that Bannatyne put together a collection of lyrics on the theme of love in order to profit from the general festive mood prevailing at that time. In 1565 the poems in this collection were not divided into the four subsections as we have them today, since the insertion of these headings dates only from the final stages in the preparation of the whole manuscript, in 1568. The so-called Draft Manuscript, which now precedes the Main Manuscript, is known to be a production of 1567 or early 1568 – the time, perhaps significantly, of the Queen's downfall. The Draft Manuscript, it may be noted, is a collection of exclusively religious and moral verse, which would also be eminently suited to the taste of these few hectic months. The usual designation of 'Draft' Manuscript suggests that this was a try-out for the main collection; this assumption, however, is unsafe – at least, without much further qualification. It might be better simply to propose that the so-called Draft Manuscript – like the initial anthology of love lyrics – be regarded simply as a second (and quite independent) collection of poems with topical appeal. In this interpretation, both the erotic verse of 1565 and the moral and religious verse of 1567/8 would have been overtaken by the events which led to the final defeat of Mary at Langside (13 May 1568) – events which led to the Bannatyne Manuscript in its ultimate form. In this final version of the manuscript religious and moral verse was privileged and expanded; comic verse was retained, albeit that it was given a new orientation through the juxtaposition of extracts from Lindsay; the love poems were equipped with suitably moralistic subheadings; and a section of moral fables was added. By a few deft strokes of the pen, the entire volume was declared at six places, if somewhat disingenuously, to date from 1568. To the present writer it seems incredible that the scribe should have resorted to such elaborate procedures if the ulterior purpose of publication had not lain behind the assembly of the manuscript.

If Bannatyne's collection had been published, it would most probably have been sponsored by either Bassandyne or Charteris (probably the latter), and printed by John Scot. The possibility that it might have issued from the press of Lekpreuik seems remote. Although Bannatyne's collection was large in bulk, it would not have defeated the technical skills of a printer who, sixteen years earlier, had been capable of producing Hamilton's *Catechisme*, and who could take Lindsay's *Warkis* in his stride. One may thus draw the following conclusions: the hypothesis that the Bannaytne Manuscript was intended to be printed is reasonable in itself, particularly within the relevant cultural context; such a hypothesis gains credibility from its power to explain many striking features of the physical make-up and lay-out of the manuscript; this hypothesis squares with contemporary technical and financial considerations.

The young George Bannatyne (he was born in 1545) was the author of a couple of uninspired love poems and a few nugatory scraps of verse. His manuscript collection, however, is a cultural document of the greatest importance in the history of older Scottish literature.[38] This is not only on account of the copiousness of the poetry which it contains, nor even of the critical categories in which that poetry is ordered, but also of the way in which the genesis of the manuscript allows one to gauge the rapid mutations in literary taste in the second half of Mary's reign. One consequence of the upheavals of the 1560s was that there was an increased interest in the classics of Middle Scots literature. Lindsay, of course, continued to be popular, since he could be presented as a poet of the Reformation. Henryson's *Morall Fabillis* were printed in 1570 (Lekpreuik, for Henrie Charteris) and 1571 (Bassandyne); so Bannatyne, when he augmented his four-part anthology with a fifth section of fables, might be said to be smartly anticipating market trends. Furthermore, Lekpreuik printed for Charteris Hary's *Wallace* (1570) and Barbour's *Bruce* (1571). John Ross published John Rolland's *Court of Venus* (written in the time of James V) in 1575, and the same poet's *Seuin Seages* in 1578; in the following year he reissued Douglas's *Palice of Honoure*. Nor should one overlook Alexander Arbuthnet's printing of the *Buik of Alexander*, in c. 1580. It would seem that the very religious and political factionalism of the period 1560–73 may have had a catalytic role in evoking a quasi-nationalistic interest in the literary achievement of mediaeval Scotland. From this perspective also the Bannatyne Manuscript may be seen perfectly to accommodate the contemporary cultural ethos.

It is easy to forget just how many poets were active during the reign of Mary; on the basis of their number alone this period might have to be ranked as the cultural apogee of the century. Gaelic poetry will here be left out of account, since it was produced in a different and largely separate cultural environment. In or near Edinburgh there are George Buchanan and Thomas Craig, writing in Latin, and Mary herself and Pierre de Chastelard, writing in French. The contemporary vernacular Scottish poets may be ranged in several categories: first, poets involved in, or contributing to the cultural life around, the court, including Henry Stewart (Lord Darnley), Sir Richard Maitland of Lethington, Alexander Scott, John Fethy, George Clapperton, John Rolland, Sir William Kirkaldy of Grange and the youthful Alexander Montgomerie; second, a group of poets associated with civic and mercantile affairs, including William Lauder, George Bannatyne, and Henry Charteris; third, a group of poets of more markedly Protestant sympathies, including Robert Norvell, John Craig, Alexander Cunningham (5th Earl of Glencairn), William Stewart (Herald), Robert Sempill, and Robert Lindsay of Pitscottie.[39] Some of these poets met violent ends: Mary Stewart and Chastelard were executed, Darnley was strangled, and William Stewart was burned as a witch. It would be nice to be certain that David Riccio's offence, for which he paid with his life, was not the composition of verses in Italian.

38 Sir Walter Scott fully appreciated this fact, as is seen in his choice of the name of Bannatyne for his antiquarian club: see Hughes and Ramson, *Poetry of the Stewart Court*, pp.22–23.
39 The list in not necessarily complete, since other poets – e.g. John Davidson, Alexander Arbuthnot (not the printer Arbuthnet), Sir John Maitland of Thirlestane – may already have been active during the reign of Mary. Note that the three categories employed here cannot be said to be absolutely exclusive.

A further dimension to the literary life of the times is that revealed by the books of poetry which Mary collected in her library. These bear witness to the continuation of literary interests which she developed at the French court, and French and Italian titles predominate.[40] In the early years after her return to Scotland, Mary made time to study classical Latin prose under the tutelage of George Buchanan.[41] While such activity would have been prosecuted within the intimate confines of Holyrood Palace, it is probable that there were other centres of learning in the country, where poetry in foreign languages and contact with the Continent was similarly cultivated; as potential candidates one might suggest such places as the Chapel Royal, the College of Justice, Seton House and the Maitland domicile at Lethington.[42] An example of an individual book-collector would be Clement Litill, many of whose acquisitions came from the libraries of the Edinburgh friaries sacked in 1559.[43] Litill was a close friend of Bishop Henry Sinclair (d. 1565), President of the College of Justice, and member of the family which in an earlier age had patronised Gavin Douglas. One might surmise that the compilation of such large poetry collections as those of Sir Richard Maitland and George Bannatyne was made possible by the existence of networks, sometimes mutually overlapping, connecting literary-minded members within the ecclesiastical, legal and official establishments.[44]

The end of the reign

As has been noted above, Mary's personal reign was inaugurated with the composition of several poems of the *speculum principis* sort; it was perhaps not inappropriate that the inglorious conclusion of her reign should have witnessed a recrudescence of poems on the public theme of the state of the nation. The murder of Darnley (10 February 1567), Mary's marriage to Bothwell (15 May 1567), her defeat at Carberry (15 June 1567), her abdication in favour of her son, Charles James (24 July 1567), her subsequent imprisonment in Lochleven Castle, and her ultimate downfall at Langside (13 May 1568) provided the inspiration for a plethora of satirical poems written by Robert Sempill *cum suis*, and published by Lekpreuik. Though it can scarcely be claimed that in these poems Sempill has raised up a monument more lasting than bronze, his polemical talents are not negligible. In *Ane Ballat declaring the Nobill and Gude inclinatioun of our King* (1567), Darnley is discovered to display formidable literary and rhetorical skills:

---

40 John Durkan, 'The Library of Mary Queen of Scots', *Innes Review*, 38 (1987), 71–104.
41 I.D. McFarlane, *Buchanan* (1981), p.208.
42 On the Chapel Royal see: Theo van Heijnsbergen, 'The Scottish Chapel Royal as Cultural Intermediary between Town and Court', in *Centres of Learning: Learning and Location in Pre-modern Europe and the Near East*, ed. J.W. Drijvers and A.A. MacDonald (Leiden, 1995), pp.299–313.
43 *Early Scottish Libraries*, ed. John Durkan and Anthony Ross (Glasgow, 1961); Charles P. Finlayson, *Clement Litill and his Library* [etc.], EBS (Edinburgh, 1980), p.6.
44 On the family networks see: Theo van Heijnsbergen, as in note 35, above.

> With Romaine hand he could weill leid ane pen,
> And storyis wryte of auld antiquitie;
> Nobill him self and Nobill of Ingyne,
> And louit weill concord and vnitie.
> He swoumit in the fluidis of Poetrie,
> And did exerse the science liberall;
> The facund Phrase did vse of oratrie:
> His gude Ingyne was rycht celestiall. (49–56)

He is furthermore given credit for being 'In pulchritude to Paris perigall' (57), with 'face formois and vult heroycall' (59).[45] The Queen, who is execrated as a latter-day Jezebel and Clytemnestra, 'did in Seton sing:/Full weill was hir that day that sho was fre' (73–4). In the following passage, though Sempill resorts to touches which hark back to Chaucer and Henryson, his advice to the sovereign and to the lords in authority is not lacking in pungency:

> O Stewartis stout, ha! benedicitie!
> War ȝe not Royis in this Regioun,
> And ay did vse Justice and equitie?
> And now ȝour glas of honestie is run.
>
> Unles ȝe now sharplie shuit out ȝour handis,
> And trewlie try the gyltie of this blude,
> ȝe wilbe repuite Lowreis ouer all landis,
> And fais to Christ, [that] deit on the Rude.
> My Lordis, thairfoir, I think for ȝow gude,
> The tresoun try and puneis equallie:
> Lat not ȝour landis defylit be with blude,
> And gif ȝe do, God shaw his Maiestie!. (77–88)

Towards the end of the poem (193) Sempill says that John Bochas, were he still alive, would write effectively on the private and public behaviour of Mary. It is interesting that Sempill has recourse to the mediaeval *de casibus* model: we might similarly in this group of poems note the use of tragedies, deplorations, and pseudo-testaments. Though the political events themselves were novel, the responses made by the poets ran along traditional lines.[46]

Scottish poetry in the age of Mary is not an easy subject to define and comprehend. Though there were many poets alive during this period, most of the poetry seems to have been written at either the beginning or the end of the reign.[47] On the Queen's return from France, one witnesses an attempt to reinvoke

---

45 *Satirical Poems of the Time of the Reformation*, ed. James Cranstoun, STS, 2 vols. (Edinburgh and London, 1891–3), I, 31–38.
46 Further on the Sempill ballads see: Gregory Kratzmann, 'Political Satire and the Scottish Reformation', *SSL*, 26 (1991), 423–37.
47 It is likely that psalm-versifications, however, are an exception to this generalisation, and that their composition continued throughout the reign.

the cultural patterns of the earlier Stewart sovereigns, and on her departure from office there was a Gadarene rush into invective. Between the two heady events there seems to have been a curious lull; during this hiatus one observes within the court circles the enthusiastic cultivation of the literary tastes of the Continental Renaissance, but the time for this to emerge as a consciously propagated movement (as it would be under James VI) was not quite ripe.

From the point of view of the social history of Middle Scots poetry, however, Mary's reign was a crucial period. This was the time during which a definite and surprisingly sophisticated awareness of literary genres first really manifested itself.[48] It was also the time in which Scottish poetry, so to speak, lost its innocence. Henceforth poetry could not be enjoyed merely for what it was, and strategies for dealing with old poetry in new contexts had to be developed. The true properties of pre-Reformation verse had to be obscured under a veil of Protestant rectitude, and collectors of verse had to be circumspect in packaging their wares. Whereas in the Middle Ages a shared cultural ideology could be taken for granted, this was after 1560 no longer the case. The factionalism of the Reformation forced poets to a *parti pris*, and condemned them to an inhibiting self-consciousness which is reflected in their literary efforts. One can only wonder to what extent Mary herself was capable of appreciating the profound cultural readjustments which her short reign precipitated.

---

48 William Ramson, 'Bannatyne's Editing', in *Bards and Makars*, ed. A.J. Aitken, M.P. McDiarmid and D.S. Thomson (Glasgow, 1977), 172–83.

THOMAS RIIS

6.   *Soldiers and Divines: Scottish–Danish Relations, 1589–1707*

The marriage of Anne of Denmark to James VI in 1589 ushered in a new era in the relations between Scotland and Denmark. Although the collaboration of the two countries had been rather close around 1500, relations between them had been allowed to dwindle under James V, Mary and the minority of James VI. Relations had never cooled, but the two countries did not need each other any more. Skippers and merchants continued to visit the other country on the basis of the treaty of 1492 which gave to Scots in Denmark – Norway and to Danes and Norwegians in Scotland the same trading rights as those belonging to the *natives*, provided that duties were paid. Moreover, Scottish mercenaries were allowed to fight for the Kings of Denmark – Norway in their wars against Sweden and the Hanseatic towns. Scottish soldiers and mariners served King John at the beginning of the sixteenth century, they took part in Christian II's conquest of Sweden in 1520, and in greater numbers under Frederik II fought against Sweden in the Seven Years' War, 1563–70.

Finally, the question of the Northern Isles had never been properly solved. Pledged as they were to Scotland in 1468–9 as security for the payment of Queen Margaret's dowry, these Norwegian islands had never been redeemed. Every time the Danish-Norwegian government offered to pay, the Scots procrastinated, arguing that such an important decision could not be taken during the minority or absence of their sovereign or that the introduction in 1548–9 of the *ad valorem* duty in the Sound was against the treaty of 1492. For the last time the issue was discussed in the 1660s,[1] and it was left to time to find a solution.

II

Most spectacular among the Scots working in seventeenth century Denmark were the mercenaries fighting in the King of Denmark's wars. Wearing leggings and plaiding, but sometimes even bare-foot and armed with bows, muskets and long knives, they formed a contrast to mercenaries of other nationalities. Their frugal needs made them enduring soldiers capable of guerrilla warfare, where their silent weapons (bow and knife) would not reveal their presence until it was too late.[2]

Some Scots did take part in the War of Kalmar of 1611–13 between Sweden and Denmark-Norway, but the most famous event was the slaughter by the

1 See Gordon Donaldson, 'Problems of Sovereignty and Law in Orkney and Shetland', *Miscellany Two*, ed. D. Sellar, Stair Society 35 (Edinburgh, 1984), pp 13–40.
2 Rigsarkivet, Copenhagen (henceforth RA). TKIA A95 III fasc. 'Skotske Høvedsmænd'. Memorandum by Capt. John Cullen, undated, but probably Autumn 1565.

Norwegians of some 300 Scots that had landed in Norway and were proceeding to fight for the king of Sweden. The event became popularised and distorted in Norwegian folklore.[3] A naturalized Dane of Scottish origin, Andrew Sinclair, who had settled in Denmark in 1591 held a key position in the War of Kalmar as commander of conquered Kalmar. When national regiments were formed after the war, he was nominated colonel of the Scanian regiment; partly for this reason he had to supervise the construction of Christianstad as a fortress town. He was a member of several embassies, mainly to Britain, and was elected to the Rigsråd (Privy Council of Denmark), probably in 1617.[4]

Christian IV took part in a phase of the Thirty Years' War, from 1625 to 1629, but Scottish units do not appear to have been engaged before 1626, although individual Scottish officers had enrolled the year before. Initially they were recruited by the Count of Mansfeld as Christian's ally, but when the Count died at the end of 1626, his Scottish regiment transferred to Christian IV's service. This regiment was led by Sir Donald Mackay of Strathnaver as its colonel and was remarkable by the fact that it had been recruited mainly on a clan basis. The following Scottish regiments (or at least regiments with Scottish officers) fought for Denmark in the Thirty Years' War: Erskine's Horse, Mackay's Foot, Nithsdale's Foot, James Sinclair's Foot, and Spynie's Foot.[5] The latter had suggested to Christian IV that Scottish noblemen and others should establish lists of their clients with the purpose of recruiting the less essential and useless people for military service.[6]

Spynie's proposal touched several important points: the recruiting agent should be a person of some standing he should have useful connections and easy access to people who would agree to volunteer. In taking less useful persons, Spynie followed the ruling of the Scottish Privy Council that had allowed the recruiting of 'idle men'. Several requests to the Privy Council during these years allow us to see the circumstances under which mercenaries were levied. Ties of friendship, family or clanship played a role in the recruiting procedure or in thwarting it. John Lindsay of Bonshaw asked the Privy Council for delivery to him of a certain Alexander Guthrie, servant to Hew Maxwell of Teiling, as he was due to enter Danish service with Lindsay. Probably, Lindsay had addressed himself to Maxwell who had seen to it that Guthrie was enrolled. This was intolerable to Guthrie's relatives, and an action led by Guthrie the Younger of Kincaldrum liberated the recruit.[7] Likewise, relatives, friends and acquaintances were always ready to take care of the deserter and the Privy Council had to forbid this practice several times. Thus deserters from Spynie's and Mackay's regiments were protected by gentlemen and others in the

---

3 RA. TKUA Alm. del 1 no. 9: Latina 1600–15, fol. 289v.–290v. (Christian IV to James VI/I 18/10 and 23/10/1612; Thomas Michell, *History of the Scottish Expedition to Norway in 1612* (London, Edinburgh, New York, Christiania, 1886), *passim*.
4 Thomas Riis, *Should Auld Acquaintance Be Forgot . . . Scottish-Danish relations c. 1450–1707* II (Odense, 1989), p. 74.
5 *Ibid.*, II, pp. 117–43.
6 RA. TKUA Skotland A II 4. The two memoranda probably belong to the beginning of 1628, cf. RA. TKUA. Alm. del 1 no. 10: Latina 1616–31, fol. 207r., 4/2/1628.
7 *Register of the Privy Council of Scotland*, ed. J. H. Burton *et al* (henceforth *RPC Sc*), 2nd Series VIII, p. 379 (5/6/1627).

Southwest (Ayr, Galloway, Nithsdale), as well as in the Northeast (Aberdeen and Kincardine). Besides the deserters certain recruits did not turn up because their masters hindered them from leaving. It is interesting to note that most of the deserters came from towns; of thirty deserters from Captain Blair's company (Spynie's regiment) recruited mainly in Angus and Fife nineteen came from towns,[8] whereas those who obstructed their servants' volunteering were mainly living in the countryside. This was perhaps due to the circumstance that in certain regions (Angus, Fife, Argyll and Lorne) there was a shortage of rural manpower. In this context one understands why the Privy Council interdicted pressganging. According to complaints to the Privy Council, travellers had been forcibly enrolled, peasants taken from the plough, and even innocent people had been hauled out of bed at night.[9]

On the other hand, there was a great many people whom the Scottish government would gladly send abroad to get rid of them. Prisoners could sometimes be released, if they would volunteer and promise not to return to Scotland, and sturdy beggars, vagabonds, idle loiterers, masterless men and gypsies could all be forced to enlist. Lists of idle and masterless men set up for this purpose have survived from a few parishes; they give both economic and moral reasons, although in the commission to the local authorities only economic criteria were mentioned. No doubt too many were enlisted who were unfit for service, but also men that *had* some occupation. Thus, at Auchindore (Aberdeenshire) the minister was delighted at the prospect of getting rid of the local troublemaker: '. . . George Tower . . . is one ewill disposed person, ane drunkard, blasphemer of Godis name, and ane continuall tuilzear, and most fitt to serwe the Kingis Majesties Varres . . .'[10] He was thus taken entirely for moral reasons. It is difficult to dismiss the thought altogether that the local authorities sometimes put Recusants, crypto-Catholics and other dissenters on the lists, but this would require detailed local research.

Our old acquaintance Lord Reay (Donald Mackay) remained faithful to his former master Christian IV of Denmark-Norway. In 1643 the King charged him with recruiting 1,000 Scots infantry, but he did not manage to levy them because of the Civil War. However, individual Scottish officers served in the wars with Sweden of 1643–5, 1657–60 and 1675–79.[11]

In 1689 Danish forces were for once sent to Scotland, on their way to Ireland as an auxiliary corps. The force – 6,000 foot and 1,000 horse – sailed from Ribe on October 7th. It had to travel across Scotland and sail to Carrickfergus in Northern Ireland. Here it fought the Jacobite rebels until 1692; after having completed its mission it went to the Low Countries where it fought the French,[12] which, however, does not concern us in this context.

8 *Ibid.*, 2nd Series VIII, pp. 389–90 (14/6/1627), cf. Riis, *Should Auld Acquaintance Be Forgot* . . . I (Odense, 1989), p. 99.
9 *RPC Sc* 2nd Series I, pp. 603–4 (16/5/1627).
10 Riis, *Should Auld Acquaintance Be Forgot* . . . I, pp. 100–3.
11 *Ibid.* I, pp. 104–5, II, pp. 118–119, 143–47.
12 *Ibid.* I, p. 105.

Several individual Scottish officers served in the Danish navy and remained in Denmark after the end of hostilities. Some of them belonged to the Scottish aristocracy and were consequently recognised as Danish gentlemen. This was the case of John Cunningham who took part in the Danish expeditions to Greenland in 1605 and 1606; in 1619 he was appointed commander of Vardøhus in Northern Norway which he governed until a few months before his death in 1651.[13] His experience as a naval officer in Arctic waters qualified him for this task of governing a vast region and of upholding Christian IV's authority against foreigners in the difficult seas north of Norway.

Other notable Scots serving Danish naval interests were the two shipbuilders David Balfour and Daniel Sinclair, who built several men-of-war for Christian IV's navy. Although both were gentlemen, they did not marry into Danish aristocratic families, nor did they acquire landed property, as far as we know.[14] They belonged more to the bourgeoisie than to the aristocracy and thus represented the type of royal servant that would become much more frequent under the Absolutism after 1660.

Speaking of soldiers, one should mention Colonel Monro whose classical work from 1637 describes the experience of Mackay's regiment in the 30 Years' War and at the same time discusses moral problems connected with warfare and the leadership of men.[15] The books left by Captain Alexander Arrat and his Scottish-born wife (both apparently died from the plague in 1654) give us a glimpse of the cultural universe of a Scottish-Danish officer. Among the fourteen books six were in Scots, while the language cannot be ascertained in two, and the others were in German. Nine books belonged to the field of religion, three to secular literature, and two were medical works. The six books in Scots were a Bible, a prayer book, and David's Psalter plus three classical literary works: two volumes of David Lindsay's works from the mid-sixteenth century and probably Blind Harry's poem from the 1470s about William Wallace.[16] It is difficult to imagine what national classics of a similary venerable age could be found among the books of Arrat's Danish colleagues.

III

A considerable number of Scots settled in Danish towns as merchants or craftsmen. For Denmark as a whole the sixteenth century was the main period of immigration, but it continued in the following century. The geography of emigration to Denmark corresponded to the pattern of Scottish trade: in Jutland Scots are found mainly in the Aalborg region and in Funen only at Odense;

---

13 *Ibid.* II, p. 58.
14 *Ibid.* II, p. 54 (David Balfour) and p. 75 (Daniel Sinclair).
15 R. Monro, *His Expedition with the worthy Scots Regiment* . . . (1637). On the author, see Riis, *Should Auld Acquaintance Be Forgot* . . . II, p. 127.
16 Landarkivet for Sjælland, Lolland-Falster og Bornholm (henceforth LAS). Helsingør Byfogedarkiv. Skifteretsprotokol E 52b, fol. 688 v. - 689r. On the Arrats, see Riis, *Should Auld Acquaintance Be Forgot* . . . II, p. 209.

clearly, they concentrated east of the Great Belt in the provinces on either side of the Sound.

In Scottish trade Denmark proper played a minor role, only in periods of bad harvests in Scotland skippers in greater numbers called at Danish ports in order to complete their westbound cargoes with grain or peas. Baltic ports like Danzig (and after about 1620 Stockholm) attracted Scottish vessels much more than those of Denmark. Before c. 1580 Swedish copper and iron was sent to Danzig and from there to Western Europe. However, Scottish ships had – like other vessels – to call at Elsinore in order to pay the Sound Toll. Thus a Scottish merchant bound for Lübeck would seldom sail directly to Lübeck; he would leave Scotland in a vessel bound for Danzig or Stockholm, and at Elsinore he would change to another one bound for Lübeck. Similarly, merchandise bound for other ports of the region would be unloaded at Elsinore and conveyed further by local and other skippers. Some of the Scots established at Elsinore were engaged in this kind of trade, such as Robert Lorimer between 1610 and 1628[17] and Albert Jack in the 1620s.[18]

Some Scottish traders were pedlars who visited Denmark for the local fairs. A few called more than once in a year which must mean that they were based in Denmark or in one of the cities on the Baltic. Thus John Lindsay who died at Elsinore in 1619 left haberdashery, gloves etc. and had allegedly been employed by Walter Aschen of Greifswald.[19] How vast an area was covered by the itinerant retailers is shown by the Bells' case. In July 1616 Albert Bell wrote from Copenhagen to his servant and probably his kinsman Thomas Bell, who stayed in the inn Zum Heiligen Geist at Rostock. Albert dissuaded him from going to Danzig, where the market would be flooded with goods, and informed him that he himself was leaving for Norway; and with whom he would deposit his remaining goods. When Thomas returned from Güstrow (in Mecklenburg), he should sail for Copenhagen, where he would find a better market for his merchandise than in Danzig. He should remain in the Danish capital for a fortnight before going to Aalborg; after two weeks there he should leave for Elsinore, where he should wait for Albert's return from Norway.[20] During his stay in Copenhagen Thomas must have tried to sell his goods in Malmø, where he suddenly died. His merchandise – according to the inventory, mainly engravings – belonged to Albert Bell[21] and covered a wide range of interests. Catholic and Protestant alike would find edifying pieces, as Bell could furnish images of saints as well as Luther's portrait; for the practical-minded there were books on sewing and lace-making; those interested in current affairs would have to do with pieces showing the funeral of the king of England's son (probably Henry Frederick, who died in 1612). The exploring mind was well served: there were the four quarters of the world, forty-two maps, a copper engraving showing the city of Cologne,

17 Riis, *Should Auld Acquaintance Be Forgot* . . . I, pp. 159–61 and II, p. 229.
18 *Ibid.*, I p. 161 and II, p. 225.
19 *Ibid.*, II p. 229.
20 Malmö Stadsarkiv (henceforth MStA). Magistratens arkiv E IIa: 7: Inkomma handlingar B 426 c 1 (12/7/1616).
21 *Ibid.* nos. B 426 c 2–4 (13/12 [two letters] and 19/12/1617).

another representing Amsterdam, another six paintings and a picture of Constantinople.[22]

Between them the Bells covered a vast region from Norway to Mecklenburg and Pomerania, travelling wherever commercial possibilities appeared most promising at the time, and working singly, but in fairly close contact with each other. For all its primitive nature this type of business organisation was remarkably effective, often more so than enterprises of a more developed kind.

IV

As could be expected the royal marriage of 1589 intensified Scottish-Danish relations, not least in the field of intellectual culture. Apparently the Danish government saw to it that Scottish men of learning and of standing met their Danish equivalents, and the frequent exchange of embassies between 1585 and 1603 furnished many occasions for encounters. The astronomer Tycho Brahe and the theologian Niels Hemmingsen were the leading Danish scholars of their day and those with the greatest international reputation. Obviously, during his sojourn in Denmark James VI both visited Brahe and discussed theological problems with Hemmingsen at Roskilde.

While Scottish visitors might call on Tycho Brahe and Niels Hemmingsen, very few established lasting contacts with Danish professors. On the other hand Nicolaus Theophilus and Niels Krag both taught in the University of Copenhagen and took advantage of their diplomatic missions to Scotland to meet learned Scots. Clearly, most of the Danish professors' Scottish friends belonged not to a university, but to the civil service. In Denmark the situation was not very different: the two internationally famous scholars, Tycho Brahe and Niels Hemmingsen, had not taught in the University of Copenhagen for many years; Theophilus and Krag did so, but their frequent diplomatic missions must have rendered their outlook closer to that of the learned civil servant than to that of the ordinary professor.[23] Krag was even admitted into the Scottish aristocracy and sealed his patent personally, while James VI entertained his guests in the garden of Holyrood.[24]

Further, in the exchanges between Scottish and Danish scholars theological concerns were almost entirely absent, with James VI and Niels Hemmingsen as the exceptions. Although in their private lives the learned civil servants were no agnostics and sometimes demonstrated a profound understanding of theological problems, Divinity was hardly a suitable discipline for a learned gentleman, only for professors and clergy.

At the centre of Scottish-Danish intellectual relations in the 1590s stood Niels Krag[25] and on the Scottish side James VI's famous preceptor Peter Young;[26] no doubt the latter's central position was due to his easy access to his

22 MStA. Rådhusrättens arkiv F IIa: 17. Bouppteckningar no. 505 (1/10/1617).
23 Riis, *Should Auld Acquaintance Be Forgot* . . . I, pp. 121–5.
24 *Ibid.* I, p. 127.
25 On Krag, see *ibid.* II, p. 289.
26 On Young, see *ibid.* II, p. 81.

learned sovereign. When, however, in 1603 the court moved to England, Great Britain's foreign affairs were conducted mainly by English diplomats. In both Denmark and Scotland, new men were taking over, perhaps less because the old generation was disappearing, than because of the changed political framework. At any rate, Christian IV took a much greater interest in architecture and music than in literature and science. It is revealing that no contacts appear to have been made between visiting Scottish scholars and the Aberdonian Andrew Robertson who studied Divinity in Copenhagen from c. 1589; he obtained his master's degree and died in Copenhagen, probably in 1592.[27]

In the decades around 1600 a number of Danes studied at Scottish universities, above all St Andrews, although two brothers were matriculated as students of arts in Marischal College of Aberdeen. The two brothers graduated as Masters in Copenhagen,[28] six Danes obtained their Bachelor degree in St Andrews, and among them two brothers continued to the Master of Arts.

The great majority of Danish students in Scotland found employment at home in the Church or in secondary schools,[29] most of them appear to have had no difficulties afterwards in Denmark because of their studies in Scotland. The greatest number of Danish students in Scotland came at a time when contacts between the two countries were frequent and when their respective churches were not too far from each other. In 1624 the last student of the Danish-Norwegian realm before the eighteenth century matriculated in St Andrews;[30] Divinity was now studied by Danes less abroad than at home (because of the growing tendency towards Lutheran orthodoxy) and the disciplines looked for abroad were better taught elsewhere than in Scotland.

Another Dane, namely James VI's Queen Anne, took an interest in the research of a professor of St Andrews. William Welwood had studied the legal question of maritime territory, distinguishing between oceans and large seas that were open to all nations, and waters near land over which sovereignty could be claimed; islands could help define the sea territory. Thus England could claim sovereignty over the Channel because she governed the Channel Islands. Queen Anne realised that Welwood's work would be useful for both the British and the Danish-Norwegian governments: the latter had since the Middle Ages claimed sovereignty over the North Sea and the Baltic as far as its island possessions in either sea, a point of view exactly corresponding to Welwood's. Queen Anne joined English lawyers and leading Scottish politicians in encouraging Welwood to refute Grotius's 'Mare Liberum'.[31] Anne was correct in thinking that Welwood's ideas were of interest to the two monarchies, especially the Dutch, who had increasingly engaged themselves from 1600 onwards in fishing off Scotland, and who gradually took over part of Scottish navigation to the Baltic.

27 *Ibid.* II, pp. 200–201.
28 Christian and Laurits Sørensen Torndal, cf. *ibid.* II, p. 296.
29 *Ibid.* I, pp. 285–288.
30 *Ibid.* I, p. 291 (the Norwegian Claudius Ericus Brun Marstrandia Arctander).
31 *Ibid.* I, pp. 130–132.

Although in most respects Thomas Kingo (1634–1703) should be considered a purely Danish divine and poet, he ought to be mentioned here, as he was the first person of his family to be born in Denmark. His father John, son of Thomas Kingo, a weaver from Crail probably moved to Denmark about 1620 where he married a Danish woman and worked as a weaver in Slangerup in North Zealand.[32] Their son Thomas finished his studies in Divinity in 1658 and was then for some years a rural 'praeceptor'. From 1661 he was a clergyman and from 1677 to his death bishop of Funen. Today he is above all remembered for his poetic works. He wrote several poems to celebrate important political events as well as religious poetry. His panegyrics to the great of this world may have paved his way to the bishopric, but in the new hymnal of 1699, 29 per cent of the hymns, by far the largest individual share – were by Kingo. Although Kingo was clearly a Lutheran, he appears to have been inspired by English theologians in his pastoral care. Moreover, his extensive libary contained 248 publications in English or by British authors. A little more than half dealt with theology, but science, history and literature were also well represented. He owned several of Francis Bacon's works, Milton's *Paradise Lost*, Shakespeare's *Hamlet* as well as a collection of his poems. The Scottish connection is represented by various works by James VI, the *Life and Acts of Sir William Wallace*, a medical work by Tycho Brahe's pupil Duncan Liddell and by Buchanan's *De iure regni apud Scotos* and *Rerum Scoticarum Historia*.[33]

To my knowledge, Kingo's works have never been studied in order to find out how much British literature influenced him. I have the impression, that he uses classical allegories much less than his contemporaries and his language is plain and straightforward.

This brief survey of part of early modern Scottish–Danish relations cannot possibly exhaust the subject. It is however my hope that it has shown that the connections were much more frequent and closer than might be expected.

32 *Ibid*. I, pp. 132–4 and II, p. 261.
33 *Ibid*. I, pp. 134–6 and II, pp. 65–6.

NED C. LANDSMAN

7. *The Foundations of Cosmopolitan Culture:
    Scottish Involvement Abroad before the American
    Colonisation*

I feel like something of an intruder into the fields of sixteenth- and early seventeenth-century Scotland and its European involvements (not to mention Medieval and Renaissance Language and Literature), since my principal subjects heretofore have all concerned the later seventeenth and eighteenth centuries. Nor have they involved Scotland and Europe, but rather Scotland and Britain, and Scotland and America. Still, it is not merely in self-defence that I will suggest that intrusions can have their advantages; the long view, it has often been shown, allows one to look beyond purely temporary circumstances to establish those features of a society or culture that appear to be integral rather than circumstantial; in short, that function as its structural foundations. For some time, I have been attempting to comprehend Scotland's quite distinctive manner of participation in the British empire in the eighteenth century and after against the background of earlier Scottish enterprises abroad. We are now developing quite an extensive literature on those foreign involvements; to date, that literature has done surprisingly little to alter our basic understanding of Scottish history in the early modern period.

I happen to believe, along with others, that one of the chief deficiencies in our understanding of my period of eighteenth-century Scotland, as it currently exists, is the lack of an adequate historical context for comprehending the very real changes that Scottish culture underwent during the age of Enlightenment, which has too often been understood as the exclusive product of eighteenth-century developments such as the Union and English influences. That is currently being remedied by some very able scholars in a number of fields, including, among intellectual historians, religion, political theory, and philosophy, who have demonstrated, for example, the vital influence of Scottish Renaissance and Presbyterian traditions upon the Enlightenment.[1] What I would like to offer here represents what might be called the under-side of that cultural history, the foundations of Scottish cosmopolitan culture, which was rooted in what came to be very real economic and demographic, but also political and cultural imperatives that developed within Scottish society and culture during a long history of involvement abroad. Those foundations, which developed principally out of Scottish contacts with Europe, would continue to shape Scottish culture long

---

1 Two useful collections that develop this theme are *The Origins and Nature of the Scottish Enlightenment*, ed. R.H. Campbell and Andrew S. Skinner (Edinburgh, 1982) and *Aberdeen and the Enlightenment*, ed. Jennifer J. Carter and Joan H. Pittock (Aberdeen, 1987).

after the specific links around which they grew up had receded in importance; indeed, I will suggest that they would decisively affect Scotland's later participation in Union and empire and help explain the surprisingly cosmopolitan character of the culture of so remote a nation. Emigration was – and has continued to be – an integral part of Scottish culture.

The immediate inspiration for this discussion grew out of a request from a branch of the North American Conference on British Studies for a paper on the subject of Scottish connections with Europe in the eighteenth century, which was chronologically, if not topically, more in keeping with what I was then pursuing. What stood out immediately in that inquiry was not the extensiveness, but rather the narrowness of such contacts during the eighteenth century. To be sure, one could discuss the numerous connections between the Scottish and European literati, as many have. There is now a substantial literature detailing the influence upon Scottish moral philosophy of such Continental traditions as Reformed Protestantism and natural law. Or one could examine the Continental correspondence of such luminaries as Hume, Smith, or Smollett, or the merchants, or anyone connected to the Jacobite Court – the last of those, in particular, a subject with much work still to be done. But overall, according to nearly every available measure, the most striking aspect of Scottish connections with Europe in the eighteenth century was not their frequency but rather their rarity.

They were rare, I would emphasise, by established Scottish standards. By almost every indicator, Scots had had more substantial involvements on the Continent a century or two earlier. They had probably traveled more on the Continent; they certainly had migrated there in far greater numbers, with perhaps as many as 100,000 migrants during the course of the seventeenth century, according to a recent survey by Chris Smout, most of it before 1650; the numbers for the later period cannot have been more than a fraction of that.[2] In the earlier period, Scottish merchants and traders lived and worked extensively in the cities of France, Sweden, Denmark, and the Low Countries, with a community of up to a thousand Scots in Rotterdam before 1700. Scots were especially prevalent in Poland during the sixteenth and early seventeenth centuries, to which as many as 30-40,000 migrated during that last half-century, representing the largest out-migration of Scots to any country during those years, exceeding even Ireland; thereafter, migration to Poland would virtually cease. Nearly as many went to Scandinavia during those years, many, though by no means all, into military service. Over a long period Scotland provided Europe with two familiar figures; the soldier and the peddler, the latter often referred to as 'Scotchmen'.[3]

For all of that, those migrants have barely affected out understanding of the

---

2 T.C. Smout, N.C. Landsman, and T.M. Devine, 'Scottish Emigration in the Seventeenth and Eighteenth Centuries', in *Europeans on the Move: Studies on European Migration, 1500–1800*, ed. Nicholas Canny (Oxford, 1994), pp. 76–112.

3 The classic account remains Gordon Donaldson, *The Scots Overseas* (1966). See also two recent collections: *Scotland and Scandinavia 800–1800*, ed. Grant G. Simpson (Edinburgh, 1990), and *The Scottish Soldier Abroad 1247–1967*, ed. Grant G. Simpson (Edinburgh, 1992), and see the works cited below.

general course of Scottish history, or even of the history of Scots overseas, unless to support such general notions as that of a national 'wanderlust.' It is as though those emigrants had fallen into an historiographical Black Hole. That is illustrated by pairing two recent collections of essays. One, on the topic of *Scotland and Europe* focuses principally on the period before 1700, covering a wide variety of subjects, including relations with France, Denmark, Poland, Sweden, and other places. The lone essay devoted exclusively to the eighteenth century discusses – typically – Smith and Rousseau. By contrast, another recent collection with the much more general title of *The Scots Abroad* confines itself to the period after 1750 and omits Europe entirely.[4] Together they make an uneasy fit. The emphasis of the latter work derives from an interpretation of Scottish history that views mass emigration as a movement of the industrial period and attributes Scotland's opening to the world to the Unions, the empire, and English connections generally. In such a view, the kind of contacts detailed in the first-mentioned volume appear as fragmentary and incidental, where they are noticed at all.

Such an interpretation has matters substantially backwards. Far from opening an isolated Scotland to overseas involvements, in several respects the British unions in fact led to a narrowing of possibilities abroad. Before the Union – exactly how far before is still somewhat sketchy – a surprisingly broad spectrum of Scots ventured and lived abroad in numbers that would not be equalled for centuries thereafter. They included merchants and traders, students and teachers at the Continental universities, soldiers, ministers, and eventually doctors with the Scottish regiments, and others. Most of the essential characteristics we associate with later Scottish involvements in the imperial world were already evident in those contacts. Moreover, instead of eradicating those traditional overseas involvements, Scottish participation in the British empire would at the outset be significantly inhibited by the strength of those earlier connections. Thus rather than Union and empire serving to open up an isolated Scotland, it might more reasonably be suggested that the existing cosmopolitan character of Scottish culture, a legacy of long involvements abroad, was itself responsible for union and empire, or at least for the particular manner in which those were experienced in Scotland.

The first question, then, that we need to address concerns the volume and pattern of emigration from Scotland over the long term. In general, it was more persistent than consistent. The best evidence we have suggests substantial emigration from the fifteenth into the sixteenth century often related to wars on the Continent, climbing in the latter half of the sixteenth, with a peak probably in the 1620s and 30s, and then, except for the famine years of the 1690s, falling off dramatically thereafter. During that period, Scots established regular connections with several sites: Ireland, although not extensively until the seventeenth century, Poland, where many began to go as peddlers from early

4 *Scotland and Europe 1200–1850*, ed. T.C. Smout (Edinburgh, 1986); *The Scots Abroad: Labour, Capital, Enterprise 1750–1914*, ed. R.A. Cage (1985); and see *Scottish Emigration and Scottish Society*, ed. T.M. Devine (Edinburgh, 1993), which establishes a context for the later emigrations but focuses on the period after 1800.

in the sixteenth century, and as soldiers and traders to Scandinavia and later the Netherlands. We can only wish our data here were more precise, but much of the fluctuation in numbers had to do with the level of the population itself. Emigration rose with the rise in population from the mid-sixteenth century and apparently peaked in coincidence with periods of crisis. The decline in emigration at the end of the period resulted from first a levelling off and, during the 1690s an actual decline in population during the years of famine. Significantly, Ireland, and especially the Presbyterian north, which attracted so many of those emigrants during the seventeenth century, including the 1690s, remained a large supplier of emigrants thereafter. Emigration thus served as something of a demographic safety-valve, as it did in other marginal economies. In that sense it was also an extension of the system of domestic mobility, which was also quite substantial and persistent. Historically, the people of Scotland moved with great frequency from farm to farm and even region to region, a behaviour was rooted in a social system that offered tenants few rights to the land, little stake in their farms, and little reason to remain attached to them, especially in times of hardship. Those were the perfect conditions for maintaining a floating population.[5]

Emigration was more than just a safety valve. Even in the best of times, Scotland exported some emigrants, and there were always large communities of both native and identifiable second-generation Scots living abroad. Moreover, Scotland attracted few foreigners and was always a net exporter of population, perhaps the most consistent net exporter of people in western Europe. If we turn those observations around and look at their implications for Scotland, the system of emigration allowed the rural countryside to produce a consistent surplus of population and to sustain a considerably higher population of Scots at home and abroad than a purely domestic and highly rooted social system would have supported. Emigration and migration functioned as economic and demographic imperatives of the social system. The population of identifiable 'Scots' has always been considerably larger than the population of Scotland. (The system was functional for the countries of Europe as well, as marginal economies such as Scotland's provided the reserve armies upon which they could call in war time)

More than just numbers made Scottish travels on the Continent significant; the emigrants contained substantial numbers of trained and educated persons, including merchants, traders, military officials, ministers, doctors, and university men, of which Scotland was a consistent net exporter also. The raw numbers, of course, were not great. But again, if we turn the question around, the significant points for Scotland are that the continual migration of such persons allowed Scotland to maintain a higher level of commerce than would have been possible

---

5 Smout, Landsman, and Devine, 'Scottish Emigration in the Seventeenth and Eighteenth Centuries'. On domestic mobility, see Malcolm Gray, 'Scottish Emigration: The Social Impact of Agrarian Change in the Rural Lowlands, 1775–1875', *Perspectives in American History*, 7 (1973), 95–174; R.A. Houston and C.W.J. Withers, 'Migration and the Turnover of Population in Scotland, 1600–1900', *Annales de Démographie Historique* (1990), pp. 285–308; and Ned C. Landsman, *Scotland and its First American Colony 1680–1765* (Princeton, 1985), pp. 29–36, 41–5.

had Scots merchants not actively ventured abroad to seek it, more active links to the Continental world of Letters to which they became notably attached, and a consistently greater number of educated men than the domestic economy could support. Thus before the establishment of Scottish medical schools in the eighteenth century, one found numerous Scottish doctors educated abroad, most famously at Leyden in the seventeenth century, and then finding employment outside of Scotland, often with the Scottish regiments. Scottish ministers regularly served Scottish congregations on the Continent and in Ireland; Rotterdam, for one, became an important post within the Church of Scotland, which often trained more ministers than it had ministries.[6] In a certain sense, the interest of Scottish elites in education, and their identification with European Letters, depended upon the ability to send people and find places abroad. For those groups, we might consider migration and travel to have been imperatives of the Scottish cultural system.

The migration of elite groups was directed into particular channels, to which they adhered with considerable persistence. For scholars in particular France was an early receiving point for a number of reasons, including, but not limited to, political alliance, and would continue so even after the Reformation. Gordon Donaldson cites 400 Scots at the university of Paris in the sixteenth century; many others went also to the Huguenot universities. Merchants ventured to the commercial centers in the Low Countries at Rotterdam and Campveere and to Poland, Denmark and Sweden. There they developed a reputation for aggressiveness and clannishness, as Donaldson noticed long ago. That was part of a general strategy employed by weak commercial powers of actively seeking out particular niches for themselves and trading principally through extended networks of their own countrymen. Thus much of Scotland's trade with the Baltic in the sixteenth century, for example, was conducted by Scottish merchants who went there to seek it, whereas England and other powers apparently traded through German intermediaries. The Scottish staple at Veere and its trading community in Rotterdam were other cases.[7]

The increasing Scottish ties to England after the Reformation did surprisingly little to alter the general pattern. In some ways it did the opposite. The growing need among Scottish merchants to compete directly with their more numerous and better-funded English counterparts probably reinforced existing commercial strategy and made them even more aggressively Scottish and clannish in their trading than before. All of this represented what might be considered a third, political and commercial imperative of Scottish culture, the persistent necessity of finding ways of combatting and competing with their consistently wealthier and more powerful neighbours to the south, whose military and commercial presence were so long of 'paramount importance' in Scottish history, to borrow William

---

6 Donaldson, *Scots Overseas*, chap. 2; and see David Hamilton, *The Healers: A History of Medicine in Scotland* (Edinburgh, 1981), chaps. 3–4.

7 Donaldson, *Scots Overseas*, chap. 2; Smout, Landsman, and Devine, 'Scottish Emigration in the Seventeenth and Eighteenth Centuries' and J. Davidson and A. Gray, *The Scottish Staple at Veere: A study in the Economic History of Scotland* (1909).

Ferguson's phrase.[8] That of course was the theory of the 'Auld Alliance,' whose importance I don't wish to overstate; it was perhaps more important in such areas as commerce and Letters, a significant theme of which was the establishment of the historical independence of the Scottish monarchy, and other related national matters, as a number of scholars have pointed out.[9] The appeal of Continental traditions derived from both positive and negative incentives.

Not until rather late in the day did England become an important recipient of Scots migrants. That was partly because they were rarely welcomed there, and partly because of the lack of any real economic purpose to setting up an extensive commerce with England other than that of the border trade; thus for many years most Scottish peddlers in England were found in the Border regions. Moreover, Scotland's continuing involvement in the worlds of Reformed religion and Continental Letters separated the interests of many Scottish men of intellect from the very different traditions emerging in England. Scots were often not especially welcomed at English universities nor did many aspire to go there, having more in common with specific European traditions in religion, law, philosophy and medicine, and having based a considerable part of Scottish identity upon those traditions.

Neither did the American colonisation significantly affect the pattern, contrary to what common wisdom suggests. For nearly a century and a half after England began to colonise the New World under the dominion of Stuart Kings, the emigration of Scots to America was rather insubstantial. The promoters of Nova Scotia and New Galloway early in the seventeenth century met with scant response from their countrymen; in fact, the evidence suggests that a majority of the small group of settlers that actually went to those colonies during the 1620s were probably English.[10] A subsequent attempt to engage a Scottish voyage to New York failed.[11] Not until almost the end of the century would Scottish promoters achieve anything like a successful settlement in the New World, at East Jersey, which would hardly compare even on a *per capita* basis to the simultaneous and related English colonisation of Pennsylvania.[12]

That unenthusiastic response on the part of potential Scottish settlers was not rooted in any unwillingness to venture abroad; the same decades that witnessed the meager Nova Scotia settlement saw perhaps 20,000 Scots depart for the plantations in Ireland and similar numbers for Poland and the Continental regiments. Both Ireland and the military continued to draw more Scots than

---

8 William Ferguson, *Scotland's Relations With England: A Survey to 1707* (Edinburgh, 1977), p. vi.
9 See, for example, Roger A. Mason, 'Scotching the Brut: Politics, History and National Myth in Sixteenth-Century Britain', in *Scotland and England 1286–1815*, ed. Roger A. Mason (Edinburgh, 1987).
10 N.E.S. Griffiths and John G. Reid, 'New Evidence on New Scotland', *William and Mary Quarterly*, 3rd ser., 49 (1992), 492–508; and Reid, *Acadia, Maine, and New Scotland: Marginal Colonies in the Seventeenth Century* (Toronto, 1981).
11 Peter Gouldesbrough, 'An Attempted Scottish Voyage to New York in 1669', *Scottish Historical Review*, 40 (1961), 56–62.
12 Landsman, *Scotland and its First American Colony*, and see George Pratt Insh, *Scottish Colonial Schemes, 1620–1686* (Glasgow, 1922).

America for the rest of the century. The irony is that far from introducing a new era in Scottish emigration, those American promotions would utterly fail to compete with established opportunities for Scots on the Continent. The level of emigration was still a function of available population. Not until the middle of the eighteenth century would the traditional mechanism of military service during the Seven Years' War begin to draw Scots to America in substantial numbers, and that was long after some of the traditional locations, especially Poland, had faded in importance.[13]

Thus early modern Scotland, before the Union or the American colonisation, had developed a distinctly and distinctive cosmopolitan character, based upon the maintaining of substantial communities of Scots abroad, sustaining commercial and educational links to the Continent that were integral to Scotland's economy and culture, and finding places abroad to employ the excess of the trained and the learned. Scots were known for, and identified, with their skills in arms, commerce, and learning. And as an isolated and somewhat vulnerable nation with a powerful neighbour upon its only border, Scottish nationals used their connections aggressively – commercially, politically, and culturally – in order to counter England's potentially dominating influence.

I return to all of this because in recent years it has become something of a commonplace to attribute the cosmopolitan character of eighteenth-century Scotland, as well as that nation's active participation in empire, to the effects of the Unions and of English relationships. Indeed, despite the demonstration by recent historians of such pre-Union innovations in Scotland as the improvement of agriculture, the reformation of university curricula, and numerous other advances in learning, that interpretive edifice has remained largely unaltered. If we view Scottish participation in imperial affairs within the wider context of the longer history of Scottish involvement abroad, we have materials to turn a part of that argument on its head. Rather than English influences opening up Scotland to active involvement abroad, it might more reasonably be suggested that the particular history of Scottish involvement abroad rather decisively affected the English relationship, helping to shape Scotland's distinctive imperial role and the way that Enlightened Scots would approach political and commercial issues generally. In short, those cosmopolitan foundations would greatly influence the nature of Scotland's British, imperial, and cultural identities.

The imperial activities of Scottish doctors provide a good example. Physicians from Scotland were ubiquitous figures in the eighteenth-century empire, and many hundreds settled in the American colonies, including the West Indies. Not only did they fill most of the important medical posts in those places, but such notable figures as William Douglass, Cadwallader Colden, and Alexander Garden all were prominent in cultural life generally and published on topics far beyond those one would strictly classify as 'medical', which would be

---

13 On those later migrations, see Ian Charles Cargill Graham, *Colonists From Scotland: Emigration to North America, 1707–1783* (Ithaca, New York, 1956) and especially Bernard Bailyn, *Voyagers to the West: A Passage in the Peopling of America on the Eve of the Revolution* (New York, 1986).

characteristic of Scottish physicians long after. The importance those physicians attained has often been attributed to the prominence of Edinburgh's medical school in the eighteenth century, in fact; the proliferation of medical men from Scotland preceded the rise of Edinburgh in that field. Most of the prominent early practitioners in the colonies had studied at Leyden, where most Scots seeking university training then went for medical degrees. Like their countrymen who had served previously in the Scottish regiments, they had to look for places abroad because of the lack of sufficient opportunities at home. For them, the American colonies provided a necessary and promising field, even at a time of reduced emigration from Scotland over all. The proliferation and prominence of Scottish doctors in the colonies had less to do with the Enlightening of Scottish medicine in the eighteenth century, which itself would follow the Leyden model of empirical medical instruction, than with a continuing Renaissance interest in Continental studies. Moreover, the rise of Scottish medical training itself – the medical Enlightenment – depended in no small part upon the continuing ability of those aspiring doctors to find the places abroad that still were not available at home.[14]

The same would be true of Scottish ministers, of which the universities would also produce a surplus. Through the seventeenth century, they regularly served the numerous congregations of Scots in Europe, as well as in Ireland. By the end of the century, both Presbyterian and Scottish Episcopal ministers would find places in America, also before many of their congregants would do so. In particular, the American colonies would provide a veritable refuge for displaced Scottish Episcopalians after 1688, whose roots in the eastern Scottish cities of Edinburgh and Aberdeen provided a background filled with Continental influences, and who included some of the most Enlightened men of the age. In fact, James McLachlan has recently confirmed the importance of America as a receiving-point for Scottish university men of all sorts during the eighteenth century.[15]

Even those Scottish merchants who flocked to the Chesapeake until they came to dominate the tobacco trade illustrate the continuity of imperial participation with previous involvements abroad. To be sure the rise of Glasgow depended heavily upon the new American commerce, but the novel commercial methods her merchants used to take over the trade were not all that novel by Scottish standards. The sophisticated 'store' system they employed, and the integrated and structured company businesses all had significant antecedents in Scottish trading at Rotterdam and at Veere. And to the extent that that form of structured trading itself became a model for most of the numerous Scottish

---

14 Hamilton. *The Healers*, chap. 4; also Raymond Phineas Stearns, *Science in the British Colonies of America* (Urbana, Illinots, 1970), chap. 11, and Brooke Hindle, *The Pursuit of Science in Revolutionary America 1735–1789* (Chapel Hill, 1956), chap. 2.
15 McLachlan, 'The Scottish Intellectual Migration to British America in the Seventeenth Century: New England and the Chesapeake', unpublished paper delivered Columbia University seminar, September, 1992. Provost R. Foskett, 'Some Scottish Episcopalians in the North American Colonies, 1675–1750', *Records of the Scottish Church History Society*, 14 (1963), 135–50.

commercial writers during the Enlightenment – Adam Smith here is the exception rather than the rule – their perspectives also may be said to have developed out of older Scottish involvements in the European sphere.[16]

Perhaps most importantly, the pattern of Scotland's European involvements also affected the *content* of national discussions during the age of Union and empire. The whole Union debate in Scotland, as it has been elaborated recently by John Robertson, suggests the legacy in Scotland of Continental traditions of political discussion and traditional Scottish concerns. Robertson has shown that both opponents and proponents of union were less concerned with the fate of Scottish nationality *per se* than with establishing a form of union that would protect the weaker power from domination by their stronger southern neighbors. To achieve that both sides drew upon the political theory of the confederation, which was taken principally from European models, at a time when the evolution of English parliamentary discussions left little space for the concept of confederation. They applied it to the problem of countering metropolitan power within a united kingdom. The opposers, led by Andrew Fletcher, set out to substitute for an incorporating union one or another variety of federal union designed to protect Scotland from English encroachment, in part by first remedying Scotland's economic deficiencies through commercial growth, on the model of the United Provinces. Fletcher, of course, even offered the radical suggestion of a trans-European confederation in which all nationalities would be suppressed and subdivided.[17]

As a number of writers have suggested, Union supporters accepted and built upon several of those premises. They shared the federal unionists' reservations about the capacity of a two-party union linking such unequal powers to protect Scottish interests, but argued instead that the best way to guarantee Scottish rights and, especially, to promote the commercial development necessary to protect Scottish interests, would be the wholesale reconstruction of the political nation, subsuming England as well as Scotland into a larger British identity. To be sure, the Union never achieved that in fact, largely because of the lack of interest in any such thing in southern Britain; it is clear that Scots would remain the most aggressive, and perhaps the only real promoters of a British identity thereafter.[18]

Probably the greatest manifestation of that sort of Britishness would be the aggressive Scottish participation in the empire. They included merchants, doctors, clergymen, and public officials of all sorts. The most notable Scots in

---

16 Jacob R. Price, 'The Rise of Glasgow in the Chesapeake Tobacco Trade', *William and Mary Quarterly*, 3rd ser., 11 (1954), 179–99; and Thomas M. Devine, *The Tobacco Lords: A Study of the Tobacco Merchants of Glasgow and their Trading Activities c. 1740–1790* (Edinburgh, 1975). A useful discussion of Scottish commercial writers is Istvan Hont, 'The Rich Country-Poor Country Debate in Scottish Classical Political Economy', in *Wealth and Virtue: The Shaping of Political Economy in the Scottish Enlightenment*, ed. Istvan Hont and Michael Ignatieff (Cambridge, 1983), pp. 271–316.
17 John Robertson, 'An Elusive Sovereignty: the course of the Union Debate in Scotland 1698–1707', in *A Union for Empire: Political Thought and the British Union of 1707*, ed. John Robertson (Cambridge, 1995), pp. 198–227.
18 *Ibid.*, along with numerous other essays by Robertson and Nicholas Phillipson, among others.

America were the imperial officials, still another group of educated Scots who set out to find their places abroad, and who appeared all out of proportion to their numbers. So aggressive were those administrators in supporting commercial and imperial ties between Britain and America that they, like the Scottish merchants, developed the reputation in America as pronounced imperialists and tools of empire. In fact, I have suggested elsewhere that those myriad officials should be viewed as educated men of the Enlightenment who developed distinctive, coherent and cosmopolitan views of imperial affairs. In several respects their goals resembled those of the Union proponents simultaneously to develop and strengthen the colonies while binding them closer to the empire. But their subject was no longer simply Scotland and England, or even Scotland and Europe, but provinces and empire, and the empire they envisioned looked less like an empire than a broad commercial union with strong federal connotations, based upon the dual principles of equity and development. Moreover in their view, the promotion of provincial growth was itself a means of securing the interests of weaker parties within the empire. That view would find its most explicit expression in Adam Smith's recommendation that the empire be preserved by the creation of an imperial parliament that would, inevitably, move to America, along with population and revenues. That seemed an unusual suggestion at the time everywhere except in Scotland, where such an eventuality was predicted quite routinely.[19] In offering such arguments, those officials managed to build upon Continental traditions and traditional Scottish concerns. At the same time, they established places for themselves as Scottish men of Letters living within a larger world of Scottish involvements abroad, and using those connections aggressively to secure national interests and prestige. All of that made those officials into a surprisingly cosmopolitan class of provincials.

---

19 Ned C. Landsman, 'The Legacy of the British Union for the North American Colonies', in Robertson (ed.), *Union for Empire*, pp. 297–317.

IAIN CRICHTON SMITH

8.   *The Experience of Being a Bilingual Writer*

I am bilingual in two languages, Gaelic and English. Gaelic was my first language, which I spoke exclusively in the house till the age of five when I went to school, where I was immediately introduced to English. Thus I spoke English in the school and Gaelic at home. The teachers in the school, though most of them would have been Gaelic-speaking, spoke English, and taught through the medium of English.

At the age of eleven I left my village school and went to the main school on the island which was situated in the only town on the island, Stornoway. There I spoke English in the school, English in the playground, since the town children didn't speak Gaelic: and Gaelic at home.

I studied Gaelic as a subject in that school, and was introduced to some of the great figures in Gaelic literature who were almost exclusively poets. There were no novels, no short stories, no books for children: there was some prose but on the whole it was not creative prose.

I began to write when I was quite young, perhaps eleven. The first poem I remember composing, rather than writing, was in Gaelic. It was in 1939 and Neville Chamberlain was touring Europe in pursuit of peace carrying an umbrella. It was about him that my poem was.

In general, however, my poems were in English. They were imitations of Keats, Shelley and other poets. One of my favourite poets was Kipling because I could read him aloud with great rhythmical verve.

As time passed, and I became an older adolescent, I discovered Auden, Eliot, etc. At this time, *Penguin New Writing* edited by John Lehmann was the magazine to get. I was writing a few Gaelic poems, but my desire was to write good English poems.

When I went to Aberdeen University at the age of seventeen, I was writing more and more in English. I had read by this time my first Gaelic book of contemporary poetry – and practically the only one – *Dain do Eimhir* by Sorley Maclean, which spoke of the Spanish Civil War and contained some great love poetry. My models were therefore on the whole English poets such as Auden and Eliot, and Spender.

Why was this? I think it was because there were few Gaelic poets at that time writing in a contemporary mode. It was also because most of my life I had been reading English literature including at various stages, Dickens, P. C. Wren, Stevenson.

Oliver Twist was a great favourite of mine. I remember also reading a book about a public school, I can't recall its exact title, which told of a boy who was dying in school hospital while he listened to the sound of cricket bats. This was me on the Island of Lewis, where of course football was the main game.

Thus, because of the paucity of literature in Gaelic, my imagination was dominated by English literature.

I studied Celtic in Aberdeen University. I had intended doing Celtic-English Honours but eventually dropped Celtic mainly because it concentrated too much on the aspect of language and too little on literature, and not at all on such little contemporary Gaelic literature as there was.

I was at that time very interested in existentialism, especially Camus and Sartre, and wanted to read them. I didn't like Anglo-Saxon literature either, apart from a few short poems, and would also have dropped that if I could. I was not interested in language, I was only interested in literature.

After my time in university was over, the family for various reasons went to live in Dumbarton, in the Lowlands, not far from Glasgow, and strangely enough I was writing a few Gaelic short stories for the BBC in Glasgow. After a few years in Dumbarton I went to Oban High School, to teach English.

Oban is a little town addicted to Bed and Breakfast. There is some Gaelic spoken there, or rather I should say there are some Gaelic-speakers there, mainly from the islands such as Barra, Uist, etc.

In Oban at that time I was writing in English and Gaelic. My Gaelic creative work was mainly in the short story, which I think I developed artistically. This has been, I think, my main contribution to modern Gaelic literature, the short story. Before I began to write we had hardly any short stories artistically developed; we had really anecdotes, some about the supernatural. I have written over the years a large number of Gaelic short stories, some poems, some plays, one or two short novels.

I began to write Gaelic plays because I was invited by an amateur Oban Gaelic company. The plays were short, usually about half an hour. Again, there is very little tradition of drama in Gaelic. Most of the plays are one-actors and not of a terribly high standard. Also, in Lewis, the island from which I come, the church was and is still opposed to drama.

Thus I was writing in Oban, in both Gaelic and English.

It is important to remember that I was not speaking Gaelic. One of the problems of the Gaelic writer, and I mean by that the writer who is writing exclusively in Gaelic, is that for economic reasons he has to leave the Gaelic heartland to come to the city, where he does not speak Gaelic. Some of our best Gaelic writers have been academics who worked in universities in the cities such as Aberdeen and Glasgow.

I have continued to write some Gaelic, but not as much as I wrote once. My main language is now English; I hardly ever speak Gaelic.

One of the problems this involves is that not only do I not feel on my pulses the problems in the Gaelic area which might develop into art, but also I lose what might be called the authentic 'blas' or taste of the language.

I suppose there are two types of Gaelic writer now. There is the Gaelic writer who no longer lives on the Gaidhealtachd but continues to write in Gaelic. There is also the Gaelic writer who lives on the Gaidhealtachd. A poet like Derick Thomson would belong to the first category, a novelist like Norman Campbell to the second category.

In the past, Gaelic writers, especially poets, who for various reasons lived in Glasgow, would write mostly nostalgic poems about their childhood. Their island was a kind of Eden from which they had been evicted to a Glasgow they never wrote about. Their island homes remained fixed, and they would hate them to change. Such poems were not of any use to developing Gaelic literature.

A poet like Derick Thomson, who has lived in Glasgow most of his life, was in the beginning writing about his island, though not in a nostalgic way. Now he is writing as a Gaelic writer about contemporary Glasgow. Thus he will write:

> Glasgow,
> wrinkled,
> with the paint cracking
> standing
> unsteadily
> on high heels

where Glasgow is drab and being rebuilt, but is also seen as a picture of a woman, perhaps a prostitute. This is very far from the nostalgic poetry of the earlier Glasgow Gaelic-writing poet who will write of the 'glen where he was young.' In Derick Thomson's new book there are poems about Rumania, Chernobyl, Freud, and even an ironic one about Princess Diana. Such a poet will have as his credo that the Gaelic poet will be able to write about any subject. And indeed during Thomson's editorship of the Gaelic magazine 'Gairm' this credo has been put into action. Along with traditional writings we have had translations of modern European poets and prose writers. Thomson has edited a book of these translations into Gaelic of some European poets.

Now, on the other hand, the writer from the Gaidhealtachd, that is to say who has remained on the Gaidhealtachd, may write while aware of modern developments, but he will write of indigenous people, sometimes in a dialect of Gaelic which will appear contemporaneously authentic.

I may say that clearly I have belonged to the first category. My mode of life has taken me away from the island and into the world outside it. Also, I write in both Gaelic and English, which these other writers do not.

I have written in modes which were not traditional in Gaelic, that is, a science fiction story, a detective story, etc. One of the problems of writing from within the Gaidhealtachd on traditional themes is that so many of these themes have been used already. Writers such as I have therefore been accused of Anglicising Gaelic literature. For instance, I wrote a story about an American president who was deciding whether or not to use the nuclear bomb. I also wrote a Gaelic play set in Troy. I was attacked for that: these were not traditional Gaelic themes. And of course they weren't. On the other hand, should Gaelic be confined to a laager of its own?

These problems would not arise if Gaelic were not a weak language. Only 65,000 people speak it, according to the latest census. We do not know how many read or write it, since many Gaelic speakers do not read or write the language. Very few of these people again would understand or appreciate a book by a modern Gaelic poet writing with a modern sensibility. Furthermore, when I went to school at the age of five, it was not a question of Gaelic having equal status with English. English was the dominant language and Gaelic was not spoken in the school at all. Even when it was taught as a subject it was taught in English.

The number of people for whom the Gaelic writer is writing is very small. Furthermore, there is a certain ethos among these people. Thus a Gaelic writer would not write sexually explicit scenes. Only recently, having reviewed a first-rate Gaelic novel, I was surprised to see that the criticism of it by a reviewer was on moral grounds and the use of certain language, even though this was only to a very limited extent.

Now there are certain people in the Gaelic world who would perhaps feel that I am being a traitor to the Gaelic language in writing in English. I feel that myself at times, there is no question of that.

On the other hand, the literature on which I grew up was an English literature. I cannot deny that as a literature I love it or that to my mind it is one of the greatest literature the world has ever known. I would never on purely nationalistic grounds say that I should never read English literature. Hugh MacDiarmid, in his defence of Scots, despised English literature. I would never do that. Associated with my childhood is, for instance, *Oliver Twist* or *Great Expectations*. And yet there is a black star of guilt pulsing inside me.

This does not mean that I do not admire the poetry of certain Gaelic poets such as William Ross, or Duncan Ban Macintyre, some of whose works I have translated, and in the present century poets like Sorley Maclean, Derick Thomson and Donald Macaulay. These poets themselves are aware of other poets from other languages and other regions of the world.

As time has passed I find that I am writing more in English than in Gaelic. Does this mean that I have been completely colonised internally, and that the English language has done its job well? I think this is probably right. This is a very delicate area and much dishonesty can be spoken about it. Maybe some years ago I would not have been so frank, or perhaps not so clear-headed.

I think one of the problems was, firstly, that there were no Gaelic books suitable to me that I could have read in my childhood. Secondly, in my adolescence there were few Gaelic poets that I could have called modern. Since adolescence is the time when our idealistic ardours for poets is at its height, this was unfortunate. My memories at university are of Auden and Eliot, as I have said already.

A curious thing happened to me when I was at university and I am a little ashamed of it. A friend of mine from my village died and I was asked to write an obituary for him. I quoted Paul Valery (in English) in that obituary. Was that me trying to show off my learning at the expense of the village? I think this is true to a certain extent.

When one is an adolescent, one becomes intellectually rebellious. It is possible that in that confusion Gaelic suffered as well. And of course Sartre and Camus were a new world to me. They seemed to be speaking to many of my concerns which were not confined to the Highlands or my island.

Such concerns as I have mentioned are now surfacing with regard to television. Recently, the Gaelic world was given £9 million to spend on Gaelic programmes, curiously enough by a Tory government. The question of subtitles arose. Gaelic programmes on BBC1 are not subtitled on the grounds that they are for an indigenous Gaelic population, who do not need subtitles. STV programmes are subtitled presumably to attract a wider audience. Here we have again in dramatic form the conflict between the purists and those who wish to reach out to a wider world, and are in effect perhaps surrendering to English. It is the question of having a few good authentic men, or a lot of 'diluted' men.

I come back to this question of colonisation. Curiously enough recently I heard in the poetry of Derek Walcott a voice that I recognised; as when recalling his kinship with Africa he writes:

> The gorilla wrestles with the superman
> I who am poisoned with the blood of both
> where shall I turn, divided to the vein?
> I who have cursed
> the drunken officer of British rule
> how choose between this Africa and the English tongue I love?
> How can I face such slaughter and be cool.
> How can I turn from Africa and live.

Derick Thomson has written very movingly about the English and Gaelic tongues in a poem called 'Coffins' and which I will translate into English.

> A tall thin man
> with a short beard
> and a plane in his hand:
> whenever I pass
> a joiner's shop in the city
> and the scent of sawdust comes to mind
>
> memories return of that place
> with the coffins,
> the hammers and nails,
> saws and chisels,
> and my grandfather bent
> planing shavings
> from a thin bare plank.
> Before I knew what death was
> or had any notion, a glimmering

of the darkness, a whisper of the stillness.
And when I stood at his grave
on a cold spring day not a thought
came to me of the coffins
he made for others:
I merely wanted home
where there would be talk, and tea and warmth.

And in the other school also
where the joiners of the mind were planing
I never noticed the coffins
though they were sitting all around me:
I did not recognise the English braid,
the Lowland varnish being applied to the wood
I did not read the words on the brass,
I did not understand that my race was dying . . .

Until the cold wind of this spring came
to plane the heart,
until I felt the nails piercing me
and neither tea nor talk will heal the pain.

What is clear here is that the world of Gaelic culture was being taken away from him at a time when he could not appreciate it, that is, at the age of five. Therefore, there was no choice involved. I have not seen this put better than by the Irish writer, Daniel Corkery:

> The difficulty is not alone a want of native moulds, it is rather the want of a foundation upon which to establish them. Everywhere in the mentality of the Irish people are flux and uncertainty. Our national consciousness may be described in a native phrase as a quaking bog. It gives no footing: it is not English nor Irish nor Anglo-Irish: as will be understood if one thinks a while on the thwarting it undergoes in each individual child of the race as he grows into manhood. Though not quite true, let us take it that the Irish born child is as Irish in his instincts, in his emotions, as the English child is English: the period of education comes on: all that the English child learns buttresses while it refines his emotional nature. Practically all the literature he reads focuses for him the mind of his own people; so also does the instruction he hears. At a later stage if he comes to read a foreign language he seizes what he reads in it with an English mind. He has something of his own by which to estimate its value for him.
>
> How different with the Irish child! No sooner does he begin to use his intellect than what he learns begins to undermine, to weaken, and to harass his emotional nature. For practically all that he reads is English. What he reads in Irish is not yet worth taking account of. It does not therefore focus his mind on his own people, teaching him the better to look about him, to understand both himself

and his surroundings. It focuses instead the life of another people ... His surroundings begin to seem unvital. His education instead of buttressing and refining his emotional nature teaches him rather to despise it inasmuch as it teaches him not to see the surroundings out of which he has sprung as they are in themselves but as compared with alien surroundings: his education provides him with an alien medium through which he is henceforth to look at his native land.

Sometimes in certain poets, as Derick Thomson, this loss becomes a sort of heartbreak.

Clearly there are disadvantages in writing in Gaelic. One of the main ones is that one's potential audience is very limited. The average Gaidheal is not a reader of Gaelic books. Furthermore, he would find modern Gaelic poetry difficult. Thus, modern texts and, generally speaking, all literary texts will be read mostly in schools or in universities. Also, because Gaelic poetry books are accompanied by English translations we have the phenomenon of a lot of modern Gaelic poets being read in translation. Not only that, but they are written about as if they were English poets. A number of the people who have written about the poetry of Sorley Maclean, for instance, are not Gaelic speakers at all, and do not read Gaelic. This leads, I think, to critical judgments being made which compare them to writers outside the Gaelic tradition. This probably wouldn't happen if the poet's original languages were, say, French or German. The problem is that Gaelic is not a major language: and yet of course Gaelic has its own tradition, its own idiosyncratic poetic instruments.

As well as this, many major Gaelic texts have been very badly translated. A great poet like William Ross has been translated scandalously by translators who have no poetic tact whatsoever, and translate in a very old-fashioned not to say incoherent manner, using all sorts of outdated poeticisms.

However, there are advantages in writing in Gaelic. Many areas have not been covered at all. The novel, for instance, is very weak in Gaelic, though more recently there have been one or two good ones. Still, there is much scope here. I myself have written a space fiction short novel for children. I have written a kind of detective story. Whole areas are waiting to be filled with forms unknown to Gaelic literature.

In the past, Gaelic poetry too was confined to the concerns of the Highlands. However, one of the most interesting aspects of Sorley Maclean's *Dain do Eimhir* was its references to the Spanish Civil War. At the heart of the book, lyrically very moving and wholly in the Gaelic tradition, is its conflict between the private and the public. Is the loved one an indulgence when great events are transforming the world? As the poet himself puts it,

> I did not take a cross's death
> in the sore extremity of Spain
> and how then should I expect
> the one new gift of fate?

or in the original Gaelic,

> Cha d'ghabh mise bàs croinn – ceusaidh
> ann an éiginn chruaidh na Spàinn,
> is ciomar sin bhiodh dùil agam
> ri aon duais ùir an dain?

The duality that is at the heart of the development of Gaelic poetry continues. Some young poets write within the tradition, some have been influenced by writers outside Gaelic altogether, and by forms which are not indigenous to Gaelic. The balancing act continues. How does one keep the 'blas' or 'taste' of Gaelic if one moves into areas outside Gaelic? This is the central hub of the matter.

I return to Walcott; he writes, in 'Codicil,'

> Schizophrenic, wrenched by two styles,
> one a hack's hired prose, I earn
> my exile . . .

Or (thinking mainly of his African blood and of English literature) he writes:

> I had entered the house of literature as a houseboy
> filched as the slum child stole
> as the young slave appropriated
> those heirlooms temptingly left
> with the Victorian homilies of Noli Tangere . . .

Or, in another poem,

> My sign is Janus
> I saw with twin heads,
> and everything I say is contradicted.

My own sign incidentally is Janus, and I look around me with double gaze.

I have written a little poem about this. It is called 'The Jester' of 'The Fool'. The idea is that the jester wore a tunic of two colours, say red and black; these represent Gaelic and English. I end by saying, what happens if it rains and the colours run into each other?

Here is the poem in an English translation:

> In the dress of the fool, the two colours that have
> tormented me, English and Gaelic, black and red, the
> court of injustice, the reason for my anger, and that fine
> rain from the mountains and these grievous storms from
> my mind streaming the two colours together so that
> I will go with poor sight in the one colour that is so odd
> that the King himself will not understand my conversation.

I have mentioned already poems that try to extend the range of Gaelic themes. Here is a poem about Freud, which I wrote a number of years ago for no other reason than that, because my work deals so much with the human mind, I have been always interested in the great psychologist. Whether you will get from this a Gaelic 'blas', in other words whether you will find it different from an English poem on the same theme, I leave you to judge. My English translation is a prose one:

> Great man from Vienna, who opened the mind with a knife keen with sore efficient happy light, and who saw the seas sweating with the blue green ghosts of plague, and uncountable riches.
>
> I follow the beasts with a joy that I cannot tell though I should be fishing from dungeon or from prison, as they move on that sea bottom in the freedom of truth with their great helmets. No one will bring them to shore.
>
> Cancer took your jaw away. But you were scanning with profundity the bottom of that sea where there are horrifying shadows. Father, mother and daughter entwined together in a Greek play, in a strangling of forests.
>
> The letter that I shall not send, the letter that I will not keep, the poetry that my head cannot put together, the history that I would not want anyone to tell of my planets, the star is below in the seaweed of the skies.
>
> Goodbye to the laughter of nature and the seas, goodbye to the salt that will bring tears to thoughts, goodbye to death which opens valuable countries, our rings are early in the weddings of our gifts.
>
> O miracle of the waves, and I tirelessly scrutinising you like a gay porpoise leaping in my country, it was you who gave us these new waves – your monument is on the bottom, and the seas are your pulpit.

Certainly, as I read the poem now the sea imagery is very traditional in Gaelic poetry, but adapted here for a new purpose, that is, representing the unconscious.

That, I think, is new and also I think within the tradition. It is, I think, a counsel of despair to say that Gaelic should not deal with great modern themes which affect the Gael as much as anyone else. Sorley Maclean saw this happening with regard to the Spanish Civil War and he also saw there echoes of the tyranny that had happened to his own people. What he did was to set the Highlands in a historical context of Europe. Thus, for instance, in his long poem *An Cuilthionn* (the Cuillins, mountains in Skye) he writes:

> I would put the awesome Cuillin
> in phosphorescence in the firmament
> and I would make the island shout
> with a cry of fate in the skies . . .
> I would keep our noble Cuillin
> head on to the waves of Europe's battle.

I do not think there is any alternative to this immersion in our own time. And this while still retaining the 'blas' of our language. It is an extraordinarily difficult task. English is very powerful and so are other languages. We might ask ourselves, Has Gaelic anything to contribute to the continual debate of the human spirit? I believe it has: that all languages have. Not only has a Gaelic poet written about Spain, but Thomson and Macaulay have written about Turkey, about Rumania, about Pasternak, about Solzhenitsyn: and George Campbell Hay about the Arabs; setting these often in a Gaelic context.

Here, for instance, is Donald Macaulay writing about Pasternak, using Gaelic imagery of sowing: the poem is called 'For Pasternak, for example.' Here it is in an English version:

> You winnow in a contrary wind
> living seed out of beard and chaff:
> since you have understood that those who hated you
> did not recognise
> your love:
> you prepare seed for planting
> since you have understood their inadequacy –
> that they consign all seed for milling.

What is it then to be a bilingual writer? It is to see double. It is to write from within two separate traditions. The danger is that writing in English will affect writing in Gaelic adversely, and that one will bring into Gaelic tactless and unfeeling imagery and concepts from the English world. It is a continual balancing act. But, as I have said, I am beginning to think that it is impossible to do both after a certain stage, and a decision has to be made. My decision more recently has been for English. It satisfies a certain complexity, and allows me to use a vocabulary which is not native to Gaelic. The major initiatives in Gaelic will come from those who write in a contemporary manner in Gaelic. Poetry is not an affair of ideas: if it were it would be much easier. It is an affair of words and of music. The music of Gaelic is different from the music of English since it has remained quite close to the oral tradition. In the middle of a poem about Spain called 'The Choice' one can hear lines from Gaelic tradition: I am speaking of the second verse of these two verses:

> I walked with my reason
> out beside the sea:
> we were together but it kept
> a little distance from me.
>
> Then it turned saying:
> Is it true that you heard
> that your fair beautiful love
> is marrying early on Monday?

Facts of the modern world can be transformed into creative power in the Gaelic language as in any other language. The problem is that by the nature of things we can have fewer poets than we need of the perception and force necessary.

I think it is possible too that because of my work in Gaelic some of that tradition may have entered my English poetry, to its advantage. I would be happy if some of that Gaelic light would shine through it, giving it colour and illumination as we find these in the Celtic world.

EDWIN MORGAN

9. *The Legacy of the Makars*

Let me begin with a couple of quotations which will show that there is a legacy of the makars, or at least one of the makars, in the late twentieth century. The Scottish poet W.S. Graham (1918–1986), who came from Greenock near Glasgow, wrote in English and was not a part of the 'Scottish Renascence' movement, as Hugh MacDiarmid called it, which aimed to revive written Scots. But Graham remained, and considered himself to be, very Scottish, and had an awareness of early Scottish poetry. A friend of his called Ronnie Duncan has written about a visit he made to the poet when he was living in Cornwall:

> We would have brought a small hamper and a large Teacher's and after a few drinks the talk would begin. I remember one Christmas after the meal Sydney and I began to read poetry to each other: the early Makars – Chaucer, Wyatt, Skelton, Dunbar. I can still hear the vibrant Scots voice now, repeating the end line from 'Lament for the Makars': 'Timor Mortis Conturbat Me'. That was a transcendent occasion, speaking to each other through the medium of other poets.[1]

My second quotation is perhaps more unexpected. After Dylan Thomas died from alcoholism in America in 1953, the American poet Kenneth Rexroth wrote an elegy for him, called 'Thou Shalt Not Kill', a long controversial poem which was much discussed at the time. In one part of it Rexroth deliberately went back to Dunbar, and laid out his own lament for the roll-call of twentieth-century American makars, and as in Dunbar he includes well-known names like Ezra Pound and Hart Crane and Vachel Lindsay, together with others that might need a footnote:

> What happened to Robinson,
> Who used to stagger down Eighth Street,
> Dizzy with solitary gin?
> Where is Masters, who crouched in
> His law office for ruinous decades?
> Where is Leonard who thought he was
> A locomotive? And Lindsay,
> Wise as a dove, innocent
> As a serpent, where is he?
>   Timor mortis conturbat me.

---

1 *Edinburgh Review* 75 (1987), 72.

> What became of Jim Oppenheim?
> Lola Ridge alone in an
> Icy furnished room? Orrick Johns,
> Hopping into the surf on his
> One leg? Elinor Wylie
> Who leaped like Kierkegaard?
> Sara Teasdale, where is she?
>   Timor mortis conturbat me . . .
>
> Harry who didn't care at all?
> Hart who went back to the sea?
> Timor mortis conturbat me.[2]

Perhaps in a way it is surprising that anything should have remained of the makars after five hundred years. Quite apart from questions of language – and most ordinary readers today would find their language unfamiliar and often difficult – these poets lived and wrote not only before the Union of the Crowns and the Union of Parliaments but also before the Reformation (though in the case of Sir David Lyndsay, on the very edge of it). Partly because of that large difference between their world and the world of twentieth-century poets, but partly also for other reasons, there was little continuity of reputation for any of these writers over the centuries. In fact, it's hardly an exaggeration to say that the two poets we most admire today, Dunbar and Henryson, virtually disappeared from view, certainly disappeared as influences, as writers establishing traditions, for most of the time between the sixteenth and twentieth centuries, whereas the other two members of the quadrumvirate, Douglas and Lyndsay, whom we tend not to rate quite so highly, continued to be relatively popular, certainly better known and more often referred to, down to the nineteenth century. The reasons for this are fairly clear, but interesting. Douglas and Lyndsay were both public figures in their time, close to and sometimes influencing political, national events. Henryson and Dunbar were private persons who vanished when their era vanished; they didn't leave their mark on their time. But Lyndsay in particular, who had made Johne the Common-weill the hero of his *Ane Satyre of the Thrie Estaitis*, was faithfully rewarded by Johne the Common-weill who for many years if his house had only two books would make sure that these were the Bible and Lyndsay's works, which became talismans to be consulted for wisdom. A common saying was 'Ye'll no find that in Davie Lyndsay!' This of course had much to do with the Reformation. Scholars today may argue about the exact point on the scale between Catholic and Protestant where Lyndsay stood, but ordinary folk had no doubt. The general feeling is nicely reflected by Walter Scott in his poem *Marmion*, where Lyndsay himself appears as a character:

2 K. Rexroth, *In Defence of the Earth* (1959), 62–3.

>He was a man of middle age;
>In aspect manly, grave, and sage,
>   As on King's errand come;
>But in the glances of his eye,
>A penetrating, keen, and sly
>   Expression found its home;
>The flash of that satiric rage,
>Which, bursting on the early stage,
>Branded the vices of the age,
>   And broke the keys of Rome.
>   (IV. vii)³

In the century before Scott, Allan Ramsay made much the same point, rather more crudely, in his poem 'An Epistle to James Clerk, Esq. of Pennycuik':

>Sir David's satyres help'd our nation
>To carry on the Reformation,
>And gave the scarlet whore a box
>Mair snell than all the pelts of Knox.⁴

But Ramsay admired Gavin Douglas too, for less partisan reasons. In the first of his verse epistles written in correspondence with William Hamilton of Gilbertfield in 1719, he compares the state of poetry in England with that in Scotland at the time, and bemoans the drastic decline of Scottish poetry since the days of the makars:

>   The Chiels of *London*, *Cam*, and *Ox*,
>Ha'e rais'd up great Poetick Stocks
>Of *Rapes*, of *Buckets*, *Sarks* and *Locks*,
>   While we neglect
>To shaw their betters. This provokes
>   Me to reflect
>
>On the lear'd Days of *Gawn Dunkell*,
>Our Country then a Tale cou'd tell,
>*Europe* had nane mair snack and snell
>   At Verse or Prose;
>Our Kings were Poets too themsell,
>   Bauld and Jocose.⁵

What is notable in these lines is not just that he singles out Gavin Douglas (who was of course, as his own footnote reminds us, Bishop of Dunkeld) as the

---

3 *The Poetical Works of Sir Walter Scott*, ed. J.L. Robertson (1904), 128.
4 *The Works of Allan Ramsay*, ed. A.M. Kinghorn and A. Law, STS, 3rd Series, 29 (1961), 273.
5 *The Works of Allan Ramsay*, ed. B. Martin and J.W. Oliver, STS, 3rd Series, 19 (1950), 120.

representative of medieval Scottish poetry, but also that he regrets the lost European connection and the cultural integration which in a small country allowed even kings – James I and James VI at least, probably others – to be part of that culture. All that has gone, and he, Allan Ramsay, is going to do what he can to remedy the situation.

When he brought out his anthology *The Ever Green, being a Collection of Scots Poems, Wrote by the Ingenious before 1600*, he did include Dunbar and Henryson as well as poems and ballads in anonymous and popular traditions. The texts were far from perfect, and were often interfered with by Ramsay himself, but at least the poems were there, and a glossary was provided to make understanding easier. Unfortunately the anthology did not do particularly well, and had little impact as far as bringing the makars back alive was concerned. The two volumes are historically important, as a signal that Scottish poetry was beginning to shake itself again, but (as it turned out) not by building bridges back to the makars, who remained of very minor significance to Fergusson and Burns, in so far as they had even read them. Would Ramsay, if he could have come back a century later, feel his work had been justified by the poetry of Fergusson and Burns, even if Henryson and Dunbar were sleeping in their graves? He certainly had no shortage of self-assurance, not to say self-conceit. In *The Ever Green* he printed Dunbar's 'Lament for the Makars', but added a 'postscript' of three stanzas of his own: it's a prophecy:

> Suthe I forsie, if Spae–craft had,
>   Frae Hethir-Muirs sall ryse a LAD,
> Aftir twa Centries pas, sall he
>   Revive our Fame and Memorie.
>
> Then sall we flourish EVIR GRENE;
> All thanks to carefull *Bannantyne*,
> And to the PATRON kind and frie,
>
>   Quha lends the LAD baith them and me.
> Far sall we fare, baith Eist and West,
> Owre ilka Clyme by *Scots* possest;
> Then sen our Warks sall nevir die,
>   *Timor mortis non turbat me.*
>
>   *Quod* DUNBAR.[6]

Perhaps it took another two centuries for that 'lad' Ramsay speaks about to really appear on the scene in the form of Hugh MacDiarmid. MacDiarmid's Scottish Renascence movement of the 1920s aimed, among other things, to draw people's attention to the forgotten virtues of the makars and to see what could be learned from the language they used. He wasn't entirely a voice crying in the wilderness; others, notably Ezra Pound, were beginning to take a keen interest in medieval poetry, and Pound's enthusiastic recommendation of Gavin Douglas is well

---

6 *The Works of Allan Ramsay*, ed. Kinghorn and Law.

known: Douglas's translation of Virgil was 'better than the original, as Douglas had heard the sea' (*How to Read*, 1931),[7] a point he expanded elsewhere when he said: 'I get considerably more pleasure from the Bishop of Dunkeld than from the original highly cultured but non-seafaring author' (*ABC of Reading*, 1934.)[8] It was the concreteness, the rich thinginess, of Douglas's style, that appealed to Pound, as it did also to MacDiarmid. In Scotland, MacDiarmid's focus was however on William Dunbar, whom he championed as a great corrective to Burns and to what he saw as the disastrous sentimentalising of Scottish poetry which Burns's nineteenth-century successors had brought about. In his long poem *A Drunk Man Looks at the Thistle* (1926) he lambasts his countrymen in this couplet:

> I widna gi'e five meenits wi' Dunbar
> For a' the millions o' ye as ye are.[9]

And this is turned into critical theory in his prose book *Albyn, or Scotland and the Future* (1927), where he writes:

> Not Burns – Dunbar! That is the phrase which sums up the significant tendency which is belatedly manifesting itself in Scots poetry today. At first it may seem absurd to try to recover at this time of day the literary potentialities of a language which has long ago disintegrated into dialects . . . Those who would try it in Scots must first of all recover for themselves the full canon of Scots used by the Auld Makars and readapt it to the full requirements of modern self-expression . . . It has been said that if Burns is the heart, Dunbar is the head, of Scottish poetry; and certainly at any time during the past century Scots literature has had desperate need to pray Meredith's prayer for 'More brains, O Lord, more brains.'[10]

Although MacDiarmid soon had his followers, not everyone agreed with his desire to revive a full canon of Scots as a modern literary medium. His insistence on it led to his famous quarrel with Edwin Muir in the 1930s, when Muir said that Scots had had its day and it must be English from now on. But rather than rehearse once again that much-told story, let me just quote a sly dig at MacDiarmid from one of the early studies of Dunbar, the poet Rachel Annand Taylor's *Dunbar: The Poet and his Period* (1931). Despite her interest in Dunbar, her having chosen to write a book about him, she keeps him firmly as a dead author:

> It is, however, but an archaic and limited kind of interest that he still possesses; and it hardly seems likely that he can be of much value as an inspiration to young Scotland, as some think.[11]

7 *Literary Essays of Ezra Pound*, ed. T.S. Eliot (1954), 35.
8 E. Pound, *ABC of Reading* (1961), 118.
9 *The Complete Poems of Hugh MacDiarmid*, ed. M. Grieve and W.R. Aitken (1985), I.107.
10 C.M. Grieve, *Albyn, Or, Scotland and the Future* (1927), 36–8.
11 R.A. Taylor, *Dunbar: The Poet and his Period* (1931), 85.

MacDiarmid himself seems to have had second thoughts, many years later. In 1973 he brought out a paperback selection of Robert Henryson and admitted in the introduction:

> When I invented and published the slogan 'Not Burns – Dunbar!', like most Scots of my age I had come late and quite inadequately to a knowledge of the makars. We were taught nothing of them in our schools and colleges. We realized at the outset the necessity *épater les Anglais* and the choice of Dunbar was shocking enough . . . But second thoughts have emphasized the greater importance of Henryson who, it is safe to say, was in nobody's mind at the time and is still far from generally appreciated.[12]

I must say I find this late conversion more dutiful than deeply felt. I cannot really see the spirits of MacDiarmid and Henryson going arm-in-arm. Dunbar and Douglas were more naturally his people. But it was a part of the general opening up of all the makars to the perception of Scottish writers (and to a wider public in the case of Sir David Lyndsay, after his *Satyre* began again to be performed and was found to be thoroughly dramatic and entertaining).

The influence of the makars is clear on the mid-century Scottish poets who used Scots: Robert Garioch, Sydney Goodsir Smith, Tom Scott, Alex Scott, to mention the most obvious names. Although this influence can be seen at work in many different ways, some of them oblique and subtle, perhaps two of the most evident examples will suffice. Robert Garioch's satirical but also celebratory poem on the Edinburgh International Festival, 'Embro to the Ploy', is a direct tribute, down to the metre and rhyme, to the old merrymaking poem 'Peblis to the Play' which is possibly by James I. Garioch obviously saw some nice parallels between the two festivals, but another part of the attraction was technical, the appeal of the 'bob-wheel' stanza with its little dancing short lines at the end: a medieval reminder, in an age of free verse, of the delights of formality. Here are a couple of stanzas, the second of them commenting on the makars and their language:

> In simmer, whan aa sorts foregether
> in Embro to the ploy,
> fowk seek out friens to hae a blether,
> or faes they'd fain annoy;
> smorit wi British Railways' reek
> frae Glesca or Glen Roy
> or Wick, they come to hae a week
> of cultivatit joy,
>   or three,
> in Embro to the ploy . . .
>
> The haly kirk's Assembly-haa
> nou fairly coups the creel

---

12 *Henryson*, Selected by Hugh MacDiarmid (1973), 8–9.

> wi Lindsay's Three Estaitis, braw
> devices of the Deil.
> About our heids the satire stots
> like hailstanes till we reel;
> the bawrs are in auld-farrant Scots,
> it's maybe jist as weill,
> > imphm,
> > > in Embro to the ploy.[13]

My other example comes from Sydney Goodsir Smith, and the tribute here is to Henryson. Smith's long sequence *Under the Eildon Tree* (1948) is a series of love elegies, a personal narrative of unhappy love being made to reverberate through various historical and legendary parallels, Antony and Cleopatra, Dido and Aeneas and so on. Among these doomed pairs we find Orpheus and Eurydice, and this section deliberately recycles Henryson's 'Orpheus and Eurydice' and uses Henryson's refrain line 'Quhar art thow gane, my luf Erudices?':

> We werena ten yairds frae the bank o' Styx
> The ferryin o' whilk was luve and libertie
> > – No ten yairds awa!
> Our braith was hechlan and our een
> > Glaizie-glentit wi the joy
> Of our twa-fauld deliverance –
> And then Jove strak with serpent subtletie:
> > – Euridicie stummelt.
>
> > (*Lauchter cracked abune. Jupiter leuch*!
> > > – *And richtlie sae*!
> > *Och, gie the gods their due,*
> > *They ken what they're about.*
> > > – *The sleekans*!)
>
> She stummelt. I heard her cry. And hert ruled heid again.
> – What hert could eer refuse, then, siccan a plea?
> > I turned –
> > > And wi neer a word,
> > > > In silence,
> Her een aye bricht wi the joy o' resurrection,
> She soomed awa afore my een intil a skimmeran wraith
> And for a second and last time was tint for aye
> Amang the gloams and haars o Hell
> > – Throu my ain twafauld treacherie!
>
> > '*Quhar art thou gane, my luf Euridices*!'
> > > > > > > (XII.iii)[14]

13 R. Garioch, *Complete Poetical Works*, ed. R. Fulton (1983), 14–15.
14 S.G. Smith, *Collected Poems* (1975), 165–6.

Smith, unlike Garioch, makes no attempt to reproduce medieval form: his poem is in free verse. Nor does he preserve Henryson's evenness of tone, his sense of stylistic harmony which has been so much admired. He interjects authorial sardonic comments, printed in italics within parentheses, to break up the narrative in the modern polyphonic manner. Yet somehow the thread from Henryson, and from the Middle Ages, is retained.

Perhaps at this point I can put myself into the picture. It's a rather depressing fact that although I came a full generation after Hugh MacDiarmid, I had to go through the same old gradual process of discovering the past of my own country's poetry. As far as the world of education is concerned, it was as if MacDiarmid had dusted off the legacy of the makars like a document, and then somebody had pushed it back into the pigeon-hole again. At school and university in the 1930s none of the makars appeared on a syllabus, and even Burns was only lightly and tangentially referred to. The subject was, as the regulations stated, 'English'. Ironically enough, at the university there was someone on the English staff who was knowledgeable about the makars, but the course I heard from her was on the English Chaucerians, Lydgate, Hoccleve, and Gower – a course that lifted few spirits! So I had to piece the jigsaw together in my own way, helped by modern editions of the principal makars which were beginning to appear, but also by some older books which came as a great revelation – I think particularly of my discovery of David Laing's *Select Remains of the Ancient Popular and Romance Poetry of Scotland* of 1822, as re-edited by John Small in 1885, a collection rich in items I found myself relishing but which my education had never mentioned, far less shown: 'The Taill of Rauf Coilyear', 'The Tale of Colkelbie Sow', 'King Berdok', 'Sir John Rowll's Cursing', 'The Gyre-Carling', 'The Wyf of Auchtermuchty', 'The Wowing of Jok and Jynny'. At the same time, because I enjoyed Anglo-Saxon poetry and was beginning to translate it, I became much interested in the persistence of the alliterative tradition which seemed to have wound its way and wielded its wealth through the north of England up into Scotland, where it affected all the makars to greater or lesser extent and gave their poetry a linguistic and aural pungence that I found attractive. But I think in a wider sense, the more I learned about the medieval poets the more I felt I could relate to this long stretch of history as a Scottish writer. I was, in shorthand terms, a modernist, but my awareness of the cutting edge of contemporary poetry, especially American and Russian, was not going to use its edge to cut me off from the bizarre energy of 'The Flyting of Dunbar and Kennedie' or the hard-won pathos of 'The Testament of Cresseid'.

I'll conclude by reading some poems which may relate to the things I've been saying.

The first is called 'The Flowers of Scotland' and was published in 1969. It's a direct socio-political poem, both angry and satirical, and you could see its approach as similar to that of Dunbar and Lyndsay in a number of their writings:

> Yes, it is too cold in Scotland for flower people; in any case who would be handed a thistle?

What are our flowers? Locked swings and private rivers –
and the island of Staffa for sale in the open market, which no one questions or thinks strange –
and lads o' pairts that run to London and Buffalo without a backward look while their elders say Who'd blame them –
and bonny fechters kneedeep in dead ducks with all the thrawn intentness of the incorrigible professional Scot –
and a Kirk Assembly that excels itself in the bad old rhetoric and tries to stamp out every glow of charity and change, most wrong when it thinks most loudly it is most right –
and a Scottish National Party that refuses to discuss Vietnam and is even applauded for doing so, do they think no lesson is to be learned from what is going on there? –
and the unholy power of Grouse-moor and Broad-acres to prevent the smoke of useful industry from sullying Invergordon or setting up linear cities among the whaups –
and the banning of Beardsley and Joyce but not of course of 'Monster on the Campus' or 'Curse of the Undead' – those who think the former are the more degrading, what are their values? –
and the steady creep of the preservationist societies, wearing their pens out for slums with good leaded lights – if they could buy all the amber in the Baltic and melt it over Edinburgh would they be happy then? – the skeleton is well-proportioned –
and by contrast the massive indifference to the slow death of the Clyde estuary, decline of resorts, loss of steamers, anaemia of yachting, cancer of monstrous installations of a foreign power and an acquiescent government – what is the smell of death on a child's spade, any more than rats to leaded lights? –
and dissidence crying in the wilderness to a moor of boulders and two ospreys –
these are the flowers of Scotland.

Next is a poem in Scots called 'The Birkie and the Howdie'. This is a flyting in the medieval tradition, with the language made as densely Scottish as possible:

> A dorty, vogie, chanler-chaftit birkie
> brattled the aizles o the clachan chimlie,
> glunched at his jaupin quaich o usquebae,
> scunnered red-wud at the clarty lyart howdie
> snirtlin by the ingle-neuk sae laithron and tozie,
> and gied the thowless quine a blaud wi his gully
> till she skrieghed like a cut-luggit houlet and dang her tassie
> aff-loof at his unco doup, the glaikit tawpie.
> The skellum callan goaved at her fell drumlie:
> 'Ye tocherless wanchancie staumrel hizzie,
> ye groazlin, driddlin grumphie, ye awnie ferlie,
> deil gie your kyte curmurrings o scroggy crowdie,

and bogles graizle ilka ramfeezl't hurdie
till aa your snash is steekit, ye duddie hoodie!'

– 'Ach, I hae warlock-briefs, stegh the collieshangie!
Aa your ier-oes sall gang sae muckle agley
they'se turn to blitters and bauckie-birds, and in a brulzie
they'se mak their joes o taeds, aa thrang and sonsie,
snowkin in aidle whaur asks and clegs are grushie:
yon is an ourie pliskie!'
 Wha wan the tulzie?

This extract from the poem 'Rider', which is about the gradual emergence of poetry in Glasgow, pays its tribute both to the fantastic quasi-surrealist imagery often found in the medieval poets and to the old bob-wheel stanza (surviving here by ghostly but still recognisable descent):

iv

butcher-boys tried to ward off sharks / the waters rose quickly / great drowned bankers
floated from bay-windows / two housemaids struggled on Grosvenor Terrace with a giant conger
the Broomielaw was awash with slime and torn-out claws and anchor-flakes / rust and dust
sifted together where a dredger ploughed up the Gallowgate / pushed a dirty wave over Shettleston
spinning shopfronts crashed in silence / glassily, massively / porticoes tilting / settled in mud
lampreys fastened on four dead sailors drifting through Finnieston / in a Drygate attic
James Macfarlan threw his pen at the stinking wall / the whisky and the stinking poverty
ran down like ink / the well of rats was bottomless and Scotch / the conman and the conned
fought on / the ballads yellowed, the pubs filled / at Anderston he reached his grave in snow / selah
the ruined cities were switched off / there was no flood / his father led a pedlar's horse
by Carrick fields, his mother sang / the boy rode on a jogging back / far back / in rags /
Dixon's Blazes roared and threw more poets in its molten pools / forges on fire
matched the pitiless bread, the head
long hangdog, the lifted elbow /
the true bloody pathos and sublime

Another poem with something of a medieval flavour, in this case an *ubi sunt* theme, is an elegy from 1977 called 'A Good Year for Death'; in that year there was an unusual procession of deaths among people famous in the worlds of entertainment and the arts:

> Where is Callas la Divina
> with her black velvet and her white passion?
> Where are the women and women and women
> she threw into life for an hour from her throat
> to float and fight? She cannot hear
> the last bravo.
> *Death has danced her tune away.*
>
> Where is Nabokov with his butterfly-net,
> his galoshes, his mushrooms, his index-cards?
> He has gone in a whiff of bilberries and blinis,
> his fire has paled, his puns have flunked.
> Shades crowd the lakeside hydrangeas and swallows
> skim quick and low.
> *Death has danced his tune away.*
>
> Where is Bolan, the elfin, now?
> Who has taken his spangles and songs,
> bongos and gongs, and his white swan?
> Who has pied-piper'd the pied piper
> into that childless, teenless wood?
> The metal shadow,
> *Death, has danced his tune away.*
>
> Where is Presley all in silver,
> with his sideburns and his quiver
> of simple rock, and what is that army
> he's uniformed for, in a white sheet,
> will the slowstep motorcade battalion
> never let him go?
> *Death has danced his tune away.*
>
> And where is Lowell that sweet mad poet
> with his rumpled suit and uranium finger?
> A giant forsythia covers the Pentagon
> with better than gold, but the magnolias
> wax the Potomac white with grief –
> in words at least. Be true, be brief:
> we lack his fellow.
> *Death has danced his tune away.*

The magazine *Agenda* brought out a special issue to celebrate the 75th birthday of the poet Tom Scott in 1993, and I contributed the following poem to it. I called it

'Macaronicon for Tom Scott', and its use of English, Scots, French, Italian, and Latin was meant as a tribute to Tom Scott's fondness for translation, especially from medieval poets:

>That night I saw a moor with scattered fires.
>Grey smoke drifted through to break the gleam
>of weapons abandoned. Figures, call them no more,
>skulked in and out of the smoke-swirls, half-crouched,
>knifed any bundles that still stirred or groaned,
>cut rings off to test any playing possum.
>No moon, only the fires. Ane barand steid,
>the flichter an the smeek, the wappins grundit,
>the besy fowk like sheddas getherin there
>tae pyke oot ony gliff o life, kickin
>corp an hauf-corp for a tellin grane,
>howkin the gowd rings, leavin the braw een
>for corbies. Nuit d'un champ de misères,
>petits feux partout, et la fumée qui roule
>parmi les armes, les mourants et les morts,
>les furtives figures qui frôlent et tuent
>ces blessés, arrachant pendant le râle
>doigt, anneau, joyau, vie et tout.
>Et la lune s'endormit. Mi ritrovai
>per uno campo oscuro che la guerra
>aveva guastato, corpo sul corpo, gemito
>sul gemito, fuoco sul fuoco, fumo
>sul fumo, ed i furfatori infernali
>robbing and hacking until the very dead
>yowlit an chirmit Oh que c'est lointain
>et fort, l'espoir des hommes, benigna pax!

In the early 1980s I wrote a sequence of 51 sonnets which was published as a book called *Sonnets from Scotland* in 1984. These poems were a reaction to the failure of the 1979 referendum to deliver a parliament or assembly for Scotland, and were a series of dramatised moments, real or imagined, from Scottish history, supposedly reported by observers from another part of the universe. The first one I shall read is 'Silva Caledonia', set at the time when the great Caledonian forest still covered a large part of Scotland:

>The darkness deepens, and the woods are long.
>We shall never see any stars. We thought
>we heard a horn a while back, faintly brought
>through barks and howls, the nearest to a song
>you ever heard in these grey dripping glens.
>But if there were hunters, we saw not one.

> Are there bears? Mist. Wolves? Peat. Is there a sun?
> Where are the eyes that should peer from those dens?
> Marsh-lights, yes, mushroom-banks, leaf-mould, rank ferns,
> and up above, a sense of wings, of flight,
> of clattering, of calls through fog. Yet men,
> going about invisible concerns,
> are here, and our immoderate delight
> waits to see them, and hear them speak, again.

The next sonnet is called 'Pilate at Fortingall', and is based on the old legend that Pontius Pilate was born at Fortingall in Perthshire. I imagine him coming back to his native place in the latter part of his life:

> A Latin harsh with Aramaicisms
> poured from his lips incessantly; it made
> no sense, for surely he was mad. The glade
> of birches shamed his rags, in paroxysms
> he stumbled, toga'd, furred, blear, brittle, grey.
> They told us he sat here beneath the yew
> even in downpours; ate dog-scraps. Crows flew
> from prehistoric stone to stone all day.
> 'See him now.' He crawled to the cattle-trough
> at dusk, jumbled the water till it sloshed
> and spilled into the hoof-mush in blue strands,
> slapped with useless despair each sodden cuff,
> and washed his hands, and watched his hands, and washed
> his hands, and watched his hands, and washed his hands.

'The Mirror' quotes the words attributed by Tacitus ('where they make a desolation they call it peace') to Calgacus, the Caledonian leader defeated by the Romans in 82:

> There is a mirror only we can see.
> It hangs in time and not in space. The day
> goes down in it without ember or ray
> and the newborn climb through it to be free.
> The multitudes of the world cannot know
> they are reflected there; like glass they lie
> in glass, shadows in shade, they could not cry
> in airless wastes but that is where they go.
> We cloud it, but it pulses like a gem,
> it must have caught a range of energies
> from the dead. We breathe again; nothing shows.
> Back in space, *ubi solitudinem*
> *faciunt pacem appellant.* Ages
> drum-tap the flattened homes and slaughtered rows.

The next poem, 'The Picts', is among other things a reminder of the linguistic and ethnic mix of the country. The names of Pictish kings are not only not Celtic but not even Indo-European, and they stir the imagination to probe that vanished life:

> Names as from outer space, names without roots:
> Bes, son of Nanammovvezz; Bliesblituth
> that wild buffoon throned in an oaken booth;
> wary Edarnon; brilliant Usconbuts;
> Canutulachama who read the stars.
> Where their fame flashed from, went to, is unknown.
> The terror of their warriors is known,
> naked, tattooed on every part (the hairs
> of the groin are shaved on greatest fighters,
> the fine bone needle dipped in dark-blue woad
> rings the flesh with tender quick assurance:
> he is *diuperr cartait*, rich pin; writers
> like us regain mere pain on that blue road,
> they think honour comes with the endurance).

'Colloquy in Glaschu' brings in a touch of macaronics again, to enliven the meeting of Saints Columba and Kentigern which did actually take place in Glasgow. As one was Q-Celtic and the other P-Celtic they either had an interpreter or used Latin. I have added some ahistorical French in a macaronic spirit:

> God but *le son du cor*, Columba sighed
> to Kentigern, *est triste au fond silvarum!*
> *Frater*, said Kentigern, I see no harm.
> *J'aime le son du cor*, when day has died,
> deep in the *bois*, and oystercatchers rise
> before the fowler as he trudges home
> and *sermo lupi* loosens the grey loam.
> *À l'horizon lointain* is paradise,
> *abest silentium, le cor éclate* –
> – *et meurt*, Columba mused, but Kentigern
> replied, *renaît et se prolonge*. The cell
> is filled with song. Outside, *puer cantat*.
> *Veni venator* sings the gallus kern.
> The saints dip startled cups in Mungo's well.

The next poem, 'At Stirling Castle, 1507', also deals with a real incident. One of William Dunbar's enemies at the court of James IV was a foreigner, John Damian, who extracted money from the royal exchequer for alchemical and other experiments and who also attempted to fly from Stirling Castle. Dunbar thought he was a charlatan and made ferocious attacks on him in his poetry. But I have tried to redress the balance, suggesting that he was a genuine experimenter, and if (as seems probable) he came from Italy, you are reminded of Leonardo da Vinci's interest in and designs for human flight at that time:

> Damian, D'Amiens, Damiano –
> we never found out his true name, but there
> he crouched, swarthy, and slowly sawed the air
> with large strapped-on bat-membrane wings. Below
> the battlements, a crowd prepared to jeer.
> He frowned, moved back, and then with quick crow struts
> ran forward, flapping strongly, whistling cuts
> from the grey heavy space with his black gear
> and on a huge spring and a cry was out
> beating into vacancy, three, four, five,
> till the crawling scaly Forth and the rocks
> and the upturned heads replaced that steel shout
> of sky he had replied to – left alive,
> and not the last key snapped from high hard locks.

My last poem from *Sonnets from Scotland* goes into the future. It is called 'The Solway Canal', and you are to imagine that a canal has been created from the Solway Firth to Berwick, so that Scotland has become an island:

> Slowly through the Cheviot hills at dawn
> we sailed. The high steel bridge at Carter Bar
> passed over us in fog with not a car
> in its broad lanes. Our hydrofoil slid on,
> vibrating quietly through wet rock walls
> and scarves of dim half-sparkling April mist;
> a wizard with a falcon on his wrist
> was stencilled on our bow. Rough waterfalls
> flashed on that northern island of the Scots
> as the sun steadily came up and cast
> red light along the uplands and the waves,
> and gulls with open beaks tore out our thoughts
> through the thick glass to where the Eildons massed,
> or down to the Canal's drowned borderers' graves.

The poems by Edwin Morgan are taken from his *Collected Poems* (1990), with the exception of 'Macaronicon for Tom Scott', which is from *Agenda* 30.4–31.1 (1993), 135.

JONATHAN A. GLENN

10. *Gilbert Hay and the Problem of Sources: The Case of the* Buke of the Ordre of Knychthede

We want to know what texts Hay worked from because knowing that would let us make judgments and draw conclusions that are otherwise impossible: estimates of the extent of Hay's reading/knowledge, for example, cannot be made with certainty unless we know what was and was not in his source(s); evaluations of his 'accuracy' or 'inaccuracy' in rendering the French can be no more than tentative unless we know fairly clearly and fairly specifically what that French actually was; conclusions about Older Scots as it manifests itself in Hay's prose could be richer if we knew more precisely what stood behind the language he uses; at times the quality of our judgments about his intentions as translator will depend on the accuracy of our knowledge about his sources. Ideally, then, the literary critic or historian or linguist working with Hay would like to be able to identify exactly which version of the French source Hay worked from – if possible the manuscript he used; failing that (as he/she certainly will), the scholar wants to know what group of French manuscripts most closely approximates the text(s) Hay most likely knew.

The *Buke of the Ordre of Knychthede* is particularly useful as a test case for source-study of Hay because of its brevity and because of the textual situation of the French *Livre de l'ordre de chevalerie*: the ultimate source, Ramon Llull's Catalan *Llibre de l'orde de cavalleria*, is well known and well edited; the known extant French manuscripts are limited in number; the text is available in a modern edition; and the various manuscripts and their relationships have received considerable attention from a variety of scholars.[1]

Fourteen manuscripts of the *Livre de l'ordre de chevalerie* are known, three of the fourteenth century, nine of the fifteenth, and two of the sixteenth. (Three prints were made in the early sixteenth-century as well.) See Table 1.[2] Of the fourteen manuscripts, one is fragmentary (B) and another is so fire-damaged as to be illegible (T). Figure 1 shows the manuscript relationships schematically. I have been able to

---

1 For the Catalan text, see Ramon Llull, *Llibre de l'orde de cavalleria*, ed. Albert Soler i Llopart, Els Nostres Clàssics A127 (Barcelona: Editorial Barcino, 1988). For the French text, see Ramon Llull, *Livre de l'ordre de chevalerie*, ed. Vincenzo Minervini, Biblioteca di Filologia Romanza 21 (Bari: Adriatica Editrice, 1971); the textual analysis in Minervini's edition must be supplemented by the following studies: Mario Ruffini, 'Un Ignoto MS. della Traduzione Francese del "Libre de l'Orde de Cavalleria" di Raimondo Lullo,' *Estudios Lulianos* 2 (1958): 77–82; Anna Cornagliotti, 'Un manoscritto sconosciuto della versione francese del "Tractat de cavalleria" di Ramon Llull (J B II 19 del 'Archivio di Stato di Torino),' *Miscellània Aramon i Serra. II. Estudios Universitaris Catalans* 24 (1980): 157–66; Vincenzo Minervini, 'Postilla lulliana,' *Annali del 'Istituto Universitario Orientale* 25.1 (Naples 1983): 333–41; and Jonathan A. Glenn, 'Further Notes on Two Unedited Manuscripts of the *Livre de l'ordre de chevalerie*,' *Studia Lulliana* (formerly *Estudios Lulianos*) 32 (1992): 39–58.

2 Tables and Figures follow the text at the end of this paper.

examine in microfilm all these manuscripts (and the prints) except for the two Turin manuscripts; statements about the *Livre de l'ordre de chevalerie* in what follows are based on these examinations and on Minervini's edition of the French text.

One feature of Minervini's study of these manuscripts (and of subsequent, less comprehensive, studies, including my own) bears mention here, since it affects what can be said on the basis of these studies about the relationship of the French manuscripts to Hay's text. Minervini established his stemma by essentially statistical study (though not exhaustive and not quantified) of the texts he worked with: by comparison of lexical items in the various manuscripts, he developed a set of 16 tables presenting shared readings and, then, unique readings of each manuscript. This method suits a relatively homogeneous group of manuscripts whose differences are, with some exceptions, differences of lexical detail rather than a clear pattern of, for example, shared errors – a more traditional approach to stemma-construction.

This situation obviously creates difficulties if one wants to study the relationship of a translation to such a group of texts: because a translator is in fact translating – substituting other words for the words of his/her original, in a relationship to that original naturally more independent than the relation between copytext and scribe – the clearest kind of evidence for a particular textual relationship (a shared or constrasting set of lexical items) is unlikely to exist consistently. When the translator treats his sources as freely as Hay occasionally appears to do, the problem of course increases.

One example will suffice to show how the independence of Hay's text tantalises the scholar, yet refuses to divulge its source. In cap. iv, Hay seems to alter significantly the French text as it exists. Hay's version reads thus:

And thar'fore knycht suld mare dout honour' na dede /– And schamefulnes suld mare chastis' a worthy knycht /– and geve him a hardar' passioun – and jt suld happin him /– Na sulde outhir hunger' or thrist / or hete or calde /– or ony dises' yat he mycht haue /– (4.157–62)[3]

Minervini's French text reads thus:

Car chevalier doit plus doubter le blasme de la gent et son deshonneur qu'il ne fait le peril de mort; et vergongne doit donner greigneur passion a son courage que fam ne soif ne chault ne froit ne aultre mesaise ne pourroit donner a son corps.[4] (Minervini 132.20–133.5)

In the first clause, Hay has made his significant change, introducing a more complex idea than the French presents. The latter simply warns against the

---

3 I quote Hay's text from my edition, *The Prose Works of Sir Gilbert Hay*, vol. III, STS (Edinburgh 1993).
4 This is a close rendering of Llull's Catalan: 'cor cavayler deu més dubtar blasme de gents que mort, e vergonya deu donar major passió a son coratge que fam ni set ni calt ni fret ni altra passió, trebayl, a son cors' (Soler 194. 119–22).

obviously undesirable 'blasme,' 'deshonneur,' and 'vergongne'; Hay, however, introduces a Boethian note with his warning also of the greater chance for dishonour when one is honoured. Since none of the extant French manuscripts or prints contains this idea here, we may safely, though not with certitude, assume that this is the translator's innovation. In addition, the Latin maxim found in Hay immediately preceding this passage – 'Quia non est tanti gaudij /– excelsa tenere /– quanti est meroris de excelso cadere' (4.156–7: For there is not so much joy in holding high offices [or honours] as there is grief in falling from a high place) – appears in none of the extant French manuscripts or prints, nor in the Catalan text (see Minervini 132–3, 196 for variants; and Soler 194); presumably, then, Hay added it, a presumption made more plausible by Hay's significant alteration of the ideas in the French passage, as noted above, creating an environment where the maxim makes sense. Such a presumption, of course, gets us no closer to Hay's source.

How, then, might Hay's exemplar be identified? As for what has been done in the past, two scholars, J.H. Stevenson and A.T.P. Byles, between them monopolise the history of source study for the *Buke of the Ordre of Knychthede*.

J.H. Stevenson's work[5] was that of a pioneer – Beriah Botfield's 1847 Abbotsford Club edition of Hay's *Buke* says nothing to the point – and as such has both its importance and its problems. Like the statements of most other scholars working in this field before 1971, the accuracy of Stevenson's observations is qualified by the incompleteness of his information about the text of the *Livre de l'ordre de chevalerie*. Thus he bases his classification of the French manuscripts and prints (as well as translations therefrom) on the somewhat limited evidence of the wording of their prologues (2: x).[6] His classification is never offered as exhaustive, but it produces the grouping indicated in Table 2, a grouping we can now recognise not only as incomplete but also as inaccurate.

Because of his incomplete understanding of the French textual situation, Stevenson's conclusions about the relationship of Hay's text to its French source(s) remain vague and impressionistic:

> Of the original used by Haye nothing is known except that at the date of his labours it was in the Castle of Roslin, and that from the internal evidence of the copy the original was in French, and . . . derived from some manuscript of the class we now speak of [i.e., Stevenson's class A]. None of the extant French manuscripts of the class . . . bears any such close resemblance to Haye's that we may say the one is meant for a mere or even generally close rendering of the other. The British Museum's Additional Manuscript, No. 22, 768 [=Miner-

---

5 In his edition *Gilbert of the Haye's Prose Manuscript*, 2 vols., STS, nos. 44 and 62 (Edinburgh: William Blackwood and Sons, 1901–14).

6 To be fair to Stevenson, his observations do imply that he knew other evidence might be to the point; thus he qualifies his remarks, 'Without going further into the differences between the examples which we have of these two versions, it is sufficient to state that the first class . . . belong to those whose Prologue begins . . .' (2: ix). The question, of course, is whether he is right that this is 'sufficient,' and the answer seems clearly to be 'no,' particularly since prologues are so easily changed for particular occasions and particular patrons.

vini's H] . . . is, so far as we have seen, the nearest in text of the French versions to the Scots; yet even it requires no exception to be made to the general statement that while all these French MS. to which we have referred, and the Caxton too, are closely related to each other, they are all verbally at least only distantly related to Haye. The criticism, however, goes no further than this, that Haye, who has in all other respects adhered to his original, has throughout his whole performance exercised so complete a freedom to amplify, expand, or paraphrase his original as to leave it more than difficult to determine how much linguistic reward is to be had from a close comparison between the Scots and any one of the French examples more than another as we have them. (2: xii)

Attitudes have obviously changed since Stevenson's day – no one today, I venture, would consider it a 'criticism' of Hay to note that it is difficult to identify his source or that his translation is 'verbally . . . only distantly related' to other versions of the text – but Stevenson's instincts seem to have been sound as far as they go: Hay's text *is*, or so scholars continue to affirm, freely adapted from his source (whatever it was), a fact that appears to render nearly moot the question of his immediate French exemplar.

The portion of A.T.P. Byles' study of the *Livre de l'ordre de chevalerie*[7] relevant to my work begins with a critique of the basis of Stevenson's classification:

Mr. Stevenson takes this variation in the prologue as the basis for a division of the MSS. into two groups, representing two independent translations from a common original. It will be shown below that the variations throughout the Royal MS. [= Minervini's I] provide a sounder basis for classification. (xxxii)

In fact, however, Byles adduces no compelling evidence for a classification, asserting only that I's 'variations . . . are sufficiently numerous to justify its classification outside the main group' (xxxiii). Byles' study is, on the other hand, more comprehensive than Stevenson's, taking into account all the manuscripts Byles knew; it is also less impressionistic, at least in appearance, than Stevenson's observations. Byles' study results in the classifications indicated in Figure 2. As a comparison with Minervini's stemma shows, Byles' classification is (1) incomplete (he did not know M, N, T, or T2) and (2) oversimplified (the Paris manuscripts are not, for example, such a homogeneous group as his schema suggests, and further research has clarified the relationship of the I-text to that in the other French manuscripts[8]).

Byles' attempt to relate Hay's *Buke of the Ordre of Knychthede* to the French texts

---

7 In his edition of William Caxton's *Book of the Ordre of Chyualry*, EETS OS 168 (London: Oxford UP, 1926). I have substituted Minervini's sigla for Byles' throughout: in quotations from Byles, I enclose the sigla in square brackets; otherwise I use the Minervini designations silently.
8 See Cornagliotti, Minervini's 'Postilla Lulliana,' and Glenn's 'Further Notes': these studies have shown that I and M belong together, both related, however, to other members of Minervini's β-group.

proves tenuous at best. Stating that 'there are some slight indications that Hay's original belonged to the group of which [I] is the only French representative,' Byles immediately adds that 'unfortunately the 'key' passage, the enumeration of the articles and the commandments [in cap. v], is omitted by Hay' (xxxv) – i.e., he admits that the evidence does not exist. Byles does nonetheless offer three instances of his 'slight indications' (xxxv–xxxvi); as Mapstone has noted, however, 'cumulatively the evidence is neither great nor conclusive'.[9] To confirm that judgment, I list Byles' evidence here:

Slight Indication 1: *sire dieu/sire/dieu*, **cap. i** (the beginning of the squire's speech praising God for bringing him to the hermit-knight)
   (1) General French reading: 'Ha, Syre Dieu'[10] (Minervini 85.5 and 184)
   (2) H: 'Ha, Syre' (Minervini 85.5 and 184)
   (3) I: 'haa dieu' (f. 339v)
   (4) Hay: 'almychtj god' (1. 178–79)

Slight Indication 2: Expanded *justice*-passage, cap. vii
   (1) General French reading: omitted (Minervini 158.3 and 204; also omitted in Llull [Soler 209.52])
   (2) I: 'car charite fait le pesant fais legier ./ ¶ Justice est vertu moult appartenante au cheuallier /' (f. 351r)
   (3) Hay: 'the quhilk cheritee makis heuy birding ly*ch*t to bere /– and grete charge soft / bathe for the vphalde of honour of knychthede /– and meryt of the saule behufe /– **jtem** justice js till all knychtis nedefull /– ffor knycht but justice . js but honoure /.' (7.64–8)

Slight Indication 3: List of seven deadly sins, cap. vii Byles claims that 'Hay, like [I], omits the list of sins and passes straight on to the remarks on gluttony' (xxxvi). As is obvious from the evidence that follows, 'I' does, *pace* Byles, include the list contained in the other French manuscripts, though the sins are listed in a different order.[11]
   (1) General French reading (with slight variations): 'Force est vertu qui maint en noble courage contre les.VIJ. pechiez mortelz qui sont voie par quoy homme va en enfer soustenir griefz tourmens sans fin. Lesquelz pechiez sont: gloutonnye, luxure, avarice, accide, orgueil, envie et ire'[12] (Minervini 160. 7–11 and 206)

---

9 Sally Mapstone, 'The Advice to Princes Tradition in Scottish Literature,' D. Phil., Oxford, 1986 (Mapstone's book is forthcoming).
10 Catalan reading: 'A Sényer Déus' (Soler 165. 115).
11 There are some other slight indications that Byles must be used gingerly as a guide to the French antecedents of Hay's translation. For example, as evidence that H and the Vérart print form an exclusive subgroup, Byles writes that 'on p. 5.7 [a reference in his edition of Caxton], [H] and Vérart have "pommier," while all the other texts have "arbre".' This seems not, in fact, to be true. See Minervini's edition of the *Livre de l'ordre de chevalerie* (78.6; 182 for variants), where the general tradition reads *pommier*, only I reading *arbre*; one may add that M agrees with I in this case (*arbre*), N and the Portunaris print with the general tradition (*pommier*).
12 Catalan reading: 'Fortitudo és virtut qui stà en noble coratge contra los.vii. peccats mortals, qui són carreres per les quals hom va a infernals turments qui no han fi: glotonia, luxúria, avarícia, accídia, supèrbia, invídia, ira' (Soler 211.85–8).

(2) I: 'force est vertu quy maint en noble courage contre les. vii pechiez mortelz par lesquelz on est dampne Et sont orgueil accide ire enuie gloutonnie luxure et auarice' (f. 351v)

(3) Hay: '**jtem** force is a grete vertu jn all noble actis. and specialy agayn the vij dedely synnis /– quhilkis quhen thai haue the maistry ledis man to the paynis of hell –/ off the quhilk sevin synnis. glutony is ane of the werst /' (omits list of seven deadly sins) (7.114–18)

The cited passages show that Hay is unique here rather than in agreement with I.

Byles' evidence, then, adds up to very little: his first instance is slight indeed, his third simply mistaken. Nonetheless, one may add further (and more compelling) instances along the same line (but without errors). In cap. v, for example, Hay appears to agree twice with unique readings in I (or the group of which I is a member):

Additional indication 1: *soit loyal* vs. *recepuoir et maintenir*, cap. v

(1) General French reading: 'par quoy il soit a l'ordre de cheualerie loyal'[13] (Minervini 136.12–13)

(2) I: 'parquoy il puisse dignement recepuoir lordre de cheualerie et icelle maintenir loyaulment' (fol. 347v)

(3) Hay: 'to ressaue and kepe / and worthily gouerne the said ordre' (5.16)

Additional indication 2: recipients of the newly dubbed knight's gifts, cap. v

(1) General French reading: 'A celuy jour convient faire grant feste de donner beaux dons et grans, et faire grans mengiers, jouster et bohorder et les autres choses qui appartiennent a feste de chevalerie'[14] (Minervini 143.7–10)

(2) French manuscripts of subgroup ι (I, M): 'A celuy iour conuient faire grant feste de donner beaulz dons et grans mengiers / iouster et tournoyer donner aux heraulz d'armes et faire tout ce quy appartient a cheuallerie comme il est acoustume danciennete' (I, fol. 348v); 'A celui iour conuient faire grant feste de donner beaulx dons & grans mengier Jouster & bahfourder et les autres choses qui appartiennent a cheualerie & donner a roys darmes & heraulz comme il est a coustume danciennete' (M, fol. 11r)

(3) Hay: 'And jn that day / suld thare be grete festyng / justing & tournay-mentis. with othir actis as lissis & behurdis /. geve grete giftis / and mak grete solempnitee jn the honoure of god and the grete feste / And yat herauldis ande kingis of armes and menstralis war' rewardit' (5.77–81)

I will cite just three more instances of unique agreement between Hay's text and manuscripts closely related to the French I:

---

13 Catalan reading: 'per la qual sie leyal a l'orde de cavaylaria' (Soler 197.11).
14 The Catalan reads, 'en aqueyl die deu ésser feta gran festa de donar, de convits, de boornar, e de les altres coses qui.s covenan a la festa de cavaylaria' (Soler 200. 104–6).

Additional indication 3: *ne peult maintenir* vs. *ne doit recepuoir*, cap. i
   (1) General French reading: 'Car nul chevalier ne peult maintenir chevalerie se il ne scet l'ordre'[15] (Minervini 83.10–11)
   (2) I: 'car nul cheuallier ne doit recepuour lordre de cheuallerie sil ne scet lordre' (fol. 339r)
   (3) Hay: 'ffor thare suld nane be sa hardy to tak that hye honourable ordre but he war' first worthy be the sicht of the prince tharetill – And syne yat coud the poyntis and articlis yat to the said ordre appertenis' (1.142–6)

Additional indication 4: *commencemens* vs. *commandemens*, cap. ii
   (1) General French reading: 'Et se tu es mauvais, tu es ennemy de chevalerie et es contraire a ses commencemens et a ses honneurs'[16] (Minervini 90. 1–3)
   (2) French manuscripts of subgroup ι (I, M): 'Et se tu es mauluais tu es contraire a cheuallerie et ennemy a ses commandemens et honneurs' (I, fol. 340r; M, fol. 4b)
   (3) Hay: 'And gif he be of wikkit / and euill lyf of tyranny and crimynous' lyfing he is contrarious' and jnymy of the ordre and / rebellour' to the commandementis of honour' (2.93–95)

Additional indication 5: *fait regarder a terre* vs. *fait baissier les yeulz vers la terre*, cap. vi
   (1) General French reading: 'aussy chapel de fer deffent homme de regarder en hault et le fait regarder a terre'[17] (Minervini 145.11–12)
   (2) I: 'aussy chapel de fer deffent homme de regarder en hault et luy fait baissier les yeulz vers la terre' (fol. 349r)
   (3) Hay: 'sa dois the stelin hat the knycht cast doune his eyne' (6.39–40)

Such examples, seen in isolation, seem, in spite of the flaws in Byles' own examples, to support his thesis that Hay's original for the *Buke of the Ordre of Knychthede* belonged to a manuscript closely related to Royal MS 14.E.ii. The same researches that cull such instances of unique agreement, however, find as well numerous instances where Hay's text agrees with the general tradition against I or uniquely with another text. Mapstone reports, for example, that she has 'also found Hay's translation to have similarities in phrasing with the group containing St John's College, Oxford, MS 102'.[18] The present evidence, then, seems not to support any definite conclusion about the French text from which Hay translated this work. Still, a comprehensive comparison of Hay's text with the French texts comprising Minervini's δ-group (C+ι [M, I]) might offer the best hope of the 'linguistic reward' of which Stevenson despaired.

Other avenues of inquiry into Hay's particular source lead to similarly suggestive but unsatisfactory results. If the particular French manuscript used

---

15 Catalan reading: 'Cor negun cavayler no pot mantenir l'orde que no sab, ni pot amar son orde' (Soler 164. 91–2).
16 Catalan reading: 'e si est àvol, tu est lo major enamic de cavaylaria, e est pus contrari a sos començements e a son honrament' (Soler 168.50–1).
17 Catalan reading: 'enaxí capeyl defèn hom de les coses altas e garda a la terra' (Soler 202. 27–8 and n. 1).
18 'The Advice to Princes Tradition' 87.

by Hay or an accurate copy of it existed, one would expect it to explain certain striking peculiarities in Hay's text. For example, at 7.225, Hay writes 'Accyde est male,' apparently copying his French original; he then proceeds to translate what he copied: 'Suereness is a vice.'[19] It should be simple, therefore, to find that text which uses these particular words and to posit that it was Hay's original. No extant text, however, uses 'male' in this passage, all reading 'Accide est (ung) vice' (Minervini 164.5 and 206; the prints agree; the passage is missing in M and N).[20] Did Hay compose the rubric himself, then? Did he substitute 'male' for 'vice'? Positive textual evidence does not exist to answer this question.

A more striking peculiarity appears at 6.71–2. Here Hay's translation interjects at the end of the discussion of 'spuris' an apparently irrelevant comment: 'Of the suerd we haue spokyn of before, jn quhat takenyng and significacioun jt is gevin.' None of the extant French texts – manuscript or print – justifies such an interjection: no mention of a sword, or indeed of any weapon, appears in this context. Indeed, Hay's treatment of the spurs is significantly different from the French treatment throughout. The general differences, however, are all possible to explain by appealing to the translator's freedom to paraphrase. The interjection, on the other hand, seems most likely to be based on some characteristic of Hay's exemplar – some phrase or word that prompted Hay to explain his omission of a particular discussion at this point.[21]

---

19 A similar instance occurs at p.6, where the scribe has copied 'de toutes choses' and then its translation, 'of all things.' In this instance, the French words are marked for expunction, but not so at 7.225. Cf. *Gouernaunce of Princis* 31.17, where 'but' is duplicated by 'sans.'

20 The Catalan reads 'Accídia és vici' (Soler 213.132).

21 Stevenson notes Hay's phrase and explains it away as indicating Hay's awareness that his list 'is not following the usual order' (xxiv), yet Hay's list accords nearly exactly to the highly consistent French list, which likewise follows Llull's list very closely. **Llull's List of Weapons, ch. 5:** (1) espaa, (2) lansa, (3) capeyl de fferre, (4) ausberc, (5) calses de fferre, (6) esperons, (7) gorgera, (8) massa, (9) misericòrdia, (10) escut, (11) la seyla, (12) cavayl, (13) fre, regnes, (14) testera, (15) guarniments de cavayl, (16) perpunt, (17) senyal, (18) senyera (Soler 201–206). **French Version's List of Weapons, Ch. 6** (This list is checked against Minervini, the variants in his apparatus, M, N, and the three prints; all agree in the 'arms' listed): (1) espee (faite en semblance de croix, taillant de deux pars), (2) lance (droite, le fer, le panoncel), (3) chapel de fer, (4) haubert, (5) chauses de fer (que chevalier avecquez fer doit tenir seurs les chemins, c'est assavoir avecquez espee, lance et mace et avecquez les autres garnemens de fer), (6) esperons (NB: et fait procurer le harnois et les despens qui ont mestier [besoing, 1510 print] a l'onneur de chevalerie; procurer au chevallier chevaulz harnois et tout ce appartient a son office pour honnourer chevalerie . . ., I), (7) gorgiere (gorgerin, I), (8) mace, (9) misericorde, coutel de croix (couseil de croix, G; coutel de clou, I), (10) escu, (11) gantelles (manie plus seurement la lance ou l'espee) (gantelles de fer, I), (12) selle, (13) cheval, destrier ('cheval et mesmement destrier'), (14) frain (les resnes du frain), (15) testiere, (16) garnemens de cheval, (17) pourpoint (cote ou paleto, L), (18) seignal (armes, L), (19) baniere (Minervini, 144–54; the French has added *gantelles* to Llull's list). **Hay's List of Weapons, Ch. 6:** (1) suerd (crossit hilt, twa egeis), (2) spere (evyn, scharp hard stelin poynt of the spere hede, pennoun), (3) chapellat of stele, stelin hat, (4) haubergeoun, haubert (maillis) (later designated 'hauberkis'), (5) leg harnais, (6) maisse, pollax, wand, (7) spuris (The *suerd* is mentioned again here in Hay.), (8) quhip, (9) gorgelin, (10) masse, fals' sterap, (11) lytill schort suerd, misericorde, (12) schelde, targe, (13) gloues of plate, (14) sadill, sete (the sadill with the grathe yat langis jt), (15) courser', destrere, (16) bridill (irne bytt, reynis), (17) hede stele of the bridill, (18) hors is enournyt with harnais before and behynd, (19) jakkis . . . of grete solempnitee of sylk, (20) takyn of armes, (21) baneris (Hay has added the first *maisse* (item 6) and the *quhip* (item 8).

Two such textual situations may be hypothesised. The first seems less likely than the second, but it has the virtue of explaining the specific weapon Hay mentions. In this hypothesis, an antecendent of Hay's exemplar divided *esperons* 'spurs' at the end of a line, thus: *espe*-. (Such a division does in fact occur in Vérart's 1504 print [not a manuscript, obviously], but without the subsequent errors hypothesised here.) The scribe's eye then skipped to following material, leaving *esperons* unfinished. A later scribe, copying this defective passage, identified an error but misread *espe* as *espé(e)* 'sword,' and filled in the gap with a brief discussion of that weapon. Hence Hay's interjection.

The second hypothesis seems more likely but fails to explain Hay's specific mention of the sword. In this hyposthesis, Hay's exemplar included an expansion of the phrase 'le harnois et les despens qui ont mestier a l'onneur de chevalerie' (Minervini 146.12–13).[22] The expansion would plainly have to include some mention of *l'espée*, a seemingly unlikely chance, given the apparent intention of *harnois* – horse-trappings or armour, but not weapons. (Cf. the reading in I, fol. 349r: 'Aussi diligence fait procurer au cheuallier cheuaulz harnois et tout ce quy appartient a son office pour honnourer cheuallerie.' The phrase 'cheuaulz harnois' suggests horse-trappings, perhaps the 'garnemens de cheval' mentioned later in the list [Minervini 151.16]; 'tout ce quy appartient a son office' leaves the intention wide open, of course, as does 'les despens' in Minervini's text.) Although we may speculate about possible textual explanations, however, discussions like this quickly show that existing evidence provides no compelling clues about Hay's motivation here.

These examples demonstrate again that the clearest potential avenues for the discovery of Hay's exemplar turn out to be blind alleys: no existing French text clarifies Hay's text in these instances. One further example may hold out a different sort of possibility for conclusion. In cap. v, Hay describes the act of dubbing the young knight:

> And than suld the squier' hald vp his handis to the hevyn / and his eyne to the hicht / and his hert to god /– syttand on his kneis /– And thare suld the prince haue a suerd redy – of honour gylt with golde and belt jt about his sides – jn takenyng of chastitee. justice – & cheritee And thare the knycht suld outhir geve him a strake with his hand – or with a drawin suerd jn the nek to think on the poyntis and defend his dewiteis // And syne suld he outhir kys him jn the mouth or ellis kys the croce of the suerd /– and geve jt him / and ger' him kis jt agayne and sa put jt jn the scalbourd /– and bid him think on his athe / ande charge yat he has vndertane / and the honour' yat he suld manetene / (5.55–66)

Most of the French copies (both manuscripts and prints) are similar in essentials to the text printed by Minervini and justify his punctuation:

---

22 See Soler 203.50 for the Catalan reading: 'l'arnès e la messió qui és master a la honor de cavaylaria.'

L'escuier se doit agenoiller devant l'autel et lever a Dieu ses yeulx corporelx et espirituelz et ses mains au ciel. Et le cheualier luy doit ceindre l'espee, en signifiance de chasteté et de justice. Et en signifiance de charité le chevalier doit baisier l'escuyer et luy doit donner une paumee, pour ce que il soit remembrant de ce que il promet et de la grant charge a quoy il est obligié et du grant honneur que il recoit et prent par l'ordre de chevalerie.[23] (Minervini 142.11-19)

A major point of contrast is obvious – the significance of the sword: in Hay the sword is girded on to signify 'chastitee. justice – & cheritee'; in Minervini's text the sword signifies 'chasteté' and 'justice,' whereas 'charité' is firmly associated with the knightly kiss. The following readings from individual manuscripts may point the way toward the sort of reading Hay's exemplar may have had, or at least toward an exemplary reading that would make Hay's translation probable.[24]

- A (fol. 38r-v): ceindre lespee en signe de chastete et en signifiance de charite ¶ le chevalier doit baisier
- C (fols. 25v-26r): ceindre lespee en signifiance de chastete & de iustice et en signifiance de charite ¶ le chevalier doit baisier
- M (fol. 10v): ceindre en signifiance de chastete & de iustice lespee / & aussi de charite. Le chevalier doit baisier
- N (fol. 96r): chaindre lespee en signifiance de chastete et de iustice et de charite / le chevalier doit baisier

A and C separate charity and the kiss only by punctuation (here the ¶ symbol); M goes further, separating charity and the kiss by punctuation (the period and the following capital letter) and by attaching charity syntactically to the sword by 'et aussi de'; N has the most straightforward series: 'de . . . et de . . . et de.' No textual development can be posited from this one passage, of course, and N belongs, after all, to a different manuscript sub-group from A, C, and M, but these manuscript readings may suggest the sort of reading Hay altered even further, separating charity and the kiss more completely by interposing between them the *paumée* ('a strake with his hand') that in all the extant French texts follows the kiss. Such an example makes a general point clear: we must include manuscript evidence in our researches – editions alone may not tell us all we need to know.

In spite of my pessimism about identifying a particular source for Hay's *Buke of*

---

23 The French has followed the Catalan closely: 'L'escuder, devant l'autar, se deu agenoylar, e que leu sos uyls a Déu, corporals e spirituals, e ses mans a Déu. E lo cavayler li deu senyr l'espaa, a significar castetat e justícia; e, en significança de caritat, deu besar s'escuder, e donar-li quexada per ço que sie menbrant de so que promet e del gran càrrec a què s'obliga e de la gran honor que pren per l'orde de cavaylaria' (Soler 200. 90-6).
24 Manuscript punctuation and capitalisation are retained, <¶> being used for various manuscript paragraph marks.

the Ordre of Knychthede (implied and justified, I believe, by the foregoing discussion), other questions about the relationship of Hay's texts to their French ancestors admit of more discussion, though because of the uncertainty of the precise textual relationships, answers to these questions must remain tentative. Useful statements can be made about many of Hay's practices (and limitations) as a translator. (I think, for instance, of Hay's tendency to simplify and sometimes confuse the syntax of French conditional clauses, exhibited twice in the third chapter of *Ordre of Knychthede* [228–30, 470–73].) One may even be fairly safe in commenting on some of the additions Hay has made to the text as he found it in French (cf. my earlier discussion of Hay's apparent addition of a Latin maxim to the text as he found it). Finally Hay's characteristic paraphrasis and expansion of the French text can be illustrated by comparison of numerous passages throughout his translations with the corresponding French passages.[25]

In my original plan for this paper, I thought of it as 'Lessons of a Dead End,' yet it seems to me now less a dead end than a road that leads to a different destination than the one at first intended. Wrestling with issues of source on the lexical level has taught me a good deal about Hay's language (though not so very much about his sources for that language); pondering possible relationships between the *Livre de l'ordre de chevalerie* and Hay's syntax – even, one may argue, his ideas – similarly demands a scrutiny of both French and Scots texts without which the scholar's statements about Hay's work remain mere impressions or little more. Perhaps our understanding of Hay's language and ideas must remain full of guesses, but these guesses should, I believe, be fully aware of the difficulties attending them – should be, in short, not *mere* guesses, but guesses educated by the full range of material with which they have to do.

Tables and Figures

Table 1: Known manuscripts and prints of the *Livre de l'ordre de chevalerie*

Manuscripts:

A   Paris, Bibliothèque Nationale, fr. 19810 (s. xiv)
B   Paris, Bibliothèque Nationale, fr. 1130 (a fragment; s. xv)
C   Paris, Bibliothèque Nationale, fr. 1972 (s. xv)
D   Paris, Bibliothèque Nationale, fr. 1973 (s. xv)
E   Paris, Bibliothèque Nationale, fr. 19809 (s. xv)
F   Paris, Bibliothèque Nationale, fr. 1971 (s. xv/xvi)
G   Oxford, St. John's College, MS 102 (s. xiv)

---

25 Several studies have worked in just this fashion. See Arthur Ferguson, *The Indian Summer of English Chivalry: Studies in the Decline and Transformation of Chivalric Idealism* (Durham, NC: Duke UP, 1960); Diane D. Bornstein, 'The Chivalric Manual in Fifteenth-Century England,' Ph.D. dissertation, New York University, 1970; and Sally Mapstone, 'The Advice to Princes Tradition.' Of these studies, only Mapstone's displays any awareness of the difficult textual situation that qualifies such studies.

H   London, British Library, Add. MS 22768 (s. xv)
I   London, British Library, Royal MS 14.E.ii (ca. 1480)
L   Edinburgh, National Library of Scotland, Adv. MS 31.1.9 (ca. 1532)
M   Toulouse, Bibliothèque Municipale, MS 830 (s. xv)
N   New York, Columbia University, Plimpton Collection, MS 282 (s. xv)
T   Turin, Biblioteca Nazionale, MS L. III. 14 (s. xiv)
T2 Turin, Archivio di Stato, MS JB.II.19 (s. xv)

Prints:
Paris, 1504, by Antoine Vérart
Paris, 1505, by Michel le Noir (reset from Vérart's edition)
Lyon, 1510, by Vincent Portunaris

Figure 1: Manuscript Relationships, *Livre de l'ordre de chevalerie*

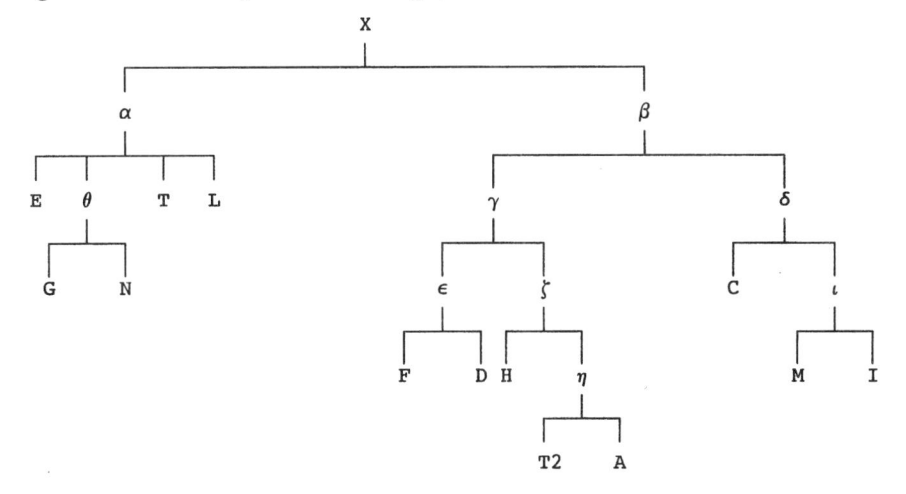

```
                          X
                          |
              ┌───────────┴───────────┐
              α                       β
              |                       |
        ┌───┬─┴─┬───┐         ┌───────┴───────┐
        E   θ   T   L         γ               δ
            |                 |               |
          ┌─┴─┐         ┌─────┼─────┐       ┌─┴─┐
          G   N         ε     ζ             C   ι
                        |   ┌─┼─┐            |
                        F   D H η          ┌─┴─┐
                                |          M   I
                              ┌─┴─┐
                              T2  A
```

Table 2: Stevenson's Class A and Class B of the *Livre de l'ordre de chevalerie* (Minervini's sigla noted parenthetically)

Class A
(Those whose prologues begin 'A la louenge et a la gloire de la pourveance devine dieu guy est sire et roy souverain par dessus toutes choses celestes et terrestres . . .' or, he adds, 'with words practically indentical')

St. John's College, 102 (G) British Library, Royal 14.E.ii (I) British Library, Add. 22786 (H) Vérart print of 1504 Hay Manuscript translation Caxton translation (1484)

Note: of the three French manuscripts in Stevenson's Class A, one (G) belongs to Minervini's α-group and two (I, H) belong to Minervini's β-group.

Class B
(Those whose prologues begin 'A Lhonneur dicelluy qui par la providence colloca la terre au centre du monde qui est cause des causes . . .')

Portunaris print of 1510
National Library of Scotland, Adv. 31.1.9 (L)

Note: L belongs to Minervini's β-group.

Figure 2: Byles' Classification of Versions of the *Livre de l'ordre de chevalerie* (Minervini's sigla substituted for Byles')

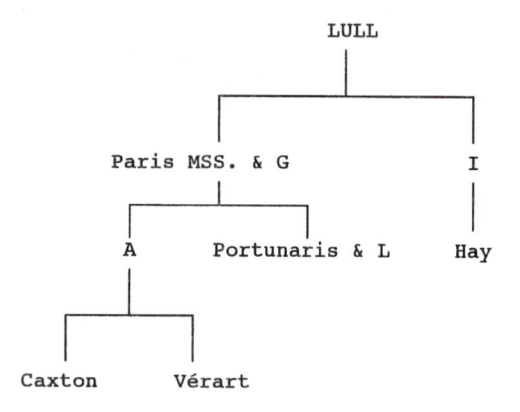

```
                        LULL
                         |
            ┌────────────┴────────────┐
     Paris MSS. & G                   I
            |                         |
      ┌─────┴─────┐                   |
      A      Portunaris & L          Hay
      |
   ┌──┴──┐
Caxton  Vérart
```

PRISCILLA BAWCUTT

11. *French Connections? From the* Grands Rhétoriqueurs *to Clément Marot*

This paper, unlike Gaul, is divided into two parts. The first is a response to an elegant lecture given to this conference at Aberdeen in 1987 by Professor Joanne Norman, when she enlisted Dunbar into 'the company of the grands rhétoriqueurs'.[1] In 1990 at Columbia her conclusions were enthusiastically endorsed by Professor Lyall: 'Dunbar', he said, 'is neither a Scottish Chaucer nor a "Scottish Lydgatian", but a corresponding member of that Continental fellowship, the *grands rhétoriqueurs*'.[2] Now one of the things that puzzles me is precisely this enthusiasm, the notion that some sort of accolade is conferred upon Dunbar by saying that he – I quote – 'at his best' is capable of 'the rhetorical pyrotechnics of the *grands rhétoriqueurs*' (Lyall, 18). These French poets, despite the epithet *grands*, are not exactly great; they are not in the class of Chrétien de Troyes or Villon. How many in this audience, I wonder, have read any of their writings, or are familiar even with their names. 'Grands rhétoriqueurs' is a convenient modern label for a number of fifteenth- and early sixteenth-century poets – important examples are Jean Molinet, Octovien de Saint–Gelais, Guillaume Crétin, and Jean Lemaire – but it was not applied to them until the nineteenth century (despite Norman, 182); it originated as a mocking reference to lawyers, not poets, and has been translated as 'pompous phrasemakers'.[3] 'Les mal aimés, les mal nommés' are the first words of Paul Zumthor's *Le Masque et la lumiére* (Paris, 1978), a brilliant attempt to rehabilitate their reputation from the onslaughts of Henry Guy.[4] Many other critics, however, remain unimpressed: one speaks of their 'imbecile ingenuity'; to another they appear 'undiscerning and immoderate in their praises, their homage tainted with false humility, in their political poems servile propagandists . . . above all, banal'.[5] Is this the company to which Dunbar belongs? Is he too mediocre, servile and banal?

In fact I remain unconvinced that there is good reason to associate Dunbar

---

1 Joanne Norman, 'William Dunbar: Grand Rhétoriqueur', in *Bryght Lanternis: Essays on the Language and Literature of Medieval and Renaissance Scotland*, ed. J. Derrick McClure and Michael R.G. Spiller, Aberdeen, 1989, pp. 179–99.
2 Roderick J. Lyall, ' "A New Maid Channoun"? Redefining the Canonical in Medieval and Renaissance Scottish Literature', *Studies in Scottish Literature*, 26 (1991), 1–13.
3 On the origin of the phrase, see Pierre Jodogne, 'Les "Rhétoriqueurs" et l'humanisme', in *Humanism in France at the End of the Middle Ages and in the Early Renaissance*, ed. A.H.T. Levi, Manchester, 1970, pp. 150–75.
4 Henry Guy, *Histoire de la poésie française au XVIe siècle, I: l'école des rhétoriqueurs*, Paris, 1910.
5 The quotations are from Derek Pearsall, *Old English and Middle English Poetry*, London, 1977, p. 219; and P.M. Smith, *Clément Marot: Poet of the French Renaissance*, London, 1970, p. 54.

with these poets, except in the most vague and general way. The proposition seems to be – I attempt to summarise it fairly – that Dunbar and the rhétoriqueurs had a similar life-experience, as well-educated churchmen, court poets serving in royal or ducal households, and that therefore they wrote in a very similar way. 'These poets shared both a common historic situation and a common poetic' is how Professor Norman puts it (183). But even if one fully accepts the literary and social determinism implicit in this argument, it commands assent only at a very general level. It would apply equally to many other poets writing at about this time: to Gavin Douglas, for instance, and later to Lindsay and Bellenden; and also to English poets, such as John Skelton and Stephen Hawes. Indeed the court of Henry VII offers plentiful evidence both of close acquaintance with Franco-Burgundian culture, and attempts to emulate it.[6]

How similar, I wonder, was Dunbar's 'historic situation' to those of the rhétoriqueurs? We know so little of his career, and of his precise relationship with James IV. But there is not a scrap of evidence that he was a paid historiographer, in the manner of Chastellain, Molinet or De la Vigne, writing chronicles and propagandist works that glorified the reputation of a king and his dynasty. Indeed, as James Goldstein has recently remarked, John Barbour, whose 'poetic practice' was inseparable from his 'royalist ideology', might better deserve to be called a court poet than Dunbar.[7] Dunbar's extant poetry contains no effusive prologues or dedications to patrons; there is no definite evidence that he was ever commissioned to write a poem, though this might be true of the two pieces on Bernard Stewart, where he shows most affinity with the rhétoriqueurs. As to the Scottish court itself, we should not be too ready to assume that it closely resembled the courts of Burgundy and France, either in wealth or atmosphere. It is surely a truism that courts reflected the character of their kings, and thus differed greatly.[8]

As for Dunbar's poetry and 'poetic', when I juxtapose him with his French contemporaries I am far more conscious of difference than similarity. I would not deny that there are indeed resemblances, but they essentially consist of the topoi and commonplaces of late medieval courtly poetry. The virtual identification of poetry and rhetoric, for instance, was no invention of the rhétoriqueurs; Lois Ebin has demonstrated its importance in fifteenth-century England.[9] The genres employed by Dunbar and also by the rhétoriqueurs – the debate, the testament, the allegorical love poem, the petition, the complaint – all had an international currency at this time. Dunbar and the rhétoriqueurs are said to exploit unspecified 'complex metrical forms' (Norman, 188); yet I observe few parallels in their practice. Where in Dunbar are the so-called 'formes fixes', i.e. the ballades and rondeaux still beloved of his French contemporaries? Why does he never

---

6 Cf. G. Kipling, *The Triumph of Honour*, Leiden, 1977, *passim*.
7 See R. James Goldstein, *The Matter of Scotland: Historical Narrative in Medieval Scotland*, Lincoln, Nebraska, 1993, p. 140.
8 Cf. David Starkey, 'Court History in Perspective', in *The English Court: from the Wars of the Roses to the Civil War*, ed. D. Starkey *et al.*, London, 1987, pp. 1–24.
9 See her *Illuminator, Makar, Vates: Visions of Poetry in the Fifteenth Century*, Lincoln, Nebraska, 1988.

employ the *prosimetrum*, a work composed alternately in prose and verse? This form was such a favourite of the rhétoriqueurs that it might almost be called their trademark. The attractive *triolet* in *The Dregie* probably had a direct French origin, but most of Dunbar's verse forms were the staple of fifteenth century English poets: the carol; tail-rhyme; and rhyme royal. Even the ornate nine-line stanza of *The Goldyn Targe*, so remarkably popular with early Scottish poets, derives from the complaint in Chaucer's *Anelida and Arcite*. The alliterative verse of *The Tua Mariit Wemen and the Wedo*, of course, is wholly Anglo-Saxon in origin.

Let me call attention to other differences, which seem to me far from insignificant. The rhétoriqueurs tend to write large-scale works, often consisting of thousands of lines; to put it less charitably, they are often extremely long-winded. Dunbar, as most critics have noted, is characterised by his brevity. It is instructive to place his elegy for Bernard Stewart (a mere 32 lines) beside Molinet's *Le Trosne d'honneur*. which runs to over 20 pages, and is filled with rhetorical set-pieces and extended commendations of the dead duke of Burgundy. In its florid eloquence it is wholly typical of many other French 'déplorations'. A favourite rhétoriqueur theme was the didactic allegorical journey, that had as its climax the vision of a temple, castle, or palace in which Honour was enthroned. This type of allegory is foreign to Dunbar; he never enters on this path to self-enlightenment, nor participates in the cult of honour. The rhétoriqueurs were learned writers, who packed their works with allusions to the Scriptures, or to antique myth and history. Some indeed should be called humanists; and several were translators from the classics – Saint-Gelais, for instance, made translations from Virgil and Ovid. Here too the contrast with Dunbar is striking; he lacks their learning as well as their pedantry. There are far better parallels to their style and subject matter in Douglas. Many readers of these French poets comment on their flattery and sycophancy; even Molinet's editor found his eulogies of various dukes and princes almost 'illisibles'.[10] Some wrote openly propagandist pieces, supporting Charles VIII's invasion of Italy and other military campaigns.[11] Contrast Dunbar again: he wrote no piece urging James IV to support Perkin Warbeck and invade Northumberland in 1496; even the poem on 'Donald Owyr' seems to contest the royal policy of clemency; and *The Thrissill and the Rois* contains almost as much rebuke and exhortation as eulogy. The petitions are humorous and often flippant, and never – I think – grovelling. The only poem of Dunbar's which is a shade sycophantic is that addressed to Bernard Stewart; despite his crushing defeat at the battle of Seminara (Calabria, 1503) he is repeatedly called 'invincible'.

We are asked to associate Dunbar 'with his brother poets of France and Burgundy' (Norman, 186). Is it not strange then that in the great poem that mourns the death of those whom he calls both 'brether' and 'makaris' Dunbar fails to include a single French poet? Why must we disregard his glowing tribute,

---

10 Cf. N. Dupire, *Jean Molinet: La Vie, les oeuvres*, Paris, 1932, 105–6.
11 Cf. Cynthia J. Brown, *The Shaping of History and Poetry in Late Medieval France: Propaganda and Artistic Expression in the Works of the Rhétoriqueurs*, Birmingham, Alabama, 1985, esp. pp. 12–25.

in *The Goldyn Targe*, to Chaucer and the 'Inglisch' tradition of poetry; there was surely no pressure upon Dunbar to write in this way emanating from James IV, who has been depicted as an anglophobe by his recent biographer, Norman Macdougall. There is good evidence, as I have argued elsewhere, in Dunbar's own poems to show that the literary 'company' or 'fellowship' that meant most to him were the poets who wrote in his own vernacular, whether Scots or English, famous or unknown, courtly or popular.[12]

To transform Dunbar into an honorary Frenchman, of course, is no new thing. Almost a century ago Aeneas Mackay asserted, with a revealing vagueness, that Dunbar borrowed 'if anywhere, from the French poetry'[13]. Since then there have been many unavailing attempts to substantiate this notion; even a distinguished scholar like James Kinsley says curiously of the seven-line stanza used in several of Dunbar's poems that it represents 'the French *chant royal* . . . associated with the poetical contests at Rouen'; only as an afterthought does he note that this stanza, which James VI termed 'Troilus verse', was used for Chaucer's *Troilus and Criseyde*. As Denton Fox noted in 1983, 'no one has ever established any specific French source for any of Dunbar's poems'.[14] Why then is this notion, which seems to me more a matter of faith than reason, so persistent? I would trace it to the mist-enshrouded glamour of the Auld Alliance, which has generated other cherished myths – from the early notion that the alliance itself originated in the time of Charlemagne to the popular belief that it explains the presence in the Scots vocabulary of such words as 'ashet' and 'gigot'.[15] The Alliance's purpose, of course, was political and military, and was directed against England. Anglophobia, alas, tends to accompany Francophilia, and is surely latent in some enthusiasm for the notion of Dunbar as either 'Scottish Villon' or 'grand rhétoriqueur'. Indeed the emphatic negatives in the remark quoted earlier – 'neither a Scottish Chaucer nor a "Scottish Lydgatian" ' – imply evident delight at removing him from the clutches of the English. I myself would not apply *any* of these terms to Dunbar, because I find such labels reductive and of little value.

12 See Bawcutt, *Dunbar the Makar*, Oxford, 1992, especially pp. 20–9.
13 See *The Poems of William Dunbar*, ed. J. Small, with W. Gregor and AE. J.G. Mackay, STS, 1884–93, I. cxlvii. Cf. also J.M. Smith, *The French Background of Middle Scots Literature*, Edinburgh, 1934, p. 60: 'he owed more of a debt to the French than to the English poets'.
14 See *The Poems of William Dunbar*, ed. J. Kinsley, Oxford, 1979, p. 237; *Ane Schort Treatise . . . in Scottis Poesie*, chapter viii; D. Fox, 'Middle Scots Poets and Patrons', in *English Court Culture in the Later Middle Ages*, ed. V.J. Scattergood and J.W. Sherborne, London, 1983, 109–27, esp. 122–3. He comments that Pierrepont Nichols wrote a Harvard dissertation, investigating 'the French verse that Dunbar might have known. The fruits of this dissertation were two articles in *PMLA*, one titled "Lydgate's Influence on the Aureate Terms of the Scottish Chaucerians", and the other, "William Dunbar as a Scottish Lydgatian" '.
15 See further, Stephen Wood, *The Auld Alliance: Scotland and France, the Military Connection*, Edinburgh, 1989, esp. pp. 8–12; cf. also G. Donaldson's Saltire pamphlet, *The Auld Alliance: the Franco-Scottish Conection*, Edinburgh, 1985. 'Ashet' and 'gigot' were both formerly current in English; see I. Macleod, 'Eighteenth-century Scots Food Terminology', in *The Nuttis Schell: Essays on the Scots Language*, ed. C. Macafee and I. Macleod, Aberdeen, 1987, pp. 219–26, esp. 223: 'throughout most of its history the word [gigot] is shared with English'; also Annette Hope, *A Caledonian Feast*, Edinburgh, 1987.

At this point I probably sound like the 'Auld Innemy' incarnate, so it should be made clear that I am well aware of the many cultural contacts between Scotland and France in the fifteenth and sixteenth centuries. But the subject is vast and complex, and J.M. Smith's book on *The French Background of Middle Scots Literature* (1934), though stimulating and pioneering, is now out of date. Much has been discovered that was not available to her; yet many of the new discoveries remain curiously neglected, their significance little studied or analysed. One small instance is *The Porteous of Nobleness*, which is preserved both in a Chepman and Myllar print and the Asloan manuscript. It was pointed out as long ago as 1950 that this translates a poem by Alain Chartier, *Le Bréviaire des Nobles*.[16] Yet a modern historian, still unaware of its French origin, treats it as original Scots work.[17] We know the name of the translator – Andrew Cadiou – and that he was no Edinburgh courtier, but an Aberdeen business-man and public notary.[18] I am increasingly impressed by the role of cultured notaries in the making and the transmission of Scottish literature at this time. (The poetry of the Scottish notary sounds far less glamorous than the poetry of the Stewart court, but might possibly be a more rewarding topic.) Cadiou graduated at the University of Paris in 1472, and this – along with similar pieces of evidence – suggests how important a factor in spreading awareness of French writing was residence in France. We should not assume that the works of the rhétoriqueurs travelled overseas to Scotland rapidly, almost as soon as they were composed.

It is interesting that Cadiou turned Chartier's popular but rather old-fashioned poem into prose; precisely the opposite occured in the case of *Lancelot of the Laik* and *Clariodus*, where French prose romances are re-cast in five-stress couplets. I suspect that these translators – and many other Scots at this time – often turned to French vernacular literature for its content, rather than the style. *Clariodus* is striking, in this respect, since its style is ornate, even aureate. Yet this does not derive from its French prose source, *Cleriadus et Meiadice*, which is notably plain and unadorned.[19] Occasional echoes in *Clariodus* of *The Goldyn Targe* suggest rather that the tradition to which it conforms is a native Scottish one. Such a spirit of independence towards a French original is sometimes voiced quite explicitly. The anonymous translator of an elegy on the dauphiness Margaret (d. 1445) ruthlessly destroyed the carefully balanced stanzaic pattern of the French *complainte*, saying:

Bot nocht withstandyng thaire is mare of this lamentacioun xviii coupill, and in the Ansuere of Resoune als mekill, this ma suffyce; for the complant is bot fenyeit thing. Bot be caus the tother part, quhilk is the Ansuere of Resoun, is verray suthfastnes, me think it gud to put mare of it.[20]

16 See *The Chepman and Myllar Prints: a Facsimile*, introd. William Beattie, Edinburgh Bibliographical Society, 1950, pp. ix–x.
17 Edward J. Cowan, *Montrose*, London, 1977, p. 24.
18 See Harold Booton, 'John and Andrew Cadiou: Aberdeen Notaries of the Fifteenth and Early Sixteenth Centuries', *Northern Scotland*, 9 (1989), 17–20.
19 See the Maitland Club edition of *Clariodus*, ed. Edward Piper, Edinburgh, 1830; also *Cleriadus et Meliadice*, ed. Gaston Zink, Geneva, 1984.
20 Cf. Bawcutt, 'A Medieval Scottish Elegy and its French Original', *SLJ*, 15, no. 1 (1988), 5–13.

It would be naive to deduce, however, that this concern for 'verray suthfastnes', or orthodox morality, was an invariable Scottish trait. Few today are likely to have read Nicol Burne's wicked travesty of a famous epigram (*Abest Candida*) by the great French Protestant, Theodore de Béze; Burne's Scottish Text Society editor decided to censor it, saying: 'It is impossible to reprint here Burne's grossly indecent translation . . . it has not even the merit of being in good Scots'.[21]

We need more and closer analysis of such cases of actual Franco–Scottish literary contact, whatever form they take – translation, imitation, or creative re-handling. In the second part of this paper I propose, very briefly, to consider Scottish responses to a French poet whose name hardly figures at all in literary histories of Scotland. This is Clément Marot (c. 1496–1544), a subtle and witty poet associated with the court of Francis I, who was, in his day – as his most recent editor tells us – 'un best-seller'.[22] He was quite as versatile as Dunbar, and far more voluminous, writing translations, allegories, satiric epistles, epigrams, and love poetry. Anne Lake Prescott, who made an excellent study of his reputation in Renaissance England, noted how Marot's very variety seemed to cause 'odd ripples and malformations in his image', as if there were several Marots who 'coexisted uneasily in mutual self-contradiction'.[23] His reputation in Scotland seems to have been somewhat similar; here I shall mention three aspects only.

The writings of Marot that had the widest cultural impact in Europe, and probably also in Scotland, were his metrical translations of forty-nine psalms. These were printed repeatedly, and included in *La Forme des priéres et chantz ecclesiastiques* (Geneva, 1542), a work which was enormously popular and influential. I cannot here investigate the complicated relationship between this publication, the Anglo-Genevan *The Form of Prayers* (1556), and subsequent renderings of the psalms in Scotland.[24] It has been suggested, however, that Alexander Montgomerie's psalm translations may have been influenced by Marot.[25] Professor Lyall has reminded us (in a paper to be found elsewhere in this volume), that such metrical versions of the psalms appealed particularly to the Reformers, and were sometimes criticised by traditional Catholics. We have late but interesting Scottish testimony to this from Zachary Boyd: 'the Papists cast in the teeth of the professors in France, that they sing the Psalms translated in

---

21 See T.G. Law, *Catholic Tractates of the Sixteenth Century*, STS, 1901, p. 144; for fuller discussion, see A.L. Prescott, 'English Writers and Beza's Latin Epigrams: the Uses and Abuses of Poetry', *Studies in the Renaisssance*, 21 (1974), 83–117, esp. 99–106.
22 The phrase comes from Marot's *Oeuvres poétiques*, ed. Gérard Defaux, Paris, 1990–93, I. clxxii. The second volume was not available, when this paper was written. Further references are to C.A. Mayer's six-volume edition: *Les Epitres*, London, 1958; *Oeuvres satiriques*, London, 1962; *Oeuvres lyriques*, London, 1964; *Oeuvres diverses*, London, 1966; *les Epigrammes*, London, 1970; and *Les Traductions*, Geneva, 1980.
23 A.L. Prescott, 'The Reputation of Clément Marot in Renaissance England', *Studies in the Renaissance*, 18 (1971), 173–202; also the chapter on Marot in her *French Poets and the English Renaissance*, New Haven and London, 1978.
24 Marot's renderings of the psalms are in Mayer's edn. of *Traductions*; for discussion, see P. Leblanc, *La Poésie réligieuse de Clément Marot*, Paris, 1955. On the English background, see R. Zim, *English Metrical Psalms: Poetry as Praise and Prayer 1535–1601*, Cambridge, 1987.
25 See R.J. Lyall, 'Montgomerie and Marot', *Etudes écossaises*, 2 (1993), 79–94.

meeter by Clement Marot, a courtly Gentleman. Etc. I can well testifie this to be of truth, for I frequently did hear such scornful givings in that land . . .'[26] Huguenot exiles, fleeing from persecution, would provide one channel by which Marot's psalm versions reached Scotland; indeed copies of some of his texts were made by Esther Inglis, the noted calligrapher.[27]

Marot made a great impact on one Reformer, Robert Norvell, a very minor poet who flourished in the reign of Mary, Queen of Scots and published a slim volume of verse in 1561, the year of her return to Scotland; most of it seems to have been composed in the 1550s when he was imprisoned in Paris, in the Bastille. He may have been known personally to Bannatyne, since one of his poems is included in the Bannatyne Manuscript. Few details survive of his life: he was a soldier in the company of the third earl of Arran, but revealingly it was to the earl of Argyle, 'the main support of the Reformers in the West Highlands', that he dedicated *The Meroure of ane Christiane*.[28] On 25 July 1561 Norvell was made an Edinburgh burgess, 'gratis for good service done and to be done'. I take this to refer less to his pious verses than to his defence of the Tolbooth a few days earlier against papistical rioters. John Knox, who refers approvingly to his actions in this and another incident, also calls him a 'mery man'.[29] Alas, little in his extant writing substantiates this, although there are a few personal touches: the dream poem in which Noah chides him for drunkenness, and he confesses to being a 'brother of Bacchus beastlie band'; and the sarcastic envoi, or New Year's gift, addressed to the archers of the Scots Guard, in which he bitterly concludes that even if he searched throughout all the world: 'I could not find so many, so vnkynde'.

Much of *The Meroure* may be traced to Norvell's reading of Marot, presumably during his captivity in the Bastille. A series of versified prayers, for instance, closely correspond to their sequence in the French – paternoster, credo, graces designed to be said before and after a meal – but there is one highly significant omission, the Ave Maria, or prayer to the Virgin (Mayer, 1980, pp. 104–8; 473–4). Another poem on the Pelican as a symbol of Christ translates Marot's ballade *De la passion Nostre Seigneur* (Mayer, 1966, 160–2). 'The Judgment of Minos' ultimately derives from Lucian, but does not mean

---

26 Quoted by Prescott 1971: 199, and Prescott 1978: 31. The quotation derives from J. Holland, *Psalmists of Britain* (London, 1843), I. 257–8; but the precise source in Boyd has not been traced.
27 See A.H. Scott-Elliot and Elspeth Yeo, 'Calligraphic Manuscripts of Esther Inglis (1571–1624): A Catalogue', *Papers of the Bibliographical Society of America*, 84 (1990), 11–86.
28 There is only one perfect copy of this work, in the Folger Library, Washington, but it is available on University Microfilms. On Norvell's debt to Marot, see William Beattie, 'Some Early Scottish Books', in *The Scottish Tradition*, ed. G.W.S. Barrow, Edinburgh, 1974, pp. 107–20, esp. 118–20. There is some discussion of his life in J. Durkan, 'James, Third Earl of Arran: the Hidden Years', *SHR*, 65 (1986), 154–66; also *Essays on the Scottish Reformation: 1513–1625*, ed. D. McRoberts, Glasgow, 1962, p. 369.
29 See *The Roll of Edinburgh Burgesses and Guild Brethren*, ed. C.B.B. Watson, Scottish Burgh Records Society, 1929, p. 384; also John Knox, *History of the Reformation in Scotland*, ed. W. Croft Dickinson, 1949, I. 358 (21 July 1561) and II. 76 (19 May 1563). Michael Lynch, *Edinburgh and the Reformation*, Edinburgh, 1981, p. 286, notes that Norvell, a merchant, was discharged from his tax contribution on 24 January 1565.

that Norvell knew Greek. It has a pedigree not uncharacteristic of the period: it is a direct translation of Marot's early poem, *Le Jugement de Minos* (Mayer, 1980, 79–92); this, in turn, derives from a French prose work, written by a Burgundian, Jean Miélot; and this derives from a corrupt Latin rendering of Lucian by 'the Italian charlatan Aurispa' (the term is Mayer's). What I find particularly interesting is the way Norvell treats one of Marot's most famous poems, the *Déploration de Florimond Robertet* (1527; Mayer, 1964, 152–8). Norvell strips from this elegy all the personal and topical passages, and isolates the impressive central section, inspired by St Paul's epistles to the Romans, in which Death addresses mankind. He translates very closely, using the same number of lines and the same stanza. Only in a few details can one see the Protestant Reformer at work, purging Marot's favourable references to saints and replacing them by 'prophets cheritable'.

Marot was also known to Scottish readers in a second, very different guise: as a witty, satirical poet, author and possibly inventor of a type of burlesque epistle, known as the 'coq-à-l'âne'.[30] The best testimony to this comes from *The Legend of the Bishop of St Andrew's Life* (after 1584), a scurrilous attack on Patrick Adamson. Seeking to find some parallel to his iniquity, Robert Sempill exclaims:

> To him I can find na compair,
> Save anes in France when I was there,
> Gud Clement Marit had a lowne –
> A knaif that cumbart all the towne,
> With spreitis employed to everie vice,
> As whoredome, drincking, cartis, and dyce;
> To sweir, to ban, to steill and tak,
> Ane never mycht trow a word he spak.
> (*Satirical Poems*, xlv. 978–85; normalised)

James Cranstoun, who edited the work in the nineteenth century, took this passage to mean that the poet had met Marot personally, and therefore used it as evidence for Sempill's birthdate.[31] But the allusion is a literary one: to Marot's Epistle XXV (Mayer, 1958), a comical complaint to the king of how his manservant stole all his possessions, including his best horse. There are other signs of Scottish interest in this aspect of Marot. Register House possesses a copy of his early poem, *L'Enfer*, which is largely a satire directed against lawyers: Chatelet (in which Marot himself had been imprisoned) is compared to Hades, and a corrupt judge to Minos. Unfortunately the exact provenance of this sixteenth-century manuscript is unknown.[32] It is revealing that the term *cokalane*, in the sense 'lampoon', was not current in English but enjoyed a short vogue at

---

30 On the 'coq-à-l'âne' see further, C.A. Mayer, in *Oeuvres satiriques*, 8–14; and *French Studies*, 15 (1962).
31 *Satirical Poems of the Time of the Reformation*, ed. J. Cranstoun, STS, 1891, I. xxxiv.
32 MS RH 13/36. I am grateful to Dr Sally Mapstone and Dr Alison Rosie for supplying me with information about this manuscript.

this time in Scots. (*DOST*'s citations belong to the end of the sixteenth and beginning of the seventeenth centuries.) The National Library of Scotland possesses an unpublished fragmentary poem (c. 1600) that is quite explicitly entitled 'The Skottish Cock a delane' (MS 1707).

I must pass rapidly over another aspect of Marot: the love poet. His elegies, epigrams and chansons were clearly known and appreciated by some Scots in the sixteenth century, a few of whom we now value more highly than Norvell and Sempill. Lois Borland demonstrated long ago that Montgomerie's 'Elegie' is based on Marot's *Elegie* III, and that his 'Admonitioun to young lasses', or 'A bony No with smiling looks agane', likewise derives from Epigram 67.[33] Both, characteristically, are free and much expanded versions of their French originals; and this is also true of an anonymous love poem in Bannatyne: 'Support your seruand peirles paramour'. This appears with a musical setting in other Scottish manuscripts (such as the Melville part book now in the Fitzwilliam Museum, Cambridge), and has been traced to a Marot chanson.[34]

I will conclude with an interesting but little-read poem in a neglected manuscript, the Maitland Quarto; its title reads 'Ane Elagie translatit out of Frenche . . . G.H' (f. 102b). Behind this lies Marot's *Elégie* XX (in Mayer, 1964; no. XXI in Defaux), in which a young woman complains of her husband's indifference and cruelty, in a kind of Renaissance variation on the medieval *chanson de mal mariée*, spiced with classical imagery and allusions to Dido and Sappho. It was also rendered by an Elizabethan poet into lugubrious fourteeners, but the Scottish version is for the most part much more sensitive and exact.[35] Only in the final section of the poem – after the option of taking a lover has been virtuously rejected – does the Scottish poet strikingly depart from the original. In Marot the woman turns for comfort to her mother:

> Doncques á qui feray ma plaincte amere?
> A vous, ma chere & honnorée Mere.
> C'est à vous seule, à qui s' offre & presente,
> Par vray devoir, la complaincte presente.
> (89–92)

But the Scottish poet says rather:

> Quhair sall I then pour out my bitter plaint
> quhomto sall I my cruell paine lament
> to plein3ie to my parentis is bot Vaine

---

33 See Lois Borland, 'Montgomerie and the French Poets of the Early Sixteenth Century', *Modern Philology*, 11 (1913), 127–34; for a fuller discussion of these poems, see Lyall, 'Montgomerie and Marot'.
34 Cf. Helena Shire, *Song Dance and Poetry of the Court of Scotland under King James VI*, Cambridge, 1969, pp. 39–41.
35 Cf. Prescott 1971: 182–3 on Humfrey Gifford's 'weepy fourteeners'; his version and Marot's text are available in D. Bentley-Cranch, 'La réputation de Clément Marot en Angleterre', *Studi Francesi*, 50 (1973), esp. 213–18.

> that quhilk is done can nocht be brocht againe
> Quhen that ye mater wes not past remeid
> o god give then thay had taine better heid
> Alace quhair then wes thair experience
> I prayis thair mynd bot curs thair negligence
> quhy wald thay not at leist seik my consent
> To friendis counsall quhy tuick thay nocht gud tent
> (116–25)

This writer expatiates bitterly – in a passage that has no parallel in the French – on the parents' failure to consult the girl over the marriage, or to take advice from friends and family. The attribution to G.H. is tantalising, and one would like to know whom these letters represent.

I am not an expert on Marot, and have only recently begun to explore this topic, drawing on the scattered researches of various scholars, in particular those of William Beattie. It seems to me, however, that Scottish awareness of Marot in the sixteenth century was much greater than is usually recognised, and would repay further investigation. It is not surprising that Marot's 'Poems' (unspecified as to edition or date) were present in the libraries of Mary Queen of Scots, and of the great bibliophile, William Drummond of Hawthornden.[36] The library of Adam Bothwell, bishop of Orkney, contained 'Oeuvres de Clement Marot'; and James VI also possessed a copy of 'les Traductions de Clement Marot', given to him by the brother of his tutor, Peter Young.[37] It would be interesting to know if Marot figured in other Scottish collections of this period. It is possible, also, that the verse satirists, writing in the later decades of the sixteenth century, may have learnt some techniques from Marot; and I suspect that those interested in Alexander Scott and Alexander Montgomerie might find it profitable to read him attentively.

---

36 See Julian Sharman, *The Library of Mary, Queen of Scots*, London, 1889, pp. 109–11; and R.H. MacDonald, *The Library of Drummond of Hawthornden*, Edinburgh, 1971, no. 1097.

37 See the inventory published in *The Warrender Papers*, ed. A.I. Cameron, 2 vols (SHS, 1931–2) II, 396–413; and George F. Warner, 'The Library of James VI, 1573–83', in *Miscellany of the Scottish History Society* (SHS: Edinburgh, 1893), p. lxv.

SALLY MAPSTONE

12. *The Scots, the French, and the English: an Arthurian Episode*

In – probably – the mid- to late 1460s two authors, one Scottish, one English, were separately at work recasting different parts of the great thirteenth-century Old French *Lancelot-Queste-Mort-Artu* prose romance cycle. The identity of the Scottish poet is unknown to us, though it has been amply speculated upon.¹ The English writer was Sir Thomas Malory, though quite who *he* was has not yet been unequivocally established.² These two writers eventually produced two highly contrasting romances: the poem we now know as *Lancelot of the Laik*, surviving incompletely in one copy made in the late 1480s; and the massive prose *Morte Darthur*, surviving also in one manuscript, from c. 1475, and in the two copies of Caxton's print of 1485.³ The choice in Scotland of verse and in England of prose for translations from prose is typical of one set of differences between Scots and English romances of this period,⁴ but the marked differences in length and narrative also reflect their respective range of sources. The *Lancelot* poet is concentrating on one relatively early part of the Lancelot French narrative, found in the same form in both the early non-cyclic romance and its cyclic successor.⁵ Malory was drawing on that romance too (though later parts of it),

---

1   Debate was at its most extensive in the early years of this century, when the detection of verbal and linguistic similarities between *Lancelot and the Laik* and *The Quare of Jelusy* prompted some critics to assert their common authorship, an interest heightened by the nature of the *Quare*'s damaged colophon, which was interpreted by David Laing, followed by (notably) Skeat and Gray as *quod auchen*, a name then linked to the 'James Affleck', or Auchinleck, in Dunbar's *Lament for the Makars*. Various Auchinlecks from the last twenty years of the fifteenth century were put forward. See W.W. Skeat, 'The Author of "Lancelot of the Laik"', *SHR*, 8 (1910), 1–4; 'Vidas Achinlek, Chevalier', correspondence from Margaret Muriel Gray, Skeat, Alexander Lawson, and J.T.T. Brown, *SHR*, 8 (1910), 321–6; Margaret Muriel Gray (ed.), *Lancelot of the Laik*, STS, New Ser. 2 (Edinburgh and London, 1912), pp. xviii–xx; and R.J. Lyall, 'Two of Dunbar's Makars: James Affleck and Sir John the Ross', *IR*, 27 (1976), 99–109. The discussion is well summarised in a valuable unpublished study of *Lancelot*, Jeanette Johnston, 'An Edition of *Lancelot of the Laik*' (B. Litt. thesis, University of Oxford, 1979), pp. 118–25. But such attributions and datings remain highly conjectural due to the illegibility of *The Quare of Jelusy*'s colophon. Alexander Lawson thought it could read *quod autor*; J. Norton-Smith and I. Pravda (eds), *The Quare of Jelusy*, Middle English Texts 3 (Heidelberg, 1976), pp. 14–17, make a case for simply *quod ane Lufar*. On the unproven shared authorship of *The Quare of Jelusy* and *Lancelot of the Laik*, see n. 24, below.
2   The most extensive and convincing study has recently appeared: P.J.C. Field, *The Life and Times of Sir Thomas Malory*, Arthurian Studies, 29 (Cambridge, 1993).
3   Quotation from *Lancelot* is from the edition by W.W. Skeat, EETS, O. Ser. 6 (2nd ed. 1870); from Malory, Eugene Vinaver (ed.), *The Works of Sir Thomas Malory*, 3 vols (Oxford, 1973).
4   See Felicity Riddy, 'The Alliterative Revival', in R.D.S. Jack (ed.), *The History of Scottish Literature, Origins to 1660* (Aberdeen, 1988), pp. 39–54 (46). Other Scots romances to convert prose into verse are *Golagros and Gawane* and *Clariodus*.
5   The non-cyclic version is edited by Elspeth Kennedy, *Lancelot do Lac, The Non-Cyclic Old French Prose Romance*, 2 vols (Oxford, 1980); the cyclic in A. Micha (ed.) *Lancelot: roman en prose au XIIIe siècle*, 9

but also on many other works in the cycle or allied to it, together with other Arthurian pieces in English, and the contrivances of his own imagination.[6] Yet for all their schematic differences these two near-contemporary recastings of Arthurian material provide equally vivid commentaries on the politics and ideologies of the kingdoms of Scotland and England in the second half of the fifteenth century, commentaries all the more telling in comparison – an approach not previously applied in any detail to these works.[7] It is this aspect upon which I intend to concentrate. *Lancelot of the Laik* is still relatively little written about, particularly in published works,[8] and many questions about it remain unresolved: its authorship, but also its curious linguistic complexion, with its hybrid mixture of Scots and southern English forms.[9] Important as these issues are, they can't be the object of my attention in this paper.

These two works form an immediate contrast in their treatment of kingship. This is distinctively focused through their presentation of the figure of Lancelot. For reasons I'll indicate anon, Lancelot comes late into prominence in the British Arthurian corpus, the only surviving work before Malory's and the Scots poem to give him any kind of comparable status being the stanzaic *Morte Arthur*, composed around 1400. Both Malory and the Scots poet are thus forging significant changes of direction in their Arthurian works. But the variations in focus they produce are not just those of scope: their approaches to the Arthur/Lancelot relationship are crucially opposed. The Scottish poet, writing a poem about Lancelot, yet recasts his French source to bring Arthur to a heightened prominence; the English writer, ostensibly shaping his material into a work in which Arthur is the central figure, creates a pronounced tension between that king and Lancelot, in which Lancelot comes increasingly to dominate the focus of the narrative.

In starting my discussion with Malory I don't wish to appear to be making a value judgement in his favour, though few people, I think, would deny that the *Morte Darthur* is a greater work than *Lancelot of the Laik*.[10] I am taking Malory first

---

vols (Paris, 1978–83). For a discussion of the relationship of these versions, Elspeth Kennedy, *Lancelot and the Grail, A study of the Prose Lancelot* (Oxford, 1986).

6 For an excellent reassessment of Malory's access to source material and the context of the *Morte Darthur*'s production, Carol Meale, 'Manuscripts, Readers and Patrons in Fifteenth-Century England: Sir Thomas Malory and Arthurian Romance', *Arthurian Literature*, 4 (1985) 93–126.

7 Malory is compared with Scots fifteenth-century chivalric works, though not in any real detail with *Lancelot*, by Alison Lee, 'Thomas Malory and Fifteenth-Century Chivalric Literature' (D. Phil. thesis, University of Oxford, 1989).

8 In addition to Johnston's thesis (above, n. 1), useful discussion is found in Flora M. Ross (now Alexander), 'A Study of the Treatment of Romance Subjects in *Golagros and Gawane, Lancelot of the Laik*, and *Rauf Coilyear*' (B. Litt. thesis, University of Oxford, 1967), some of which appears in Flora Alexander, 'Late Medieval Scottish Attitudes to the Figure of Arthur: a Reassessment', *Anglia*, 93 (1975), 17–34. Other discussions of the poem include Walter Scheps, 'The Thematic Unity of *Lancelot of the Laik*', *SSL*, 5 (1967–8), 167–75 and John MacQueen, 'Poetry – James I to Henryson' in Jack (ed.), pp. 55–72 (60–3).

9 Gray, 'Vidas Achinleck', 323–4, and (ed.), *Lancelot of the Laik*, pp. xx–xxxi; Johnston, pp. 107–17; A.J. Aitken, 'The Language of Older Scots Poetry' in J. Derrick McClure (ed.), *Scotland and the Lowland Tongue* (Aberdeen, 1983), pp. 18–49 (26–31).

10 Disparaging assessments of *Lancelot of the Laik* are numerous, but often uninformed. Representative are the comments of Robert W. Ackerman, 'English Rimed and Prose Romances', in Roger

for the practical reason that the contrast between his romance and *Lancelot of the Laik* shows better that way, and shows up most markedly the far greater degree of optimism in the Scots work.

At the very end of the *Morte Darthur* Malory signs off from his work in the following fashion:

> For this book was ended the ninth year of
> the reygne of Kyng Edward the Fourth, by
> Syr Thomas Maleoré, Knyght. . . . [III, p. 1260]

The ninth regnal year of King Edward IV was March 1469 – March 1470, a particularly contentious time within the protracted and divisive struggles of the Wars of the Roses. It was in fact the year during which at one point the ruling King Edward IV was being held prisoner by Warwick and his rebels; and the previous king and continuing Lancastrian claimant, Henry VI, was being held prisoner by the Yorkists. It was against this disruptive background that Malory was completing the *Morte Darthur*. He was completing it, moreover, as the earlier part of his conclusion makes clear, in prison. There is still dispute over the details of Malory's life, but in so far as they can now be reconstructed they constitute a career whose twists and turns and changes of loyalty seem to reflect the larger course of disordered events on the political stage. The highlights of this life see Malory installed as a member of parliament for Warwickshire around 1445, but shortly afterwards becoming involved in a catalogue of crimes of various degrees of sensation including ambush, rape, and cattle-stealing, in relation to some of which he was imprisoned (though not brought to trial) for several years. Malory appears in the 1450s and later on to have been involved with the Yorkist cause. But by the last years of the 1460s it appears that he had given up support for Edward IV and become party to some kind of Lancastrian plot, for which he was being imprisoned. He seems to have been released during the brief period in which Warwick had Henry VI restored during 1470, and he died in 1471 shortly before Edward IV regained control of the kingdom.[11]

As far as his own relationship to kings goes, then, Malory's behaviour would seem to have more in common with Sir Aggravayne than with Sir Bors. And while his *Morte Darthur* makes much of the ideal of loyalty towards one's ruler, it is also a work that deals at length with disloyalties, discords, failures in kingship. It is possible that this cycle of stories culminating in civil war and disputed kingship appealed to Malory in part because of its felt relevance to his own environment. I do not mean by this that Malory drew a one-to-one set of correspondences between what was happening in England and what he was reading and transforming into his own narratives, but that the shape he gives to his materials

---

Sherman Loomis (ed.), *Arthurian Literature in the Middle Ages* (Oxford, 1959), pp. 480–519 (491–3); attempts to rehabilitate the poem include those of Johnston (who writes interestingly on it as a 'social romance'), Scheps and MacQueen.
11 The definitive account is now that of Field (n. 2, above).

takes much of its ideological bearing from the political complexion of the period during which he was writing.[12]

For, as has been indicated already, kingship is a key issue in the *Morte Darthur*. As the narrative progresses, Arthur is perceptibly less assertive. This is the more striking because in the first two books he is such an active and successful figure. Malory's comment at the end of the second book: 'Here endyth the tale of the noble kynge Arthure that was Emperoure hymself throw dygnyté of his hondys' (I, p. 247), is a reference to the major role which Arthur plays in this book, continuing the interventionist image which he had attained in the first one; and a reference as well to one of the major alterations Malory makes to his source in actually showing Arthur installed as emperor in Rome. The other important change he has made is to shift the Roman war story back from its more customary position in Arthurian tradition as an event occurring towards the end of Arthur's rule. In Malory's direct source for the last part of his *Morte Darthur*, the French *La Mort le roi Artu*, the Roman war takes place while Arthur is already abroad in pursuit of Lancelot. Malory moves it from here to a far earlier position, to appear as a logical continuation of the career of the young and ambitious Arthur. And in moving it back he swopped the elliptical French version for the more extended English alliterative *Morte Darthur* account.[13] In this version, moreover, Lancelot was not an outstanding figure. The attractions of this distribution of emphasis for Malory are obvious. He does not yet need a powerful Lancelot; he does want a dominant Arthur. But not for long. The same conclusion which so praises Arthur then adds 'And here folowyth afftyr many noble talys of Sir Launcelot de Lake' (I, p. 247), and it is with the emergence of Lancelot into the course of the narrative that the nature of Arthur's role begins palpably to alter. By the time of the Tristram, two books later, Arthur is a slightly diminished figure, knocked off his horse in jousting by both Sir Tristram and Sir Palomides, and increasingly directing jousts rather than participating in them; and he is given other moments of discomfiture, as when Tristram bears to him a shield on which the malicious Morgan la Faye has had engraved 'a kynge and quene ... and a knyght stondynge aboven them with hys one foote standynge uppon the kynges hede and the othir upon the quenys hede', an image of the 'bondage and ... servage' (II, p.554) in which Morgan claims Lancelot holds Arthur and Guinevere.

There are, naturally, also intended strengths in Arthur's passive role. His kingship symbolises the heart of the accord of the Round Table, in terms of which all knights define themselves. Their adventures only really acquire significance when they return to the king in Camelot. Yet the firmness of this precept, too, is under challenge in the book that follows the macho Tristram, the pious Grail expedition. There the significance of a knight's actions is no longer to be defined in relation to his chivalric achievements for a court with Arthur at its head; it is instead spiritual achievements in relation to a heavenly king that matter. And the

---

12 Cf. the approach in Elizabeth T. Pochoda, *Arthurian Propaganda: Le Morte Darthur as an Historial Ideal of Life* (Chapel Hill, 1971).
13 Felicity Riddy, *Sir Thomas Malory* (Leiden, 1987), p. 42.

best knights, those, Galahad and Percival, who attain the Grail, can no longer return to Arthur's court. Their perfection takes them beyond it. In the last two books Arthur becomes an ever more embattled figure, in conflict finally both with Lancelot, the man who has served him best as a knight, and with his son Modred, in the civil war. It is a moment of intense irony that a reassertion of his old aggressive forcefulness in the last stages of battle, when he rushes out against his own son, leads to his death.

This paradox in the representation of Arthur, both as the renowned strong and central monarch, and the strangely passive one was one that, seen in a European context, was not peculiar to Malory. It had been a feature of the Arthur of the French tradition from early on. Elspeth Kennedy sees the paradox, for instance, as 'at the very heart of the first part of the prose Lancelot', and indeed it is Lancelot who dominates the French prose cycle.[14] But in an English context what Malory is choosing to do is striking. For not before Malory had this treatment of Arthur come in an English work into such prominent juxtaposition with the ascendancy of Lancelot. Lancelot is a late arrival in the English tradition probably because the granting of greater dominance to him would, as has recently been suggested, have 'disrupt[ed] the position of Arthur from the centre of the story of the line of British kings'[15] – more of a problem, obviously, for an English writer than for a French one. But this is precisely what Malory does elect to do. One of the most conspicuous ways in which he enhances the idea of the fallible Arthur is through his representation of Lancelot.

As Arthur's active role decreases, so Lancelot's increases. He is quickly the best knight, a position which he only loses in the different world and different way of judging in the Grail. In the temporal Camelot-centred world, where ethical and criminal disputes are frequently solved by armed combat, Lancelot is equally invincible. Moreover, many of his actions bring Arthur and his court greater glory.

But there are very considerable tensions within this schema. Their local cause is a simple one: Lancelot's adulterous relationship with Arthur's queen, Guinevere. Malory is coy about this, to the point of near-bowdlerisation of his sources, but the fact of the relationship remains.[16]

And the insufficiency of Arthur's rule becomes more and more pronounced as he comes more and more into opposition with Lancelot. In the earlier books Lancelot is not so much Arthur's threatening 'double', the man who can take his place as a knight and a lover, as his active side. While Arthur must remain often

---

14 Elspeth M. Kennedy, 'King Arthur in the First Part of the Prose *Lancelot*' in F. Whitehead, A.H. Diverres, and F.E. Sutcliffe (eds), *Medieval Miscellany Presented to Eugene Vinaver* (Manchester, 1965), pp. 186–95 (187); also Rosemary Morris, *The Character of King Arthur in Medieval Literature*, Arthurian Studies, 4 (Cambridge, 1982).
15 Riddy, *Malory*, p. 41; Morris, esp. pp. 116–18.
16 See, for instance, the discussion in two articles in *Arthurian Literature*, 3 (1985), Derek Brewer, 'The Presentation of the Character of Lancelot: Chretien to Malory', 26–52, and Irene Joynt, 'Vengeance and Love in "The Book of Sir Launcelot and Queen Guinevere" ', 91–112; and now J.D. Pheifer, 'Malory's Lancelot' in Eileán Ní Cuilleanáin and J.D. Pheifer (eds), *Noble and Joyous Histories, English Romances 1375–1650* (Dublin, 1993), pp. 157–93.

in the court, Lancelot performs deeds of worth in a way that enhances the prestige of that court. There is another aspect of this function, too, which Lancelot himself points up as the harmony of the Round Table is being finally fractured: 'And well I am sure' he says, 'I knew many rebellyons in my dayes that by me and myne were peased' (III, p. 1204). Lancelot's presence has been essential for the social order of the realm. But when he has to act to defend himself against Arthur, the harmony of their active and passive roles is destroyed.

Nor should it be forgotten in this context that Lancelot is himself a king. He is made a knight of the Round Table by Arthur but he is, as son of King Ban, independently a ruler in France in his own right. His kingship is in fact another thing that emphasises Lancelot's closeness as a form of 'double' for Arthur, but its re-emphasis in the final scenes of conflict and division also serves to enhance that atmosphere. Knights are now divided in their loyalties between two different kings, with a further would-be king emerging in the form of Modred. But for all the fact that Lancelot is in many ways a better knight and a better man than Arthur, as episodes such as the healing of Sir Urry – Malory's own invention – are designed to illustrate, his kingship does not make him, in the world that Malory presents, clearly the better king. Much as Malory admires Lancelot, much as he does all he can to protect him from criticism, he must finally accept the consequences of Lancelot's relationship with Guinevere. Neither Arthur nor Lancelot matches up to quite what a king should be. Lancelot may be the better knight and man but he cannot, either in conjunction with Arthur or on his own, supply the 'stable' centre, to use diction similar to Malory's own, of values in the work. Its locus of values, in other words, adheres finally and completely in *no one* character.

All of this, I would argue, Malory perceives. The fact that Malory so often unpicks the careful interlacing of his sources is of considerable significance in this connection.[17] Malory does not see order in these events; he sees disorder. He does not judge because he cannot see a resolution. It is revealing that the most carefully patterned parts of his writing are the last two books, which are heading for the final collapse of the Camelot society. A course which leads to the last apocalyptic division is one he can keep.

The absence of an abiding value-carrying character who can exist in the social world is the strongest admission of this. Malory remains admiring, in different ways, of both Arthur and Lancelot, but both die in retreat from the world, Arthur being taken away over the seas, Lancelot having retired into a monastery even before his death.

What Malory's writing powerfully articulates is the desire for a society with a strong centrally governing king and a clear and hierarchical order, in which destructive individualistic elements are contained. But what he shows instead is a society ever more fragmented, where real moral perfection is only attained outside the dominant social nexus.

What he makes of the *Morte Darthur*, then, reflects his own perception of an England confused and warring over the nature of its monarchy, where no one for

---

17 Cf. the discussion in Riddy's final chapter, 'Divisions' (*Malory*, pp. 139–65).

a long time had been able to hold the country together. How strongly he feels about this is revealed in a sudden outburst in the narrative, all the more remarkable for its unusualness, just after the point when Modred's rebellion against Arthur has been reported.

> Lo, ye all Englysshemen, se ye nat what a myschyff here was?
> For he that was the moste kynge and nobelyst knyght of the worlde, and moste loved the felyshyp of noble knyghtes, and by hym they all were upholdyn, and yet myght nat thes Englyshemen holde them contente with him. Lo thus was the olde custom and usayges of thys londe, and men say that we of thys londe have nat yet loste that custom. Alas! thys ys a greate defaughte of us Englysshemen, for there may no thynge us please no terme. [III, p. 1229][18]

This is Arthur Malory is talking about. And it is thus very telling that he should call him 'the nobelyst knyght of the worlde', the kind of epithet generally reserved for Lancelot. In order to make these statements Malory effectively sets Lancelot aside here. He sees vividly in the past a reflection of the instabilities of his own day. And he has no answer for them. The notion that 'there may no thynge us please no terme' is one of the most melancholy statements in this last book, for it suggests no prospect of resolution. Malory's own switching of allegiances from the Yorkists to the Lancastrians is indicative enough of the fickle pragmatism that was at work in the 1450s and 1460s. The sense of exhaustion and an enfeebled starting again with which the *Morte Darthur* ends is an atmospherically apt evocation of what the country's state must have felt like in 1469 – particularly if you were in prison at the time.

The date of composition of *Lancelot of the Laik* remains uncertain, but the present state of knowledge about it appears to justify localising it within a period of thirty years between the end of the 1450s and the end of the 1480s and then narrowing down from that.[19] As I've mentioned, and here I must note my debt to the unpublished work by Roderick Lyall on the makeup of the manuscript, Cambridge, CUL Kk.1.5 in which *Lancelot* appears, the particular unit containing our poem can be dated as copied around 1484–90 and probably 1489–90.[20]

18 On the political ambiguity of this passage, Field, pp. 145–7.
19 There is little critical concurrence in dating *Lancelot of the Laik*. The poem is still occasionally dated later than its manuscript: *DOST* cites it as c. 1500; M.P. McDiarmid describes it as 'end-of-century' ('The Metrical Chronicles and Non-alliterative Romances' in Jack (ed.), pp. 27–38, 35). Johnston (p. 117) places it on linguistic grounds as c. 1485–90 – the period now known to be that of its copying. In a paper given a decade or so ago to the Edinburgh Bibliographical Society Roderick J. Lyall posited the controversial theory that the *Lancelot* prologue was a later fifteenth-century addition to a poem composed before 1460 and possibly as early as the second quarter of the century. Regrettably, this paper has not been published.
20 Information from R.J. Lyall's 'Fifteenth-Century Scottish Manuscripts: a Further Revised Checklist' presented at the Fourth International Conference on Medieval and Renaissance Scottish Literature, University of Mainz-Germersheim, July 1984, and private communication, 20 September 1985. Greater discussion in Sally Mapstone, 'The Advice to Princes Tradition in Scottish Literature, 1450–1500' (D.Phil. thesis, University of Oxford, 1986), pp. 144–54.

But we should not assume that the composition of the poem is contemporary with this particular copying of it – which is after all incomplete. Kk.1.5 is compiled from a number of manuscript units of various dates of composition and copying.[21] Other material in the unit preceding our poem, copied by the same scribe who did *Lancelot* and containing moral works like *Ratis Raving* and the *Thewis of Gud Women*, can be shown to have been copied around the same date,[22] but the composition of *Ratis Raving* is put as early as the 'opening decades of the fifteenth century' and that of the others 'c. 1450 at the earliest', and no more precisely than that.[23] *Lancelot* is probably not as early as *Ratis Raving*, but the reasons for putting it earlyish in the second half of the fifteenth century are just as good, if not a bit better, as those for putting it later.

Lancelot of the Laik shows some similarities to two other datable Scottish works of the second half of the century, one from c. 1456 and one from 1474–6. (I am not including here its similarities to *The Quare of Jelusy*, since the dating of that work is still even more unstable than *Lancelot* itself. I might add, though, that I find the claims for their shared authorship unconvincing.[24]) *Lancelot*'s advice to princes section has some verbal resemblances to phrasing in two of the works in Sir Gilbert Hay's prose MS, *The Buke of Knychthede* and *The Buke of the Governaunce of Princis*.[25] The resemblances aren't decisive enough (because the matter is very conventional) to demonstrate unequivocally a borrowing, but if one were to be present the

---

21 Ibid; R. Girvan (ed.), *Ratis Raving and Other Early Scots Poems on Morals*, STS, 3rd Ser. 11 (Edinburgh and London, 1937), pp. vii–lxxiv; Tauno J. Mustanoja (ed.), *The Good Wife Taught her Daughter . . .* (Helsinki, 1948), pp. 140–7.

22 Lyall, 'Checklist' and private communication, 20 September 1985. The paper in these units is different, and in Lyall's opinion 'there is no codicological reason to suppose that their common scribe intended the two units to occur together'. Girvan (p. xii) reaches a similar conclusion on the compilation of these two items. The legend '*per manum V de F*' appears at the end of one item in the unit preceding *Lancelot*, the *Dicta Salominis*. Lyall thinks him very likely to have been a notary public.

23 Girvan, pp. lxxii, lxxiv. These datings are largely accepted by subsequent commentators, though see the important qualifications in Denton Fox, '*DOST* and Evidence for Authorship: Some Poems Connected with *Ratis Raving*', in Caroline Macafee and Iseabail Macleod (eds), *The Nuttis Schell, Essays on the Scots Language* (Aberdeen, 1987), pp. 96–105.

24 *The Quare of Jelusy* is contained in Oxford, Bodleian Library, MS Arch. Selden. B. 24, written c. 1488–1510. Its similarities with *Lancelot*, pointed up most notably by M.M. Gray (see n. 1, above), lie primarily in the most stylised and formulaic parts of these poems. Brown's comment ('Vidas Achinlek, Chevalier', 326) that the similarities 'do not *prove* the common authorship of *The Quare of Jelusy* and *Lancelot of the Laik*. They establish the relationship and nothing more' may be reinforced by Johnston's, 'These resemblances suggest that to a considerable extent the language and idiom of these poems is a shared form of literary expression, and that echoed phrases are not adequate proof of common authorship for *Lancelot* and *The Quare of Jelusy*' (p. 123). Nonetheless, their common authorship continues to be asserted, e.g. MacQueen, p. 60.

25 Cf. *Lancelot*, ll. 1836–58 and *The Buke of Knychthede*, pp. 58/30–59/7; *Lancelot*, ll. 1864–6, 'larges . . ./Amyd standing of the vicis two,/Prodegalitee and awerice also' and *Buke of the Governaunce of Princis*, p. 81/5–6, 'largess, quhilk is the myddis betwix prodigalitee and avarice'; this section on prodigality and largess in the poem and pp. 80–5 in Hay's work also have much thematically in common, especially *Lancelot*, ll. 1905–8 and *Buke of the Governaunce of Princis*, p. 83/27–31; *Lancelot*, ll. 1637–44 and the section on 'How punicioun suld be maid eftir the cass and state of personis' in *The Buke of the Governaunce of Princis*, pp. 98–100 (especially the idea of 'diligent enquiry'). Quotation from Hay is from J.H. Stevenson (ed.), *Gilbert of the Haye's Prose Manuscript*, vol. II, STS, 1st Ser. 62 (Edinburgh and London, 1914).

context would make it more likely that the *Lancelot* poet was borrowing from Hay than vice versa; though both are translators, the *Lancelot* poet has far more freedom. It has also been noted that *Lancelot's* use of the decasyllabic couplet, its prologues, stylised complaints, and, one could add, its battle-speeches and division into books, show similarities with the *Wallace*.[26] But here it is really not clear enough which way the debt lies, if indeed it can be called that. These works may rather be illustrating a shared set of influences, in which Chaucer obviously plays a large part, but they do at the least testify to a common currency of taste in writing which might point to a similar period of composition.[27]

If we tentatively take 1456 as a *terminus ab quo* for the poem that locates us in the reign of James II; the mid-1470s, when the *Wallace* was composed, would see us into the reign of James III, but not yet in its most controversial period. I mention this because one of the reasons it has been common to date *Lancelot of the Laik* as written late in the 1480s is the desire to associate its criticism of kingship with the reign of James III.[28] There is, however, nothing apart from the date of its copying to link the poem with the last decade of that reign, the years in which James III's unpopularity is most demonstrable.

This surely goes for the content of the poem too. Rather than constructing through the criticisms of Arthur a specific critique of the practice of one particular king, the approach is one of detailing what are presented as a series of common dangers in the execution of kingly power. This kind of generalised approach is typical of the fifteenth-century Scottish advice to princes tradition,[29] but that statement is itself more significant than it might appear. There are texts that address specific problems or events (the *Wallace* could be said to be one), but the more usual advisory posture is to address particular sets of recurrent issues and to do so in a way (and even the *Wallace* finally does this) which is largely supportive and constructive towards the institution of Scottish kingship.

Scottish political literature of the fifteenth century reflects in its own way the continuity of the Stewart dynasty. Chequered as several of the James' reigns were, it was that line of succession that was accepted by the majority of the political community, in stark contrast to the disputed succession of the country over the border.[30] Scottish advice to princes literature thus focuses more on issues

---

26 Scheps, 'Thematic Unity', 169, and 'William Wallace and his "Buke": Some Instances of their Influence on Subsequent Literature', *SSL*, 6 (1969), 220–37 (223–6).
27 Stimulating discussion of *Wallace* as a 'post-Chaucerian text' in R. James Goldstein, *The Matter of Scotland, Historical Narrative in Medieval Scotland* (1993), pp. 257–62. The inclusion of extensive advice to princes within a Scots romance also prompts comparison of *Lancelot* and *The Buik of King Alexander the Conquerour* (ed. John Cartwright, 2 vols, II–III, STS, 4th Ser. 16, 18, Aberdeen, 1986, 1990). But the disputed dating and authorship of that poem reduces its use in this discussion.
28 E.g. Bertram Vogel, 'Secular Politics and the Date of *Lancelot of the Laik*', *SP*, 40 (1943), 1–13; Karl Heinz Göller, *König Arthur in der englischen Literatur des späten Mittelalters*, Palaestra, 238 (Gottingen, 1963), pp. 130, 137–43. R.W.M. Fulton, 'Social Criticism in Scottish Literature, 1480–1560' (Ph.D. thesis, University of Edinburgh, 1972), p. 180; Alexander, 'Late Medieval Scottish Attitudes', 27.
29 Mapstone, 'Advice to Princes', *passim*.
30 The classic statement is by Jenny Wormald, 'Taming the Magnates?' in K.J. Stringer (ed.), *Essays on the Nobility of Medieval Scotland* (Edinburgh, 1985), pp. 270–80.

of kingship handed on from reign to reign, notably the exercise of justice and the balance in kingly rule between intervention and restraint. *Lancelot of the Laik* is a classic case of this kind. But this is not to suggest that such texts are blandly unhistorical. My own view is that the *Lancelot*'s composition is more likely to be from the first decade of James III's mature rule, i.e. from the late 1460s onwards, than from the second. The ultimately optimistic line it constructs on the practice of kingship and some of its more specific comments make more sense within that dating; and they form a strong contrast to the negative standpoint in the English close contemporary Malory.

Lancelot of the Laik is a free translation of a sequence of episodes from the prose *Lancelot*.[31] The Scottish poet draws on the first part of the work, a part never used by Malory, whose own book of *Tale of Sir Lancelot du Laik* is based on later episodes in it.[32] But Malory's *Lancelot* book is incorporated in his *Morte Darthur*. The Scottish *Lancelot of the Laik*, whether it is earlier or later than Malory, is thus the first Scottish or English work to stand as a separate Lancelot romance. But for all that it proclaims, particularly in its prologue, that this will be a poem about Lancelot, it is in fact a work which gives a great deal of attention to Arthur, and in which the execution of the kingly role is an essential element. Thus while the Scottish writer is interested in Lancelot, he is as much if not more drawn by the role of king Arthur – almost the reverse of the axis of Malory's interests. The episodes the Scottish poet selects create a narrative structure designed in terms of repeated intercutting between scenes featuring Arthur and scenes featuring Lancelot, but for the first two of the three books into which the Scottish poet has arranged his material, it is with Arthur that he is primarily concerned.

And Arthur, odd as this may initially seem, is clearly being used to provide a form of commentary on Scottish kingship, though he is, manifestly, an 'English', or rather non-Scottish, king. There was admiration for Arthur in medieval Scottish literature as a renowned chivalric monarch at the same time as there was a tradition of dislike and condemnation of him; and it is to that first branch that *Lancelot of the Laik* largely belongs.[33]

The lengthy prologue to the poem summarises *Lancelot*'s life thus far and takes us to a point in the source where he is being imprisoned by the lady of Melyhalt who is refusing him release. At this stage in the narrative, we should bear in mind, Lancelot is powerfully in love with Guinevere, but that love is not yet consummated. However, his imprisonment has coincided with a growing crisis at

---

31 Discussed in most detail in the theses by Johnston (n. 1, above) and Mapstone, pp. 144–200.
32 See Vinaver (ed.), III, pp. 1398–1404.
33 For references to Arthur as a chivalric hero see *Bruce*, I, 1. 549 (vol. II, ed. Matthew P. McDiarmid and James A.C. Stevenson, STS, 4th Ser. 12, Edinburgh, 1980); *Wallace*, VIII, 11. 845, 886–7, 967–8 (vol. I, ed. Matthew P. McDiarmid, STS, 4th Ser. 4, Edinburgh and London, 1968). An alternative tradition depicted him as the illegitimate ruler who had displaced the rightful heir, Modred, from the English throne. This is the argument of, for instance, *The Cronycle of Scotland in a Part* (1461); but as Alexander ('Late Medieval Scottish Attitudes', 19) notes, it is not until the sixteenth-century chroniclers that really antagonistic accounts become dominant. Fordun and Bower, for instance, note Arthur's illegitimacy but quote Geoffrey of Monmouth's comments that he was the best equipped to rule at the time: John and Winifred MacQueen (eds), *Scotichronicon by Walter Bower* (Aberdeen, 1989), vol. 2, pp. 64–7.

Camelot. Book one opens during a period of strange lull there. Arthur has been away from the court at Carlisle and his knights request him to come back to liven things up. But that night he is disturbed by a nightmare in which he dreams that all his hair has fallen out. A few days later an even more disturbing nightmare follows, in which he dreams that his bowels fall out and lie beside him on the ground. It is obvious that the dream images of physical decay and decomposition are indicative of something being badly wrong in the body politic, of which Arthur as king is the key member. Under duress, Arthur's wise men inform him that the prognosis for him and his country is a dire one, a warning that is shortly followed by the arrival of a messenger from king Galiot, who claims that this king is threatening to invade Arthur's lands. Arthur rebuffs the messenger and goes hunting, but soon another messenger arrives, this time from the lady of Melyhalt, to say that Galiot has entered the country and is conquering its castles. As Arthur sets out for battle against Galiot, the narrative switches to the imprisoned Lancelot, who is lamenting his situation and his love for Guinevere.

The juxtaposition here, which has involved the Scottish poet in considerable recasting of his French source, heightens the sense of Lancelot's 'potential importance for Arthur's struggle to maintain his kingdom'.[34] But it is only one of a range of strategies used to emphasise Arthur's imperilled state. For the Scots poet also elaborates an episode in which one of Arthur's knights, who knows the enemy Galiot, describes him in admiring terms as a man endowed with all the estimable kingly virtues: wisdom and courage, along with gentility, humility and largesse. The cumulative suggestion is that Galiot is a more complete king than Arthur.[35]

The attention of the first book of *Lancelot of the Laik* then continues to be devoted to Arthur. After Lancelot's brief appearance the narrative switches back to the first battle between Arthur's troops and Galiot's, in which while Gawain performs nobly on Arthur's behalf that king's troops are vastly outnumbered. At this point the lady of Melyhalt permits Lancelot temporary release in order to fight on Arthur's side, and he performs characteristically magnificent deeds. But it remains clear that Galiot has overwhelming superiority in numbers of troops. His might is in fact matched by his magnanimity, as he then announces to his council that it would be no honour for him to win victory against a king with such depleted troops, and he declares a truce for a year in order to give Arthur time to build up his power. As the end of the first book approaches, Arthur begins to see that there is some relationship between the forebodings of his dream and the paucity and poor performance of his army, but he does not yet perceive that his own practice is the cause of the problem. We should note also another difference from the Lancelot of much of Malory's narrative here: valiant as the Scots Lancelot is, he alone cannot solve the problems of Arthur's kingdom. It is with the king that their resolution must begin.

---

34 Johnston, p. 18, with further discussion of the surrounding material.
35 Useful comparative comments on the significance of this in the French romance in Kennedy, *Lancelot and the Grail*, pp. 73, 228–31.

It is this that dominates the second and central book which opens with Arthur anxiously brooding on events.[36] Now a new figure appears, a wise clerk called Amytans, who rebukes Arthur for his ill-government, tells him that the failings in his kingdom are due to the wrath of God which will destroy him if he does not reform, and then proceeds to offer him systematic advice on how he may effect the necessary reformation. While the advice to princes section in *Lancelot of the Laik* does have its origins in the French source, it extensively and dramatically develops the material there.[37]

One important alteration the Scots poet makes is in the relationship between Amytans and Arthur. In the French source the counsellor is only identified as a 'preudhomme', who appears mysteriously at Arthur's court. In *Lancelot of the Laik* Amytans is someone the king already knows and respects. He is a well qualified counsellor, whose advice therefore has an added pragmatic weight to it, being based on empirical observation of the king's malpractice. Amytans is clearly distinguished from the king's other advisers who had earlier been incapable of fully explaining the meaning of his bad dreams. This in itself is perhaps designed to enhance another prominent feature of the recasting in *Lancelot of the Laik*. The fact that only one counsellor can really offer Arthur effective advice contributes to the sense of the importance of the king as the central member of the realm from whom all good government should emanate.

The dialogue between Amytans and Arthur opens, as I mentioned, with Amytans' accusations that the failings of Arthur's subjects stem from the bad rule of the king himself.[38] Moving into a fall of princes mode he expounds vividly on what happens to a tyrant-like king, who is shown to face a three-fold danger. Disaffection in his subjects may incite neighbouring kings to move against him; his people themselves may turn against him. And the wrath of God, already present in the permission of such rebellions, may be turned more actively still upon a ruler. That such theorising may be amply borne out in practice is immediately signified through a structural shift worked by the Scottish poet in the ordering of this scene. For just as Arthur is being warned that bad kings attract other kings to make war upon them two messengers from Galiot arrive, bearing the news that Galiot, amazed at the feeble performance of Arthur's troops, has offered peace for a year, but then intends to attack him again. As Arthur rejoices in the reprieve, Amytans sharply states that this is a providential act of God, who is testing Arthur to see if he can really reform sufficiently to rescue his country. In the French source, the arrival of the messengers occurs at the very end of the counselling session.[39] Their transposition to an earlier point in the Scots narrative indicates more sharply the seriousness of Arthur's position.

36 Ibid, pp. 20, 72, 226, 242–3, 247 on the significance of recurrent 'royal broodings'.
37 On the French advice, Elspeth Kennedy, 'Social and Political Ideas in the French Prose *Lancelot*', *MAE*, 29 (1957), 90–106.
38 While expanding the advisory section, the Scots poet reduces the degree of actual dialogue between Amytans and Arthur, perhaps with the view of creating the effect of the advice of Aristotle to Alexander in the *Secretum Secretorum*, a work that lies broadly behind much of the advice given here.
39 With more detail, Mapstone, p. 177, Johnston, p. 15.

But it also conveys his innate if obscured worth as a monarch, by implying that God is ready to withhold his anger, should Arthur make amends. From this point of view, an essentially positive approach lies behind the treatment of the kingly crisis in *Lancelot of the Laik*.

There is another radical way in which this conception of Arthur differs from that familiar from Malory. Arthur's inadequacies are here highly politicised, even more strongly in the Scots version than in its French original. This is in part because Lancelot's relationship with Guinevere is not yet a fully realised and threatening force, but it remains that the Scottish poet has chosen to constitute the principal subject of his first two books as Arthur's political failings as a king. This assumes even more significance and the Lancelot factor commensurately less in the Scottish work than in its French source because the French romance thereafter pursues its huge account of the life and works of Lancelot. The focus of the shorter Scottish work is quite different. While Lancelot assumes a greater prominence in its third book, what continues to take dominant narrative shape is the account of how Arthur is allowed to redress his faults and work towards a more positive control of his people. In Malory, by contrast, his course is one towards ever more fragmentation of the Round Table and finally of the kingdom.

The reordering of the advice puts it into a form of a movement through the virtues of wisdom, justice, truth, liberality and honour, designed to turn Arthur into the sort of 'complete' king characterised earlier in the description of Galiot.[40] And some of the additions made by the Scottish poet indicate an even more specific sense of the wider reference of his Arthurian material to the kingship of his own day. Discussing justice, he follows his French source in urging that kings should pass throughout their realms administering the law.[41] This was traditional advice to princes, but it was also something that Scottish parliaments regularly urged on their rulers, as did James III's in 1473, for instance.[42] That the poet is thinking of a recurrent situation in Scotland is pointed up in the lines that immediately follow the injunction on the active manifestation of royal justice:

> But kingis when thei ben of tender ag,
> [i.e. when still in their minorities]
> Y wil not say I trast thei ben excusit,
> Bot schortly thei sall be sar accusit,
> When so thei cum to yheris of Resone,
> If thei tak not full contrisioune.
> And pwnyss them that hath ther low mysgyit,
> That this is trouth it may not be denyit ... (1658–63)

There is no precedent for this disquisition on the consequences of minorities in the original, and it is a very apt addition. By the mid-fifteenth century in Scotland a

---

40 Cf. Johnston, pp. 8–11.
41 *Lancelot*, 11. 1645–54 and *Lancelot du Lac*, I, p. 286.
42 *APS*, II, p. 104/6; Norman Macdougall, *James III: A Political Study* (Edinburgh, 1982), p. 95.

pattern had been established whereby kings on assuming power after their minorities had to assert themselves in order to demonstrate and confirm their authority.[43] It is this for which the Scottish poet is pressing here, a strong demonstration of royal rule over those who are commonly likely to have attempted to abuse the rule of law during a minority. This was the situation in which, for example, both James II and James III found themselves.[44] If this poem does date from James III's reign these comments make it more likely to be from the late 1460s, when he was in this sort of position, than later.

The balance of advice proffered in *Lancelot of the Laik* is thus quite a delicate one. For while monarchs are warned against the misuse of power, they are also encouraged to assert it. A similar anxiety characterises the Scottish poet's added excursion on the dangers of flattery. Kings must distance themselves from flatterers, in order properly to administer the course of justice. This is again traditional material, but the *Lancelot* poet persistently works over the attainment of this right balance between assertion and restraint. Amytans concludes his advice by re-emphasising the interrelation of king and people and stressing that the king's wisdom is dependent upon the reasoned exercise of his will.

In arguing that the convergence of will and wisdom in a king ensures the stability of a realm the *Lancelot* poet is affirming the fundamental integrity of a kingship in which the monarch strikes the classic mean between being, as he puts it, 'not . . . our fameliar' (1699) with his subjects and yet sufficiently conspicuous to confirm his people's sense of his divinely established authority.

Lancelot of the Laik thus is on balance, and especially in comparison with Malory, a hopeful work. One of the alternatives to a failure in kingly rule posited in Amytans' speech, the take-over of the country by alien kings, was certainly for the Scots a continuing fear (if not a particularly genuine danger) from the English.[45] The other that Amytans mentions, that a king could be destroyed by his people, was never a very strong threat in fifteenth-century Scotland. But it is significant that both of these dire warnings of manifestations of the wrath of God are juxtaposed with a hint of his willing benevolence to a king who will mend his ways. Rebellion against Arthur of a successful and damaging type gets much further in Malory's *Morte Darthur* than it finally will in *Lancelot of the Laik*. This Arthur has a chance to change himself, and by the end of the second book we are being informed that he is starting to do it and his people to love him in return. In the other strand of the narrative the lady of Melyhalt does a deal with Lancelot in which she agrees to release him on the day of the big battle with Galiot.

But not everything is quite plain sailing, narratively or ideologically, and the Scottish poet's treatment of his book III indicates some abiding doubts about the

---

43 See, for instance, Jenny Wormald, *Court, Kirk, and Community, Scotland 1470–1625*, The New History of Scotland, 4 (1981), pp. 13–14. The argument here that minorities also provided a 'safety-valve' in preventing the emergence of an over-mighty or autocratic monarchy is entirely consonant with the judicious balancing of kingly power evoked in *Lancelot of the Laik*.
44 Christine McGladdery, *James II* (Edinburgh, 1990), pp. 49–74; Macdougall, pp. 70–87.
45 Norman A.T. Macdougall, 'Foreign Relations: England and France' in Jennifer M. Brown (ed.), *Scottish Society in the Fifteenth Century* (1977), pp. 101–11.

execution of kingship as characterised through his Arthurian figure, now pointed up through comparisons with Lancelot, and again with Galiot.[46]

Book III opens with the end of the truce approaching. The strengthened loyalty of Arthur's people to him is evident in the speech that Gawain makes to his fellow men, emphasising the interdependence of king and people 'for we but hyme no thing may eschef' (2513). But though Gawain makes it clear that he fights, as the troops do, for the honour of his king and country, Lancelot, on whom Arthur still remains highly dependent, is motivated differently. His conscious inspiration, emphasised in several scenes, is his love for Guinevere. Thus Lancelot does not directly see the defence of the kingdom as a prime reason for his participation in the battle, and the woman he serves is the wife of Arthur.

Arthur himself is not on the field, counselled by Gawain not to bear arms because Galiot will not be doing so. His passivity, in other words, is a response to Galiot rather than of his own initiation, a comparison not entirely flattering and one continued in the course of the battle where the advantage switches from one side to another. While Galiot does intervene to encourage his men, Arthur's dispirited troops are not similarly encouraged by their king. As they in turn despair, it is Lancelot who assumes the hortatory role. His actions have previously heartened them, now his words serve a similar function, in a rousing speech vastly expanding a far more short and to the point series of commands in the French original.[47] It is just after this that, regrettably, the Scots poem breaks off.

As the third book has progressed Arthur has in fact been eclipsed by Lancelot. This was inherent in the source, but the Scots poet who has elsewhere shown such a willingness to make alterations does little to tamper with this. It is probable that in the remainder of the Scottish poem Arthur did assume a more active role, since in the prose *Lancelot* Arthur takes to the field himself in the final battle with Galiot. Nevertheless the conclusion of this episode (and doubtless of *Lancelot of the Laik*) Galiot's surrender, is prompted by his extraordinary admiration for Lancelot rather than Arthur's supremacy. Arthur himself believes the army to be at the point of defeat.[48]

To an extent then, *Lancelot of the Laik* has in common with Malory's *Morte Darthur* the fact that no one figure fully and lastingly encapsulates perfect kingship. Galiot looks a better king than Arthur, but he will be finally defeated. Arthur certainly improves in the course of the poem, but he is not a decisive knight on the field of battle. Lancelot is less Arthur's 'double', but nor is he wholly his right-hand man. The separateness of his motivation renders his identification with the patriotism of the Arthurian cause less than complete.

Nevertheless, *Lancelot of the Laik* shows a greater belief in the potential for

---

46 On the wider implications of this in the French romance, Kennedy, *Lancelot and the Grail*, pp. 228–31.
47 Cf. *Lancelot of the Laik*, 11. 3445–76 and *Lancelot do Lac*, I, p. 319. Lancelot's speech and the people's response have much of the tenor of the exchanges between Bruce and his troops at Bannockburn (*Bruce*, XII, 11. 171–329, vol. III, ed. Matthew P. McDiarmid and James A.C. Stevenson, STS, 4th Ser. 13, Edinburgh, 1981).
48 See the account in Kennedy, *Lancelot and the Grail*, pp. 98–100.

effective kingship than was achieved in Malory's narrative, or more especially its last parts. The nature of good government is programmatically defined in Book II and the poem reaches towards an optimistic conclusion in Arthur's victory that differs dramatically from the mood of defeat and exhaustion with which Malory concludes the *Morte Darthur*. Arthur is a redeemable ruler and Lancelot is still working for the harmony of the Arthurian kingdom. And the issue of *his* kingship, the sense of him as a kind of kingly alternative to Arthur, is not, by this writer, played up. For the Scottish poet there is to be no alternative. The Scottish poem moves from crisis to the restoration of order; the English Arthurian cycle moves from the establishment of order to crisis and division. That the Scottish poet chooses to select a part of the Arthurian narrative in which a king is under threat from an alien nation and – more strongly – from his own need to find the right kind of assertive government, and that the English writer chooses to select a cycle that culminates in factionalism and civil war and with both a king-figure and his best knight dead, are perhaps less surprising and more comprehensible when set against the political climate and patterns of succession in fifteenth-century Scotland and England.

BERTHOLD SCHOENE-HARWOOD

13. *A Story of One Faith and Blood
    – Orkneyinga saga and the Poetics of
    Historical Continuity**

* This conference paper evolved into a chapter of my study on literature and the Orkney identity: *THE MAKING OF ORCADIA. NARRATIVE IDENTITY IN THE PROSE WORK OF GEORGE MACKAY BROWN* (Frankfurt a.M.: Peter Lang, 1995)

No doubt, it is our indefatigable human desire to make sense of time and our own existence in time which must be regarded as the main impetus behind the creation of all narratives, historical as well as pseudo-historical or fictional. In his article 'Narrative Time' Paul Ricoeur takes 'temporality to be that structure of existence that reaches language in narrativity and narrativity to be the language structure that has temporality as its ultimate referent.'[1] He points out that by emplotting time, narrative endows our human reality with a structure and hence with a meaning that is relatable and consistent. As Peter Brooks explains,

> [n]arrative is one of the ways in which we speak, one of the large categories in which we think. Plot is its thread of design and its active shaping force, the product of our refusal to allow temporality to be meaningless, our stubborn insistence on making meaning in the world and in our lives.[2]

This narrative making of meaning is a particularly urgent issue when it comes to answering the question 'Who are we?'. As Ricoeur argues, 'to answer the question 'Who?' [. . .] is to tell the story of a life',[3] meaning that only by dint of narrative can human identity ever be adequately grasped and expressed. The problem here is that human identity is never static and immutable. Permanently exposed to the vicissitudes of historical change, it is caught up in a continuous process of having to rectify and readjust itself. It is always in quest of a more authentic narrative expression of itself, leaving behind innumerable versions of what will paradoxically never cease to be basically always the same identity-bearing story. Disaster lurks in a time of sudden and fundamental change when this identity-bearing story is in danger of losing track of its own red thread and consequently, an individual or a whole community faces a severe identity crisis. Then, it is essential that the story can be skillfully restored and thus salvaged from oblivion.

1 Paul Ricoeur, 'Narrative Time', in: W.J.T. Mitchell (ed.), *On Narrative*, Chicago and London 1981, 165.
2 Peter Brooks, *Reading for the Plot. Design and Intention in Narrative*, Oxford 1984, 232.
3 Ricoeur, *Time and Narrative*, tr. by K. McLaughlin and D. Pellauer, 3 vols, Chicago and London 1984–8, vol. 3, 245.

Medieval Scandinavian historiography

In this paper I shall argue that the compilation of *Orkneyinga saga* is precisely such a work of 'restoration' and as such, it has to be regarded as a direct narrative response to the religious and cultural identity crisis suffered by the young Viking nation of Orkney after its Christianisation.

The first literate historians of the Scandinavian Middle Ages were primarily compilers of oral traditions. They collected as many as possible of a community's co-existing 'rival' narratives about certain historical events, compared them with one another, and then, for their own reasons, either favoured one of the versions in particular and completely discarded the rest, or neatly dovetailed two or more of them into what they deemed a more authentic and informative whole. As likely as not, they also sought to iron out ostensible inconsistencies and imaginatively filled up inconvenient gaps that might have left their own historical accounts questionable. Or – least disputable against the backdrop of modern academic standards of historical research – they overtly hinted at different oral traditions and sources of reference.[4]

It was the saga compilers' task to reconcile the Viking ethos, with which the whole indigenous oral tradition of the North was instilled, with the new Christian world picture that had gradually become established in the Scandinavian countries since the last decades of the tenth century. The saga compilers may have considered literary attempts to obliterate all pagan narratives or work on their transformation into historically insignificant folktales and heroic lays. Yet as members of relatively young nations on the outermost periphery of medieval Europe, Norse scholars – some of them educated at universities on the Continent – were proudly aware of their highly identity-bearing historical heritage and eager to emulate their European counterparts in an attempt to consolidate their national distinctiveness by telling elaborate stories about their origin.[5]

Obviously, a great amount of ingenuity and skill was required to transmute the barbaric Vikings, who had not long ago haunted the whole of Europe with their notorious raids, into acceptable ancestors of pious and sophisticated Christians.

---

4 Cp. Dietrich Hofmann, 'Die Einstellung der isländischen Sagaverfasser und ihrer Vorgänger zur mündlichen Tradition', in: Hans Bekker-Nielsen et al. (eds.), *Oral Tradition – Literary Tradition. A Symposium*, Odense 1977, 17f. See also the accounts of St. Magnus's brother's death and Earl Paul Hakonarson's destiny after his abduction from Orkney by Svein Asleifarson, in the context of which the compiler of *Orkneyinga saga* openly refers to contradictory oral traditions (*The Orkneyinga Saga*, tr. and ed. by Alexander B. Taylor, Edinburgh and London 1938, chapters XLII and LXXV). The saga also gives an intriguing description of how a group of Vikings comes to settle on one and the same narrative interpretation of a historical event in which they had all participated but of which each of them told a different version. According to the saga, they unanimously accepted their leader's account: 'There was much talk about the exploit they had just performed. Each man was giving his version of it. And the talk turned upon who had been first to board [the dromond of the Saracens] and they could not agree upon it. Then some said that they would cut a fine figure if they did not all have the same story to tell about so great an exploit. And the upshot was that they agreed that Earl Rognvald should settle the matter, and that afterwards they would adopt his version of it' (ibid., chapter LXXXVIII, 297).

5 For an interesting discussion of the role of literature in medieval Iceland, particularly as to the development of a specific national identity, see Kurt Schier, 'Iceland and the Rise of Literature in 'Terra Nova'. Some Comparative Reflections', *Gripla* 1 (1975), 168–81.

For example, as Rosalie Wax sketches out, the Christian historians of twelfth- and thirteenth-century Scandinavia must have had considerable difficulties in fully understanding their forbears' mythic train of thought:

> [. . .] it is most unlikely that Snorri Sturluson [1179–1241] believed such incidents in the tales he recorded as that a young man might mate with a Being whose shape might change into a swan. But his ancestor, Egil Skallagrimsson [c. 910–990], did likely believe such things could happen, and some of Egil's ancestors almost certainly knew people who believed they had undergone this kind of experience.[6]

Yet as the sagas prove, although the civilisational rift seemed fundamental, it was by no means insurmountable. The main problem was how to detect and establish continuity in spite of seemingly all-embracing change. It had to be made plausible how the later layers of Orcadian history could have grown quite naturally out of the more ancient ones; also, that it was actually the dynamics of an indigenous tradition rather than a coarsely disruptive imposition at foreign hands that had instigated all the religious, ethical and cultural changes in the first place. Fortunately, the historians of medieval Scandinavia were familiar with certain historiographical patterns and techniques that enabled them to salvage their pagan heritage from total oblivion without ineluctably infringing upon medieval notions of Christian piety. As Joseph Harris and Gerd Weber outline in their articles, the method saga compilers generally opted for in order to instill in their readership a sense of historical continuity was that of typology.[7] As a popular interpretative pattern, typology was frequently employed by medieval scholars for relating events of a long bygone past to less remote events as well as the immediate present, especially when two historical periods were incisively separated by a great cultural – mostly religiously motivated – change. For the Scandinavians such a change was evidently given in their conversion to Christianity which modern Icelanders still tellingly refer to as the *siðaskipti*, meaning 'change of customs'.[8] It does not need an academically sound familiarity with the sagas to realise after the reading of only three or four of them that a lot of their action hinges on that pivotal historical moment, 'the locus for the epoch', as Harris quite aptly calls it.[9]

Seen through the eyes of a medieval Scandinavian historian time presented itself as significantly divided in two parts: the pagan past before the *siðaskipti* (or *forn siðr*) and the far less remote Christian past (or *inn nyi siðr*) of which the immediate present stood as the most recent emanation. These two epochs could now be reconciled by means of a typological *interpretatio christiana* of history: pre-Christian

---

6 Rosalie H. Wax, *Magic, Fate, and History. The Changing Ethos of the Viking*, Lawrence/Kansas 1969, 47.
7 Joseph Harris, 'Saga as Historical Novel', in: John Lindow et al. (eds.) *Structure and Meaning in Old Norse Literature. New Approaches to Textual Analysis and Literary Criticism*, Odense 1986, 187–219; Gerd W. Weber, 'Irreligiösität und Heldenzeitalter. Zum Mythencharakter der altisländischen Literature', in: Ursula Dronke et al. (eds.), *Speculum Norroenum. Norse Studies in Memory of Gabriel Turville-Petre*, Odense 1981, 474–505.
8 Cp. Arngrimur Sigurðsson's *Islenzk-Ensk Orðabók* (Reykjavik 1983) in which *siður* is translated as 'custom, habit' and *skipti* as 'change'.
9 Harris, 'Saga as Historical Novel', 195.

events and historical persons were identified as *types* correspondent to the *anti-types* of the Christian era. This meant in terms of the belief in a natural heathen perception of God (as represented in medieval literature by the topos of a *naturalis gentium religio*) that certain heathen practices and narratives were interpreted as foreshadowings or dim reflections of the one and only true Christian canon, and that certain historical persons, first and foremost of course those that had played an important part in the Conversion, were regarded as forerunners of later saints.[10] Such a stylisation of history is reminiscent of the practices and conventions of medieval Biblical exegesis, especially its commonly accepted division of time into B.C. and A.D. and correspondingly, the division of Scripture into the Old and New Testaments.[11] Yet as Harris points out, there is an intriguing difference between Biblical typology and medieval Icelandic historiography:

> When we consider Icelandic medieval historiography [. . .], we notice an interesting twist: Biblical typology ultimately meant interpreting the present to conform with the sacred past (the 'Geschichtsmythos' of the Jewish past). But in twelfth- and thirteenth-century Scandinavia it meant re-'writing' (revising) the past to create antecedent types for the Christian present [. . .] twelfth- and thirteenth-century, Christian-medieval concepts are projected into the past. Such projection, however, [. . .] is not random but patterns roughly according to typological principles to constitute a 'historical myth'.[12]

The historiographical achievement of *Orkneyinga saga*

Like a great amount of Old Norse Literature, *Orkneyinga saga* – compiled sometime between 1190 and 1230[13] – can by no means be unequivocally defined as either history or fiction. As Einar Sveinsson propounds, saga literature in general has to be appreciated as 'a literature that is extremely various, complex and full of subtle nuances' and 'does not permit a judgement to be made in terms of: 'the saga is history', or, 'the saga is fiction'.[14] Accordingly, although *Orkneyinga*

---

10 Weber, 'Irreligiösitat und Heldenzeitalter', specifically 474f.: 'Jede genealogische, ethnische, nationale und politische Kontinuität der nordischen Völker von der Vorzeit bis zur Gegenwart des 12., 13. und 14. Jahrhunderts ist auf die heilsgeschichtliche Peripetie des Übertritts zum Christentum bezogen. Dieser *Baptismus*-analoge Vorgang teilt die nordische Geschichte (in *forn siðr* und *inn nyi siðr*). Kontinuität und Einheit stellen sich erst auf dem exegetischen Umweg über die *typologische* Deutung der Geschichte wieder her: Die typologische Geschichtsdeutung 'erkennt' in den 'vor'-christlichen Ereignissen und historischen Personen den *Typus* zum *Antitypus* der christ-lichen Zeit und ermöglicht so den Anschluß jener an diese.'
11 For an exemplary case study of how skilfully medieval Scandinavian scholars applied the theological device of typology to a thorough re-interpretation of their pagan ancestors' mythology cp. Heinz Klingenberg's analysis of Snorri Sturluson's *Gylfaginning* ('Gylfaginning. Tres Vidit Unum Adoravit', in: Bela Brogyanyi and T. Krömmelbein (eds.), *Germanic Dialects. Linguistic and Philological Investigations*, Amsterdam and Philadelphia 1986, 627–89). For a more general discussion cp. John Lindow's 'Mythology and Mythography' in Carol J. Clover and J. Lindow (eds.), *Old Norse-Icelandic Literature. A Critical Guide*, Ithaca and London 1985, 21–67.
12 Harris, 200f.
13 Cp. Kurt Schier, *Sagaliteratur*, Stuttgart 1970, 31f.
14 Einar Sveinsson, 'Fact and Fiction in the Sagas', in: Victor Lange and H.-H. Roloff (eds.), *Dichtung – Sprache – Gesellschaft. Akten des IV. Internationalen Germanisten-Kongresses 1970 in Princeton*, Frankfurt a. M. 1971, 306.

saga is often numbered among the so-called kings' sagas, which Fritz Paul defines as a non-fictional genre, it is far from being 'realistic' in the modern sense of the word.[15] Rather, it represents a 'pseudo-realistic' work of art that principally seems to value structural smoothness and self-contained integrity much higher than absolute historical authenticity.[16]

As will be shown in the following, the structure of *Orkneyinga saga* is quite obviously informed by the attempt to reconcile Orkney's pagan warrior past with the ideological propositions of the new Christian era. No doubt, the compiler of *Orkneyinga saga* tried to do for Orkney what his fellow historians did for Iceland and also – in *Faereyinga saga* – for the Faroe Islands, namely to create a historical myth in order to moderate the identity-menacing cultural incongruence that had been brought about by the relatively sudden official introduction of Christian values in the Northern Isles. As Herman Pálsson and Paul Edwards outline, even as early as at the time of the saga's first compilation in written form, the history of Orkney must already have presented itself to the discerning eye as rife with contradictions and thus in great want of an integrative re-'reading'. How could a warrior-earl end up as martyr, saint, and miracle-worker? And how is it to be explained that on Earl Rognvald's expedition to the Holy Land, the Bishop of Orkney himself featured as one of the hardiest viking-captains? With respect to these questions Pálsson and Edwards manage to capture the intrinsic socio-psychological intention of *Orkneyinga saga* remarkably well without in any way mitigating its integrity as a literary work of art:

> The purpose of the saga is, partly at least, to explore [. . .] social and psychological tensions [. . .] in the history of the people of Orkney, and to help them understand themselves through a knowledge of their origins. Though based on fact, it is only partly governed by what actually happened: like other inspired chronicles, *Orkneyinga saga* has its own coherence even when it departs from the historical facts.[17]

---

15 Fritz Paul, 'Das Fiktionalitätsproblem in der altnordischen Prosaliteratur', *Arkiv för nordisk filologi* 97 (1982), 61. A.B. Alexander does not wholly agree with Paul's classification of *Orkneyinga saga* as a typical kings' saga but would rather it was seen as some intricate convolution of several different saga genres: '[. . .] the *Orkneyinga saga* is a clever compilation made on the model of the Collections of Kings' Lives, but in its various parts it has affinities to all the other classifiable types of Saga literature – in the Mythological Introduction to the 'Sagas of olden time,' in the Sagas of the early Orkney Earls to the Kings' Lives themselves, in the Sagas of Saint Magnus to the ecclesiastical Saints' Lives, and in the Saga of Rognvald Kali to the typical Family and Outlaw Sagas and the later Romantic Saga' (*The Orkneyinga Saga*, 9). Cp. also Taylor, '*Orkneyinga saga* – Patronage and Authorship', in: Peter Foote *et al.*, *Proceedings of the Fifth International Saga Conference – University of Edinburgh 1971*, London 1973, 396.
16 Cp. Paul, '*Das Fiktionalitätsproblem*', 63, where even Paul who ascribes a high degree of historicity to the kings' sagas concedes that '[. . .] der Pseudorealismus der Sagakunst in Wirklichkeit mit all seinen stereotypen Verfahren, etwa den genealogischen Anfangs- und Schlussteilen, den oft wortwörtlichen Einleitungs- und Schlussformeln, eine hochartifizielle manieristische Kunstform wan, deren Gesetzmässigkeiten keinesfalls durch Verfahrensweisen objektiver Geschichtsschreibung durchbrochen werden durften.'
17 *Orkneyinga saga. The History of the Earls of Orkney*, tr. by Herman Pálsson and P. Edwards, London 1981, 19.

The most conspicuous fictional device in *Orkneyinga saga* is its recurrent leitmotif of a division of the earldom of Orkney among two or even three eligible aspirants which is given a mythological root in the folktale-like exposition of the saga. But whereas the division of Norway between mythic Nor and Gor was a peaceful settlement, most of the subsequent arrangements are only made after periods of fierce strife entailing war and murder. The saga tradition grounds this new violent quality of the recurrent division of Orkney in an anecdote concerning Einar Buttered-Bread, a grandson of Thorfinn Skull-Splitter. The saga seeks to make us believe that it is only because this man would not listen to a seer's doom-predicting prophecy and postpone his murder of Earl Harvard the Fecund, his uncle, that strife, hatred, and bloodshed should later prevail over the whole of his family's undertakings:

> 'Don't do your work today,' he [the seer] said, 'leave it till tomorrow. If you won't, there are going to be killings in your family for years to come.'[18]

Thus employing a clear historiographical embellishment of what actually happened, the saga compiler explains the dynamics of conflict and war which underlie the entire history of Viking Orkney by hinting at the inexorable workings of fate. The embellishment as such is residual of the pagan origins of the saga; only for purely narratively motivated reasons, that is, as a brief exposition of the main plot of the saga, does it seem to have survived the compiler's Christian and – what is even more important – consciously Christianising redaction.

That there can be no doubt whatever about the overtly Christian outlook of the saga becomes evident in such sections as that about the conflict of heathen and Christian practices in Sweden. In its context, the saga compiler points at both the absurdity and blasphemous dangerousness of divination and soothsaying customs apparently quite similar to the one called on by Einar Buttered-Bread in the exposition of the saga. It is interesting to note that what was further above welcomed by the saga compiler as a structuring device of narrative foreshadowing is here now disdainfully rejected as a naive and – due to its pagan nature – outrageous act of barbarism:

> In Sweden, Christianity was in its infancy, so there were still a good many people practising paganism in the belief that by it they would gain wisdom and knowledge of many things yet to happen. King Ingi was a devout Christian and every heathen was abhorred by him. He made great efforts to put down the evil practices which had been for long a part of heathen worship, but other leading men and landowners grew so resentful when their barbarism was criticised that they installed another King who still adhered to the pagan rites, the Queen's brother Svein, nicknamed the Sacrificer.[19]

18 *Ibid.*, chapter 9, 34.
19 *Ibid.*, chapter 35, 79f. For another clearly anti-pagan reference in the saga cp. also the episode on Svein Asleifarson's murder of Svein Breast-Rope, Earl Paul Hakonarson's forecastleman, who 'was keen on the old practices and had spent many a night in the open with the spirits' (ibid., chapter 65, 120f.). The saga writer makes explicit mention of the fact that 'the bishop thanked him [Svein Asleifarson] for killing Svein Breast-Rope and called it good riddance' (chapter 66, 127). Obviously, even an act of heinous murder could find the sanction of the Church, only provided that the victim had been an inveterate heathen.

The contrast between Pagan and Christian sacrifices

The subject of sacrificial practices, mentioned for the first time in connection with the so-called 'Thorri's Sacrifice', represents a recurrent point of interest in *Orkneyinga saga*. The changing modes of and attitudes toward religious sacrifices over the centuries supply the saga writer with a suitable field within which he can illustrate the ethical differences between paganism and Christianity.

Torf-Einar's atrociously gory and cruel sacrifice of Halfdan Long-Legs[20] is a document of his deep faith in Odin and the Germanic pantheon. In this context it seems to be no sheer coincidence that Einar himself has previously been described as 'tall and ugly, and though he was one-eyed he was still the most keen-sighted of men'.[21] One-eyedness (sometimes correlated with references to an impressive sagacity) represents an indispensable ingredient of the majority of Odin-descriptions in medieval literature and iconography.[22] When he dies in battle holding a magic raven banner in his hand Sigurd Hlodvisson the Stout is equally identified with the chief god of the Germanic tribes who was also known as the raven-god. And eventually, Thorfinn the Mighty strikingly takes after Odin, the god of war, when he sets out to fight the Scots at Tarbat Ness: '[. . .] Thorfinn marched before his ranks, a golden helmet on his head, a sword at his waist, wielding a great spear in both hands.'[23] Not only are there many iconographic documents showing Odin as a horseman with a spear in his hand, the Germanic warrior custom of hurling a spear over a troop of enemies is also said to signify the latter's dedication as a sacrifice to Odin.

In direct contrast to all the heathen practices of sacrificing an enemy in the name of Odin, St Magnus sacrifices himself and dies a martyr: '[. . .] he prostrated himself on the ground, committing his soul to God and offering himself as a sacrifice.'[24] Confronted with the exact wording of the original Old Norse text, learned Norse readers cannot have missed its obvious allusive parallelism to stanza 138, 5–6, of the monological Eddic poem 'Hávamál' which describes Odin's mythic self-sacrifice.[25] By means of this parallelism, *Orkneyinga saga* clearly identifies St Magnus with Odin but not at all in the way that Einar, Sigurd, and Thorfinn are identified with him. Magnus's genuinely altruistic Christian self-sacrifice in imitation of the Crucifixion not only sets him on a par with Odin but superiorises him to the pagan godhead who sacrificed himself – as it were, autistically – to himself and also to a purely selfish end, namely the acquisition of supernatural knowledge.

---

20 *Ibid.*, chapter 8.
21 *Ibid.*, chapter 7, 29.
22 As a source of reference for information on Germanic mythology cp. Rudolf Simek's *Lexikon der germanischen Mythologie*, Stuttgart 1984.
23 *Orkneyinga saga*, chapter 20, 54.
24 *Ibid.*, chapter 50, 95.
25 Cp. 'Hann fell til jarðar ok *gaf sik guði* ok foerði *honum sjálfan sik* i fórn' (*Orkneyinga Saga*, ed. by Finnbogi Guðmundsson, Reykjavik 1965, [Islensk Fornrit 34], 110) with '[. . .] ok *gefinn Oðni/siálfr siálfom mér* [. . .]' (= '. . . and given to Odin/myself to myself . . .') in *Edda. Die Lieder des Codex Regius nebst verwandten Denkmälern*, ed. by Gustav Neckel, Heidelberg 1914, 39.

Antagonistic character constellations

The most admirable artistic feat of the compiler of *Orkneyinga saga* is to be found in the way he renders the relationships and feudal constellations among its main characters semiotically meaningful. In the culturally transitional eleventh and early twelfth centuries, Orcadian society was characterised by a highly problematic co-existence of diametrically opposed ideals, defined by John Mooney as follows:

> [. . .] (a) the old warlike spirit, the spirit of strife and revenge, defiance of danger, whether from man or the elements, dauntless courage, indifference to human suffering; and (b) the Christian life, guided by the laws of God found in the Bible, and taught by His servants, the priests and bishops; the gospel of love and brotherhood – love for everything that is good, hatred of everything evil (except a fellowman), obedience to the will of God, and Christian courage capable of the highest and noblest heroism.[26]

Viking and Christian ethics had not yet stopped vying for predominance and sometimes blended into curious hybrid forms of conduct and self-expression. In the islands fierce warriors used to raiding, raping, and pillaging could frequently be found living cheek by jowl with pious monks.

That personal antagonisms in saga literature should illustrate the competition of civilisationally incompatible strands within one and the same society at one and the same time is not a particularly new finding. Paul Schach has pointed out that as 'manifestations of the gradual transvaluation of the heroic ideal', the sagas often confront representatives of different generations 'to portray the clash of antagonistic cultures', brought about by great civilisational changes such as that of the Conversion.[27] But in order to demonstrate the utter confusion of the Viking society of early Christian Orkney our compiler goes a step further than that. In *Orkneyinga saga*, it is not representatives of different generations but exact contemporaries that epitomise the heavily contrasting sets of ideals. The most prominent antagonistic couple to be named here are certainly the cousins Hakon Paulsson and St Magnus in respect to whom O. Duncan Macrae-Gibson is fully entitled to speak of 'this neatly opposed contrast between warrior and Christian behaviour'.[28] The clash between the two of them could scarcely be stylised as more fundamental: on the one hand, there is the perfect Viking statesman with a clear eye for political necessities which potentially include even murder as a last resort, 'a shrewd practitioner of *real-politik*';[29] on the other, we are confronted

---

26 John Mooney, *St. Magnus–Earl of Orkney*, Kirkwall 1935, 43.
27 Paul Schach, 'Some Observations on the Generation-Gap Theme in the Icelandic Sagas', in: Harald Scholler (ed.), *The Epic in Medieval Society. Aesthetic and Moral Values*, Tübingen 1977, 381.
28 O. Duncan Macrae-Gibson, 'The Other Scottish Language – *Orkneyinga saga*', in: J. Derrick McClure and M. R. G. Spiller (eds.), *Bryght Lanternis. Essays on the Language and Literature of Medieval and Renaissance Scotland*, Aberdeen 1989, 423.
29 George Mackay Brown, 'The Real Earl Hakon', *Rockpools and Daffodils. An Orcadian Diary 1979–1991*, Edinburgh 1992, 254.

with the extremism of saintly Christian faithfulness. This striking collision of ethical ideals comes to a kind of synthesis in the personality of St Magnus's nephew, Earl Rognvald, the later Saint. As Marlene Ciklamini argues,

> Rognvaldr's [*sic*] retention of the jarlship depended [. . .] upon a compromise of values. He often practised the virtues of a Christian ruler; yet he understood and tolerated, whenever necessary, the violence inherent in a society which adhered to the heroic code of ethics.[30]

Quite naturally, the saga compiler himself prefers the pious Christian part of Rognvald's character to its indigenous Viking strands which repeatedly cause considerable havoc in the future saint's *curriculum vitae*. On their pilgrimage to the Holy Land, for instance, Rognvald and his men conquer a dromond and kill the whole of its Black African crew apart from the leader whom they then try to sell in the land of the Saracens. Eventually, their captive turns out to be a Saracen aristocrat who in spite of his heathendom – which was to justify the Vikings' onslaught on his crew and possessions as a clear case of Christian duty – behaves astoundingly nobly towards them. The Vikings' Christian presumptuousness, hypocrisy, and arrogance is deliberately unmasked here by the saga compiler; the Norsemen and their saintly leader appear much more barbaric and considerably less civilised than the 'infidels of Mohammed'.[31] This account lends credence to Kaaren Grimstad's assumption 'that the saga audience in the thirteenth century associated the word Viking primarily with a pirate and malefactor' and invariably frowned upon exploits like the one related above as despicably heathen and barbaric.[32] Nevertheless, they could by no means afford to see the whole of their Viking heritage consigned to oblivion. Vindications had to be searched for, vindications that could successfully outweigh their forbears' atrocities which they so mindlessly, and often hypocritically, committed. In this respect, the mere fact that Earl Rognvald and his retinue found themselves on a pilgrimage to Jerusalem and assumed they were fighting for a Christian cause when they attacked the dromond must perhaps be regarded as a mitigating circumstance.

As a *saintly* historical figure Rognvald is only visibly contoured against the immediate presence of his most irrepressibly Viking contemporary, Svein Asleifarson. Whereas St Magnus personifies the extreme of Christian saintliness, Svein embodies an impressive exemplar of unattenuated Vikingdom. He is 'the ultimate viking', as Eric Linklater so aptly put it, downright atavistic in his attitudes and doings but nonetheless a glorious personality:

> He [Sweyn] outlived his age [. . .] The pirate force with which he raided towns and shipping [. . .] kept Gairsay noisy till the autumn of 1171; when in Oxford

---

30 Marlene Ciklamini, 'Saint Rognvaldr and Sveinn Asleifarson, the Viking', *Scandinavian Studies* 42: 1 (Feb. 1970), 52.
31 *Orkneyinga saga*, chapter 88.
32 Kaaren Grimstad, 'A Comic Role of the Viking in the Family Sagas', in: Evelyn S. Firchow *et al.* (eds.), *Studies for Einar Haugen. Presented by Friends and Colleagues*, The Hague and Paris 1972, 252.

a university had lately been founded. Sweyn was the last of the great vikings, and long before he died the Norsemen had turned from piracy and taken to architecture [. . .] It was in 1137 that Earl Rognvald began to build the cathedral of St. Magnus, but thirty-four years after its foundations had been dug, and the pious stones had been laid, Sweyn and his narrow ship still went to private warfare oversea.[33]

In the antagonistic constellation Svein vs. Rognvald the contradictions characteristic of late Orcadian Viking history come to a final climax. In a sometimes disturbingly ambivalent way the lives of the two men are inextricably entwined: they are friends and allies, then enemies, then friends again. Yet although the conflict pagan/Christian is apparently still an issue as far as the medieval identity crisis of the people of Orkney is concerned, the die has long been cast: the future of Orkney is a Christian one. As Linklater points out, '[. . .] crusading and the road to Jerusalem were now [at the beginning of the 12th century] held in more esteem than the viking path [. . .]'.[34] In fact, Svein Asleifarson himself is said to have succumbed to the superiority of the Christian faith before he was killed on a raid in Dublin. Typically of the semiotic style of the saga, even this 'ultimate conversion' is rendered in terms of a personal relationship when Svein movingly renews his vow of vassalage to Earl Rognvald the Saint:

'Whether or not I'm to fall today,' he said, 'I want everyone to know that I'm the retainer of the holy Earl Rognvald, and now he's with God, it's in him I'll put my trust.'[35]

Conclusion

It now seems necessary to modify Gerd Weber's statement that sagas in general contain an intrinsic division into two parts embracing the heathen and Christian periods of Old Norse history subtly set in contrast by dint of typological devices.[36] *Orkneyinga saga* clearly differs from other medieval Norse sagas in that its final achievement is not a mere remoulding of the past into a kind of pagan mirror-image of the Christian present. Rather, it manages to contrive a sense of linear historical continuity interlocking past and present through an almost completely riftless organic development. According to *Orkneyinga saga*, Christianity in Orkney activates potentials already existing in the Orcadian people, for instance, the potential capacity of bringing forth individuals of a saintly stature. *Orkneyinga saga* must be regarded as an attempt to present Christianity as coming from within Orkney where, as a seminal entity, it has been lying uncatalysed for centuries. This impression is reinforced by the fact that all the major protagonists of the saga, whether heroic heathens or pious Christians, are of one and the same kin. The implication is that if only Christianity had been introduced earlier in

33 Eric Linklater, *The Ultimate Viking*, London 1955, 7f.
34 *Ibid.*, 74.
35 *Orkneyinga saga*, chapter 108, 218.
36 Weber, 'Irreligiösität', passim.

Orkney cruel Torf-Einar might have been a much more recognisable relation of his pious descendant St Magnus.

No doubt, the typological principle lies at the narrative heart of the saga. It can hardly be called in question that across the cultural rift caused by the Conversion, the motif of changing sacrificial practices is meant to connect Torf-Einar's gross barbarism with St Magnus's Christian martyrdom: the *tertium comparationis* here is the basic human need to worship a supernatural power by way of sacrifices, compellingly felt even by the fiercest pagan warrior. Of course, Magnus's self-sacrifice outshines all prior and posterior sacrifices in Orkney. As we have seen, the obviously stylised wording of the original saga text also presents it as merging the sacrificial practices of the new and old belief systems. In the personality of St Rognvald, the devoutly Christian and heathen warrior strands of the family come to an acceptable synthesis to which even the ultimate Viking Svein Asleifarson, who – significantly – is an outsider to the kin of the Orkney earls, must eventually give in.

As demonstrated above, in *Orkneyinga saga* the collision of civilisationally antagonistic ethical standards is not illustrated by an implementation of the generation-gap theme but rather by the competitive interplay of exact contemporaries. This is why a blatant rift between past and present cannot be detected. The historical layers of the societal palimpsest of medieval Orkney seem to grow into and out of one another almost organically. The civilisational change is not presented as being suddenly enforced from outwith Orkney but, on the contrary, as taking place in a gradual process of catalysing hidden potentials within Viking Orkney itself.

Like all narratives, *Orkneyinga saga* combines two aspects, one chronological and the other configurational. The chronological aspect sets the facts and incidents of Orcadian history in a neat episodic sequence while the configurational aspect superimposes a plot on them, thus transforming the simple chronological succession of historical events into a meaningful and consistent narrative whole – what we call a story.[37] In *Orkneyinga saga*, the act of configuration marks the narrative process *per se* as a highly creative organisation of real-life events and reveals it as rather more than a one-hundred-percent accurate means of mimetic reproduction. In the act of configuration, the fictional component of narrativity influences the factual authenticity of history. Quite obviously, the plot of *Orkneyinga saga* is informed by its compiler's preconceived view of Orcadian history as a story of historical and religious continuity rather than disruptive change. Orcadian identity is imaginatively construed against the background of an intricate process of historical selection and narrative contrivance which confirms Ricoeur's proposition that '[i]ndividual and community are constituted in their identity by taking up narratives that become for them their actual history.'[38] In *Orkneyinga saga*, fact and fiction collapse into one and create what could only be appropriately described as an 'authentic myth', that is, in the words of M. I. Steblin-Kamenskij, something 'as impossible as a cross between a camel and a tiger'.[39]

---

37 Cp. Ricoeur, 'Narrative Time', 174, and idem, *Time and Narrative*, vol. 1, 65.
38 Ricoeur, *Time and Narrative*, vol. 3, 247.
39 Cp. M. I. Steblin-Kamenskij, *The Saga Mind*, Odense 1973, 24.

BENJAMIN HUDSON

14.   *The Literary Culture of the Early Scottish Court*

Little attention has been given to the literature of Scotland before the late middle ages and the earlier centuries have been considered a literary desert, even by those well-disposed towards the Scots.[1] Therefore it is somewhat surprising to read in the biography of the Welsh scholar and bishop Sulien of St. David's, written by his son Ieuan in the last years of the eleventh century, that determined to study outside Wales,

> Moved by gusts of wind, he landed in the country which they call by the name of Scotland. And remaining there for five years, unwearied he pursued his desire . . . persisting diligently (in his studies) by night and day, extracted continuously from the pure stream of the sevenfold fountain [i.e. the seven liberal arts] cupfuls fragrant with mellifluous aroma. For, learning and writing with immense effort, whatsoever he investigated during the night, having been retained in his mind, arising at the clear light of the day he wrote down intelligently.[2]

This estimation is echoed in the introduction to the earliest extant life of St. Kentigern, written by an anonymous non-Scottish cleric at the orders of Bishop Herbert of Glasgow (1147–69),

> When at length I came to the kingdom of the Scots, I found it very rich in the relics of the saints, illustrious in its clergy and glorious in its princes.[3]

Not only did the Scottish kingdom possess an intellectual culture that was admired, but also one that was being deliberately sought out by non-Scots. This leads to the question, what kind of literary culture did it have? Certainly an aspect of this was ecclesiastical, and one assumes that Bishop Sulien pursued his unwearied studies in some religious environment, possibly St. Andrews where the scholars of the church would gather to greet the bishop-elect Eadmer in 1120.[4] At the same time, one can begin to discern the outlines of a literary culture at the

---

1 Kathleen Hughes, *Celtic Britain in the Early Middle Ages* (Woodbridge, 1980), p. 20.
2 This poem has been edited several times, the most recent edition and translation is by Michael Lapidge, 'The Welsh-Latin Poetry of Sulien's Family,' *Studia Celtica*, viii-ix (1973–4), 68–106 (at lines 95–114; text on pages 84 & 86, translation on pages 85 & 87); this translation follows Lapidge.
3 *Vita Kentegerni Imperfecta, Auctore Ignoto* in *Lives of S. Ninian and S. Kentigern*, edited by Alexander Penrose Forbes, Historians of Scotland volume v (Edinburgh, 1874), pp. 243–52 (at page 243).
4 Eadmer, *Historia Novorum*, ed. Martin Rule (London, 1884), p. 284.

royal court of Máel Coluim III, better known as Malcolm Canmore, beginning with the king and his queen Margaret, then continuing through the reigns of his sons Alexander I and David I. This dynasty has received much attention in other matters and what follows is only a preliminary survey of a topic that could bear much more scrutiny by those better qualified for the task.

I. The Celtic background

Any inquiry into the literary traditions at Máel Coluim's court must acknowledge that it belonged to a Gaelic-speaking cultural area that extended from southwest Ireland to northeast Scotland. The literature presented at these royal courts seems to have been largely oral in presentation, although it was written down at some stage. There was a pronounced historical tint to this literature, and one should remember that 'history' was interpreted far more broadly then than now. Sagas such as the Cattle Raid of Cooley or hagiographical writings such as the legends of St. Patrick were considered as much a part of the historical canon as versified genealogies, lists of kings and historical narratives. A ninth century description of an ale-feast at an Irish court notes that the assembled company was entertained by a chanted recitation of genealogies.[5] Ale had a particular importance for the Gaels as the drinking of ceremonial ales was a mark of sovereignty. They played an important rôle at courts in what would become Scotland. An eighth century list of royal ales included the ales of Dál Riata, the ancestral home of the Scottish kings, and Angus, an important Pictish province. For Dál Riata it is noted that 'warriors performed great feats for the sake of the drinking,' while the Picts had 'ales red like wine.'[6] After the merger of the Picts and Scots in the ninth century the Scottish kings took an interest in the history of the Picts and it has been suggested that the poem 'Why came the Picts to Britain' was commissioned by the eleventh-century monarch Macbeth.[7]

By the late eleventh century there was a general increase in literary production, in which royal courts were active, found throughout Europe. The German historian Adam of Bremen notes that much of the Scandinavian material in his *History of the Archbishops of Hamburg-Bremen* was given to him by the Danish king Sveinn Estriðsson; the contemporary English king, William of Normandy, was patronising historians, albeit for his own political purposes. For Máel Colum, there are three extant pieces that appear to have been composed during his reign and probably intended for an initial performance at his court. The first is a king list designated B, which lists the kings of the Picts and then the Scottish rulers from Cináed mac Alpin.[8] The second piece, a verse history of Máel Coluim's pre-

---

5 The entire poem concerning an evening's entertainment at an Irish court is printed and translated in W. Stokes and J. Strachan, *Thesaurus Paleohibernicus*, 2 volumes (Dublin, reprint 1975), ii, 295.
6 *Scéla Cano meic Gartnáin*, edited by D.A. Binchy, Mediaeval and Modern Irish Series no. xviii (Dublin, 1975), p. 18; Dál Riata at lines 478–9 and Gerginn (i.e. Angus) at lines 484–5.
7 B.T. Hudson, 'Historical Literature of Early Scotland,' *Studies in Scottish Literature* xxvi (1991), 141–55 (at p. 149).
8 *Ibid.*, pp. 148 and 151 discusses the relevant texts.

decessors first in Dál Riata and then in the united kingdom of the Picts and Scots, is called 'The Scottish Poem' or *Duan Albanach*. The final text is the historical poem 'Prophecy of Berchán,' which included Irish as well as Scottish kings in a 'pan-Gaelic' survey. These tracts are part of the usual Celtic courtly literary tradition that delighted in lists of kings, royal genealogies and historical poems.

There was, however, a second aspect to the literary culture at the court of Máel Coluim and that was provided by his wife, the Anglo-Hungarian St. Margaret, the earliest queen in Britain for whom there is any indication of her literary interests. What we know of her is largely from her biography, or more appropriately hagiography, that seems to have been written by her confessor, and later bishop of St. Andrews (1109–15), named Turgot.[9] This tract was not written for a disinterested audience and the preface states that it was commissioned by Margaret's daughter, and Queen of the English, Matilda. According to that narrative, King Máel Coluim was illiterate, but Margaret was literate and after reading sacred texts, would discuss them with learned men (chapter 8). The queen was also an avid collector of manuscripts and the author of her biography writes from first-hand experience since she often employed him as her agent in procuring volumes and building up a royal library (chapter 6). Among the many signs of her sanctity, there is one miracle that involved a book from her personal collection. Margaret would take books with her, during her travels throughout the kingdom, and they were wrapped in leather coverings. Once, while crossing a river, the queen lost her gospel-book, which fell into the water. Upon reaching the opposite shore, the volume was found unharmed, with no trace of damage from the water (chapter 11). This is a rather typical miracle, found often in hagiography; while the book's safety was attributed to the queen's sanctity, one could reasonably suggest that the leather wrapping which covered the volume was waterproof.

Clearly the multi-lingual king and queen of the Scots allowed their court to be a meeting-ground for diverse literary traditions. Margaret spoke English, read Latin, and possibly spoke a continental language from her years in exile. Máel Coluim was a native Gaelic speaker who also spoke English, learned during his exile in England as a youth, and on occasion he would translate for his wife's English-speaking visitors. Gaelic historical verse and Old English liturgical texts were both welcomed, as were the enthusiasts of the Norman culture to the south, such as Turgot.

II. Royal patronage

The literary interests of Margaret and Máel Coluim were passed on to their children. For three of them – their elder daughter Matilda, and younger sons Alexander and David – those interests can be addressed directly. Two of the three, Matilda and David, lived for long periods away from Scotland. At the age of about

---

9 This follows the translation in A.O. Anderson's *Early Sources of Scottish History*, 2 volumes (Edinburgh, 1922), ii, 59–88; references to the narrative will be by chapter.

8 Matilda, with her sister Mary, was sent south to be educated at the convents at Wilton and at Romsey, under the supervision of their aunt Christine. Little is known of Alexander's early years; apparently he usually remained in Scotland, but much of David's youth was spent in the care of his older sister Matilda after her marriage to the English king Henry I. David lived at court among the other noble youths, where his enthusiasm for things French could be cultivated.

It may seem odd to begin with Matilda, who from childhood lived her life in England. Yet she was keenly interested in the literature and history of her native land, which had the additional attraction of being, in large measure, her family history. As noted above, Turgot's biography of St. Margaret was written at her express command and it is sad to learn that the reason for the commission was because she remembered so little of her mother. Yet, Matilda may have remembered something of the literature circulating round her parent's court, such as the marvelous adventures of the saints. The argument has been made that she commissioned the *Voyage of St. Brendan* to be translated into Anglo-Norman, and at least one dedication of it to her survives.[10] Her great passion was, however, music and an international group of poets and composers sought her patronage at her court at Westminster. Not all approved of these gatherings and her contemporary William of Malmesbury disapproved of the rabble of foreigners at Matilda's court, noting sourly that anyone with a novel song could find a patroness in her.[11] For the queen, these may have revived dim memories of listening to the chanting of tales at court. The Scots were famed for their musical prowess and even the acid-tongued Gerald of Wales, in one of the few kind words he had for anyone other than himself, considered Scottish music superior to either the Welsh or Irish.[12] Matilda's younger contemporary, Ailred of Rievaulx would note that as a youth he had shed tears while listening to these heroic ballads.[13]

While Matilda may have been bringing bits of Scottish and Gaelic literary culture to the English court, her brother Alexander exhibited a similarly cosmopolitan attitude at his court. He was literate and seems to have encouraged book production in Scotland.[14] Alexander shared his sister's interest in hagiography, especially in the lives of the Gaelic saints. He and his queen Sibylla commissioned some verses on the great saint of Scotland, Columba. Twenty-five lines of verse can be reconstructed and they are appended to a life of St. Columba, which was damaged in the fire at the Cotton library.[15] An interesting feature is

---

10 See R.L.G. Ritchie, 'Date of the Voyage of St. Brendan,' *Medium Aevum* xix (1950), 64–6.
11 *Willelmi Malmesbiriensis monachi De Gestis Regum Anglorum . . .*, edited by William Stubbs, 2 volumes (London, 1887–89), ii, 493–5.
12 Gerald of Wales, *History and Topography of Ireland*, ed. & trans. John O'Meara (London, rep. 1985), p. 104.
13 R.L. Graeme Ritchie, *Chrétien de Troyes and Scotland* (Oxford, 1952), p. 16.
14 Ailred of Rievaulx, *Genealogia regum Anglorum* in J.P. Migne, *Patrologiae cursus completus. Patres . . . ecclesiae latinae*, 217 vols (Paris, 1844–55), cxcv, columns 711–38 (col. 736).
15 The manuscript is now British Library MS. Cotton Tiberius D. III; the verses are at folio 217aa. The damaged lines can be partially restored from a transcript of the first five and final six lines made by Bishop Ussher, who saw the manuscript before it was damaged, which are printed in *Britannicarum Ecclesiarum Antiquitates*, chapter xv, in *The Whole Works of the Most Rev. James Ussher, D.D.*, ed. C.R. Elrington and J.H. Todd, 17 vols. (Dublin, 1847–64), vi, 230 & 239.

that their author was a monk named Simeon from Iona. He worked under the direction of a William, who could have been an early bishop of the Isle of Man or his contemporary, Bishop William the Old of the Orkneys. So the poem is truly cosmopolitan as the commemoration of an Irish saint was written for a Scottish king by a monk with an English name under the direction of a Manx or Orkney bishop. The goodwill of a member of Iona towards Alexander is less surprising in light of the patronage extended to the monastery by his parents, when they gave revenues for rebuilding and for the maintenance of the community.[16]

When we turn to the youngest of Máel Coluim and Margaret's children, David, there is much more to be learned. Most histories of medieval Scotland begin in earnest with his reign. King David is the first for whom we begin to get comparatively full and accurate accounts of his career and his court. His personal interests ran to the law, fostered while he resided at the court of his brother-in-law Henry I of England. This manifested itself when he became king and, compared to his predecessors, David's reign saw a comparative flood of administrative materials. He also shared his family's devotion to the Church and, like his brother Alexander, patronised the reformed continental monastic orders. Those interests, together with the nationality of some of his circle of intimates, has led to the stereotyping of David as a mere 'Francophile'. Certainly there is some truth to this, but, as a survey of the literary interests at his court suggests, David's interests were broader than that.

One writer who gives some idea of the literature at the royal court is Ailred of Rievaulx, King David's steward, who abandoned the life of the king's court for the cloister. With Ailred one can glimpse, almost for the last time, the Old English literary and intellectual culture of Northumbria. For almost a century it had found shelter with the Scottish kings. Ailred was born about the year 1111 and came from a literary family. His father, Eilaf, was the hereditary priest of Hexham who died in religious retirement at Durham. One of the books owned by Eilaf was a life of St. Brigit, the famous Irish saint of Kildare, and it was given to Laurence of Durham. Laurence wrote a letter to Ailred, mentioning his father's gift in terms that suggest he (Laurence) had been Ailred's tutor.[17] At the time of this letter, Ailred was still the steward at David's court, so it must be dated prior to 1134, when Ailred left. One of the books that Laurence's letter implies they both knew was Cicero's *On Friendship*. Not all his interests were classical and Ailred confessed that in his youth he neglected his chores in order to listen to the tales of Arthur.[18]

Ailred was not the only person interested in vernacular literature at the Scottish court, for another was King David himself. His court became a meet-

---

16 Orderic Vitalis, *Historia Ecclesiastica*, book 8, chapter 20 in J.P. Migne, *Patrologia*, vol. 188, columns 620–1.
17 The book is mentioned in a letter from Laurence to Ailred, edited by A. Hoste, 'A Survey of the Unedited Works of Laurence of Durham with an Edition of His Letter to Aelred of Rievaulx,' *Sacris Erudiri* vii (1960), 249–65 (at page 263).
18 After D.L.T.Bethell, 'English Monks and Irish Reform in the Eleventh and Twelfth Centuries,' *Historical Studies* viii (1971), 111–35 (at page 123).

ing-ground for Gaelic, Old English and French literary interests. A famous visitor to the court was St. Malachy, the sometimes archbishop of Armagh and confidant of St. Bernard of Clairvaux. He was one of the individuals by whom the Scottish court was connected with continental intellectual centres. One of the visits recorded in the *vita* of the saint, written at Clairvaux sometime within four years of his death in 1148, found the saint visiting David at a castle that is generally assumed to be Carlisle in the autumn of 1140, when Malachy ministered to David's ill son, Henry of Huntingdon.[19] Malachy may have brought more than just comforting words for an invalid. Laurence of Durham claimed,

> We have heard some of the greatest men, and not a few Irish bishops, tell about the [Irish] birth of St. Cuthbert . . . St. Malachy told King David of Scotland many things on this matter, and Maurilius his successor afterwards asserted confidently and Bishop Eugenius of Ardmore discussed it more exactly, and so did two other bishops whose names have been forgotten and so did their companions, priests and clerks at different times.

What this little passage tells us plainly is what one would be tempted to infer from the writings of Ailred of Rievaulx, that the Scottish king was not merely supporting literature for his own amusement and edification, but, also, that his court was acting as a literary meeting ground. How did a monk of Durham learn of a conversation between an Irish bishop and a Scottish king? Possibly from the king himself, for David was a guest of the monks of Durham at the end of September in the year 1141 and may have 'sang for his supper' by telling his hosts the information he had received about their founder.[20]

Malachy also travelled with books that had been given him during his stay on the continent, among which was a copy of the famous constitutions of Arrouaise. The foundation of an Arroasian house at Carlisle shortly after Malachy's departure has been attributed to that visit, and it has been suggested that he left a copy of the constitutions there.[21] Contacts ran both ways and Malachy's entourage brought news of his Scottish visit to Clairvaux, where the occasion was remembered in his biography. David's support of the reformed monastic orders may have been a contributing factor in the distribution of current continental theological writings among the supposedly conservative Celtic religious houses. When the community of *Celi Dé* at Loch Leven was suppressed *circa* 1152, an inventory was made of the library and among the expected

---

19 Bernard of Clairvaux, *Liber de Vita et rebus gestis S. Malachie* in Migne, *Patrologia* volume clxxxii, columns 1095–1096. For a discussion of this visit see B.T. Hudson, 'Gaelic Princes and Gregorian Reform,' in *Crossed Paths*, ed. B. Hudson and V. Ziegler (Lanham, 1991), 61–82 (at pages 62 and 63).
20 *Historia Dunelmensis Ecclesiae, Continuatio Prima*, in *Symeonis Monachi Opera Omnia*, ed. Thomas Arnold, 2 vols. (London, 1882–5), i, 145–146.
21 G.W.S.Barrow, 'Scottish Rulers and the Religious Orders 1070–1153,' *Transactions of the Royal Historical Society*, fifth series, vol. 3 (1953), 77–100 (p. 94).

liturgical texts is unexpectedly found a copy of the *Sentences* of St. Bernard of Clairvaux.[22]

III. Literary influence of the Scottish court

The stray bits of information about the literary currents at the Scottish court lead one to ask the question, what influence did it have? The question of influence is a difficult one to answer even in later and better documented times. Yet, some speculation might indicate those avenues for enquiry that could prove fruitful. One such influence seems to have been a revived interested in the history of Northern Britain in earlier times. The interests in saints' lives by kings Alexander and David, seen in the poem on St. Columba directed towards Alexander, and in the enquiry on the birth of St. Cuthbert, may have contributed to the interest in the early Church. The literary interests at the royal court also could have contributed to a general improvement in writing. Beginning at least by the reign of David, there was in Scotland a deliberate re-working of materials on the lives of saints. This led to the seeking of older volumes and their reworking; literary preservation and improvement were not only common throughout Britain and Ireland during this century, but throughout Europe. Laurence of Durham claims that he was given the *Life* of St. Brigit by Ailred of Rievaulx's father Eilaf so that he would rewrite it in a more elegant style. One should remember that Laurence wrote to Ailred to tell him of this at a time when Ailred was still attached to the Scottish court; did Laurence know of King David's interest in hagiography and hope to gain a royal patron? Laurence's commission to improve his exemplar is mentioned repeatedly in prefaces to revisions of older materials. The anonymous author of the earliest life of St. Kentigern, whose praise of Scotland was noted at the beginning of this essay, states that he assembled his book from 'a little book of his virtues and from the oral testimony of the faithful'.[23] That little volume might or might not be the narrative in the Scotic style that later would so horrify Jocelin of Furness when he wrote his longer version of St. Kentigern, 'seasoning the barbarous language with Roman salt'.[24]

Literary influence occasionally may have followed politics. Prior to his ascension, David ruled the old British kingdom of Strathclyde as the lieutenant of his brother King Alexander. In 1124 David held an inquisition on the problem of the extent of the lands anciently belonging to the St. Kentigern's cathedral, at Glasgow.[25] Testimony came from the older and wiser men of the whole region, who gave the names of the churches belonging to the See. Ritchie made the suggestion that David's Norman friends, who witnessed the report of the

---

22 Sir Archibald Lawrie, *Early Scottish Charters* (Glasgow 1905): the inventory of the library is given in a grant made by Bishop Robert of St. Andrews to the priory printed at pp. 210–1, and a discussion of the list is given at pp. 445–6.
23 *Lives of S. Ninian and S. Kentigern*, p. 243.
24 *Lives of S. Ninian and S. Kentigern*, p. 160.
25 The result of the investigation was entered in the *Registrum Vetus* of the Bishopric of Glasgow; it is printed in Lawrie, *Early Scottish Charters*, pp. 44–7 (with notes at pages 299–305).

proceedings, may have collected some of the materials from southern Scotland that eventually found their way into Geoffrey of Monmouth's *History of the Kings of Britain*.[26] Was it there that information about another saint, Ninian, came before the king and circulated around the court, 'in a barbarous language that obscured the life of the most holy Ninian';[27] leading King David's former steward, some years later, to write a biography of Ninian? Unlike those who would write a biography of Kentigern, Ailred had a good historical framework for his additional materials from two eighth-century historical records: the *Ecclesiastical History* of Bede and the versified 'life' of Ninian written in the eighth century. The suggestion has been made that the Scottish historical materials found in the so-called Chronicle of the Canons of St. Mary's, Huntingdon, now extant only in a transcript made on the orders of the English king Edward I, came into the possession of the Augustinian community through the royal Scottish connections with the Honour of Huntingdon.[28] The story of the destruction of the Pictish nobles at Scone, found in a list of important Irish tales in the Book of Leinster, went into Ireland in the late eleventh or early twelfth century.[29] Was it transmitted during the making of an alliance between Edgar, the elder brother of Alexander and David, and the Irish king Muirchertach Ua Briain when in 1105 Edgar sent the gift of an elephant into Ireland?[30]

When one turns to popular literature and folklore, the contacts are less easy to see and the ideas usually had an international circulation. In at least one instance, however, the origin of a particular tale can be suggested. In his *History of the English Kings*, William of Malmesbury relates a tale about two tenth-century kings: Edgar of the English and Cináed II mac Máel Choluim of the Scots.[31] This story begins with a banquet given by Edgar at which Cináed was a guest. Cináed, having taken more drink than was good for him, made a joke about Edgar's short stature and said it was odd that so many princes were subject to a midget. This was told to Edgar and the next day he took his rival on a walk. When the two kings were alone, Edgar produced two swords and offered Cináed a duel with the chance to prove whether or not a midget could fight like a man. At this Cináed apologised for his remark. A similar story is told by Ailred of Rievaulx in his *Letter on the Genealogy of the English Kings* about the Scots king Máel Coluim Canmore.[32] In that story, Máel Coluim is at a banquet when he learns of an assassination plot by one of his nobles. The king takes his would-be assailant hunting and when the two men are alone, Máel Coluim produces two swords and challenges the noble to a duel. The noble repents of his evil intent and throws himself at the mercy of the king.

---

26 Ritchie, *Chrétien de Troyes and Scotland*, p. 8.
27 *Lives of S. Ninian and S. Kentigern*, p. 137. Skene suggests that the rubric in one manuscript claiming the work to a translation from English into Latin was merely an effort to preserve the fiction of the antiquity of the volume, pp. 255–6.
28 E. Cowan, 'The Scottish Chronicle in the Poppleton Manuscript,' *Innes Review* xxxii (1981), 3–21 (at p. 18).
29 P. MacCana, *The Learned Tales of Medieval Ireland* (Dublin, 1980), pp. 145.
30 *Annals of Inisfallen*, ed. Sean Mac Airt (Dublin, 1951).
31 *Gesta Regum*, i, 177–178.
32 Aelred of Rievaulx, *Genealogia Regum Anglorum*, in Migne, *Patrologia*, vol. cxcv, col. 735.

Little attention has been given either story, but William's story has been considered as part of the folklore of the tenth century. One would expect, then, that Ailred's story is a borrowing from this earlier authority, reworked with a Scottish setting. In this instance, however, we know that this is definitely not the case. Ailred tells us that he was told the story by King David, who seems to have been told the story as a very young boy by his father, Máel Coluim. It does not stretch the imagination to suggest that this story was circulating round the English court in the first two decades of the twelfth century, possibly when David lived at the English court and slept among the other noble youths. From there it could have come to the attention of William of Malmesbury who either changed the characters, or heard the story in its changed form. Far from being a relic of tenth-century folklore, William's story might be an example of twelfth-century literary borrowing from the Scottish royal family.

IV. Continuity and culture

By the end of the reign of David I, the Scottish court had many of the attributes that made it similar to the English and continental courts. Yet, the meeting-ground provided by David would continue and the older, Gaelic, element would not quickly disappear as traces would remain until the late middle ages. For example, the highest grade of poet among Gaelic society was the *ollamh* and he is found on a seal of Alexander III, together with his harpist or *clársach*.[33] John of Fordun records that at the coronation of King Alexander III at Scone in 1249, at the end of the ceremony a Highlander, clearly a *senachaid*, stepped forth from the crowd and began the recitation of the king's genealogy.[34] Although this material was presented orally, it was preserved in writing and Fordun notes that he himself had read the genealogy in Gaelic.

This brief survey of the literary culture at the Scottish court and in Scotland itself during the late eleventh and early twelfth centuries leaves more questions than answers. What other literary counsels did St. Malachy and King David have? Were there verses on other saints commissioned by King Alexander and Queen Sibylla? How many of the foreigners crowding the court of Matilda were Scots hoping to receive a welcome for songs that might contain a childhood memory for her? One would like to know where in Scotland the Welsh scholar Sulien studied, or what else was in the volume written in the Scotic dialect used by the anonymous author of the life of St. Kentigern. Enough survives to suggest that the early Scottish court had an importance in literary preservation and transmission that would bear further study. The surviving remains of the literary culture at, and in contact with, the Scottish court suggest a sophisticated and cosmopolitan court led by literate and humane monarchs with genuine interests both in current literature as well as the productions of an earlier period. The

---

33 John Bannerman, 'The King's Poet and the Inauguration of Alexander III,' *Scottish Historical Review* lxviii (1989), 134.
34 *Johannis de Fordun Chronica Gentis Scotorum*, edited by W.F. Skene, Historians of Scotland volume i (Edinburgh, 1871), p. 294–5 (*Gesta Annalia*, xlviii).

charge that the children of Máel Coluim and Margaret were just 'Francophiles' or 'Anglophiles' is unfounded. There is no denial of their admiration for the culture and accomplishments of their neighbours. One should remember, however, that it was David who queried an Irish bishop on the origins of an Old English saint. Alexander and his Norman queen Sibylla commissioned the verses on the Irish saint who laboured among the Picts. Perhaps a fit coda for this survey comes from Matilda who, as a queen living most of her life in England, would yearn for the stories and music of her homeland.

R. L. KINDRICK

15. *Turning Law into Literature: The Influence of the* Ars Notaria *on Fifteenth-Century Scottish Literature*

The medieval arts of rhetoric exerted a profound influence on both the day-to-day discourse and the poetry of the period. Medieval rhetoric largely has its basis in the work of Cicero and built selectively on the classical tradition. *De inventione*, a youthful work which does not reflect the wisdom of his later writings, was a basic source as medieval rhetoric developed its own three approaches. Even, however, with Ciceronian dominance, other influences are clearly evident. From the schoolroom tradition, Donatus' *ars grammaticus* and Priscian's *Institutio grammatica* both had an influence on the later development of the arts of poetry. Even though Aristotelian influence was uneven, Aristotle had an impact, especially in the 12th–15th centuries.[1]

Yet medieval rhetoric was not slavish in its imitation of classical models. In point of fact, three major distinguishable traditions existed, each with its own advocates and major texts. The first of these traditions was the *ars praedicandi*. The art of preaching developed its own goals and rhetorical techniques, first pragmatically through the works of Christian preachers attempting to save souls and later, more theoretically, in the monasteries and universities of Europe. Because this school of rhetoric attempted to reach a diverse audience, its techniques involved the reinforcement of multiple levels of meaning to enhance widespread understanding of doctrine.[2] The *ars poetriae* was devoted in greater part to aesthetics than to the widespread audience appeal of the *ars praedicandi*. Based in large measure on the *ars grammatica*, it had its origins in the schoolroom and focused on prosody, invention, and organisation.[3] Finally, the third major area of medieval rhetoric was the *ars dictaminis*, which probably reveals more closely than the other two its Ciceronian roots. The *ars dictaminis* is sometimes misleadingly translated as 'the art of letter writing'. In point of fact, while letters were a substantial portion of its focus, the art itself extended much further, and ultimately spawned the *ars notaria*.[4]

---

1 For an overview of classical influences on medieval rhetoric, see James J. Murphy, *Rhetoric in the Middle Ages* (Berkeley, 1974), pp. 3–42; Harry Caplan, 'Classical Rhetoric and the Medieval Theory of Preaching,' *Classical Philology*, 28 (1933), 73–96; and John O. Ward, 'From Antiquity to the Renaissance: Glosses and Commentaries on Cicero's *Rheotorica*,' in *Medieval Eloquence*, ed. James J. Murphy (Berkeley, 1978), pp. 25–67.
2 A good summary of rhetorical techniques is provided by Caplan, 'The Four Senses of Scriptural Interpretation and the Medieval Theory of Preaching,' *Speculum*, 4 (1929), 282–90, and Murphy, pp. 269–355.
3 See Douglas Kelly, *The Arts of Poetry and Prose* (Turnhout, 1991), *passim*.
4 On the *ars dictaminis*, see Martin Camargo, *Ars Dictaminis, Ars Dictandi* (Turnhout, 1991), *passim*. The *ars notaria* is also completely explored in Murphy, pp. 263–6.

The political dimensions of the *ars dictaminis* are evidenced by its courtly lineage. One of the earliest students of this school of rhetoric is Cassiodorus Senator, who discusses the plight of the *quaestor*.[5] The *quaestor* was a literate minister of the king who had responsibility for transmitting the monarch's thoughts, sometimes in public audiences but more often through written communications when the king himself could not be present. As the main communication channel for the monarchy, the *quaestor* developed increasing authority as the *ars dictaminis* grew in influence. Its goals were largely political, but they also reflected a significant interest in audience psychology, organisation, delivery, and literary realism, all effective elements in transmitting political messages.[6] The courtly origin of the *ars dictaminis* made it the perfect medium for royal decrees and laws. In small cohesive social groups, where most matters might reach the royal court for a decision, the *ars dictaminis* was effectively the rhetorical tool for law and legal judgements. However, with the development of the nation-state and diffuse legal centers in consistory and ecclesiastical courts, the *ars dictaminis* had to be sharpened and refined in an effort to insure equal justice when hearings might be held on similar cases in diverse locations by a multiplicity of judges. It is this pressing political development, rather than any innate failing of the *ars dictaminis* (as Murphy suggests[7]), which ultimately led to the development of the *ars notaria*.

The *ars notaria* appears to have originated in Italy, either Pavia or Bologna, depending upon which theory one believes. There is no doubt that this school of rhetoric 'concerned itself with the physical forms of documents',[8] but it also involved itself with a great deal more. There was a special emphasis on fixed diction and sentence structure in an effort to establish accuracy and ensure repeatability of judicial procedures. As a result, the language of the *ars notaria* became quite static. Indeed, parts of it appear in legal rhetoric to this day. In addition to its use of static diction and figures developed from Latin and sometimes French, *ars notaria* developed structural formulae for a wide variety of common court documents, including the petition (which appears in numerous forms in fifteenth-century poems). Careful attention is also provided to other aspects of organisation, precise realism in legal description, and procedural regularity. In all of these senses, it is perhaps best understood as an extension of the *ars dictaminis*, and it also gives considerable attention to both audience and setting, natural factors in courtroom situations.[9] The critical nature of this rhetoric in Scotland is perhaps best illustrated by the fact that two of the Makars – Henryson and Dunbar – likely had legal training of some type. In addition, Scottish legal historians point very clearly to the 'developing' nature of the system

---

5 See Cassiodorus, Senator, *Variae*, ed. T. Mommsan, *Monumenta Germaniae Historica, Auctorum Antiquissimorum*, XII (Berlin, 1894), pp. 178–9.
6 In addition to Camargo, see Giles Constable, *Letters and Letter-Collections* (Louvain, 1976), *passim*.
7 Murphy p. 265.
8 *Ibid.*, p. 264
9 See, for instance, Aegidius Fuscarariis, *Der Ordo Iudicarius des Aegidius de Fuscarariis*, ed. Ludwig Wahrmund (Innsbruck, 1916), p. 5.

of law in the country during the fifteenth century.[10] The Scottish Education Act of 1496 indicates that legal education is a priority:

> It is a statute and ordanit throw all the realme that all barronis and frehaldaris that are of substance put thair eldest sonnis and airis to the sculis fra thai be aucht or nyne yeiris of age and till remane at the grammer sculis quhill that be competentlie foundit and have perfite latyne and thereftir to remane thre yeris at the sculis of art and jure sua that thai may have knawlege and understanding of the lawis. Throw the quhilkis justice may reigne universalie throw all the realme sua that thai that ar schireffis or jegeis ordinaris under the kingis hienes may have knawlege to do justice that the pure pepill sulde have na neid to seik our soverane lordis principale auditouris for ilk small injure.[11]

Scotland imported part of its legal expertise from Italy, where studies in the *ars notaria* had developed as early as the 14th century. R. D. S. Jack and John McQueen have already explored many of the literary and intellectual relationships between Scotland and Italy.[12] Clearly the importation of the *ars notaria* should be numbered among those relationships.

In fifteenth-century Scotland, then, there was an increasingly decentralised legal system which extended 'the King's justice' to remote areas, based in part on efforts of the early Stewarts to expand the scope of royal power at the expense of baronial power. Uniform laws and courts were critical, yet Scottish courts were notoriously corrupt.[13] Given the fact that two of the Makars likely had legal roles, how did this emphasis on the legal habit of mind and legal procedures influence the poetry of the late Middle Ages and early Renaissance? A few examples illustrate how the *ars notaria* had a significant impact on major and minor poets of the fifteenth century.

The Kingis Quair reflects the development of the *ars dictaminis* into the *ars notaria*, at least in its early stages. The poem is pervaded with references to law and government (see, for instance, stanzas 82, 105, 107, 115, 123), as might be expected from an author familiar at first hand with the administration of justice. In addition, the Boethian prologue and conclusion extend the meaning of the poem beyond a treatise on love.[14]

Fixed phrases from the courts reflecting the set language of the *ars notaria* are also to be found in the poem. The lover's oath of fealty to Venus is in language much in keeping with standard legal forms:

---

10 On the history of this development in Scotland, see David M. Walker, *A Legal History of Scotland* (Edinburgh, 1988), I, pp. 212–45 and James J. Robertson, 'The Development of the Law,' in *Scottish Society in the Fifteenth Century*, ed. J. M. Brown (1977), p. 139.
11 Gordon Donaldson, ed., *Scottish Historical Documents* (New York, 1970), pp. 92–3.
12 R. D. S. Jack, *The Italian Influence on Scottish Literature* (Edinburgh, 1972) p. 1–28; John MacQueen, 'Neoplatonism and Orphism in Fifteenth-Century Scotland,' *Scottish Studies*, 20 (1976), 69–89.
13 Campbell H. Paton, *An Introduction to Scottish Legal History* (Edinburgh, 1958), pp. 18–24.
14 For an overview, see Matthew P. McDiarmid, ed., *The Kingis Quair of James Stewart* (Totowa, NJ, 1973), pp. 36–8.

> 'O Venus clere, of goddis stellifyit,
> To quhom I ȝelde homage and sacrifise,
> Fro this day forth ȝour grace be magnifyit,
> That me ressauit haue in suich a wise,
> To lyve vnder ȝour law, and do seruise.
> Now help me furth, and for ȝour merci lede
> My hert to rest, that deis nere for drede.'[15]

This passage compares well with real oaths of homage from a formulary from Tours.[16] Such formularies were designed as books of models to prepare notaries in the use of proper and legally-binding language. There are parallels between the oath of *The Kingis Quair* and legal oaths which indicate the heritage of such oaths in the love literature of the fifteenth century.

The crowd thronging the court of the gods seeks justice just like any less supernatural group of petitioners, and their conduct is described in legal terms:

> A warld of folk, and by thaire contenance
> Thaire hertis semyt full of displesance,
> With billis in thaire handis, of one assent
> Vnto the juge thaire playntis to present. (ll. 571–4)

An unhappy throng grasping 'billis' or legal petitions was surely common in Scottish consistory courts. It is, however, in the lover's meeting with Venus that the full impact of dictaminal-notarial rhetoric comes to the fore. Having been transported through the crowds that besiege the court of the gods, he finally approaches Venus with his appeal. The organisation of his presentation reflects perfectly the pattern of organisation developed in the *ars dictaminis* and encompassed by the *ars notaria* as a basis for legal petitions. By the early fifteenth century, standard organisational formats had developed for a variety of legal documents. Among them was the petition, originally an appeal to a monarch or lord but later a standard form in the decentralised system of justice. The formula for the petition consisted of five parts: the salutation with a *captatio benevolentiae* (the greeting, showing proper deference to the person addressed), *exordium, narratio, petitio*, and *conclusio*. The *exordium* was the introduction proper, setting forth the nature of the case in general terms. In the *narratio*, the petitioner related as many of the facts of the case that would reinforce the *petitio*, the actual appeal for redress. Finally, the *conclusio* made use of a variety of appeals to reinforce the plight of the petitioner in the judge's mind. Each part had its own highly structured variations that were illustrated in detail in the formularies of the day.[17]

---

15 McDiarmid edition, p. 88, ll. 358–64. This edition will be used throughout; hereafter line numbers only will be provided.
16 Karl Zeumer, *Formulae merowingici et Karolini aevi, Monumenta Germaniae Historica, Legum V* (Hanover, 1886), see especially pp. 157–9.
17 See 'The Art of Letter Writing' (*Rationes dictandi*), trans. James J. Murphy in *Three Medieval Rhetorical Arts*, ed. Murphy (Berkeley, 1971), pp. 6–19.

170   *The European Sun*

The lover's petition for relief to Venus follows perfectly this organisational scheme. He begins with a duly differential salutation and a humble *captatio benevolentiae*, noting appropriately both her high rank and virtues.

> Hye quene of lufe, sterre of beneuolence,
> Pituouse princes and planet merciable,
> Appesare of malice and violence
> By vertew sure of 3our aspectis hable,
> Vnto 3our grace lat now bene acceptable
> My pure request, that can no forthir gone
> To seken help bot vnto 3ow allone. (11. 687–93)

His ending, asking her to consider his 'pure request,' then leads into an *exordium* which states his needs and explains her power to deal with his case:

> As 3e that bene the socoure and suete well
> Off remedye, of carefull hertes cure,
> And in the hugë weltering wawis fell
> Of lufis rage blisfull havin and sure,
> O anker and keye of oure gude auenture
> 3e haue 3our man with his gude will conquest.
> Merci therefore and bring his hert to rest! (11. 694–70)

This *exordium* also contains elements of the *narratio* or statement of fact. However, the lover formally treats the *narratio* in the next stanza:

> 3e knaw the cause of all my peynes smert
> Bet than my self, and all myn auenture.
> 3e may conuoye and as 3ow list conuert
> The hardest hert that formyt hath nature. (11. 701–4)

His statement of fact is brief for practical reasons. First, he assumes Venus is omnipotent in matters of love and that it would be presumptuous and time-consuming for him to repeat what she already knows. His literary audience, of course, has previously been acquainted with the nature of his plight, which does not once again require rehearsal.

The lover then proceeds to the *petitio*, the formal statement of what he desires:

> Sen in 3our handis all halë lyith my cure,
> Haue pitee now, O bryght blissfull goddesse,
> Off 3our pure man, and rew on his distresse.
> And sen I was vnto 3our lawis strange
> By ignorance and nought by felonye,
> And that 3our grace now likit hath to change
> My hert to seruen 3ow perpetualye,

> Forgeue all this, and schapith remedye
> To sauen me, of ȝour benignë grace,
> Or do me steruen furthwith in this place. (11. 705–13)

The petition itself is also properly humble, even confessing the lover's fault in having been 'vnto ȝour lawis strange'. In exchange for the boon sought in this petition, the lover pledges 'to seruen ȝow perpetualye'. Such 'barter' was commonplace in courts of law where petitioners often found that judgements were more often favourable when compromise or reciprocity prevailed. In the *conclusio*, the lover restates his request to reinforce it in Venus' mind:

> And with the stremes of ȝour percyng lyght
> Conuoy my hert, that is so wo begone,
> Ageyne vnto that suetë hevinly sight,
> That I, within the wallis cald as stone,
> So suetly saw on morow walk and gone,
> Law in the gardyn, ryght tofore myn eye.
> Now, merci, quene, and do me nought to deye! (11. 715–21)

He adds emotional appeal (a common technique for the *conclusio* in Ciceronian rhetoric) with a pitiful description of his condition and the exclamation that his anguish is killing him. None of the other petitions, to Minerva or Fortune, in the poem contains all five parts of the notarial pattern. The petition to Minerva contains basically an *exordium*, *narratio*, and *petitio*. The appeal to Fortune is basically *petitio*, pure and simple. Yet both refer back to the more complete statement of the argument through the five-part formula.

Even Venus' judgement is couched in the language of the law. Her response to the lover opens with a statement that she has inspired him to 'knawe my lawe' (1. 105). She then goes on to take account of accidents of both person and circumstance, an admonition in legal rhetoric extending back to Aristotle and Quintilian. She further goes on to inform him that while she can give him good will, the redress of his petition is not within the scope of her authority. Finally, she makes clear that his case has major social implications for the others who are 'negligent' about keeping her 'lawis':

> Quhen thou descendis doune to ground ageyne,
> Say to the men that there bene resident,
> How long think thay to stand in my disdeyne,
> That in my lawis bene so negligent
> From day to day, and list thame nought repent,
> Bot breken louse and walken at thaire large?
> Is nought left none that thereof gevis charge? (11. 799–805)

Her admonition to him to use his plight to help others avoid similar results is paralleled by comments in real judgements handed down in consistory courts, where judges were fully cognizant of the impact of their decisions in establishing 'examples'.[18] In sum, her response is judicial in tone and substance, reflecting the realities of legal procedure and the rhetoric of the *ars notaria*.

I have already addressed Henryson's use of the *ars notaria* elsewhere.[19] Surely, however, he must be mentioned as well in this overview. Henryson's use of the *ars notaria* is among the most pronounced of any poet in the century, with elements of the rhetoric appearing in a number of works, including *The Testament of Cresseid*. In fact, *The Morall Fabillis* illustrates better than any other work the evolution of the *ars dictaminis* into notarial rhetoric. A number of Henryson's fables, in part because of their political intent, include the full range of dictaminal techniques. Perhaps 'The Lion and the Mouse' is the outstanding example. The maister mouse's petition contains all five parts of the dictaminal and notarial formula for such documents and illustrates precise parallels with other historical petitions and dictaminal records. Even the lion's dialogue reflects the figures and tone of authentic court records. The diction of the poem is permeated with dictaminal language. In its remarkable parallels with authentic historical documents and its close attention to an almost textbook accommodation of dictaminal rhetorical form, 'The Lion and the Mouse' illustrates Henryson's ability to adapt a variety of rhetorics to his poetic purposes.

Yet other fables, such as 'The Trial of the Fox,' illustrate more transitional stages in which Henryson combines dictaminal rhetoric with a greater number of elements from the rhetoric of law. Perhaps, however, his outstanding example of notarial rhetoric is 'The Sheep and the Dog.' In the first stanza of the poem, Henryson establishes the court setting:

> Esope ane taill puttis in memorie
> How that ane doig, because that he wes pure,
> Callit ane scheip vnto the consistorie,
> Ane certane breid fra him for to recure.
> Ane fraudfull volff wes iuge that tyme and bure
> Authoritie and iurisdictioun,
> And on the scheip send furth ane strait summoun.[20]

The establishment of the consistory court as a setting, along with language such as 'authoritie' and 'iurisdictioun' and 'ane straite summoun,' provide the perfect milieu for further development of the notarial arts. In the succeeding stanza, Henryson goes on to provide detail on the summons itself, making use of common court rhetoric. His accuracy in the formulation of the summons and the procedures involved has been well attested. Henryson's animal court consists of all of the officers of a real Scottish consistory court:

---

18 See Norman Doe, *Fundamental Authority in Late Medieval English Law* (Cambridge, 1990), pp. 37–8.
19 *Henryson and the Medieval Arts of Rhetoric* (Garland, 1993), pp. 143–76.
20 Denton Fox, ed. *The Poems of Robert Henryson* (Oxford, 1981), p. 47, ll. 1146–52. This edition will be used for all citations; hereafter only line numbers will be provided.

> Schir Corbie Rauin wes maid apparitour,
> Quha pykit had full mony scheipis ee;
> The charge hes tane, and on the letteris bure;
> Summonit the scheip befoir the volff, that he
> 'Peremptourlie within the dayis thre,
> Compeir vnder the panis in this bill,
> To heir quhat Perrie Doig will say the till.'
>
> This summondis maid befoir witnes ancw,
> The rauin, as to his office weill effeird,
> Indorsat hes the write, and on he flew.
> The selie scheip durst lay na mouth on eird
> Till he befoir the awfull iuge appeird.
> The oure off cause quhilk that the iuge vsit than,
> Quhen Hesperus to schaw his face began.
>
> The foxe wes clerk and noter in the cause;
> The gled, the graip vp at the bar couth stand,
> As aduocatis expert in to the lawis,
> The doggis pley togidder tuke on hand,
> Quhilk wer confidderit straitlie in ane band
> Again the scheip to procure the sentence;
> Thocht it wes fals, thay had na conscience. (ll. 1160–80)

The depiction of these 'officers of the court' reinforces Henryson's vision of the difficulties of finding justice in a Scottish court.[21] All of the animals are predators or, worse yet, scavengers, and their presence bodes ill for the sheep. Once the sheep appears, the poem contains a formal charge and response. The sheep is called by the clerk of the court and the 'aduocatis' begin to 'propone' their arguments. The pleadings on both sides are pervaded by the language of law and give close attention to fine points of law. The sheep chooses the clever legal tactic of 'declining' the judge, the time, and the place. He goes on to indicate that the judge is a 'iuge suspect' because he has always been at enmity with the sheep's kin. He further notes that other members of the court have been 'ennemies mortall' to him and all his kinfolk. He then goes on to argue 'The place is fer, the tyme is feriate' (l. 1198). The sheep's plea that the court should not have jurisdiction reflects authentic Scottish legal history.[22] Defendants did indeed have the ability to request a change of venue or to question other court proceedings at the outset. Interestingly enough, the wolf takes the sheep's objection into consideration and initiates a legal search for a way to handle the matter. Henryson's legal search is as realistic as it possibly can be:

---

21 See Mary Rowlands, 'Robert Henryson and the Scottish Courts of Law,' *Aberdeen University Review*, 39 (1962), 219–26. For other details on the accuracy of Henryson's depiction of the court, see Fox, pp. 251–62.

22 See *The Rhetoric of Alcuin and Charlemagne*, ed. and tr. W. S. Howell (Princeton, 1941) p. 75 and W. C. Dickinson, ed. *Sheriff Court Book of Fife 1515–1522* (Edinburgh, 1928), pp. 315–16.

> The beir, the brok, the mater tuke on hand,
> For to discyde gif this exceptioun
> Wes off na strenth, or lauchfully mycht stand;
> And thairupon as iugis thay sat doun
> And held ane lang quhyle disputatioun,
> Seikand full money decretalis off the law,
> And glosis als, the veritie to knaw.
>
> Of ciuile money volum thay reuolue,
> The codies and digestis new and ald,
> *Contra et pro*, strait argumentis thay resolue,
> Sum a doctryne and sum a nothir hald;
> For prayer nor price, trow ʒe, thay wald fald,
> Bot held the glose and text of the decreis
> As trew iugis. I schrew thame ay that leis. (11. 1209-22)

The legal terms in this passage hardly need elaboration – suffice it to say that they are completely accurate insofar as our knowledge of fifteenth-century Scottish legal practice makes it possible for us to judge them. Even following such legal formalities, the conclusion seems foregone. Henryson's sheep is judged to be subject to the jurisdiction of the court. That final judgement is itself predicated on real legal judgements of the time:

> The scheip agane befoir the volff derenʒeit,
> But aduocate, abasitlie couth stand.
> Vp rais the doig, and on the scheip thus plenʒeit:
> 'Ane soume I payit haue befoir the hand
> For certane breid.' Thairto ane borrow he fand,
> That wrangouslie the scheip did hald the breid;
> Quhilk he denyit, and thair began the pleid.
>
> And quhen the scheip this stryif had contestait,
> The iustice in the cause furth can proceid.
> Lowrence the actis and the proces wrait,
> And thus the pley vnto the end thay speid.
> This cursit court, corruptit all for meid,
> Aganis gude faith, gude law, and conscience,
> For this fals doig pronuncit the sentence. (11. 1230-43)

The only term not commonly found in the language of consistory courts is 'derenʒeit,' which seems otherwise to be unattested.[23] Clearly, however, the term means 'arraigned'. Whether Henryson is using a new legal term or whether he is simply engaging in poetic wordcraft has not yet been determined with certainty.

---

23 See Fox, p. 259.

Nonetheless, throughout this poem his knowledge of law and ability to use the *ars notaria* for poetic purposes seems clear. That the *ars dictaminis* and the *ars notaria* play such an important role in *The Morall Fabillis* is an indication of Henryson's familiarity with the Scottish court system, whether or not he himself was a notary or practised law or not.

There is perhaps less attention to the *ars notaria* in the work of William Dunbar than might be expected, given his legal background. Nonetheless, Dunbar does make use of this rhetorical approach, particularly in matters of organisation, while simultaneously transmogrifying and remolding it in his verse. Unlike Henryson, Gavin Douglas, and the author of *The Kingis Quair*, Dunbar seems less influenced by the vocabulary of the *ars notaria*. Perhaps given his own creativity in diction and his dedication to shorter narratives, legal language simply did not suit his purposes. He occasionally touches on the language of law, but his use of such language is usually not technical. Legal terms are used in a general sense and are most often integrated into his general diction, as illustrated by this passage from 'The Thrissill and the Rois':

> Exerce justice with mercy and conscience,
> And lat no small beist suffir skaith na skornis
> Of greit beistis that bene of moir piscence;
> Do law elyk to aipis and unicornis,
> And lat no bowgle, with his busteous hornis,
> The meik pluch ox oppress, for all his pryd,
> Bot in the ʒok go peciable him besyd.[24]

His courtly *milieu* and audience demand that he employ the language and realistic description of the *ars dictaminis*, but there is little movement towards the more specific diction of the *ars notaria* in his verse.

His most pronounced use of the *ars notaria* is to be found in organisational formulae. Dunbar's 'petitions' all in one way or another make use of the five-part pattern of organisation for legal 'documents of this type'. Sometimes virtually the entire poem may be structured around the *petitio*, as is the case in 'Complane I wald . . .' In other instances, such as 'Of Discretioun in Taking,' the poem incorporates a prolonged *narratio*, emphasising circumstances in the court that affect the poet. While it is possible to make the case that every one of Dunbar's petitions contains modified elements of the formula of the *ars notaria*, the only principle of modification seems to be the occasion of the poem.

There are, however, a few instances in which he adheres closely to the formula of the *ars notaria*. Both 'Schir, ʒe have mony servitouris' and 'Schir, ʒit remembir as of befoir' contain elements of all five parts of the formula. The latter poem, however, is the more interesting example. Dunbar begins his work with a salutation and personal *captatio benevolentiae*, but provides an interesting twist:

---

24 James Kinsley, ed., *The Poems of William Dunbar* (Oxford, 1979), p. 144, 11. 106–12. This edition will be used for all future citations; hereafter only line numbers will be provided.

> Schir, ȝit remembir as of befoir,
> How that my ȝouthe is done forloir
> In ȝour service, with pane and greiff;
> Gud conscience cryis reward thairfoir:
> Exces of thocht dois me mischeif. (ll. 1–5)

Instead of praising the magnificence of his sovereign, he emphasises his own plight and worthy service. Such personal and emotional appeals were judged to be a legitimate approach in both the *ars dictaminis* and the *ars notaria*. The main goal of this rhetorical device was to make the audience well disposed to hear the petition, whether such good will came as a result of extolling the judge's honour or reporting on one's own virtues. The *captatio benevolentiae* sets the tone for the entire *exordium*, which seems to conclude with line 10 and provides a transition into the *narratio*. Dunbar's *narratio* runs 35 lines and describes the conditions of court life in terms of aviary metaphors. Each court personality is given its own bird as a representative, with James, of course, emerging as the 'gentill egill' addressed in line 26. Dunbar has clearly taken full advantage of poetic licence in this section – extended metaphors were suspect in the *ars notaria* because of their ambiguity. Nonetheless, in so far as the allegory of the passage reflects the poet's perception of the facts of life at court, it fulfills the function of the *narratio*.

Dunbar's *petitio* is lengthy. In line 36 he moves from allegory to a more direct statement of his case, reintroducing the first person pronoun in a sustained tone of personal appeal that lasts throughout the remainder of the poem. The first part of the *petitio* continues to develop the poet's problems using emotional appeals based on litotes, including comments about his 'few vertewis' and the 'lycht' nature of his service. All of this leads up to the real object of the petition – the benefice requested in lines 56–8. The poet even goes so far as to cite precedent, invoking the names of others who have received better treatment than he, even though possessed of more limited virtues. The *conclusio* occupies the last two stanzas of the poem (ll. 76–85). It contains devices standard to the *ars notaria*: a summary of comparisons with the precedents, an expression of respect for authority, and a reinforcement of the petitioner's distress:[25]

> How suld I leif and I not landit,
> Nor ȝit withe benefice am blandit?
> I say not, sir, ȝow to repreiff,
> Bot doutles I go rycht neir hand it:
> Exces of thocht dois me mischeif.
> As saule in to purgatorie,
> Leifand in pane with hoip of glorie,
> So is my selff ȝe may beleiff
> In hoip, sir, of ȝour adjutorie:
> Exces of thocht dois me mischeif. (ll. 76–85)

---

25 See 'The Principles of Letter Writing,' pp. 16–18, 19.

Dunbar was clearly familiar with this petitionary formula from the *ars notaria* and demonstrated in this poem, as in 'Schir, ʒe have mony servitouris . . .' that he could use it to good effect.

One final example may be adduced, from the work of Gavin Douglas. While *The Palis of Honoure* was likely written shortly after the turn of the sixteenth century, it provides an excellent capstone in reviewing the literary influence of the *ars notaria* in the fifteenth century. The poem is one of the most self-consciously rhetorical works of the period. Cicero, Quintilian, Lorenzo Valla, and Poggio Bracciolini appear as characters, with the latter two even engaged in a quarrel (ll. 1232–33). The court of the Muses is described as 'the court rhetorical/Of polit termys',[26] and the garden of the palace itself is a place marked by 'The swete florist colouis of rhetoreis' (l. 2066). It is hardly surprising that the *ars notaria* should intrude among the other forms of eloquence in the work.

Dictaminal rhetoric is pervasive in the poem, especially emphasised in the descriptions of the courts and entourages, the historical and literary events, and even the palace itself. The most pronounced use of the *ars notaria*, however, occurs in the confrontation between the dreamer and the court of Venus in Part I. Having deliberately offended the court with his rendition of a song attacking love, the dreamer is ultimately discovered and dragged before Mars, Cupid, Venus and her court. He is aware immediately of serious trouble on the horizon because of the formal structure of the proceedings.

> Entronit sat Mars, Cupyd and Venus.
> Tho rais a clerk wes clepit Varius
> Me tyl accusyng of a dedly cryme
> And he begouth and red a dittay thus:
> 'Thou wikkyt catyve, wood and furious,
> Presumptuusly now at this present tyme
> My lady here blasphemed in thy ryme.
> Hir sonne, hir self and hir court amorus
> For till betrais awatit here sen prime.' (ll. 664–72)

The intonation of the charges by a 'clerk' is the appropriate legal procedure for indictment for a 'dedly cryme'. The dreamer reacts accordingly, with coldness in his heart and a quaking voice. He kneels and submits himself without 'any langer pley' (l. 676), but Venus herself uses the *ars notaria* in ordering 'chargis till procede as before' (l. 679). Varius then orders the dreamer to maintain silence, shortly thereafter demanding 'myn answere' (l. 682) in perfect legal protocol. To this point the scene has been replete with the language of the *ars notaria* and the formal procedure of the court. But the poet is just beginning to explore the uses of this school of rhetoric.

The dreamer's response intensifies the legal rhetoric and moves the poem

---

26 Gavin Douglas, *The Palis of Honoure*, ed. David Parkinson (Kalamazoo, 1992), p. 40, ll.835–36. This edition will be used for all future citations; hereafter only line numbers will be provided.

further into the technicalities of legal procedure. His initial response uses the rhetoric of law and touches on a fine point of legal procedure:

> 'Set of thir pointis of cryme now on me laid
> I may me quyte giltles in verité,
> Yit fyrst, agane the juge quhilk here I se,
> This inordenat court and proces quaid
> I wyll object for causys twa or thre.' (ll. 686–90)

Phrases such as 'pointis of cryme' and 'me quyte giltles' were intrinsic parts of the legal rhetoric of the period. In addition, Douglas uses as a part of his defence the same legal tactic employed by Henryson's sheep in 'The Sheep and the Dog' – he argues that the court does not have proper authority in his case. He elaborates the argument with appropriate rhetorical flair:

> Inclynand law, quod I with pietuus face,
> 'I me defend, Madame plesyt your grace.'
> 'Say on,' quod sche, than said I thus but mare:
> 'Madame, ye may not syt in till this cace
> For ladyis may be jugis in na place
> And, mare attour, I am na seculare.
> A spirituall man (thocht I be void of lare)
> Clepyt I am, and aucht my lyvys space
> To be remyt till my juge ordinare.'
>
> 'I yow beseik, Madame with byssy cure,
> Till gyf ane gracius interlocuture
> On thir exceptionys now proponyt late.' (ll. 691–702)

First, his 'pietuus face,' as Parkinson has noted, accords well with rhetorical advice offered by Cicero for pleading.[27] In addition, his diction in this passage is full of set phrases from the *ars notaria*, including 'plesyt your grace,' 'syt in till this cace,' 'juge ordinaire,' 'interlocuture,' 'exceptionys,' and 'proponyt.' This language becomes the means for an appeal based on real legal procedure. His argument that Venus may not sit as judge because 'ladyis may be jugis in na place' (l. 695) may jolt readers who are steeped in the courtly tradition. Venus indeed commonly renders such judgements. Yet the argument is based on real legal practice in Scotland and would be a legitimate basis for arguing against the authority of a court. Just as this approach may be jarring in what is ostensibly a 'love' dream-vision, so his next argument also takes the reader by surprise. He pleads for 'benefit of clergy' because he is 'A spiritual man.' This argument reinforces his request for a change of venue to a 'juge ordinare'.[28] His conclusion

27 *Ibid.*, p. 96.
28 But for information on an example that would seem to provide 'precedent' for Venus' ruling, see Doe, pp. 67–8.

intensifies the use of the *ars notaria* in its technicality. He requests an 'interlocuture/On thir exceptionys now proponyt late' (11. 702-3). The finely legal language of this proposal infuriates Venus and she erupts in a torrent of anger against such a 'subtle smy' who would dare to decline her as judge. Her anger leads her away from notarial rhetoric and legal procedure, but she cannot completely forget the legal setting.

She warns him that he shall 'thoill jugement' (1. 709) at her hands, and she dismisses his legal expertise with the assertion that 'Ye clerkis bene in subtyle wordis quent' (1. 716). She notes he is an example of the men that 'bewrays my commandis' (1. 718), and when she finally calms herself and returns once again to procedural proprieties, she says:

> 'Have doyn,' quod sche, 'syr Varius. Alswyith
> Do writ the sentence. Lat this cative kyith
> Gyf our power may demyng his mysdeid.' (11. 727-29)

It is fortunate indeed for the dreamer that the proceedings are interrupted by Caliope and her court. However, even after Venus pardons him, she continues to think of the incident and the dreamer in legal terms, referring to him at their next meeting as 'my presoner' (1. 1735). Like Henryson, Douglas indicates clearly his knowledge of the *ars notaria* and the finer points of law.

These examples are not exhaustive. Both the *ars dictaminis* and the *ars notaria* appear in other, lesser known works in the fifteenth century. For instance, an anonymous poem that McKenzie reprints in his edition of *The Poems of William Dunbar* as item number 92, 'To the Gouvernour in France,' is in the form of a perfect governmental petition, based on royal and legal documents of the fourteenth and fifteenth centuries.[29] In similar fashion, Richard Holland's *The Buke of the Howlat* contains an exceptional share of dictaminal rhetoric. Its description of the assembly of fowls as well as the description of contemporaneous Scotland (11. 300-455) well demonstrate Holland's familiarity with standard dictaminal approaches in the description of nobility and court assemblages. The emphasis on heraldry and pomp further reflects the same tone to be found in many examples of the *ars dictaminis* emanating from real courts. His use of legal rhetoric, however, is limited. References to the law, unlike those found in either Henryson or *The Kingis Quair*, are infrequent. The appeals of the owl to the pope (poppenjay) contain certain elements of the *ars notaria*, such as the *exordium*, *narratio*, and *petitio*, as illustrated in lines 93-131 and lines 250-61. Neither of these appeals, however, shows the conscious attention to organisational principle found in other poetry of the period. In this respect, *The Buke of the Howlat* represents a close interest in dictaminal rhetoric with the slightest brushmarks of the *ars notaria*. Nonetheless, because it represents

---

29 See W. Mackay Mackenzie, ed., *The Poems of William Dunbar* (London, 1932), pp. 181-2. For parallels in this petition form, see E. L. G. Stones, ed. and trans., *Anglo-Scottish Relations 1174-1328* (Oxford, 1965), especially pp. 88-101, 106-11, and 280-5.

an early stage in the development of this movement, the work is worthy of note.

The influence of the *ars notaria* is uneven. Its impact on the poetry of Henryson and the author of *The Kingis Quair* is quite evident. In fact, in view of the total corpus of his writings, Henryson may be the outstanding exponent of the *ars notaria* in the period. Additionally, the pointed use of such legal rhetoric in Douglas' *The Palis of Honoure* and the petition form in Dunbar indicate that legal rhetoric was pervasive. As noted above, the widespread nature of its influence may indeed be due to certain social conditions, most notably the attention in fifteenth-century Scotland to law and legal education as consistory courts developed in an avowed Stewart effort at consolidation. The influence of Italian culture may be another factor. The widening development of the *ars notaria* originating in Italy provided for a great social need throughout Europe and the British Isles: an effort to ensure equal justice by embodying legal terms and judgements in static language which would likely always gain the same results in a court of law. Finally, there is the innate appeal of this school of rhetoric for those who 'play with words'. Bridging Latin and the vernacular as access to the system of justice became more widespread, the *ars notaria* proved a fascinating intellectual playing field for students of language. Its easily-learned formulae and its reduced inventory of figures also made it a form of rhetoric more easily and completely mastered than, say, the *ars praedicandi* or the *ars poetriae*. Moreover, any learned person who wished to play a role in the active life of court or society would have been obliged to become familiar with the language of law. For all of these reasons, and perhaps many others, the greatest Scottish poets of the fifteenth century saw fit to adapt and blend legal rhetoric into their verse.

ROSEMARY GREENTREE

16. Who Knows if all that Critics Wrote was True? Some thoughts on Robert Henryson's 'biography'

> Of Robert Henryson's life almost nothing is known for certain except that he was schoolmaster in Dunfermline, probably of the Abbey School there.

So David Murison begins the introduction to his *Selections from the Poems of Robert Henryson*, and the thoughts are expressed, with striking similarity, in other editions of Henryson's poems.[1] We may wonder why editors stress first the lack of biographical information about our poet and then his profession, which has, from the first, been attached to Henryson's name, particularly if they heed the admonition from G. Gregory Smith:

> We know so little about Henryson's life that the task of an editor who is expected to offer the customary 'Memoir' resolves itself in the main into warning the reader against the surmises and fictions of his predecessors.[2]

The Harleian manuscript and Bassandyne, Charteris and Hart prints of the *Moral Fables* refer to 'the schoolmaster of Dunfermline,' and the Charteris and Anderson prints of *The Testament of Cresseid* style him 'Master Robert Henryson.' Both traditions were observed by H. Harvey Wood, who called his edition *The Poems and Fables of Robert Henryson, Schoolmaster of Dunfermline*, and began his introduction: 'Of the life of Robert Henryson little is known.'[3]

Information is scanty, but not confined to the matter of Henryson's vocation of schoolmaster. There are records of the signature of a Robert Henryson, a notary public, yet this respected title seems never to be used with the poet's name. The admission of a Robert Henryson as a member of the University of Glasgow is also noted. The name 'Robert Henryson' was not an unusual one, and these records are not accepted by all editors as applying to the poet.[4] It is prudent to heed the first sentence of Charles Elliott's biographical note:

---

1 David Murison, *Selections from the Poems of Robert Henryson* (Edinburgh: The Saltire Society, Oliver and Boyd, 1952).
2 G. Gregory Smith, ed., *The Poems of Robert Henryson*, 3 vols (Edinburgh: Scottish Text Society, Blackwood, 1914), 1: xix.
3 H. Harvey Wood, *The Poems and Fables of Robert Henryson, Schoolmaster of Dunfermline*, rev. ed. (Edinburgh: Oliver and Boyd, 1958) xi.
4 Denton Fox accepts both, as stated in his edition *The Poems of Robert Henryson* (Oxford: Clarendon, 1981) xiii. W.M. Metcalfe accepts the admission, with some reservations about its value, in *The Poems of Robert Henryson* (Paisley: Gardner, 1917) xiii. Wood cautiously refers to Laing's list of numerous contemporary Henrysons (xiii). Smith, is frankly sceptical about records found in 'the homeland of the Hendersons' (xxiv).

Information concerning the life and person of Robert Henryson is limited and vague, taking on the nature of inference rather than of evidence.[5]

The most specific references are made by other poets. Dunbar, in his 'Lament for the Makars,' shows that Henryson's death, or at least a serious illness, had occurred before the death of Stobo, in 1505.[6] In 1530, Sir David Lyndsay includes Henryson (as Henderson) in a list of dead poets, in *The Testament of the Papyngo*.[7] A more exuberant reference comes in the 'merry though somewhat vnsauory tale' of Henryson's deathbed, which Sir Francis Kinaston added to his translation into Latin of *Troilus and Criseyde* and *The Testament of Cresseid*. Sometimes the tale is quoted doubtfully, because of Kinaston's proven inaccuracies about 'aged schollers' and the 'tradition of flippant last words,' but we should heed Douglas Gray's comment that it is, '[i]n the light of *Sum Practysis of Medecyne* . . . not as fundamentally unHenrysonian as has been alleged'.[8] We could easily imagine the jaunty abuse of the witch being given by the genial charlatan in that poem of medical chicanery.

Eventually we may think that Smith's sharp estimate of the value of Laing's biographical research is the soundest made on this kind of endeavour for Henryson scholars:

> Laing followed up every clue, only with the result that we have but a halfpenny-worth of evidence to an intolerable deal of free conjecture.[9]

In cases such as Henryson's, all biographical fragments are cherished and ruthlessly probed to yield more treasures of information. He falls into an awkward category, between those anonymous poets of whom we can know nothing at all, and those who have left letters, diaries and other records that illuminate the study of their writings. The task for anyone who wants to discern how much importance should be attached to what we know of Henryson's life is to identify fact and separate it from conjecture.

It is generally accepted as fact that Henryson was a schoolmaster. This leads to conjecture, perhaps coloured by readers' ideas of schoolmaster, as suggested in Smith's tart warning:

---

5 Charles Elliott, ed., *Robert Henryson: Poems* (Oxford: Clarendon, 1963) xvii.
6   In Dumfernelyne he [Death] has done roune
    With Maister Robert Henrisoun;
    . . .
    And he has now tane last of aw
    Gud gentill Stobo and Quintyne Schaw
James Kinsley, ed., *The Poems of William Dunbar* (Oxford: Clarendon, 1979) 180, lines 81–6.
7   Quintyng, Mersar, Rowle, Henderson, hay, & holland,
    Thocht thay be ded, *tha*r libells bene leua*n*d
    Quh[i]lkis to reheirs makeith redaris to reioise.
Douglas Hamer, ed., *The Works of Sir David Lindsay of the Mount 1490–1555*, 4 vols. (Edinburgh: STS, Blackwood, 1931), vol. 1, lines 19–21.
8 Smith, xxi; Fox, ed., *Poems*, xv: Douglas Gray, *Robert Henryson* (Leiden: Brill, 1979) 3.
9 Smith, xix.

It is easy for any one who merely skims the poems in these volumes, and brings
with him prejudices derived from his reading of the English Chaucerians, to say
that Henryson is no better than his neighbours, that he is a tedious moralist,
and by habit, as by title, plain schoolmaster.[10]

Harsher than this is the assessment of Hanna, who writes of *The Testament of
Cresseid* and

> a large group of critics who find the poem too scrupulously moral. Although
> they admit the justice of Cresseid's fate, they suggest that Henryson, as a result
> of his dour Scottish school-teacher's mentality, shows too much interest in
> purely retributive chastisement.[11]

The thought echoes Grierson's, that Henryson is 'a Scot and a Schoolemaister,
with a Scot's and a schoolmaster's belief in retribution'.[12]

The style expected of a schoolmaster seems to be that of a rather prim pedant,
an instructor by word and example, and a believer in punishment for misdeeds.
The work most likely to demonstrate such a style is the *Moral Fables*, which may
confirm or deny the expectations. There is much to maintain the reader's first
impression of a didactic work. No one could ignore the stern moral messages
found in tales and *moralitates*, and no one would expect not to find them in a work
with such a title. Other aspects of the *Moral Fables* seem to attach them to a
teacher. Aesop's *Fables* were among the first texts used in the schools, and any
schoolmaster could be expected to know them well. So, of course, could a former
student. The accomplished telling of Aesop's *Fables* suggests an educated person,
although not necessarily a teacher. The restrained pathos and penetrating wit
which enrich the stories told in the classroom also remove them from that setting.
Grierson qualifies his earlier comment to say

> if the schoolmaster in Henryson prompted him to translate the Fables and add
> an appropriate moral, it in no way interfered with his dramatic and humorous
> rendering of them.[13]

Fox is cautious in his assessment of the tone of the work and the inferences that
can legitimately be drawn from it:

> The pedagogical tone that occasionally appears in Henryson's poetry is no very
> good evidence that he was a schoolmaster, but it is worth noting that Gualterus
> Anglicus, the source for some of his fables, was an author with whom a

---

10 Smith, xiv.
11 Ralph Hanna III, 'Cresseid's Dream and Henryson's *Testament,*' *Chaucer and Middle English Studies in Honour of Rossell Hope Robbins*, ed. Beryl Rowland (London: Allen, 1974) 288–97, 296.
12 'Robert Henryson: An Address to the Scottish P.E.N. Club,' Sir Herbert Grierson, *Essays and Addresses* (London: Chatto, 1940) 105–17, 109.
13 Grierson, 110.

schoolteacher would perforce be very familiar. A more convincing argument, however, is that a degree in canon law would be an appropriate one for a notary public, and we know that notaries public were sometimes schoolmasters.[14]

Several fables, in particular 'The Sheep and the Dog' and 'The Wolf and the Lamb,' furnish evidence of the poet's familiarity with legal matters, yet he is never described as 'Robert Henryson, the notary public of Dunfermline'. Is this perhaps because so many people have had contact with a schoolmaster and feel they can recognise a schoolmaster's voice, but relatively few are familiar with notaries public?

We should also consider the unusually important position of the schoolteacher. For many, the schoolteacher is the first significant adult they encounter who belongs outside the family circle. To the child, the first teacher has a barely questioned authority, beyond that of parents; and a vivid image, often exaggerated, remains in the pupil's mind for many years. It can be a surprise to realise that one's first teacher has no magical properties, such as eyes in the back of the head, or an ability to read minds or predict the future: it is almost disappointing to find that he or she leads an ordinary human existence outside the school. Of course, these are irrational stereotypes, the kind we no longer hold consciously, the kind devised and perpetuated in the classroom – the first classroom. Can we be sure that the myths of teachers do not linger? I shall be guilty of speculation if I suggest that such thoughts influence the preference for calling Henryson 'the schoolmaster of Dunfermline' rather than 'the notary public', but the idea is tempting. It finds a vestige of encouragement in H. Marshall Leicester's book *The Disenchanted Self: Representing the Subject in the 'Canterbury Tales'*, in the dedication of the work to those he calls 'teachers, colleagues, friends, my significant others, and my other selves'.[15]

Why should we need or want to know about the lives of poets? It can seem legitimate and even unavoidable. The letters and diaries of the Romantic poets shed light on their poetic works: Coleridge's *Ode on Dejection* seems incomplete without the *Verse Letter to Asra*, and his notebooks give many insights. Elegant acrostics and graceful play with names and details would be lost to us if we knew nothing of the poets. We would not appreciate the significance of the lines by Charles of Orléans which spell out 'Anna Molins:' we would miss the effects of Donne's witty play with his name.[16] These matters could remain secrets if we had no biographical knowledge, if we could read only anonymous fragments, but they are secrets made to be discovered. They are rather like art forgeries whose creators cannot show their talents without revealing their crimes, or hoaxes where

---

14 Fox, ed., *Poems*, xvi.
15 H. Marshall Leicester, Jr., *The Disenchanted Self: Representing the Subject in the 'Canterbury Tales'* (Berkeley: U of California P, 1990) xii.
16 See Eleanor Prescott Hammond, 'Charles of Orléans and Anne Molyneux,' *Modern Philology* 21 (1924): 215–16; Donne's word-play is found particularly in 'A Hymn to God the Father' and 'To Christ'.

the joke cannot be shared if it has been too successful. It is reasonable to wonder how many other references are hidden because we know so little of many medieval poets, and just as reasonable to hope that more will be discovered. It is not reasonable to add conjectures unsupported by reliable evidence.

The lack of biographical knowledge about medieval authors gives us freedom in dealing with their works. We are liberated from the need to interpret works in the light of what we know of a poet's circumstances – of ambitions, illnesses, anxieties or love – something we can hardly avoid when we have letters and diaries, although too much information may puzzle us and suggest contradictory interpretations. As well as freedom from the details of biography however, a lack of material gives freedom to produce biographies of the kind in which literary theory, conjecture and the creative linking of a few details may produce results limited only by the imagination of the biographer. We can compare John Gardner's frankly speculative work *The Life and Times of Chaucer* with the entirely unexceptionable chapter in which Douglas Gray surveys records of the 'barely subdued chaos of ordinary life' of Dunfermline in Henryson's era, scrupulously setting the scene for a study of the works.[17] We can only guess at a life of Henryson written by someone with fewer inhibitions than those who have honourably said that little is known of it.

The lack of biographical details gives us freedom to look at the poems themselves, with fewer distractions than the works of more recent poets allow. It does not mean that we will not investigate every treasured scrap of additional knowledge. But we must be guided in our readings by all that the *poet* gives us, dealing with the face that individual presents, rather than a construction from known fact and some plausible stereotypes – external additions from our picture of the poet's private life. Henryson shows the riskiness of such speculation by presenting his poems in the mouths of very different characters. We have already considered the presenter of *Sum Practysis of Medecyne*; it is hard to imagine this cheerful fraud giving the moral lessons of the *Fables* or an alternative ending to the story of Criseyde. The sombre resignation of *The Abbey Walk* is far removed from the urgent pleading of *Ane Prayer for the Pest*, and the rigour of *The Thre Deid Pollis* from the acerbic wit of *Robene and Makyne*. We may accept that the schoolmaster of Dunfermline has created the speakers, but not that they are all in his everyday image.

It is salutary to observe that the narrator of the *Testament of Cresseid* has impressed readers in various ways, none of them necessarily schoolmasterly in any usually accepted sense. In his edition of the *Testament*. Fox describes an 'extremely Chaucerian,' but 'imbecilic' and 'stupid and passionately involved narrator'.[18] This opinion is somewhat softened by the qualification that

> [a] fifteenth-century reader, trained to recognise conventions and to value poetry for its rhetoric and, in the best sense, its contrivance, would not be likely

---

17 John Gardner, *The Life and Times of Chaucer* (London: Cape, 1977); Gray, *Robert Henryson*, 'Dunfermline and Beyond,' 1–30, 11.
18 Denton Fox, ed., *Testament of Cresseid* (London: Nelson, 1968) 21, 2, 23.

to confuse the narrator with the poet, or to think that Henryson's concealed art was clumsiness or an amiable *naiveté*.[19]

He concludes that the narrator is 'an unintelligent, low-minded and agreeable old man'.[20] In her reply to Douglas Duncan, Sydney Harth asserts that 'Mr. Duncan is mistaken in seeing the narrator as a medieval Yeats: he is much more like a medieval Noel Coward.'[21] Del Chessell's notion of 'a mature man, who has tried the game of love and knows it all too well,' may be shared by many readers of the poem.[22] We may agree with any of these ideas or none of them, but it is hard to reconcile this range of figures with popular ideas of the demeanour of schoolmasters.

When we consider the personality of the narrator of a poem it is hard to dismiss our notion of the poet, but we should be guided by what the poet presents, and so discover topical references, acrostics and the like not only *as* but also *if* the poet wishes, and not grudge any secrets. Expectations of reliability or sincerity are not helpful in this context, since usual ideas of trustworthiness or consistency are simply irrelevant. (We may, for instance, enjoy the exposure of an unreliable narrator in conflicting accounts given by other narrators in a work.) The view expressed by Robert C. Elliot, writing of the Roman elegists, applies here:

> For them sincerity is a function of style, involving a relation between the artist and the public; it has to do with the presentation of a self appropriate to the kind of verse being written, to the genre, not with the personality of the poet.[23]

It is then entirely reasonable and legitimate to think of Henryson, or any other poet, as presenting the most suitable public face whenever such a face is required, with no regard to consistency with the poet's personality or the face presented in other works. This face may be called a persona (although there are some objections to the use of this convenient term) or, where a story is being told, a narrator.

A celebrated and analogous case is the face presented by Chaucer in the *Canterbury Tales*, called 'Chaucer the pilgrim' by E. Talbot Donaldson, but denied by Leicester, who nevertheless suggests 'Chaucer the poet' and eventually 'Chaucer the poem'.[24] Leicester objects to an excess of 'narrative entities' and 'unimpersonated artistry' and proposes 'Leicester's razor' to remove them.[25]

---

19 Fox, ed., *Testament*, 2.
20 Fox, ed. *Testament*, 53.
21 Sydney Harth, 'Henryson Reinterpreted'. *Essays in Criticism* 11 (1961): 471–80, 474. She writes in reply to Douglas Duncan, 'Henryson's *Testament of Cresseid*,' *Essays in Criticism* 11 (1961): 128–35.
22 Del Chessell, 'In the Dark Time: Henryson's *Testament of Cresseid*,' *Critical Review* 12 (1969): 61–72, 63.
23 Robert C. Elliot. *The Literary Persona* (Chicago: U of Chicago P, 1982) 43.
24 E. Talbot Donaldson, 'Chaucer the Pilgrim,' *Speaking of Chaucer* (London: U of London, Athlone, 1970) 1–12; first published *PMLA* 69 (1954): 928–36. H. Marshall Leicester. Jr. 'The Art of Impersonation: A General Prologue to the *Canterbury Tales*,' *PMLA* 95 (1980): 213–24, 221.
25 '*Narratores non multiplicandi sunt praeter absolutum necessitatem*,' first mentioned in 'The Art of Impersonation,' 215, and later in *The Disenchanted Self*, 6.

Chaucer's narrator describes, with apparently innocent admiration, characters later shown to be deplorable, such as the fraudulent Pardoner and the unwholesome Cook; he seems to be 'Chaucer the silly duffer,' rather than any popular ideas of 'Chaucer the collector of customs,' such as Kittredge's, that 'a naïf Collecter of Customs would be a paradoxical monster'.[26] Here we are using stereotyped ideas of customs officers as very observant, even suspicious people, looking for the worst as well as the best. Such characteristics would also be helpful to those who tell stories that expose the characteristics of humanity revealed in a work such as the *Canterbury Tales*. A collector of customs could be a proficient observer of and commentator on his fellows, but such a pilgrim is not mentioned in the *General Prologue*.

Stereotyped notions, even those not consciously held, may interfere with our acceptance of a work as the poet presents it and of the poet as he or she is. Indeed, some stereotypes of a poet can only interfere with our perceptions. Among these are thoughts of frantic scribbling of endless drafts, while the poet freezes and frets by the light of a flickering candle in a miserable garret. This pale, feverish young man (whose image owes much to stereotypes of Keats) may be racked by a consumptive cough. With those ideas go assumptions that suffering and a mind devoted to unworldly things are essential for the production of poetry of any value. The stereotype, of course, excludes many poets of the past and present, the most obvious exceptions being all who are not suffering young men. A particular exception we might examine against the notion is Wallace Stevens, who pursued his profession of lawyer with the Hartford Insurance Company, arriving at his office punctually after composing poetry as he walked to work, then dictating the poems to his secretary, who presented him with typed copies from her shorthand notes, so that he could make further adjustments.[27] It would be absurd to dismiss Stevens as insensitive, absorbed only in actuarial matters or points of law, hence incapable of creating poetry of any worth.

It is just as absurd to imagine any poet as one whose existence is bounded by occupation, a flat character deprived of the life of imagination, writing only the thoughts of mundane life: for Chaucer as a collecter of customs, for Stevens as a lawyer, for Keats as a surgeon, for Henryson as a schoolmaster. We may agree with Leicester that 'there is only one speaker of the entire poem and . . . he is also the poem's maker'.[28] He refers to Chaucer in the *Canterbury Tales*, but we can apply the thought to other cases, and add that the poem's maker appears in the form he or she chooses.

Thus we can confidently think that Henryson presents his version of Aesop's *Fables* as he wishes to do, using a narrator who has many characteristics of a schoolmaster, shown in the choice of subject, the pedagogical tone he often uses, and his clear wish to teach. There are also many other characteristics, the most conspicuous being that narrator's clear intention to admonish, entertain and

---

26 Noted by Donaldson, 2.
27 Peter Brazeau, *Parts of a World: Wallace Stevens Remembered* (New York: Random House, 1983) 34, 39.
28 Leicester, 'Art of Impersonation,' 220.

persuade *adults*, sometimes called his friends, rather than children. The atmosphere of the 'Prologue,' for example, is not that of the schoolroom; its tone suggests conviviality and amusingly exaggerated deference, unexpectedly undercut by harsh condemnation. The lessons taught in the *Moral Fables* are not for beginners; they are for adults who already know the stories but need the surprises of a fresh telling, such as the unexpected lessons the narrator draws when he appears to ignore the most obvious messages in his idiosyncratic readings.

How then can we distinguish and strike a balance between biographical fact and conjecture when we examine Henryson's works? We can accept that he was a schoolmaster and notary public, and the *Moral Fables* confirm his familiarity with works in the school curriculum and points of law. We should not try to find particular local or political references unless we can be absolutely sure. It has been suggested, for example, that 'ane abbay . . . fair to se' in the fragment of 'master Robert hendersonnis Dreme On fut by forth' is a reference to Dunfermline Abbey, and that the spital house of *The Testament of Cresseid* was also to be found in Dunfermline.[29] Such references gain no more force from being particular than they do from being general or typical. Similarly the warnings to those in power found in 'The Lion and the Mouse,' 'The Wolf and the Wether' and 'The Wolf and the Lamb' actually lose strength when they are considered only as temporary, topical, political satire rather than general teachings to apply for other generations.[30] We may accept Agnes Mure Mackenzie's perception of the tone of *The Testament of Cresseid*: 'The whole thing has a stark sense of the east wind – one of those bleak Fife days with white water on the Firth,' but feel some regretful doubt about Maurice Lindsay's notion of Henryson's 'warm and kindly personality' and his confidence that '[t]his schoolmaster of Dunfermline must have been a good person to know'.[31] Specific references may be obscured by our lack of dependable biographical knowledge, but we are spared unjustified assumptions.

The distinctions we can make between fact and conjecture resemble those set by Wimsatt and Beardsley, in their essay 'The Intentional Fallacy'.[32] They distinguish between internal and external evidence for the meaning of a poem, where 'internal' comes from the examination of text and context, and 'external' is 'private and idiosyncratic' coming from 'revelation . . . about how or why the poet wrote the poem – to what lady while sitting on what lawn, or at the death of what friend or brother.'[33] They also consider

---

29 Smith refers rather dubiously to Laing's assertions, xxiv.
30 These ideas have been canvassed by John MacQueen, *Robert Henryson: A Study of the Major Narrative Poems* (Oxford: Clarendon, 1967) 170-3, and by R.L. Kindrick, 'Lion or Cat? Henryson's Characterization of James III,' *Studies in Scottish Literature* 26 (1979): 123–36. They are rejected by R. J. Lyall, 'Politics and Poetry in Fifteeth and Sixteenth Century Scotland', *Scottish Literary Journal* 3 (1976): 5–29, especially 7–10.
31 Mackenzie and Lindsay are quoted in the introduction to *Henryson, Selected by Hugh MacDiarmid* (Harmondsworth: Penguin, 1973), Poet to Poet, 13, 15.
32 W.K. Wimsatt, Jr., and Monroe C. Beardsley, 'The Intentional Fallacy', *The Verbal Icon: Studies in the Meaning of Poetry*, W.K. Wimsatt, Jr., (London: Methuen, 1970) 3–39.
33 Wimsatt and Beardsley, 10.

an intermediate kind of evidence about the character of the author or by a coterie of which he is a member. The meaning of words is the history of words, and the biography of an author, his use of a word, and the associations which the word had for *him*, are part of the word's history and meaning.[34]

These thoughts find analogies in Leicester's that

> the voicing of individual tales [of the *Canterbury Tales*] has almost always been interpreted on the basis of something external to them, usually either some aspect of the historical background of the poems (what we know from other sources about knights, millers, lawyers, nuns) or the descriptions of the speakers given in the Canterbury frame, especially in the *General Prologue*.[35]

Our use of biography must be rigorous and sceptical, as free as possible of any assumptions, even inadvertent ones, or we shall certainly be guilty of a biographical fallacy. We may feel dubious even about the enthusiasm of Wood for the *Fables*:

> What will rejoice Scottish readers more than anything, I believe, will be to find in this fifteenth century Dunfermline schoolmaster the same distinguishing features that mark out the Scotsman, in any company, to-day.[36]

This thought depends as much on the reader's notions of schoolmasters and Scots as on the text of the poem, and would have unexpected and undesired effects if they were the disapproving ones noted earlier. Wood then invites the reader to compare the 'peremptory note' in the mourning of the sheep with the tone to be heard from the 'north-country pulpit,' and the questioning of Aesop with that to be expected from a native of the Kingdom of Fife, encountered on a train journey.[37] How are we served by such editorial assumptions? The comments are surely made to enhance the reader's understanding and pleasure, but in ways available only to those who have, already installed, ideas corresponding to the critic's. A knowledge of the historical and linguistic background does increase the enjoyment of a text, but unjustified assumptions can be at best harmless and at worst misleading; they can lead to incorrect interpretations, along paths blending knowledge with stereotype, towards sweeping assumptions such as 'Henryson was a schoolmaster, but in his heart he was a poet.' We could delude ourselves that we had reconciled available facts if we do not recognise assertions that have no sure foundation in the poet's works. We must decide that assumptions that cannot be shown to be true could be misleading, and that we cannot readily identify them. Thus we need to make cautious assessments of the value of biographical comment, and can often give only a Scottish verdict – not proven.

34 Wimsatt and Beardsley, 10.
35 Leicester, *The Disenchanted Self*, 7.
36 Wood, xvii.
37 Wood, xvii–xviii.

We cannot expect that Henryson was not influenced by his surroundings, family, occupation, familiar customs, things that influence everybody, but we cannot say how much. Thus we can welcome both Gray's account of life in Dunfermline and his refraining from drawing conclusions from this about Henryson's life. We should approach the poet's works prepared to be influenced by all that he has given us, but not to import our attitudes. Although we recognise a pedagogical tone in the *Fables*, it should not mask the poet's other notes. Perhaps Henryson *was* exactly like the narrator of his *Moral Fables*; he must then have been rather unlike his other voices. If we have no more grounds for making such a decision than Henryson's profession, our evidence is incomplete and unsafe.

Any insistence on consistency between the narratorial face seen in a poem and the poet's own life suggests restriction and undervaluing of the poet's talents. His imagination must be hobbled indeed if it cannot devise a narrator who differs from the poet's everyday face. In Henryson's case, there is no need to consider such a possibility. No poet who could create the presenters of his other poems could lack the imaginative skills needed to find a persona to narrate his *Fables* with an individual style. That narrator's mood changes from genial deference, to be tinged with revulsion and compassion, darkening to pessimism for this life but hope for the next, and he is closer to his audience at the end of the *Fables* than in the 'Prologue'. He gives novel variations on traditional teachings, and instructs the audience in pedagogical style, but he does more. Even in his most schoolmasterly work, the limited stereotype of a limited schoolmaster does not suffice. Kinsley's words are apposite:

> The common portrait of the schoolmaster of Dunfermline, a quiet, elderly 'serious good man', is inadequate. It is easy enough to see the moralizing dominie in Henryson's works; but the hard ironist is also there[38]

Finally, we must endorse Grierson:

> Of Robert Henryson's personal life we know really nothing. But this absence of knowledge has certain advantages . . . We are concerned with the poet alone, his work and its significance and interest for us today.[39]

From the material presented, we must choose what to accept as truth, and accept too that we can never have the whole truth, nor yet nothing but the truth.[40]

---

38 James Kinsley, ed., *Scottish Poetry: A Critical Survey* (London: Cassell, 1955) 21.
39 Grierson, 105.
40 I thank Dr T. L. Burton for kindly reading and commenting on an earlier draft of this paper.

JOANNE S. NORMAN

17. *William Dunbar's Rhetoric of Power*

Of all the great Scottish poets, William Dunbar is most distinguished by his close association with a royal court, that of James IV. While other poets enjoyed royal patronage to varying degrees, and none remained unaffected by current political and social changes, only Dunbar lived his entire professional life intimately bound to one king and his immediate circle. His circumstances obviously influenced the nature of his poetry – its themes, style, and intention – so much so that in a very real sense his work may be said to embody the court culture of fifteenth-century Scotland.

While William Dunbar's situation may be apparently unique in Scotland, his career presents close analogies with other court poets both in England and on the Continent. The various tantalising references to Dunbar's travels indicate that he, in common with many other Scots courtiers, experienced at first hand the international court culture of Europe that was so prominent during the late middle ages and Renaissance. The world of international diplomacy provided ample opportunity for personal contact between individual courtiers so that Italian-French-English courts became loci of transmission of both ideas and texts.[1] I have argued in an earlier paper that Dunbar did more than simply observe the role of court poets elsewhere; he actively imitated them by sharing their precarious way of life and their literary preoccupations.[2]

One of the chief of those preoccupations was the identification of poetry as a 'second rhetoric'. Dunbar clearly makes this association in some famous passages in 'The Goldyn Targe' and the 'Flyting',[3] and his contemporaries commend him in turn for his 'language at large' and his 'rethorik'.[4] It would be impossible, in fact, for a university graduate, as Dunbar was, not to be fully conversant with formal rhetorical theory and practice.[5] Dunbar's technical training is apparent in his brilliant use of rhetorical figures.

However, his understanding of rhetoric goes beyond simple application of technique. The association of poetry with rhetoric is part of a new emphasis on

---

1 Michael Hanly, 'The Order of the Passion: Courtiers, Poetry, and the Peace Movement,' Eighth International Congress of the New Chaucer Society, University of Washington, Seattle, WA, August, 1992.
2 Joanne S. Norman, 'William Dunbar: Grand Rhétoriqueur,' *Bryght Lanternis*, eds. J. Derrick McClure and Michael R.G. Spiller (Aberdeen, 1989), pp. 179–93.
3 All reference to titles and texts of William Dunbar's poems are to *The Poems of William Dunbar*, ed. James Kinsley (Oxford, 1979). 'The Goldyn Targe' (K. 10), ii. 253–79 and 'The Flyting of Dunbar and Kennedie' (K. 23), 1. 97.
4 Sir David Lyndsay of the Mount, *Papyngo*, ii. 15–18, quoted by Priscilla Bawcutt, *Dunbar the Makar* (Oxford, 1992), p. 37.
5 See Robert L. Kindrick, 'Politics and Poetry at the Court of James III,' *Studies in Scottish Literature*, 19 (1984), 40–55 and Ian Simpson Ross, *William Dunbar* (Leiden, 1981).

the social and political role of rhetoric promoted by the humanists throughout western Europe, especially in the courts and other centres of power. Political developments in the fifteenth century fostered an increased prestige for rhetoric, and its proponents developed new possibilities of discourse, including a perception of aesthetic form as having value and power, speech as the expression of personality, and ordinary language as a tool for the exploration of reality.[6] According to Struever, the 'distinctive contribution of fourteenth-century Humanism . . . is the defence of poetry'[7] that recognises and approves of the sensual and imaginative qualities of poetic discourse[8] because it can move its audience through their senses and their passions – the primary goal of rhetoric itself. It is a humanist commonplace that eloquence 'fires' the spirit to action, that it is capable of swaying multitudes, and that form radically alters content.[9] Therefore, 'the rhetor is a mediator between exemplary action and action imitative of the exemplar'.[10] In a similar way, Castiglione later defined the courtier as a poet of public life who connects the good with the pleasurable by means of artful, well-directed flattery.[11] The 'grands rhétoriqueurs' (the group of poets associated with French and Burgundian courts in the late middle ages), as their name suggests, also conceived of their role primarily as orators, whose work necessarily involved persuasive rhetoric. The poet as rhetorician creates pleasing pictures or images of the good and the true that by their very beauty persuade his audience to identify with them and to act out, and thereby make real, the illusion.

This form of the art of persuasion has carried with it a political dimension from its origins in classical Greece. Attempts to co-opt the poet-orator with his potentially dangerous power begin with Plato who sees that the duty of the poet is to provide good stories or 'mythologeia' for the masses that will promote the policies of the state.[12] The work of the court poets of the fifteenth century, especially the 'grands rhétoriqueurs' implements a comparable view of the social function of poetry that can be directly related to their position as court polemicists who provided a professional service to the state/crown.[13] From this perspective, the orator/poet may be seen to go to either extreme: he may believe completely in whatever causes he supports, or he may sell his literary skill to the highest bidder regardless of truth or integrity. In between is the professional whose duty is to do the best he can in an assigned task.[14]

Perhaps one should not immediately assume that all court poets were closet rebels or hypocrites. They viewed their position and work as an integral part of a system

---

6 Nancy S. Struever, *The Language of History in the Renaissance* (Princeton, NJ, 1970), p. 43.
7 Struever, p. 46.
8 Struever, p. 47.
9 Struever, p. 61.
10 Struever, p. 61.
11 Richard A. Lanham, *The Motives of Eloquence* (New Haven and London, 1976), pp. 154–5.
12 John Poulakos, 'Plato's *Statesman* and the Control of Rhetoric,' Conference of the Canadian Society for the Study of Rhetoric, Ottawa, May, 1993.
13 Michael F.O. Jenkins, *Artful Eloquence: Jean Le Maire de Belges and the Rhetorical Tradition* (Chapel Hill, NC, 1980), p. 59.
14 Jenkins, p. 67.

that they willingly supported and served. Their ethos as poets of persuasion may have rested largely on the unconscious formation and then expression of a common ground or set of lived values, that is, an ideology, that involved a 'forgetting to remember' its artificial construction. However, when a particular ideology is losing ground or fragmenting, which seems to have been the case in fifteenth-century Europe, the repression of dissent or contradiction can create internal conflicts or schizophrenic splits between public and private life.[15] Zumthor has characterised the expression of this divided self in the rhétoriqueurs as 'fête' and 'monde à l'envers', the same dualism that pervades the poetry of William Dunbar.[16] In other words, a political awareness informs all court poetry, and is not limited to the direct expression of political concepts, or references to specific historic events, or explicit political and social satire.[17] For example, Arlyn Diamond shows in her analysis of Chaucer's *Troilus and Criseyde* how inherent contradictions in the ideology of courtly love and 'patriarchal feudalism' may be seen setting up the unresolved and unacknowledged conflicts in that very courtly narrative.[18]

The main vehicle used to express ambiguous reality in court poetry was epideictic rhetoric – the expression of praise and blame. This form of rhetoric with its ceremonial associations has often been defined as superficial display of verbal virtuosity on the part of individual orators without immediate practical interest and thus of less value than the supposedly more serious deliberative and/or forensic rhetoric. However, Lawrence W. Rosenfield in 'The Practical Celebration of Epideictic' argues against this prevalent modern view.[19] According to him, Aristotle himself coined the term to define the use of language to reveal or illuminate the intrinsic nobility or excellence of the subject, not the virtuosity of the speaker. Since the nobility of the described subject is part of its essential nature and is not created by outward signs or actions, epideictic rhetoric is involved not with a critical assessing of good qualities, but more with recognising and appreciating those which are already emanating from the subject. One of the most important issues, then, in the use of epideictic rhetoric is the establishment of the ethos of the speaker as he creates a common ground or consensus.[20] This is

---

15 This definition of ideology is based on Lynnette Hunter, 'Ideology: Ethos of the Post-Renaissance Nation State,' Conference of the Canadian Society for the Study of Rhetoric, Ottawa, May, 1993. Although Hunter is commenting on a different historical period, her analysis of how an ideology can work in a particular social institution seems unexpectedly apposite to European court culture of the fifteenth century.
16 Paul Zumthor, *Le masque et la lumière* (Paris, 1978).
17 I would agree with Robert Kindrick's general statement in 'Politics and Poetry at the Court of James III' that all fifteenth-century Scots poets are 'dramatically influenced by Scotland's political problems' (p. 43). However, I do not consider 'courtly literature' or 'romance' apolitical, as Kindrick's comparison of explicitly political satire to courtly literature would suggest.
18 Arlyn Diamond, 'Troilus and Criseyde: The Politics of Love,' *Chaucer in the Eighties*, eds. Julian N. Wasserman and Robert J. Blanch (Syracuse, NY, 1986).
19 Lawrence W. Rosenfield, 'The Practical Celebration of Epideictic,' *Rhetoric in Transition: Studies in the Nature and the Uses of Rhetoric*, ed. Eugene E. White (University Park, PA, 1980).
20 Lynnette Hunter uses Aristotle as a frame of reference for her analysis of the role of ethos in developing political consensus. For key passages on the importance of the character of the speaker in persuasive discourse, see Aristotle, *On Rhetoric: A Theory of Civil Discourse*, ed. George A. Kennedy (New York and Oxford, 1991), 1.2.3–4; 1.8.6; 1.9.1; and 2.1.5–6.

obviously more easily done within a smaller, more homogeneous group, such as that provided by the structure of a court. At the same time, the pressure of new tensions in the social fabric at the end of the middle ages made stabilising an ideology both more difficult and more urgent.

For Dunbar, poet of the court of James IV, the ground of all social and political life lay in the person of the king. In keeping with a broadly based trend among most European rulers, especially those old allies and enemies, France, Burgundy, and England, the Scottish crown persevered with relative success in a gradual attempt to centralise royal power and extend the king's own rule and prestige. The royal court became the single most important focus of this political change, and the self-conscious images of the court were created by its makars both as part of this process and as a response to it. Yet Jenny Wormald in her careful analysis of the historical development of the power of the crown remains curiously ambivalent towards the ideological aspect of effective royal rule in Scotland. On the one hand, she argues that the enhanced prestige of the Scottish court and the 'idea of personal kingship' was an essential aspect of a balance of power between the king and local nobility that accounts for Scotland's relative political stability for two centuries.[21] However, she then denies that Scottish kings, despite the 'supreme importance of personal contact within a political structure that was institutionally underdeveloped,' ever used 'quasi-religious propaganda' or a 'personality cult' like their [dare we insert 'more corrupt'?] fellow rulers in England or France.[22] Yet it was James VI, heir to the Stewart line, who produced one of the most definitive expressions of the divine right of kings, despite an exposure to political theories that limited royal rule.[23] His treatise can be viewed as a logical outcome of the well-known medieval tradition of the king's two bodies: one natural and subject to all the normal human infirmities; the other a transcendent body politic beyond error. E. Kantorowicz and Colette Beaune, among other historians, have drawn in extensive detail the development of this concept in its many varied forms to its final apotheosis during the late middle ages and Renaissance in the rival national monarchies of western Europe.[24] Dunbar's highly coloured portraits of his king and court do not suggest a puritan restraint from the extravagant adulation that was inherent in the social and linguistic codes of any sophisticated fifteenth-century court. If, as Wormald seems to be saying, Scottish monarchs relied more on persuasion and attraction rather than actual force to bolster their authority, then royal propaganda was absolutely necessary and, obviously, very persuasive.

William Dunbar's celebration of court festivities and formal ceremonies, that in themselves formed a complex series of political and cultural codes, resulted in some of his more elaborate and brilliant poems. Their object would seem to be to

---

21 Jenny Wormald, *Court, Kirk, and Community: Scotland 1470–1625* (Toronto, 1981), pp. 3–19.
22 Wormald, pp. 18–19.
23 Wormald, pp. 146–9.
24 Ernst H. Kantorowicz, *The King's Two Bodies: A Study in Mediaeval Political Theology* (Princeton, NJ, 1957) and Colette Beaune, *The Birth of an Ideology: Myths and Symbols of a Nation in Late-Medieval France*, trans. Susan Ross Huston, ed. Fredric L. Cheyette (Berkeley, 1991).

recreate in language the ideal already evoked in conspicuous visual display and theatrical gesture. Just as each court event would centre around the royal person, so each poem focuses on the representation of that figure. When Queen Margaret enters Aberdeen in 1511, the 'beriall of all tounis' (1.1) is transformed – literally in some ways – into a symbol of the new Jerusalem.[25] The pageants presented to her clearly draw analogies between her as the hope of the royal dynasty and the Virgin Mary as mother of the Messiah. The pageant of the royal family tree is a deliberate echo of the tree of Jesse with its prophetic overtones of redemption and renewal. Another encomium to Margaret herself, 'Gladethe thoue, Queyne of Scottis Regioun' (K. 31), begins and ends with a hyperbolic series of lapidary images that have common Marian associations and attributes a quasi-divinity to Margaret in such apostrophes as 'O hevin in erthe of ferlifull suetnes' (1. 15). In 'The Thrissill and the Rois' (K.50) Margaret the bride is again described with Marian imagery (ii. 150–2) and the royal marriage is celebrated as a political triumph of Scottish power.[26] Even in 'The Dregy' (K. 22) the king is described in cosmic terms and given close association with the Christian divinity.[27] The identification of the royal house with that of Christ Himself was, in fact, a common topos for royal entries throughout Europe that emphasised the king as the source of all peace and justice, the creator of a renewed world order.[28]

Other typical examples of the idealisation of the monarch occur in Dunbar's petitionary poems. Most critical attention, often negative, has been focused on the role of the poet in these pieces. However, their emphasis is as much on the king as on Dunbar. Helena Shire pointed out some time ago in 'Images of Monarchy' that these poems were rituals tied to a specific public occasion, and their purpose was to emphasise the dependent relationship between *servitour* and *maister*. They were actually intended primarily as encomia of the king's largesse and power. In one of the longest and most complex of these poems, 'This hinder nycht halff sleiping as I lay' (K. 51) the king is given a flattering allegorical portrayal as 'Nobilnes,' who sends help to the melancholy poet, and whose benevolence is the only remedy for the poet's disease caused by the lack of a benefice. In conclusion, the poet is assured by Patience of the king's 'nobill intent'.[29] Similarly, after a long catalogue of complaints against the decay of the world, 'Quilk to consider is ane pane' (K. 39), James appears in this rather apocalyptic context as

> The formest hoip yit that I have
> In all this warld, sa God me save,
> Is in your grace, bayth crop and grayne . . . (11. 97–9)

---

25 'Blyth Aberdeane, thow beriall of all tounis' (K. 48).
26 Louise O. Fradenburg, 'Spectacular Fictions: The Body Politic in Chaucer and Dunbar,' *Poetics Today*, 5 (1984), 511–12.
27 Helena M. Shire, 'Images of Monarchy: Three Royal Stewarts,' Fifth International Conference on Scottish Language and Literature, Medieval and Renaissance, Aberdeen, August, 1987.
28 See Fradenburg, pp. 498–99 and Joanne S. Norman, 'Image-Making at the Court of Francis I: Rondeaux for Louise de Savoie,' *Proceedings of the Canadian Society for the Study of Rhetoric*, 4 (1991–92).
29 These comments are a reflection of Bawcutt's analysis of the poem, pp. 119–21.

Even at the end of one of the most scathing attacks on false courtiers and unjust patronage, 'Complane I wald, wist I quhome till' (K. 45), Dunbar can still address the king, without any apparent sense of incongruity, as 'prince maist honorable' (1. 67). He goes on from there to ask directly for the king's favour. A clue to this contradiction may be found in comparing the opening stanza of the poem to its conclusion. The poet sees an analogy between the 'God, that all thing steiris,/All thing seis and all thing heiris' who inscrutably allows injustice and evil to exist, and the 'wardlie prince heir downe' who also unaccountably has refused to act. Yet, just as God's grace may bring comfort and justice to a suffering individual, the king may finally reward the poet with his royal favour:

> Bot efter danger cumis grace,
> As hes bein herd in mony plece. (ii. 75–6)

Such poetry is not exclusively or even primarily interested in the person of James IV as an individual. Dunbar is more concerned with constructing a series of visual figures of kingship. Some, like the lion, eagle, and thistle, are allegorical and therefore obviously more abstract.[30] But even the apparently human representations of James IV easily move towards an artificial construct of the ideal king that has religious overtones.

Why does epideictic poetry used in this way seem so distasteful to Wormald and, indeed, to literary critics of Dunbar and other court poets? Perhaps it is the reaction of a modern sensibility that is jaded through continual exposure to media of persuasion dealing with everything from politics to floor polish and a resulting impatience with an attitude that seems naively uncritical. The deployment of religious and moral allegory for political ends, a favourite technique of the 'grands rhétoriqueurs'[31] that is present in Dunbar's allegories of 'The Thrissill and the Rois' (K. 50) and 'The Goldyn Targe' (K. 10), seems to an audience of unbelievers shockingly blasphemous. Poetry and 'high art' should be at least one refuge from a crassly utilitarian function.

However, it is precisely 'utilitarian' ends that poet/orators pursued. They are engaged in representing not a psychological or 'realistic' view of an individual, but rather the figure of the ideal. In providing a living picture of that ideal they encourage the human king to perform or act out the virtues and values necessary for political and social order. Ideology is amplified through these images so that one is deflected away from the personal and the concrete to the public and abstract. Although Dunbar is quite correctly described as 'select[ing] the ingredients of his poems from the flux of actual life,' he is not engaged in the purely mimetic representation of 'real places, people and events'.[32] Indeed, he and his contemporaries seem to have a postmodern awareness that all experience of reality is mediated; that is, we

---

30 'The Thrissill and the Rois' (K. 50).
31 Cynthia Jane Brown, *The Shaping of History and Poetry in Late Medieval France: Propaganda and Artistic Expression in the Works of the Rhétoriqueurs* (Birmingham, AL, 1985).
32 Bawcutt, p. 39.

only know the 'real' through representations of it.[33] The humanists regularly argued for the essential relationship between thought and the language that actualised it:

> For indeed, reason itself lies hidden in the obscure processes of the intellect before it has been drawn forth by speech; it has just so much light or brilliance as the fire hidden in the flint before the iron strikes it: indeed, while it is hidden, no one would think to call it fire.[34]

Richard Lanham asserts in *Motives of Eloquence* that what is at stake for the humanists in metaphors like this one is that language itself creates reality – in practice, multiple realities. Such a consciousness permeates Dunbar's 'Goldyn Targe' (K. 10) that has been described as a poem about language and its limitations.[35]

Therefore, instead of limiting his poetry to a problematic illusion of objective sense experience, Dunbar recreates vivid concrete entities that become progressively generic or symbolic. Andro Kennedy, whatever his now unrecoverable individual historic identity was, has become the traditional drunken goliard. His 'Testament' (K. 38), like most of Dunbar's poetry, is a palimpsest of meanings; local topical references are layered over with a series of literary and cultural allusions until they become progressively more universal and general. In Dunbar's more specific praise poetry, a similar transformation of historic figures occurs through the amplification of a theme in visual metaphors. This technique Finkelstein has identified as the basis for Dunbar's aureate style.[36] Furthermore, the means of representation that he has chosen produce of themselves a particular ideology.[37] 'The Ballade of Bernard Stewart' (K. 35) is one extreme case in which language is used to mediate between an historical figure and the 'golden world.' Although there seems to be good documentary evidence to suggest that the praise of the Lord of Aubigny was merited, as Bawcutt points out, 'we learn more facts from the elaborate title of this "ballade" ' than from the poem itself, which is a tissue of eulogistic commonplaces and traditional topoi as well as apparently imaginary scenes of suitable historic events that never actually happened.[38] Bernard Stewart, like James IV, Queen Margaret, and other courtly personages of power, has been transformed through a dizzying series of hyperbolic analogies into an icon of 'knightheyd' and 'chevalry.' The acrostic in the concluding stanza is an imitation of a favourite device of the 'grands rhétoriqueurs' for whom it served an important symbolic function: 'le nom acrostiché constitue la devise du "dessin" qu'est le poète ou son client, de sorte que le poème entier, d'une certaine manière, en devient la glose.'[39]

33 Linda Hutcheon, *Politics of Postmodernism* (London and New York, 1989), pp. 33–4.
34 Quoted by Streuver, pp. 60–1.
35 John Speirs, *The Scots Literary Tradition*, 2nd ed. (London, 1962), p. 194.
36 Richard Finkelstein, 'Amplification in William Dunbar's Aureate Poetry', *Scottish Literary Journal*, 13, No. 2 (1986), 5–15.
37 See Linda Hutcheon's discussion of Althusser's theories about the politics of representation, pp. 33–4.
38 Bawcutt, pp. 82–3.
39 Zumthor, *Le masque et la lumière*, p. 13.

Although eulogies like this one seem to present at first glance a purely static picture whose generality frees its subject from any ties to a specific person or place, Dunbar is in effect writing for his audience a series of roles to be performed in that most theatrical of milieux, the court. And one of the most prominent of his performers is himself. If there seems to be 'no fixed or immutable relationship between the world in which Dunbar lived and the poetic world that he created,'[40] this fluidity is the largely the result a shifting series of roles that are used to create a self. Rhetorical training during the Renaissance provided an education in politics and social surfaces so that the trained courtier became a 'rhetorical man'; that is, an actor whose reality was public and dramatic and whose self depended on a constant reenactment: 'A rhetorical view of life begins with the centrality of language. It conceives reality as fundamentally dramatic; man as fundamentally a role player.'[41] Such a human figure becomes 'form without content, or rather form as content; style as thought; self-conscious personification rather than sincerity; surface rather than depth; conscious, deliberate unreality; the writer as declared poseur.'[42] For scholars such as Lanham and Greenblatt, Castiglione exemplifies this Renaissance theory of self-construction as a conscious process in which the rhetorical man has no central self but a series of scripts that he acts out.[43] Or as a prominent Elizabethan dramatist expressed it in the mouth of another courtier: 'All the world's a stage,/ And all the men and women merely players:/. . . And one man in his time plays many parts . . .'[44] However, Lee Patterson, H. Marshall Leicester, and Elaine Hansen, among others, recognise the emergence of the 'performative self' in the fourteenth century, primarily in the poetry of that other great court poet, Chaucer.[45]

The effect of such a dramatic view of reality is that all genres are open to be used/abused by the writer while he disappears into his text. Truth is always present in appearances but is also always 'elsewhere'.[46] Lanham has suggested that the self-construction in the Renaissance foreshadows, or is in fact the origin of, the modern awareness of self-representation as essentially problematic. Such self-consciousness tends to foreground the unacknowledged politics, for example, questions of gender, class, and race, that lie behind representations of the self.[47] So in Dunbar's case, we have an extravagant multiplying of selves or roles, from the faithful 'auld hors' to the 'pillie wanton' who 'hoppet' in the 'Quenis chalmer,' to the angelic messenger in 'The Dregy'. These self-dramatisations fluctuate uneasily between what seems to be authentic individual experience and

---

40 Bawcutt, p. 39.
41 Lanham, p. 4.
42 Lanham, p. 222.
43 Greenblatt, Stephen. *Renaissance Self-Fashioning: From More to Shakespeare* (Chicago, 1980).
44 *As You Like It*. II.vii. 139–40; 142.
45 Lee Patterson, ' "For the Wyves Love of Bathe": Feminine Rhetoric and Poetic Resolution in the *Roman de la Rose* and the *Canterbury Tales*,' *Speculum*, 58 (1983), 656–95; H. Marshall Leicester, *The Disenchanted Self: Representing the Subject in the 'Canterbury Tales'* (Berkeley, 1990), and Elaine Tuttle Hansen, *Chaucer and the Fictions of Gender* (Berkeley, 1991).
46 Michel Beaujour, *Miroirs d'encre: Rhétorique de l'autoportrait* (Paris, 1980), pp. 280–1.
47 Hutcheon, p. 40.

rhetorical construct. The question can be summed up by referring to a familiar critical debate: Did Dunbar's head really 'yak yester nicht'?[48] Such self-fashioning may offer an apparently infinite freedom, yet the courtier often found his performance directed according to the 'rules' and his recognition of the limits of role-playing may be seen in self-ironising characterisations like Chaucer's and Dunbar's.

One of Dunbar's most frequently assumed roles – and one that has been frequently commented for its literary effectiveness – is that of the detached onlooker or observer, especially in the dream poems that are among the most elaborate celebrations of the courtly 'fête.' Louise Fradenburg has pointed out how this topos in Dunbar reveals an underlying ambiguity in the poet's position at the court. For one thing, the poet presents himself as often reluctant or recalcitrant to the demands of the occasion. In 'The Thrissill and the Rois' (K. 50) the poet lies sleeping and responds to the demands of 'fresche May' in a rather ungracious manner until he is almost dragged out of bed to perform his duty of creating the golden world appropriate for an epithalamium (ii. 1–49).[49] In 'The Goldyn Targe' (K. 10) the poet insists on his poetic limitations, his inability to write or describe what he sees, even as he does so. Both in this poem and in 'Ane Dreme' (K. 51), Dunbar remains essentially passive and helpless before the action that nevertheless involves him as its central focus. Fradenburg sees these kinds of responses as characteristic of a court poet who must produce a poem 'on demand' for a special occasion yet whose offering must seem to be freely given and spontaneous.[50] In a sense Dunbar gives up expression of his own desire and subjugates it to something 'other,' 'the discourse of sovereignty'. The initial resistance that seems to exist only to be overcome provides a tension in these poems that is a way of acting out Dunbar's political position at court. The topos becomes a vehicle for the subjugation of his individual difference to the totalising discourse of the 'fête.' Such a submission is but another revelation of the power and the glory of the corporate community of the sovereign and his court.

But was Dunbar always the willing accomplice of the court of James IV? What place do his nightmares and satires exposing the dark underbelly of the golden world have in his rhetoric of power? Several critics have recently identified in Dunbar's poetry various motifs that belong to the 'monde à l'envers' or 'carnival' that opposes itself to the dominant court culture or 'official' hierarchy.[51] Dynamic and ironic poetry that speaks in cynical, worldly, or disillusioned tones

---

48 Summaries of the arguments over this poem, 'My heid did yak yester nicht' (K. 21), which seems to have become a 'test case' for determining questions of Dunbar's 'sincerity' or his 'realism' versus his use of convention are summed up in Bawcutt, p. 116, and argued more extensively by Edmund Reiss, *William Dunbar* (Boston, 1979) and Ian Simpson Ross, *William Dunbar* (Leiden, 1981).
49 Fradenburg, pp. 506–7.
50 Fradenburg, p. 506.
51 Deanna Delmar Evans, 'Dunbar's *Tretis*: The Seven Deadly Sins in Carnivalesque Disguise,' *Neophilolgus*, 73 (1989), 130–41, and 'Bakhtin's Literary Carnivalesque and Dunbar's "Fasternis Evin in Hell",' *Studies in Scottish Literature*, 26 (1991); Joanne S. Norman, 'Elements of the Grotesque in William Dunbar's "Dance of the Sevin Deidly Synnis," ' *Scottish Studies* (1989), and Bawcutt, p. 185.

has frequently been treated as more 'authentic' (or at least more enjoyable!) than the static idealisation of the poetry of praise.

However, epideictic rhetoric includes both praise and blame; the poet/orator is simply engaged in another series of roles. Even the frequently asserted, and bleakly powerful, *contemptus mundi* topos or rejection of worldly and courtly values that runs like a black thread through any number of 'moralitees' and 'fantasyis' reflects an essentially rhetorical stance, as conventional in its way as the exaggeratedly positive picture of harmony and order. While the world upside down seems at first to be an instance of extreme transgression of the cultural norms in a hierarchical society, it is dependent upon the official culture that it subverts. It is a *licensed* release[52] that actually engages in a 'complicitous critique'.[53] After all, the most powerful social and economic groups at the centre of cultural power designate what is to be considered 'high' and 'low'; the top must include the low 'as a constituent of its own fantasy life'.[54] Such an ambivalent relationship explains why the carnival always exists within the extremes of a class society and yet never emerges into social action or change.

Dunbar both by profession and, possibly, by birth[55] remained firmly attached to the perspective of the nobility. Donald Mackenzie makes the astute observation that of all Dunbar's Tudor counterparts, the one he most resembles is Surrey in his comparatively confident acceptance of his place at court.[56] His satirical targets are usually those that are opposed to the chivalric and aristocratic values of that class. For example, it is possible to read a subtext in 'The Turnament' (K. 52B) that expresses the illogicalities and contradictions embedded in the practices of chivalry. However, the most obvious point of the poem is a scathing attack on bourgeois pretenders, like the hapless 'telyour' and 'sowtar,' who imitate aristocratic behaviour without any real understanding of its true meaning. Dunbar's most bitter venom seems reserved for a variety of low-born upstarts like the 'pykthank in a prelottis clais' of 'Complane I wald, wist I quhome till' (K. 45) and the *nouveau riche* second husband of the Wedo who suffers appropriately for his misplaced social ambition in the 'Tretis'[57] or declared enemies of James IV like the outlaw, Donald Owyr.[58] Other apparently mocking portrayals of the royal court often contain within them implied praise or compliments, such as 'Ane Dance in the Quene's Chalmer' (K. 28); 'Schir for your grace bayth nicht and day' (K. 25); and even 'The Dregy' (K. 22). A more complex situation obtains in Dunbar's great comic poems, 'The Tua Mariit Wemen and the Wedo' (K. 14), 'The Dregy' (K. 22), 'The Testament of Maister Andro Kennedy' (K. 38), and 'Fasternis Evin in Hell' (K. 52). In the first of these poems, Dunbar begins by inscribing the official or courtly codes that he then opposes. A great deal of the

52 Peter Stallybrass and Allon White, *The Politics and Poetics of Transgression.* (London, 1986), pp. 16–26.
53 Hutcheon, pp. 1–2.
54 Stallybrass and White, pp. 4–5.
55 Bawcutt, p. 6.
56 Donald Mackenzie, 'Review of *Dunbar the Makar,*' *Scottish Literary Journal*, Supp. No. 37 (Winter 1992), 3.
57 'The Tretis of the Tua Mariit Wemen and the Wedo' (K. 14), II. 296–358.
58 'In vice most vicius he excellis' (K. 34).

effect of 'social realism' or apparent 'verisimilitude' in the 'Tretis' depends on genre crossing. The opening frame of the *locus amoenus* evokes the ordered and chivalric courtly world in terms that are almost identical to those employed in the poetry of celebration. However, the assumptions – illusions, if you will – are then undermined by the grotesqueries of the anti-feminist characterisation of the bourgeois female speakers. The rhetorical question posed by the narrator at the end of the poem deliberately blurs the limits between art and life, fiction and non-fiction. The parodies as well must first incorporate and in a way authenticate the very texts and genres that they challenge. In order to do this, Dunbar weaves a network of intertextual allusions between high and low styles and genres including the liturgy, goliardic verse, legal and literary wills and confessions, penitential treatises, estates satire and *sermones ad status*, court masque and dance macabre – all building on and on in an almost infinite series of echoes.

In his skilful deployment of the wide range of discourse allowed within epideictic rhetoric, William Dunbar shows a sophisticated awareness of the political and social currents of his courtly environment. He participates in the creation of the political ideology that the Scottish court shared with its European counterparts. Like his contemporary poet/orators in those other courts, he wrote poetry that uses language to give form and significance to a particular reality – even while acknowledging, indeed, underlining through role-playing its fleeting and illusory nature. Truly, 'thair was nane frackar' than 'Dunbar the mackar'[59] at the 'great game of rhetoric.'[60]

---

59 'Sir Jhon Sinclair begowthe to dance' (K. 28). ll. 22–23.
60 Phrase used by Zumthor in 'The Great Game of Rhetoric,' trans. Annette and Edward Tomacken, *New Literary History*, 12 (1981).

MAURY McCRILLIS III

18. *Narrative Subjectivity and Narrative Distancing in James I of Scotland's* Kingis Quair

Implicit in any discussion of literary subjectivity is the question as to what constitutes the individual and what relationship exists between the individual and the way that it is constructed grammatically. The problem with attempting to articulate a theory of the individual is that any such theory is ultimately dependent upon language for its articulation and is thus, for the poststructuralist at least, always suspect. It might be argued, for example, that an essentialist theory of the individual must posit *a priori* a transcendental notion of self which language may be capable of pointing to but which it cannot define in absolute terms. Similarly, it might be said that a poststructuralist theory which would describe the individual as the ever-shifting nexus of various stabilising and destabilising forms of discourse intersecting with and dissecting one another in a continual process of self-redefinition is itself a theory that is invested with a truth value that proves to be just as elusive as that of the essentialist position. For this reason I will not attempt to articulate a theory of self except to say that it is possible to know oneself, if nothing else, without having to rely upon a theory of the individual at all.

The question as to what relationship exists between the individual and the way in which the individual is constructed linguistically is a far more difficult question to answer and one which perhaps demands the use of theory. However, a theory of the grammatically constructed subject-position in a work of literature need not and, I will argue, ought not invest too much faith in the assumption that what is true of the grammatically-constructed self must necessarily also be true of the author himself or herself.

What I think is important about the struggle between essentialist and deconstructionist/poststructuralist notions of self is that these competing ideas reflect the struggle of the individual author to articulate the self in spite of the polysemous nature of language. In the case of the *The Kingis Quair*, the author's struggle to articulate the self is undertaken first by locating himself within literary tradition by appropriating the conventions of his predecessors for his own artistic purposes and second by synthesising those conventions into something which ultimately differentiates the work from that of his predecessors. The location of the subject within literary convention ultimately for the purpose of distinguishing the self from that convention is, in some respects, complimentary to Caroline Bynum's notion that the rise of subjectivity in the Middle Ages results from the burgeoning of institutionalised forms of life from the 12th century on.

In her essay 'Did the Twelfth Century Discover the Individual?' Bynum argues that the 'intense competetiveness' and the 'growing sense of the positive value to be given to "diversity in unity" ' ultimately contributes to the emergence of the self in twelfth-century literature.[1] The medieval conception of self, however, is not one that is developed in terms of a direct opposition of the individual to institutions, but rather in a willing participation in those institutions.[2] For Bynum, the former, an essentially modern conception of selfhood, ought not be confused with a medieval conception of the self. The medieval conception she defines in two ways that she regards as precise:

> [T]he twelfth century discovers the self in the sense that interest in the inner landscape of the human being increases after 1050 in comparison to the immediately preceding period; second, the twelfth century discovers the self in the sense that knowing the inner core or human nature within one's own self is an explicit theme and preoccupation in literature of the period.[3]

Bynum, however, never adequately explains what she means when she speaks of an 'inner landscape' or an 'inner core.'[4] But then that is not the central focus of her essay. Rather, Bynum is interested in correlating the idea of a discovery of self with the 'proliferation of forms of institutionalized religious life', a proliferation that ultimately leads to an 'articulation of differences'[5] among groups and the acknowledgement on the part of those groups that 'within any religious community there are complementary roles and talents for various individuals.'[6] What is important about Bynum's thesis is that she attempts to balance the essentialist position of the self as *individuum* (indivisible, permanent and unchanging), with the deconstructionist position of the 'decentered subject' who, according to Sarah Kay, is governed by the social codes of language.[7] 'In the twelfth century,' Bynum explains, 'turning inward to explore motivation went hand in hand with a sense of belonging to a group which not only defined its own life by means of a model but also was itself . . . a means of salvation and evangelism.'[8]

In deference to deconstructionist and poststructuralist notions of the self, however, I am inclined to agree that 'deep structures of desire and institutional power that move through and constrain the individual subject'[9] can and ought to

---

1 Caroline Bynum, 'Did the Twelfth Century Discover the Individual?' *Journal of Ecclesiastical History* 31.1 (1980): 5.
2 Bynum, p. 4.
3 *Ibid.*
4 The language here is far from precise, but Bynum attempts to clarify her description of an 'inner landscape' and an 'inner core' by paraphrasing John Benton's 'Consciousness of Self and of "Personality" ' (a paper delivered at RTC Conference) to the effect that 'what the [medievals] thought they were discovering when they turned within was what they called "the soul" (*anima*), or "self" (*seipsum*), or the "inner man" (*homo interior*).' The discovery of the *homo interior*, Bynum continues, was 'the discovery within oneself of human nature made in the image of God – an *imago Dei* which is the same for all human beings.'
5 Bynum, p. 5.
6 Giles Constable quoted in Bynum, 7.
7 Sarah Kay, *Subjectivity in Troubadour Poetry* (Cambridge University Press, 1990), p. 2.
8 Bynum, p. 14.
9 H. Marshall Leicester, Jr., *The Disenchanted Self: Representing the Subject in the Canterbury Tales* (University of California Press, 1990), p. 22.

be revealed. The self and its grammatical constructions are in many ways contingent upon structures of desire and institutional power. However, by contingent, we ought to acknowledge that we are ascribing truth value to propositions that are derived from facts that are apart from the propositions themselves. To confuse contingency with predication, which would imply *a priori* notions of causality in which representations of self are entirely 'based upon' or 'founded upon' structures of desire and institutional power, would be a mistake. Anthony Giddens is, I think, absolutely right when he argues that 'It . . . is necessary to insist that the de-centering of the subject must not be made equivalent to its disappearance' because, after all, 'the modern critique of the subject has not provided a satisfactory account of the agency of the subject.'[10] The idea that the linguistic or – in the larger sense – literary presentation of the self is formed in part by the self as it exists essentially need not be opposed to the notion that the linguistically constructed self is shaped by the rules of language, social codes and institutions, or literary conventions. The opposition between the so-called modern theory of the self and essentialist notions of self is, I think, the result of an unnecessary and egregious encroachment of the former upon the latter.

It is with this prolegomenon that I approach James I's *Kingis Quair*.'[11] Some thirty-two years ago Professor MacQueen wrote that 'Most critical readings of the *Kingis Quair* have emphasized that the narrative is personal' and that each of those critics who have regarded the narrative as such have 'play[ed] down the conventionalism and stress[ed] the realism of the *Quair*.'[12] Nearly a decade later, though, Matthew McDiarmid argued in the introduction to his edition of the *Quair* that,

> Too often critics have considered the poem simply as an attractive collocation of topics, symbolized or conventionalized themes or doctrines to be identified, abstracted, and re-presented with much the same significance as they have in works of a generally similar content.[13]

Interestingly, Mr. McDiarmid then goes on to say that 'recent critics have indeed been reluctant to consider the *Quair* as a personal document at all. They do not actually say that the history it contains is irrelevant but they write as if it were.'[14] Thus, in 1961, when Professor MacQueen published his essay 'Tradition and the Interpretation of the *Kingis Quair*,' he observed how most readings emphasised the personal elements of the text, but by 1973 Mr. McDiarmid had observed that critics have been reluctant to consider the text as personal at all. Both observa-

---

10 Leicester, p. 22.
11 I am in full agreement with John Norton-Smith, ed., *The Kingis Quair* (Leiden, 1981), p. xix, that '[t]he repetitious contesting of James's authorship of *The Kingis Quair* . . . is largely of academic manufacture: *clericus amat mysterium*.'
12 John MacQueen, 'Tradition and the Interpretation of the *Kingis Quair*,' *RES* 12.46 (1961): 8.
13 Matthew P. McDiarmid, *The Kingis Quair of James Stewart* (Rowman and Littlefield, 1973), p. 49.
14 McDiarmid, pp. 49–50.

tions reveal two important qualities about the poem: namely that a remarkably personal subject position is effectively sustained in a highly conventionalised narrative structure. True, there are many instances 'to which a fairly definite conventional and traditional meaning may be attached'[15] but nevertheless, as Gregory Kratzmann notes, 'the narrative of the Scots poem is, from the outset, centered unobtrusively but quite firmly in the experience of one man'.[16]

Michael Cherniss has argued that the inclusion of autobiographical details in the *Quair*, personal or not, is itself attributable to Boethian convention. Cherniss explains that 'one should not lean all too heavily upon the poem's supposedly autobiographical nature' because '[a]ll writers of Boethian Apocalypse from Boethius himself onward claim to be recounting personal experience.'[17] 'Whatever the historicity of the personal experience of King James in the *Quair*,' he explains, 'that experience has been transformed into an artifact composed primarily of conventional literary elements'.[18] Cherniss is, of course, right about this. After all, the *Kingis Quair* is a poem and not a historical narrative. But what Cherniss seems to underestimate in his evaluation of the work is the degree to which this 'spiritual autobiography' or 'allegory of love' finally gains its authority not from antiquity (ie, the authority of the author's predessessors) but from the direct testimony of the author himself. The same, I think, is true of Boethius.

Boethius is preoccupied throughout the *Consolation of Philosophy* with the question of agency in the individual. Lady Philosophy, for example, early in the text asks of the narrator 'whether there is anything more precious to you than your own self' and then goes on to explain that 'if you were in possession of yourself you would possess something you would never wish to lose and something Fortune could never take way.'[19] But the best evidence of Boethius's fundamental concern with the principle of agency in the individual is his attempt throughout the entire fifth book of the *Consolation* to overcome theological fatalism. Theological fatalism effectively eliminates the possibility of free-will in the individual if only the necessary and seemingly harmless premise is granted that God is omniscient.[20] The problems faced by the removal of the property of individual agency are numerous. To remove free-will is to make Boethius's suffering unbearable, his impending execution meaningless, Theodoric ultimately inculpable, the possibility of achieving salvation hopeless, and the writing of the *Consolation* itself pointless. To eliminate free-will is to eliminate the self, since

15 MacQueen, p. 8.
16 Gregory Kratzmann, *Anglo-Scottish Literary Relations, 1430–1550* (Cambridge University Press, 1980), p. 38.
17 Michael Cherniss, *Boethian Apocalypse: Studies in Middle English Vision Poetry* (Pilgrim Books, 1987), pp. 193–4.
18 Cherniss, p. 194.
19 Boethius, *Consolation of Philosophy*, trans. V.E. Watts (London, Penguin Books, 1969), p. 63.
20 For a detailed outline of the argument for theological fatalism, see S. Cahn, *Fate, Logic, and Time* (Yale University Press, 1967), p. 69. Briefly stated, if one grants that God is omniscient and, thus, that God knows at T1 (t = time) that a person X will do action A at T2, then X must do A at T2 since to do otherwise would be to confute God's foreknowledge. To be able to confute God's foreknowledge, though, effectively means that God is not omnisicient. In order to have free-will, though, X must be able to choose to do A at T2 or not to do A at T2.

the property of agency is the essential quality that defines the self for Boethius.

While James's situation does not seem to have been as dire as was Boethius's, nonetheless he has undertaken the similar task of contemplating his own imprisonment. The Boethian concern with the question of the extent to which events are governed by either God's will or chance is apparent to some degree early in the poem, but what is interesting is that that larger philosophical issue only very gradually becomes a central concern in the poem. James first recollects details from his own life, specifically how at about the age of ten he left Scotland for France, supposedly under the advisement of his caretakers, Bishop Wardlaw, Walter Forstare, and Sir David Fleming:

> Noght ferr passit the state of innocence
> But nere about the nowmer of yeris thre –
> Were it causit throu hevinly influence
> Of goddis will or other casualtee
> Can I noght say – but out of my contree,
> By thair avise that had of me the cure,
> Be see to pas tuke I myn auenture. (*ll.* 148–54)[21]

The question as to whether circumstances are controlled by God's will or some other contingency is more closely examined in the dream vision when Minerva explains that '. . . sum clerkis trete/ That all your chance causit is tofore/ Heigh in the hevin' (*ll.* 1016–18) and 'other clerkis haldin that the man/ Has in himself the chose and libertee/ To cause his awin fortune' (*ll.* 1023–7). Outside of the context of the author's own experiences, however, the question bears little relevance. It is the author's experiences that are central to the text:

> Vpon the wawis weltering to and fro,
> So infortunate was us that fremyt day
> That . . . quhethir we wold or no
> With strong hand, by forse (schortly to say)
> Of inymyis takin and led away
> We weren all, and broght in thair contree.
>   (*ll.* 162–7)

It is certainly indicative of James's knowledge of Boethian convention that the particular detail of 'the wawis weltering to and fro' is reminiscent of Boethius's use of similar metaphors such as the 'storms of life . . . surging up the weight of care'[22] and Boethius's 'commit[ting] [his] boat to the winds'[23] and the 'north wind churn[ing] the deep with raging storms and mad unrest.'[24] However, the

---

21 James I of Scotland, *The Kingis Quair*, ed. John Norton-Smith (Leiden, 1981). All quotes are taken from this edition of the poem.
22 Boethius, p. 37.
23 Boethius, p. 55.
24 Boethius, p. 61.

artistic effect that is achieved by evoking the image of the ship tossing at sea does not ultimately lie in how reminiscent of Boethian convention it is, but rather in how it, like Boethius's philosophy, functions in relating the experiences of the author.

John Norton-Smith regards those instances in which James relates his individual experiences as instances which reflect the 'amateurish quality' of the *Quair*.[25] Yet surely the development of the authorial subject in the *Quair* is no more amateurish than what G.L. Kittredge regards as the ridiculously obtuse dreamer in the *Book of the Duchess* who 'understands nothing, not even his dream'.[26] James's development of the author's personality as author is definitely 'a literary quality quite distinct from that of Chaucer',[27] but I don't think that it's quite distinct because of James's 'unsophisticated delight in a direct, easily communicated sense of the enjoyment of experience'.[28]

The development of the author's personality as author strikes me as a deliberate misreading of Chaucer and Chaucer's very skilful development of fictional personae.[29] I think that James wants the reader to ponder whether the opening of the poem is some sort of 'literary preface' as C.S. Lewis explained or 'something prefixed to the main body of the poem' which sets the theme as Professor MacQueen explains.[30] He seems to want the reader to question whether his poem is allegorical or autobiographical, whether it's a courtly romance, a Menippean satire, or a *consolatio*, or even whether it's a narrative or lyric poem, precisely because such attempts to define the poem ultimately lead the reader right back to the subject position as author. Rather than undertake his literary project for the purpose of locating himself within literary tradition, he locates literary tradition within himself by appropriating the conventions of his predecessors for the purpose of illustrating his own experiences both past and present.

Were the autobiographical details of the *Quair* just a conventional means of making a transition to the Boethian themes of the poem, it seems that James would have used the earlier opportunity presented by the narrator's inability to sleep to make such a transition. He does indeed begin with Boethius, but not with a *consolatio* 'full of fruyte and rethorikly pykit' (*l*. 45). Interestingly, he begins with various biographical details concerning Boethius's own life. James explains that the book he read was 'Compilit by that noble senatoure . . ./ [Who] from estate by Fortune . . . Foriugit was to pouert in exile' (*ll*. 17–21). It is noteworthy that

---

25 Norton-Smith, *The Kingis Quair*, p. xiv.
26 G.L. Kittredge, *Chaucer and His Poetry* (Harvard University Press, 1970), p. 49.
27 Norton-Smith, *The Kingis Quair*, p. xv.
28 *Ibid*.
29 Harold Bloom, in *The Anxiety of Influence* (Oxford University Press, 1973), p. 5, argues very persuasively that 'strong poets make [poetic history] by misreading one another, so as to clear imaginative space for themselves.' The strong poets, Bloom states, are 'major figures with the persistence to wrestle with their strong precursors . . . Weaker talents idealize; figures of capable imagination appropriate for themselves.' While James, like all of the Scottish Makars of the High Middle Ages, remains marginalised in a profession that is overwhelmingly Anglo-centric, he strikes me as being a strong poet.
30 MacQueen, p. 119.

James chose the epithet 'noble senatoure' here rather than philosopher. The epithet is I think suggestive of James's identification with Boethius's role as a political figure and his identification with the misfortune that sometimes befalls those who hold such office. James does not initially identify with Boethius as Neo-Platonic philosopher but as 'worthy lord and clerk' (*l.* 22).

Little attention is paid early on to Boethian philosophy except insofar as it relates to Boethius's own fall from prosperity into misfortune. 'Therefore,' says James, 'I lat him pas, and in my tong/ Procede I will agayn to my sentence/ Of my mater, and leue all incidence' (*ll.* 47–9). Yet he is not able to dispense with Boethius entirely because as he reflects upon his own life he discovers how Boethius's misfortune is similar to his own. And after he has fully reconsidered his own individual predicament the philosophical and theological questions of the *Consolation* become more significant to the poem. For example, he first reflects upon his own imprisonment and explains how,

> Without confort, in sorowe abandoun . . .
> Quhare as in ward full oft I wold bewaille
> My dedely lyf, full of peyne and penance. (*ll.* 171; 176–7)

He realises how his own grief is analogous to that of Boethius 'who once composed with eager zest/ [and was] driven by grief to shelter in sad songs'.[31] Moreover, Boethius's lament 'First fickle fortune gave me wealth short-lived, Then in a moment all but ruined me'[32] also begins to take on added significance in the context of James's own experiences.

To say, then, that James's development of the subject position as author is the one quality of the poem that is unfortunately amateurish and unsophisticated is to imply that the poem would be more professional and more sophisticated perhaps – and by implication successful – if only James had developed a more ambiguous subject position like that of Chaucer where, according to Norton-Smith, 'style and poetic manner . . . are always the result of a calculating intelligence'.[33] That notion strikes me as being one step removed from the notion that James would have been a better poet if only he were Chaucer. Yet what is remarkable about James is how he is unlike Chaucer. While he does recommend his book to Chaucer and Gower, and while the influence of Lydgate and Boethius and others is indisputable, he is not finally memorable because of the ways in which he resembles any of them but in how he appropriates them to create 'sum newe thing to write' (*l.* 89).

What I think is problematic about the poem lies in that part which Norton-Smith seems to find most successful – the dream vision. What is problematic about the dream vision is that the grammatical subject in the dream is obfuscated by the aesthetic distancing that is required for the allegorical effect. That is, the

---

31 Boethius, p. 35.
32 *Ibid.*
33 Norton-Smith, p. xv.

'I' of the poem in the allegory needs to be objectified in order for the reader to fill the space assigned for the subject otherwise the didactic function of the allegory will be lost. The more developed the allegorical journey toward an understanding of the relationship of love and wisdom to God's law becomes, the more difficult it is to regard the 'I' of the poem as successfully sustaining its earlier position as the centre of the poem. The first person position, gradually uprooted from the factual experiences of the author, begins to slip away from the author himself toward that of a more ambiguous persona who is suddenly 'araisit vp into the air, Clippit in a cloude of cristall clere and fair,/ Ascending vpward ay fro spere to spere/ Through air and water and hote fyre' (*ll.* 524–7).

At the same time, however, the subject position in the dream vision becomes ontologically indistinguishable form the personified abstractions. 'Of gude folkis that fair in lufe befill,' the narrator says, 'There saw I sitt in order by thame one/ With hedis hore, and with thame stude Gude Will/ To talk and play' (*ll.* 554–57). Along with Good Will is Courage 'amang the fresche folkis yong' (*ll.* 559) and Repentence 'degysit in his wede' (*l.*564) as well as the 'blynd God Cupide' (*l.* 654) and so on. The objective distancing is accompanied by various details which constantly refer back to James himself. Venus, for example, explains that 'the cause of thyne inward sorowe/ Is noght vnknawin to my deite' (*ll.* 729–30). She is not referring to an objectivised sorrow felt by an objective narrator. She is referring to the inward sorrow that James speaks of earlier in stanza 25 (*l.* 171).

We can be reasonably sure, too, that the James that Venus is speaking to when she says that he must question those who have been negligent in obeying her laws when he descends to the ground again (*l.* 799) is the same James from the beginning of the poem. The grammatical subject, it seems, struggles to maintain a position 'half sleeping and half suoun' (*l.* 510) somewhere between personal experience and philosophical abstraction, between action and contemplation. Yet what is true of Troubadour lyrics is also true of James's dream vision: 'reorienting the allegory around the subject position erodes the distinction between inside and outside, self and other.'[34] In doing so, though, it 'problematizes notions of the self'[35] because 'establishing an 'individual' ground for allegory does not produce a stable and coherent account of "individual" psychology.'[36]

James finally relocates the grammatical subject of the dream vision firmly in the author's personality as author and the poem ends where it begins – with the author. Awakening he says, 'there with sone, I dressit me to ryse,/ Fulfilld of thoght, pyne, and aduersitee' (*ll.* 1219–20). He then contemplates the significance of his dream, asking 'Is this of my forethoght impressioun,/ Or is it from the hevin a visioun?' (*ll.*1224–5).

It would be nice to think that James was the first poet to experiment with subjectivity in his writing, but his experiment would still be remarkable if he were

---

34 Kay, p. 55.
35 *Ibid.*
36 Kay, p. 53.

among the first to experiment in the vernacular with a tradition that had been developed primarily by the Troubadours and later by the Northern French Trouverses. Whether James's attempt at articulating the self in the *Quair* was in any way influenced by Northern French tradition or whether that influence possibly came through Lydgate is largely a matter of speculation.[37] All that we can reasonably assume at this point is that James spoke French both because 'Henry IV was alleged to said that there was no need for the boy to go to the continent for lessons in French, as he himself could teach that language' and because 'both his mother and his brother corresponded in that tongue.'[38] The concurrence of King Charles and Queen Isabeau to the alliance with Henry V that was formed by the murdered son of the Duke of Burgundy, and the subsequent marriage of Henry to Catherine in 1420[39] may have provided James with an opportunity to examine some of the poetry of Northern France. Norma Goodrich goes as far as to speculate that since James was a poet 'one might suppose that he and Duke Charles had a bond.'[40] The question as to whether each had any influence on the poetic style of the other is a subject that needs to be considered in detail.

James's sophisticated use of convention and the traditional meaning that may be attached to such convention should not be underestimated. One the other hand, though, the emergence of the subject as author in the text should also not be underestimated. Yet neither need be mutually exclusive. The self as it exists essentially and the self as it is constructed linguistically are separable in concept but actually constitute a unified whole.

---

37 H.J. Chaytor, *The Troubadours and England* (Cambridge University Press, 1923), p. 120, notes that 'when we consider the close political and commercial relations existing between England and Southern France, it is reasonable to assume that some influence was directly exerted [on English lyrics] by Provencal lyric poetry.'
38 Gordon Donaldson, *Scottish Kings* (B.T. Batsford, Ltd., London, 1967), p. 63.
39 Ranald Nicholson, *Scotland: The Later Middle Ages* (Harper and Rowe, 1974) p. 250.
40 Norma Goodrich, *Charles, Duke of Orleans: A Literary Biography* (New York, 1963), p. 131. Whether such a bond may have influenced James's poetic style or even whether there was a bond at all is again purely a matter of speculation.

ANNE M. McKIM

19. *The European Tragedy of Cresseid: the Scottish Response*

The title of my paper is of course prompted by the recently published book of essays, *The European Tragedy of Troilus*, edited by Piero Boitani. Few would disagree that there's also a European tragedy of Criseyde: as early as the fifteenth century the Scottish poet Robert Henryson articulated precisely this aspect of the story of the ill-fated lovers when he composed *The Testament of Cresseid*. and identified his work as a 'tragedye'.[1] The contributors to Boitani's book concentrate on the personal fate of Troilus, the central importance yet changing significance of his death in almost all versions of his story from antiquity on. The sometimes radical changes to the end of the Troilus story prove, Boitani concludes, that 'after antiquity the end of the story is felt to be unsatisfactory, disturbing, and hence open to debate and reinvention.'[2]

The most significant innovation to the Troilus story was the introduction by Benoit de St. Maure and his imitators of Brisseida/Criseida and the love-and-betrayal plot which not only complicated the story but changed the sense of Troilus's tragedy from an epic to a romantic one.[3] Chaucer's role in introducing this European figure into English Literature, and from there into Scots, has long been recognised. It was clearly Chaucer's portrayal of Criseyde that inspired Henryson to compose a tragedy in which he graphically presents her suffering and death as a companion piece to the English poet's tragedy of Troilus, and the account there of his suffering and death.

The nature of Henryson's tragedy has been the subject of a number of studies which have explored the *Testament* as a tragedy in the Boethian sense of a fall from prosperity to misery, as a Senecan tragedy, and in his article, 'Henryson's "Tragedie" of Cresseid', Steven R. McKenna has described the heroine's progress as a 'downfall into enlightenment' and Cresseid herself as a tragic figure 'who must not only discover, but must bear the burden of her own identity'.[4] My focus is narrower: how the *Testament* and another late medieval Scottish poem derived from Henryson's poem, offer quite radical responses to, even revisions of, the Troilus story.

The Testament of Cresseid is unmistakably a reworking, a reinventing, of the ending, specifically the fifth book, of Chaucer's five-book *Troilus*. While in a number of respects Henryson's poem picks up and develops Chaucer's account,

---

1 *The Poems of Robert Henryson* ed. Denton Fox (Oxford, 1981), line 4. All subsequent quotations from the *Testament* are taken from this edition.
2 *The European Tragedy of Troilus* ed. Piero Boitani (Oxford, 1989), p. 299.
3 Boitani, p. 281.
4 *SLJ*, 18 (May 1991) p. 29.

notably with respect to Cresseid's fate in the Greek camp, he makes some changes to his source, the most remarkable of which is to *ignore* Troilus's death so that a poignant last meeting between the two former lovers can take place. Not only is this a particularly striking instance of reinventing the ending of the received story, but radical in that Henryson's concern with 'the consequences to herself of Criseyde's infidelity, and her end,'[5] means Cresseid becomes the focus of narrative interest and her death provides the poem's climax.

Indeed the death of Cresseid is such a notable feature of Henryson's poem that the title by which it has been known, since at least the early sixteenth century when it was first printed,[6] *The Testament of Cresseid* (even though strictly speaking her final will or testament occurs only at the end of the poem), clearly prepares readers for this significant narrative event. It is not without interest then that the one other surviving, but less well-known late medieval Scottish version of the tragedy of Cresseid also has a title that portends her imminent death. This is *The Laste Epistle of Creseyd to Troyalus*, a late sixteenth- or early seventeenth-century poem preserved with others in the same hand in one of the gatherings in the Hawthornden MSS collection held in the National Library of Scotland, which contains works by Drummond of Hawthornden as well as poems and prose by his uncle William Fowler (c. 1560–1612) and others. In his edition of William Fowler's works, Henry Meikle attributed *The Laste Epistle of Creseyd to Troyalus* to Fowler, but in the category 'Poems of Doubtful Authenticity', largely because the hand in which it is written is not the poet's.[7] While authorship of the poem has yet to be established, there are strong grounds, assessed by Meikle, for accepting it as a Scottish work.[8]

The Laste Epistle of Creseyd was clearly inspired by Henryson's *Testament*. As the title suggests, this poem takes the form of a final letter, rather than a will or testament, supposedly written by Creseyd just after the last meeting of the lovers so vividly imagined and presented by Henryson. Like the *Testament*, the *Laste Epistle* presents Cresseid's perspective, one might even say her retrospective account of the events associated with the end of her relationship with Troilus, and it culminates in her death. There's also an obvious debt to Chaucer. In the English poet's work a number of letters are exchanged by the lovers, which may have given the author the idea of composing a final one in the series. More than that though, *The Laste Epistle* is largely a reworking of the endings of the two earlier works, a sophisticated and remarkable achievement, considering that the author requires only 305 lines to accomplish this, 305 lines that resonate with quite specific allusions to Henryson's *Testament* and Chaucer's *Troilus*.

The purpose of this paper is to consider whether these Scottish works which respond to the European tradition, and specifically to Chaucer's version, of the Troilus and Criseyde story by according to Cresseid the status of tragic heroine

---

5 Anna Torti, 'From "History" to "Tragedy": The Story of Troilus and Criseyde in Lydgate's *Troy Book* and Henryson's *Testament of Cresseid*' in *The European Tragedy of Troilus*, p. 171.
6 By Francis Thynne in *Chaucer's Workes* in 1532.
7 *The Works of William Fowler*, 3 vols. STS, 6,7,13 (1914–40), vol. III, pp. xlvi-xlvii.
8 Vol. III, pp. 31–3.

and which apparently provide us with her viewpoint, offer what Jill Mann has called 'imaginative retrievals . . . [of] the female perspective'.[9]

In contrast to other medieval versions of the love-and-betrayal story, including Chaucer's, in which Criseyde is, as one critic has put it, 'something that happens to Troilus',[10] in Henryson's poem the focus is very much on Cresseid's reactions to her experience, voiced reactions at that, most notably in her outcry against her gods, her complaint in the leper hospital and, most powerfully of all, her testament.[11]

While 1/4 of the lines in the poem are spoken by Cresseid, all of the lines in the *Laste Epistle* are Creseyd's. There is no frame, no narrator to mediate her words. Her viewpoint is presented just as the epistles of Ovid's classical heroines, in the *Heroides*, on which the *Laste Epistle* is evidently modelled, express their perspectives. There's a strong sense of immediacy, a dramatic quality, about her monologue which invites the reader to see things from her point of view, to share her feelings as she writes this letter.[12] In other words, both these Scottish works explore the potential pathos of Criseyde's situation and in doing so they develop more fully than any previous accounts what has been recognised as 'an abiding element in the stories of Criseyde.'[13] In Benoit and Chaucer the heroine's interior monologues enlist a good deal of sympathy for her plight when she finds herself, against her will, in the Greek camp and importuned by Diomede, but in various ways from Benoit's 'constant interruptions to the narrative . . . [which] impugn any good motive she might conceivably have had'[14] to Chaucer's more subtle and ironic commentary on Criseyde's thoughts and conduct, her position has been undermined.

Recently in an essay on Shakespeare and the tradition of complaint, John Kerrigan noted there was a resurgence of female-voiced plaints or laments at the beginning of the sixteenth century, most of which were by male authors, and E. Talbot Donaldson has also reminded us 'that the origin and development of Criseyde has [sic] been exclusively the work of males'.[15] Indeed, one could regard Henryson's memorable depiction of himself as the elderly writer of Cresseid's

---

9 Jill Mann, *Geoffrey Chaucer* (London & New York, 1991), p. 16. She argues that in *The House of Fame* and *The Legend of Good Women* Chaucer, influenced by Ovid's *Heroides*, rediscovers Dido's viewpoint in the *Aenead's* essentially male heroic story.
10 Jennifer Strauss, 'To Speak once more of Cresseid', *Scottish Literary Journal* vol 4, no. 2 (Dec. 1977), p. 8.
11 Douglas Gray has noted 'The ending of the poem has a peculiar nobility and force. Cresseid becomes an active figure again – if only to write her testament and to prepare for death'. *Robert Henryson* (Leiden, 1979), p. 205.
12 John McKinnell has made the interesting observation that Criseyde's final letter to Troilus in Chaucer's poem actually manages to distance us from Criseyde's thoughts largely because 'we see the letter as received by Troilus, not as Criseyde is writing it (whereas we are shown Troilus writing his letter V, 1303–16)'. 'Letters as a type of formal level in *Troilus and Criseyde*', *Essays on Troilus and Criseyde* ed. Mary Salu (Cambridge, 1991), p. 88.
13 'Briseis, Briseida, Criseyde, Cresseid, Cressid: Progress of a Heroine' in *Chaucerian Problems and Perspectives* ed. Edward Vasta and Zacharias P. Thundy (London, 1979), p. 11.
14 *Ibid.*, p. 6.
15 Introduction to *Motives of Woe: Shakespeare and 'Female Complaint'. A Critical* Anthology (Oxford, 1991), p. 1; 'Briseis, Briseida, Criseyde, Cresseid, Cressid: Progress of a Heroine', p. 4.

tragedie in the opening lines of the *Testament* as a particularly apt image of masculine construction of the feminine.[16]

Framed plaints frequently exploit the differences between the usually male narrator's frame and the reported voice of the female so that, as Kerrigan has explained, 'these differences are . . . developed in ways which depend integrally on gender':

> When these settings are employed, a potentially infinite complication, by virtue of the speaker's ambiguous and the narrator's reporting stance, ensues. The plaintful subject becomes an object, the narrator's 'I' a refracting medium. . . . It is the pregnant difference between reported voice and the script that conveys it (through a narrator) to the world which underpins contrasts between lamenter figures, and the 'I's who describe them.[17]

Cresseid's voice in the *Testament* is conveyed to us through just such a refracting medium, in a way, I believe, that exploits the contrasts more than the often remarked resemblances between the narrator and Cresseid. The narrator as writer reports her angry outcry against Venus and Cupid, her complaint in the leper house, and finally her testament.

While gender-based contrasts are less likely to occur in unframed plaints, like letters, subversion of the female speaker remains a possibility when the writer is male. Ovid's witty 'counter-rhetoric' in the *Heroides* amply demonstrates this. Of further relevance in the present case is the fact that the *Heroides* was frequently used as a model for exercises in persuasion in the Middle Ages, so a letter written as the *Laste Epistle* so clearly is in this style, might draw attention to itself as an essay in persuasion. An awareness of the model also suggests the irony inherent in the betraying woman, Creseyd, uttering the kind of epistolary lament long associated with betrayed women because of the *Heroides*. Moreover, if such betrayed and abandoned women can be parodied by Ovid, as a recent study of the *Heroides* cogently argues,[18] one wonders whether a figure who from her creation was regarded as a type of inconstancy could ever be sympathetically presented by poets working in the medieval and Renaissance tradition.[19]

Laying aside for now the question of subversion of female speakers in poems by male poets, one can see how, with no mediating narrator, the *Laste Epistle*

---

16 In the *Testament*, as a number of readers have noticed, Henryson 'develops a portrait of his narrating and creating persona in a way which ultimately suggests the resemblance between his experience and that of Cresseid's [and] raises the possibility of the text being read as an old man's view of the subject . . . [as he] makes her end merely a reflection of his experience'. Lesley Johnson, 'Whatever happened to Criseyde? Henryson's *Testament of Cresseid*' in *Courtly Literature: Culture and Context* ed. K. Busby and E. Kooper (Amsterdam, 1990), p. 319.
17 *Motives of Woe*, p. 11.
18 Florence Verducci, *Ovid's Toyshop of the Heart* (Princeton, 1985). See especially the chapter on *Heroides* 3, Briseis to Achilles, pp. 98–121.
19 Gretchen Mieszkowski, 'The Reputation of Criseyde 1155–1500', *Transactions of the Connecticut Academy of Arts and Sciences* vol. 43 (December, 1971), 71–153, p. 87.

consistently offers Creseyd's point of view. Much more remarkable still is that the poem explicitly presents Creseyd's perspective on, and challenging of, the literary tradition, the male rhetoric, which has both created and destroyed her reputation.

Chaucer's Criseyde, like Benoit's Briseida before her, laments in one of her best-knowm monologues that her good name can never be retrieved.[20] Henryson responds by having his narrator defend Creseid against her detractors and accuse the men responsible of destroying her reputation with 'scornfull language' (86), but in a way that defies readers to take his exculpation at face value.[21] The author of the *Laste Epistle* makes a further contribution to the issue of Creseyd's literary representation as an essentially destructive process, and it's to this that I wish to turn in the second part of my paper.

At the beginning of the poem, Creseyd is presented as not only the speaker in the poem, but as the composer of this verse epistle. After a conventional greeting to her erstwhile lover, she refers to her closing life and the writing of this final letter as simultaneous in a play on the word, 'lynes':

> Healthe, healthe to worthy Troylus dothe
>   His sometyme Creseyd send,
> If so she may whose lothed lyfe
>   and lynes at ones must end.
>
> $(1-4)^{22}$

The conventional idea that her life is a fragile line is developed a short time later in the references to the two fates, Clotho and Lashesses, who spin and the third fate, Atropos, who evetually cuts, the 'fatall threid' (11–16),[23] but then a more novel idea is introduced as Creseyd's 'lynes', the verse letter itself, challenge all those other reproachful lines written by male poets 'Faire Creyseydes treuthe to blame' (26).[24] She welcomes her death, regretting only that she has lived long enough to become a woman, convinced that it would have been preferable to have died a child, devoured by 'some sauage beaste' or been returned prematurely to the earth's 'wombe', than to suffer the more dreadful savagery of 'cruell

---

20 *Troilus and Criseyde*, V, 1054–64 ed. Larry D. Benson, *The Riverside Chaucer* (Oxford, 1988). *Roman de Troie*, 20238–41, 20255–62 ed. Léopold Constans, Sociéte des Ancíens Textes Français (Paris 1904–12).
21 Mieszkowski, pp. 138–40.
22 Cf. Hugh Holland in Prefatory verses to Shakespeare's first folio (1603) cited in *OED* s.v. *line*:
Though his line of life went soone about,
The life yet of his lines shall neuer out.
23 Cf. similar references in other contemporary Scottish works, *The Testament and Tragedie of King Henry Stewart* (1567) ed. Sir John Graham Dalyell, *Scottish Poems of the Sixteenth Century* (Edinburgh, 1801), line 161, and in another work in the same hand as *The Epistle* in the Hawthornden Mss., XIII, f. 26^r, an elegy, edited by Meikle, vol. I, p. 367.
24 According to the *MED line* occurs in the sense of a row of written letters as early as 1000, and specifically in the sense of writing or verse by 1390. Although the earliest recorded use of *lynes* meaning a letter is 1647, it is not unlikely that it was a synonym for letter long before then: it occurs in the sense of written message or record in the fifteenth century (*Alexander*, 1932) according to the *OED*.

goddes' and unkind poets alike (16-24).[25] Because these relatively merciful deaths were not her fate, because, in other words, she became a woman, poets have accused her of inconstancy in undeniably anti-feminist terms. Creseyd complains that she is classed with other 'ladyes falce', her name becoming synonymous with falseness in love so that men, thanks to the poets who perpetuate the image of Creseyd as fickleness personified, can upbraid other fickle women by citing her as a bad example:[26]

> Then should no poet haue the cause
>   Faire Creyseydes treuthe to blame,
> nor after this with ladyes falce
>   Remember Creysedes name;
> Ne yet no mann his fickle dame
>   With Creysed should vpbraid,
> Nor by examples bringe me in
>   How Troyolus was betrayde.
>   (25-32)

One can of course regard her as merely self-pitying here, but as Jill Mann has argued in her discussion of the famous lines in Chaucer's *Troilus* (V, 1057-67) which inspired the view expressed by Creseyd here, the writer's responsibilty for the literary fiction that is Creseyd is also effectively foregrounded.[27]

In the *Testament*, Cresseid makes discernable progress from blaming others – her gods, Fortune, fate – to eventual self-blame in the testament itself; in the *Epistle* she could perhaps be seen as attempting to minimise her own guilt – after all 'fair Creyseydes treuthe' was not irreproachable! – by blaming the very poets who invented and perpetuated her crime. But, while the pseudo-defence of Cresseid by Henryson's narrator had served to highlight how morally questionable his sympathy was, this challenging of the received literary representation of Criseyde by the figure herself contributes to a sense of her autonomy and prepares the reader for a perspective which is uniquely hers. And in her account of the exchange for Antenor we have a particularly clear instance of how her viewpoint is carefully recuperated, or retrieved, by the author of the *Laste Epistle*, from Chaucer's *Troilus*.

In Book V of *Troilus and Criseyde* the exchange of Criseyde for Antenor is seen entirely from Troilus's point of view: we are told of his wretchedness and suffering as Diomede leads Criseyde's horse off towards the Greek camp (39-40); we are privy to his thoughts, and the questions he asks himself about why he does not

---

25 Cf. Ovid's Briseis, who in her letter to Achilles wishes the earth to open and swallow her in its gaping mouth (*devorer ante, precor, subito telluris hiatu*), line 63. Text, with translation, by Verducci, *Ovid's Toyshop*.
26 C. David Benson discusses 'chauvinistic' Renaissance English works 'in which [Criseyde] usually appears only as a horrible *exemplum* with which the poet can threaten his lady or console himself when he has been played false.' 'True Troilus and False Cresseid: The Descent from Tragedy' in *European Tragedy*, ed. Boitani, p. 165.
27 *Geoffrey Chaucer*, p. 17.

prevent the departure of his beloved (40–9); and we are treated to the narrator's sympathetic views, in the form of replies to these self-same questions. Troilus apparently fears that Criseyde could be slain in the tumult that would be precipitated by his intervention at this point (53–59). We are given *no* idea of Criseyde's state of mind, her thoughts and feelings; significantly, the only word she utters in Chaucer's acccount is 'allas' (58), the cry of countless hapless women in medieval lyrics; she has, after all, no choice: 'But forth she moot, for aught that may betide/Ther is non other remedie in this cas' (59–60). Once the despondent Troilus rides off, Chaucer turns to the thoughts and then words not of Criseyde, but Diomede (92–175), and again the muteness of Criseyde is striking:[28]

> Criseyde vn-to that purpos lite answerde.
> (176)

Lines 109–72 of the *Epistle* re-enact the same scene, but from Creseyd's point of view. There are clear echoes of the *Troilus* in Creseyd's imagined questions to the absent Troilus:[29]

> Howe could thy knightly harte consent,
>   Or eyes abyde the sight,
> To see me vnder DIOMEDES guarde
>   From TROY to GREIKES so stray?
> Why slewest thou not thy mortall foe,
>   And fled with me awaye?
> (111–16)

She seems partly to identify with *his* suffering as he watches her departure and partly to reproach him with her question about his failure to prevent this by dispatching Diomeid and escaping with her. In this version *she* provides the answer, one different from Chaucer's yet influenced by the English poet's depiction of Criseyde's belated appreciation of the extent and steadfastness of Troilus's nobility and possibly too by Henryson's wording of his Cresseid's similar acknowledgement of Troilus's 'gentilnes', especially his solicitude for the 'opinioun' of 'all wemen' (556–7):

> No, thou extemed myne honour soe,
>   Myne honestye to blott
> Thou was affrayde, or ellis thou shouldst
>   Haue done it well, I wote.
> (117–20)

---

28 Barry Windeatt in his edition of *Troilus and Criseyde* (London, 1984) notes how selectively Chaucer represents Criseyde's response to Diomede so as not to incriminate her in the way Boccaccio does. See his note to V, 183–9.
29 Cf. *Troilus* V, 46–47, 78, 92. There are also echoes of lines which occur later in Book V: 173, 932, 934, 1025, 1471–93.

Then follow *her* impressions and reaction to Diomeide's first attempt at seduction on the ride into the Greek camp, impressions imbued with resentment arising from Diomeide's subsequent callous treatment of her:

> For thou no sooner tooke thy loue
>   Of me, nor from me went,
> When DIOMEDE with his sleated lipps
>   Hathe faste my bridle hent.
> And then he sharpes his subtill will,
>   And faste his brayne he fyles,
> And tipps his tongue with RETHORICKS sweit,
>   Bewitchinge me with wyles,
> And layethe me forthe his loue alonge,
>   he no persuasion spares.
> Sometymes he Piteous tears dothe shedd,
>   Some tyme as madd he stayres;
> Then dothe he bragg of Parentes stout,
>   And in these eares of myne
> He ringes me out his royall race,
>   And tells his stately lyne.
>
> (121–36)

It is interesting that Creseyd sees herself, as many other female speakers in complaints and laments saw themselves, as the one who is left by her lover. No sooner is she placed in this vulnerable position than the wily Diomeide with his 'sleated lipps' moves into the offensive – the art of seduction is here represented as a carefully-laid strategy involving military-like preparations of the necessary weapons: his words.[30] Not only is the tenacious will of Diomeide effectively conveyed, but the art of persuasion itself, from the 'Rhetoricks sweit' and deceit, to the carefully devised performance requiring tears and mad stares, is also brutally exposed.

Creseyd recalls being little impressed by Diomeide's various efforts to win her over: all his talk, she says, simply went in one ear and out the other (149–50), but she is moved to confess that before they reach the Greek host, she succumbed to his entreaties 'T'accept him as my seruant' (159). With bitter regret she craves Troilus's forgiveness for the unseemly haste with which she yielded to Diomede. However one may choose to regard her remorse here, it is worth noting that Creseyd represents herself as, on the one hand a woman cajoled by the 'painted wordes' (161)[31] of Diomeide and, on the other hand, as weighed down by what she imagines to be the 'cursinges' (171) of Pandarus brought on her head by her inconsistent conduct towards her two suitors.

30 There is possibly an echo of Chaucer's depiction of Will, as the daughter of Cupid, in Chaucer's *Parliament of Fowls*, lines 214–16.
31 Cf. *Troilus*, II, 424 where Criseyde accuses Pandarus of employing 'all this painted proces' in his attempts to persuade her to consider Troilus as her lover.

The reader is inevitably reminded on the one hand that the seductively 'painted wordes' of Diomeide were all too soon succeeded by his 'cursinges', what Henryson called the 'lybell of repudie' (74) or bill of repudiation by which Diomeide expelled Cresseid from court, a prelude to the retributive 'cursinges' of the predominantly male gods in the *Testament*; and at the same time the allusion to Pandarus and the part he played in Troilus's courtship of Criseyde recalls the 'painted proces' he too had employed and reinforces the suggestion that Cresyd has been the object of male rhetoric, the language of seduction or praise on the one hand, and the language of denunciation or blame on the other.[32]

The fate of the character Cresseid mirrors her fate at the hands of the various poets who created, inherited and embellished her story. The object of their occasional praise and frequent blame, she has also been freely passed among these male poets in a literary exchange. Yet the *Laste Epistle* manages to set alongside the established image of Criseyde the betrayer another view: that of Cresyd betrayed, betrayed and ultimately destroyed by male rhethoric, the kind that tips the tongues of Pandarus and Diomede and then conveys the vengeful sentence of Saturn and the other gods. That same power of the male word is then attested by Creysed in her epistle, when she alludes to the poets and other men who destroy and will continue to destroy her name.

Which brings me back to Creseyd's word and the issue of *her* point of view. That her literary representation has been largely if not exclusively the work of men becomes a crucial consideration. The *Laste Epistle* is a poem of 'doubtful authenticity', but for reasons Henry Meikle may not have had in mind: hers is not an authentic female voice but is part of a fictional construct in which the female voice of Creseyd is impersonated, probably by a male poet, just as Henryson more obviously is the ventriloquist in the *Testament*. Elizabeth D. Harvey, in a study of ventriloquism in the poetry of Donne, has argued that such fictional reconstruction of the Other, of the feminine voice 'functions as a poetic enactment of the mechanism of censorship at work within the broader cultural context'.[33] In western patriarchal culture what is censored is women's speech, which of course many clerical writers in the Middle Ages regarded as being as 'untrustworthy as her sexuality.'[34]

Cresyd's word, like the original female betrayer Eve's, was identified by Guido of Colonna and John Lydgate, for example, with the double-tongued speech of the serpent. What Sidonie Smith, writing on the poetics of women's autobiography, has said of Eve, is equally true of Criseyde:

> The father's curse successfully denies her the authority of her own word as the medium through which to articulate her desire. Subject to the authority of her

---

32 In the *Testament* Cresseid is effectively exiled from the community by a process that begins with the exchange of prisoners and ends with her death as a leper.
33 'Ventriloquizing Sappho: Ovid, Donne, and the Erotics of the Feminine Voice', *Criticism*, Spring 1989, Vol. XXXI, No. 2, 115–38, p. 129.
34 A phrase Lee Paterson uses in an essay on feminine rhetoric and the Wife of Bath, *Speculum*, 58, 3 (1983), 656–95, p. 657.

husband, Eve, and after her all women, will be the object of male representation and will thereby be recuperated as the mother of the phallic order.[35]

So, while it seems to me that the *Testament* and the *Epistle* do reconstruct or recover Cresseid's perspective, these 'imaginative retrievals', to come back to Jill Mann's expression, cannot and do not aim to provide an authentic female voice. In the *Testament* Cresseid's voice, her speaking, is not only transmitted by a male narrator but is enclosed within a frame in which that narrator introduces himself as the writer of her tragedy and brings his account to an end with a reminder of his role as maker of this 'ballet' (610). Within that frame, however, Cresseid is presented as a woman writing when 'with paper scho sat doun,/ And on this maneir maid her testament' (575–6). This image of Cresseid as woman writing is in turn taken up and adapted by the author of the *Laste Epistle*, who, like his predecessor, understood that the privileged position of writer could only be safely assigned to an abject and dying woman.

The *Testament*, and the *Epistle* may not offer us feminine rhetoric, but the female perspective they provide suggests that the words of men – Hector, Pandarus, even Troilus, and the arch example Diomede – cannot be trusted. So even while the traditional function of Cresseid was to show that her words, and all women's words, were not to be trusted, both works raise interesting questions about whether poet's words are to be trusted or relied on. The last word has to be Henryson's, or to be precise, his narrator's:

> Quha wait gif all that Chauceir wrait was trew?
> Nor I wait nocht gif thia narratioun
> Be authoreist, or fen ʒeit of the new
> Be sum poeit, throw his inventioun
> Maid to report the lamentatioun
> And wofull end of this lustie Creisseid,
> And quhat distres scho thoillit, and quhat deid.
>
> (64–70)

---

35 *A Poetics of Women's Autobiography: Marginality and the Fictions of Self-Representation* (Bloomington and Indianapolis, 1987), p. 30.

R.D. DREXLER

20. *Cresseid as the Other*

Gretchen Mieszkowski argues in her monograph *The Reputation of Criseyde: 1150–1500*[1] that Robert Henryson was working within a well articulated tradition when he wrote *The Testament of Cresseid* and for that reason the poem does not represent anything new. Specifically she is arguing against the article by Hyder Rollins, *The Troilus – Cressida Story*,[2] in which he implies that Henryson's poem was, indeed, something new and was responsible for the tradition that made Shakespeare's *Troilus and Cressida* an 'unattractive play.' In this article I would like to argue that Henryson's poem is new but not in the way Hyder Rollins thought, that the *Testament of Cresseid* changed the way we look at the character of Cresseid and was the harbinger of a distinctively modern way of looking at character generally.

Mieszkowski, after she has discussed Henryson's poem, turns back to Chaucer's treatment of the story and argues that Chaucer's treatment of Criseyde[3] depends on understanding that she is a type, the 'false Criseyde who takes pleasure in loving two men,'[4] and thus Chaucer's treatment, while it seems more sympathetic on the surface, is in fact firmly a part of the false Criseyde tradition. While I agree with Mieszkowski about the tradition,[5] I think that the fact that Criseyde is false is not what is most important about her in either Chaucer's or Henryson's treatment.

Chaucer, it seems to me, was working inside two traditions – anti-feminist satire, as Mieszkowski recognises, and courtly love – and that this is crucial to how he treats Criseyde. Criseyde is false, and, in so far as Chaucer is working within the anti-feminist tradition, he is at pains to show her so, but more importantly he is working with the courtly love tradition. Chaucer does not take either tradition very seriously, and he creates a narrator who is completely overwhelmed by the courtly love aspects of the story; thus Criseyde is viewed sympathetically even though she takes little time in breaking her vows to Troilus

---

1 Gretchen Mieszkowski, 'The Reputation of Criseyde, 1155–1500', *Transactions of the Connecticut Academy of Arts and Sciences*, 43 (December, 1971), pp. 71–153. Hereafter referred to as *Mieszkowski*.
2 Hyder E. Rollins, *The Troilus-Cressida Story from Chaucer to Shakespeare*, PMLA, XXXII (1917), pp. 383–429.
3 I will use the convention of spelling Cresseid's name differently when referring to different treatments of the story. Thus Henryson's character is Cresseid, Chaucer's Criseyde, and Shakespeare's Cressida.
4 See Mieszkowski, p. 102.
5 I should note, however, that her sense of the tradition depends on rather arbitrary chronological limits. The seed of the story in Homer supposes a quite different Criseyde and the subsequent treatment by Dryden in 1679 views her quite specifically as virtuous.

once she is with the Greeks. Troilus' 'male suffering,' because of Chaucer's detachment, is made to look more than a little foolish.

Henryson, on the other hand, while he is familiar with anti-feminism, is much more concerned with a Cresseid caught up by fortune, or, as it comes out in the poem, the play of opposites, and with the Christian tradition of repentance and redemption. The entire poem is framed as an elaborate play of opposites. The weather at the beginning is 'doolie' even though readers of Chaucer might expect just the opposite from the information that 'Aries [was] in middis of the Lent'.[6] The planetary gods are carefully paired opposites – Saturn against Jupiter, Mars against Phebus, Mercury against Cynthia – and Venus, the odd planet both in number and because of her relationship to Cresseid, is portrayed as an opposite in herself. She is dressed in 'ane half grene, the vther half sabill blak,' (1.221) and 'ane eye lauch, and with the vther weip.' (1.231).[7] Cresseid herself, in terms of this concern, is interesting to Henryson primarily because her transformation from a lady of 'greit fairnes and all . . . bewty gay' (1.313) to a leper whose face is 'ouirspred with spottis blak' (1.339) conforms to this pattern. Henryson is also greatly interested in the traditional pattern of sin, recognition of sin, confession, repentance, and redemption and how well he can make the Cresseid he discovered in the anti-feminist tradition conform to that pattern. I suspect that some of the apparent inattention to detail for which Henryson has been taken to task is because he is interested in these wider patterns and not narration as such.[8] For example, Henryson tells us that after Diomeid 'had all his appetyte' he sent Cresseid 'ane lybell of repudie' which caused her to 'walkit vp and doun' 'amang the Greikis air and lait' as a prostitute. (II. 71–84) In the next stanzas, however, Henryson gives the impression that Cresseid 'passit far out of the toun' immediately after being repudiated and went to her father's 'mansioun' because when he asks her why she has come, she says: 'Fra Diomeid had gottin his desyre/He wox werie and wald of me no moir.' (II.92–102). It seems that Henryson wants to get Cresseid to the 'secreit orature' where she can have the vision of the planetary gods which brings on her leprosy and that this is the reason he gets he out of town immediately. On the other hand the general pattern of the poem – the play of opposites – leads him to show her falling from felicity in the arms of Diomeid into despair as a common prostitute. That this general pattern seems to conflict with the narrative purpose at this point is ultimately not important for the poem. The fact that Chaucer is much more careful about narrative details is an interesting difference between the two poems but nothing more.

6 All quotations are taken from *The Poems of Robert Henryson*, ed. Denton Fox (Oxford: the Clarendon Press, 1981).
7 See Jill Mann, 'The Planetary Gods in Chaucer and Henryson', *Chaucer Traditions: Studies in Honour of Derek Brewer*, ed. Ruth Morse and Barry Windeatt (Cambridge: Cambridge University Press, 1990), pp. 91–106 for a further discussion of this pattern.
8 See for example the exchange between J.A.W. Bennett and Peter Godman in J.A. W. Bennett, 'Henryson's' *Testament*: a flawed masterpiece', *Scottish Literary Journal*, I(1974), pp. 5–16 and Peter Godman, 'Henryson's Masterpiece', *Review of English Studies*, 35:139 (August, 1984), pp. 291–300.

There is, however, a difference between the two poems that is important. Henryson, in fact, has done something with the character of Cresseid that has never been done before. In order to see this we need to consider the possible ways to treat her character. In the *Iliad* the daughter of Chryses, Chryseis, is a point of conflict between the Trojans and the Greeks. Chryses, who like Calchas is a priest of Apollo, wants his daughter returned, and Apollo in support of his wish rains 'foul pestilence' on the Greeks until they force Agamemnon, who has taken Chryseis, to return her. Agamemnon subsequently takes Briseis from Achilles, occasioning his anger and withdrawing from the battle. The two names Chryseis and Briseis suggest the Briseida in Benoit de Sainte-Maure's poem *Le Roman de Troie*, the first (c. 1155)[9] version of the Troilus and Cressed story, and the subsequent confusion between the names – Briseida and Criseida, the spelling Boccaccio adopts in his version of the story *Filostrato* (1336), Chaucer's proximate source.

What is important to notice about the treatment of Chryseis and Briseis in the *Iliad* is that neither can be seen as the 'false Criseyde who takes pleasure in loving two men.' Both in fact are women reduced to the status of possessions by the disorder of war. Even in Chaucer's poem it is possible to see Criseyde in this way. When Calchas defects to the Greeks in Book I because he 'knew wel that Troye sholde destroyed be,'[10] he leaves Criseyde in an extremely difficult position. She is the daughter of a traitor, without social or political backing in Troy, and with no real way of protecting herself except through a love relationship but with no way of establishing a relationship that is socially acknowledged. Troilus, we must remember, keeps his affair with Criseyde secret and does not let anyone know of his relationship with her, except Pandarus, even when she is repatriated. One explanation for this is that love affairs according to the strictures of courtly love must remain secret.[11] But the effect of this secrecy from Criseyde's point of view – courtly love always being a male view of love – is that she is left defenseless. When Criseyde is transferred to the Greeks, she is in a scarcely better position. Her father in spite of the fact that he has helped the Greeks is still in their eyes a Trojan and worse yet, since he has defected, a man not to trust. That Criseyde should consider seriously Diomede's expression of interest is a sign of her realism and a symptom of her extremely precarious state. We further need to remember that Troilus offered Criseyde words but little else. Clearly for him, in so far as what he actually does, the return of Antenor in the exchange that sent Criseyde back to her father was more important than the loss of Criseyde. Looked at then from a women's point of view – freeing the poem from the cant of courtly love, a male view of the

---

9 See Mieszkowski for an excellent account of the development of the story and a specific treatment of Benoit.
10 All quotations from Chaucer are taken from *The Complete Poetry and Prose of Geoffrey Chaucer*, ed. John H. Fisher (New York: Holt Rinehart and Winston, 1977).
11 Andreas Capellanus in *De arte honeste amandi* counsels that 'Love increases, too, if it happens to last after it has been made public; ordinarily it does not last, but begins to fail just as soon as it is revealed.' See Andreas Capellanus, *The Art of Courtly Love*, trans. John Jay Parry, ed. Frederick W. Locke (New York: Frederick Ungar, 1957), p. 27.

centrality of male suffering – Criseyde has not in fact behaved badly. We need to remember that Chaucer tells us that his interest in the story is

> The double sorwe of Troylus to tellen
> That was the Kyng Priamus sone of Troye,
> In lovynge, how his aventures fellen
> Fro wo to wele, and after out of joye,
> My purpos is, er that I parte fro ye.
>
> (I, 1–5)

Chaucer is interested in male suffering and not the difficulties of Criseyde. Chaucer, however, allows Criseyde to remain recognisably herself. This is also true of the earlier versions of the story by Benoit, Guido de Columnis[12] and Boccaccio. They all disapprove of Criseyde and tell us so but allow us to see her as herself. This is not true of Henryson's treatment of Cresseid in *The Testament of Cresseid*.

Mieszkowski points to 'a change in Cresseid's attitude towards herself as the central event' in the poem and admits that this 'material is not suggested in any of the earlier versions.'[13] This must strike most readers of her monograph as an odd comment since Cresseid's leprosy would seem to be the 'central event' of the poem as well as the most obvious change in the tradition.[14]

At this point I would like to have recourse to the concept of the Other in order to make clear what I think is revolutionary about Henryson's treatment of Cresseid. The Other occurs in texts when 1) one character or set of characters is portrayed in terms of what a second character or set of characters is not[15] or when 2) one character or set of characters is portrayed not as a character in her/himself but as a character seen in terms of the fears and insecurities of another character or set of characters in the same work. Thus in Herodotus' history of the Persian wars the Scythians are portrayed as what the Greeks are not, and in *Beowulf*, to illustrate the second definition, Grendel and Grendel's mother are quite clearly 'indigenous peoples,' as we might say, who are unhappy about Hrothgar's marauding band having decided that Grendel's traditional hunting grounds would be a good site for a hall and who do not share common customs, or language, with Hrothgar and his men. (The scop tells us that they do not pay 'fea

---

12 See a summary of Guido's treatment in Mieszkowski, pp. 89–93.
13 See Mieszkowski, p. 132.
14 Cresseid's death is introduced earlier as is suggested by poems from which Mieszkowski quotes. In a short poem by Lydgate, *That Now is Hay Some-Tyme Was Grase*, he says of Cresseid, in a list that also incudes Polixene, Helen, and Dido, that 'dethe came laste and can disdeyne/Their freshness, and made them full base.' She also quotes a similar *memento mori* passage from a poem by Charles d'Orléans. See Mieszkowski, pp. 128–9. Leslie Johnson points out that Cresseid's 'leprosy . . . literally produces the conditions of old age' suggesting that the *memento mori* tradition may indeed have been an intermediate step between Cresseid as a false, fickle woman and Cresseid as a leper. See Lesley Johnson, 'What happened to Criseyde? Henryson's' *Testament of Cresseid: Courtly Literature: Culture and Context*, ed. Keith Busby (Amsterdam: Benjamins, 1990), p. 314.
15 See Francois Hartog's discussion of otherness in *The Mirror of Herodotus* (Berkeley: University of California Press, 1988), pp. 61ff.

þingian,' that is, *wergild*, see l. 156). As a result they are seen in the poem as the embodiment of the fears of the sea-faring peoples that are the audience and at the centre of the poem. They attack from the land at night. They live under the sea. They inflict night-mare like damage. They cannot be communicated with or appeased, and they are entirely outside the norms of civilised society as Hrothgar's men defined them. This affects how they are depicted in that they are not given faces or human bodies, and emotions that would normally be praised – Grendel's mother's desire to revenge her murdered son, Grendel's desire to protect his hunting ground – are discounted.

The Other is not always negative. Beatrice for Dante and Laura for Petrarch are also manifestations of the Other. In these cases, the fears and insecurities of the two poets conjure up women who by their very perfection alleviate the poet's fears and insecurities. Or looked at in another way the two poets incorporate the two women in their symbolic systems in such a way that their essential nature is entirely understood from a male point of view. Another way to look at how the Other functions is to see that when character is seen in its own terms we say that a person is more or less good, more or less bad. The Other causes a radical disjunction to occur between the terms more or less so that when character is seen as the Other it is either more or it is less but never more or less.

The matter of the 'poleist glas' (1.348) into which Cresseid looks after she has been turned into a leper is a good point at which to start our examination of how this concept of the Other illuminates Henryson's treatment of Cresseid.[16] Understanding this episode depends on our appreciating the role played by narcissism in ego formation and love.[17] Narcissism, Julia Kristeva argues, is 'the means for protecting that emptiness . . . which is at the root of the human psyche.'[18] Cresseid makes clear in her *Complaint* that her identity has been determined by her narcissistic attachment to her own beauty. When she embarks on the *ubi sunt* section of the *Complaint*, we see that she has seen herself in terms of the material possessions that have reflected, like the 'poleist glas,' her self love:

> Quhair is thy chalmer wantounlie besene,
> With burely bed and bankouris browderit bene;
> Spycis and wyne to thy collatioun,
> The cowpis all of gold and siluer schene,
> Thy sweit meitis seruit in plaittis clene
> With saipheron sals of an gude sessoun;

---

16 See the debate over this mirror in J.A.W. Bennett, pp. 5–16 and Godman, pp. 291–300. Bennett argues that 'an oratory is an unlikely place to find a mirror' (p. 6) and Godman counters that by saying that the mirror serves the purpose of 'provok[ing] a sense of tragic paradox' whatever the likelihood of its being in an orature (p. 293).
17 See the discussion of this point by Julia Kristeva in her essay *Freud and Love: Treatment and its Discontents*, trans. Leons S. Roudiez, reprinted in *The Kristeva Reader*, ed. Toril Moi (New York: Columbia University Press, 1986), pp. 240–71.
18 Kristeva, p. 242.

> Thy gay garmentis with mony gudely goun,
> Thy plesand lawn pinnit with goldin prene?
> All is areir, thy greit royall renoun!
>
> Quhair is thy garding with thir greissis gay
> And fresche flowris, quhilk the quene Floray
> Had paintit plesandly in euerie pane,
> Quhair thou was wont full merilye in May
> To walk and tak the dew be it was day,
> And heir the merle and mawis mony ane,
> With ladyis fair in carrolling to gane
> And se the royall rinkis in thair ray,
> In garmentis gay garnischit on euerie grane?
>
> Thy greit triumphand fame and hie honour,
> Quhair thou was callit of eirdlye wichtis flour,
> All is decayit, thy weird is welterit so;
> Thy hie estait is turnit in darknes dour . . .
>
> My cleir voice and courtlie carrolling . . .
> My pleand port . . .
>   (ll. 416–37, 443, 446)

I have quoted at length because what Cresseid says about herself is so telling. She describes her 'chalmer' and the 'garding' in great detail before she gets to what is obviously the central issue, how she has been deformed by leprosy. She even sees herself as being part of the garden 'callit of eirdlye wichtis flour' and not as a person herself. Before she actually talks about what has happened to her physically in lines 443 and 446 she laments her loss of 'hie estait.' By extension we can see that her love for Troilus was based not on character traits in her or in him but rather on the fact that Troilus reflected in his admiration of her her own love for herself. Thus her character before she is afflicted by leprosy has been determined by the narcissism that acts to protect the emptiness 'at the root of the human psyche'.

 The punishment inflicted on her by the planetary gods, therefore, is not really a case of the punishment being the crime stripped of its glamour, as it is in Dante, for example, but a complete destruction of her personality. She has been rendered nothing or, to put it another way, she has become the Other (in the first sense of the term) to herself. We notice when Cynthia 'red ane bill on Cresseid quhair scho lay,' in the process describing her for us as readers, we get what amounts to an anti-blazon:

> 'Thy cristall ene mingit with blude I mak,
> Thy voice sa cleir vnplesand hoir and hace,
> Thy lustie lyre ouirspred with spottis blak,

> And lumpis haw appeirand in thy face:
> Quhair thow cummis, ilk man sall fle the place.
>
> (ll. 336–41)

The blazon of the courtly love sonneteers was, of course, an attempt to make the women which it described more than she was while this anti-blazon makes Cresseid less. (Shakespeare's blazon 'My mistress' eyes are nothing like the sun' works to defeat the blazon by restoring the woman described as more and less.) We also notice that this antiblazon recognises its purpose because after describing Cresseid it makes clear that her presence now will make all men 'fle the place.'

The reason, then, why Cresseid's first act after she has awakened from 'this doolie dreame, this vglye visioun' is to look into the 'poleist glas' to find out whether she exists.[19] The fact of her non-existence is underlined by two things which subsequently happen. After she has realised that it was a mistake 'with my goddis for to chyde,' a child 'come fra the hall' knocks at the door of the orature. This child has been often praised because its appearance underlines the pathos of the scene. But more importantly the child appears because the play of opposites demands it. Leprosy has made Cresseid in effect old which in turn demands that someone young appear. Cresseid is now 'maculate' which calls forth the child 'immaculate'. But also Cresseid has ceased to exist in her father's household and has been replaced. This is made clear immediately after when she meets her father. He is clearly unhappy. He is described as 'wringand his handis, oftymes said allace/That he has leuit to se that wofull hour' (ll. 373–4), but he does nothing else except think that there is 'na succour'. Indeed somewhat later we are told that she must '3eid/Fra place to place, quhill cauld and hounger sair/ Compellit hir to be ane rank beggair' (ll. 481–3).

When we make recourse to the construct of the Other, it is clear why all this has happened. In Chaucer's version of the story, which Henryson claims to be continuing, Troilus was the one who suffered from not knowing who he was. When we first see him in Book I, he is like a school boy with his friends making fun of girls, love and lovers. He falls in love suddenly, because of his total inexperience. When he enters a temple his eyes search through the 'rout' and:

> His eye percede, and so depe it wente
> Til on Criseyde it smot, and ther it stente.
>
> And sodeynly he wax therwith astoned,
> And gan hire bet biholde yn thrifty wyse.
> 'O mercy God,' thoughte he, 'wher hastow woned,
> That art so fair and goodly to devyse?'

---

19 Douglas Gray in *Robert Henryson* (Leiden, E.J. Brill, 1979), p. 193, points out that Venus is often seen as 'that 'self-regarding goddess' and depicted as looking at herself in a mirror. He reproduces a picture of Venus with a mirror from Rawlinson MS D. 1220 f. 31v in the Bodleian Library in plate 10. Subsequently as he pointed out on p. 199, Cresseid urges others to 'ane mirrour mak of me' (1, 457) in order to know who they really are as they approach death.

> Therwith his herte gan to sprede and ryse,
> And softe sighed lest men myghte hym here,
> And caught ayen his first pleyinge chere.
>   (I, 272–80)

Unlike Cresseid he has not fallen in love with a narcissistic projection of himself, and for this reason he has no defence against Criseyde. This of course is the pathology generally of the man in the courtly love tradition. Troilus' lack of defense is made clear subsequently in Book III when he becomes so overwrought with emotion – 'the sorwe so his herte shette' – that he 'fel al sodeynly aswowne' (III, 1086, 1092), and in Book V, after he is convinced that Criseyde has betrayed him, how Chaucer has him killed in a line – 'Despitously hym slowh the fiers Achille' (V, 1086), as if there was really nothing left to kill.[20]

Henryson has created Cresseid to right the excesses of the courtly love tradition, to speak to the fears of vulnerability and non-existence (the second sense of the Other) to which the treatment of male amatory feeling in the courtly love myth give rise. Henryson resurrects Troilus:

> That samin tyme, of Troy the garnisoun,
> Quhilk had to chiftane worthie Troylus,
> Throw ieopardie of weir had strikken doun
> Knichtis of Grece in number meruellous;
> With greit tryumphe and laude victorious
> Agane to Troy richt royallie thay raid
> The way quhair Cresseid with the lipper baid.
>   (ll. 484–90)

Troilus is now bathed in 'greit tryumphe and laude victorious' and no longer dead on the battle field and, more importantly, Cresseid is quite literally at his feet. We notice that Troilus is no longer the one who faints. Cresseid falls 'doun in ane extasie' in line 141 to signal the beginning of the 'dreame' of the planetary gods, but more importantly to signal the end of Cresseid as a person. After Cresseid is told who the 'chiftane worthie' is whom she sees above her we are told:

> Quhen Cresseid vnderstood that it was he,
> Stiffer than steill stert ane bitter stound
> Throwout hir hart, and fell doun to the ground.
>   (ll. 537–9)

---

20 Troilus' death reminds us of later male victims of courtly love who at the end of the fiction in which they find themselves, will their own deaths – Pechorin in Lermontov's *A Hero of Our Time* and Vronsky in *Anna Karenina* come to mind. Julien Sorel in *The Red and the Black* not only wills his own death but is seen at the end of the novel transformed into the ideal lover for Mathilde, a head without a body, an image of the male fear of what the devouring female, 'la belle dame sans merci' secretly wants to do to every man.

Henryson has transferred this sign of non-existence from Troilus to Cresseid. The often debated section just preceding this where Troilus recognises Cresseid, in spite of her disfiguring leprosy, and Cresseid needs to be told who Troilus is is also made clear by reference to the concept of the Other. The narrator tells us that Troilus recognises Cresseid because

> Na wonder was, suppois in mynd that he
> Tuik hir figure sa sone, and lo, no quhy:
> The idole of ane thing in cace may be
> Sa deip imprentit in the fantasy
> That sa appeiris the wittis outwardly,
> And sa appeiris in forme and lyke estait
> Within the mind as it was figurait.
> (ll. 505–11)

Fox and others explain these lines by reference to Aristotle,[21] but what Henryson has done is given Troilus a psyche that is now intact and unaffected by outward mischance, a psyche radically unlike the one Chaucer pictures him as having. Cresseid, on the other hand, has been destroyed both physically and mentally. There is no longer anything 'deip imprentit in [her] fantasy' and so she is unable to recognise even faces that she knew well a short time ago.

As others have noticed,[22] once Cresseid has been robbed of her identity, Troilus is able to have sex with her on his own terms. When he recognises her he becomes sexually aroused – 'ane spark of lufe than till his hart culd spring/ And kendlit all his bodie in any fyre' (ll. 512–3) – and a disguised version of copulation occurs:

> For knichtlie pietie and memoriall
> Of fair Cresseid, ane gyrdill can he tak,
> Ane purs of gold, and mony gay iowall,
> And in the skirt of Cresseid doun can swak;
> Than raid away and not ane word he spak . . .
> (ll. 519–523)

The unexpected word 'swak' underlines the sexual nature of this act, but what is more striking is the position of the 'lovers'. He is on horseback and she is at his feet. He acts, not out of desperation as he does in Chaucer, but for motives of 'knichtlie pietie and memoriall/ Of fair Cresseid.' In other words the male lover of the courtly love myth whose entire identity depends on his passion for a woman is now able to function confidently. He is able to have sex – albeit rather odd sex – without threatening his identity.

If any reader at this point should think I am overstating my point that

---

21 See Fox, pp. 377–8.
22 See Malcolm Pittock, 'The Complexity of Henryson's 'The Testament of Cresseid'', *Essays in Criticism*, 40:3 (July, 1990), pp. 198–221, especially p. 206.

Henryson's project in this poem is to destroy Cresseid's identity, to turn her into the Other who is less, let me turn back to the trial of Cresseid by the planetary gods. This trial is, of course, a travesty.[23] It is called by Cupid, who, as Cresseid rightly claims and as Chaucer makes clear, caused the problem in the first place. Mercury, whom Henryson tries to support by saying that he was 'honest and gude, and not ane word culd lie' (l. 252) when we know he is the patron of liars, announces that the case will be decided by Saturn and Cynthia, the two gods least sympathetic to Cresseid. (Their choice is also dictated by the play of opposites since they are, as Mercury points out, the 'hiest planeit heir' and the planet 'the lawest of degre.') Saturn is depicted as the opposite of sexuality; the narrator tells us that he 'gave his sentence/ Quhilk gaue to Cupide litill reuerence' (ll. 151-2). Saturn, we also remember, has had considerably difficulty with sex (as shown in his misadventures with his own children) and especially with disobedience. Cynthia is depicted as a kind of leper herself. Her 'haw [was] as the leid' and her cloak is described as 'grey and full of spottis blak' (ll. 257, 260), a description which reminds us of the 'spottis blak' which soon appear on Cresseid's face. What, of course, is happening here is that the forces hostile to sexuality are allowed to judge Cresseid who has lived and known herself only through her sexuality. (Jupiter, who is described as 'nureis to all thing generabill' (l. 171) and 'far different' from Saturn, is excluded. Venus, as I have mentioned, who might have been expected to support sexuality if not Cresseid, is denied her usual identity and seen as 'variant,' more like Fortuna than the traditional Venus.)

The point about all this, however, is not that it is unfair but that the trial is not a trial at all but a ceremony in which Cresseid is stripped of her identity. She emerges no longer the 'false Criseyde who takes pleasure in loving two men' of anti-feminist satire or 'la belle dame sans merci' of the courtly love tradition, but a name with no identity of her own. She has been denied her narcissism which was the foundation of her ability to love.

The ending of Henryson's poem which is usually praised because is allows Cresseid to repent and thus allows her the possibility of redemption is in reality rather sinister.[24] She has been, in the terms we have been using, fully incorporated into the system of symbols Troilus ascribes to, that is that women are false and dangerous when alive and only capable of salvation when dead. (Beatrice and Laura, two good women in the courtly love tradition, are safely dead, or in Laura's case perhaps a symbolic construct from the beginning.) Cresseid is made to say that her body, which was the source of her narcissism and by extension her identity and which was, in Chaucer, the source of her power, is now 'carioun/ With wormis and with taidis to be rent' (ll. 577-8). Her final act is to give Troilus

---

23 See Mairi Ann Cullen, 'Cresseid Excused: A Re-reading of Henryson's *Testament of Cresseid*', *Studies in Scottish Literature*, 20 (1985), pp. 149ff.

24 E.M.W. Tillyard in *Five Poems, 1470–1870* (London: Chatto & Windus, 1948) is the most forceful statement of the argument that the ending of the poem should be taken as a positive setting forth of Cresseid's redepmtion. Many later critics want to agree that the ending is positive but not necessarily Christian. See, for example, Gray, pp. 203ff.

the 'royall ring, set with . . . rubie reid' which had been part of her dowry. What has happened is that Troilus who in Chaucer gave Criseyde gifts because he was in her power (as the lover in courtly love tradition always was), is now in power and receives gifts instead. He has taken back his identity. Significantly it is only after Cresseid actually dies – that is only after Troilus is safe – that he is allowed to feel again the emotions that so wracked his soul in Chaucer's poem. We are told that when he heard of her 'greit infirmitie' 'he swelt for wo and fell doun in ane swoun' (ll. 596, 599).

What Henryson has done with the traditional character of Cresseid is something altogether new. Interestingly it is something that Shakespeare does not do with Cressida. Even in V, ii when Troilus in hiding watches her being seduced by Diomedes she retains her identity; she remains more or less good, more or less bad:

> Troilus, farewell! One eye yet looks on thee,
> But with my heart the other eye doth see.
> Ah, poor our sex! This fault in us I find:
> The error of our eye directs our mind.
> What error leads must err. O, then conclude:
> Minds swayed by eyes are full of turpitude.
> (V, ii, 110–5)[25]

Henryson's treatment, on the other hand, reflects the fears and insecurities that we have come to understand often are used to define character in modern texts. In robbing Cresseid of her identity in order to deal with the fears and insecurities implanted in males by the courtly love tradition, in transforming Cresseid into the Other, Henryson foreshadows an important practice of later writers.

---

25 All quotations taken from *The Compete Works of Shakespeare*, ed. Donald Bevington, 4th ed. (New York: Harper Collins, 1992).

STEVEN R. McKENNA

21.   *Robert Henryson, Pico della Mirandola, and Late Fifteenth-Century Heroic Humanism*

The humanistic idealism put forth by Pico della Mirandola (1463–94) regarding human self-determination, as articulated especially in his *Oration On the Dignity of Man*, was in the European intellectual environs in the latter half of the fifteenth century, though the *Oration* itself was not published until 1496, being composed probably ten years prior in 1486.[1] Pico's fundamental humanistic idealism contains as its essence a human dignity which rests in the human capacity for self-determination. In effect, Pico forwards the notion that we become what we will to be – particularly in the realm of moral freedom. In rewriting the Genesis myth, Pico has God tell Adam that humanity and the soul are godlike and limited only by the individual, that the earthly and mortal confines must be and can be transcended. In recasting the Genesis myth, Pico has God say to Adam,

> 'In conformity with thy free judgment, in whose hands I have placed thee, thou art confined by no bounds; and thou wilt fix limits of nature for thyself . . . Thou, like a judge appointed for being honorable, art the molder and maker of thyself; thou mayest sculpt thyself into whatever shape thou dost prefer. Thou canst grow downward into the lower natures which are brutes. Thou canst grow upward from thy soul's reason into the higher natures which are divine.'[2]

Pico then proclaims,

> Let a certain holy ambition invade the mind, so that we may not be content with mean things but may aspire to the highest things and strive with all our forces to attain them: for if we will to, we can. Let us spurn earthly things; let us struggle toward the heavenly. Let us put in last place whatever is of the world; and let us fly beyond the chambers of the world to the chamber nearest the most lofty divinity. There, as the sacred mysteries reveal, the seraphim, cherubim, and thrones occupy the first places. Ignorant of how to yield to them and unable to endure the second places, let us compete with the angels in dignity and glory. When we have willed it, we shall not at all be below them.[3]

---

1 On the dating of Pico's *Oration* and other works, see Charles Trinkaus, *In Our Image and Likeness: Humanity and Divinity in Italian Humanist Thought* (Chicago, 1970), p. 507.
2 Giovanni Pico della Mirandola, *On the Dignity of Man, On Being and the One, Heptaplus*, trans. Charles Wallis, Paul Miller, and Douglas Carmichael (Indianapolis, 1965), p. 5.
3 Pico, p. 7.

These issues of human dignity comprise only about the first sixth of Pico's *Oration*, the last five-sixths functioning as a defence of his 900 theses on the subject of the unity of all knowledge. Yet an important characteristic of Pico's thinking regarding human dignity is that death represents the key to this transcendence – a transcendence wherein souls can unite with each other and God.[4]

This high humanistic ideal stems from a more general notion that humanity has in its evolution achieved essential equality with God, an idea that owes its origin to Genesis 1:26 where humanity is described as being created in the image and likeness of God.

There is no concrete or convincing evidence that Henryson read Pico, though it is possible, especially considering Pico's notoriety after 1486 when the Church condemned his 900 theses. And if the reference to Cresseid found in 'The Spectacle of Luf' in the Asloan Manuscript is in fact a reference to Henryson's poem, then *The Testament of Cresseid* can be assumed to have been composed in or before 1492.[5] Rather than argue for a direct influence of the Italian on the Scotsman, I intend to show that *The Testament of Cresseid* displays many of the same heroic and humanistic elements as those voiced by Henryson's Italian contemporary – which would suggest Henryson's connection, however proximate or remote, with these intellectual currents on the Continent.

Perhaps the most important figure in this humanistic thinking is Marsilio Ficino (1433–99), who undertook complete translations of Plato and the Neoplatonists. As a result, Ficino's influence spread far and wide in the second half of the fifteenth century.[6] Ficino's philosophy, which is later upheld and epitomised by Pico himself, exalts human greatness in our being the crown of creation and masters of the world we inhabit.[7] Such an emphasis marks the human as the centre of the universe (as the book of Genesis would suggest), and is a hallmark of Renaissance humanism. This is not to say that the medieval preoccupation with the miseries of the human condition were suddenly abandoned for a deified conception of humanity.[8] Rather, the humanistic philosophies that reemerged in the fourteenth and fifteenth centuries due to the rediscovery of the Greeks allowed for an assimilation of classical humanism with medieval Christianity,[9] a point

---

4 Brian P. Copenhaver and Charles B. Schmitt, *Renaissance Philoshopy* (Oxford 1992), p. 167, elaborate on this aspect of Pico's philosophy.
5 The 'Spectacle of Luf' describes 'how quyte cresseid hir' trew luffar troyelus his lang service In luf quhen scho forsuk him for dyomeid And þareefter went common amang þe grekis And syn deid in gret myssere & pane' (*Asloan Manuscript*, ed. W. Craigie. Scottish Text Society, New Series vol. 14 [Edinburgh, 1923], p. 279, 11. 21–4), and claims to be a 1492 translation from a Latin source. This is not necessarily an allusion to Henryson's poem, and may in fact be a reference to a tradition on which Henryson himself drew. On this question of the Asloan Manuscript and Henryson's poem, see Douglas Gray, 'Some Chaucerian Themes in Scottish Writers,' eds. Ruth Morse and Barry Windeatt, *Chaucer Traditions: Studies in Honour of Derek Brewer* (Cambridge, 1990), p. 82.
6 For a discussion of Ficino's influence, see P.O. Kristeller, *The Philosophy of Marsilio Ficino* (New York, 1943), pp. 18–19.
7 Jean Delumeau, *Sin and Fear: The Emergence of a Western Guilt Culture, 13th–18th Centuries*, trans. Eric Nicholson (New York, 1990), p. 163, elaborates on this aspect of Ficino's thinking, especially in regard to Ficino's *De Triplici Vita*.
8 Trinkaus dwells at length on this duality of the concept of humanity.

made as part of Pico's 900 theses. In essence, humanistic philosophy attempted to resolve the givens of life with the Christian conception of human greatness in the cosmos; the optimistic and pessimistic visions had to be harmonised and to an extent were so in a recognition of a god-like human potential. The significant point here is that human life in this world achieved a significance in its own right. The result was an expanded conception of admirable human behaviour and 'a new inducement to faith and religious fervour within a point of view which made the Christian religion compatible with the more human values history had imposed . . .'[10] In other words, in contrast to earlier notions that humanity was incapable of bettering the world, the emergence of humanism brought with it the notion that humanity is charged with the ability and responsibility to improve the world. Otherwise, it won't get done. And Walter Ullmann speculates that this sort of Renaissance humanism emerged in Italy because of the extensiveness of the Church's influence and the intensity of scholarly activities in the mundane matters of human life: law, government and universities.[11]

Professor Jack, in addressing the Italian influences on Scotland, makes several important points regarding Henryson's potential links with the humanistic ideas I've outlined here: Henryson is mentioned in the records of the University of Glasgow in 1462 as being on a postgraduate level; his earlier education may very well have been on the continent, where humanistic thought would have been more pervasive; and at the time there were close links between the University of Glasgow and the University of Bologna.[12] Professor MacQueen even offers the tantalising suggestion of the possibility that Henryson 'was a graduate of an Italian university, and that he may actually have met, or at least sat under, Ficino or one of his disciples.'[13] Though matters of biography such as Henryson on the continent must remain in the realm of speculation, nevertheless if Henryson were indeed trained in law at an Italian university, the humanistic influences of Italian culture would have been unavoidable, just as they were for Chaucer in his diplomatic missions a century or so prior to Henryson.

Furthermore, a continental education would not have been the *sine qua non* of Henryson's exposure to Italian humanism. Chaucer, Lydgate, and Italian writers and philosophers from Petrarch onward would have served such purposes.[14] As

9 See, for example, Beverly Kennedy, 'The Re-Emergence of Tragedy in Late Medieval England: Sir Thomas Malory's *Morte Darthur*,' ed. Anna-Teresa Tymieniecka, *The Existential Coordinates of the Human Condition: Poetic-Epic-Tragic: The Literary Genre* (Dordrecht, 1984), p. 364, who discusses this matter especially in light of the possibilities for the reintroduction of tragedy.
10 Trinkaus, p. 464.
11 Walter Ullmann, *Medieval Foundations of Renaissance Humanism* (Ithaca, 1977), p. 11.
12 R.D.S. Jack, *The Italian Influence on Scottish Literature* (Edinburgh, 1972), pp. 7–8.
13 John MacQueen, 'Neoplatonism and Orphism in Fifteenth-Century Scotland: The Evidence of Henryson's "New Orpheus," ' *Scottish Studies* 20 (1976), p. 86. Cf. also MacQueen's *Robert Henryson: A Study of the Major Narrative Poems* (Oxford, 1967), pp. 17, 20–1.
14 Jack, p. 1–28, cites in detail Scotland's access and links to Italy from James I to the early 16th century. Douglas Gray, *Robert Henryson* (Leiden, 1979), pp. 22–5, likewise discusses humanist influences in fifteenth-century Scotland.

Professor Jack and others have shown, Italian humanism was known in fifteenth-century Scotland (particularly through the works of Poliziano, Valla, Pico della Mirandola, and Ficino), and its influence on the literature was only slightly less pervasive than the influence of French. The evidence for Henryson's direct knowledge of these Italian philosophers is inconclusive, but at the turn of the sixteenth century and shortly thereafter the Italian humanists were widely known in Scotland.[15] Suggestions have been made, though, that the ending of Henryson's 'Orpheus and Eurydice' might be a direct echo of a portion of Ficino's *De Amore*,[16] that the poem itself could be based on Poliziano's version of the story,[17] and that the music of the spheres in the poem derives directly from Plato's *Timaeus*.[18]

Returning to Pico and the lines from the *Oration* I quoted previously, we can detect a dual purpose in his humanism and the tradition out of which it arises: an expanded perception of human nature and its potential is afforded, and this in turn serves to reinforce the worship of God. In other words, inherent in Pico's thinking is the notion that human beings can discover human divinity, linked as it is with the claim in Genesis that we are created in God's image, and the no less profound conception that God is in part discoverable through the human image. The key to this is bound up with the immortality of the soul, its capacities in the afterlife, and the dignity the soul's immortality confers on mortal existence. Since Pico places so much potential, and thus responsibility, in human hands, he thus implies that inherent in human consciousness is the necessity for humanity essentially to create its image of itself, for if we are indeed created in the image of God, we cannot even begin to know the divine and transcendent without first knowing the human – in all its manifestations, from brute to divine, as Pico suggests.[19] Emphasised here is the function of the individual's consciousness and what might be termed the subjectivity of human experience. As Charles Trinkaus has put it,

> The 'dignity of man' . . . was held by Pico to consist in the condition that man was not created as a fixed part of the structure of the universe, but was given a role by God, after the universe itself was completed, of viewing it and admiring its Maker. Man was to be in this view the earthly image of God, and the being that helped the deity maintain the subjectivity of His own being by sharing it to some degree with a creature whose nature was to rise above nature into subjectivity. This subjectivity comprised man's freedom to participate in the universe at whatever level and in whatever condition he chose. Man could debase himself to the pure materiality of the elements, . . . rise with reason to the spheres of the heavens, ascend beyond them to the supercelestial realm of

---

15 Gray, *Robert Henryson*, pp. 24–5.
16 MacQueen, 'Neoplatonism,' pp. 84–5, citing lines 401–4 of Henryson's 'Orpheus' and Ficino's *De Amore* II.323.
17 Jack, pp. 8–14.
18 MacQueen, 'Neoplatonism,' *passim*.
19 Pico, p. 5 (quoted above).

the intelligences or angels, by using his intellect. Here he would closely approach towards becoming akin to God Himself.[20]

Therefore, of no small importance is human will and its ability to control the soul, and in a roundabout way determine fate itself. In other words, Pico implies that the origin for action, wisdom, and human destiny is nothing other than the self – particularly the self endowed with autonomy and charged with the resulting responsibility. The end of such humanistic thinking is nothing less than the recovery of what in the fallen condition has become the lost image of humanity and each individual self. If the edenic fall and original sin represent a form of self-inflicted wound, Pico suggests that the heroic dimension of humanism is bound up in the human attempt to recover a prelapsarian image of a god-like capacity.[21]

How is this to be achieved? Most directly, for the humanists such as Ficino and Pico, a knowledge of God becomes the highest form of human wisdom, and this notion is echoed in Henryson's 'Preaching of the Swallow,' wherein human reason, though inadequate to discover the secret of God, can nonetheless give insight into the nature of God. Specifically, Henryson says that

> Nane suld presume be ressoun naturall
> To seirche the secreitis off the Trinitie,
> Bot trow fermelie and lat all ressoun be.
>
> 3yt neuertheles we may haif knawlegeing
> Off God almychtie be his creatouris,
> That he is gude, fair, wyis, and bening. (ll. 1647–52)[22]

As Professor Kindrick observes, 'This is one of the most humanistic . . . tenets of [Henryson's] philosophy.'[23] Of importance here is the idea that all creation, and not just humanity itself, is in one way or another an image of God.[24]

The drive to recover the image of God, and thus the image of self, is not meant to be seen as retrograde motion, any more than Dante's nostalgia for and attempt to recover Eden can be seen as a movement backward through the physical and spiritual cosmos;[25] nor, I would argue, should Cresseid's blasphemy and longing for her lost love life be so viewed. In fact, Saint Paul in 1 Corinthians 13:12 and 2 Corinthians 5:1–8 describes the feeling of seeing God as a movement forward for the individual, and Pico also views this recovery of the rightful place of humanity

---

20 Trinkaus, p. 506.
21 Richard Neuse, *Chaucer's Dante: Allegory and Epic Theater in* The Canterbury Tales (Berkeley, 1991), sees such a humanistic theme embedded in Dante's *Divine Comedy*.
22 Robert Henryson, *The Poems of Robert Henryson*, ed. Denton Fox (Oxford, 1981). All quotations from Henryson are from Denton Fox's edition and will be cited parenthetically within the text.
23 Robert L. Kindrick, *Robert Henryson* (Boston, 1979), p. 96.
24 For an analysis of this aspect of Ficino's philosophy, see Kristeller, p. 60.
25 Franco Masciandaro, *Dante as Dramatist: The Myth of the Earthly Paradise and the Tragic Vision in the Divine Comedy* (Philadelphia, 1991), elaborates at length on this element in Dante's *Divine Comedy*.

in the celestial hierarchy as an evolutionary movement forward. In other words, the recovery of the human image is bound up with spiritual transformation and growth.

Yet such a movement is not without its risks, for the recovery of the image entails a breakdown of the hierarchical distance between the human and the divine, and it is also a breakdown prompted, as I've suggested earlier, by human consciousness, will, needs and desires. And so the element of the tragic is never far off from the humanistic and the heroic aspects of the search for the image. We can see especially in the case of Cresseid that her desire for a stable and enduring position as Fortune's favorite and for stability in a mutable world lead to a blasphemy which in effect causes the divine to enter into closer proximity with the mortal, thus graphically illustrating such a loss of hierarchical distance – in this case, sin rather than piety being a movement toward an origin (namely Venus and Cupid, who, Cresseid believes, endowed her with the material wherewithal for a rewarding love life). The blasphemy suggests a reaching out for the divine realm and an encroachment or a superimposition by the human onto that realm. In this, Cresseid becomes more like a god, and Cupid's reaction displays a petty and all too human sense of outrage and wounded vanity.

Though Cresseid doesn't really become a god herself, she nevertheless clings potentially heroically to an essentially godlike aspect of her own character – that she is a being who deserves and tacitly demands better treatment from the gods. Her condemnation of Venus and Cupid indicates that rather than abandon the gods she wants instead to intrude on the gods' realm out of her profound sense of frustration and feeling of having been abandoned in and by both the mortal and divine realms. This blasphemy is thus a heroic and sublime act. By directing her ire at the divine realm from within the confines of the mortal sphere, she implicitly indicates that despite the gods' powers to control human reality the individual need not endure fate passively or with deep humility. This action interrogates the nominal powers in her universe, and this interrogation further reinforces the notion that the human subject and the metaphysical object are brought into closer proximity by human action. In short, she rebels against her destiny as she perceives it.

This god-like element of Cresseid's character is vividly portrayed in the portion of her dream where Cynthia and Saturn pass judgement on their victim (ll. 330–343) and shortly thereafter when the leprous Cresseid wakes to her 'sciknes incurabill' (l. 307). The punishment renders Cresseid cold, gray, mottled, and remote from human society. And in addition, at least in appearance she resembles these two gods, just as in her former days she bore a certain resemblance to Venus and Cupid in her amorous affairs. In calling the gods to account as she does, Cresseid effectively (if not literally) meets the gods face to face. In her desire not to accept humbly her lot in life, her actions impose her presence on the gods and attempt to hold them responsible, this based on a human system of values and ideals. In contrast to Pico's heroic notions, Cresseid's heroism is premised on defiance of the metaphysical realm. But what Henryson and Pico share is a vision of humanity attempting to maintain the integrity of the human realm and the self *vis-à-vis* that metaphysical realm. And significantly for Cresseid, the punishment she receives from the gods, assuming that the leprosy is literally administered by real deities, has no apparent overriding effect on her feelings toward the gods or the blasphemy. In fact, her suffering with the disease further brings her inward and further removes the gods from the central concerns of her world. The gods, in effect, become irrelevant to her.

Perhaps the most critical moment in the poem for the general approach I'm pursuing here is the point where Cresseid recovers from her swoon and gazes at her image in the 'poleist glas' (l. 348). Her lament immediately following begins a process wherein she comes to acknowledge and accept her responsibility for her situation:

> Weiping full sair, 'Lo, quhat it is', quod sche,
> 'With fraward langage for to mufe and steir
> Our craibit goddis; and sa is sene on me!
> My blaspheming now haue I bocht full deir;
> All eirdlie ioy and mirth I set areir.
>
> (ll. 351–5)

Here she begins to understand that she bears the burden of being the agent of her destiny, and this finally encompasses more than merely being punished for blasphemy. As her character progresses and develops from this scene onward, she discovers that she has always been the agent of her destiny. Where initially she sees herself as being misled, mistreated and abandoned, after the vision of the gods her self-perception increasingly shifts from passive victim to active participant.[26] This process comes to completion when she in the end learns that the passing knight was in fact Troylus. Castigating herself, she laments:

> 'Thy [i.e. Troylus'] lufe, thy lawtie, and thy gentilnes
> I countit small in my prosperitie,
> Sa efflated I was in wantones,
> And clam vpon the fickill quheill sa hie.
> All faith and lufe I promissit to the
> Was in the self fickill and friuolous:
> O fals Cresseid and trew knicht Troilus!'
>
> (ll. 547–53)

This intrinsic equation of herself with Fortune suggests what I would call a heroic demystification of Fortune as a cosmic determinant that imposes itself on impotent humanity. Cresseid comes to see that she herself is essentially a metaphysical force, or perhaps even more to the point, metaphysical forces are indeed and in fact quite human, that destiny is self-created.

---

26 E. Duncan Aswell, 'The Role of Fortune in *The Testament of Cresseid*,' *Philological Quarterly* 46 (1967), *passim*, points out that in the post-visionary part of the poem Cresseid's actions are described through the use of active verb forms, underscoring her responsibility for her fate. See also Gray, *Robert Henryson*, p. 174.

The blasphemy of the gods functions as a catalyst which sets in motion physical and psychological events that help clarify and elucidate the heroine's character. The blasphemy, both religious and courtly, precipitates the events that get her out of the protection of the Greek camp to a point where she is able to meet Troylus and thus see herself for what she is and what she was before the action of Henryson's own poem begins.

In Henryson's poem, the demystification of the metaphysical realm focuses attention on the heroic capacity in the mortal sphere. In *The Testament* the gods become a reflection of the human, and thus for the human figure to aspire to a god-like stature is for that figure to know the self. In the metaphysical mirror is the self only.

As the poem intimates, in that supreme moment of self-assertion the heroine breaks down the walls between the human and divine realms, and the distinctions are thus for a time levelled. The transcendental conception of Fortune is dismantled by virtue of a metaphysical conflict that undermines the absolute authority of that notion. Its relativity and lack of distinction from the mortal herself offer a partial decoding of its mythological status, hence a demystification of what makes it function. To put it slightly differently, to demythologise the notion of Fortune as a divine and uncontrollable force in the universe is to (re)mythologise the being who dismantles the myths. Furthermore, Cresseid's final disposition and Henryson's treatment of her as an example of how not to behave suggest also that the responsibility for improving human amatory affairs (and by extension all else) in this world is finally a human responsibility.

In sum, I would suggest that as Pico's notions of human spiritual evolution imply a movement of the human to a union with the divine, so Cresseid's blasphemy likewise and paradoxically brings her to a god-like status. For Pico, human dignity derives from the human origin, in theological terms, and from the movement of humanity toward that origin. In other words, for Pico, the soul desires to become God.[27] I would argue likewise that Cresseid's dignity derives from her movement toward the gods that 'made' her, and as a movement toward an origin and a recovery of the image, this becomes no less than a recovery of a conception of the self as being god-like, as being fate itself. The heroic dimension in this, and the potentially tragic dimension as well, is that human striving for the recovery of the image is in effect a striving for the infinite by attempts to overcome the finite, which in human terms can never be accomplished. Desire is always capable of surpassing ability.

Yet the recovery of the image in Pico and in the case of Cresseid is premised on human will. In both cases, autonomy and its resultant responsibility are required. Instead of passive acceptance of the human condition, the recovery of the image is premised on the active superimposition of human will on the self, on the world and on the cosmos. In humanistic terms, the exercise of human will valorises human activity, desire for change, for growth, and implicitly the human

---

27 Ficino's *Theologia Platonica* dwells at length on this idea, and curiously it is not that far from Sartre's existentialist dictum to the effect that 'man is the desire to be God.'

dissatisfaction with the physical and metaphysical *status quo*. For both Pico and Cresseid, passions and desires are fundamental and driving forces in human nature, and there is virtue in acting on desire. This activity allows for transcendence of determinism, for in its god-like capacity human will itself becomes the agent of destiny.[28] As Pico implies in his *Oration* and as Cresseid laments in her blasphemy, humanity does not occupy a fixed place or status in the cosmos. As a result, human apotheosis becomes theoretically possible. For Pico, humanity literally ascends in and through the metaphysical realm. For Cresseid, a collapsing of distinction between the physical and metaphysical occurs and she becomes an object moral lesson situated beyond time at the poem's conclusion. But in both cases, each conception of the self represents simultaneously a transcendence of self in the movement toward union with the image.

For Pico and Henryson, humanity exists in and must function with a struggle for autonomy. In the process, the human image may appear overtly glorious, in Pico's case, or overtly deformed, as is the case of Cresseid's image in the mirror. But what unites these conceptions into a common humanistic and heroic vision of the human image is the notion that the human being embodies the ultimate freedom, and the ultimate burden, of moral autonomy. Both Pico and Henryson hold forth the possibility that the human being can recognise the limitations of existence, and by the supreme act of will overcome those limits. Whether we view such striving as piety or sin is, I feel, ultimately irrelevant. What matters is that in both Pico and Henryson fate is self-inflicted, and because of this humanity bears the responsibility for its own disposition. In both, humanity strives to recover its image, and in doing so strives to achieve a vision of order and freedom – even if this quest is finally doomed to fall short of allowing the human to become God.

The vision of the heroic held by these writers involves intellectual and moral struggle, the battlefield being within the self, with will and desire. The self-mastery and equation of the self with fate both writers value point to the god-like capacity of the human being. More importantly, the recovery of the human image suggests the human ability to construct its image of itself. If such action entails punishment, the punishment does not of necessity invalidate the action, and in Cresseid's case the celestial powers would appear to uphold the limiting structures of the cosmos and balk at the breakdown of difference that Cresseid's blasphemy precipitates. In other words, full realisation of the image may ultimately be denied by the very source of that image. But an important point to keep in mind about Cresseid is that despite the apparent human vulnerability at the hands of divine powers, she 'is the most important creature the planet-gods have to exercise their power on'.[29] In humanistic terms, this suggests a vision of an anthropocentric cosmos, and Henryson's poem can be read as a cosmological displacement in that 'The seuin planetis [descend] fra thair spheiris' (l. 147) and

---

28 In 1494, Pico wrote a lengthy tract against astrology (*Disputations Against Astrology*, published in 1496), the thesis being that because human consciousness transcends the physical reality it cannot thus be subject to that reality.

29 L.M. Sklute, 'Phoebus Descending: Rhetoric and Moral Vision in Henryson's *Testament of Cresseid*,' *English Literary History* 44 (1977), p. 194.

revolve around a human being. In short, the human, not the divine, becomes the center of the universe. Henryson portrays Cresseid as an essentially noble figure who cultivates a benevolent and utilitarian power on the world at large by way of her capacity to suffer and through the truth that suffering reveals. Her actions lead to a realm of higher meaning, and this shows that despite her destruction and death all is not destroyed with her. There remains a conception of fate that rests squarely within the human sphere of action and will, and this becomes part of the divine image of humanity. This displays Henryson's fundamental faith in mortal existence and a possibility for heroic grandeur even if that leads to self-annihilation.

MATTHEW P. McDIARMID

22. *Robert Henryson on Man and the* Thing Present

My previous writings on Henryson have not addressed themselves simply and directly enough to what Matthew Arnold would have called his criticism of life. Henryson sees the common condition of man as one of subjection to the 'thing present', his phrase in that great poem, 'The Preiching of the Swallow' (1865).[1] By this he means betrayal of the forward-looking mind and spirit by the self that sees only present need, real or assumed, present convenience, present desire, a self that if it looks where mind and spirit point, too seldom the case, turns away.

It is a criticism that, as Henryson's poems illustrate, can have a comic, a pathetic, a tragic, expression, and is his dominant theme. Its relevance to our present-day society should be apparent. For us present needs are polluting motor cars and polluting factory chimneys. It was as far back as 1946 that my brother-in-law, the physicist Stanislas Broderick, today famous for his Theory of Probability, informed me that the heating of the planet may now be irreversible. In the previous year I had returned from a war in which the atomic bomb, now outmoded by the nuclear missile, and the terrible potential of that, a present for our grandchildren, was the present need.

Henryson goes straight to his theme in the first of his fables. A careless housemaid sweeps a 'jasp', a jewel, into the barnyard where the cock busily pecks for grain. In what follows we must not make the mistake of dismissing the cock as altogether a fool. Henryson calls him that, but this refers to his ultimate choice. He is a person, as intelligent as most of us. He recognises the jewel for what it is, the Word of God, and sadly rejects it. His livelihood, the corn, comes first. Indeed I find myself thinking of that excellent young man with all the virtues, who could not pass Christ's final test of giving up his great possessions, so went off sadly, watched still more sadly by Christ. Henryson's despair over the cock's all too human choice, comes out in the abrupt ending of his Moralitas, 'Ga seik the jasp quha will, for thair it lay.'

In the following tale of the two sisters, country mouse and town mouse, sympathy naturally goes to the former fleeing from dangerous luxury to 'Blythnes of hart with small possessioun', and yet some pity might be kept for the town mouse, the inevitable victim of her luxurious present, for 'the cat cumis and to the mous has ee', a sinister line that suggests both death and the

---

[1] The text quoted here is that of Charles Elliott, Clarendon Press (Oxford, 1974). For a more religious interpretation of *The Morall Fabillis* than my own see Marianne Powell, *Fabula Docet* (Odense University Press, 1983).

devil. Where the country mouse knows freedom with 'small possessioun', her sister is slave to fearful wealth.

That comic predator the fox, too clever for his own good, now enters these tales. I pass over the pure farce of his brief capture of Chanticleir, his flight from the household knights of the cock's mistress, for so she seems to address her hounds, for his more remarkable confession. But first I must note how Renard, nothing if not conventional, allows Henryson to comment on man's similar subjection to 'consuetude and ryte', customs and habits of his inherited present, however bad, that possess him and govern his unconsidering behaviour: 'Use drawis nature swa in propertie/Of beist and man that neidlings thay man do/As thay of lang tyme hes bene hantit to'. The moralist who considers man's history of warfare, and violence at home must agree.

The influence of custom is well illustrated by Renard who, despite some eccentric practices, is only too conventional. We are introduced to him by night, from a hilltop[2] scanning the heavenly signs and finding cause to bless his father for giving him a university education, for he reads there some unhappy fate impending. Confession is indicated, and he finds a very understanding confessor, Freir Wolf Waitskaith. Honesty will not allow him to bring a full repentance for, as he says, 'hennis ar sa honie-sweit/And lambes flesche that new ar lettin bluid', but imperfect penitent and experienced confessor are agreed that 'neid may haif na law', a very human sentiment.

Full remission is granted, yet the conscientious Renard feels that some further gesture towards atonement is required, perhaps he should vary his diet of meat with a fish. He makes for the river, on his way seizes a young kid, and combining solemn ceremonies of baptism, conferring of a new knighthood on the spiritually new man, perhaps with the transubstantiation of the Communion Table also remembered, says, 'Ga down Schir Kyd, cum up Schir Salmond agane!' It is all a somewhat eccentric grace to the meal.

But he had read the heavens aright. Later under a bush, stroking a full belly in the sun he recklessly says, 'Upon this wame set wer a bolt full meit', that is, now would be the perfect time to die, and the watchful goatkeeper obliges him. Renard is surprised, gazing at the bolt he protests, 'Me think na man may speik ane word in play/Bot now on dayis in ernist it is tane'. Of his two worthy sons, equally clever and conventional, I can only say that like him they are unable to pass up a present opportunity.

Some fables relate particularly to the political and social state of Scotland. Of the former kind is 'The Taill of the Wolf and the Wedder', plainly written after the rebellious hanging at Lauder in 1482 of the king's lowborn, too influential favourite Cochrane. James III was warded in Edinburgh castle, and the citizens of Edinburgh who liberated him are the mice who freed the lion-king in 'The Taill of the Lyon and the Mous.' The king had been trapped, warded, because

---

2 The fox's heavenly studies, like some other incidents in Renard's career, are from *Le Roman de Renart le Contrefait*, 23569–601. Lines 416–20 of the *Testament* use a reference to the death of Queen Candelus in the same *Roman*, 23791–8.

'hurt men wrytis on the marbill stane.' All parties are the victims of a new, demanding, present world, the Renaissance.[3]

The tales of the 'Scheip and the Doig' and the 'Wolf and the Lamb' deal with present-day injustice in the Scots courts of law, civil and ecclesiastical, that Henryson, himself a lawyer, a notary public, sees as universal. Judgements are given by the powerful in favour of their own kind, the victims are the 'puir and innocent'. The intensity of Henryson's response is unequalled in his other moral fables. And more than the justice of man it is the justice of God that is at issue. True that the suffering innocent in a particular case may once have sinned, a justification of God's wrath in 'Ane Prayer for the Pest', but in neither case does it satisfy the poet, and his true feeling speaks in the winter-time cry of the shorn sheep, 'Lord God, quhy sleipis Thow sa lang?'

If these tales do not touch our subject explicitly, in 'The Preiching of the Swallow' his central theme has its full and perhaps greatest statement. It begins with a remarkably stark and bold contrast between the faculties of God and those of his creature man. God sees all times and things as 'ay present', and with His foresight cannot err. His judgement, therefore, infinitely excels that of his creature, whose 'presoun corporall . . . Blindis the spirituall operatioun', so that, as Aristotle says, man is like the bat, blinded by light, seeing only in a shadow-world. Error thus being natural to man, Henryson bids us in matters of faith 'trewe fermelie and let all resoun be'. This is not an orthodox position. It does, however, agree with, is reflected in, his attitude to the unreason about him. His faith tells him that it must be censured, but his conviction that error is natural to man tells him that he is above all to be pitied.

Since reason does not help, the poet gladly finds his troubled faith corrected and renewed by what the senses report of the creative goodness of God as seen in the flower, the fish, the fowl – 'sa forcelie thay flee' – and especially in the order of the seasons, their sure procession from Spring to Spring, the 'secretar of somer with his seil,/Quhen columbie up-keikis throw the clay'. Sadly we cannot find or put such order in our lives, for wanting the divine foresight we cannot always see beyond the 'thing present'.

The illustration of this defect and its consequences is preceded and emphasised by the introduction of the poet, light-hearted and happy for the busy labour and promise that he sees in the fields of Spring: 'It was grit joy to him that luifit corne'. And his happiness seems shared by the marvellous multitude of birds that settle on the hawthorn tree beneath which he lies, but not shared by one of them, the Swallow. It has seen the fowler sowing linseed to make nets that will trap and kill his kind. The lark, however, laughs at and scorns her warning with a series of so-called wise saws, all of which say, this is the present, let the future look after itself. Wondering the poet goes home. In June he is there again. The young shoots barely show, but he hears the Swallow's impassioned plea, still you can pull them up before they grow to height, and the same scornful answer of the birds, content

---

3 For the above see Ranald Nicholson, *Scotland: The Later Middle Ages*, Oliver & Boyd (Edinburgh, 1974), pp. 505, 509.

in the season. It is winter when he takes his walk that way again. Now the birds are desperate for food, they have not seen as the Swallow did, and will not heed her, the fowler covering his nets with chaff that looks like corn. They swoop down, to be gathered in the fowler's nets, and bloodily butchered.

Foolish deaths, though not tragic, can be greatly pitiable. The tragic note comes in with the despairing cry of the Swallow that cared so much and so hopelessly, and with the poet's final sight of her, as if with her went his hope too:

> 'This grit perrell I tauld thame mair than thryss,
> Now ar thay deid, and wo is me thairfoir.'
> Scho tuke hir flicht, but I hir saw no moir.

It is not a hopeful estimate of man that this tragic narrative of his subjection to the 'thing present', as represented by the lamented fatal want of foresight in the birds offers. It says exactly what was said so starkly at the beginning of the poem.

The last of the moral fables, 'The Taill of the Paddok and the Mous', is very amusing in its beginning, if not in its ending. Again the theme is the treacherous present. The vision of the tempting field of corn, that is so near, yet so removed from the desirous mouse by the stream, summons to a disastrous end. The comment on it is made with force and precision: the spirit 'Into this warld with cairis implicate' is 'Bundin and fra the body may not wyn'. This is not the orthodox position in any Church. Henryson was no heretic, but his view of the natural difficulty, to the point of inability, that the spirit knew in its effort to free itself from corporal bonds, made him look at the supposed example set by authorities in his Church, in much the same way that he looked at the professors of the law. His pity for the human condition also readied him for the more fundamental questioning of the ways of God to man. It is this critical habit of mind, which he may have considered only proper to a truly religious man, that gives to Henryson an intellectual interest lacking to Chaucer or his own fellow 'makars'.

Thus in *Orpheus and Erudices* is criticism of all the ranks of the Church, and we need not doubt that it is the Church as he has known it in his own day of which he speaks. In hell he puts 'mony pape and cardinale/In haly kirk quhilk dois abusione', with them ironically 'bischoppis in thair pontificall', and so down to abbots, perhaps guilty of symony, as was his own Lord Abbot. One wonders if it is of his abbot, and for this sin that at the beginning of his fables he speaks dismissively of a 'lord/Of quhome the name it nedis not record'.

As in the tales of the sheep and the lamb, so also in 'Ane Prayer for the Pest', it is the goodness of God that is at issue. How can He be so pitiless, even if there is sin, and that so natural, that 'nane dar mak with uthir residence', and men 'dye as beistis without confessioun'? Why punish with 'violence' and not with pity? Pity, as Henryson's understanding of the natural limits and weaknesses of humanity, illustrated in both animal and human fable, shows is for him the great virtue.

There are clear indications in concept and wording – not noticed in my little book on the poet[4] – that the Moralitas appended to the *Orpheus*, as I shall call the poem, was written with the last of the animal fables and its moralitas still fresh in mind.[5] The *Orpheus* is conceived indeed as just another fable, at least more that than as the story of a very human person. It is given a moral expressed in Henryson's characteristic way, not at all derived from the *Commentarius* of Nicholas Trivet.[6] Henryson's statement is this: 'Perfyte resoun wepis wounder saire/Seand our appetit thusgate misfaire . . . It is so fast into the body bund'. It is the sexual appetite of Orpheus talking of 'play', and so at last looking at Erudices and losing her that is meant.

There was little room for invention within the received limits of the classical fable, and so little room for development of Orpheus as a tragic and not merely pathetic figure, something more than the moral that he is made to point. Henryson could only fill in his canvas with what may be called poetical accessories, and this procedure diverts attention from his subject.

Such accessories are the divine genealogy given to his hero, the vain questioning of gods and goddesses about the whereabouts of his queen, the pointless listing of Greek musical terms, suggested by Plato's fancy of a 'hevinlie melodie . . . Passing all instrumentis musicall', the arbitrary naming of famous inhabitants of hell, the several symbolic guises of temptation such as the narrow bridge over a wondrously deep flood, a fairly obvious test, not so obvious the thorny moor of ballad tradition, every thorn a sting of deceiving pleasure, the road fearful for 'slidderness', all these dangers to be passed on his way to hell. One act that Henryson treats with some feeling, that reflects Orpheus' own need, and gives him briefly a more human aspect, is his mercy to the three criminals endlessly tormented by the gods. However, as when she was on earth, so in hell, the opportunity to give Erudices a personal voice is not taken, and at the close the merely generalising talk of how indefinable is love, how various the fortunes of lovers, distracts from our concern with the 'waefu wedowe' on his 'hamwart' way.

In sum, there may be moments of beauty, moments that win a response of pity such as the refrain 'Quhar art thow gane, my luf Erudices?', though even here one may ask if lyricism is the best mode of expression for grief, but the poem, more poem than narrative, is not felt as a humanly affecting unity. The typical Henrysonian subject defined in the commentary, that might have supplied the unity, is assumed evident and not developed.

In vital respects *The Testament of Cresseid* is very different. All is relevant, all is intense, descriptions, speaking characters, and not only Cresseid. The final effect of this narrative of 'the fatall destenie/Of fair Cresseid that endit wretchitlie' is tragic, and not simply because of humiliating physical events. The term tragic applies properly to a small number of writings in the early literatures of western

---

4 Matthew P. McDiarmid, *Robert Henryson*, Scottish Academic Press (Edinburgh, 1981).
5 Compare the up-and-down motif, and the theme of the soul bound in the body, in the moralitas of 'The Paddok and the Mous', 2939, 2949–50, with the same in the moralitas of *Orpheus*, 432, 451–2.
6 For Trivet see *The Poems of Robert Henryson*, ed. by Denton Fox, Clarendon Press (Oxford, 1981), pp. 384–91. Fox's notion of two storytellers has no basis in the text and makes no sense.

Europe, and as such the *Testament* stands alone between certain tales of Dante in his *Inferno* and the tragedies of Shakespeare.

The storytelling is initially given a significant setting, a scene of extreme winter weather in Spring, 'the blastis bitterly/Fra Pole Artick come quhisling loud and schill' (shrill), an inhospitable scene, and so Cresseid will find life. The storyteller, a 'man of age', with his 'fadit hart of lufe', the hot blood of youth gone, fits with the setting and the tale he is to tell. He is driven to his fire and his books. The prayer that he had meant to make to Venus, 'bewtie of the nicht', is countered by cold, as Cresseid's devotion to Venus, her desire, will be countered by cold, a killing cold. This idea of an inimical cold in life recurs. The two gods who decree her leprosy were reputed the coldest, Saturn and Cynthia the moon, and the idea is used, as we shall see, in her complaint.

To understand Cresseid, however, we take note of the storyteller's first choice of reading, *Troilus and Criseyde*, and Chaucer's hints that she left Troy and Troilus with Diomede not unwillingly. Not unwillingly, because in giving herself to the Greek she gave herself to her conception of the 'thing present', an ever-present world in which, so she imagined, just as in Troy, she would be 'the flour of lufe', that is, the most desired of women. Her belief in that imagined ever-present world, and the shock of disillusionment that came with rejection by Diomede and the disfigurement of leprosy, are all in these lines from her bitter complaint to the gods of this physical world:

> 'Ye causit me alwayis understand and trew
> The seid of lufe was sawin in my face,
> And ay grew grene throw your supplie and grace,
> Bot now, allace, that seid with froist is slane,
> And I fra luifferis left and all forlane.'

Complete disillusionment about one's world, as in *Hamlet*, is a tragic theme, and Cresseid 'all forlane', quite alone, the outsider, has expressed her disillusionment about the world in which she imagined herself to be. Yet her hurt and hopeless state are given additional effect by the caring responses of others. These make her and her story more real to us. It is a pity that for reasons of courtly convention in their stories of Troilus, Boccaccio and Chaucer could not use the same means to produce the same effect.

Thus the narrator of Cresseid's fate, who at every point shows his concern, can censure her degradation in the Greek camp, and yet say, 'I haiff pity thow suld fall sic mischance'. The father who welcomes her with the pathetic commonplace, 'Peraventure all cummis for the best', must later look on her as what he knew Scots law would consider her an outcast, in its term one of 'the living dead':

> He luikit on hir ugly lipper face
> The quhilk befor was quhite as lillie-flour,
> Wringand his hands of times he said allace
> That he had levit to se that wofull hour,

> For he knew weill that thair was na succour
> To hir seiknes, and that dowblit his pane,
> Thus was their cair eneuch betuix thame twane.

The words of the 'lipper lady' are all the more affecting for their dreadful practicality: 'I counsall the, mak vertew of ane neid,/To leir to clap thy clapper to and fro/And leve efter the law of lipper leid.'

It should be said here that the gods, yet other voices on her case, do not decree the leprosy as a moral judgement, they being merely the physical powers that determine physical events. What angers them, the wilful Cupid in particular, is her unrealistic complaint that they had no right to change that present, and to her pleasant, world once determined by them. But even the gods are subject to the ruling goddess Fortune, whom the 'variant' Venus is made to resemble.

The one significant judgement is Cresseid's self-judgement, made when she learns that unknowing she has met Troilus. She understands then that she has never had love to give, only the beauty that once made her 'the flour of lufe'. Self-knowledge is a virtue, hers so painful that it kills her. It is death with the attainment of that knowledge that makes Cresseid's story tragic.

Thus Henryson consistently in his tales, movingly in the despairing cry of the Swallow and killing self-criticism of Cresseid, expresses his theme of man's subjection to the 'thing present', the spirit 'so fast into the body bund'. Cresseid's ending is tragic because it comes in the very act of freeing herself from that subjection, that imprisonment. Let me end with the simple words of Henryson that say so much: 'Sen scho is deid I speik of hir no moir'.[7]

---

[7] The following words from the moralitas of *Orpheus*, 517–18, might be read as his idea of catharsis: 'our complexioun/Waxis quyet in contemplacioun'.

L.A.J.R. HOUWEN

23. Lions Without Villainy: Moralisations in a Heraldic Bestiary

> Wherever romances of knighthood and of courtly love were read or recited, wherever crowds gathered to witness jousts and tournaments, wherever families looked back over their record of honourable achievement and association, heraldry was in consequence a significant science. This encouraged its practitioners to infuse all sorts of symbolic meaning into its colours and devices and to read back its history into the chivalrous past as they knew it, and so to make of it the erudite branch of secular learning that, in the late medieval heyday of the heralds, it was ultimately to become.[1]

Maurice Keen here aptly summarises one of the most characteristic features of late medieval heraldic treatises, namely breadth of learning and the incorporation of this learning into heraldic symbolism. Nowhere is this more clear than in the so-called heraldic bestiaries where animal lore is used in a heraldic rather than the moral-religious context encountered in the bestiaries. One such example of a heraldic bestiary is to be found in the late fifteenth-century Middle Scots *Deidis of Armorie*.[2]

The *Deidis of Armorie* is the name given in the *explicit* to a loose collection of heraldic and chivalric treatises which have been separated from the surrounding – and quite similar – material by formal *explicits*. Some attempt has also been made to integrate some of the material into a distinct treatise, although I suspect this had already been done at a much earlier stage. The *Deidis* is a translation from the French and a copy of the French text, also known as 'Banyster's French Treatise,' is in the possession of the College of Arms in London.[3] The heraldic bestiary section of the *Deidis* forms the bulk of its 2557 lines. On a previous

---

1 M. Keen, *Chivalry* (New Haven, 1984), p. 128.
2 BL, Harley 6149; three later copies are also extant (1) Oxford Queen's College MS 161, from c.1500; (2) the so-called Scrimgeour MS (NLS, Adv. Lib. 31.5.2), copied in the first half of the sixteenth century by John Scrymgeour of Myres (Fife); (3) the Lindsay MS (NLS, Adv. Lib. 31.3.20), owned by Sir David Lindsay of the Mount, who was Lord Lyon from 1591 to 1620, 2 vols (Edinburgh, 1994). The Harley text is edited as: *The Deidis of Armorie: A Heraldic Treatise and Bestiary*, ed. L.A.J.R. Houwen, STS, 2 vols (Edinburgh, 1994).
3 MS. M. 19. The treatise is discussed by R. Dennys, *The Heraldic Imagination* (London, 1975), pp. 73–4. Dennys divides the treatise into 10 parts of which sections iv-ix would seem to correspond with the Middle Scots *Deidis of Armorie*. Dennys's division should be treated with some caution since he does not refer to any of the treatises which appear on ff. 130v–54 (between parts ix and x). A more reliable description of the contents of this manuscript appears in L. Campbell and F. Steer, *A Catalogue of Manuscripts in the College of Arms, Collections, Volume 1* (London, 1988), pp. 161–66. In their description of part ix the inanimate charges which follow the 'fishes' are not mentioned.

occasion I have discussed the more general aspects of this work;[4] here I would like to narrow the topic down to the moralisations which accompany the descriptions of the animals in particular. It is important to bear in mind that all remarks made about the *Deidis of Armorie* also apply to the French treatise on which it is based. When the 'author' is referred to, this should be understood to indicate either the author of the French text or the author of the treatise or treatises which make up this French text.[5]

As far as we know the oldest heraldic treatise is the Anglo-Norman *De Heraudie*, also known as the 'Dean Tract',[6] which may be dated to between 1280 and 1300.[7] This brief work, which only runs to some 144 lines, does include some animals, those which the text says: 'sount de custome portez en armes.'[8] The animals mentioned are the lion, leopard, griffin, martlet, popinjay, crow, swan and heron; fish do not appear. The animals are followed by leaves and flowers and inanimate charges. There are no moralisations and there is only one example of a non-heraldic element entering a description. The griffin, the text asserts in line with the encyclopaedias, is both a bird and a beast (eagle and lion). The only other detail given about the griffin is that Alexander the Great bore one in his arms.[9]

De Bado Aureo's *Tractatus de Armis*, probably composed towards the end of the fourteenth century, and its derivatives such as the Welsh translation – the *Llyfr Arfau*, is a much more substantial work. It discusses some eighteen beasts, birds and fishes.[10] Many of these are accompanied by moralisations. These moralisations normally follow the animal description, but sometimes the moralisation is all that is offered. The horse, for example, is only interpreted figuratively and is described entirely from the perspective of its first bearer in arms. Its animal characteristics only serve to help define the nature and character of the first knight who bore him in his shield.[11] Its description starts as follows:

> Equum in armis portare etiam significat hominem benevolum ad bellandum pro minima causa; quia equi solo et modico tubae sono ad bellum excitantur. Significat etiam hominem bene formatum, et habentem quatuor proprietates equorum, quae sunt hae, forma, pulchritudo, meritum, et color.[12]

4 L.A.J.R. Houwen, 'A Scots Translation of a Middle French Bestiary,' *Studies in Scottish Literature* 25 (1991), 207–17.
5 I strongly suspect that the French source of the *Deidis* is itself an amalgam of a number of different treatises.
6 CUL, MS Ee.4.20; see R.J. Dean, ed., 'An Early Treatise on Heraldry in Anglo-Norman', in *Romance Studies in Memory of Edward Billings Ham*, ed. U.T. Holmes (Hayward-California, 1967), pp. 21–9.
7 Dennys, *Heraldic Imagination*, p. 61.
8 *De Heraudie*, 11. 85–6.
9 *Ibid*. 11. 87–8: 'Griffoun: et si est griffoun oiseal et beste./ Le Roy Alexandre porta l'escu de goules ove un griffoun d'argent.'
10 E.J. Jones, ed., *Medieval Heraldry* (Cardiff, 1943), pp. 95–143. See also Richard Tracksler, 'Das "Heraldische Bestiarium" Johannes' de Bado Aureo', *Reinardus* (1996), 145–60, which appeared after this article was written.
11 Other examples of bare moralisations are the entries for the dog, dragon, swan, and crab.
12 Jones, *Medieval Heraldry* (*Tractatus I*), p. 116. Cf. also p. 163 for the virtually identical version found in BL Add. MS 28791.

A horse borne in arms signifies a man who is willing and prepared to fight with little cause; for at the faint sound of the clarion is the horse provoked to battle. It also signifies a well-formed man, who has four attributes which are found in the horse, namely, form, beauty, prowess, and colour.[13]

Sometimes an entry starts with the moralisation after which the general description follows. This is the case for the hawk which, like the horse, is described from the perspective of its first bearer, but its description also includes details from 'natural history' taken largely from Alexander Neckam's *De laudibus*:

> Accipitrem portare in armis est signum quod portans fuit gracilis vir, non fortis, sed anima pocius armatus quam corpore; quia accipiter est [avis] que plus anima quam ungulis est armata, et quod in quantitate corporis derogatur, hoc in virtute, prudencia, et cum audacia recompensatur, ut dicit Ysidorus, Plinius, et Aristoteles, libro XIV°.
>
> Alexander Nequam [*De Laudibus*].
> Accipitris preda ditatur mensa potentum,
>   Huius pre cunctis laudibus una placet.
> Frigoris insidias brumali tempore vitans
>   Unam consequitur providus hostis avem.
> Nocte tenet gelida captam, que luce sequenti
>   Permissam gaudens gaudet inire fugam.
> Invigilat prede predo, venator at illam
>   Sepius occurrat, gratus abire sinit.
> Officii memor est nocturni nobilis ales,
>   Hac vincit claros nobilitate viros.[14]

A hawk borne in arms signifies that the first to assume it was a slender, weak and daring man, better armed with courage than with bodily strength: for this bird is armed rather with courage than might and talons, and what it lacks in strength is made up in skill, cunning, and courage. This is maintained by Isidore, Pliny, and Aristotle. Alexander, too, in his *De Naturis Rerum*, states that on a cold night in winter the hawk seizes a bird and keeps it under its feet until the next day to save being cold; and then it sets it free. And if during the next day it should meet that bird several times it would not cause it any harm because of the help and comfort derived from it, and because of that noble nature the hawk is superior to the lords and proud men, as Alexander says.[15]

---

13 Jones, *Medieval Heraldry* (*Llyfr Arfau*), p. 29.
14 Jones, *Medieval Heraldry* (*Tractatus II*), p. 167; for other such examples see the descriptions of dragon, jackdaw, and griffin. Cf. also Alexander Neckam, *De naturis rerum et De laudibus divinae sapientiae*, ed. T. Wright, Rolls Series (London, 1863), pp. 379–80.
15 Jones, *Medieval Heraldry* (*Llyfr Arfau*), pp. 37–9. An almost identical moralisation and description save for the story based on Alexander Neckam's *De naturis rerum* is found in the *Deidis*, 11. 1087–95.

It is tempting to regard such 'inverted' examples as an intermediary stage between the exclusive moralisations and those which, like the *Physiologus* and the bestiaries, present a general description with the *moralitas* following rather than preceding it.

A later treatise known as 'Mowbray's French Treatise' enumerates some eighteen beasts, six serpents, five fishes and twenty-three birds, and, just for good measure, also lists some twenty-two precious and semi-precious stones.[16] None of the animals, however, are accompanied by a 'chivalric moral' and we have to turn to 'Banyster's French Treatise' and the Middle Scots translation for another example of a heraldic treatise in which the animals are accompanied by moralisations. The number of entries has also increased dramatically: the *Deidis* deals with some seventy-seven beasts, birds, fishes and reptiles and some fifty-seven inanimate charges. Dennys explains this increase in the later heraldic treatises as follows:

> The greater use of heraldic devices by the junior knights and even squires towards the end of the fourteenth and early fifteenth centuries, is borne out by the need which King Henry V found in 1417 to clamp down on the indiscriminate and unauthorised use of armorial devices. As arms were used in war and tournaments, it was necessary to keep the design of a shield as simple as possible and, as the Ordinaries and the traditional creatures of heraldry were used up, the newly armigerous gentleman had to make do with the more unusual creatures and fabulous beasts.[17]

One of the characteristics of the *Deidis of Armorie* which reminds one of the bestiaries is its overall structure. The *Deidis* is subdivided into 'chapters' on beasts, birds, 'fishes' and inanimate charges, each of which is headed by the 'king' of that particular section (lion, eagle, whale and cross). The section on 'fishes' also incorporates serpents and reptiles. A similar arrangement is found in many bestiaries and ultimately derives from Isidore's division of book twelve of his *Etymologies*. The inclusion of inanimate charges is, of course, peculiar to the heraldic bestiaries, but even this is paralleled in the *Physiologus* and some of the more traditional bestiaries which sometimes include chapters on stones (*lapides igniferi, adamant*) or trees (*arbor peridexion*). Although the broad outline of the topics in the *Deidis* is similar to that of Isidore's, the author motivates his own subdivisions by pointing to the relative merits of each group. Beasts come first, he says, because living things are more worthy in themselves than inanimate things (except for the fleur-de-lis and the cross, both of which are gifts from heaven) and he will therefore start with the beasts, followed by the birds (757–60).[18] The

16 This treatise is described by Dennys, *Heraldic Imagination*, pp. 72–3.
17 Dennys, *Heraldic Imagination*, p. 74.
18 Birds are introduced in 11. 1059–61, fish in 11. 1654–5 and inanimate charges in 11. 2059–60. The *Tractatus* uses a similar subdivision though a gender distinction is included in the argument. This is reflected in the *Llyfr Arfau* which introduces its animate charges as follows: '. . . of these charges those which are animate are of greater dignity than those which are inanimate, and of the living charges males are of greater dignity than females. Therefore it is proper to begin with a treatment of male creatures . . .' (Jones, *Medieval Heraldry*, pp. 20–1).

'chapters' on beasts, birds and fishes all end with a note advising the reader that if he wants to know more about the animals in questions he should consult the 'buk þat spekis of propirteis, þe quhilk may be gottin in mony places' (1054–8).[19] The pattern is repeated at the end of the section on inanimate charges except that the reader is not advised to consult an encyclopaedia, but the old and experienced heralds (2552–5).

The entries for individual animals and inanimate charges also follow the familiar pattern found in the *Physiologus* and the bestiaries. They open with a description of the particular charge, listing its characteristics, followed by an allegorical interpretation of these characteristics. The moralisation is set apart from the preceding by a standard phrase which, with very few variations, opens with: 'And [the above] signifies that he who first bore this [charge] in arms was . . .' Compare the entry for purplefish:

> Murne is a gret fische with coquille, þe quhilk quhen / he is cuttit or schorn with yrn he puttis out of him / reid teeris or of purpre coulour; and has blud alanerly in a / vane; and eftir þe effusioun of þat sammyn blud he deis. And signifies at he þat first bur him in armes wes off / nobill blud and in sum part of þe ligne of a hie prince;/and þat be his blud he wald schaw to þe ded aganis his enemys. (1965–71)

Only rarely does the author forget to mention that the ensuing moralisation only applies to the *first* bearer of this particular coat of arms and not necessarily to his descendants. Since the *Deidis* was used by heralds or Kings of Arms as a reference work which would help them find an appropriate charge to be used in a new coat of arms, this emphasis on the first bearer of the particular charge makes good sense.

Unlike the *Tractatus* where moralisations follow, precede or even constitute the entire description, the *Deidis* only has one or two examples which deviate from the standard order. The description of the dog amounts to no more than an allegorised account of the animal's loyalty and willingness to fight for his lord and master (818–22), and in the case of the heraldic blackbird or martlet (1565–9) no encyclopaedic information on the habits and characteristics of this bird is offered at all since its use is restricted to heraldry. Both descriptions are similar to those found in the *Tractatus*.

Sometimes the author does not bother to allegorise certain elements of the characterisation of the animal and assigns them (almost) literally to the bearer without any adaptation, which can lead to rather absurd results. At other times, however, the animal's characteristics and habits are properly (if crudely) given new meaning. The pelican is a good example of both these types. There are two kinds of pelicans, we are told, the land- and the aquatic birds; the latter feed on fish, the former on serpents and lizards. The fish-eating bird is compared to a man

---

19 The reference is most likely to *De proprietatibus rerum* by Bartholomaeus Anglicus, who is also referred to by name on several occasion. See also lines 1651–3 and 2056–8.

who reaps his profits from fishing, but the feeding habits of the land-pelican are allegorised: the serpents and other venomous beasts it feeds on represent men who lead an evil life and who cannot otherwise be corrected, and the man who bears this pelican in his shield is thus a kind of medieval Terminator (1342–8). Both types of interpretations can also be found in the *Physiologus* and the Bestiaries.

Slavish following of descriptive parts of the text in the moralisation can lead to quite ridiculous results. One such example is that of the man who first bore the crocodile in his shield. He is said to have been a great man of different colours who preferred water over land, was hard skinned and a man of few words, who weeps when he destroys his enemies; a man, moreover, who needed another man who lived on filth and who would flatter him without realising that this same man would destroy him:

> And signifies þat he þat bur him first in/ armes wes a gret man and had his armes and leggis/ of iiii paires of maneris or coulouris; and he desirit/ mair to be in wattir na in erd, and clerar seand/ in wattir þan in erd; and wes hard of skyn/ and litil spekand and destruyt his enemys/ gretand; and wald haue a man liffand of filth/ quhilk flatteryt him sa mekle þat wnder colour þarof ane/ oþiv com and distruyt him . . . (1695–1703)

In descriptions such as this one it is often easier to reconstruct the characteristic features of the animal from the moralisation than it is to make sense of it in human terms.[20] And this is only a small part of the description which continues for another six lines. Unfortunately the interpretation of the crocodile is not the only example of a description which is interpreted literally and one wonders whether such passages would have been of any help to a herald who is trying to fit the arms to the person.

However, the author can also be quite discriminative in his interpretations as well. Sometimes he selects only those characteristics for which he has a use, as in the case of the deer where an account of its breeding habits and parental devotion is omitted in the moralisation which concentrates on the significance of the stag shedding its antlers and its prudence when it refuses to fight other stags before they have grown again (802–7). At other times the author dispenses with the *moralitas* altogether, as in the case of the dolphin, where all the reader is told is that the Dauphin bears it in his arms because it suits him (1825–30).[21] Additions also occur,

---

20 Compare the corresponding animal description: 'Corcodrille is a fische, as Ysidore sais, with iiii feit,/ ȝaulow of coulour, habitant in þe ȝerd be day/ and the nycht in watteris; and is ner xx^ti futis of lenth, rycht/ starkly armyt with teith and leddir, for he has the/ skin sa hard þat harions, na strakis, na stanis dois/ him nane evil; he makis eggis for generacioun apon/ land at the famelle and the male lais þe tan eftir/ þe toþir, as sais Plitone; and has na tong; and gif/ he may vectus a man he ettis him gretand; ande/ hapinnis quhen a foull, callit surofillos, wil haf a/ caroingne til eit he puttis him in þe mouth of a/ corcodrille and clawis him softly quhil he opinnis/ al his thrott for þe delit of his clawing; than/ cumis ane vthir fische, callit ydre, and entris within/ his body and passis furth be a hoill at he makis/ in his sid be sic maner þat he slais him . . .' (*Deidis*, ll. 1669–84).
21 The dolphin is not moralised in the Ashmole and Cambridge bestiaries either; cf. F. Unterkircher, *Bestiarium* (Graz, 1986), f. 87^v (pp. 190–1) and T.H. White, *The Book of Beasts*, pp. 200–1 (New York, 1954).

particularly when the characterisation of the animal is brief or contains few useful facts. The only 'fact' given about the tiger, for example, is its etymology (straight from Isidore), namely that it is a very fast animal, which is why the Persians call them 'arrows' (856–7). This is thought to signify that the bearer of a tiger in his coat of arms is insincere, crafty, sly and deceitful, and, perhaps worst of all, a coward who would rather flee from the battlefield than stay (858–61).

Even though many descriptions of animals betray the influence of the bestiaries and encyclopaedias, the same cannot be said about their moralisations. In keeping with the different purpose of the heraldic bestiary these moralisations tend to concentrate on matters chivalric in which such issues as knightly virtues, wealth and status, good governance and the like predominate. In one instance only does part of the *moralitas* as found in the *Physiologus* and bestiaries carry over, namely in the description of the pelican – which is based on Brunetto Latini's *Livre dou Trésor* – where it is noted that as 'Holy Church bears witness, Christ represents the pelican' (1333–5).[22] The chivalric moralisation which follows the description subsequently explains the story of how the pelican kills its young in terms of a man who kills his neighbours because they wronged him, only to repent of his deed later and expiate himself by spilling his own blood.

Despite the lack of direct influence of the bestiaries on the heraldic moralisations the latter often do share the moral preoccupation of their bestiary counterparts. In some of the moralisations in the *Deidis of Armorie*, the chivalric purpose is entirely lost sight off and a purely moral one replaces it. The peacock, for example, is described by the *Deidis* as having a serpentine neck and feet, a voice which resembles that of the devil, a thief-like gait, and wings which resemble those of an angel and which the peacock displays only too willingly. The man who first bore this bird in his arms resembles it in these respects, but the moralisation also contains an implicit warning in its assertion that such ostentatious display and vanity made its first bearer the object of scorn and destroyed him (1483–8).

Moreover, there are a few animals which can hardly be discussed other than in a moral fashion. It would be very difficult, for example, to give a chivalric slant to the moralisation which accompanies the description of the turtledove, not only because it has few characteristics which could be considered suitable to a knight, but also, and perhaps most importantly, because its characteristics had become more or less standardised, largely due to the exegetical commentaries on a passage in the Song of Songs [2.12]: 'the voice of the turtle is heard in our land.' Both the Y and the B version of the *Physiologus Latinus* open with this verse despite the fact that both represent two completely different traditions with respect to the turtledove.[23] The turtledove which remains chaste after it loses its mate thus

---

22 The symbolism goes back to Ps. 101.7 (Vulgate): 'similis factus sum pelicano solitudinis factus sum sicut nycticorax in domicilio.' From the point of view of typological exegesis both David and the pelican were considered types of Christ, i.e. they were symbols in the Old Testament of what was to pass in the New.
23 Cf. *Physiologus Latinus Versio B*, ed. F.J. Carmody (Paris, 1939), pp. 49–50 and F.J. Carmody, ed., 'Physiologus Latinus Versio Y', *University of California Publications in Classical Philology* 12 (1941), 95–134 (p. 131). See also the bestiaries, and W.B. Clark, ed. & tr., *The Medieval Book of Birds: Hugh of Fouilloy's Aviarium* (Binghamton, 1992), pp. 154–5. Bernard of Clairvaux, *Sermones in Cantica*,

becomes a symbol of the knight who turns his back on the world and all its pleasures after he loses his mate, and leads a solitary life devoted to prayer (1498–1501). This type of moralisation not only reminds one of knights who retire from active service in order to become hermits but also of those religious-didactic treatises which advocate the solitary life such as the *Ancrene Wisse*, where the ⟨turtle⟩ dove is presented as a symbol of the anchoress, both on account of its solitary life and its proverbial meekness.[24]

This concern with moral issues is apparent in many of the other moralisations as well. Particularly noticeable are the many instances where animals are explained in terms of vices and virtues. Among some of these vices one can recognise a few of the Seven Deadly Sins. One such is embodied in the example of the griffin guarding his mountain of gold in Asia, which Solinus had already linked to avarice in his *Collectanea rerum memorabilium*:

> In Asiatica Scythia terrae sunt locupletes, inhabitabiles tamen: nam cum auro et gemmis affluant, grypes tenent universa, alites ferocissimi et ultra omnem rabiem saevientes. quorum inmanitate obsistente ad venas divites accessus rarus est: quippe visos discerpunt, velut geniti ad plectendam avaritiae temeritatem.[25]

> In the Asiatik Scythia are rich Lands, but notwythstanding vninhabitable. For whereas they abound in gold and precious stones: the Gryffons possesse all, a most fierce kinde of foule, and cruell beyond all cruelnesse: whose outragiousnesse is such a stoppe to all commers, that hardlie and seldome arryue any there: for as soone as they see them they teare them in peeces, as creatures made of purpose to punish the rashnesse of couetous folke.[26]

The *Deidis* expands on this and explains that the man who first bore the griffin in arms was so covetous that he would refuse to distribute his gold among his soldiers. The lizard or *saura* is also associated with this Deadly Sin when it is explained that the man who first bears it in his arms is virtuous but becomes greedy with age when he puts himself in a 'little place' full of riches which becomes his only pride and joy until he is 'robbed' of his wealth when he dies (1734–7). Similarly, in the moralisations which accompany the descriptions of the pike (1989–96) and otter (964–72) avarice is also mentioned, but in these

interprets the text as follows: ' "Your cheeks are beautiful as the turtle dove's' [Song 1:9] III. 4. ... you I say who are moved by the urgings of the Holy Spirit and long to perform all that is required of one who would be the bride of God ... in imitation of that most chaste of birds, and following the advice of the Prophet, abide in solitude because you have raised yourself above yourself ... Live alone therefore like the turtle dove. Avoid the crowds, avoid the places where men assemble; forget even your people and your father's house and the king will desire your beauty ...' *The Works of Bernard of Clairvaux, Volume Three*, tr. K. Walsh (Kalamazoo, IV 1986).

24 Cf. *The English Text of the Ancrene Riwle: Ancrene Wisse edited from MS Corpus Christi College Cambridge 402*, ed. J.R.R. Tolkien, EETS OS 249 (Oxford, 1962), p. 151, 11. 26–8.

25 C. *Ivlii Solini. Collectanea rervm memorabilivm*, ed. Th. Mommsen (Berlin, 1864), p. 97, 11. 9–15.

26 *The Excellent and Pleasant Worke of Caius Julius Solinus (1587)*, tr. A. Golding (Gainsville, 1955), pp. nii–nii^v.

instances the gluttonous appetite of the animals is re-interpreted as avarice in the moralisation.

In addition to the sin of *avaritia* there are references to envy in the description of the raven (1149–51) and the wolf (926–9) – although in the latter case this is not reflected in the moralisation. Lechery is commonly associated with the goat which, according to Isidore, explains why it squints and why its blood can soften the diamond.[27] These details are repeated in the *Deidis* (952–9) although, unlike Isidore, the author does not mention Suetonius as their source. Moreover, the account of the goat is moralised in terms of knightly (and courtly) love, with a knight fighting for his lady in tournaments and jousts. Noticeable in the moralisation is the extent to which the lecherous aspect is played down:

> And betakinnis he þat/ bur it [he-goat] first in armes wes rycht iolius, amorious in/ lechory, abilland him weil in armes, and desirand/ mair to get renoun for þe luf of wemen þan of men;/ and fynd him-self with gud will at iustis and tournais. (959–63)

The partridge (1414–18; 1431–4), the tench and the mermaid are also associated with *luxuria*. The tench earned the epithet lascivious because it was thought to engage in lechery with the paddock (1983–8). Aspects of the mermaid are moralised both within and outside of the moralisation proper: her wings and claws are explained as symbols of 'fleeting love', her natural abode of the sea is associated with the weakness of lechery, and the man who first bore her in his shield is someone who deceives people with his pleasant speech and behaviour in order to achieve his own lecherous ends (1718–19, 1721–5). Finally, there may just be a hint of pride in the moralisation following the description of the antelope (1614–17).

Even when no particular virtues or vices are mentioned there are many references to the bearers of this or that animal or other charge being a virtuous or evil person solely because the animals has positive or negative connotations. Some of the virtuous animals are familiar ones, like the sagacious elephant (1046–50), and the loyal dog (818–22); others are less well known, such as the ermine, whose white fur is interpreted as signifying the virtue of its bearer (899–904) and the scallop (1848–60). Evil creatures have always existed but it is remarkable how often they are discussed in more or less neutral or even positive terms in the *Deidis*. Even the description of that evil monster *par excellence*, the dragon, is followed by a more positive interpretation when we read that the man who first bore it in arms was a great fighter, a conqueror wherefore, the author adds, it is borne by many men of great courage (827–30).

Another notion encountered in many didactic treatises and elsewhere in literature also appears regularly in the moralisations, namely that of the wits or senses. Of the five senses speech and sight are met with most often. Speech is by far the most important since most animals produce some sound and should he so

---

[27] Isidore of Seville, *Etymologiae XII/ Etymologies Livre XII Des Animaux*, ed. & tr. J. André (Paris, 1986), pp. 46–7 (XII.1.14).

desire the author could incorporate it in the moralisation. He does so often. The asp was first borne by a man who often opened his mouth to grieve others, but he was smart enough to stop his ears against the deceptive words of enchanters (1785–6, 1789–92); the basilisk comes to symbolise a man who was so full of wrath that he could even slay people with his speech if he so desired (1760–2), while the crow represents a great deceiver who tried to increase his standing by mere words (1548–52). The man who first bore a raven in his arms must have had a terrible croaking voice (1161–2), whereas the voice of the man who first bore the turtledove was sweet (1496–7). Even such an animal as the sea turtle with its strong jaws with which it can break rocks, becomes the symbol of a strong-mouthed man, a man full of virtuous language (1958–9). Even though all these men are described as being extremely adept at using their tongues, silence may still be golden. The man who first bore the sturgeon in his arms reflects the fact that this fish was thought to lack a mouth and survive exclusively on the south wind: he was loath to talk of dishonourable things, but when he did open his mouth he spoke only on virtuous and honorable subjects (1943–47).

The references to sight are fewer and less interesting in that they tend to repeat the animal characteristic without properly allegorising. Thus, since the crocodile sees clearer in the water than outside of it, so does the man who first bore the animal in his arms (1698–9); the same straight transference of characteristics with respect to sight is applied to the moralisation of the cat who sees clearly in the dark (920–1). More interesting is the example of the raven which conceives simply by being looked at by its mate. This turns the man who first bore it in his arms into someone who practised lechery more with his eyes than in deed (1159–60).

That 'speech' of the Five Senses appears more often in the moralisations than 'sight' is perhaps not surprising in view of John 1.1, but it is interesting to see its *abuse* highlighted in so many passages. At moments such as these the moralist takes over from the heraldist just as elswhere in the same text the author includes narrative stories about animals in his treatise which have little or no relevance to the heraldic matter in hand.[28] In fact, the treatment of the senses in the moralities is remarkably similar to that by the authors of such didactic treatises as the *Ancrene Wisse* and *The Fyve Wyttes*.[29]

The wealth of the bearer of a particular coat of arms as well as his rank in society are two other topics which stand out in the moralisations. The importance of the former in late medieval England is brought out in the Letters Patent issued by Henry VIII to Thomas Benolt, Clarenceux King of Arms, on 19 April 1530. In this document the qualifications for ennoblement and the subsequent granting of a coat of arms are directly linked to the wealth of its future bearers:

> And also the said Kyng at armes to gyve to any persone or persons spirituall the which be preferred by grace vertue or connynge to rowmes and degrees of

---

28 Cf. the discussions of the friendship between dolphins and boys (1816–20, 1821–24) and those of the aldulterous (1234–43, 1243–60) and grateful storks (1260–72).
29 See particularly the second part of the *Ancrene Wisse* on the five senses; *The Fyve Wyttes*, ed. R. Bremmer (Nijmegen, 1987).

honor & worshipp armes accordyng to their merites And likewise to any person or persons temporall the whiche by the service doon to us or to other *that be encreased or augmentid to possessions & riches hable to manteyne the same* So that they be not issued of vyle blood rebelles to our persone not heritiques contrary to the faithe But men of good honest Reputacyon, And all suche whiche shal be enoblished to have their armes regestred in the Erle Marshalles boke[30]

In the well-known controversy between the Garter and Clarenceux Kings of Arms of the same year the conditions are explained in greater detail when Garter states that 'every persone beynge of good name and fame and good Renoune And not vyle borne or Rebells myght be admyttyd to be enobled to have armes *havynge landes and possessyons of free tenure to the yerlye value of X pounds sterlinge or in movable goods iii c. li. sterlynge.*'[31] It will be clear that only those owning land or having enough 'portable property' were thought to be fit to be raised to the nobility and to be given a grant of arms.

Many of the moralisations reflect this concern with wealth. Some of the animals borne in arms simply indicate that its bearer is wealthy. The basilisk which shines with venom lends its light to the man who is apparently so bedecked with gold and jewellery that he 'shines with great treasure' (1757). A horse depicted in a coat of arms can symbolise a fighting man, but it can also be indicative of its owner's wealth or 'good fortune' (865–7). Sometimes an animal's life is characterised by periods or cycles which are then interpreted as a turn of the Wheel of Fortune in its bearer's life. The colour of the tench is sometimes black and sometimes a golden hue, just as its bearer sometimes appears poor and at other times wealthy and clad in gold (1984–7). And the stag's shedding of its antlers symbolises the man who was poor in his youth ('first age') but whose wealth increased as he grew older (802–4). When a man is without any possessions but sly as a fox he might even consider adopting that animal for his arms, since it symbolises a man who knows how to steal and rob lords and princes (881–3). We even encounter a man who lives way beyond his means because although he was great of body and stature like the ostrich, he owned no land to 'sustain his state in accordance with his deeds' (1314–16).

However, as the author of the *Llyfr Arfau* sagely notes about the men who bear martlets in their arms, 'It is not by wealth and riches alone that nobility is acquired, but by deeds of prowess and other good habits.'[32] The martlets, he states, signify that their bearers 'have to live on the bounty of their lords.' Not every knight can be a rich landowner but they can distinguish themselves in jousts, tournaments and battle and their bravery may well be rewarded in the form of a grant of arms. Consequently, many animals in the *Deidis of Armorie*

---

30 The actual text is based on a contemporary certified copy of the Letters Patent contained in Benolt's Deputation to Hawley. It is quoted from A.R. Wagner, *Heralds and Heraldry in the Middle Ages: An Inquiry into the Growth of the Armorial Function of Heralds* (London, 1956), pp. 9–10; the emphasis is mine.
31 *Ibid.*, p. 79; my emphasis.
32 Jones, *Medieval Heraldry*, pp. 46–7; for the Latin versions see pp. 122, 137.

appear to be chosen on account of their real or imagined association with knightly virtues like strength, courage, military skills, loyalty and honour. Such virtues are found first and foremost in the descriptions of the more traditional heraldic animals such as the courageous cock who 'sings' to celebrate the victory over an opponent (1554-5), the valiant lion (762-3), and the cruel leopard, which in heraldry had to face the spectator (778-9),[33] but they also appear as characteristics of many other animals. One of these is the boar: the knight who first bore him in his shield is characterised as a cunning fighter, who like the boar, would rather die than flee (813-16). The bearer of a crane in his arms has the same solid military skills as the cranes which fly in battle formation and run their entire migration to Asia with military precision; these same skills make him eminently suitable to lead others in battle (1188-93). The first bearer of the pilgrim's token of St James, the scallop, is not just a natural leader of men but a spiritual guide, not quite a saint yet, but certainly a good shepherd:

> And signifies / þat he at first bur him in armes wes a man of grace and/consavit of noble lignaige; and of him sprang precious and / noble verteus; and þat he wes a gret convoyar of folkis þat / with gud will followit him of his conduit; and vas þe / first þat put him in danger to saif his fallowis; and quhen / he wes tane al his cumpany wes eith to discumfye / and to tak, for his conduit did mair na þe mychtis of his/ fallowis; and of his natur he luffit to haue a lord/ and king; and wes man mar hard, mair stark, and mar / vaillande and bettir luffit in strange landis þan in the / propre land of his natur; and wes richt weill / luffit with þaim þat followit him. (1848-60)

Honour and reputation are of paramount importance to the first bearer of the stork in arms, who punishes his relatives or servants when they have acted dishonourably but who would generously reward those who had done him a good turn (1280-5). A curious emblem of bravery is represented by the lion 'sans vilainie [fierceness]', the French term for what is now called a demi-lion (rampant), the upper half of the body of which is cut off straight but which still shows the upper half of the tail (2474-6). Godefroy explains this heraldic term as follows: 'Un lion sans vilenie, cest un lion sans membre ni testicules.'[34] Despite the animal's questionable ancestry the author manages to give the

---

33 The idea that the leopard in heraldry should be depicted 'guardant' (facing the spectator) was a common one. Nicholas Upton said that 'a Leopard ought to be painted with his whole face shewed abroad openly to the lookers on' (quoted by Dennys, *Heraldic Imagination*, p. 135). H. Stanford London, 'Lion or Leopard?', *The Coat of Arms*, 2 (1952-3), 291-2, observed that: 'In the middle of the next, the 14th century, Bartholus de Saxo Ferrato is positive that the lion is distinguished by his shaggy mane, whereas the leopard has no mane and is spotted. Fifty years later, c.1394, Johannes de Bado Aureo, after quoting Bartholus, turned and rent those heralds who would distinguish the two beasts merely by the position of their head (p. 291).' The illustrator of the *Deidis* ignored this and depicted him 'statant' (standing on all four legs, both for and hind-legs being in a straight line). He also ignored the well-known fact that the leopard was 'speckled like its father' (Jones, *Medieval Heraldry*, pp. 24-5; cf. also *Deidis*, line 783), and painted him brown throughout.
34 F. Godefroy, *Dictionnaire de l'ancienne langue française*, 10 vols. (Paris, 1881-1902), *vilenie*.

moralisation a positive twist by interpreting the demi-lion as a courageous and magnanimous man who lost some of his limbs defending his honour on the battlefield:

> And signifies at he þat first bur him in armes be his / vaillance of courage in dedis of batall had tynt sumpartis of membres; and þat wilfully departit of his gudis to gar ho-/nour be maynteinyt. (2476–9)

The moralisations also tell us something about politics and the issue of kingship in particular. This is particularly true for the discussion of the bees. This entry is one of the longest in the *Deidis of Armorie* largely because their system of government is discussed at great length. The organisation of the bee-hive, in which each member has its place, with dukes and a king[35] to govern them, reflects that of medieval society. The king, we are told, is chosen from amongst the best and wisest but also from amongst the lowest-ranking 'citizens', thereby assuring his humility and piety. But he rules like a divine king and his bees owe him their undivided loyalty, and obey him in every respect. In war the bees are more than willing to die fighting for their king. Should any of them ever violate any of these unwritten rules he will punish himself by breaking his own sting. And if the king were to die the whole hive would be in disarray. These issues are reflected in the moralisation in which the first bearer of a hive in his arms is said to be someone of middle rank who desires to be governed by a lord and master whom he serves loyally and is willing to die for. He is, however, ambitious, which is shown by the fact that he has a great house built for himself and his family (1355–1412). The discussion of the bees and the ideal social organisation of the hive has a history which stretches as far back as Homer's *Iliad* and Virgil's *Georgics*, but, as other writers were to do after him, the author of the *Deidis* has adapted the *moralitas* to reflect some of the major issues of contemporary society.[36] With respect to the kingship-debate he favours those who prefer an elected king above a hereditary one, but he also accepts the king's divine right to rule. The moral interpretation, moreover, reinforces one of the corner stones of feudal society with its emphasis on the allegiance a knight owes his (feudal) lord:

> And signifies þat he / þat first bur þe ruches in his armes wes desirand til / haf a king, lord, and maistir; and at he wes of myd / stait without feit or wyngis, þat is to say, without lordschip; / and þat he maid gret diligens to grow þarto and till / edifie and big hous and propir placis til his plesans for / him and for all his; and he knew in him-self þat he / ves bot porretur and rottinnes and he wes rycht

---

35 The notion of a *queen* bee rather than a king bee was not generally accepted until the eighteenth century.
36 *Il.* 2. 87–90; *Georg.* 4.149–227. One of the most poignant examples of these must surely be Bernard Mandeville's *The Grumbling Hive, or Knaves Turned Honest* (1705) also known as the *Fable of the Bees*. That similes based on such social creatures as bees and ants have lost nothing of their force has recently been shown by A.S. Byatt in her novella *Morphi Eugenia*, published together with *The Conjugial Angel* as *Angels & Insects* (London, 1992).

amyable and / obeissand till his lord with gret reuerens; and wald mak / nan enterprins to pas befor his lord and followit him in all / his dedis of battell; and be þe sowndis of trumpettis and of / all-armes he had lever be ded þan leiff him; and giff / be aventour he tynt him, for displeissans þarof all his / gud he had lever tyn and waist þan till eke it for þe / tynyng of his maistir and lord and his defaultis he wald / correk with < out > biding of iustice; and for na-thing wald he / brek þe law na commandment of his lord bot himselff / walde he pwnys þarfor. (1395–1412)

The descriptions and interpretations of other animals complement this picture. In the section on the eagle, for example, we can read that the eagle as king of the birds is entitled to feast on his own citizens if hungry and the other prey is not sufficient to satisfy his appetite, but his main characteristic is his liberality. He will happily share his food with those birds that follow him around; these characteristics, the author adds, make the bird an appropriate symbol for a (Roman) emperor since he ought to posses those same characteristics (1062–73). Another example of a reference to good leadership is represented by the bunch of grapes which signifies that the man who first bore them was valiant in noble deeds but someone who would not flourish himself until he found a lord and master to hold him in check and govern him wisely, observing all his actions, correcting them where necessary, and supporting his good deeds (2480–9).[37]

The concepts of knighthood and nobility were often closely linked to that of 'the common profit' as Hay explains in the *The Buke of the Ordre of Knychthede*,[38] and it is also one of the topics touched upon the *Deidis of Armorie*, where it appears exclusively in the section on inanimate charges. In the moralisation accompanying the description of hands borne in arms the hands signify that its bearer was a tough and valiant man, a man of faith who worked principally for the common profit:[39]

And signifies þat he þat bur it first in / armes wes a man hardy and intromettand of vaillance, / and a man of faith and luffand þe body of man for þe / quhilk to withald and keip oft-tymes wrocht his handis / in noble dedis, in gret hardynes, and principaly for þe common/ profit mair þan ony vthir thingis. (2294–9)

Many of the issues mentioned above are discussed at much greater length and depth in the *regimen principe* literature. Book seven of John Ireland's *Meroure of Wysdome*, for example, deals with the issue of hereditary kingship (which Ireland advocates) as well as with the need for wise rulers, all of which are also touched upon here.

---

37 See also the discussion of the chequered design in lines 2221–32.
38 'jtem till knychthede afferis principaly tobe amorous of the commoun prouffit / and of the commouns / – ffor quhy be the commouns / and for the commoun proffit/ knychthede was foundyn stablyst and ordanyt'; *The Prose Works of Sir Gilbert Hay, Volume III*, '*The Buke of the Ordre of Knychthede*' and '*The Buke of the Gouernaunce of Princis*', ed. Jonathan A. Glenn, STS 21 (Edinburgh, 1993), chapter 7, lines 408–12.
39 For further references to the common profit see lines 2174, 2444, 2448, 2525.

The animal symbolism encountered in the moralisations is not limited to moral or chivalric issues, animals can also function as symbols of particular professions and trades. In the *Deidis* we encounter couriers, lawyers, monks, usurers and heralds themselves. The hare is here depicted as the ideal messenger (a task often performed by the heralds themselves), because of its great speed. But with the hares these messengers also share a natural urge to flee from their enemies (947–51). The magpie, on the other hand, is thought to be a good symbol for a lawyer, since both are characterised by their verbal powers. Lawyers, the author reasons, can argue about anything and from any perspective:

> And/ signifies þat he þat bur þat first in armes wes a man/ of prattik þat couth spek of al materis and til al pur-/pos, and with richt or wrang couth suttelly do þat/ with his prattikis; and wes sa doubtit for his spech/ þat quhar he duelt nan durst conuers to do him scaith,/ ffor in his langage he wes son providit; and as the / pye makis hir nest in hie treis, sa maid he his hous/ besid gret lordis til avance him be his caquet;/ and þai ar bettir armyt to be aduocatis than oþir persons (1508–17).

The dove, on the other hand, is thought to be an appropriate charge for those messengers of peace, the heralds themselves, who, like the dove who abandons the company of fellow creatures once it has lost its mate, give up the practice of arms for the office of arms (1539–42). Fortunately for the monk the only correspondence between him and the sea-monster known as the monk fish or *monachus marinus* is his tonsure (1977–9) but its inclusion among the fishes carries a faint echo of the notion that all creatures found on land have their equivalent in the sea (and, to a lesser extent, in the air). Usurers, finally, could bear a lizard in their arms (1738). The *Deidis* recounts how, when the lizard becomes old, it creeps through a narrow slit in a wall, facing the sun (the east), by which process it manages to renew its youth. The same story is found in the *Physiologus* and the bestiaries in the description of the first nature of the serpent and the lizard otherwise known as the *saura*.[40] However, the moral significance is quite different from that found in the *Physiologus* and the bestiaries, where it represents the relinquishment of the old sinful clothes (Old Testament) and the acceptance of the new garments of life (New Testament) in the form of Christ.[41] In the *Deidis* the garments are abandoned and the narrow crack facing the sun becomes a treasury full of riches, but the approach is similar to that in the books on beast:

---

40 A simplified version of this story is told about the saura in the Bodley bestiary (MS 764), recently translated (in part) by Richard Barber (London: Folio Society, 1992), p. 194; cf. also the edition and translation (in German) of the famous Ashmole 1511 bestiary by F. Unterkirchen, *Bestiarium*, f. 84v; it also appears in the chapter on serpents in the *Physiologus* (cf. *Versio Y*, Carmody, chapter 13 (p. 110–11), and P.T. Eden, *Theobaldi "Physiologus"*, Leiden, 1972).
41 Cf. *Physiologus Versio Y*, Carmody, chapter 13, 6–7 (p. 111), *Bestiarium*, Unterkirchen, f. 84^r (pp. 184–5), White, *Book of Beasts*, p. 187.

... and quhen he [man bearing the lizard] worth auld put / him in a litil place schynand of riches quhar-in wes/ all his felicite; thar-of he wes dispulzeit and syn/ he leit him de; and na man wist quhar becom his gudis;/ and ar bettir armes for vsueris þan ony oþir þersonis. (1734–8)

What rôle do the interpretations play within the larger framework of the heraldic bestiary? Right from the beginnings of Christianity the moral-didactic interpretations of animal characteristics have been more important than the animals themselves. This is particularly true for the hexameral writings of St Basil and St Ambrose and it became institutionalised in the *Physiologus* and early bestiaries in which the *moralitas* often exceeds the description proper in length. In the later bestiaries this *sensus moralis* starts to lose its importance and occasionally disappears altogether. The didactic approach, however, gained a new lease of life when it was applied in a heraldic and chivalric context. For a herald and / or an author on heraldry the (figurative) interpretations are the life-blood of the animal-emblems; without them no association between animal and bearer would be possible. It would seem reasonable therefore to assume that an animal's potential to be moralised in chivalric terms helped to determine its inclusion in this treatise.[42] We only have to examine the texts themselves to find proof that such a figurative reading of the animals in a heraldic treatise like the *Deidis of Armorie* is indeed of crucial importance to the treatise as a whole. De Bado Aureo is quite explicit about this in his *Tractatus* when he explains the purpose and significance of its animal symbolism. He adds the following explanation to the description of the dog:

... and thus it often happens in the case of other animals that the bearer has the same habits as the animal which he bears, because whenever a man makes petition for arms or some device, it is necessary to know about the man's habits, and thus can arms be suggested for him, as the Civil Law testifies in the book called *Digest*.[43]

The issue reappears in the form of an imaginary discussion between the King of Arms and a sceptical member of the public which is incorporated in the discussion of the swan:

Cignum in armis portare signat primum assumentem catatorem [fuisse], quia cignus a canendo dictus, in cuius alis maxima est fortitudo. Quidam tamen

---

[42] However, other factors such as the availability of source material as well as a first-hand knowledge of animal charges in existing blazons no doubt also left their marks on the *Deidis*.

[43] Jones, *Medieval Heraldry (LLyfr Arfau)*, p. 33; it is not among the description of the dog in the Latin texts (pp. 115, 163).

portaverunt cignum in armis qui non fuerunt cantatores. Cum interrogatur Rex Haraldorum quare talibus cignum in armis assignavit, respondeat quia fuerunt viri pulchri, vel quia habuerunt longa colla.[44]

A swan borne in arms as learned people maintain, signifies that the first to assume the arms was a good singer, for in Latin the two words are similar. Yet there are many who bear swans in their arms who are not singers. And when the herald king of arms is asked why he has granted such a charge to them, he replies that it was because they were handsome men of good countenance and long-necked, and for that reason they were granted these arms.[45]

Yet not all the animals are equally suitable to be borne in arms. At times the heralds must have had some misgivings about the appropriateness of some of the animals which make an appearance in the *Deidis*. What knight – sworn to defend women and churches – would want to bear the owl in his arms, a bird which is associated with dishonour and the pillage of churches and one that is hated by all (1526–9, 1522)? Moreover, who would want to be associated with the cruel and voracious wolf (929–30; 965–6) or the weak and servile hedgehog (998–1003)?

Sometimes an awkward situation is avoided by adapting the 'moral' somewhat.[46] The author gives an interesting twist to the story of the partridge about which the bestiaries relate that it is such a lecherous animal that it will even mate with fellow males, thereby ignoring its own 'nature'. In the moralisation there is no hint of homosexuality; instead the first bearer of arms charged with a partridge is blamed for disowning its own parents (1414–18, 1435–6). That such discretion as is shown here was not always practised by others is shown by Sir Nicholas Upton in his adaptation of De Bado Aureo's *Tractatus* when he reveals that the reason for the three partridges given to a knight for his bravery in the field is that 'to bear partridges in arms betokens the first bearer to be a great liar or a sodomite.'[47] A selective approach to the description is another means open to the author to avoid potentially embarrassing moralisations. Although the dove was often associated with lechery and this detail is also mentioned in its description in the *Deidis*, it does not appear in the moralisation where the reader is only told that the man who first bore it in his shield was a simple person who relied more upon others than upon his own strength (1536–8).

Heraldic treatises such as the *Deidis of Armorie* are a veritable store-house of information from which the herald could pick and choose the charges he thought

---

44 Jones, *Medieval Heraldry (Tractatus II)*, pp. 169–70. The imaginary discussion also touches upon such issues of whether one man may bear the arms of another and who is entitled to bear arms. The latter question is answered with the familiar argument of Bartolo de Sassoferrato in his *De insigniis et armis*, that arms, like names, can be taken and changed at will; see Jones, pp. 221–52 (here, pp. 228–9) and Wagner, *Heralds and Heraldry*, p. 68 & Appendix A (14).
45 Jones, *Medieval Heraldry (LLyfr Arfau)*, pp. 41–3.
46 Compare the case of the he-goat referred to above (p. 257).
47 As related by Keen, *Chivalry* (pp. 130–1), who uses it to show not just how canting arms may illustrate a name, but also as an example of 'erudition beginning to find its way into heraldry, as it found its way also into so many other aspects of knightly custom and observance.'

were appropriate for a particular person. What the animal symbolism in the *Deidis of Armorie* and related treatises shows above all, however, is the extent to which the science of heraldry had become professionalised and had even been turned into that 'erudite branch of secular learning that, in the late medieval heyday of the heralds, it was ultimately to become.'[48] One only hopes that the authors of these works also experienced some of the pleasure involved 'in pure seeing-of-similitude, taken in as immediately as an echo, while conceiving the literal story, as one sees a pebble under water with more significance than a pebble. Neither water nor pebble offers any great novelties; what pleases is merely to observe the nature of the world and correspondences one can see in it.'[49]

---

48 Keen, *Chivalry*, p. 128.
49 R. Tuve, *Allegorical Imagery* (Princeton, 1966), p. 10.

R. JAMES GOLDSTEIN

24. The Freiris of Berwik *and the Fabliau Tradition*

Despite occasional praise from a few critics, *The Freiris of Berwik* has suffered undue neglect in recent years. C. S. Lewis devoted a mere two sentences to the poem, suggesting that 'This excellent *fabliau* . . . is by a real Chaucerian and ranks above all other attempts to continue the tradition of the comic Canterbury Tales.'[1] Kinsley praises its 'structural finish, characterization and sheer zest,' suggesting that its 'vivid comic narrative' is unrivalled in Middle Scots poetry.[2] Kratzmann has briefly commented on the 'tone and structural sophistication' of the poem, which he finds reminiscent of the *Miller's Tale* and *Reeve's Tale*.[3] R. D. S. Jack has examined some suggestive Chaucerian parallels in the only detailed study of the poem in recent years.[4] A fresh re-examination of this remarkable poem is therefore long overdue.

Part of the reason for the poem's neglect is due to the vicissitudes of its treatment by editors. After Pinkerton's suggestion in 1786, the poem was long held to be a possible Dunbar composition and was included in editions of his works by Laing (1834), Small (1893), Schipper (1894) and Mackenzie (1932), even if some of these early editors expressed serious doubts as to his authorship. Since Mackenzie's rejection of the poem from Dunbar's canon, little scholarly attention has been given to the anonymous work.[5]

Although future examination of its language may provide further help in dating the poem, for now we may only roughly date it between c. 1450 and 1540.[6] The *terminus ad quem* has been suggested on the grounds that the poem 'refers to

---

1 C. S. Lewis, *English Literature in the Sixteenth Century, excluding Drama*, Oxford History of English Literature (Oxford, 1954), p. 99.
2 James Kinsley, 'The Mediaeval Makars,' in *Scottish Poetry: A Critical Survey*, ed. James Kinsley (London, 1955; rpt. Folcroft, Penn., 1974), pp. 14–15.
3 Gregory Kratzmann, *Anglo-Scottish Literary Relations, 1430–1550* (Cambridge, 1980), p. 99.
4 R. D. S. Jack, '*The Freiris of Berwik* and Chaucerian Fabliau,' *Studies in Scottish Literature*, 17 (1982), 145–52. For other studies, see Everett C. Johnston, 'The Transmutation of Friar Johine in ' "The Freiris of Berwik",' *Studies in Scottish Literature*, 5 (1967–8), 57–9; Walter Morris Hart, 'The Fabliau and Popular Tradition,' *PMLA*, 23 (1908), 329–74.
5 The fullest critical edition is in *Ten Fifteenth-Century Comic Poems*, ed. Melissa Furrow (New York & London, 1985), pp. 315–62. It also appears in *Poetry of the Stewart Court*, ed. Joan Hughes and W. S. Ransom, (Canberra, 1982), pp. 562–73, essentially a transcription of B with modern punctuation and glosses. (Since this paper was submitted, the poem has been edited in *The Mercat Anthology of Early Scottish Literature, 1375–1707*, ed. R. D. J. Jack and P.A.T. Rozendaal (Edinburgh, 1997).)
6 Furrow, pp. 321–4, provides a preliminary study of the language, finding the lexicographic evidence in particular to be equivocal. She concludes: 'the poem is as likely to have been written during the period 1461–82 [i.e., when Berwick was a Scottish possession] as later' (p. 323).
7 Denton Fox, in a typescript reproduced in Priscilla Bawcutt, 'A First-Line Index of Early Scottish Verse,' *Studies in Scottish Literature*, 27 (1991), p. 269.

the monasteries in Berwick, which were supressed no later than 1539,'[7] though there is no reason in principle why it could not have been written slightly later. The poem was evidently popular among early modern audiences, since it survives in the late sixteenth-century Bannatyne and Maitland Folio manuscripts and in an early seventeenth-century print.[8] The two manuscripts often provide widely different readings, thus offering a striking example of *mouvance*, a term coined in 1972 by Paul Zumthor in his *Essai de poétique médiévale* to call attention to the 'essential instability in medieval texts' in a manuscript culture. In the case of fabliau, Zumthor notes, 'considerable instability is observed'.[9]

Because the *Freiris* has been so infrequently studied, a brief summary of the narrative may be helpful at this point. After an extended description of the fortified town and castle of Berwick, the narrator traces the adventures of the Dominican friars Allane and his younger, more robust companion, Robert. Returning from an unspecified journey 'vpaland',[10] they are unable to enter the gate before curfew. They find 'a fair manar' 'without þe toun' (52), which belongs to one Symon Lawrear, a 'gude hostillar' (51) who has been away for some time in search of corn and hay. His wife Aleson offers them meagre refreshments but is reluctant to put them up for the night because (as we soon discover) she has previously arranged to entertain the rich Friar Iohine (whom I'll call John for convenience).[11] Eventually she agrees to let them spend the night in a loft upstairs. She spruces up while her maidservant prepares a feast. Friar John arrives with additional delicacies; affections are exchanged. But in the meantime, the high-spirited and suspicious Friar Robert cuts a hole in the floorboard that allows him to witness the entire scene below. Just as the couple sit down to enjoy their feast, however, Symon unexpectedly returns home. She quickly hides her panic-stricken lover in a kneading tub and directs the maid to smother the fire and hide the food in a cupboard while she undresses and pretends to be asleep. When she finally admits her exasperated husband, she offers some cold left-overs, and his mood soon lightens. The convivial but naive husband

---

8 Bannatyne MS, fo. 348b–54b; Maitland Folio, pp. 113–29; *The Merrie Historie of the Thrie Friers of Ber [wi]cke*, printed by Edward Raban (Aberdeen, 1622) survives in one copy (new STC number 7349.5) owned by the Huntington Library, San Marino; see Furrow, pp. 320–21. For the two manuscript witnesses (which I cite as 'B' and 'M'), see the Scolar Press facsimile edition, *The Bannatyne Manuscript, National Library of Scotland Advocates' MS. 1.1.6*, introduction by Denton Fox and William A. Ringler (London, 1980); *The Bannatyne Manuscript, Writtin in Tyme of Pest, 1568*, ed. W. Tod Ritchie, STS, 2nd Series, 22, 23, 26; 3rd Series, 5 (1928–34), IV, 261–77; *The Maitland Folio Manuscript*, ed. W. A. Craigie, 2 vols., STS, 2nd Series, 7, 20 (1919–27), I, 133–48. Unless otherwise indicated, all quotations will be taken from the STS edition of B, with abbreviations expanded and capitalisation and punctuation modernised; I have checked Ritchie's transcriptions against the facsimile of B.
9 Paul Zumthor, *Toward a Medieval Poetics*, translated Philip Bennett (Minneapolis, 1992), pp. 45–6; Bennett suggests translating *mouvance* as 'mutability.'
10 B, line 31; M reads 'vpon land.'
11 B, lines 126, 470, 501, consistently refers to Iohine as a 'blak freir' (i.e., a Dominican like the other two), while M consistently makes him a 'gray' or Franciscan friar; Johnston, 'Transmutation,' argues for the B reading on questionable grounds. Furrow believes John should be Franciscan but also observes: 'The poet is clearly confused on the colors pertaining to the different orders of friars' (p. 324), since line 24 describes the Jacobins (Dominicans) as 'freiris of þe quhyt hew.'

wishes for some company, whereupon Robert coughs to make their presence known. Symon invites them downstairs to share his modest supper. The comic climax of the fabliau involves a carefully stage-managed scene where Robert pretends to employ occult skills and a supernatural helper to conjure up the extravagant meal, which is hidden in the cupboard. Aleson tries to contain her alarm when she realises her secret is out, though Symon suspects nothing. Instead, he asks to see Robert's secret servant, who the friar explains is too 'fowll and vgly for to se' (448) in his usual state, so Symon requests him to appear in the guise of a friar. Robert directs John's escape from the tub and the stout blow he receives in the neck from Symon, who falls and cracks his head on a stone, while John falls in a mire outside the entrance before fleeing in chagrin.

The Freiris of Berwik is the most elaborate and skillful version of a widely disseminated variety of the trickster tricked motif.[12] None of the other known versions is close enough to be considered a direct source of the poem, whose anonymous author could have learned the basic story line from a variety of sources, from clerical Latin tradition to popular oral lore.[13] The best known literary analogue, however, is the thirteenth-century French fabliau, *Le Povre Clerc*.[14] Briefly, this fabliau centers on a student whose poverty forces him to leave Paris. Arriving after a day's journey at a village inn, the wife refuses him lodgings because her husband has gone to have the wheat ground; that the innkeeper has to travel some distance to a mill suggests a seigneurial monopoly on milling rights. Outside the door, the student notices that the maidservant is making a cake and cooking some pork; he also sees a manservant carrying two casks of wine into the house. A priest passes him without greeting and is admitted to the house. When the clerk wonders aloud where he can spend the night, the husband overhears him on his way home and offers him hospitality. Once inside, the clerk exacts revenge on the wife in a central episode we shall examine in a moment.

Professor Jack has recently shown that a comparison with the French fabliau helps suggest that the *Freiris* employs 'many of the devices initiated or perfected' in Chaucer's fabliaux,[15] such as the highly particularised setting that is closely integrated with the action; a greater elaboration of character and the use of internal monologue; and the presence of complex irony and satire. The decasyllabic couplets of the *Freiris* provides an obvious metrical link to Chaucerian verse. Furthermore, all the characters in *Le Povre Clerc* are unnamed, while the characters' names in the *Freiris* appear in Chaucerian fabliaux.[16] Perhaps the most suggestive of all the parallels that Jack discusses, however, is the satirical presentation of the

---

12 See Furrow, pp. 315–17 for a discussion of the known analogues; cf. Joseph Bédier, *Les Fabliaux: études de littérature populaire et d'histoire littéraire du moyen age*, (1894; 6th ed., Paris, 1969), pp. 453–4.
13 Janet M. Smith, *The French Background of Middle Scots Literature* (Edinburgh, 1934), p. 84, inconclusively argues for a French source; cf. Furrow, p. 317.
14 A. de Courde de Montaiglon, *Recueil général et complet des fabliaux* (Paris, 1872–90), V, 192–200; all references to Old French fabliaux are to this edition by page number; translations are my own.
15 Jack, p. 143.
16 Jack, p. 146; Hart, p. 368 also believes the names are derived from Chaucer, though unlike Jack he points out that they all appear elsewhere in the French fabliau tradition.

superstitious John in the *Miller's Tale* and Symon in the *Freiris*, who both fall for elaborate supernatural rituals staged by clerical figures.[17] While the influence of Chaucer's fabliaux on the *Freiris* is not conclusively established, it does seem a likely enough possibility. If so, the Scots fabliau would then provide a virtually unprecedented case of a later medieval writer responding to such twentieth-century favourites as the *Miller's* and *Reeve's Tale*, when most other fifteenth- and sixteenth-century poets almost exclusively imitated and praised Chaucer's dream visions, chivalric romances and moral tales.

Yet it would be a mistake, I believe, either to overemphasise the resemblences between the *Freiris of Berwik* and Chaucerian fabliau, or to restrict discussion of literary relations to matters of plot and style in a single French fabliau that provides the closest analogue. Recent scholars have shown that writers of Old French fabliau were working in a highly sophisticated and self-conscious literary genre whose linguistic and narrative economies cannot be measured by Chaucerian standards.[18] Although surely no one would claim that *Le Povre Clerc* is among the most brilliant fabliaux, a knowledge of the French tradition suggests that it is far wittier and sophisticated than previous scholars have indicated. Much of the humor of both *Le Povre Clerc* and the *Freiris of Berwik* relies on the excessive nature of the feasting.[19] The specific form taken by the subversive or carnivalesque preference for what Bakhtin famously calls the 'material bodily lower stratum' of 'the genital organs, the belly, and the buttocks' links the *Freiris* more closely with the French narrative than with either the *Miller's* or *Reeve's Tale*.[20]

Much of the wit of *Le Povre Clerc*, however, depends on what it leaves unsaid. Indeed, nowhere does the French jongleur tell us the purpose for the meeting between the wife and priest, because the author could count on the audience's generic expectations to fill in that silence. Ménard estimates that about a third of the existing corpus of fabliaux involves an unfaithful wife, while Nykrog adds, with only a little exaggeration, that 'in such triangles the lover is *always* a priest.'[21] Neither oral nor sexual pleasure, however, is the real focus of this relatively mild French tale, which instead devotes its greatest energies to exploring, albeit in a highly condensed form, the opposition between literate clerical culture and lay ignorance to celebrate the ingenuity of the unbeneficed Paris clerk whose poverty forces him to leave university. His identity as a university scholar is highlighted in his first words of direct dialogue: 'je viens d'escole' (V, 193). After instructing the

---

17 Oddly, Jack neglects the lay-clerical opposition of the *Summoner's Tale*.
18 See R. Howard Bloch, *The Scandal of the Fabliaux* (Chicago, 1986), and Alexandre Leupin, *Barbarolexis: Medieval Writing and Sexuality*, translated Kate M. Cooper (Cambridge, Mass., 1989), pp. 79–119 ('The Impasse of the Fabliaux') for two of the most provocative recent studies; my indebtedness to both scholars will be clear.
19 For the respective dinner menus, see *Recueil*, V, 193; B, lines 134–5; 157–60. Hart, p. 364 n. 2, observes that 'Freir Robert conjures a good deal more out of the cupboard than Aleson put in,' but the variant readings in M suggest a need for greater caution.
20 Mikhail Bakhtin, *Rabelais and His World* (1965; Bloomington, 1984), p. 21; see also chapter six.
21 P. Ménard, *Les Fabliaux: contes à rire du moyen âge* (Paris, 1984), p. 14; Per Nykrog, *Les Fabliaux: étude d'histoire littéraire et de stylistique médiévale* (Copenhagen, 1957), p. 62, both cited Bloch, pp. 62–3.

maidservant to prepare bread from the flour he has brought with him, the husband invites the poor clerk to pass the time with a story:

> Mainte chose avez ja oïe,
> Car nos dites une escriture
> O de chançon o d'avanture.

(You have already heard many things; tell us something you've read, either a song or an adventure.)

(Recueil V, 196)

The clerk replies that he doesn't know any fictive tales ('de fablel ne sai je rien'), but he offers instead to narrate a fear that he has recently experienced (V, 197). The clerk's apparent seriousness seems to motivate the husband's unintentionally ironic comment: 'je sai bien que fableor / N'estes vos mie par nature' (I know that it is not at all your nature to make things up, tell fictions [V, 197]). By narrating his fictional encounter with a wolf, the clerk exacts his revenge on the wife for her refusal to lodge him, using fiction to reveal the truth – that she has hidden the meal and the priest. In the struggle between the husband and the priest at the end of the tale, the priest loses his coat and mantle, which the husband hands over in reward to the poor clerk.

The literary self-consciousness of this storytelling episode at the center of *Le Povre Clerc* clearly reveals that the tale is a self-reflexive exploration of the poet's power to create fiction while placing its central character in the same social role as the anonymous jongleur who composed the tale. The gift of the coat is a witty allusion to a French literary commonplace whereby the aristocratic patron rewards the jongleur by clothing him.[22] This commonplace simultaneously gestures toward the performer's relation to his audience and to symbolic links between texts and textiles, coats and linguistic representation, which were widely exploited in medieval literature.[23] *Le Povre Clerc* thus provides further evidence for Bloch's striking thesis that the 'scandal' of the fabliaux 'is not that they contain dirty words, celebrate the body in all its concavities and protrusions, revel in scatology, or even that they poke fun at villainous aristocrats, lecherous priests, and insatiable women, but that they expose so insistently the scandal of their own production.'[24]

While *Le Povre Clerc* alludes to the social opposition between unbeneficed, university-educated clergy and the more economically secure parish priest, *The Freiris of Berwik* subtly draws on an established tradition of anti-mendicant satire. So far as I am aware, the Old French fabliaux never mention friars, which suggests they were mostly composed by the mid-thirteenth century, since their irreverent authors could hardly have resisted drawing on the anti-fraternal satire that proliferated after the controversies at Paris broke out in the 1250s.

---

22 For a witty example, see *Les Lais de Marie de France*, ed. Jean Rychner (Paris, 1983), *Lanval*, line 211.
23 See Bloch, pp. 22–58.
24 Bloch, p. 35.

Yet the reputation of the friars for gluttony and lechery and for elaborating fictions would have been familiar to Scottish audiences long before the composition of *The Freiris of Berwik*.[25] The poet suggests familiar stereotypes when we learn that Allane and Robert 'with wyffis weill cowld gluder' [flatter] / Rycht wondir weill plesit þai all wyffis / And tawld þame tailis of haly sanctis lyffis' (34–6). Our suspicions are raised by the introduction of Alesone, whom the narrator describes as 'Ane fair blyth wif' (54) who was 'sumthing dynk and dengerous' (55). The author toys further with our expectations when he has the older friar say to the wife: 'Cum hiddir, deme, and sett ȝow doun me bye / And fill the cop agane anis to me' (72–3). Our suspicions may increase when the younger man immediately adds, 'Full weill payit sall ȝe be' (74), followed by the narrator's observation that 'The freiris wer blyth and mirry tailis cowld tell' (75). Yet if the poet raises our expectations, it is only to frustrate them, since within a few lines the friars are sent to the loft. Robert, however, is not ready to sleep: 'I hecht to walk this nicht. / Quha wait perchance sum sport I ma espy?' (116–17). At this point the narrator introduces us to Friar John, who 'govirnit alhaill the abbacy' (127) and had silver and gold in abundance, as well as 'a prevy posterne of his awin' (129), which he uses to slip out of the friary in secret. Aleson is after bigger game.

After she thrusts the 'fatt caponis to þe speit / And fatt cunyng to a fyre culd scho lay' (134–5), we may soon suspect that the 'cunyng' carries a double meaning. When she retires to her chamber to prepare for her tryst, Bannatyne gives four lines that are expanded to eight in Maitland. Mackenzie omits this brief passage from his edition, he tells us, because of 'their coarseness and apparent character as an interpolation':[26]

> Scho pullit hir cunt and gaif hit buffettis tway
> Vpoun þe cheikis, syne till it cowd scho say:
> 'ȝe sowld be blyth and glaid at my requeist
> Thir mvllis[27] of ȝouris ar callit to ane feist.'
>
> (B, 139–42)

This brief passage is intended to violate linguistic propriety; it is the outrageousness of the humour, not its textual authority, that troubles Mackenzie. The Maitland MS makes the conflation of feasting and sexual activity even more explicit by adding: 'or I sleip I think ȝe salbe pleisit / ȝour appetyt and myn sall

---

25 In addition to Dunbar's well-known anti-fraternal satires, see *The Poems of Robert Henryson*, ed. Denton Fox (Oxford, 1981), *Moral Fables*, lines 2969–71.

26 W. Mackay Mackenzie, *The Poems of William Dunbar* (1932; London, 1970), p. 233; cf. Jakob Schipper, ed. *The Poems of William Dunbar* (Vienna, 1894), p. 392, who also rejects the authenticity of the passage because of its obscene tone.

27 According to *DOST*, s.v. *Mull, mwl (1)*, the word probably denotes 'The lips of an animal; applied to the labia of the vulva.' In addition to this occurrence, the word is recorded in Kennedy and Dunbar, which may suggest the *Freiris* is not much earlier than c. 1500. The same conclusion seems supported by the word *libberla* (B, line 481), meaning 'cudgel'; *DOST*, s.v. *Libber-lay* describes this word as current c. 1500–40; cf. Furrow, 323.

both be easit' (M, lines 145–6).[28] This little episode, so clearly central to the narrative economy of the *Freiris*, suggests close links with what Bloch identifies as a 'general fetishization of body parts' in French fabliaux.[29] Alesone's vagina may not be detachable (as in *De l'Escuiruel*) or get a speaking part of its own (as in *Du Chevalier qui fist les cons parler*), but the Scottish fabliau nonetheless isolates her genital organs from the rest of her body as an autonomous subject of desire that momentarily takes on a fictive personality.[30]

While the flesh roasts on the fire downstairs, Aleson dresses herself in a costly 'kirtell'[31] (145); 'Hir uper garmentis as the reid gold did schyne; / On every finʒer scho weiris ringis two. / Scho was als prowd as ony papingo' (146–8). The redness of her dress (and her 'kirtell' in the Maitland text) is reminiscent of Alisoun of Bath.[32] In both cases the excessive decoration of the female body corresponds to the linguistic improprieties that drive the narrative.[33]

In both the French and Scots fabliaux, images of feasting stand metonymically for sexual pleasure. *Jouissance* is doubly deferred: *coitus interruptus* is replaced by *cibus interruptus* as each couple is surprised by the unexpected arrival of the husband before the couples may enjoy the oral pleasures that were to whet the appetite for more illicit ones. After John temporarily usurps Symon's position of authority in the household ('So prelat lyk sat he in to þe chyre' [183], the reassertion of masculine authority, which in Lacanian terms marks a return to the symbolic order of patriarchal law, is ironically figured in the image of Symon standing with his 'libberla' (481) or cudgel in hand, waiting to punish the transgressing friar whom he misrecognises as nonhuman. Although some of you may hestitate to embrace what may seem an unacceptable imposition Lacanian theory at this point, an important, though previously unnoticed, link between the Scottish poem and the corpus of French fabliaux invites such a reading. According to the narrative logic of French fabliaux, when a priest and an unfaithful wife form a dangerous liaison, as Bloch observes, 'the priest is almost always dismembered – castrated, beaten, or killed – for his concupiscence.'[34] Castration anxiety is especially evident in a surprising number of fabliaux: *Du Prestre crucifié, D'Aloul, Du Connebert*, to name just a few.[35] The relevance of a psychoanalytic approach to the Scottish fabliau becomes especially clear through

---

28 For another Scottish example of the common image of the vagina as mouth, see 'I saw me thocht this hindir nycht,' *Bannatyne MS*, ed. Ritchie, III, 34, line 12 (fo. 143b); cf. Evelyn S. Newlyn, '"Of Vertew Nobillest" and "Serpent Wrinkis": Taxonomy of the Female in the Bannatyne Manuscript,' *Scotia*, 14 (1990), 1–12 (2–3).
29 Bloch, p. 63.
30 A selection of other relevant French fabliaux would include *Le Souhaiz desvez, Du Moine, De la Sorisete des estopes, De Porcelet, Des. IIII. Souhaits*. As Bloch suggests, 'The preoccupation with sexual members is at once the product of and a fascination with narrative and not its referent. Narrative is the catalyst of desire and not its simple reflection or representation . . .' (p. 90); see pp. 59–100 for a stimulating discussion of 'The Body and its Parts.'
31 M, line 147 describes it as 'fyne reid.'
32 Jack, p. 147 makes this comparison (and also mentions Simon's wife in the *Reeve's Tale*), though without specifically commenting on the colour symbolism.
33 M, line 150 suggests an image of the phallic women: 'With ane proud purss and keyis gingling syn.'
34 Bloch, p. 63.
35 See Bloch, pp. 61–5, for discussion of these and other examples; cf. Leupin, pp. 106–19.

a close scrutiny of the Maitland Folio. In that version, when Friar John realises that Symon has returned, he speaks four lines that are absent in Bannatyne:

> In to this case, Lord, how sall I me beir?
> For I am schent and Symond fynd me heir;
> I dreid me sair and he cum in this innis
> And find me heir þat I loss both my quhynnis!
> (M, 209–12)

Quhynnis, which literally denotes a hard variety of stone, is being used metaphorically for what a French writer would call *coilles*.[36] Unlike the French examples mentioned earlier, in this tale the loss of the male member exists only in John's understandably panic-stricken imagination, for the only cutting edge used as a tool of domination is the one Robert wielded earlier: 'throw þe burdis he maid with his botkin / A littill hoill' (175–6). Yet John's castration anxiety clearly indicates the Scottish writer's familiarity with a central motif from the French tradition that is entirely absent in Chaucerian fabliaux.[37] Perhaps Bannatyne (or an anonymous scribe before him) was sufficiently troubled by the threat of castration to repress it from his copy of the text.

In the end, it is finally Friar Robert – and the poet he ultimately stands for – whose wit triumphs and whose linguistic transgressions reign supreme. Aleson seems subject to lack from beginning to end. In the Maitland version, she initially tells John, 'ȝe ar weill mayr wylcum heir / Than Symon is or salbe all this ȝeir' (169–70), clearly suggesting that her husband fails to satisfy her; John's response to her greeting is to 'thrist hir hand agane full preuilie' (171). At the end, Alesone 'on na wayiss gat hir will' (565). Friar John receives a harsh beating before falling into the mire as punishment for his transgression. Symon cracks his head open as the price he must pay both for not being firmly possessed of the phallus and for restoring the fragile patriarchal order whose temporary disruption he never suspects. The return to a threatened patriarchal order depends on a fiction so preposterous as to reveal the precariousness of that order. This conspicuous dependence on an elaborate stage-illusion – the functional equivalent of the story-within-the story in *Le Povre Clerc* – unmasks, as Leupin argues in a similar context, how 'phallic dominion announces its own dubiety'.[38]

Yet if French fabliaux, as Leupin believes, 'evoke the fundamental law of representation both as fiction's power and as a fiction *of* power,' *The Freiris of Berwik* further adds a uniquely complex symbolic and historical dimension to that general law by setting the action in that marginal space just outside the heavily

---

36 DOST, s.v. *Quhin*, n^2, definition 2 ('testicle'). This instance provides the only citation in DOST of the metaphorical meaning. Cf. Leupin, p. 83, who argues that the endlessly metaphorical naming of male body parts in the fabliaux reveals a 'metaphorical mask intended to foil . . . the inability of language to name the sexual relation' due to the absence of any 'master-signifier.'
37 Only with the Pardoner does Chaucer express castration anxiety; see the *General Prologue* portrait (I. 691) and in the Host's angry insult (VI. 952–5).
38 Leupin, p. 104.

fortified town and castle of Berwick-upon-Tweed, 'wallit weill abowt with stane' (9). The opening description of 'wallis wrocht craftely withall' and the portcullis standing ready to fall 'most subtelly' (13–14) provides a solid emblem for the craft of poetic fiction, while also offering a reminder that Berwick was long a contested site of Anglo-Scottish hostilities. Held almost without interruption by the English from 1333 to 1461, when it was briefly ceded to the Scots, Berwick was recaptured in 1482, never to revert to Scottish rule again.[39] The historiographic effect of the opening lines is poignantly recapitulated in the final verse of the Maitland text, when after the comic violence of the denouement, the poet prays: 'Chryst send ws peice and lat ws nevir haue weyr' (M. 564). Codicological evidence may support a reading that would relate *The Freiris of Berwik* to the history of Anglo-Scottish conflict, for the Maitland Folio places the poem in the context of a brief series of historiographic texts that focus on questions of political authority and national identity. The *Freiris* is immediately preceded by a well-known Scottish advice to the king poem, 'Richt as all stringis ar cupillit in ane harpe'; an excerpt from Wyntoun, 'The Duke of Orleans' defence of the Scots'; and 'The Ring of the Roy Robert,' attributed to one David Steil. I must concede that the original arrangement of this section of the Maitland Folio may not have agreed with its present one, since its leaves are now mounted separately, thus destroying evidence for the original quires.[40] But we can at least be sure that the *Freiris* was preceded by the 'Ring of the Roy Robert' since they share a leaf. Bannatyne, however, seems to have preferred the relative safety of including the poem under the far less threatening rubric of 'fabillis'. The effect of encountering it immediately after Dunbar's *Goldyn Targe* is thus a very different one.

Although *The Freiris of Berwik* seems to draw on Chaucerian fabliau, its skillful handling of motifs from the French tradition suggests that other works of this genre circulated in late-medieval Scotland. The evident sophistication of the anonymous author and his original audience makes it difficult to believe that he worked in isolation; the poem thus offers valuable evidence for the existence of specifically French influences on comic verse narrative in Scotland that were perhaps made possible by the close cultural and political ties during this period. At the same time, I would emphasise, the Scottish poet manages to achieve effects that are all his own.[41]

---

39 Ranald Nicholson, *Scotland: The Later Middle Ages*, Edinburgh History of Scotland (Edinburgh, 1974), pp. 400, 505–7.
40 See *Maitland Folio*, ed. Craigie, II, 1–2.
41 Some of research for this essay was made possible by a Research Grant in Aid from Auburn University and by funding from the National Endowment for the Humanities, which allowed me to participate in a Summer Seminar for College Teachers on 'Old French Fabliaux and the Medieval Sense of the Comic,' led by R. Howard Bloch at the University of California, Berkeley, in 1992. I gratefully acknowledge the generous support of these agencies and would like to dedicate this piece to Howard Bloch and the other members.

DEANNA DELMAR EVANS

25. *Re-evaluating the case for a Scottish* Eger and Grime

According to an entry in the *Accounts* of the Lord High Treasurer of Scotland, on 19 April 1497, James IV rewarded 'tua fithelaris that sang Graysteil'. The work performed was apparently some version of the romance *Eger and Grime*. With this record in the Scottish *Accounts*, the romance was given a place in Scottish literary history. In the twentieth century *Eger and Grime* has received occasional mention by those concerned with the history of Scottish literature.[1] Moreover, James Caldwell published a critical edition of it in 1933,[2] and Mabel Van Duzee the only scholarly book about it in 1966.[3] Caldwell, in his introduction, investigated likely sources and included a brief linguistic study of rhyme words, concluding that 'the dialect of the original was Northeastern or Central Scottish . . .,' and the plot was 'based on a Celtic, probably Scottish, version of the folk-tale, *Die Zwei Brüder*'.[4] Caldwell's linguistic argument, however, was seriously challenged by his reviewers who faulted his tendency to base conclusions on rhymes found in only one version of surviving texts. Subsequently, one of Caldwell's critics, H.A. Basilius, made a study of the 127 rhymes common to both existing versions; he pointed out that since a few of these bore 'northern characteristics', there is a strong probability that the 'common ancestor' of the extant versions 'was written in a northern English or Scottish dialect'.[5] Van Duzee expanded on Caldwell's study of the Celtic background of the romance and from this was persuaded that 'in a stage considerably earlier than that of the extant versions, *Eger and Grime* may conceivably have been an Arthurian romance.'[6] She claimed that certain names, such as *Gallias* (Wales), *Kay*, and those of the two heroines, are evidence of that connection, and other names, including that of the co-hero *Eger*, indicate a

---

1 Among the most prominent literary histories to mention *Eger and Grime* are those by Agnes Mure Mackenzie, *A Historical Survey of Scottish Literature to 1714* (London: Alexander Maclehose & Co., 1933), pp. 24 & 26; C.S. Lewis, *English Literature in the Sixteenth Century* (Oxford: Clarendon Press, 1954), p. 68, finding its adventures 'as palpable as those in Homer'; and, most recently, Matthew P. McDiarmid, 'The Metrical Chronicles and Non-Alliterative Romances,' *The History of Scottish Literature: Origins to 1660*, Vol. 1, ed. R. D. S. Jack (Aberdeen: Aberdeen Univ. Press, 1988), pp. 34–5, describing the author as 'a story-teller of genius'. I owe a considerable debt of gratitude to the late Mr McDiarmid who suggested that I undertake the present study of *Eger and Grime* and offered much encouragement and advice along the way.
2 *Eger and Grime: A Parallel Text Edition* (Cambridge, Mass.: Harvard Univ. Press, 1933); Caldwell, p. 6, makes mention of the Treasurer's Accounts record cited at the beginning of this essay.
3 *Medieval Romance of Friendship*: Eger and Grime (New York: Burt Franklin, 1963).
4 Caldwell, pp. 42–52, provides his rhyme word study; on p. 157, he asserts that the plot 'is based upon a Celtic (probably Scottish) version of the very widespread folk-tale, *Die Zwei Brüder* . . .'.
5 H.A. Basilius, 'The Rhymes in *Eger and Grime*,' *Modern Philology*, 35 (1937–8): 129–33.
6 Van Duzee, p. 16; this argument dominates the book, and one of her central ideas is that the basic plot of the romance is derived from the *Pwyll* tradition of early Welsh literature.

tinge of 'slight Bohemian coloring'.[7] Indeed, it is ironic that after two centuries of scholarly exchange about the Scottish romance of *Eger and Grime*, Van Duzee's book and reviews of Caldwell's edition have created doubt about whether the romance is Scottish at all.

During the last thirty years *Eger and Grime* has received little critical attention, a result, I suspect, of such uncertainty. The only recent journal article halfway focused on it (a comparative study) calls *Eger and Grime* a Middle English romance, and its author quotes exclusively from the sole English manuscript.[8] Not everyone, of course, has quit believing that *Eger and Grime* is a Scottish romance. Both M.P. McDiarmid and R.J. Lyall at a recent triennial conference spoke of it as being Scottish.[9] Basilius had said that he found 'nothing inherently improbable in Caldwell's assumption that the romance was versified in the fifteenth century in Scotland,'[10] and even Van Duzee, who was convinced that *Eger and Grime* was not of Scottish origin, nevertheless endorsed the idea of a probable Scottish version by the late fifteenth century.[11] Surely it is time to reassess what is known about *Eger and Grime* and, if possible, to make secure its place in the canon of late medieval Scottish literature.

One factor preventing a positive identification of *Eger and Grime* as a Scottish romance is the unreliability of existing texts. There are two extant versions, both quite late and 'so corrupt and modernized that they may well be very different in language and even in details of incident from the romance which the fiddlers sang to James IV . . .'.[12] One, bearing the title *Eger and Grime*, is found in the Percy Folio Manuscript (c. 1665), and this anglicised version consisting of 1,474 lines was described in the fourth edition of Bishop Percy's *Reliques* (1794) as 'a well invented tale of chivalry, scarce inferior to any of Ariosto's'.[13] The other version, bearing the title *The History of Sir Eger, Sir Graham, and Sir Greysteil*, is in a Scottish or Northern English dialect; containing 2,860 lines, it is approximately twice as long as the Percy. Yet Caldwell and Van Duzee both consider it a patched job, perhaps the fusing together of earlier versions. Referred to as the Huntington-Laing (HL), in honour of a library and an early editor, this version has survived

---

7 Van Duzee, p. 122.
8 David E. Faris, 'The Art of Adventure in the Middle English Romance: *Ywain and Gawain*, *Eger and Grime*,' *Studia Neophilologica* 58 (1981): 91–100; this is the only article on *Eger and Grime* listed in the *MLA Bibliography* between January 1981 and January 1993.
9 McDiarmid, p. 17, 'The Scots Makars and the Ballad Tradition,' in *Bryght Lanternis*, ed. J. Derrick McClure and Michael R.G. Spiller (Aberdeen: Aberdeen Univ. Press, 1989); Lyall, p. 41, 'The Lost Literature of Medieval Scotland,' also in *Bryght Lanternis*.
10 Basilius, p. 133.
11 Van Duzee, p. 10, states that the many 'indications, though conflicting and inconclusive, point nevertheless to the probability that by the fifteenth century there was a Scottish romance of Sir Eger, Sir Grime, and Sir Graysteel,' and on p. 141, states, 'There is little to tell us when *Eger* became a Scottish romance. Internal evidence of material and names would indicate that the Scottish stage was late.'
12 Van Duzee, p. 6.
13 As quoted by Caldwell, p. 14, who publishes this version in his 1933 edition; Van Duzee, pp. 5–6, also describes this MS; it was not published until 1867 when it was included in *Bishop Percy's Folio Manuscript*, edited by J.W. Hales and F.J. Furnivall.

in three nearly-identical Scottish black-letter prints, the earliest dated 1669.[14] However, an inventory record from 1577 indicates that a Scottish printer had three hundred 'Gray Steillis' in his possession,[15] and other legal citations show that at least four Scottish printers obtained permits to publish it between 1599 and 1628.[16] Hence, there is considerable proof that black letter prints of the romance existed in Scotland before the Percy Manuscript was written, but there is no way of knowing how much these varied from the extant texts. It has been generally agreed that both P and HL are revisions of an earlier Scottish romance and that neither derives from the other, although both apparently 'descend' from the same earlier romance.[17] Controversy continues as to which is closer to the 'original'.[18]

The two versions are quite distinct from each other, differing considerably even in plot. M.P. McDiarmid, who insists that HL be treated as a separate and 'Scottish' romance, has summarised the primary differences between it and the Percy:

> There are the formal differences, the Scots tale [HL] being twice as long, not ending in happy marriages all round, introducing new characters, a figure of warning for Sir Eger, a hospitable burgess, his wife (we enter her kitchen) with an obliging son, a Sir Hew . . . A substantial difference, a stroke of genius, is the death of Sir Gryme, the real hero . . . so that Sir Eger, standing with his wife Winliane of Bealm above his friend's grave, is moved to confess to her that it was Sir Gryme and not he that slew . . . Sir Graystiel; and she, who had proudly sworn never to wed a defeated knight, leaves him for a convent, while he goes to Rhodes to fight the invading Turk. When Wynliane dies he returns to share life with the also widowed Lillias.[19]

---

14 Van Duzee, pp. 6–7, is the only one to discuss the earliest of these prints which she discovered in the British Library; contained in a badly worn book, this version, with two leaves missing, seems to have been printed in Glasgow by Robert Sanders in 1669; Caldwell, p. 13, describes the print of 1687 which he discovered in the Huntington Library, indicating that it is nearly identical with the copy printed by James Nicol in Aberdeen in 1711; the latter, now in the Bodleian Library, was published by David Laing in 1826 in a volume entitled *Early Metrical Tales including the History of Sir Egeir, Sir Gryme, and Sir Gray Steill*; Laing's edition was reprinted twice before the turn of the century, and his introductions contain much of the historical information cited here. I have examined the 1669 and 1711 prints and have compared them with the editions published by Caldwell and Laing, and agree that the three texts are nearly identical.
15 Caldwell, p. 10, cites the inventory record of 18 October 1577 of Thomas Bassandyne, the first printer of the Bible in Scotland.
16 Caldwell, pp. 10–11, notes the names of Robert Smyth of Edinburgh, his sons and heirs, Thomas Finlayson and his son and successor, Walter Finlayson.
17 Georg Reichel, 'Studien zu der schottischen Romanze: The History of Sir Eger, Sir Grime, and Sir Gray-Steel,' *Englische Studien* (1894): 21, first makes this argument; Caldwell, pp. 40–2, refines Reichel's argument and designs an elaborate *stammbaum* showing the hypothetical 'original' *Eger and Grime* at the top with a lost recension and two later versions leading to H and then 17.17 on the left and a separate line of descent to P on the right.
18 Caldwell, pp. 20–40, drawing upon the work of Reichel, presents an elaborate argument to prove that HL represents the earlier version; Van Duzee, pp. 7–9, summarises the controversy and aligns herself with those who favour P as the earlier.
19 'Metrical Chronicles,' p. 34.

If we can agree momentarily that HL seems likely to have derived from an earlier Scottish romance – it is, after all, in the Northern dialect and was printed several times in Scotland – there is still a question of when such a Scottish romance could have been written. Van Duzee suggests the latter half of the fifteenth century. M. P. McDiarmid concurs and provides a more precise date, basing his choice on the 1497 entry in the Scottish *Accounts* and details within HL, particularly Eger's going off to Rhodes to fight the Turks. Noting that the Turkish attack on Cyprus took place in 1479, McDiarmid concludes that the romance must have been written c.1485.[20] The validity of this date, of course, depends upon the 'Graysteil' rewarded by King James being an earlier version of HL and the reference to Eger's fighting in Rhodes *not* being a later addition by a transcriber. Elsewhere McDiarmid suggests an additional reason to support the 1485 date: he points out that HL contains phrases and lines from Barbour and Hary.[21] If true, then any written version of *Eger and Grime* containing 'echoes' would have to have been written after the *Wallace* (c. 1476–78).[22]

As the reaction of critics to Caldwell's rhyme word study indicates, it is next to impossible to prove on linguistic evidence alone that *Eger and Grime* is a Scottish romance, even though such evidence does not exclude that possibility. Earlier scholars who believed *Eger and Grime* to be a Scottish romance based their judgments on several other kinds of evidence – geographical, historical, literary – and their claims are worth reviewing.

There are, first of all, many allusions to *Eger and Grime* in sixteenth-century Scottish literary works. These occur in Sir David Lindsay's *Squyer William Meldrum* (1548–50) and *Ane Satyre of the Thrie Estaitis* (1552) in a portion known as the 'Cupar Banns,' which earlier scholars referred to as *The Auld Man and his Wife*. In addition, *Eger and Grime* is listed along with other popular works of the period by the shepherd in *The Complaynt of Scotland* (c. 1550) and in some later works, including a memorial poem by John Davidson (1595).[23] Then F. J. Child noted more than a century ago, that the romance seems to have influenced the ballads of 'Sir Lionel' and 'Sir Cawline'.[24] Secondly, there are external, non-literary facts, including references to a tune called 'Old Graysteel'[25]

20 'Scots Makars,' p. 22, n.14.
21 'Metrical Chronicles,' p. 34.
22 Matthew P. McDiarmid, ed., *Hary's Wallace*, STS (Edinburgh and London: William Blackwood & Sons, Ltd., 1968), p. xvi, contends that the *Wallace* 'was almost certainly written in the years 1476–78.'
23 Caldwell, pp. 9–10; Van Duzee, pp. 2–3, 9; many earlier critics, including Laing, noted these literary allusions. The Lindsay allusions may be found in the most recent edition, *The Works of Sir David Lindsay of the Mount, 1490–1555*, ed. Douglas Hamer, STS (Edinburgh and London: William Blackwood & Sons, Ltd., 1931) as follows: the *Squyer Meldrum* allusion to Sir Gryme's victory over Graysteill is found in Vol. 1, p. 181, ll. 13–17, and the *Satyre* allusion in Vol. II, p. 30, ll. 242–3; the reference to 'sir egeir and syr gryme' in the *Complaynt* may be found in *The Complaynt of Scotland* (c.1550) by Robert Wedderburn, ed. A.M. Stewart, STS (Edinburgh, 1979), p. 50.
24 *The English and Scottish Popular Ballads*, Vol. 1 (Boston, 1882–4), p. 209; Vol. 2 (Boston, 1885), p. 56 (rpt. New York: Dover Publications, 1965); Caldwell, pp. 58–62, provides a full discussion, indicating that the ballad most closely related is *Sir Cawline*.
25 Caldwell, p. 12; Van Duzee, p. 3.

and accounts of three Scottish knights being given the sobriquet 'Graysteel.'[26]

Geography provides additional clues. The character *ffyndlaw* in Lindsay's *Ane Satyre of the Thrie Estaitis* observes: 'I wait he faucht, that day, als weill / As did Sir Gryme aganis Graysteill' (Hamer, Vol. 2, p. 30). Edith Rickert considered this a reference to Kinnell, a stream in Dumfriesshire; however, it seems more likely that Lindsay was referring to Kinneill, a well-known castle in West Lothian. More helpful is Rickert's careful study of the topography of the romance which convinced her that it was set in the border district above Solway between Esk and Sark.[27] A study of maps of Cumberland county, such as those printed in the *Victoria History of the Counties of England*,[28] supports Rickert's suggestion, especially in the case of the HL text. Many names in HL correspond with Cumberland place names; moreover, words like *fell* (windy hill) and *law* (hill), both frequent in Border place names, figure prominently in the meticulously described landscape of HL.

On the other hand, Van Duzee used place names and historical names to argue against the origins of the romance being Scottish, as already noted. Yet, there are Cumberland place names which offer alternatives for some of those names Van Duzee suggested were Bohemian. For example, the name of Sir Eger, which Van Duzee argued 'was the German name of a well-known city in medieval Bohemia, a city on the Eger river,' seems more likely to come from Egremont, a place name on the Cumberland map near the West Coast and the Irish Sea, and the site of an ancient castle associated with the Barony of Egremont.[29] Van Duzee also considered the Land of *Beam*, as it is called in P, and the place name *Vaclaw* in HL (1. 852) to be Bohemian in origin: the former, she says, is a Middle English spelling of Bohemia, and the latter was named for King Vaclav II.[30] Yet, in HL, Winliane's home is in *Bealm*, and this name could be derived from *Beal*, a word of Gaelic origin according to *Jamieson's Scottish Dictionary* meaning 'an opening between hills, a narrow pass'. As for *Vaclaw*, it seems significant that its second syllable is the word *law*, a word for 'hill' common in Cumberland place names; moreover, since *V* was often used for *W* in medieval Scottish orthography, the

---

26 Caldwell, pp. 7–9, gives the fullest description; Van Duzee, p. 3, and earlier scholars also mention this evidence; the three men were Archibald Douglas of Kilspindie, serving under James V; William, first Earl of Gowrie, serving under both Queen Mary and her son James VI; and Alexander, sixth Earl of Eglin, who served under James VI.
27 *Early English Romances in Verse Done Into Modern English by Edith Rickert: Romances of Friendship* (London: Chatto and Windus, 1908), pp. xxi–xxii.
28 *A History of Cumberland*, ed. James Wilson, Vol. 2, in *The Victoria History of the Counties of England* (Haymarket: James Street, 1905), facing p. 276, map of castles and fortresses; all references to the map of Cumberland will refer to maps in this edition.
29 Van Duzee, p. 123; Egremont is on the maps of Cumberland in *A History of Cumberland*; the etymology of the name of the Eger river also argues against Van Duzee's claim, for according to C.F. Ingerslev, *Lateinisch-Deutsches Schul-Wörterbuch* (Braunschweig: Friedrich Vieweg und Sohn, 1869), the name derives from *Egeria, – ae* (f.), 'eine italische weissagende Nymphe, von welcher der König Numa Rathschlage erhielt,'; A.M. Armstrong, A. Mawer, F.M. Stenton & Bruce Dickins, *The Place-Names of Cumberland*, Vol. 20, English Place-Name Society Series (Cambridge: University Press, 1950), p. 2, describe the Barony of Egremont and how the Fitz Walters came into possession of it in the fourteenth century.
30 Van Duzee, pp. 122–3.

name could have been something like *Watchlaw (watch hill), and there is a Watchclose on the Cumberland map.

Of course, Cumberland is in England, not Scotland. A study of Border history, however, reveals that during the fifteenth and sixteenth centuries, the area was inhabited by both English and Scottish families; their loyalties to rulers were shifting, and boundaries were the subject of continual dispute.[31] The Esk was 'the old boundary of the Scottish kingdom'.[32] At the center of much of the fighting was an 'international family, part English, part Scots,' named Graham.[33] Contemporary ballad scholars argue that national loyalties were not as pronounced in the Border country as eighteenth-century ballad collectors have led us to believe: 'Much of the action of the ballads does not work along chauvinistic lines,' declares Stephen Knight, and he supports that claim by noting that 'the Graham family in particular revelled in having homes in both countries'.[34]

Certainly the importance of the Graham family in the Border country has significance for the HL text of *Eger and Grime*, for, of course, the name of its principal hero has been changed from Grime to Graham. It is noteworthy that this family name was spelled in at least five different ways in early documents, including *Grame, Graeme, de Graeme, Greyme*; it was not written as *Graham* until 1361.[35] The name seems to be derived from *Grayn*, the father-in-law of Fergus II, King of Scots, who had come over with the monarch from Denmark.[36] Thus, the author of HL, or of a text that preceded it, may not have considered himself to be changing a name at all, only normalising its spelling.

The name of Graysteel's land in the HL text is called the Land of Doubt, and this name offers perhaps an additional connection to the Border country and the Grahams. Edith Rickert believed it a likely reference to the so-called Debateable Land, that much disputed section between the two countries named officially in 1552, although the term was in common parlance much earlier.[37] The Grahams had many holdings in this area as Victorian genealogist Burke pointed out: 'These Border Grahams could scarce be called pure Scotch, yet still their country was the "Debateable Land," and the root of their old tree lay very deep in

---

31 W. Mackay Mackenzie, 'The Debateable Land,' *Scottish Historical Review* 30 (1951): 109–25, focuses on the history of that much disputed area; George MacDonald Fraser, *The Steel Bonnets* (1971; rpt. New York: Alfred A. Knopf, 1972), presents a thorough history of the Borderlands in the sixteenth century.
32 Mackenzie, p. 111.
33 Fraser, p. 178, describes the feuds of the Grahams.
34 Stephen Knight, 'The Borders and their Ballads,' in *Jacobean Poetry and Prose: Rhetoric, Representation and the Popular Imagination*, ed. Clive Bloom (Houndmills, Basingstoke, Hampshire, and London: Macmillan, 1988), p. 64; see also Fraser, who gives the Grahams much attention and on p. 364, points out that 'they had been a thorn in the side of two kingdoms for as long as anyone could remember.'
35 Bernard Burke, *Vicissitudes of Families*, Third Series (London: Longman, Green, Longman, and Roberts, 1863), p. 131, indicates, 'the name is spelt five different ways in ancient documents'; Louisa G. Graeme, *Or and Sable: A Book of the Graemes and Grahams*, (Edinburgh: William Brown, 1903), p. xvii, lists some of the early spellings.
36 Graeme, p. xvii.
37 Rickert, pp. xxi–xxii; *The Place-Names of Cumberland* Vol. 20, p. 38, indicates earlier variations of the term: 'the Batable landez' (1449), 'the Batabil lands' (1451), 'the Batable Lande' (1510).

Scottish soil.'[38] W. M. Mackenzie describes their settlement into the area: 'About 1516 William Graeme, called "Long Will", and his eight sons . . . left Scotland under banishment and squatted on land along the English side of the Esk.'[39] The vastness of the Graham holdings in the Borders is evident from the Division of Debateable Land in 1552. There is a rough outline of the defences of the West Border in the Cotton MS (Calig. B. viii, 239); in the English portion of the district between Esk and Sark, south of the dyke, there are five towers and between Line and Esk, nine towers, thus explained: 'All these little stone houses or towers ar betweene Serk and Eske and betwene Eske and Leuen and belong to the Greyms [sic].'[40] A further testimony to the importance of the Graham family in the 'Debateable Land' is the fact that the Graham name appears in some Border ballads.[41]

Several other names in HL have probable links with Cumberland place names, and most of these have some connection with the Graham family as well. McDiarmid notes a few: 'The name Gryme . . . is given in 1555 to a Sir Fergus Gryme, one of the Graemes about the Solway that won the lands of Garrieston and Alston (Sir Alistoun) [in HL] in Cumberland mentioned in the poem.'[42] Garrentine, another character in HL, may be linked with Garriestown or Garistown in Cumberland, a place thought to be associated with the family of Georgius Grame.[43]

Since an earlier version of *Eger and Grime* apparently was performed for James IV, it is perhaps significant that an earlier Scottish branch of the Graham family was related to the royal Stewarts. This relationship came about at the beginning of the fifteenth century. About 1400 Sir William Graeme, Knight of Kincardine, married the Lady Mary Stewart, daughter of King Robert III, and they had five sons, 'all entitled to wear the double treasure on their coats, signifying their royal descent'.[44] Sir William held a Charter of Entail from Robert, Duke of Albany, of the lands of Auld Montrose.[45] Sir William was succeeded around 1444 by his grandson, Patrick, the fourteenth in line; Patrick, one of the Lords of Regency during the reign of James II, was created a Lord of Parliament in 1445 with the title 'First Lord Graeme'.[46]

The names of the two heroines of *Eger and Grime*, especially as they appear in P (Winglayne and Loosepine), have been linked with the Matter of Britain,[47] not with place names or with family names. The change of Loosepine's name, as it is

38 Burke, p. 136.
39 Mackenzie, p. 117.
40 *A History of Cumberland*, Vol. 2, p. 279, note 2.
41 Knight, p. 58, discusses two: 'Hughie the Graeme' and 'Graeme and Bewick'.
42 McDiarmid, 'Metrical Chronicles,' p. 34.
43 *Place-Names of Cumberland*, Vol. 1, p. 147.
44 Graeme, p. xxxi.
45 Graeme, p. xxi.
46 Graeme, p. xxxi.
47 Van Duzee devotes Chapter V to Loosepine, identifying her with 'the lady of the thorn' in the traditional ford combat and inheriting the traditions of Morgain la Fée; she devotes much of Chapter VI to drawing parallels between Winliane and Guinevere, showing a relationship between her name and that of Welsh *Gwenllian*.

in P, to Lillias in HL possibly has its explanation in Graham family history, for there was a sixteenth-century Graham lady named Lilias. She was the fourth and last daughter of Graeme of Inchbrakie and his wife Marian Rollo. As did Lillias in the romance, she married twice: Colville of Condie in 1601 and afterwards Laurence Oliphant of Gask.[48] It is possible that the HL poet deliberately changed the heroine's name in order to honour Lilias Graham on some special occasion, a second wedding perhaps. This would account for the unusual present-tense ending of HL, a prayer for the marriage of Eger and Lillias:

> I pray to Iesus Heauens King,
> To grant them grace and good to spend,
> And love ay while their latter end. (H 2858–60)[49]

Graysteel, the mysterious villain of the romance, like the two heroines, seems a character borrowed from Celtic folklore, especially since he is of gigantic size and his strength waxes and wanes with the sun. Yet, his name remains enigmatic, and perhaps the author of the HL text or of its immediate predecessor, saw some connection between this character and another important Border family. Caldwell believed Graysteel's name referred to his armour, even though that armour is *red* in both HL and P. I believe it as likely that the name refers to the sword which Graysteel used to cut off the little fingers of his victims. If so, there could be some connection between this character and the Greystokes of Greystoke, another prominent Border family who 'became conspicuous as fighting families.' at a time when records of the Border lands 'teem with deeds of incursion and reprisal.'[50] (The *OED* indicates that one meaning of the word *stoke* around 1400, was 'a thrust with a weapon, a stab.') The Greystoke castle, located in the English West Marshes and having for protection 'the treacherous Solway tides,'[51] bears some resemblance to Graysteel's domain. To add to the intrigue of this admittedly highly speculative association, *A History of Cumberland* makes mention of an effigy in a Greystoke church, where are joined the 'arms of Greystoke (ancient) and Grymethorpe' [a name suggesting 'village or hamlet' of Gryme] with the figures of a large knight and a small one, the larger clad in plate armour of the early fifteenth century.[52]

Geographical and historical facts, as the last examples indicate, sometimes tease the critic into a kind of speculative fantasy land. Nevertheless, the many possible Cumberland associations in HL make a strong case for its being a romance of the Borders. Yet, they can account only partially for that elusive quality of *Eger and Grime* that persuaded earlier readers to 'feel', seemingly by intuition, that this romance was Scottish. This latter phenomenon, I suspect, is a

---

48 Graeme, p. 31.
49 This and all other citations of the romance are from Caldwell's edition of the Huntington print.
50 *History of Cumberland*, Vol. 2, pp. 259–60, including note 3.
51 Fraser, p. 39.
52 *History of Cumberland*, Vol. 2, p. 214; it is noted, 'As the knights are of quite different sizes, it is certain that they were originally on the same tomb.'

result of literary attributes of the romance that are not exclusively Scottish, but which nevertheless remind readers of other Scottish literary works. Caldwell, Van Duzee, and others have demonstrated satisfactorily that much of the story material in *Eger and Grime* derives from Celtic folklore, including some Scottish folk tales.[53] There are also the analogues in some popular Scottish ballads; in fact, M.P. McDiarmid has argued that 'several ballad themes or symbols' are recognisable within the HL text.[54]

While *Eger and Grime* has characteristics of popular tales and ballads, it is a more complex and sophisticated literary work. Graysteel is vanquished in the romance, but Grime's motivation is not the desire for personal fame. Nor is the victory simply a matter of the triumph of good over evil. Grime challenges Graysteel so that his 'sworn brother' may win a bride. In HL, as already noted, the plot is further complicated by the unexpected death of Graham (Grime), the real 'hero'. In those passages focusing on defeat and death, the HL poet introduces the theme of fortune and thereby adds a philosophical dimension. This addition, I believe, is further indication of the HL poet's familiarity with Hary's *Wallace*, for in that great Scottish narrative of 'shield friendship,' the theme of fortune was of great importance, as McDiarmid recently demonstrated.[55] Of course, such themes are universal, so the HL poet could have found them elsewhere, perhaps in Chaucer's *Knight's Tale*. Yet since the fortune theme is not a part of P, but is quite pronounced in HL, its inclusion there suggests the poet's familiarity with the earlier Scottish poem.

Although much fuller development is possible, a few examples will illustrate the importance of the fortune theme in HL. Lillias, that nearly perfect and wise woman who possessed knowledge of medical lore, explains to Graham as he anxiously awaits his battle with Graysteel, that fortune will determine the victor:

> I trow to God ye shal do well,
> And if that ye do win the gree,
> It is but fortune, and not ye,
> And fra fortune against him rin,
> There is no more defence in him,
>
> If ye have hap the knight to slay,
> I trow to God ye shal do swa. (H 1370–4; 1377–8)

This portrait of Lillias delivering the fortune speech no doubt was modelled after the passage in Hary's *Wallace* where a mysterious 'qweyne' (the Virgin Mary or Lady Fortune) speaks prophetically in Wallace's vision.[56] Fortune is

---

53 Caldwell, pp. 151–5, notes the importance of several Scottish folk-tales, including 'Lod, the Farmer's Son' and two variants of 'The Sea Maiden,' which, in part, led him to conclude that the plot of *Eger and Grime* is based upon a probably Scottish version of *Die Zwei Brüder*.
54 'Scots Makars,' p. 17.
55 '*Rauf Colyear, Golagros and Gawane*, Hary's *Wallace*: Their Themes of Independence and Religion,' *Studies in Scottish Literature* 26 (1991): 530.
56 Hary's *Wallace*, Book VII: 89–107.

referred to again in *Eger and Grime* at the conclusion of the fight which ends Graysteel's life:

> In world there is no bale nor bliss,
> Or whatsoever that it is,
> But at the last it will overgang
> Suppose that many think it lang.
> This tale I tell by sir Gray-steel,
> That fortune long had led him well. (H 1619–24)

There must surely have been another, similar passage about the capriciousness of fortune in HL, that is missing in the existing text; that would be the passage describing the death of Sir Graham. The unexpected death of the hero comes at a time when he is at the apex of Fortune's wheel: newly married to Lillias and the host of a magnificent tournament. All that he lacked was fame for having killed Graysteel, but that was not to come until Eger stands at his grave. By adding the philosophical theme of fortune to an already complex plot, the HL poet exhibited his literary sophistication and considerable talent.

Without an earlier version of the romance, ideally in a Scottish manuscript written before 1600 with the name of a Scottish poet attached, there will always be some question as to whether *Eger and Grime* should be called a Scottish romance. From the evidence assembled, it seems safe to assert that HL is a Border romance: this conclusion is confirmed by dialect, geography, and history as well as by its similarities with ballads. Some recent studies of Border ballads have also been concerned with the problem of nationality. Stephen Knight, for example, argues that a sense of nationalism was not pronounced in the early ballads: 'It is later simplifications which develop reductive ideas such as English traitors and brave true Scots. The Borderers may have been scoundrels, but at least they were not patriots.'[57] Hamish Henderson, commenting on the problem of determining which Border ballads were Scottish, points out the need to 'allow for extensive interpenetration between contiguous folk cultures' and to recognise that 'an ancient Celtic substratum likely underlies much of the folklore of England, as well as that of Lowland Scotland.'[58] Henderson also comments on the obscure origins of ballad plots:

> Many of the narrative songs which were to find their way into Child's . . . *Ballads* were . . . incomers from across the North Sea, or 'land- loupers' which came up from the South, after crossing the English Channel – in some cases starting their fabulous migration in the Mediterranean world.[59]

---

57 Knight, p. 64.
58 'The Ballad and Popular Tradition to 1660,' *The History of Scottish Literature: Origins to 1660*, Vol. 1, ed. R.D.S. Jack (Aberdeen: Aberdeen Univ. Press, 1988), pp. 267–8.
59 Henderson, p. 268.

What has such ballad theory to do with *Eger and Grime*? A great deal, perhaps. As has been shown, the HL version of the romance has much in common with the Border ballads: its roots are in Celtic folklore, an oral folk tradition, and many proper names within it derive from the Border country. Once the connection is made between *Eger and Grime* and the Border ballads, it seems obvious that we probably have been asking the wrong questions about its origins. Whether HL represents an earlier version of *Eger and Grime* than Percy is not important. Nor is the solution to find some *ur-text* from which both versions descend. In fact, I doubt that an 'original' version will ever be found, not because the manuscript has been lost or destroyed, but because it never existed. Just as the texts of the popular Border ballads derive from a common *oral* tradition, so also, I suspect, do the Percy and HL texts of *Eger and Grime*, even though each seems to have been preceded by one or more written versions. But I see no reason for believing them to have derived from a *common* written text. What King James rewarded in 1497 was, after all, what two fiddlers *sang*, an oral rendition, and the technique of those singers was, no doubt, that of the traditional balladeer:

> The traditional singer does not learn individual songs as fixed texts, but learns instead both a method of composition and a number of stories. By this method he re-composes each individual story every time he performs ... each rendering of the story is, then, an 'original text'.[60]

Hence, I submit that Percy and HL both stem from separate written texts, but are fruits of a common oral tradition, one with roots deeply grounded in Celtic folklore and branches sprouting out on both sides of the Esk.

The question remains as to whether *Eger and Grime* should have a place in the canon of Scottish Literature. The answer is an emphatic yes, with HL being the representative text. The romance, not necessarily in the exact form of HL, obviously enjoyed a popularity in Scotland unparalleled anywhere else. This is affirmed by the record in the *Accounts* of James IV, the early references to the tune 'old Graysteil', the Scottish knights bearing the sobriquet 'Graysteel,' and the allusions to the romance by Lindsay and other Scottish writers along with the analogues in popular ballads. Moreover, as has been suggested, the HL text is itself a distinctive literary product of considerable merit and deserving of critical study and appreciation. It is almost certainly the product of an accomplished Scottish writer, as evidenced by the text itself: the features of a Scottish or Northern English dialect, the probable 'echoes' of earlier Scottish chronicles and romances, the sophisticated technique not unlike Hary's of combining the themes of fortune and 'sworn brotherhood,' the use of place names and family names of the Border country, and the use of several ballad themes and symbols. If that were not enough, there is the historical evidence provided by early prints and

---

60 David Buchan, *The Ballad and the Folk* (London and Boston: Routledge and Kegan Paul, 1972), p. 52.

records of permits to printers, proving that during the sixteenth and seventeenth centuries, there was a demand in Scotland for repeated and frequent printings of the romance, *Eger and Grime*.

KATHRYN SALDANHA

26.   The Thewis of Gudwomen: *Middle Scots Moral Advice with European Connections?*

Denton Fox has observed of Medieval poems of moral advice that

> people seem to have regarded them, fairly enough, as miscellaneous collections of good advice rather than poetic masterpieces, and writers seem to have felt completely free to make additions, deletions and changes as they saw fit.[1]

Support for Fox's view is provided by the Middle Scots moral advice poem known as *The Thewis of Gudwomen* which is found in three different MS versions. The textual instability of the *Thewis* extends to the poem's title. Only the version found in Cambridge University Library, MS. Kk.1.5. has the title *The Thewis of Gudwomen*. The version found in Cambridge, St. John's College, MS. G.23 is introduced with the words *Incipiunt documenta matris ad filiam*.[2] I am indebted to Sally Mapstone of St. Hilda's College, Oxford, for bringing to my attention the existence of a third version of *The Thewis* which is contained within the British Museum, Additional MS. 40732, and The Scottish Register House, Edinburgh, MS. GD 112/7/9. This third version of *The Thewis* is untitled since it is not found as a separate poem, but inserted within the work known as *The Book of King Alexander The Conquerour*.[3] As this third version of *The Thewis* is not treated as an independent work, but is instead adapted to form part of a much longer poem, I propose to discuss it separately at the close of my paper.

In this paper I will attempt to consider the place of *The Thewis* within the European tradition of didactic vernacular literature. In an article entitled 'The Fourth Lateran Council and Manuals of Popular Theology',[4] Leonard Boyle

---

1 Denton Fox, 'DOST and evidence for authorship: some poems connected with *Ratis Raving*', in *The Nuttis Schell; essays on the Scots language presented to A.J. Aitken*, ed. by Caroline Macafee and Iseabail Macleod (Aberdeen, 1987), pp. 96–105, p. 101.
2 The two Cambridge versions of *The Thewis* are edited alongside each other by Ritchie Girvan in *Ratis Raving and Other Early Scots Poems on Morals*, STS, 3rd Series, 11 (London, 1939), pp. 80–100, and by Tauno F. Mustanoja in *The Good Wife Taught her Daughter; The Good Wyfe Wold a Pylgremage; The Thewis of Gud Women*, Annales Academiae Scientiarum Fennicae, BLXI,[2] (Helsinki, 1948), pp. 176–96. References are to Girvan's edition, and, unless otherwise stated, to the Kk.1.5. version of *The Thewis*. I silently normalise thorn and yogh.
3 *The Buik of King Alexander the Conquerour*, ed. by John Cartwright, STS, 4th Series, 13, (Edinburgh, 1986), 16 (Aberdeen, 1990). Lines from *The Thewis* are found in Vol. 1, pp. 215–18, ll. 8477–596.
4 Leonard E. Boyle, 'The Fourth Lateran Council and Manuals of Popular Theology', in *The Popular Literature of Medieval England*, ed. by Thomas J. Heffernan, *Tennessee Studies in Literature*, 28 (Tennessee, 1985), pp. 30–43.

discusses the enormous stimulus that this Church Council of late 1215 gave to the production of works of 'popular theology'. Within the umbrella term 'manuals of popular theology' Boyle includes manuals of pastoral care, manuals of confession, *summae* of moral teaching, expositions of the Ten Commandments, compendia of the vices and virtues, collections of sermons and sermon exempla. By contrast to the large number of works of popular theology extant in Middle English, there are very few such works extant in Middle Scots. While there are several translations of Friar Laurent's influential *Somme le Roi* into Middle English[5] there is no extant translation of the *Somme le Roi* into Middle Scots. However, this does not mean that works of popular theology were unknown in Scotland. Roderick Lyall has discovered that there are fragments in Middle Scots orthography of two separate MSS. of the *Speculum Vitae* – a work in Middle English verse which draws extensively upon the *Somme le Roi*.[6] A number of Middle Scots works also provide evidence that 'manuals of popular theology' such as the *Somme le Roi* were not unknown in Scotland.[7] During the course of the Middle Scots paternal advice poem known as *Ratis Raving* the author instructs his audience that if they wish to know all the 'condiscions' of sin they should 'ga to the buk of confessions' (*ll.* 723–4). The author of *Ratis Raving* observes of this 'buk of confessions' that it gives details of all the 'branchis' of sin and of the 'commandmentis ten' (*ll.* 726,732). Unfortunately, it is impossible to identify this 'buk of confessions' exactly from the description offered in *Ratis Raving* – both the *Speculum Vitae* and the *Somme le Roi* provide this information. The only extant copy of *Ratis Raving* is contained in Cambridge University Library, MS. Kk.1.5., and it is interesting that the version of *The Thewis* contained in Kk.1.5. includes a passage that Ritchie Girvan suggests may have its origins in the *Somme le Roi* or one of its Middle English adaptations. Both the Cambridge MSS of the *Thewis* contain a passage warning women to be modest in their dress and to avoid the sin of pride. Women are advised not to parade themselves in public, but to humbly take the lower place at a public gathering. However, this warning against female pride is followed by the concession that women should nevertheless

> . . . be honest ay
> Eftir thar stat euirilk day, (*ll.* 53–4)

At this point the Cambridge MSS diverge completely, each offering a very different definition of what it means for women to 'be honest ay / Eftir thar stat'. For the author of the St. John's version this means that women should dress

---

5 *A Manual of the Writings in Middle English*, Vol. 7 (1986), pp. 2258–61.
6 R.J. Lyall, 'The Lost Literature of Medieval Scotland', in *Bryght Lanternis, Essays on the Language and Literature of Medieval and Renaissance Scotland*, ed. J. D. McClure and M. Spiller (Aberdeen, 1989), pp. 33–47 (pp. 35–6).
7 Roderick Lyall has discovered that one of the sources for Book I of John Ireland's *Meroure of Wysdome* is the *Somme le Roi*, a discovery which indicates that Ireland at least had access to a copy of this work. See R.J. Lyall, 'A New Maid Channoun'? Redefining the Canonical in Medieval and Renaissance Scottish Literature', *Studies in Scottish Literature*, 26, pp. 1–18 (p. 4).

according to their social status. In the Kk.1.5. version of *The Thewis* however, the statement that women should be 'honest ay / Eftir thar stat' is followed by the explanation

> Fore god commendis honestee,
> quhilk of al gud is best of three;
> and eftir honore cummys profyt,
> And of al gud leist is delyt. (*ll.* 55-8)

As Girvan points out, the *Somme le Roi* also offers a definition of three kinds of good and in the Middle English translation of the *Somme le Roi* known as the *Book of Vices and Virtues*, the French text is rendered as follows: 'Many men deuysen thre manere of goodes: honourable good, delitable good, & profitable good'.[8] The *Book of Vices and Virtues* then goes on to speak of virtue which is 'thing wel honourable, profitable, and delitable' (p. 79). Although I have been unable to obtain an authoritative text of the *Speculum Vitae*, I have examined the versions of this work contained in Cambridge University Library, MS. Ff.4.9. and Cambridge University Library MS. Ii.1.36. In neither of these MSS of the *Speculum Vitae* is the idea of the three goods expounded. As with the identity of the 'buk of confessions' described in *Ratis Raving*, it is not possible to give an exact source for the reference to the three goods in the Kk.1.5. version of *The Thewis*, although it does not appear to be drawn from the *Speculum Vitae*. These lines seem to indicate that in addition to the knowledge of the *Speculum Vitae* in Scotland, there was also knowledge of the *Somme le Roi* or of some other work which, like the *Somme le Roi*, treats of the three goods.

It is generally accepted that the moral advice poems known as *The Foly of Fulys and the Thewis of Wysmen*,[9] and *The Consail and Teiching at the Vys Man Gaif his Sone*,[10] both of which are only extant in Cambridge University Library, MSKk.1.5., show strong evidence of a common authorship with *The Thewis*. However, in an examination of the vocabulary of the moral advice works in Kk.1.5. Denton Fox also produced evidence linking *Ratis Raving* to three shorter moral advice works (p. 99-101). Since *Ratis Raving* is usually dated to the late fourteenth or very early fifteenth century, while the three shorter moral advice poems have been dated to the mid-fifteenth century,[11] Fox's linguistic evidence suggesting the possibility of some form of common authorship appears puzzling. As a solution to this puzzle Fox suggests

> ... that *Ratis Raving* and the other shorter poems are not, as we now have them, works that were composed by single authors, but the results of revisions, additions, and deletions made by various hands. (p. 102)

I would suggest that the fact that the Kk.1.5. version of *The Thewis* contains lines that appear to be drawn from a 'buk of confessions' such as the *Somme le Roi* adds

---

8 Edited by W.N. Francis, EETS (London, 1942), p. 79.
9 Edited by R. Girvan in *Ratis Raving*, pp. 52–65.
10 Edited by R. Girvan in *Ratis Raving*, pp. 66–79.
11 Girvan, pp. xxxii–lxxiv.

further support to Fox's argument. While the discussion about female dress in the St. John's version of *The Thewis* appears to follow logically from the assertion that women should 'be honest ay / Eftir thar stat', the discussion of the three goods found in the Kk.1.5. version of *The Thewis* does not really address the question as to why women's honesty should be connected to their social estate. The fact that *Ratis Raving* includes a description of a 'buk of confessions', and the Kk.1.5. version of *The Thewis* contains lines which seem to belong within such a 'buk' appears to support Fox's contention that both works may have been revised by the same person at some point.

Although it is impossible to identify exact sources for most of the moral advice offered by *The Thewis*, it is possible to examine this poem, not only within the very broad context of 'manuals of popular theology', but also within the more restricted context of the medieval tradition of instructional literature addressed to women. In a survey entitled *De la Litterature Didactique s'addressant specialement aux femmes*, Alice Hentsch lists over sixty works which she considers to have been addressed to medieval women.[12] Even a more restrictive survey such as Diane Bornstein's account of *Medieval Courtesy Literature for Women* contains a list of over twenty works of practical advice on conduct and morals addressed to women.[13] Of the works addressed to lay women that are listed by Hentsch and Bornstein, a high proportion are in French, and many of these French works seem to be addressed primarily to women of the nobility.[14] *The Thewis*, which is the only extant instruction for women, lay or religious, to be written in Middle Scots, is therefore perhaps slightly unrepresentative of the main European tradition of advice literature for women, as it appears to be addressed primarily to women of the middle class, and probably to women of the urban middle class, since among the advice offered is the injunction to 'Nocht oys na tratlynge in the toune' (*l.* 17).[15]

In its concern with the morals and conduct of lay, middle-class women, *The Thewis* has much in common with the Middle English poem known as *The Good Wife Taught Her Daughter*.[16] While five of the six extant versions of *The Good Wife* employ a stanzaic verseform, the version of *The Good Wife* contained in Oxford, Bodleian Library, MS. Ashmole 61 is written in octosyllabic couplets[17] as are the

---

12 Alice A. Hentsch (Cahors, 1903).
13 Diane Bornstein, *The Lady in the Tower: Medieval Courtesy Literature for Women* (Connecticut, 1983).
14 Diane Bornstein lists seventeen works of female instruction written in French. Although several of these works include advice addressed to women other than the nobility, almost all are concerned primarily with the conduct of noblewomen, and are written from an 'aristocratic' bias. Even the work known as *Le Menagier de Paris*, which was written by a wealthy Parisian merchant, is not addressed to a 'middle-class' female audience, since the merchant writes for his young wife who belonged to the nobility.
15 In my discussion of the class of woman addressed by *The Thewis* I have benefited greatly from the criticism of Felicity Riddy of the Centre for Medieval Studies, University of York, and from the opportunity to hear her paper entitled 'Lady be Good: Conduct Books and the Independent Woman', delivered at the Conference on 'Women and the Book in the Middle Ages' which was held at St. Hilda's College, Oxford, August, 1993.
16 Edited by Tauno Mustanoja in *The Good Wife Taught her Daughter*, pp. 157–75 and 197–221.
17 Mustanoja, pp. 216–21.

two Cambridge versions of *The Thewis*. The version of *The Good Wife* contained in MS. Ashmole 61 is immediately preceded by a version of the Middle English paternal advice poem known as *How the Wise Man Taught his Son*,[18] just as the version of *The Thewis* contained in Kk.1.5. is immediately preceded by the Middle Scots paternal advice poem known as *The Consail and Teiching at the Vys Man Gaif his Son*. Furthermore, the versions of *The Good Wife* and *How the Wise Man Taught his Son* contained in MS. Ashmole 61 are both followed by the colophon 'quod Rate', while as Denton Fox points out the title *Ratis Raving* which is given in the scribal colophon to this work in Kk.1.5. 'presumably means 'Rate's Raving' (p. 102). There appear to be a number of interesting coincidences therefore, between some of the poems contained in Ashmole 61 and some of the poems in Kk.1.5., although whether these are more than coincidences is not entirely clear. The most obvious difference between the Ashmole version of *The Good Wife* and *The Thewis* is that while the Middle English poem takes the form of a mother's address to her daughter, the Middle Scots poem does not take the form of a maternal address. Despite this difference in form however, *The Thewis* does share much basic subject matter with *The Good Wife*. Both works advise women how to behave in public, and how to manage a household. However, there are also certain differences in subject matter between the *Thewis* and *The Good Wife* which may perhaps be related to the fact that the former is not cast in the form of a maternal address. While the *Good Wife* is mainly composed of practical advice as to how the daughter should behave, *The Thewis* intersperses advice of this nature with more general pronouncements such as the statement that

> women that has a thowlas hart,
> ane houre ore twa thinkis bot a start. (*ll.* 145–6)

The first piece of moral advice offered by *The Thewis* is that '. . . men suld considyr/ That womenis honore is tendyr & slyddir' (*ll.* 7–8), and the first instruction offered to women by the poem is that

> A woman suld ay have radour
> Of thinge that gref mycht hir honoure. (*ll.* 11–12)

The Thewis as a whole is very concerned with the question of how a woman may maintain her 'honestee' and 'honore', and avoid 'dishonore' and 'schame'. In its obsession with 'honore' and 'schame' *The Thewis* resembles *The Foly of Fulys* and *The Conseil and Teiching* both of which are concerned with these concepts. However, it is in *The Thewis* that the most frequent references to 'honore' and 'honestee' are made, perhaps because female 'honore' is felt to be more vulnerable than male 'honore'.

Although I suggested above that the intended audience for the *Thewis* may

---

18 *How the Wyse Man Taught hys Sone*, edited by R. Fischer, *Erlanger Beiträge zur Englischen Philol.*, II (Erlangen, 1889). The version of this poem found in MS. Ashmole 61 is on pp. 42–9.

well have been composed of middle-class, urban women, there is a passage at the close of the Kk.1.5. version of *The Thewis* which suggests that the author of this version may have been addressing an audience of women of a slightly higher social status. The author of the Kk.1.5. version speaks of the need to provide for young women who unlike young men 'have na craft' (*l.* 261) which would enable them to earn their own living. The reference to a 'craft' here seems to suggest once more a middle-class, urban context for *The Thewis*. However, in the Kk.1.5. version of *The Thewis* the author then proceeds to observe that

> . . . mony lordis ar nocht larg,
> Thinkand thai have our-gret charge
> To mary thar barnis to thar estat. (*ll.* 265–7)

with the result that young women 'forfalt', and are ruined. The reference to 'lordis' in these lines and to the cost of providing dowries could perhaps be addressed to a middle-class audience, but it does seem to suggest the wealthier middle-class, or perhaps even the lesser nobility. In the last hundred lines of *The Thewis* the author discusses the education of 'madenis yhinge' and urges that they should be

> In teching with a gud maistres,
> Quhilk knawis gud thewis mar & les. (*ll.* 203;205–6)

The author of *The Thewis* argues that youth always inclines to vice and that it is for this reason that

> . . . yonge lordis ar put to cur
> quhill wysdome cum thaim be natur,
> Or ellis throw documentis ore age,
> To gouerne weill thare heritage; (*ll.* 213–6)[19]

Once again it is slightly difficult to gauge the class of audience that these remarks are addressed to, partly because of a lack of information about the forms of education available to women in medieval Scotland.[20] In *The Physician's Tale* Chaucer addresses

> . . . ye maistresses, in youre olde lyf,
> That lordes doghtres han in governaunce, (*ll.* 72–3),

which gives an indication that daughters of the nobility were probably expected to be 'In teching with a gud maistres'. However, Felicity Riddy has persuasively argued that the phrase 'In teching with a gud maistres' might also apply to the

---

19 The last two lines of this passage are only found in the Kk.1.5. version of *The Thewis*.
20 I am indebted here to Felicity Riddy's criticism of my reading of this section of *The Thewis*.

instruction of girls who worked in prosperous middle-class households, such as the households of merchants. Very little is known about the form of education which such girls received, but the lines from *The Thewis* which argue that a girl should be taught by a 'gud maistres' who 'knawis gud thewis mar & les', suggests that for the author of this poem at least a major aim of such an education was moral instruction. The fact that the author of *The Thewis* compares the education of 'madenis' who are 'In teching with a gud maistres' with the education of 'yonge lordis . . . put to cur', is interesting since it suggests that the author of *The Thewis* considers that the moral education of young women is as necessary as that of young noblemen, and he also seems to suggest that the education of young noblemen may offer something of a model for female education.

During the course of this paper I have described *The Thewis* as a work addressed to women. However, there is no definite evidence that the poem had a female audience, and it is not impossible that, in its present form, *The Thewis* was addressed as much to a male as to a female audience. Lines such as the instruction to

>Dant nocht women our-wantonly,
>Na feid thaim nocht our-delygatly (*ll.* 71–2),

are addressed not to women themselves, but to the men who provide for them. For as the closing lines of *The Thewis* make clear, since women 'have na craft' they must ultimately depend upon 'thriftee men' to give them 'gudly, suet, neidfull lewynge' (*ll.* 248–9). However, elsewhere in *The Thewis* the instruction does seem to be addressed to women themselves, as in the lines which urge women

>. . . eftir nwne one the haly day
>owthir pray or play at honest play,
>To reid bukis or lere wefinge. (*ll.* 167–9)

Although the instruction 'To reid bukis or lere wefinge' is only found in the Kk.1.5. version of *The Thewis*, the line is interesting, since alongside the traditional injunction to women to 'lere wefinge' is an encouragement to female literacy. The instruction to women 'to reid bukis' in the Kk.1.5. version of *The Thewis* also provides useful evidence that the author of this version envisaged women as being capable of reading his work. It is difficult to decide therefore, how far *The Thewis* is a poem written about women, and how far it is a poem addressed to women themselves.

I would now like to turn to the third version of *The Thewis* contained within *The Buik of King Alexander the Conquerour*. There is considerable controversy concerning the authorship of this work, which is attributed to Sir Gilbert Hay in a confusing scribal epilogue. While I do not wish to enter into the controversy over authorship in this paper, I do intend to use the title *Hay's Buik* to refer to *The Buik of King Alexander the Conquerour*. The version of *The Thewis* contained within *Hay's Buik* has been adapted from the octosyllabic couplets in which the two Cambridge versions are written, to the very uneven decasyllabic couplets in which the rest of *Hay's Buik* is composed. The version of *The Thewis* contained in *Hay's Buik* might almost be described as a 'selection' rather than a separate version, since it is only about a third of the length of the Cambridge versions. The version of *The Thewis* found in *Hay's Buik* contains two lines which appear to be based on lines unique to the St. John's version,[21] and two lines based on lines unique to the Kk.1.5. version.[22] Therefore, it is unlikely that the version of *The Thewis* found in *Hay's Buik* is based on either of the Cambridge MSS. The version of *The Thewis* found in *Hay's Buik* also contains several lines which do not appear in either Cambridge MS.

The Thewis is introduced into *Hay's Buik* during the course of a Court of Love which is held in the Castle of Effesoun by a group of young noblemen and noblewomen. The Court of Love in *Hay's Buik* is based upon the Court of Love which occurs within the branch of the French *Roman d'Alixandre* known as *Les Voeux du Paon*.[23] However, *Hay's Buik* treats its French sources very freely. Much of the Court of Love in *Les Voeux du Paon* is concerned with questions of who various characters love, although there are also four *demandes d'amour*. By comparison with *Les Voeux du Paon*, *Hay's Buik* presents the Court of Love as a much more organised event in which the nobleman chosen as the King of Love has to ask each of the participants three questions, and the participants themselves are able to ask the King of Love three questions. *Hay's Buik* does not make use of one of the *demandes d'amour* found in *Les Voeux du Paon*. However, it does make use of the remaining three *demandes d'amours* found in *Les Voeux du Paon*, and also adds a further twenty-one *demandes d'amours* for which there is no source in the French text. In *Hay's Buik* it is a female character, 'Dame Ydory' who asks

> At yow schir king, I spere, sen best ye can,
> Quhilk ar the thewis of ane gud women, (*ll.* 8477–8)

In the Cambridge MSS of *The Thewis* the opening lines announce that

> The gud Wyf schawis, fore best scho can,
> quhilkis ar thewis of gud women, (*ll.* 1–2)

In *Hay's Buik* therefore, the King of Lufe is attributed with moral advice which in the Cambridge MSS of *The Thewis* is attributed to the persona of the 'gud Wyf'. This leads to the slightly bizarre situation in which it is The King of Lufe who urges

---

21 Although the evidence is not conclusive, *Hay's Buik*, *ll.* 8505–6 appear to be based on the St. John's version of *The Thewis*, *ll.* 67–8.
22 *Hay's Buik*, *ll.* 8511–12, are based upon the Kk.1.5. version of *The Thewis*, *ll.* 77–8.
23 MS. Bibliothèque Nationale, No. 12565 of the *Voeux du Paon* is edited by R.L. Graeme Ritchie in his edition of *The Buik of Alexander*, Vols II-IV, STS, n.s. 12, 21, 25, (London, 1921, 1927, 1929).

> Off mette or drink be nocht oure liccorous,
> For lichery oft followis, men sais thus;
> Na drowryis gif, na giftis to ressave,
> Na sangis of plesance for to gif na craif; (*ll.* 8507–10)

The definition of the 'thewis of gud women' offered by the King of Lufe seems to directly contradict the definition of a 'good woman' offered by 'Merchiane' only a little earlier in the Court of Love. For in response to the question whether a '. . . lady may but velany / Lufe may na ane vnfendyeand lelely' (*ll.* 8335–6), Merchiane replies ' "ya" schortlie' (*l.* 8363), since he argues that 'ay the better woman, mare benyng' (*l.* 8369), and that

> The wourthiest ay, and gretest of degre,
> Has maist of piete and benignitie,
> For pietie in ladyis hart is wele semand,
> As in the gold ring is the diamand; (*ll.* 8371–4)

It could be argued that the difference between Merchiane's defintion of the 'better woman', and the King of Lufe's definition of the 'thewis of gud women', is the difference between the kind of behaviour expected of 'wourthy ladyis' and the kind of behaviour expected of middle-class 'gud women'. One effect of the insertion of lines from *The Thewis* into *Hay's Buik* is to bring into juxtaposition the ideal of the 'wourthy' lady full of 'pietie and benignitie' towards those who request her love, and the ideal of the middle-class 'gud wyff' who is aims to strive 'In hussychip . . . ay with hir nychtboure / Quha can maist thrifty be' (*ll.* 8515–16). The introduction of lines from *The Thewis* into *Hay's Buik* raises the question as to whether these lines from *The Thewis* are intended to offer some form of critique upon the ideal of the 'wourthy' lady in the Court of Love. However, the fact that the next questioner of the King of Lufe asks him 'Quhilkis ar the thewis of a fare woman' (*l.* 8608), seems to suggest that the introduction of lines from *The Thewis* into *Hay's Buik* may not have had an entirely serious and moral intent.

The version of *The Thewis* found in *Hay's Buik* also includes a passage of advice which is clearly directed to men, and which is not found in the Cambridge MSS. of the poem. This is the advice that

> . . . quha likis owthir lufe or lady cheis
> Behald first of quhat burgioun that scho beis,
> For gude mother, dochter gude is to presume, (*ll.* 8573–5)

The advice that a man should choose his wife according to the morality of her mother is a commonplace in Middle Scots didactic works. This same basic counsel as to how to choose a wife is also found in *The Buke of the Chess*,[24] *Ratis Raving*, *The Conseil and Teiching*, and the Middle Scots prose work known as *The*

---

24 Edited by Craigie in *The Asloan Manuscript*, Vol. 1, pp. 81–152 (*ll.* 620–4).

Spectacle of Luf.[25] The phrasing of the above lines from *Hay's Buik* is very close to that found in *The Consail and Teiching*, where the son is instructed by his father that

> . . . quhen a wyff thow takis for the,
> Se fyrst of gud burgione scho bee. (*ll*. 251–2)

When allowance is made for the alteration from the octosyllabic couplets of *The Consail and Teiching* to the decasyllabic couplets of *Hay's Buik*, then I would suggest that five lines in the version of *The Thewis* found in *Hay's Buik* are based on lines found in *The Consail Consail and Teiching*.[26] I would therefore suggest that the author of *Hay's Buik* knew *The Consail and Teiching* as well as *The Thewis*. Since the author of *Hay's Buik* does not appear to draw his version of *The Thewis* from either of the Cambridge MSS, I would suggest that *The Consail and Teiching* and *The Thewis* may have existed together in a MS. other than Kk.1.5.

Hay's Buik contains another passage which is of interest to a discussion of *The Thewis*. An important feature of *Hay's Buik* is that it gives much greater prominence to the role of Aristotle than is found in either the various branches of the *Roman d'Alixandre*, or in the *Historia de Preliis*. One instance of this expansion of the role of Aristotle in *Hay's Buik* is its inclusion of an account of how Aristotle's love for an unnamed woman led him to agree to be saddled and ridden by her, to the mockery of hidden onlookers. This episode is recounted in different forms in the *Lai d'Arioste*,[27] *Aristoteles und Phillis*,[28] and in various Latin exempla.[29] A reference to the bridling of Aristotle is also found in the anonymous Middle Scots prose work *The Spectacle of Luf*. In the *Spectacle of Luf* the author asks

> Was nocht arrestotill . . . inschantit sa with the bewte of the quen of grece that scho maid him to be sadillit . . . schorand him lyk a hors? For the quhilk deid clerkis haith tane sic vengeance that thai haif ryddyn mony a thowsand in contrar that of wemen & yit thinkis nocht that trespas recompensit. (p. 278)

In *Hay's Buik* it is Aristotle himself who initiates the literary revenge of 'clerkis' upon women. For in his rage at the woman who mocked him Aristotle writes to Alexander

> . . . how lufe ourcummys all thing;
> And thareof made a buke into that place,
> How many kyndis of paramouris thare was,
> And of gude women and thare gude thewis,
> And how vise men are dissauit with schrewis.

---

25 Edited by W. A. Craigie in *The Asloan Manuscript*, Vol. 1, pp. 271–98.
26 *Hay's Buik*, *ll*. 8573–7, are based on *Consail and Teiching*, *ll*. 251–5.
27 Edited by Anatole de Montaiglon in *Recueil general et complet des fabliaux*, volume 5 (Paris, 1872).
28 Edited by John L. Campion in *Modern Philology*, XIII (1915–16), pp. 347–60.
29 The anecdote is in Jacques de Vitry, *Exempla*, edited by J. Greven (Heidelberg, 1914).

And sic ane vengeance ordand he to take,
Sen hiddirwart that neuer was sene the make,
For money a thousand sic wemen sen that day
Was with his clerkis oure-riddin, I dar wele say.
And daly dois, and euermare sall do,
Bot sum assith be made the party to. (*ll.* 7230–40)

It is interesting that in both *The Spectacle of Luf*, and *Hay's Buik* the bridling of Aristotle leads to a 'literary' revenge which continues to this day in the animosity between women and 'clerkis'. This idea of a literary revenge for Aristotle's humiliation at the hands of a woman is not found in the *Lai d'Arioste*, nor in the Latin exemplum of Jacques de Vitray.[30] The phrasing of the idea of the revenge of the 'clerkis' upon women is so close in both the Middle Scots works that it seems very likely one may have influenced the other. However, at this stage I have been unable to ascertain whether any influence is from *Hay's Buik* upon the *Spectacle of Luf* or vice versa. The reference in the lines from *Hay's Buik* to Aristotle's composition of a work containing material about 'gude women and there gude thewis' is also of interest since a little later in the narrative the author of *Hay's Buik* will introduce material from *The Thewis of Gudwomen*, which is just such a work as Aristotle is here said to have written. However, the lines from *Hay's Buik* are of further interest since they place Aristotle's composition of a work concerning 'gude women and thare gude thewis' within the narrative context of his revenge upon an individual woman. In the closing section of this paper therefore, I would like to very briefly consider how far *The Thewis* belongs within the extensive tradition of medieval misogyny, and how far it offers women any alternative to this misogynistic tradition.

Although *The Thewis* contains a conventional warning against women who 'cowet the maistry' (*l.* 148), it is less declaredly misogynistic than many Medieval works written about women such as *The Spectacle of Luf*. The author of *The Spectacle of Luf* offers as an alternative title for his work the heading the 'delectatioun of luf of women' (p. 271). The 'delectatioun of luf of women' turns out to be a slightly ironical title however, since *The Spectacle of Luf* proves to be a work with strong affinities in subject-matter to the more appropriately titled Latin poem *Fuge cetus feminarum*.[31] While *Fuge cetus feminarum* argues in turn against loving a virgin, wife, widow, beghine and nun, *The Spectacle of Luf* argues in turn against loving a virgin, wife, widow and nun. *The Spectacle of Luf* supports its anti-feminist arguments by the extensive use of *auctoritates*, and of illustrations of evil women drawn from history and literature, especially from Ovid's *Metamorphoses*. By contrast, *The Thewis* does not refer to a single named *auctor*. The fact that *The Thewis* does not use *auctoritates*, and does not give examples of good and

---

30 The closest parallel that I have been able to find to the idea of Aristotle's literary revenge is in the Middle German romance of *Aristoteles und Phillis*, in which a humiliated Aristotle leaves the court and writes 'ein michel buoch' (*ll.* 534–41).

31 I owe my reference to this poem to *Chaucer and Medieval Estates Satire: The Literature of Social Classes and the General Prologue to the Canterbury Tales* by Jill Mann (Cambridge, 1973), p. 265, note 72.

bad women drawn from history and literature, but instead offers moral advice to contemporary women, means that the poem is not within the mainstream of sophisticated clerical misogyny to the same extent as a work like *The Spectacle of Luf*.

While it would be ridiculous to claim that *The Thewis* is a feminist work, the statement in the opening lines of the poem that the 'thewis of gud women' make '... pouer women princis peir' (1.4), suggests an equality of moral worth between men and women, even if in all other spheres the sexes are unequal. The idea that virtue can make a poor woman a prince's equal is not to my knowledge a common feature of medieval works of instruction addressed to lay women. Another feature of *The Thewis* that is not typical of advice work for women is the consideration which the poem gives to the economic situation of women. In *The Thewis* the author remarks that 'pouertee tynis mony gud woman', and he observes that many young women act dishonourably not because they want to, but out of economic necessity. The author of *The Thewis* remarks of these young women that

> Thai have na craft – how suld thai leif?
> and frendis will thaim na-thing gif;
> than is thar nocht bot do ore dee.
> One fors thus mone thai fulys bee. (ll. 261–4)

This is a very different argument from that of traditional anti-feminism, which sees women as dishonourable and voluptuous by nature. This traditional anti-feminist argument is put forward in the *Spectacle of Luf* whose author employs numerous *auctoritates* to support his case including Secundus who 'says that wemen are the veschell of adultre, a stynkand rois, a box full of venum' (p. 276). By contrast, the author of the Kk.1.5. version of *The Thewis* attacks those 'lordis' who are slow to marry their daughters because of the need to provide them with dowries. When the daughters lose their honour through this delay in marriage, the author of the Kk.1.5. version of *The Thewis* suggests that while their fathers pretend to be grieved they are really glad at the expense spared. While the author of *The Thewis* opens with the statement that 'gud thewis' can make 'pouer women princis peir', he closes with the idea that a woman's virtue may in fact depend upon the willingness of men to provide for her. Unlike the author of *The Spectacle of Luf* the author of *The Thewis* does not suggest that women are by nature a 'veschell of adultre' and a 'box full of venum'. Instead the author of *The Thewis* suggests that women act dishonourably not out of choice but out of economic necessity. The author of *The Thewis* is no social revolutionary, and he offers no challenge to the economic *status quo* in his poem. However, he does suggest how far female virtue may finally be a question of male economics.

C. MARIE HARKER

27. 'Chrystis Kirk on the Grene': Dialoguic Satire in Fifteenth-Century Scotland

The anonymous Middle Scots poem known as 'Chrystis Kirk on the Grene' has been known primarily as the object of a long-standing controversy concerning its authorship and date. What little critical attention it has attracted has been largely content to admire its rollicking, slapstick comedy. A small proportion of the commentary has suggested that the work – a burlesque treatment of a country fair, probably dating from the second quarter of the fifteenth century[1] – is informed by class-specific satire, in which the social pretensions of peasants are mocked by an aristocratic narrator. However, this fails to acknowledge the dialoguic nature of the work, in which a variety of competing fifteenth-century subject-positions critique one another. This is a polyvocal work, whose referential object is the heterogenous world of the late medieval Scottish burgh, with its increasingly excluded craftsmen, its ascendant merchant class, and its largely absent aristocrats. 'Chrystis Kirk on the Grene' speaks the social agon of urban Scotland in a period of considerable flux; its satiric voices present a carnival bringing-together of the high and the low.

Obscured by the broadly visual 'Punch-and-Judy' comedy of a village mêlée, with screeching wives and groaning champions, 'Chrystis' satire is so understated as to have been generally ignored.[2] When noted, its satire has been read as a simple containment of an undifferentiated lower class – 'a good-natured burlesque of peasant customs and peasant character, written by a conscious and intellectual artist, and addressed to an upper-class audience'.[3] This is satire informed by a binary paradigm of the nobles versus the commons:

> ... the alleged belligerence of the lower orders was a welcomed argument for the propertied classes ... the upper classes could keep their hegemony

---

1 Attributed to both James I (1406–37) and James V (1513–42), the evidence, while equivocal, supports the former. David Irving, *The History of Scottish Poetry*, ed. J. A. Carlyle (Edinburgh, 1861), pp. 134–5, points out that in 1521 the historian Major detailed James I's literary achievements: an 'artificiosum libellum de regina' ('Kingis Quair'), 'Yas Sen,' and 'At Beltayne.' Alexander Lawson, *The Kingis Quair*, (London, 1910), p. lii, notes that 'Chrystis Kirk''s companion poem, 'Peblis to the Play' begins with 'At Beltane...', while 'Yas Sen' is a likely corruption of 'Chrystis Kirk''s 'Was nevir ... sene.' Dating from the last quarter of the fifteenth century, the sole exemplar of 'Kingis Quair' attributes that work to James I (Bodl. Arch. Selden Ms B. 24); the most authoritative witness of 'Chrystis Kirk' attributes it also to James I.
2 John Speirs, *The Scots Literary Tradition* (London, 1940), p. 98; and Roderick Watson, *The Literature of Scotland* (London, 1984), p. 52.
3 Allan H. MacLaine, 'The "Christis Kirk" Tradition: Its Evolution in Scots Poetry to Burns,' *Studies in Scottish Literature*, 2 (1964–5), p. 13.

only as long as they could keep the numerically stronger masses disarmed . . .[4]

The nobility laughed at the lewdness of the lower classes because it confirmed their own cultural superiority; yet their laughter probably betrayed subconscious fear of the vigor and fertility of the lower orders, who ever threatened to engulf and overwhelm them.[5]

This kind of uncritical historicism gives little credit to the complexities of either the poem or its context; neither was so monolithic as these readings would suggest.

Early fifteenth-century Scotland had already begun to enjoy a period of international peace and domestic security. The War of Independence was over, and the monarch – who was to prove an able ruler – had returned from eighteen years of English captivity. However, this century was to see wide social changes and redistributions of wealth; 'social and economic distinctions between the greater and the lesser were . . . becoming blurred and challenged'.[6] While the large majority of the Scottish population continued to live as tenant farmers, urban Scotland was growing increasingly powerful.[7] In growing numbers merchants purchased 'gentle' status,[8] and the growth of a money economy was 'further reducing the gulf between the aristocracy and the gentry'.[9]

In large part, the new mercantilism was centered in and dependent upon the institution of the royal burgh. Mainly established in the early twelfth century, these market towns were nearly autonomous settlements, free from local lords' jurisdiction – indeed, actively resistant to political influence by the gentry.[10] Inhabited by merchants and craftsmen, the burghs exerted monopolies on trade and crafts over a wide region: markets and fairs were restricted to burghs until the sixteenth century, and no foreign trade could exist outside a royal burgh.[11] Consequently able to supply the considerable revenue levies necessitated by the English ransom payments established on James' release, the burghs enjoyed increasing parliamentary representation, and a concomitant influence on legislation.[12]

However, these circumstances did not affect all burgesses alike; throughout the fifteenth and into the sixteenth centuries, the merchant class systematically excluded craftsmen from local, hence national, polity.[13] The 'merchant burgesses

---

4 George Fenwick Jones, ' "Christ's Kirk," "Peblis to the Play," and the German Peasant Brawl,' *PMLA*, 68B (1953), p. 1115.
5 *Ibid*, p. 1122.
6 Jenny Wormald, *Court, Kirk and Community* (London, 1981), p. 32.
7 Ranald Nicholson, *Scotland in the Later Middle Ages* (Edinburgh, 1974), p. 17.
8 Alexander Grant, *Independence and Nationhood: Scotland 1306–1469* (London, 1984), p. 71.
9 Wormald, *Court*, pp. 48, 50.
10 Thomas Johnston, *The History of the Working Classes in Scotland* (Wiltshire, 1974), p. 15; Jenny Wormald, *Lords and Men in Scotland: Bonds of Manrent 1442–1603* (Edinburgh, 1985), p. 138.
11 I. F. Grant, *The Social and Economic Development of Scotland Before 1603* (Edinburgh, 1930), p. 368.
12 Wormald, *Court*, p. 47; I.F. Grant, p. 372.
13 I.F. Grant, p. 410; S.G.E. Lythe, 'Economic Life,' in *Scottish Society in the Fifteenth Century*, ed. Jennifer M. Brown (London, 1977), p. 71.

... dominated the burghal hierarchy and controlled the burgh'.[14] Burgh councils were dominated by merchant oligarchies; the election of new councils was increasingly determined by the old.[15]

The parliaments of this period produced an escalating series of acts of restriction of the craftsmen. From 1424–7, craft-governance by a deacon selected by and from within the ranks of the craftsmen was replaced by external governance by a warden chosen by the merchant-dominated council; this warden was to establish both prices and wages.[16]

The fourth parliament, which rescinded the position of deacon – curiously, and unlike preceding and following parliaments, recorded in Latin – directly alleges craft conspiracies:

> Rex . . . ipsus ordinationes revocavit, et . . . annulavit . . . ne tales Decanni in aliquibus regni Burgis inter artificies eligantur, nec etiam alias electi, ulterius exerceant officia Decanorum, nec faciant suas congregationas consuetas, qua conspirationes sapere praesumuntur.[17]

The craftsmen were increasingly marginalised by both literal exclusion from influence, and figural construction as conspirators; this agon was to come to fruition in the craft uprisings of 1555.[18]

However, while the merchant hegemony constructed a picture of craftsmen as dishonest and conspiratorial, the merchants were themselves not free from censure. A constricting economy, in conjunction with the social tensions occasioned by shifting status, effected growing aristocratic criticism of the merchant class – criticism that was expressed not least in parliamentary legislation.[19]

The medieval Scottish economy – largely based on the export of raw materials and the import of manufactured and luxury items, such as fine cloth and wine – had, by the last quarter of the fourteenth century, begun to suffer a trade imbalance, brought about by a severe reduction in exports.[20] The chain of results – a net outflow of bullion, a series of debased coinages, a resultant state of inflation – affected all levels of Scots society.[21]

General economic hardship joined with class-specific resentment to produce sumptuary legislation. Supposedly responsible for the net outflow of bullion, luxury imports, '. . . like the expensive colored cloth which husbandmen were supposed not to wear' were discouraged.[22] In 1429, Parliament decreed that '. . .

---

14 Nicholson, p. 263.
15 W. C. Dickinson, *Scotland: from the earliest times to 1603* (London, 1965), p. 202.
16 *Laws and Acts of Parliament Made By King James the First* (Edinburgh, 1682), II, 39; III, 77, 78; V, 102.
17 *Laws*, IV, 86.
18 Dickinson, p. 201.
19 For further discussion of the discursive figuration of this resentment, see, Louise Fradenburg, *City, Marriage, Tournament* (Madison, Wisconsin, 1991), pp. 16–19.
20 Alexander Grant, p. 71; Wormald, *Court*, p. 43.
21 Lythe, p. 81; Alexander Grant, pp. 80–2, 238–9.
22 Alexander Grant, p. 72.

na man sall weare claithes of silk, nor furrings . . . bot allanerlie Knichtes & Lordes . . .'.[23] The following year, burgesses, with the exception of 'aldermen, baillies and councillors' were prohibited the wearing of fur.[24] Ostensibly enacted to prevent the export of bullion, legislation prohibiting imported cloth continued to appear throughout the century; however, considerable quantities of foreign textiles continued to enter the country.[25] While seldom explicitly targeting the merchant-class, these repeated acts point to the growing affluence of the merchants, 'the nearest approach to a middle class in Scottish society'.[26]

For all the crown's economic reliance on the burghs, there is considerable evidence of upper-class resentment, often focused on the burgesses' putative luxury. The critical perspective of the landholders and minor gentry made little distinction between burgh dwellers:

> Shoemakers, tailors and all such craftsmen they reckon as contemptible . . . Townsfolk are accustomed to luxurious eating and drinking . . .[27]

The same insistence on the inappropriate luxury of the Scottish people appears in de Ayala's 1498 description:[28]

> . . . vain and ostentatious by nature . . . They spend all they have to keep up appearances. They are as well-dressed as it is possible to be . . . they are envious to excess.

By the reign of James IV, this resentment of the 'pretentious strutting of the merchants'[29] surfaced in Dunbar's 'To the Merchantis of Edinburgh':[30]

> Your proffeit daylie dois incres,
> Your godlie workis les and les; . . .
> Think ye not schame,
> That ye sic substance dois posses
> And will not win ane bettir name.

All of these elements – the shifting national polity, intraburghal power dynamics, the general desire for foreign luxuries opposed by a contracting economy – are at play in the multiple utterances of 'Christis'. While the ostensible satiric object of the work is the wooings, dancings, and brawlings at a burghal fair, these are always presented by the framing voice of an interested narrator, himself a satiric butt. The nature of the satiric models – both social and literary –

---

23 *Laws*, VIII, 118.
24 Nicholson, p. 305.
25 Lythe, p. 73, 76.
26 *Ibid*, p. 81.
27 John Major, *A History of Greater Britain*, trans. Archibald Constable (Edinburgh, 1892), p. 47.
28 P. Hume Brown, ed., *Early Travellers in Scotland* (Edinburgh, 1891), p. 44.
29 Lythe, p. 72.
30 *Poems*, ed. James Kinsley (Oxford, 1958), p. 76.

implicates a variety of objects much wider than the specifically identified townsfolk. The satirising subject-positions are detected not simply through their referential objects, but through their conflicting utterances; the discursive variety of 'Chrystis' voices the heterogenous politics of the Scottish fifteenth century.

Most obviously, 'Chrystis' is a world of satiric reversals based on disjunctions between the activities of courtly romance and those of burgh experience. It is as noteworthy that 'damsellis' have washed themselves as that they are decked out in 'new kirtillis' (7,8).[31] The poem begins with a heroine, 'Gillie', described with the stock similes of romance tradition; with cheeks red as roses and skin lily-white (21-2), she is willing to brave death to remain true to her love (25). Yet her hair is not golden, but the more prosaic 'yellow' (23); although loveliest of the 'madynis myld as meid' (21), she is a mocking fish-wife ten lines later, 'murion[ing]' Jok for his spindly physique (32-8).

Similarly, the dancing and fighting that follows the courting is satirically portrayed as a courtly feasting and tournament. Thome Lular may sing sweetly in the French manner, but he nevertheless concludes with a rural Morris dance, 'Full lowd' (39-44). Robene and Jok might scuffle 'manly' over a point of honor, but their encounter includes some less than heroic hair-pulling (53-62). The obligatory list of the champions' weapons describes such entirely homely implements as 'forkis . . . flailis . . . bowgaris of barnis . . . rungis (131-3). The combatants are characterised as absurd combinations of belligerence and cowardice; Heich Hucheoun may not have been a 'barty bummil', but the loss of a thumb-tip sends him howling for safety (154-67). 'Chrystis' concludes with a parody of heroic loyalty; Dik comes forward 'to fell a fidder' (a multitude) who would have slain his brother, yet turns to drubbing his wife and mother in fear of greater foes (222-8). The narrator, who reminds us of his presence throughout the work with stock distancing tags, 'as I wene' (5, 71, 86), invites us to appreciate the contrast between the trappings of courtly romance and the characters whom he paints as rude, physically coarse, clumsy, aggressive, and fearful.

The broad strokes of this canvas are aimed at an entire community. The social pretensions of a wide variety of characters are exposed: the lasses so careful of their fashionable attire (13-16), yet squealing 'lyk ony gaitis' (18); a doughty dancer, 'no rynk micht him arreist' (51), who then 'oistit (farted) at baith the ends' (56); amorous young men fighting for the honor of a girl's attention nevertheless hauling on each other's ears (61-6); dauntless archers joining an accelerating fray, yet unable to effect any injury (95, 105, 124); matrons encouraging the fighters with the ballad-like, 'Lo, quhair my lyking liggis' (138), then grimacing and groaning (141). Almost without exception, the inhabitants of a Scots burgh – minstrels, cobblers, archers, millers – are subjected to the scrutiny of a detached and superior observer. The one burghal group not exposed to overt ridicule is the class historically most interested in the containment of craftsmen, the merchants.

'Chrystis' is perfumed with the social and economic issues of the mid-fifteenth

---

31 C. Marie Harker, Chrystis Kirk of the Grene, unpub. M.A. thesis (Victoria, 1990).

century, especially the concern with luxury spending by the lower orders. Though 'full gay', the lasses' kirtils are initially of grey, the legal colour of everyday use for the lower classes, appropriate for burgh girls at a fair.[32] However, these same girls sport 'gluvis . . . of the rafell richt/ . . . schone . . . of the straitis/ . . . kirtillis . . . of lynkome licht / weill prest with mony plaitis' (13–6). Gloves were more commonly an aristocratic item; mittens would have been more appropriate.[33] 'Rafell', or roe-fells, were produced for an export market, and were therefore another satiric luxury.[34] 'Schone of the straitis' probably refers to the Straits of Gibraltar, Morrocan leather goods being yet another luxury import.[35] The initially grey kirtills have become lincoln green, permissible only on holidays.[36] The plaiting of the kirtills was an innovation generally dated from the sixteenth century; allowing for flexibility in the dating, this suggests the modish vanity of the lasses.[37] The portrayal of sumptuary excess of a group legislatively victimised throughout the fifteenth century by the very group most guilty of that excess suggests that the narrator voices, in part, the utterance of merchants.

Yet the narrator's is a voice that undermines its own authority with contradictions. The 'fechtaris' are both eager to join the fray – firing on one another with scant provocation – and desperately timid, retreating with scant injuries; with such names as Downie and Lowrie, they are connotatively dishonest and crafty[38] – yet dull and oafish, mindlessly brawling until 'als meik as ony mulis / that mangit wer . . .' (183–4). The representation of the commons as 'generally intemperate, lustful and lazy' is found in other works of the period, such as Barbour's *Bruce* and *The Complaynt of Scotland*;[39] however, the combination of these characteristics with wilful violence is less common.[40] The narrator's satiric treatment of the village folk is openly interested, sacrificing mimesis to class-containment.

'Chrystis' is a tapestry of rebelliously fraying strands: assuming the standards of gentility, merchant interests criticise lesser burgesses for their own literary and sumptuary pretensions; yet that subjectivity is betrayed both by the absence of its own representation and by agonistic self-contradictions. The assumption of absence, the seeming transparency of the narrator's subject-position, is a bid for immunity from social critique. Yet this is a 'normative' transparency that continues to collapse under examination: in displacing its own excesses onto lesser

---

32 Jones, p. 1110.
33 *Ibid*, p. 1112.
34 George Chalmers, *The Poetic Remains of Some of the Scottish Kings* (London, 1824), p. 139.
35 Jones, p. 1112.
36 P. Hume Brown, *History of Scotland* (Cambridge, 1902), I, 244.
37 Dorothy K. Burnham, *Cut My Coat* (Toronto, 1973), p. 5.
38 Jones, p. 1123.
39 Joachim Schwend, 'Nationalism in Scottish Medieval and Renaissance Literature,' in *Nationalism in Literature: Literature, Language, and National Identity*, eds. H. W. Drescher and Herman Volkel (Frankfurt, 1989), p. 37.
40 It is not insignificant that the name of one character characterised as both fierce and timid, 'Heich Hucheoun', carries connotations of an insurrectionary commonalty; for further discussion of 'Hochon', see Paul Strohm, *Hochon's Arrow* (Princeton, 1992), p. 16.

burghal inhabitants, this merchant-locus discursively assumes an aristocratic voice with the language of romance and the criticism of luxury. Yet here again strands escape. Although the escalating mêlée of drunken villagers is couched in the courtly terms of romance battles – even employing many of the stock collocations of heroic alliterative diction – the fight grows in the manner of the noble bloodfeud which was 'greatest potential cause of disorder in the localities'.[41] After 'ane' and 'the toder' have attempted to 'cheir' (wound) one another with arrows (71–6), another, 'a freynd of his' cries 'Fy' and joins in (81). Indeed Bloodfeud is explicitly invoked, as another fears his injury done for 'auld done feid' (163), and flies to safety. The poem concludes with Dik, determined to fell 'yone hangit smaix, / Rycht now wald slane my bruder' (223–4). Still, this feuding is not free from satiric treatment, as the 'wyffis' join the fray armed with sticks and stones (137, 143), and Dik beats his wife and mother, 'for he durst ding nane udir' (228). These clownish satisfactions of honour and fulfilments of fealty-obligations satirise both the rustic louts of the poem, and the unwritten gentry whose 'government by faction' so often played out the rituals of bloodfeud.[42]

In this work there is a variety of discourses, none fully subordinated to any other's authoritative centre.[43] Historical dialogues may be traced in these layered utterances. The lexicon of alliterative heroic verse and its romance values is opposed by both coinages imported with the cloth and wine of continental trade, and the earthy, local vernacular of flyting.

The characteristic collocations of alliterative romance are, throughout 'Chrystis' employed to provide a lexical contrast with the boorish tableaux they represent. The sound effects that evoke the clamour of battle in 'Golagros and Gawain' highlight with bathos this rustic battle:

> Athir berne braithly bet with ane bright brand;
> On fute freschly thai frekis feghtin thai fang.[44]
> He ettlit the bern in at the breist;
> The bolt flew our the byre . . .
> Als fers as ony fyrflawcht fell,
> Freikis to the feild thay flokkit.

In 'Chrystis' ' primary satiric reversals, 'bernis' are felled to make bridges (134), and a 'heynd' archer misses his mark (92).

However the narrator would align himself with the gentle viewpoint, his merchant context continues to reveal itself. The import recession notwithstanding, this period saw a growth in trade with the Low Countries and the Hanseatic League;[45] Flemish trade was largely responsible for the increased affluence of the

---

41 Wormald, *Court*, p. 35.
42 I. F. Grant, pp. 194–5.
43 Bakhtin, Mikhail, *Problems of Dostoevsky's Poetics*, ed. and trans. Caryl Emerson (Minneapolis, 1984) p. 189.
44 Anon., 'The Knightly Tale of Golagros and Gawane,' *Scottish Alliterative Poems*, ed. F.J. Amours (1897; rpt. New York, 1966) p. 20.
45 Nicholson, p. 266.

merchants.⁴⁶ Dealings with these foreigners occured almost exclusively within a burgal context, and a resultant lexical exchange is reflected in the neologisms of Dutch and Lower German derivation in the poem. Stevin dances in, 'platfute' (MDu: platvoet); Hary catches up a 'taikle' (MLG); and while the wives shriek, their 'yunkeris' battle (MDu: 'jonc' + 'her', young master).

Further, this is a work spiced with the living vernacular. 'Chrystis' is the first, and in many cases only, attestation of a variety of contumely expressions, of either Gaelic or unknown derivation – 'Javell' (63), 'dirdum-dardum' (74), 'Barla-fummyl' (158), 'grit glaiks' (225). The vernacular idiom, with its characteristic phrases – 'ga chat him' (35), 'gaif thame . . . thair paiks' (227) – undermines a monologic satire of lower classes by dependance on their discourse. Such use of the vernacular had the potential to rebound against its user: 'the ability to use [latinisms] freely . . . marked one as a member of an elitist in-group of cultivated persons';⁴⁷ speaking broad Middle Scots, the narrator entertains association with the very objects of his satire. While the manners and dress of the elite may have been adopted by the merchant-burgesses, the satiric objectification of the commons by a narrating perspective that participates, implicitly, in that very mercantile subjectivity, nevertheless relies on the vulgar idiom. This reliance, this employment of the aggressive vernacular, implicitly criticises both rarified aristocratic taste and the merchant-position that would ape that taste.

Bakhtin suggests that the use of others' utterances is always potentially dialogic:

> . . . the life of the word is contained in its transfer from one . . . social collective to another . . . the word does not forget its own path and cannot completely free itself from the power of these concrete contexts into which it has entered . . . ⁴⁸

'Chrystis' represents the dialogic extreme, in which the subjects, values, and discourses of a variety of concrete social contexts interact as the irresolvable historic class positions that inform them.

'Chrystis' presents a dialogue of competing subject-positions, defined by their satiric objects, rather than overtly identified: the satirist of the craftsmen / peasants, the satirist of the merchants, and the satirist of the aristocracy. Such shiftily opposing positions are represented not only by their referential objects, but also by their various linguistic styles, 'perceived as semantic positions, as language worldviews'.⁴⁹

While earlier appraisals of the satiric in 'Chrystis Kirk on the Grene' fully grasped the use of aristocratic literary models to provide an absurd contrast with the rude antics of villagers, they fell afoul of a limited binary model of social

---

46 Lythe, p. 81.
47 A. J. Aitken, 'Language of Older Scots Poetry,' in *Scotland and the Lowland Tongue*, ed. J. Derrick McClure (Aberdeen, 1983), p. 35.
48 Bakhtin, p. 201.
49 *Ibid*, p. 184.

interaction in the Middle Ages. Unlike England, Scotland never experienced as strict a division of serf and noble as that which characterises English social history; late medieval Scotland was peopled by a full array of intermediates, 'a tenurial pyramid'.[50] Indeed, unlike most of Europe, Scotland was largely free from violent class antagonism;[51] merchants and wealthy landholders were more likely to support the nobility than lesser commoners, while peasant resentment was most commonly directed against the 'Auld Ennemie' than the landed classes.[52] These multiple and shifting class alliances and oppositions of James I's Scotland find expression in a dialoguic text in which various interests are simultaneously spoken and undermined – craftsman, merchant, and noble alike.

50 Nicholson, p. 7.
51 Wormald, *Court*, p. 47.
52 Alexander Grant, p. 87.

K. D. FARROW

28.   *Scottish Historiographical Writing: The Evolution of Tradition*

At the outset, it would perhaps be useful to develop some elementary analytical tools. Let me begin by defining my terms. 'Historiographical', the adjectival form of 'historiography', is considerably less daunting than it sounds, and easier to define than it is to say! It denotes simply 'written history' as a literary genre. By 'evolution' I mean 'redaction': that specific process whereby written material undergoes purposive, often systematic and continual reshaping as it spirals from text to text and is restructured from author to author.[1] 'Tradition' refers to the basic material which has initially undergone a conversion or reification process from pre-existing oral narrative to written account, and also represents a hardcore of material usually common to all the various redactions of a narrative, no matter how highly developed from their original versions. In the process of narrative transmission, however, 'tradition' too is an ever-evolving factor.

Having defined my terms, it remains for me to outline my subject matter. Of course, Scottish historiographical writing is, with regard to its word-bulk, an enormous field, encompassing works such as John Barbour's *Bruce*, John Fordun's *Chronica Gentis Scotorum* and Walter Bower's continuation *Scotichronicon*, right through to the ecclesiastical histories of David Calderwood and John Spottiswoode. Therefore, given the short time available to me, I intend to confine this paper to a discussion of only a few authors: Fordun, Bower and Hector Boece initially, before further analysis of a Boecian narrative, as it is presented by one of his less well-known translators, William Stewart. Other verse histories, for example Andrew of Wyntoun's *Orygynal Chronykil of Scotland*, and Barbour's work, have regrettably been excluded. For readers who are not as familiar with my chosen topic as they might wish, I shall say a little about the authors themselves and comment generally on their works.

Rather less, perhaps, can be said of John Fordun than the other writers within my sphere of investigation. His date of birth is unknown and the date of his death (ca. 1384) can be determined only as the result of informed speculation. He has always been associated geographically with Fordun, following the medieval custom with names, but there is no hard evidence to tie him to the ascription. He was a secular priest and, in all probability, chaplain at Aberdeen Cathedral. His chronicle holds a unique place in the canon of Scottish literature as the

---

[1] 'Redaction', of course, is a term more closely associated with biblical scholarship than mainstream literary criticism, but it is essentially a literary tool, and ought to be more commonly used. J.A. Cuddon's one line definition in his comprehensive *Dictionary of Literary Terms*, Harmondsworth, 1976, p. 558, is hardly adequate.

earliest surviving substantive attempt to write a continuous and comprehensive history of Scotland. It identifies the origin of the Scots (not at all credibly) and, although Fordun evidently drafted more material, his main narrative terminates with the death of the saintly David I in 1153.

Edward I, of course, had removed from Scotland many documents relating to matters of national interest, and obviously, this act partially fired the patriotic spirit which can be detected in the work, and we know that, like the best of the later historians, Fordun travelled (to England and Ireland) in an attempt to gather or recover information. *Chronica Gentis Scotorum* contains five full books, and an incomplete sixth, of which the first three are historically fabulous, while the remaining two combine an admixture of fable with much more reliable historical material. It was first printed over three hundred years after the author's death, in Thomas Gale's *Scriptores quindecim* around 1690, and again by the editors Thomas Hearne in the early 1720's and W.F. Skene in the late nineteenth century.

But this is to say nothing of Walter Bower's fifteenth-century continuation of it as the early part of *Scotichronicon*, which brought Scotland's story down to the assassination of James I in 1437. We should note that such wholesale appropriation (with additions) was by no means an uncommon practice, and testifies to a belief that with this type of medieval writing at least, the narrative and not the author was of supreme importance. The same process is discernible within continental historiography. For example, a glance at French literature reveals that Enguerrand de Monstrelet's *Chronique* is a continuation of Froissart, and that Monstrelet's own work was, in turn, continued by other authors.[2] And so on.

We can say more about the life of Walter Bower (ca. 1385–1449) than we can of his predecessor in the composition of history. He became Abbot of Inchcolm in 1418, and seems to have been something of a diplomat, since he was involved in the negotiations between Scotland and France concerning the marriage of James I's daughter to the Dauphin. Additionally, he took part in the Council of Perth in 1432 as a defender of the Scottish cause. So, like Fordun, he was a man of affairs and a patriot, two very useful qualifications for his endeavour. With the completion of the *Scotichronicon* in 1447, he began the task of shortening it to manageable proportions, and the result was *The Book of Cupar*. Another title, referring to the whole text, is *The Black Book of Paisley*.

As a literary figure, Hector Boece (ca. 1465–1536) has not yet received the attention which he thoroughly deserves, although I am aware that this situation is, even as I speak, being rectified. Born in Dundee, he is most commonly associated with the University of Aberdeen, where he was a founder and its first Principal. He enjoyed the intimacy of William Elphinstone, Bishop of Aberdeen, whom he advised with regard to the foundation of the University, and whom he celebrated as the most 'sagacious man of our times' in his first work *Episcoporum*

---

2 Among Monstrelet's successors we can number, for example, Georges Chastellain and Olivier de la Marche.

Murthlacensium et Aberdonensium per Hectorem Boetium Vitae (Paris 1522).³ Exactly like his great contemporary and fellow historian, John Major, he was for his time a distinguished academic who took his first degree at Paris and who taught philosophy there as a young man. He was an acquaintance of Erasmus and a couple of letters to Boece from the Dutch humanist survive. Boece is referred to as 'great scholar and great friend'⁴ with typical exaggeration, but another comment on, or rather assessment of the Scotsman, that he 'knew not what it was to tell a lie',⁵ must be taken with a greater degree of seriousness, especially when we come to consider Boece's major work *Scotorum Historiæ a prima gentis origine cum aliarum et rerum et gentium illustratione non vulgari*, (Paris 1527).

The critics usually have only one or two points to make about Boece. The main accusation against him is as follows: his work is historically untrustworthy to an extreme degree. Lewis grants him only eight lines and concludes that if he is 'as fabulous as Geoffrey of Monmouth' he is 'not so interesting'.⁶ The generally more sympathetic P. Hume Brown does little better. Of two paragraphs devoted to Boece, one berates his accuracy, and the other concentrates on John Bellenden's 1536 translation of his work.⁷ For the record: yes, *Scotorum Historiæ*, in its early stages particularly, can only be described in a casually pejorative sense as fiction, or worse, fiction which purports to be truth not just within its own parameters. Adopting I. A. Richards' terminology, we might even call it a pseudostatement in referential language. But the notion that this automatically disqualifies Boece from detailed and careful study is an absurdity all too readily embraced. We might just as well discard Hardy's *The Mayor of Casterbridge* or Dickens's *Bleak House*. The historian J.B. Black points us in the right direction:

> . . . those who love a good tale well told, whether it be true or merely a figment of the fancy, may perhaps be inclined to pardon the shortcomings of the *Historiæ* . . . I can also conceive the student of historiography, or the art of history in its evolutionary setting, finding it profitable to look within its pages for the light they throw on the state of historical learning in late medieval Scotland . . .⁸

This is precisely the way to approach *Scotorum Historiæ*, and, with the above concessions made, we can build very constructively on Black's observations. We have acknowledged its faults. What are the strengths of Boece's primary work and what makes it special?

---

3 This text was edited and translated by James Moir, Aberdeen, 1894. Boece actually wrote '*homo (quod sine invidia licet dicere) omnium qui nostro fuerunt tempore prudentissimus*', p. 57.
4 See *The Collected Works of Erasmus* (Letters 1–141, 1484–1500), tr. R.A.B. Mynors and D.F.S. Thomson, Toronto, 1974, p. 94, and, for the original: *Opus Epistolarum Des. Erasmi Roterodami*, ed. P.S. Allen, Oxford, 1906, Vol. I, p. 154.
5 Erasmus, ed. Allen, Vol. VIII, p. 373.
6 C.S. Lewis *English Literature of the Sixteenth Century (Excluding Drama)*, Oxford, 1955, p. 116.
7 P.H. Brown *The Cambridge History of English Literature*, eds. A.W. Ward and A.R. Waller Cambridge, 1909, pp. 155–6.
8 See J.B. Black's essay 'Boece's *Scotorum Historiæ*' in A *Quatercentenary of the Death of Hector Boece*, Aberdeen, 1936, p. 31.

Well, for one thing, it is the earliest full-length history of the Scottish nation ever to be addressed to a European audience in the language and style of the Renaissance, and consciously modelled on the best writers of classical antiquity, Livy in particular. As Benedetto Croce reminds us, (if we need reminding), the really substantial achievements and advances in this 'humanistic type of historiography' were Italian works.[9] In the fifteenth century alone Italy could point to such carefully documented writings as Leonardo Bruni's *History of Florence*, even before Nicolo Machiavelli and Francesco Guicciardini seized upon the genre as a vehicle for political comment of the most rigorous kind. And in the sixteenth century, the impact of these two enormously influential figures can be seen in a whole host of successors: Jacopo Nardi, Giovanni Battista Adriani and Paolo Giovio, to name but a few.

In France, admittedly, the country in which *Scotorum Historiæ* was published and made a deep impression, historiography had seen a decline after the substantive writings of Geoffrey de Villehardouin, Jean Joinville, Froissart and Philippe de Comines, but even so, it was not long before memoir writers began to excel there.[10] So it is all the more remarkable that a lone Scot took his pen in hand in a noble attempt to lift his national prose literature into a new climate of learning, breaking away at the same time from the methods of history-writing so recently adopted by John Major. Boece, moreover, saw history as an instructive model, and while he is not unique in this (Bower and Major, for example, had the same perception), none of his predecessors had sought to educate their readers with as much elegance, dignity and distinction as Boece.

If we cannot speak as glowingly of the comparatively obscure William Stewart, we can, however, still speak constructively. His translation of the *Historiæ*, entitled *The Buik of the Chroniclis of Scotland* bears no author's name, but internal evidence allows us to determine exactly who is writing, and when.[11] Stewart seems to have studied at the University of St. Andrews, and initially found some success as a poet in the court of James V. In all probability, he ultimately took up an ecclesiastical appointment in the jurisdiction of Lanark and was dead by 1560, since he is commemorated in the prologue to Rolland's *Buik of Seven Sages*.[12]

I think, however, that I have been on my soapbox long enough. It is time now to turn to textual analysis. I have decided to explore initially a narrative common

---

9 See Benedetto Croce *Theory and History of Historiography*, tr. Douglas Ainslie, London 1921, p. 229. Indeed, an Italian rendering of Boece's introductory *Scotorum Regni Descriptio*, under the title *Descrittione del Regno di Scotia et delle Isole sue Adjacenti*, Antwerp, 1588, by Petruccio Ubaldini, testifies to a direct link between Boece's work and European vernacular literature, as does Jean Desmontiers' *Summaire de L'Origine Description et Merveilles D'Escosse*, Paris, 1538. This French text, too, is largely a rendering of Boece's geographical introduction to Scotland. I am indebted to Mrs. Priscilla Bawcutt for drawing my attention to the translation by Ubaldini.

10 I am thinking, for example, of Francois de Lanoue or Pierre de Bourdielles Brantôme.

11 See William Stewart, *The Buik of the Chroniclis of Scotland*, ed. William B. Turnbull, London, 1858, Vol. I, pp. v–viii. Major line references to the poem will appear in the text hereafter.

12 See Stewart, ed. Turnbull, Vol. I. p.ix.

to *Chronica Gentis Scotorum*, *Scotichronicon* and *Scotorum Historiae*: the story of how King Fergus III was murdered by his Queen.[13] My purpose in doing so, is, as I have already implied, to establish not just *where* but *why* the versions differ, and how the redaction process can be classified as systematic. While I shall be attempting to identify the earliest layers of a narrative, I have no particular interest in whether the events described 'actually happened', or even if the characters mentioned ever existed. These are matters for the historians to determine. In other words, my interests, for the time being, are textual and inter-textual, but not extra-textual (in a historical sense, anyway).

What of the narrative itself? As D.E.R. Watt's team asserts, it definitely has 'no earlier authority' than Fordun, and 'it may ultimately be based on oral saga . . .'[14] What evidence is there for these points? The former can be accepted after a detailed study of pre-Fordunian Scottish literature. But what of the latter? After Fergus's Queen indulges in one of her many vocal outbursts, the author observes that she spoke in these, *or some such words*, ('. . . *haec seu simila verba*') (*Chronica* I. 132, II. 125). Any scholar who has studied literature in its essential early processes of development and transmission will automatically identify this kind of comment as evidence that the author does not have access to an authentic eye-witness tradition. However, let me develop the narrative more fully for you.

Fordun, in Book Three of his chronicle, tells how a jealous Queen fatally poisoned her adulterous husband, but afterwards, smitten by remorse, savagely incriminated herself and attempted to commit suicide by drinking from the same poisoned chalice with which she dispatched her unfortunate spouse. Not content with this apparently inconclusive act of self-destruction, she finished the job with her own dagger, secretly concealed about her person. Fordun, then, is actively investigating the concept of poetic justice in the same way as Shakespeare, when the latter dramatises Hamlet's final actions against Claudius. Similarly, Fordun's tragic Queen doubtless feels emotions akin to those of Laertes when he reflects 'I am justly kill'd by mine own treachery' (*Hamlet*, 5.2.299). Her definitive dagger thrust provides an unexpected but highly dramatic conclusion, and has, perhaps, a Lucretia-like nobility about it. But more of that shortly.

Certainly, what we have here transcends 'story' and constitutes 'plot', at least as E.M. Forster would define the latter, primarily because its sense of causality supersedes the simple time sequence progression of events. But it also satisfies the more traditional Aristotelian model. There is, for example, a profound moment of *anagnorisis* when the Queen views the corpse of her husband. She ruthlessly tears her hair and laments wildly. The whole scene in fact is developed extensively. Her

---

13 See John Fordun, *Chronica Gentis Scotorum*, (Latin edition) ed. William F. Skene, Edinburgh, 1871, Vol. I, p. 132, and for the English translation by Felix J.H. Skene, see Vol. II, pp 125–6. The revised versions can be found in Walter Bower, *Scotichronicon*, eds. John and Winifred MacQueen, (General Editor, D.E.R. Watt), Aberdeen, 1989, Vol. II, pp. 155–7, and *Scotorum Historiæ a prima gentis origine*, Paris 1527, Folio 189r. All subsequent references are to this edition of Boece, by Joss Badius. In the interests of space, I have not made mention of the versions in the *Extracta e Variis Cronicis Scocie* ed. William B. Turnbull (Edinburgh 1842) or *Liber Pluscardensis*, ed. Felix J.H. Skene, Edinburgh, 1880), with regard to this narrative or the other considered in the course of the paper.
14 Bower, ed. the MacQueens, Vol. II, pp. 255–6.

immediate response, which embodies a considerable degree of psychological verisimilitude, is self-questioning disbelief: 'What hast thou done?' (I. 132, II. 126). She answers her own question in the form of other questions, and supplies for us her own motives. We learn from her recorded words that she was driven on by lustful fury (*'libidinose furore'*) (I. 132), although we cannot judge from the evidence of the text whether this accusation is justified. Perhaps it is an element which survives from an earlier pre-literary version of the narrative. Only one possibly pejorative word is applied to her behaviour in the earlier stages of the tale: that she was *over*-jealous of her husband for sleeping with other women ('. . . *nimium in ipso zelata mullierum concubinata'*) (I. 132). This does not substantiate the Queen's subsequent claim to have acted out of lasciviousness or wanton madness. In fact, it is a charge which could more properly be levelled against her victim.

The Queen's lament splits itself into two related but divergent strands (exaltation of her husband and deprecation of herself), thereby creating and maximising the hiatus between him and her. That some of the praise applied by her to Fergus is manifestly unfounded appears to bother neither the Queen nor Fordun. Her eulogistic comments may strike us as rather incongruous, especially if we have read Boece's later version. She calls the adulterer Fergus the most loving of men *'amantissimum virorem'* (I. 132), and unless we understand this language ironically (a reading not in keeping with the mood of the tale), we must place it within the 'exaltation of the dead process' which is so integrally a part of the scene. The same classification must be applied to her assertion that Fergus was extremely beautiful 'beyond the love of women' (II. 126), with its vestiges of biblical rhetoric.[15]

Alternatively, we can interpret the positive aspects of the Queen's speech as psychologically realistic. Indeed, I have already noticed a degree of such authenticity. After all, the boundary between love and hatred within a sexual relationship can easily become blurred, especially when emotions such as jealousy are involved, and when one character at least entertains a strong belief in fidelity. Indeed, what we have is an example of the 'Othello-syndrome', although the Queen's motivating grievances are actual and not imaginary, unlike Othello's. And so she acts determinedly but inadvisedly, and must shoulder her grief thereafter. Her self-deprecation is severe to the point of radical masochism. She calls herself a snake, a witch, and a betrayer, and demands to be punished. She thinks it fitting that she be dragged to the gallows by horses and her body burnt to ashes. She seeks, in other words, to eradicate every last trace of a 'self'. And it is after these utterances that she takes her life.

Walter Bower's adaption of Fordun's primary narrative is minimal. However, he adds an extra episode to the original text. In fact, he attaches to Fordun's account a story which, he says, is not remotely like it, but which is nevertheless salutary to readers. The redaction process here, then, is purely edificatory, with little or no regard to thematic links? We should, of course, be wary when we

---

15 See Bower, ed. the MacQueens, Vol. II, p. 257. The biblical reference is to 2 *Kings* 1:26 (*Vulgate*), 2 *Samuel* 1:26 (*N.E.B.*).

encounter this kind of authorial statement. If Bower's additional material is not related to that of his source writer, why should he include it in the first place? And a study of his own text reveals that his fusion of narratives is *not* wholly arbitrary, as he would have us believe. The plot with which he chooses to supplement Fordun's writing is an account of Lucretia's suicide, a parallel already hinted at in the course of this paper. Bower, moreover, tells us that his source is Augustine's *De Civitate Dei*, but his knowledge is evidently derived from the original: Livy's *Ab Urbe Condita*.[16] Augustine, in fact, does not tell the story at all. He merely reflects upon it in order to vilify the act of suicide. What he writes is a commentary.

Why does Bower, then, link the two narratives? There are several reasons. Both stories focus primarily on isolated noblewomen whose men-folk are marginalised to a considerable degree. Both women are in a very tangible sense the victims of male lust. Both take matters into their own hands. Both behave in a way which, in Christian terms, is reprehensible and damnable. Tarquin's unremitting cruelty to Lucretia represents human activity at an extreme matched by Fordun's Queen when she denigrates her own person. And so on.

Lucretia, as we know, ultimately gives way to her ravisher, Tarquin Sextus, when he threatens to cut the throat of a slave and attach the corpse to her dead body, thereby creating the unjustified rumour that she slept with one of low birth, was caught in the act, and paid the price. More terrorised by dishonour than death, she succumbs to his advances. Bower, then, is exploring the behaviour of compromised individuals in crisis situations, and, like Livy and Fordun before him, he chooses an example where an otherwise blameless character is curiously implicated in what would ordinarily be regarded as outright sin. Lucretia, of course, does not wish her behaviour in giving consent to become part of a test-case for similar situations, and therefore, she warns other women not to neglect the example of her punishment, which is, sadly, identical to that of Fordun's Queen.

What does Boece bring to this plot, which, as we can see, has taken on a considerable amount of flesh since it was oral saga? We know, of course, that he had access to, and used, *Scotichronicon*. His modulation of detail, for one thing, is extremely skilful. He excels Fordun and Bower in his own attempt to paint a picture of the abused spouse. In the *Historiæ*, moreover, the author more fully illustrates the corruptive power of sin. The Queen approaches Fergus repeatedly and gives him clear, unequivocal warnings that if he does not amend his life he cannot escape sudden punishment. The advice is much in keeping with orthodox historiographical morality, but we suspect that the Queen will be an agent in any act of retribution, divine or otherwise.

It is important to Boece that we note the frequency of the Queen's efforts to reform her husband. A King must be given every fair chance to amend. The advice however only serves to inflame Fergus further, so we can be in little doubt about his imminent fate. Again, Boece has to emphasise that the Queen takes her action only as a last resort, but the author also hints that her motivation, while

---

16 See Titus Livius, *The Early History of Rome, or Books I–V of the History of Rome from its Foundation*, tr. Aubrey de Sélincourt, ed. R.M. Ogilvie, Harmondsworth, 1960, pp. 98–9.

understandable, is not altogether commendable. Boece, unlike his predecessors, tells us that the deed was carried out at night by strangulation. This does not lessen our impression of the deed as treachery and we *do* feel that the King is pitiably vulnerable, so it is safe to say that Boecian adaptions do function purposefully.

Written into Fordun's plot is the detail that none suspected the Queen, and this early component survives through to Boece. However, he adds material which becomes an interlocking counterpart and triggers her confession. Others are arrested, interrogated and tortured. As Dickens reminds us, there is little that is as keenly felt as injustice,[17] even when we are not ourselves the victims of it. The Queen's subsequent speech in Boece is very much the kind of set-piece which is so appealing to him as a humanist author in the tradition of Livy. He has a stage: the Queen addresses her own audience, presumably made up of courtiers, but over and above, there is Boece's audience too.

He edits Fordun's less tasteful material, but like Bower, he does not end this section of his history with the suicide. The morality of the Queen's actions both in killing her husband and taking her life are keenly debated by those around her. Some, who praise her, draw attention to her concern for the innocent suspects, but others, Boece tells us, condemn her unequivocally. This debate, however, is really between the dictates of the ancient Roman world, and Christianity, with their conflicting codes of conduct. If, in conclusion, Boece sounds ambivalent it is because he has, as it were, a foot in both camps.

Overall, however, we should also remember that the redaction process in Boece has been governed by other factors. His material on Fergus III falls within the period covered by a lost history, allegedly written by one 'Veremundus',[18] which almost certainly makes fraudulent claims about its own antiquity,[19] and upon which Boece placed a very misguided emphasis. (Thus, when, Erasmus calls him the most honest of men, he is ultimately testifying only to Boece's credulous integrity.) What this author, or group of authors, added to such stories cannot be satisfactorily determined, so one of our 'layers of evolution' is missing. What we can be sure of, is that the 'Veremundus-source' was written to illustrate the fallibility of Kings and the people's right to depose them if justified by circumstance.[20]

But it is time to leave this contentious issue and move on to a study of William Stewart. What I propose to do now is examine the subsequent story of King

17 See Charles Dickens, *Great Expectations*, Oxford, 1963, pp. 66–7. Dickens, admittedly, is speaking of the world of childhood, but, of course, many an impression formed therein remains with us always.
18 This author has been tentatively identified as Richard Vairement by John and Winifred MacQueen, see *The History of Scottish Literature*: Vol. I (*Origins to 1660*), ed. R.D.S. Jack, Aberdeen, 1988, p. 237.
19 The really substantial proof of this is offered by Father Thomas Innes in his pioneering work *A Critical Essay on the Ancient Inhabitants of Scotland*, Edinburgh, 1879. See also Hugh Trevor-Roper, *George Buchanan and the Ancient Scottish Constitution* in *The English Historical Review*, Supplement 3, Aberdeen, 1966, for a more modern commentary on Innes and on Humphrey Lhuyd's critique of Boece, (which, according to Trevor-Roper, also deflated Buchanan's beliefs), pp. 25–39.
20 See Black, p. 51.

Kenneth III as it occurs in his *Buik of the Chroniclis of Scotland*.[21] This gives us the opportunity to examine an extremely well-knit plot. I think a semiotic or semiological analysis brings this out most effectively for reasons which will hopefully become evident. What makes Stewart's adaption of *Scotorum Historiæ* so interesting, more interesting indeed than John Bellenden's, is the fact that, not only are we moving from one language to another, we are changing medium, from prose to verse, and this 'double-shift' undoubtedly has an effect on the material which is ultimately presented to the reader. I would argue, too, that while Stewart's version is by no means a stylistic advance on Boece's, it is still worthy of attention and interpretation in its own right.

In the early part of the story, the character Cruthlinthus slaughters his own grandfather, the similarly named Cruthnethus, after a quarrel.[22] Stewart develops Boece's handling of this opening incident, from some ninteen lines of prose, (twelve in Bellenden), to nearly fifty in verse, with much greater concern to elucidate related incidents and render them more explicable within the context of the story. The central figure in both narratives is a woman, named Fenella. She is the daughter of Cruthnethus and the mother of Cruthlinthus, and therefore in a special sense, an intermediary character.

The incident from which all the subsequent action unfolds is described very vaguely by Boece. He tells us that Cruthlinthus was visiting 'Delbogin' where his grandfather holds a royal office. They quarrel; about what, and why, Boece has no information: '. . . *causa in arce*', (*Historiæ*, Fol. 238v). But we know the consequences. Boece tells us that Cruthnethus expels his kinsman from his castle in a rage. The results are the same in Stewart's narrative, but there is a second controversy, contingent upon the first. When the grandson argues defiantly, the elder figure, in response, makes short work of him:

> Sayand, himself had all the wyte
> Quhairof that tyme he sold na mendis haue,
> And callit him bayth harlot, loun and knaue,
> War nocht he wes his dochteris sone so neir,
> He maid ane vow he sould haif bocht it deir.
> (37,116–20).

We need not assume that Stewart had access to historical traditions which escaped his source author. Rather, the changes and expansions are due partly

---

21 Earlier examples of this narrative can be traced back to Fordun, see Skene, Vol. I, pp. 174–6, and Vol. II, pp. 165–7. Bower's presentation varies little, see Bower, ed. the MacQueens, Vol. 2, pp. 375–9. Internal evidence from Stewart's text makes it clear that he was familiar with the work of Fordun, (as well as that of John Major, Blind Harry and Froissart) see Stewart, ed. Turnbull, preface, Vol. I, p. xxiv. There is also a version in Andrew of Wyntoun's *Orignyal Chronykil of Scotland*, ed. F.J. Amours, Edinburgh, 1914, Vol. IV, pp. 197–9. The King is called 'Kynnede', and 'Fembel' or 'Sibill' is the daughter of 'Conquor' or 'Comequhare'. The narrative is linked to Dunsinane and Fettercairn. Boece's account can be found in *Scotorum Historiæ*, 237v–242r.
22 Stewart in fact presents the two characters as exact namesakes, and thereby enhances the symmetry of the narrative. The Boecian text offers him no precedent. In Fordun's text the elder's name is 'Cruchne', while the younger remains anonymous. See Stewart ed. Turnbull, Vol. II, p. 555, Fordun ed. Skene, Vol. I, p. 174, II, p. 166.

to his imagination. Of course, one cannot deny that he writes rather ordinary iambic pentameter lines, but his compositional process seems to involve the coalescence of organic and mechanic form. This is to say that his imagination is in fact *stimulated* by his obligation to metre and rhyme. They too are 'generative'.

For instance, the series of insults 'harlot, loun and knave', delivered by the grandfather is not justified by the Latin, even if Stewart's 'harlot' has not yet picked up suggestions of sexual delinquency. Our poet here also introduces credible motivation. The grandfather moderates his response to Cruthlinthus, out of deference to his own daughter, even though he is 'richt fureous'. So, in Stewart's version we can better appreciate why the grandson narrowly escaped with his life. Boece's text contains situations with numerous gaps which a writer with a keen eye for expansion can exploit, and this is precisely what Stewart is doing.

Now we come to the role of Fenella within this particular narrative unit. Applying semiotic analysis to the story, we can see that semantic axes exist which depend on opposition, in the original as much as in Stewart's development of it. The first major opposition is between male characters, actually a slightly modulated version of the traditional father / son controversy which is so common. The female character is the pivot between them. Female characters are, not invariably, but very often, presented negatively in Boece. This presentation is not only shared by Stewart it is perceptibly enhanced. (His redaction process is, then, gender-hostile).

Cruthlinthus' actions follow recurrent rules in both accounts. Initially he complained to his grandfather. Now he complains to his mother *about* his grandfather, and this time the grievance has a definable form. Her response to him is, in turn, the opposite of her father's. She encourages and indulges him. Fenella's negative characteristics involve being 'richt hie and het' and the fact that she is an effective, dominant woman (which makes her all the more loathsome to Stewart) is strongly emphasised, again in each version. She *commands* her son to avenge himself, and he responds without *delay*.

Fully armed and supplied by his mother, he attacks his grandfather's castle. Signals in the Latin and Scots texts indicate that this is done dishonourably. It is a surprise night-time attack which does not discriminate between its targets and it violates ruthlessly the bonds of consanguinity. As Stewart says: 'Bayth ill and gude that war thairin ilkane / He slew thame all . . .' and 'his grandsire gat no mair girth nor the laif' (11.37,142–5). Boece's matter-of-factness and the concision of his narrative underplay the sense of outrage which Stewart focuses on.

The act of slaughter in turn encourages Cruthlinthus to provoke a full-scale rebellion in Scotland, and it is at this point that the narrative interfaces with the larger one of King Kenneth, who, of course, acts to suppress the rising. When the King has rounded up those involved, however, *he does* distinguish very clearly between those noblemen who are guilty of treason and the commons, who merely obeyed orders. 'The men of gude that had auctorite

/ With Cruthlynthus condampnit war to die', Stewart tells us, and '. . . the pepill quhilk war till excuiss / For that same caus vnpuneist [he] lat thame pas' (37,187–8, 191–4).[23]

The fact that this information has to be teased out through rhyming verse makes it more memorable and resonant than it is in the original Latin, although in both, these details are important. They are part and parcel of how historiography 'works', as a morally instructive medium. The juxtaposition of exemplary behaviour with that which is reprehensible, serves to highlight both. Boece, in other words, shows his readers *how* to behave and *how not* to behave, and Stewart follows suit. (We should remember that *Scotorum Historiæ*, as well as its translations, is dedicated to a young King).

Boece's King Kenneth, however, does not always behave in such a pristine fashion. One heinous act laid to his charge is the poisoning of Prince Malcolm Duff, the ultimate heir to the throne, and son of Kenneth's predecessor. Like Macbeth's, Kenneth's sceptre appears a barren one, unless he is willing to take rather drastic actions. He succeeds in these, but faces the pangs of conscience thereafter. The King reaches a crisis point when he becomes the recipient of a prophetic nocturnal vision. Therein, an apparition warns Kenneth that his sins are not hidden from God, accuses him of hypocrisy insofar as his own mandate would have rigorously punished such actions in others, and prophesies both the King's own death and that of his sons. Not surprisingly, he has trouble sleeping thereafter. Obviously, in a character not wholly corrupt, the only realistic course of action after such an experience is repentance and submission to the will of God. The King enlists the aid of 'Ane haly bishop . . ./ The quhilk to name wes callit Mouean' (37,469–70).

In the original Latin, the advice offered by this character to Kenneth is presented in *oratio obliqua*, (see *Historiæ*, 241v), but Stewart builds it up into an elaborate example of *oratio recta*,[24] and this is something which Stewart will do where other translators like Bellenden will not. Moreover, what the bishop says performs an important function in Stewart's version of the story. The advice rests on the following premise, which is, in fact, crucial.

> Sic ordinance is ay in Goddis will,
> Nothing in erth uvpuneist to lat pas,
> Decretit hes for all vice and trespas,
> Ane cruell pane correspondand thairtill,
> For euirilk falt quhilk force is to fulfil.
> (37,486–90).

---

23 Fordun's information on this point is scanty. He says of Fenella's son 'whether [he were put to death] by the severity of the law, or for what he had done, or in some other way, I know not', see Fordun ed. Skene, Vol. II, p. 166.

24 The distinctive uses of these two rhetorical forms can be admirably illustrated by the works of Livy. See, moreover, P.G. Walsh, *Livy: His Historical Aims and Methods*, Cambridge, 1961, pp. 232–3.

We can pass over these lines for the time being, but we shall return shortly to illustrate their relevance. One other incident remains. It contains, of course, the account of Kenneth's death. A hunting trip carries him to Fettercairn. It is here that Fenella dwells: 'that wickit wife baith bellicois and bald' (37,538), who, as we might expect, harbours somewhat lethal intentions for him.

Boece makes it clear that the King's death, which occurs shortly after this in the narrative, is linked with his former sin in killing Malcolm Duff, and Fenella's character again supplies the link. Kenneth, of course, was responsible for the execution of her evil son, but as if that weren't enough, Boece also depicts her as a cousin to the slaughtered prince, and related to Constantine and Gryme, two characters with valid claims on the throne which were suppressed by Kenneth. Stewart does not mention these details, but the omission here is compensated for by his enhanced account of the holy Bishop's speech.

In both versions, Fenella apparently lives in a splendid tower decorated with many silk and gold tapestries, but one decoration, a pillar with a golden apple bearing an image of the King, is a triggering device rigged to a loaded crossbow which is concealed behind all the finery. More than Boece, Stewart gives us the impression that the tapestries are before his eyes at that very moment. Even if he uses conventional language to describe them, his vision is much more clearly defined than Boece's (see 37,561–85). He even notes the scenes which are depicted: they are 'depanetit all with greit plesance and joy' showing 'The ald story of Thebes and Troy' (37,557–8). Boece is more interested in precious stones.

It is to this place that Fenella invites the King when he becomes separated from his men. She invites him in, knowing 'richt weill' that 'this nobill king greit pleasance and delyte / Had alway for to se sic coistlie werk of curiositie'. Stewart enhances a little on Boece when he tells us that a meal to which Fenella treated the King was complete with 'coistlie spycis and mony mychty wyne / Of diuerss cullouris into cowpis cleir' (37,628–9).[25] Certainly, the reader is given an opportunity to reflect upon the insidious evils of luxury and epicurism, a theme very close to Boece's heart. The strong dramatic irony of Stewart's comment 'weill ma ye wit scho made him rycht gude cheir;/Bot syne allace! scho gart him pa weill ford' (37,630–1) is decidedly un-Boecian in its flavour, and marks Stewart out as an intrusive and slightly sardonic narrator.

Kenneth's curiosity brings him to the brink: 'Of euirilk thing he speirit hes the quhuy' (37,639), says Stewart, and both he and Boece are implying that the King's frivolity is not an attractive characteristic. When Kenneth comes to the golden apple and asks its function, there is a further delightful irony in Fenella's response, albeit one which is evident in Boece's text too. The image, she says, is to signify that 'scho wes traist and trew / And lovit him at all power of mycht'

---

25 This is a detail which is perhaps ultimately derived from John Major's account of the narrative. There are in fact two versions, one referring to Edmund Ironside, the other to Kenneth II, in his *History of Greater Britain*, ed. Archibald Constable, Edinburgh 1892, p. 112, p. 118. In both cases, the traitor invites the victim to breakfast. Stewart is quite specific that the King eats 'dennar . . . at ganand tyme' (37,635, and 627). Fordun and Bower do not mention a meal.

(37,644–5). The apple, she further elucidates, is *'ordand* for his heines alone' (37, 652). The verb here, with its theological overtones, (from Boece's *decrevi*), directs us back to the speech of Mouean, when he warned of divine ordinances and decrees which led to very specific retribution.

The religious symbolism of woman offering man an apple (or at least a luscious fruit with sexual associations) is hardly stimulating, but it is certainly consistent with the gender-hostile approach adopted by the authors, and by their age in general. Stewart's verse also leads him into some pardonable hyperbole at this juncture. When the fruit is lifted by Kenneth and the trigger activated, Stewart tells us '. . . al the hous begouth to rok / And all the stringis slippit out of nok' (37,661–2). The arrow, of course, finds its target with all the unwelcome exclusivity of a heat-seeking missile. The moment at which the King meets his end is rendered by Stewart with a greater degree of pathos than by Boece. Stewart's King dies alone and his death is a considerable loss: '. . . suddantlie without help or remeid / Doun on the fluir this nobill king fell deid' (37,665–6). Stewart maintains our involvement with the story by describing Fenella's escape, then records first the confusion of the King's few servants as they belatedly pick up his trail. They knock on Fenella's door with increasing anxiety, then, after a forced entry, they find their master 'with bludie woundis reid / Upon the fluir . . . liand deid'. Stewart, rather typically, modifies pathos with *meiosis*: 'Ye ma weill wit that tha war rycht wnfane' (37,687).[26]

Stewart in fact is recognisably over-emotional in a way which Boece simply is not, even if, again, the poet's mode of expression lacks the depth to find original language for high emotion: 'Suppois ane hart had bene all of hard steill . . ./ It wald haif burst to heir thair piteous mone' (37,691–2). Fenella, Stewart tells us, is pursued with diligence, but in the end escapes earthly retribution: 'And quhair awa I can nocht rycht weill tell' (37,674). However, by this time he has so thoroughly assassinated her character and sex that a retribution scene is unnecessary. But the whole narrative is appealing to us because its theme is revenge, always an exciting subject. Moreover, the plot is luridly sanguinary and therefore sensational. And once it gets underway, it develops naturally and inevitably towards its climactic conclusion. Blood will have blood, they say.

In the course of this paper, then, we have seen how a Fordunian narrative has gone through a three-fold process of adaption, culminating in the sophisticated humanist Latin version by Boece. Moreover, we have seen Boece acting as a redac*tor* and his own work being redac*ted*. Hopefully, I have established that governing factors within the redaction process are many and varied: mechanical, personal, political, gender-related, genre-related, and so forth. Also, it should be clear that historiography is a complex mode of writing, and that an exaggerated focus on the questions of historicity or factuality, can actually detract from our

---

26 At this juncture in the narrative, Fordun chooses to use *aposiopesis*: 'Why say more? Why dwell on so sad a tale?', see Fordun ed. Skene, Vol. II, p. 167.

literary appreciation of the genre. Questions of style, while relevant, might also obscure our understanding of plot. But these are just some ways of responding to the art of historiography. Scotland, of course, can offer world literature a fine collection of histories which surely hold their own against any continental parallel. I hope that other scholars will be encouraged to undertake similarly detailed and specific literary studies of them in the future.[27]

---

27 I very gratefully acknowledge financial assistance from the British Academy during the production of this paper.

ULRIKE MORÉT

29. *Some Scottish Humanists' Views on the Highlanders*

To put the attitudes of the Scottish humanist historians towards the Gaelic Scots of their own times in context, we should perhaps remind ourselves briefly of what other people in Scotland tended to think of the Highlands then, and of the relationship between Highlands and Lowlands from the later Middle Ages onwards.

We know that relations between the Gaelic-speaking and the Scots-speaking parts of the country had deteriorated. Even if we dismiss the older notion of a clear-cut so-called 'Highland line' where nobody that lived on one side of it was able or even willing to speak with anybody that lived on the other side, we still have to state a certain degree of alienation. There is ample evidence that from the later fourteenth century onwards, Scotland saw itself as divided into two different languages and cultures, and that this linguistic and cultural division corresponded to a geographic division between Highlands and Lowlands.

This feeling of being a divided nation is one that did not arise in Scotland until after the Wars of Independence. But then, in the course of the fourteenth century, mutual prejudice seems to have built up quickly, probably going along with various historical and linguistic developments. By the middle of the fourteenth century the Gaelic language on the mainland had retreated to the less accessible, mountainous parts of Scotland. The terms 'Highlander' (in a literal sense) and 'Gaelic speaker' at this time began to be used interchangeably. The cultural and linguistic division became even more significant after the Scottish court ceased to use French as its official language and began to use Scots rather than going back to Gaelic. In the 1370s the royal court moved its main seat from Perth to Edinburgh. This meant that the centre of government moved decidedly away from the Highland population into an area where no Gaelic was spoken.

On the other hand, many Gaelic Scots, especially those of the western Highlands and Islands, might not have considered this an overly great loss. Their interests lay to the west anyway where they maintained strong links with Ireland which shared their language and culture. Also in the fourteenth century, the powerful Lordship of the Isles emerged which by 1376 held nearly all the Western Isles as well as Lochaber. It formed a growing, self-contained and consciously Gaelic institution that showed a certain aloofness in attitude towards the Scottish government. When it came to royal writs or demands, for example, the Gaels tended to be evasive and often altogether ignored the Scottish king and his attempts to rule the Highlands more effectively. This again was typical of the Celtic approach to kingship in general. The Gaels still to some extent adhered to a system which contained different grades of kingship, and although they recognised the superiority of the Scottish king as their high-king, they resisted his efforts to govern them directly because this they considered to be the responsibility of their own local sub-king.

To the Scottish king, whose government (like that of the English king) had long since become Anglo-Norman in character and to whom direct authority in all parts of his realm was therefore very important, this kind of attitude was highly irritating. He was also unhappy with the enthusiasm with which the Highlanders fought out and kept alive their feuds and quarrels and which resulted in a general impression of lawlessness and disorder in their part of the kingdom – even if such disorder could also be found in the Borders. The church in the Highlands, finally, was too loosely organised to act as a steadying influence.

It is well documented what the Scots-speaking Lowlanders in this late medieval period thought of their Gaelic-speaking neighbours. Not surprisingly perhaps, they tended to express adverse criticism, seeing themselves as civilised, law-abiding and governed by reason – the thinkers among them placing an Aristotelian emphasis on the importance of civilisation – and the Highlanders as primitive, unruly and devoid of reason. In poetry, chronicles and acts of parliament we usually find disapproving comments, concerning especially the hostility of the Highlanders towards their own countrymen, their status as savages and troublemakers, the Gaelic language with its boastful way of speech, or the Highland dress which was thought to be ugly and undignified. Nobody seemed to know very much about the Highlands, but everybody seemed to agree that the Gaelic Scots were culturally inferior, and that they were not behaving the way they should.[1]

If we then look at the sixteenth and earlier seventeenth centuries, we find that the Highland situation has not much changed. In fact, it seems to have become even worse. Not only did the sixteenth century start off with a series of revolts of the former Lordship of the Isles, but it was also the great time of the growth of clanship. Besides the usual feuds and cattle raids which were going on all the time anyway, a new reason for which a Highlander could fight now was the expansion of the territory of his own clan. More than ever the Highlanders were engaged in aggression and violent conflicts, and their constant warlike occupation became a kind of philosophy. One scholar, David Stevenson, writes:

> The Highlands were experiencing a heroic age in which the warrior was the dominant element of society, in which the warrior bands of neighbouring communities fought each other and individuals gained renown in warfare of an aggressive and predatory character, [and] in which literature [. . .] was much concerned with the deeds of warriors, with the feats of strength and courage of individual heroes.[2]

---

1 A very good survey on this subject – although I believe it needs some slight modification in places – is Ranald G. Nicholson's article. 'Domesticated Scots and Wild Scots', *Scottish Colloquium Proceedings*, i (1968), 1–20.
2 David Stevenson, *Alasdair MacColla and the Highland Problem in the Seventeenth Century*, Edinburgh 1980, 15–16.

Such a situation would have driven any king to despair. We know that King James VI, probably the king with the most extreme views regarding the Highlands, would have liked to see the Gaelic Scots disappear altogether. In his reign various schemes were tried out to make the Highlands a more profitable part of the kingdom, but none of them was successful. James also tried to integrate Highland magnates into national Scottish politics – in which they had not been very interested so far – but as a result they promptly joined in the general scheming and plotting that was rife in the kingdom, and everything became worse than before.[3] In 1597, parliament felt the need to propose that 'the saidis Inhabitantis of the saidis hilandeis and Iles may the better be reduced to ane godlie honest and ciuill maner of living',[4] but three years later the same parliament states that this has

> [. . .] heirtofoir [. . .] bein very difficill to be accomplischit / be ressoun of the evill disposition and barbaritie of the Inhabitanttis thairof directlie opponeing thame selffis to suffer or permitt ony policie or civilitie to be establischit amangis thame naturallie abhorring the samyn being persounes altogidder destitut of the feir and knawledge of god and of his trew religioun / continewalllie applying thame selffis to all kynd of Inhumanitie daylie declairing the effectis thairof nocht onelie be thar tressonabill practeissis and attemptattis aganis his maiestie his estait and quyetnes of his hienes realme Bot also be maist detestabill damnabill and odious murthouris fyiris reveisching of wemen / witchcraft and depredatiounes maid amangis thame selffis extendit maist vnmercifullie to all sorttis of persounes without ony pitie or mercie ather of yhoung or auld [. . .].[5]

There is no doubt that in the sixteenth and seventeenth centuries, too, the majority of the Lowlanders were inclined to look upon the Highlanders with suspicion and disrespect. There is additional evidence for this – a half-Gaelic derisory poem by Alexander Montgomerie,[6] for example, or that nasty anonymous poem called *How the first Helandman, of God was maid/Of ane horss turd, in Argylle, as is said*;[7] there is also a letter written by Sir Alexander Hay in 1610; it concerns the rebel Neill Macleod from Lewis whom Sir Alexander would like to see shipped over to America to live amongst the Indians of Virginia, because, he says.

> There would be no suche danger there as of his being in Iyireland, for albeit both the speiches be barbarous, yit I hope he shall neid ane interpretour betwix him and the savaiges.[8]

---

3 On James VI's difficulties with the Highlands cf. esp. Maurice Lee, *Government by Pen: Scotland under James VI and I*, Urbana, Chicago and London 1980.
4 *Acts of the Parliaments of Scotland*, edd. T. Thomson and C. Innes, Edinburgh 1814–75, iv, 139.
5 *Ibid.*, iv, 248. (For technical reasons, '*th*' and '*y*' are used here to represent the letters 'thorn' and 'yogh'.)
6 Cf. Alexander Montgomerie, *Ane Answer to ane Helandmanis Invective*, in: *The Poems of Alexander Montgomerie*, ed. J. Cranstoun (Scottish Text Society, 1885–7).
7 Cf. Anon., *How the first Helandman* etc., in: *ibid*.
8 *Collectanea de Rebus Albanicis*, the Iona Club, Edinburgh 1847, 49.

In view of all this, even if some of it represents an exaggerated view of the Highlanders' conduct, a striking contrast is formed by a small group of Lowland authors in the sixteenth century who went to similar extremes to present a positive image of the Gaelic Scots. These are the three Scottish historians, Hector Boece, John Leslie and George Buchanan.

Hector Boece, whose *Scotorum historiae*[9] was published in Paris in 1527, is the first historian to approach his subject from a humanistic point of view. This also affects his perception of the Highlands. Scottish historians before him – John of Fordun, Walter Bower, Andrew Wyntoun and John Mair – had been negative and unsympathetic towards them. Or sometimes, they had used a scientific approach, for example when they explained the typical combative Highland behaviour by the antique concept that nations who lived higher up north had stronger blood and greater courage, but were rather less subtle of wit.[10] But Hector Boece's humanistic literary ideals and interest in classical literature provide an important background for his new positive image of the Highlanders.

His work has not been studied much. Apart from being criticised for its confusion of fact and fiction and highly imaginative approach to history writing, Boece's history has sometimes been compared to Livy's history of Rome, *Ab urbe condita*; but it would not be fair to say that Boece simply modelled his own book on Livy's. Rather one should say that both Livy and Boece were faithful followers of certain literary and historiographical ideals the ultimate source of which was Cicero. Cicero's suggestions on the proper way of writing a history were set down in his book *De oratore*.[11] Here Cicero, in order to initiate a Roman historiographical tradition, names certain requirements for history writing which go back to earlier Greek concepts. He suggests that a history should be sober, accurate and scientific, but also didactic, and pleasant to read. Thus along with his demands for truthfulness, impartiality and accuracy, he also instructs future historians to write in an elegant style. Cicero did not object if, in order to display his eloquence and rhetorical ability, a historian included some material in his work that was not strictly necessary. Such 'unnecessary' rhetorical material in ancient histories often took the form of speeches (made by historical protagonists in important moments, and especially before battle), and long digressions, preferably ethnographical ones about subjects like the character and customs of foreign cities or peoples. As for these ethnographical descriptions in ancient historiography, from very early onwards one can often find in them an element of what has been called 'primitivism'. This is the belief that a simpler or even primitive way of life – to be found either in the past of one's own country or in extant foreign savage nations – must be a purer and better way; it originates in the belief that one's own civilised surroundings are corrupt and decadent and

9 Cf. Hector Boece, *Scotorum historiae a prima gentis origine*, Paris: Badius Ascensius 1527.
10 Cf. e.g. Walter Bower, *Scotichronicon* XVI, xvii (ed. D.E.R. Watt, Aberdeen 1987–98), or John Mair, *Historia majoris Britanniae tam Angliae quam Scotiae* (Paris: Badius Ascensius 1521), I, viii.
11 Cf. Cicero, *De oratore*, esp. II. 55–7.

very remote from the Golden Age, and that it might be worth making certain adjustments to one's own lifestyle.[12]

That Hector Boece was attracted by such primitivistic notions becomes very obvious in his own ethnographical description, which is about the ancient Scots and extant Highlanders. It is prefixed to his history, where it functions as an exhortation to the reader.[13] In it Boece argues that many centuries back in time, the Scots were a brave and successful nation, but then half of them (the Lowlanders) suffered contamination by the effeminate ways of the southern neighbours, and gave up the ancient Scottish ways as well as the language. This change took its beginning in the late eleventh century, when king Malcolm III committed the reprehensible act of marrying an English princess and introducing English customs. From then on. Boece believes, Scotland has often embarrassed herself in military and cultural failure, while the Highlanders alone faithfully preserve the ancient Scottish language, manners and customs.

Thus when Boece compares Highland and Lowland Scots, this has completely new results. While Lowland historians before him saw the Gaels as backward savages and were eager to draw attention to their own level of civilisation, Hector Boece interprets this Lowland civilisation as decadence, and the simpler culture of the Highlands as the key to the former strength of the Scottish nation.

Unfortunately, however, he does not seem to have known very much about ancient or even present Highland life. This is the kind of information that he gives on the Gaels.

Their way of life, he says, has always been characterised throughout by the virtue of *temperantia* (moderation). It showed especially in their eating and drinking habits. The ancient Scots were happy to live on what was yielded by their own land, and never imported any fancy food or other goods. From domestic herbs they distilled themselves a drink called 'aqua viua', but their more common daily drink was beer. When food was scarce they subsisted on dried fish or a paste made of flour, butter, milk, cheese and vinegar. Great importance was attached to military bravery and discipline. In times of peace they kept their bodies exercised and did not allow them to soften and become prone to ill-health. They shaved all hair off their heads, leaving only a little tuft standing up on the forehead, and this is the reason, says Hector Boece, why no bald person has ever been seen in Scotland. They were hardened against heat and cold, and their clothes were meant to be practical, not elegant. Most of the time they went without shoes. About their women Boece informs us that they often fought in battle, and that this was of no small support to the men; he also writes that mothers were expected to nurse their children themselves, and that if their milk was not sufficient this would cast very grave doubts on their faithfulness to their husbands. Boece's ancient Scots were pure not only in lifestyle, but also in character. Simplicity and sincerity were valued highly. They would never, in war

---

12 On the subject of primitivism cf. esp. Arthur O. Lovejoy. *Primitivism and Related Ideas in Antiquity*, Baltimore 1935 (repr. New York 1973).
13 This description, called *De Scotorum priscis recentibusque institutis ac moribus paraenesis Hectoris Boethii accommodatissima*, takes up fos. 17^V–20^V of the 1527 edition of the *Scotorum historiae*.

or in private quarrels, employ trickery or deceit, or hide enmities only to attack from behind. Everything was decided in open conflict. A man was considered a noble on the grounds of personal excellence only, and not because of his wealth or the brave deeds of his ancestors.[14]

Boece's account continues for a little longer, but one does not have to read any further to form an impression. It is not as if he did not know anybody who could have told him something about the Highlands, quite on the contrary – but whether he actually consulted them is another matter. Boece's own links with the Highlands must have been more than tenuous. He does include information which has a vaguely Scottish feel about it, but most of his report is a combination of elements adopted from classical ethnography – especially Tacitus's *Germania* – and wishful thinking. Other elements are plainly mysterious, such as the ancient Scottish haircut. But on the other hand, Boece's image of the Highlanders is only a by-product of his two main intentions here: one is to create a respectable past for Scotland by giving it respectable ancestors, and the other is to compare ancient and contemporary Scotland in order to make his own fellow Lowlanders see their own shortcomings. While the Highlanders are used to emphasise both these points, the main focus of interest is nevertheless not on them but on the ancient Scots. And as far as these are concerned, Boece must have felt free to improvise.

Boece's successor in the field of Scottish historiography was certainly much better informed. John Leslie, bishop of Ross, who in 1578 published a history called *De origine, moribus et rebus gestis Scotorum*,[15] had grown up in Kingussie, a place which in his day was well on the Gaelic side of the linguistic boundary. Leslie was familiar with Boece's work, and as far as his attitude towards the Highlanders is concerned, he adopts Boece's didactic and primitivistic approach; however, he adds to it a new dimension. When he wrote his history it had not been long ago that Scotland had adopted the Protestant faith, and the Catholic bishop Leslie therefore praises both the Scottish forefathers and the Highland Scots of his own time for their steadfast adherence to the Catholic religion. He compares Highland and Lowland Scots in a way that is aimed to make the Lowlanders see their own corruption mainly on a religious level.

But leaving aside this religious aspect, Leslie's presentation of ancient Scottish and Gaelic life is a great improvement on Hector Boece's. In the Scottish forefathers of his description we can actually recognise the Highlanders of the sixteenth century.[16] Leslie throws out details which he finds unlikely – there is no mention of a punk hairstyle – and he also transforms Boece's vague and stereotyped Noble-Savage description into an account that is based on detailed knowledge of the Gaelic way of life. He even shows a certain insight into the Gaelic way of thinking.

As for his knowledge of Gaelic everyday life, Leslie gives us accurate informa-

---

14 Cf. *ibid.* for the whole of this description.
15 Cf. John Leslie, *De origine, moribus ac rebus gestis Scotorum libri decem*, Rome: In Aedibus Populi Romani 1578.
16 For this description cf. esp. *ibid.* I, pp. 56–9.

tion, for example, about their clothes and weapons. He mentions the long saffron shirt worn by the Highlanders of his own time, the short woollen jacket-like garment with sleeves that could be opened length-wise, the occasionally worn tight trousers, the woollen mantle, and the women's long tunics and wide cloaks; he also mentions bows and arrows, lances and two-edged swords, and mailshirts and tough leather garments as serving them in times of war. Leslie is also among the first to comment on the Highlanders' famous practice of cooking their meat in the stomachs of the killed animals, and he is also familiar with their way of baking bread. Furthermore, he must have had some knowledge of Gaelic poetry and music. He tells us that the ancient Scots would, like the Highlanders, educate their young sons to be warriors, and that the little ones would learn about exemplary heroic persons in poetry and in what he calls 'rhythmical song' (*rhythmus quidam*). It seems that Leslie was not only aware of the existence of Gaelic heroic praise song, but also knew that Gaelic music contained (and still contains) a number of highly rhythmical songs which were designed for the accompaniment of manual work such as waulking cloth, rowing, or dandling little children.

As for Leslie's insight into the Gaelic psyche, he ascribes to the ancient Scots sentiments which he can only have observed in his own Gaelic-speaking neighbours. He mentions, for example, the unconditional devotion with which they would follow their chiefs, or the excessive vengefulness with which they handled their internal quarrels. About his Highland contemporaries he says that they all aspire to be considered nobles, or at least strenuous warriors, and that they object to the idea of working as mere farmers, craftsmen or labourers, even if this reduces them to poverty and starvation. We remember that in the sixteenth century the Highlanders were experiencing their 'heroic age' – this is of course the other side of the coin. In a society in which the dominant figure was the warrior, no other occupation seemed respectable.

Moving on from Leslie's well-informed report, we finally have to look at the presentation of somebody who was probably even better informed. George Buchanan, whose *Rerum Scoticarum historia*[17] appeared in 1582, was a Gaelic speaker from the Lennox. His account therefore could have been the most interesting of the three. However, the way in which Buchanan handles the Gaelic question indicates a really difficult personality.

He has hardly written three pages of the first book of his history when he declares already that it would not bother him in the least if Gaelic was to die out and if 'those barbarous sounds' (*barbaros illos sonos*) were to vanish and be replaced by the sweet sounds of a Romance language.[18] But a little later one finds that Buchanan has in fact a very keen interest in 'those barbarous sounds'. The *Rerum Scoticarum historia* contains his famous linguistic analysis of the relationship between the Celtic languages,[19] and in this analysis, but also when he describes

---

17 Cf. George Buchanan, *Rerum Scoticarum historia*, Edinburgh: Alexander Arbuthnot 1582.
18 Cf. *ibid*. I. fo. 2^V.
19 Cf. *ibid*. II, *passim*.

the various parts of Scotland in the beginning. Buchanan makes much use of Gaelic place-name etymology. His linguistic interest is after all stronger than his humanistic distaste of all things barbarous. Still he appears to wish to remain at a distance from the language. He refers to it in a way that totally obscures his own connection with it; mostly he calls it 'the language of the ancient Scots', and he never includes himself as a speaker of it.

As for his views on the Highlanders, his presentation is different from that of Hector Boece and John Leslie in that it avoids the historical dimension. There are no ancient Scottish forefathers in Buchanan's description of the Gaelic Scots: although he is clearly familiar with Boece's and Leslie's approach, he only writes about the Highlanders of his own time. The reason is that Buchanan was not only a humanist but also a political author. So was, of course, John Leslie; but to a much greater degree than he, Buchanan is concerned to create a certain image of Scotland. He was suspicious of the idea of an Anglo-Scottish union, and when he wrote his history, it was partly in answer to certain claims put forward by both English and Scottish unionists. These claims included the argument that Scotland's language and culture was so similar to that of England that Scotland's wish to remain independent was hardly justifiable on the grounds of any substantial difference in culture.[20] But this argument only worked if the term 'Scotland' was understood to mean mainly Lowland Scotland, and if the Gaelic population was seen as an odd, marginal group that did not quite fit in. Boece's and Leslie's approach confirmed such a view. Although it saw the Highlanders in a positive light, it marginalised them all the same. It saw them as a group that was dramatically different and – which is more important – as a group that was by no means representative of the whole of Scotland. Although they were primitivists, they did not want their readers to get a wrong impression of Scotland. Buchanan must have realised the inconsistency and the dangers inherent in their views. If one presented Highland culture as the original Scottish culture, the whole world was going to laugh at an anachronistic nation of Noble Savages. If one therefore insisted that nevertheless the Lowlanders formed the dominant element in Scottish culture, then according to the Boecean definition Scottish culture was not really distinctly Scottish. The safest way was to avoid elaborating this point. In Buchanan's work therefore, Scotland seems strangely homogenous. Scotland in his book is different from England because it looks back on an ancient Scottish (that is, Gaelic) culture, but then what happened to this ancient Scottish culture is left unexplained. There is no mention of anybody giving it up at any point. Even Malcolm III, the king under whose rule Scotland allegedly became corrupt, is rehabilitated by Buchanan. Although he married an English princess, Buchanan simply denies that he introduced English decadence.[21]

On the whole, Buchanan makes it clear that in his own time there are two

---

20 On this concern of Buchanan's cf. also Arthur Williamson, *Scottish National Consciousness in the Age of James VI*, Edinburgh 1979, chap. 6.
21 Cf. George Buchanan, *Rerum Scoticarum historia* VI, fo. '74^V' according to page numbering, but in fact fo. 76^V.

different languages and cultures in Scotland, but he does not say exactly which is where, and he never compares them with each other. One does not hear where the differences lie. The whole affair is effectively blurred. Scotland emerges as a country with a Scottish culture – this seems to be Buchanan's main message. In a uniquely vague fashion he emphasises the importance of Gaelic culture within the culture of Scotland as a whole, and thus he argues against the statement that Scotland's culture is almost English.

As for his description of Highland life, it is a bit of a disappointment. Although he was presumably an insider, Buchanan says hardly anything that John Leslie. Hector Boece or even John Mair have not said before him. He gives so little additional information that it is hardly worth going into detail. His presentation is positive, however, and like that of John Leslie combines primitivistic elements with accurate information.

To sum up, three idealised descriptions of the Highlanders emerge in the sixteenth century. The classical learning of the humanist historians had produced a new interest in positive aspects of primitive life, and this, combined with their wish to create a respectable ancient past for their country, plays an important part in their interpretation of the culture of Gaelic Scotland. Boece and Leslie see the Gaels as mirroring ancient Scottish life in all its attitudes, manners and customs and political principles, and George Buchanan joins them in their almost enthusiastic description of the Highlanders. Their culture is no longer regarded as savage and inferior but as a singular manifestation of dignified simplicity. In contrast to the authors before them, the humanists include the important aspect of consciousness: Highland culture is no longer presented as the result of backward ignorance and incomplete human development, but as a deliberate keeping up of valuable traditions.

However, in the sixteenth and seventeenth centuries, this interpretation of Gaelic culture did not leave a substantial impression. One would have expected the Highlanders at least to embrace it with great joy, but they were not at all impressed. They had been thinking along these lines for centuries, seeing themselves as the true original Scots, and the Lowlanders as a foreign entity which stole their land and encroached on their culture. Walter Kennedie, for example, the Gaelic-speaking opponent of Dunbar in the *Flyting of Dunbar and Kennedie*, expresses these ideas quite clearly.[22] Apart from that, very few of them would of course have been familiar with the works of the Scottish humanists. We know of one early Gaelic author who had actually read Boece and Buchanan, and he complains that neither Boece nor Buchanan ever 'spoke a favourable word of the Highlanders, much less of the Islanders and Macdonalds'.[23] He is partly right

---

22 Cf. *The Flyting of Dunbar and Kennedie*, vv. 345–52: 'Thou lufis nane Irische, elf, I understand, Bot it suld be all trew Scottis mennis lede; It was the gud langage of this land. And Scota it causit to multiply and sprede Quhill Corspatrik, that we of tresoun rede, Thy fore fader, maid Irisch and Irisch men thin, Throu his tresoun broght Inglis rumplis in: [. . .].' (Ed. J. Kinsley, *The Poems of William Dunbar*, Oxford 1979.)
23 *History of the MacDonalds*, in: *Highland Papers*, ed. J.R.N. MacPhail (Scottish History Society 1911–34), i, p. 10.

– if one applies this statement to what the two authors had to say about the historical deeds of the Gaelic Scots – but this is a different story.

Perhaps less surprisingly, the idealised view of the Highlands did not appeal to the Lowlanders either: it did not agree with public opinion. The Highlanders were still regarded as troublesome, aggressive and potentially dangerous, and a highly intellectual and idealistic approach such as that of the humanists is easily considered to be of secondary importance when the political situation is perceived to be one of tension or crisis. It took considerable time to become accepted on a larger scale: in fact, it was not until the Highlands had been 'pacified' and made safe after 1745, and their original culture had virtually been destroyed, that it became widely popular. Then, a romanticised image of the Gaels appeared in Macpherson's epic *Ossian* or in the works of Sir Walter Scott and was welcomed with excitement all over Europe; but in fact it revives, and owes much to, the views which the Scottish humanists had expressed two hundred years before.

J. HADLEY WILLIAMS

30. *Lyndsay and Europe: Politics, Patronage, Printing*

Through the eyes of an early sixteenth-century Scot, what was Europe? This is the place to begin, for David Lyndsay's particular interaction with that Europe, the concern of this paper, is an integral part of the larger question.

Lyndsay himself gives the standard answer, when in *The Dreme* he sets out for James V some of the information he will need as sovereign.[1] Europe, he says, is one of the three major divisions of the Earth. It is found in the Occident, with Africa; both being more than balanced by Asia, in the Orient (666-8). The surviving, imperfect, texts of *The Dreme* go on to list only the first three of the four principal regions of Europe (Spain, France, Italy and Germany), but as far as can be discovered, Lyndsay is following the view of the classical sources, such as the two he mentions by name, Pliny and Ptolemy.[2] Lyndsay certainly appears to see Scotland as part of Europe, though in this section as it stands it can only be one of the unnamed 'Yles'. He separates these from the 'ferme land' that is continental Europe. Later, he returns to the 'braid Yle of Bertane' (791), mentioning also England and Ireland, but only as a means of giving a closer setting to Scotland, for it is that country alone that he is concerned to show the king from various geographical and moral viewpoints.

Another far more challenging and politically aware answer to the question may be found in the scheme of the heraldic ceiling of St Machar's Cathedral, Old Aberdeen. This was completed 1520-1, near the beginning of James V's reign. In layout from east to west, the ceiling consists of three rows of forty-eight carved and painted shields, which represent the secular and spiritual leaders of contemporary European nations. The scheme takes serious account of political and religious precedence and, in the process, of how each European nation is associated with Scotland, and with each other, and especially, of how these Christian nations are related to the Holy Roman Emperor and to the Pope; yet, too, how all these leaders stand before God at the high altar.

---

1 *The Works of Sir David Lindsay of the Mount*, ed. D. Hamer, 4 vols, STS (Edinburgh and London, 1931-6), I, 3-38. (All quotations are from this edition).
2 Ptolemy named the island of Albion as the first of his four regions of Europe; Pliny (Books II-IV of the *Historia Naturalis*) begins with Baetica, North-east Spain and Italy, includes Germany and also ninety-six North Sea islands, Britain among them. Bower, citing Isidore, Vincent of Beauvais and Lucan, also describes a similar set of regions: *Scotichronicon*, Vol. I, ed. J. and W. MacQueen, Books 3-6. For further discussion see *The Works*, ed. Hamer, III, 33-9, and S. Cairns, 'Sir David Lindsay's *Dreme*: poetry, propaganda and encomium', *The Spirit of the Court*, ed. G.S. Burgess and R.A. Taylor (Cambridge, 1985), pp. 110-19 (112).

Such intricate patternings are discussed at length elsewhere, as they deserve.[3] One feature of the ceiling's heraldic panorama of Europe, however, draws immediate attention to the Scottish point of view of its local designers. In the southernmost row, the shield of the king of Scots, fittingly, leads those of St Margaret and the Scottish nobles. It is thereby also separated from the series of European monarchs and nobles in the northern row. The monarchs are: Charles V (Holy Roman Empire); Francis I (France); Carlos I of Spain (that is, Charles V) (Leon and Castile); Henry VIII (England); Christian II of Denmark according to the printed designation under the shield (arms of Norway);[4] Louis II (Hungary); Emmanuel the Fortunate (Portugal); Carlos I of Spain (that is, Charles V) (Aragon); King of Cyprus (office only, since still vacant at this time); Henri II (d'Albret) (Navarre); Carlos I of Spain (that is, Charles V) (Sicily); Sigismund I (Poland), and Louis II (Bohemia). It is the open crowns above the shields of these European monarchs that are so noticeable, for they indicate that all so designated are subject to the Emperor, whose shield leads the series. By contrast, Scotland's crown, similarly-placed above James V's shield, is the closed crown of imperium, adopted from the time of James III to assert independent sovereignty. This is also expressed in the central and principal row, where the arms of Scotland's ecclesiastical leaders again display an independence of jurisdiction: there is nothing between the arms of the Archbishop of St Andrews and the leading shield of the Pope, which is surmounted by the three-fold crown, the tiara of papacy.

Many lacunae, revealed on closer examination, also denote a Scottish bias. England, for example, fares badly. Not only does it give way to France, and Leon and Castile of Spain, but the arms depicted are not those normally used by the reigning monarch, Henry VIII. They lack the fleurs-de-lis quartering that was introduced from the time of Edward III to assert England's claim to the French crown.[5] The shield of the dukedom of Charles of Bourbon, the first of only two continental dukedoms included, signals future royal family ties: Scotland's proposed matrimonial association with this house was already the subject of serious negotiation. The second, the shield of the duke of Gueldres, recalls Scotland's links with this region through Mary of Gueldres, Queen of James II.

Selective though it is, the present survey of the heraldry of St Machar's ceiling

---

3 W. Duguid Geddes and P. Duguid, *The Heraldic Ceiling of the Cathedral Church of St Machar Old Aberdeen* (Aberdeen, 1888); D. McRoberts, *The Heraldic Ceiling of St Machar's Cathedral, Aberdeen* (Friends of St Machar's Cathedral Occasional Papers No.2), 1974; rpt. (Aberdeen, 1981); L.J. Macfarlane, 'The Liturgical Significance of Gavin Dunbar's Ceiling', *Annual Report 1992*, Friends of St Machar's Cathedral (Aberdeen, 1992), pp. 7–9; H.M. Shire, 'The King in his House: Three Architectural Artefacts Belonging to the Reign of James V', *Stewart Style 1513–1542: Essays on the Court of James V*, ed. J. Hadley Williams (East Linton, 1996), pp. 62–96 (63–72).

4 Norway, with Sweden, was under the Danish crown at this time (Treaty of Kalmar still valid). Denmark is given unusual prominence; it seems likely that this is because James V's grandmother, Queen Margaret, was Danish. See Geddes and Duguid, *Heraldic Ceiling*, pp. 24, 91 and adjacent plate. See also T. Riis, *Should Auld Acquaintance Be Forgot . . . Scottish-Danish Relations c. 1450–1707* (Odense, 1988), I, 29, who notes that Aberdeen was the port closest to Norway, which thus to Aberdonians was more important than Denmark for trade.

5 Geddes and Duguid, *Heraldic Ceiling*, pp. 22–3.

goes some way, it is to be hoped, towards providing an answer to the opening question (what was Europe, to a Scot, in the sixteenth century?) and, as well, a context in which Lyndsay may be viewed. Indeed the two merge, for there were Lyndsay family connections to be found upon the ceiling: the shield of David eighth Earl of Crawford, from whose line David Lyndsay's was a cadet, appears tenth (and first of those dating from after the Stewart accession),[6] in the row headed by James V. Here is evidence of how this noble house was regarded, not only locally in Aberdeenshire – since distant earldoms do not figure – but also by the king and realm as a whole. Unanswered, however, are some tantalising and basic questions: did the Lyndsays have connections of their own with any part of Europe? And if so, how did David Lyndsay regard them?

In his armorial record book (c.1536–42), with its interesting snippets of genealogical commentary as well as blazons, Lyndsay states that the 'Lyndesays' were among 'yame that come furth of England with Sanct Margaret'.[7] Again, it is the ceiling that reveals St Margaret's importance to Scotland. Since the king was as yet unmarried, the shield of his mother, Margaret Tudor, might in the circumstances have followed his, but with a certain diplomatic evasiveness, it is St Margaret's that is given the honour. Within Lyndsay's armorial manuscript, the Lyndsay-family link to St Margaret is therefore evidence not so much of a Saxon family origin as of a most honourably Scottish ancestry, dating from the even-then ancient and stabilising time of Malcolm III and his Queen. Lyndsay's poetic references to the subject, emphasising family loyalty to the monarch, support this reading: the out-of-favour royal hound Bagsche, for example, appeals for help to 'gude brother Lanceman, Lyndesayis dog,/ Quhilk ay hes keipit thy laute' (*Complaynt of Bagsche*, 89–90). On the same basis, Squyer Meldrum appoints Lyndsays as his executors: 'That Surname', as he puts it, 'failȝeit neuer to the Croun' (*Testament of Squyer Meldrum*, 19).

Lyndsay stresses this aspect of his relationship to James V in his opening to *The Dreme*, written c. 1526, at about the time of the king's second formal elevation to office.[8] The choice to write the poem in Scots, at a dignified but not elaborate stylistic level, could be viewed as another indication of Lyndsay's attitude: first and last the poem was to be highly accessible to his king and to the Scottish audience of his subjects.[9] The choice of Scots therefore was appropriate and also practical – James's education had been neglected in later years – yet it was, at the

---

6 Ibid., pp. 77–8 and A. Grant, 'Extinction of Direct Male Lines Among Scottish Noble Families in the Fourteenth and Fifteenth Centuries', *Essays on the Nobility of Scotland*, ed. K.J. Stringer (Edinburgh, 1985), pp. 210–31 (213).

7 The armorial is most easily consulted from the *Facsimile of an Ancient Heraldic Manuscript Emblazoned by Sir David Lyndsay of the Mount*, ed. D. Laing (Edinburgh, 1822), but caution should be maintained, as later additions are not differentiated; for the 'Lyndesay'-St Margaret passage: Laing, fol. 133ʳ. By contrast, Lord Lindsay (*Lives of the Lindsays*, London, 1849), I, 1–6) attributes to the Lyndsays a Norman origin.

8 See C. Edington, *Court and Culture in Renaissance Scotland: Sir David Lindsay of the Mount* (Amherst, Mass, 1994), pp. 24–5.

9 It is argued by Hamer, 'The Bibliography of Sir David Lindsay', *The Library*, X, No. 1 (1929), 1–42 (7–11) and *The Works*, IV, 15, that *The Dreme* was first published c. 1528 by the Scottish printer Thomas Davidson, from which Jean Petit's 1558 text was reprinted line-by-line.

same time, an early indication of Lyndsay's belief in the value of the native language. There was a well-established tradition of skilful writing in the vernacular behind him, but Lyndsay's attitude – and *The Dreme*'s well articulated structure bears this out – was also forward and outward looking, in touch with that of contemporary writers in other European countries. It was not, all the same, the internationalising approach of a Latinist, though to some extent both were products of humanist thinking. An anonymous *Strena*, possibly written for the same occasion, underlines the difference, initially in its contrasting title page in Roman type, and throughout in its Latin expression. These automatically sought out for that poem a different, scholarly and largely continental, audience in a way that *The Dreme*'s approach did not.[10]

In attempting to grasp what Lyndsay's particular connections with Europe were, it is important to keep this difference in mind and advisable also to remember that at the time Lyndsay wrote *The Dreme* he had neither studied nor travelled abroad. Indeed, although some of the sources Lyndsay mentions in *The Dreme* were university textbooks at the time, there is no conclusive evidence that Lyndsay had studied at a university at all, even one of those within Scotland.[11] In the 'Exclamation . . . twycheyng the wryttyng of Vulgare and Maternall Language', in the much later *Dialog betuix Experience and ane Courteour*, Lyndsay suggests that the study of ancient languages by 'cunnyng men' (595) is necessary, yet he does not seem to be counting himself among those 'cunnyng men': 'That I am nocht of that sorte sore I rew', 599).

On the other hand, Lyndsay's court service began in James IV's cosmopolitan household.[12] There, Lyndsay who had been quick to display his talent in theatre and music, had many opportunities for cultural exchange, whether or not he was present at court early enough to have taken supportive part in such high points of that reign as the internationally attended tournaments of the Black Lady (1507–8), or to have met members of French knight Bernard Stewart's retinue.[13] The impact of James IV's court is apparent when Lyndsay later writes of this time in

10 See further, *Ad Serenissimum Scotorum Regum Iacobum Quintum de suscepto Regimine a diis feliciter ominato Strena*, Edinburgh, Thomas Davidson, [1528], STC 14435. It is reproduced in *The Bannatyne Miscellany* II, ed. D. Laing and T. Thomson (Edinburgh, 1836), [ix–xvi], 1–8, with an Augustan translation by Archdeacon Wrangham; J. IJsewijn and D.F.S. Thomson, 'The Latin Poems of Jacobus Follisius, or James Foullis of Edinburgh', *Humanistica Lovaniensia*, XXIV (1975), 102–52 (103, 105–6, 135–7, and notes 151–2). See also the most useful discussion in L.O. Fradenburg, *City, Marriage, Tournament: Arts of Rule in Late Medieval Scotland* (Madison and London, 1991), pp. 47–64.
11 See, for example, the discussion of Aberdeen University's Liberal Arts course in the early sixteenth century in L.J. Macfarlane, *William Elphinstone and The Kingdom of Scotland 1481–1514: The Struggle for Order* (Aberdeen, 1985), pp. 362–72. A 'Dauid Lin[d]esay' was incorporated as a student at St Andrews University c. 1508, *Early Records of the University of St Andrews*, transcr. and ed. J.M. Anderson (Edinburgh, 1926), pp. 202–4. For information on Lyndsay's possible earlier education, see J. Durkan 'Education in the Century of the Reformation', *Essays on the Scottish Reformation 1513–1625*, ed. D. McRoberts (Glasgow, 1962), pp. 145–69.
12 See *Accounts of the Lord High Treasurer of Scotland*, ed. T. Dickson and Sir J. Balfour Paul (Edinburgh, 1877–1916) [*TA*], IV, 269 (1511); 313 (1511); 442 (1512).
13 A reference in the *Exchequer Rolls*, to 'uno vocato Lyndsay in averia quondam domini principis' is found in the year 1508, and must be dated after the prince's death in February 1508. It may be relevant that during the visit to France of 1536, Lyndsay looked after the king's horses and saddles; see *TA*, VI, 455 and 456.

the *Testament of the Papyngo* (1530). His prefacing catalogue of poets 'in tyll our vulgare toung'(10) finds Gavin Douglas pre-eminent, above all for his translation of Virgil into Scots. (And a contemporary and newcomer, John Bellenden, is next highly praised – for his promise as a 'cunnyng Clerk' (50)). Thereby Lyndsay marks his own approval of such learned and forward-looking studies in Scotland and in Scots, and his poem does the same. In it, there is a witty blending of traditional genres with those of more recent writing abroad – from *chanson d'aventure* to Jean Lemaire's Ovidian epistles, *L'Amant Vert* (1505) – and allusions also to writing within Scotland, including that of Richard Holland, Robert Henryson and William Dunbar. Lyndsay's deftness, built upon the more tentative beginnings made in *The Dreme*, asserts Scotland's growing international status, political and literary, and does so on its own terms.

It is in this self-aware setting of the *Papyngo* that Lyndsay makes the confident statement that the fame of James IV's court, of its 'tryumphand tornayis, iustyng and knychtly game' (508) 'sprang' (500) through Europe. There was truth in the claim, for contemporary and modern commentators are in agreement that James IV himself deserved such an assessment.[14] Yet the words come within an extended *ubi sunt* passage (350–625) – the greater the glory the greater the loss – and from the pen of a man who could be looking with some idealising regret to events of his early twenties, before the 'murthur, & myschance' (529) of the minority. Embedded there, moreover, is a desire to suggest to James IV's son, presently ruling, the way to a 1530s renaissance.[15] And informing the claim, or perhaps distorting it, must be that factor noted earlier but not yet discussed: Lyndsay had no first-hand knowledge of continental Europe, and with that a less-than-perfect ability to make informed comparisons of Scotland and other European countries, until 1531, the year after the *Papyngo* appeared, when as a trusted herald he travelled to the court of Charles V in Brussels.

Something of Lyndsay's reactions to the matters and style of the 'court imperiall' has survived, in his official letter to secretary Thomas Erskine.[16] The closely written, page-long letter is full of interest, all the more so because it is the only such still extant. Just a few aspects can be considered here. First it is evident that Lyndsay writes with the knowledge – set out so clearly on St Machar's ceiling – that Scotland is not subject to the Emperor; indeed, that Scotland holds a position of strength. At that time, when Henry VIII had begun moves to divorce the Emperor's aunt, Catherine of Aragon, the alienated Emperor was vying with France for Scotland's support. Thus in Lyndsay's first paragraph, there is brisk reference to the successful conclusion of the main

---

14 N. Macdougall, *James IV* (East Linton, 1997), pp. 282–312 and P. Bawcutt, *Dunbar the Makar* (Oxford, 1992), pp. 78–81.
15 In a letter to Hector Boece, 15 March 1530, Erasmus was expressing the same hope: see *Opus Epistolarum Des. Erasmi Roterodami*, ed P.S. Allen et al, 12 vols (Oxford, 1906–58), VIII, 2283.
16 B.L. Cotton Caligula B. I. f. 313. For a full discussion of the letter, see J. Hadley Williams, ' "Of officiaris serving thy senyeorie": David Lyndsay's diplomatic letter of 1531', in *A Palace in the Wild*, eds L.A.J.R. Houwen, A.A. MacDonald and S. Mapstone, Groningen, 1999, pp. 125–40.

business – the ratification of the renewal of an ancient trade treaty.[17] He continues with a summary of the then-prevalent rumours of James V's death, 'send for werrite furth of Ingland'. Lyndsay reports that on the basis of these rumours, the Emperor had promptly ordered prayers for the King's soul, and that the Queen Dowager, then a possible marriage partner for James, was glad at the scotching of the report.[18] For a moment Lyndsay has been a key player in the game of international politics, and is aware of it: the rumour, he says, 'war haldin for effect ay quhill my cumin to ye cowrt'.[19]

The final paragraph concerns news of less formal importance but usefully up-to-the-minute. Court movements are noted; Lyndsay reports, for example, that the 'emprior purposis to depart at the fyn of yis moneth and passis wp In almanʒe for reformation of ye luteriens'. Lyndsay uses the word 'luteriens' laconically, with every assurance of ready understanding. The rapid word-of-mouth spread of Lutheran teachings and other doctrines at first associated indiscriminately with them is evident: by this time, indeed, Denmark and several German principalities had adopted Lutheranism officially.[20] But also evident in Lyndsay's use of the word is an interesting linguistic connection with Europe. His Scots spelling of 'luterien' suggests an indirect transmission, perhaps through the French word 'Luthérien', whereby it would have gained for Lyndsay association with the rather free thinking attitudes of the French reformers before 1534.[21] By contrast, the equivalent English word 'Lutheran', first recorded in use ten years earlier, is built directly on the German reformer's name, with the suffixes 'an' or 'ane' added to 'Luther'. This is a tiny piece of information, yet it assumes some importance as it helps to depict the picture of Lyndsay's, and certainly Scotland's, particular links with Europe.

Also in this final paragraph, Lyndsay refers at length to the 'triwmphand Iustynis', 'ye terribill turnementis' and the 'feychtyn on fut In barras' that he has witnessed at court since his arrival. He promises separately-written articles, to be shown to the king on his return, covering one 'gret towrnament', which, it is plain, has deeply impressed him. This is worth marking: we remember Lyndsay's expansive estimate of James IV's 'triumphand tornayis'. Yet the actual importance of the Brussels event can be questioned. No study of such tournaments so far

---

17 See *The Letters of James V*, collected and calendared by R.K. Hannay, ed. D. Hay (Edinburgh, 1954), pp. 191–2: James V to Charles V, and Confirmation, 25 May 1531; pp. 193–4, James V to Charles V, 30 June 1531; p. 194, Instructions to David Lyndsay [30 June 1531].
18 See further, *Letters of James V*, ed. Hay, pp. 203–4: the Secretary to Benedict, Cardinal of Ravenna, Edinburgh, 10 December 1531. This letter also reveals that during his Brussels visit, Lyndsay played a part in the marriage negotiations, though this is not mentioned explicitly by him.
19 Such rumours were not uncommon. Gavin Douglas, for example, discusses the unconfirmed report that Louis XII was dead in a letter to Adam Williamson, 21 January 1515 (*The Poetical Works of Gavin Douglas*, ed. J. Small, (Edinburgh, 1874), I, xl).
20 In 1525, the importation of books by Luther and his followers was banned; in 1535, their possession by persons within the realm was added to the import restriction: *Acts of the Parliaments of Scotland*, ed. T. Thomson (Edinburgh, 1814), II, 295 and 341.
21 See R.J. Knecht, *Francis I* (Cambridge, 1982), pp. 141–5 and 248–52, and P. Burke, 'Humanists, Reformers and French Culture', *French Literature and its Background*, ed. J. Cruikshank (London, 1968), pp. 32–45 (41).

examined has mentioned this one.²² The absence underlines obvious differences between the small poorer kingdom of Scotland and one of the great European empires. It also confirms the limited extent of Lyndsay's own knowledge of spectacle to this date.²³ This was so soon to change, with the repeated missions to France that began in the following year, that it has obscured the fact that, in 1531, Lyndsay was witnessing the kind of event he had only, quite possibly, heard about. Lyndsay's interest was nonetheless professional: he has, he also reports, recorded the names of those 'lordis and kny^{tis} y^t war hurt' that day. This was a long-used and truly international practice among heralds: similar records of the feats of battle by particular combatants were made from earlier times, in at least one instance from an observation post that was shared by officers of arms from the opposing sides.²⁴

His professionalism, in turn, raises the question of how much contact Lyndsay had with other European heralds and works of heraldry on the Brussels and subsequent missions. One result of such contact may have been the incentive they gave to Lyndsay to compile Scotland's own heraldic record book. He would have found a definite need for an armorial originating in Scotland: of the many European rolls of arms and armorial books to that time, only that of the herald Gelre, compiled in the later fourteenth century, approached either comprehensiveness or reliability in its record of Scottish arms.²⁵ Lyndsay certainly began one in this period, completing what is now the first folio – the royal arms of Scotland – before 1536.²⁶ Others, now following these arms, could have been painted earlier, since Lyndsay set out out his work after the continental pattern and included mythological blazons – Prester John, the Three Wise Men, and the Nine Worthies. The beautiful lozenges of James V's two French Queens were of course not to be dated earlier than the middle of 1538,²⁷ but arms of some Scottish nobles could have been painted before that. Beaton's, distinguished by the lavish full-page allocation given them, are those to which he was entitled only very late in 1538.²⁸ Lyndsay appended the date 1542 to his own arms, thus indicating a spread in the

22 Among others, *Fêtes and Cérémonies au Temps de Charles Quint*, ed. J. Jacquot (Paris, 1975), and R. Strong, *Splendour at Court: Renaissance Spectacle and Illusion* (London, 1973).
23 Lyndsay was not included in the embassy to England in 1524/5, when Scottish visitors were lavishly entertained at Greenwich over Christmas with combats and a mock assault: E. Hall, *The Union of the Two Noble and Illustre famelies of Lancastre and Yorke*, ed. H. Ellis (London, 1809), pp. 587–91 and S. Anglo, *Spectacle, Pageantry and Early Tudor Policy*, (Oxford, 1969), pp. 115–16.
24 *A European Armorial: an armorial of Knights of the Golden Fleece and Fifteenth Century Europe* [Bib. de l'Arsenal MS 4790], ed. R. Pinches and A. Wood (London, 1971), p. 12.
25 See J. Stevenson, *Heraldry in Scotland*, 2 vols (Glasgow, 1914), I, 113–14, 195 and Plates xii, xiii, and xiv; M. Keen, *Chivalry* (New Haven and London, 1984), pp. 139–40.
26 The depiction records the first additions to the arms under James V (two saltire banners on flagstaffs held by the unicorn supporters), but not the subsequent changes seen after the redesigning of the sceptre in 1536, those afterwards incorporated into the woodcut used for Bellenden's *Chronicles* and the *New Actis . . . of Parliament Maid be . . . James the Fift*. See C.J. Burnett, 'The Development of the Royal Arms to 1603', *The Double Tressure*, I (1977–8), 7–19 (16–18).
27 For a facsimile reproduction see Stevenson, *Heraldry*, I, Plate XVI.
28 Laing facsimile, fol. 49; compare the arms on the title verso of Beaton's copy of Archibald Hay's *Ad Reverendissimum in Christo patrem D. Iacobum Betoun, pro Collegii erectione* (Paris, 1538), illustrated in J. Durkan and A. Ross, 'Early Scottish Libraries', *Innes Review*, IX, No. 1 (1958), Plate V.

manuscript's making of at least seven years. These years were those of Lyndsay's direct and frequent contact with the continental heralds, and those when the making of a splendid armorial book was a particularly fitting and useful way of enabling the Scotland of James V to take its proper place among the Western European nations.

A Scottish armorial record would have been very useful in France in 1537, at the wedding tournament in which James V himself took part,[29] but there were other aspects of the French missions that had an influence upon Lyndsay, and Scotland in turn. Lyndsay's state poem of mourning, *The Deploratioun of the Deith of Quene Magdalene* (1537), has been discussed as the formal lament of the Scottish nation, but the many valuable details it contains of the scale and form of the official reception planned by Edinburgh for Madeleine de Valois in 1537 have gone largely unnoticed. Similarly, the fact that these were reported by a Scotsman who had been in France for lengthy visits, several between 1532 and 1537, and who was closely involved with the entry and celebrations in Paris for James V, has also been insufficiently considered.[30]

James's entry into Paris, as described in the French President Liset's official report,[31] was most punctiliously ordered, by profession, estate, and regulation of dress. In addition, by the command of Francis I, the court of Parliament wore the fine red robes previously worn only to honour the French king himself. Lyndsay does not mention this fact, made much of at the time,[32] in his own shorter poetic description of James's reception, but when he describes Madeleine's entry into Edinburgh as it had been planned, Lyndsay reveals it was to have had similar emphases – the careful ordering by profession, rank, and colour of dress. Lyndsay also heightens the contrast to the mourning black of the actual event by noting the greater variety of colours of the planned Scottish celebration: the craftsman's green, the 'purpure, blak, and brown' of the Senators (122), the gold of 'knychtlie Barroun and baurent' (124), the tinctures of the heralds' 'aufull Vestimentis' (138), and he refers, too, to the 'scarlot' and 'claith of grane' of the burgesses (118).[33] Notably, the word 'grane' is not, as might be supposed, a reference to a grainy-textured or-coloured fabric but to a scarlet dye. The use of two words, 'scarlot' (a fine cloth often scarlet in colour) and 'grane', quietly emphasises the wearing of red garments.[34] Scotland's poetic artifact, balancing France's ceremonial reality, thus became a skilled piece of international diplomacy relying heavily upon Lyndsay's first-hand experience abroad.

29 *Letters and Papers, Foreign and Domestic of the Reign of Henry VIII*, arranged and catalogued by J. Gairdner (London, 1888), XI, 1315.
30 See *TA*, VI (1531–2), 44; (1532), 46; (1534), 232; (1538 [1536]), 455, 456, VII, 16 and see references to Lyndsay in A.J. Mill, *Medieval Plays in Scotland* (New York and London, 1924).
31 A. Teulet, *Papiers d'Etat, pièces et documents inédits ou peu connus relatifs à l'histoire de l'Ecosse au XVIe*, I (Edinburgh, 1852), 123–4.
32 Teulet, *Papiers d'Etat*, I, 122.
33 For further discussion on this topic of ceremonial dress, see T. Innes of Learney, 'The Robes of the Feudal Baronage of Scotland', *Proceedings of the Society of Antiquaries of Scotland*, LXXIX, Seventh Series, VII (1944–5), 111–63 and plates.
34 See *DOST*, s.v. *Grain(e, Grane*, n^1, II.6.

Where there is such an awareness of balance and parallel gesture, any reported differences between French and Scottish ceremonies deserve close attention. The choice of the language of oratory, central to the political messages conveyed between nations, is one of them.[35] Liset had noted that after the addresses made to the Scottish king by President and estates representatives, James had embraced the parliamentary representatives without actually speaking to them because, it was reported, he knew little of the language.[36] It is surprising, perhaps, that James V did not delegate the part of spokesman to Cardinal Beaton, as he had earlier in his visit.[37] Lyndsay himself could with some aptness have spoken for Scottish king and kingdom.[38] But the silent action preserved and even increased kingly status, where a speech by a stand-in would have lessened both. Lyndsay's *Deploratioun*, in its turn, mentions Edinburgh's 'ornate Oratouris' (162) drawn from clergy, town and council. The language spoken is not divulged, though there is perhaps a touch of asperity in the brief allusion to the harmonious and definitely French '*Viue la Royne*' that Scottish virgins and burgess wives were to have cried.[39]

The burgh records of Marie de Guise's entry into Edinburgh in the following year, however, are more forthcoming: at least on that occasion, the culmination was a formal welcome 'in Fransche'. Also recorded, and of near concern, is David Lyndsay's direct involvement, for although his participation in the devising of Madeleine's earlier entry has been long-assumed, there is no surviving evidence to prove it. Moreover, Lyndsay's role of only a year later was vital: 'all ordour and furnesing' of seven stations along the Queen's High Street progress were to be done with Lyndsay's 'avyse'. Lyndsay himself, with a local furrier Robert Bischope, was responsible for one of the scaffolded 'rowmes' or spaces that were to be prepared for undescribed 'personages'. And the climax, the French oration, was to be 'devysit with avyse of Maister Adame Otterburne, Maister James Fowlis and Dauid Lyndsay'.[40]

Why was it that Lyndsay was also specifically named here, when he was already, by right of office as senior herald, heavily involved in the entry's devising as a whole? As other scholars have noted, Foulis and Otterburn, their academic qualifications gained on the continent, were prominent advocates, and senior burgh officials of the city. They were also learned poets in Latin (Foulis with an international reputation). And somewhat like David Lyndsay, these men were closely associated with James V: Otterburn repeatedly had been his ambassador

---

35 French and Latin, though languages of international diplomacy, were no longer, it would seem, used as a matter of course. See Anglo, *Spectacle*, p. 240, for an English instance where French was used to make a diplomatic point.
36 Teulet, *Papiers d'Etat*, I, 124. Compare also, for example, *LP HVIII*, XI, 1173, Bishop of Faenza (Papal Nuncio in France) to Mon. Ambrogio (Papal Secretary and Prothonotary), in which James's lack of French fluency is noted.
37 *LP HVIII*, XI, 1173, 1194.
38 On Lyndsay's position, see T. Innes of Learney, 'Heraldic Law', *An Introductory Survey of the Sources and Literature of Scots Law*, ed. H. McKechnie (Edinburgh, 1936), pp. 379–95.
39 Notably, the 1558 French prints of Lyndsay's poem substitute 'Veua la royna'.
40 *Extracts of the Records of the Burgh of Edinburgh AD 1528–1557*, ed. J.D. Marwick (Edinburgh, 1871), II, 88–91.

to the English court; Foulis had been secretary to the King in 1529 and was clerk register in 1538.[41]

Several other matters, however, could have had some bearing on the specific mention of Lyndsay here. Lyndsay was neither burgess nor provost, but he also had strong ties with Edinburgh, of which its magistrates could not have been in ignorance. Since 1511 the burgh had been the base for much of his court service and from 1513, the location of his own property. Interestingly, this was part of a tenement on the south side of the High Street, where, incidentally, it would have been well positioned to provide one of the scaffolded areas mentioned in the 1538 records.[42] Edinburgh, too, was where much of Lyndsay's heraldic work was carried out: the business of Lyon Court, and of Parliament, where Lyon was 'the Royal *alter ego* for proclamatory purposes'.[43] He had also recently displayed these skills in public speaking at St Andrews, in an address made to Marie de Guise, within the 'triumphand frais' of welcome.[44] Apart from this, there was also Lyndsay's appropriateness in terms of learned reputation. He, too, was in contact, though not exclusively, with the circle of humanist scholars known by Foulis and Otterburn. The scholars Ferrerio and Buchanan, for example, were both, at different times during the 1530s, at the Scottish court. Lyndsay was abroad for part of this period, but Ferrerio knew Sir Walter Lyndsay, a near relation of David's. Thus, in manuscript, Ferrerio's treatise on the true meaning of comets (*De vera cometæ significatione [contra astrolgorum omnium vanitatem libellus]*, (Paris, M. Vascosan, 1540)), written for the superstitious James V in 1531, was either directly or indirectly likely to have reached the poet, who had shown some interest in the subject of 'heuenly influence' and James's sensitivities to it, in the *Complaynt* of 1529.[45] And with Buchanan, who had also written of Madeleine's death, in Latin verses, Lyndsay's contact is well known.[46] Otterburn, Foulis and Lyndsay were all definite individuals, but by 1538 they formed a threesome where talents and various qualifications were shared equally. Arguably, it was Lyndsay's recent official contact with Europe that set him apart, for he alone, as

41 For Otterburn, see J.A. Inglis, *Sir Adam Otterburn of Redhall, King's Advocate 1524–1538* (Glasgow, 1935), and I.D. McFarlane, *Buchanan* (London, 1981), pp. 49–50. For Foulis, see note 10; J. Durkan, 'The Beginnings of Humanism in Scotland', *Innes Review*, IV, No. 1 (1953), 5–24 (7–9), and 'The Scottish Nation in the University of Orléans 1336–1538', ed. J. Kirkpatrick in *Miscellany of the Scottish History Society Second Volume*, various editors (Edinburgh, 1904), 45–102 (64, 82–3, 97, 102).
42 *Protocol Book of John Foular, 1503–1513*, I, Part ii (1509–1513), ed. M. Wood (Edinburgh 1953), 168, No. 886.
43 T. Innes of Learney, 'The Scottish Parliament: its Symbolism and its Ceremonial', *Juridical Review*, XLIV (1932), 87–124 (114, continuation from 113, note 3).
44 R. Lindesay of Pitscottie, *The Historie and Cronicles of Scotland*, ed. Æ.J.G. Mackay, 3 vols (Edinburgh, 1909–11), I, 378–9.
45 See J. Durkan, 'Giovanni Ferrerio, Humanist: His Influence in Sixteenth-Century Scotland', in *Religion and Humanism*, ed. K. Robbins (Oxford, 1981), pp. 181–94 (183, 189–90); Durkan, 'Beginnings of Humanism', 14–17.
46 McFarlane, *Buchanan*, pp. 48–77; I.D. McFarlane, 'George Buchanan's Latin Poems from Script to Print: a preliminary survey', *The Library*, 5th Ser., XXIV, No. 4 (1969), 277–332 (277–80); *TA*, VI (1531–38), 353. Gavin Dunbar provides another example. He mentioned Foulis with affection in his will, and was also close to Lyndsay during the first twelve years of the king's life, the one his tutor, the other his companion after school. See Lyndsay's *Complaynt*, 79–100.

the keen observations in the *Deploratioun* make clear, possessed the detailed knowledge of the conduct, and oratory, of the latest state events abroad.

Missions to European countries involved their envoys, including Lyndsay, in a great deal of patient waiting. There were delays of the kind Beaton experienced in France and reported to James V: '. . . I have evir differit to writ to 3our grace sen my cummyne . . . because ye king 3our gracis fadir wes euir removand and I culd neuir gett him and his counsal togiddir'.[47] There were administrative setbacks, some associated with political strategies or personal ambition. In June 1518, for example, Papal Legate Cardinal Campeggio had arrived at Calais to cross to England, but by Wolsey's design was kept waiting there until late July, thereby enabling the English cardinal to win from the Pope a mandate for himself for equal legatine authority.[48] For Lyndsay in Brussels on his first mission, all had gone well at face-to-face meetings, but to some written questions Lyndsay was given 'na answar . . . quhill I was reddy to depart furth of ye cowrt imperiell', some seven weeks later.[49] And not to be forgotten, there were those delays caused by the misadventures of travel itself. On his last embassy, to Protestant Denmark, Lyndsay had already spent three months abroad when the first attempt to leave, in February 1549, nearly cost him his life through shipwreck in icy seas.[50] Forced to wait until spring, but with his rather difficult negotiations brought to satisfactory conclusion, Lyndsay had a number of unexpected opportunities.

Looking from Denmark, with time to ponder, Lyndsay might have been struck first by the incongruities in his position. Soon after his arrival at court, an ambassador from England had also presented credentials. This man had put England's counter-appeal, based heavily on community of religion, beside still-Catholic Scotland's requests for Danish military and trade support against English attack. The envoy had been a trump card for Protector Somerset, none other than the expatriate Scot, Sir John Borthwick, formerly the familiar servant of James V and Lyndsay's past colleague. Borthwick's position reflected Scotland's present religious 'miserie'. He had been forced to flee to England in 1540, ahead of the trial that had condemned him *in absentia* for heresy. His Scottish library, which had included a vernacular Bible and volumes of Melanchthon and Erasmus, had been held against him, yet in Denmark, as Lyndsay would have known, the same works were all sources for open discussion and study.[51]

Such circumstances are conducive to a loss of political optimism, and indeed such a state of mind seems to have been Lyndsay's if it may be judged from the

---

47 A. Laing, 'Letters of Cardinal Beaton 1537–41', *Scottish Historial Review*, XXI (1908), 150–8 (152), Add. MS 19401 1541, fol. 35.
48 See Anglo, *Spectacle*, pp. 126–8.
49 See also the account of the path through the formalities trodden by Bishop Robert Blacadder in Rome: L.J. Macfarlane, 'The Elevation of the Diocese of Glasgow into an Archbishopric in 1492', *Innes Review*, XLIII, No. 2 (1992), 99–118.
50 T.L. Christensen, 'John Borthwick og hans plan om et samlet protestanisk Nordeuropa', *Kirkehistoriske Samlinger* (Copenhagen, 1976), 44–66 (51–2 and references). I am indebted to the author for this reference, and for translation of key extracts from it.
51 J. Durkan, 'The Cultural Background in Sixteenth-Century Scotland', *Innes Review*, X, No. 2 (1959), 382–439 (408–9); J. Durkan, 'Scottish 'Evangelicals' in the Patronage of Thomas Cromwell', *Records of the Scottish Church History Society*, XXI, Part 2 (1982), 127–56 (132).

sober tone of his longest, most scholarly work, the universal history *Ane Dialog*, which dates from about this period.[52] Did Lyndsay begin or finish part of it while waiting in Denmark? Or – inspired by the congenial ideas he was encountering there – did he at least invest some of his waiting time in arousing sympathetic interest, or gaining financial assistance for the publication of *Ane Dialog*? What evidence there is – of imprint, dating, sources used, extensive Biblical translation – suggests that one or both of these processes occurred.

In the 1540s there was underway in Denmark a project to print a Danish translation of the Bible. It had royal patronage, and was the work of a group of eminent Danish theologians, but another expatriate Scot, the former Perth Dominican prior, John Macalpine, was overseeing it.[53] Known in Denmark as Macchabæus (a name said to have been given him by Philip Melanchthon), Macalpine, now a doctor of theology, was the respected professor of the University of Copenhagen and a man with the ear of the king.[54] Scottish contact had been maintained with him during the Marian minority. Letters and records of meetings survive between Macalpine and George Leslie, the Earl of Rothes, as does official correspondence from Governor Arran.[55] Macalpine's own testimony of continuing interest in Scotland can also be found in a letter in which he referred to his willingness to act as adviser to Scottish students travelling to Denmark.[56] Consequently it would be the more remarkable if Macalpine and Lyndsay had not met, though the piece of the jigsaw directly connecting them is so far still missing.

It seems likely that it was Macalpine who encouraged Lyndsay's biblical translation, and gave him introduction or access to copies of the scholarly texts he drew upon in *Ane Dialog*.[57] For instance, one of its sources, Carion's *Chronica*, was not in English until 1550, but had been published in German in 1532. This was the edition Melanchthon had used for his lectures. These, in turn, had been heard by the student Macalpine, who had achieved his present teaching position partly through Melanchthon's warm recommendation.[58] Delayed in Denmark, Lyndsay was in reach of this scholarly network and it seems he embraced it. When the first edition of *Ane Dialog* appeared in 1554, it bore the words: 'And Imprentit at the Conmand and Expensis off Doctour Machabeus, In Copmãhouin'.

Was Macalpine its patron? Though the various editors of Lyndsay have

---

52 See Durkan, 'Cultural Background', 422.
53 See F. Bredahl Petersen, 'Dr Johannes Macchabæus John MacAlpin: Scotland's Contribution to the Reformation in Denmark', Diss. Edinburgh, 1937, pp. 204–14.
54 See T.L. Christensen, 'Scots in Denmark in the Sixteenth Century', *Scottish Historical Review*, XLIX, No. 2 (1970), 125–45 (137–8); T. Riis, *Auld Acquaintance*, I, 114–20.
55 *TA*, IX, 386–7; T.L. Christensen, 'The Earl of Rothes in Denmark', *The Renaissance and Reformation in Scotland*, ed. I.B. Cowan and D. Shaw (Edinburgh, 1983), p. 65.
56 H. Ilsøe, 'Christian og Johannes Macchabæus', *Kirkehistoriske Samlinger*, Ser. 7, V (1963–5), 454–71.
57 See Durkan's pertinent discussion of Macalpine's views on the church and its ministry, 'Cultural Background', 415–17.
58 A detailed discussion of the nature of Lyndsay's debt to Carion is found in A.M. Stewart, 'Carion, Wedderburn, Lindsay', *Aberdeen University Review*, No. 147 (1972), 271–4.

dismissed the possibility,[59] Macalpine's nationality, interests and standing (which had its financial rewards)[60] all lend support. The evidence of the Danish Bible's printer, Ludwig Dietz, confirms that Macalpine, lacking Danish as a first language, was concerned chiefly with 'having [the Bible] published and distributed'.[61] Perhaps Macalpine saw *Ane Dialog* as a more modest, yet equally needed, Bible-based project in his native Scots, in which he could take a similar role?[62]

The evidence assembled and examined here suggests that Lyndsay gained professionally, as senior herald, and intellectually, as a morally based reformer, rather more than as a poet, from his continental European encounters. It seems possible that what Lyndsay learned abroad had its impact on his devisings in Scotland for the king's French marriages and on his official heraldic compilation, the first native armorial. Travelling the distances, encountering the linguistic, social and religious barriers and freedoms, observing the scale of public events, and actually participating on behalf of Scotland in the power-plays of international political bargaining, Lyndsay would have been in a position to modify his own initially theoretically- and hearsay-based understanding of Europe. If the direct evidence of his realisation of the difference is lacking, it is, nonetheless, reflected in his later poetic works. In *Ane Satyre*, for example, Lyndsay is able to offer through the words of his character Folie (4553–95 [1554]), a view of contemporary Europe, and an assessment of Scotland's involvement in it, that has something of the intelligent if partial dynamism of St Machar's ceiling, and that is Erasmian in its emphasis on the need for peace. Literary influence, however, cannot be tied similarly to Lyndsay's exchanges with continental countries, though the effects, somewhat uneven, of Lyndsay's foreign contact while still in Scotland, are just glimpsed. There is the influence of French theatre convention on the later work, *Ane Satyre*,[63] yet Lyndsay opened his last poem, *Ane Dialog*, using the dream vision form he employed in the first poem now extant, *The Dreme*. Though he is inspired in part by Gavin Douglas (*Eneados*, Prologues, x and xii), Lyndsay's traditional rejection of the classical Muses reflects a change in degree in his religious preoccupations. These had always been part of his writing, and do not necessarily indicate European influence. Added to the differences in theme and content of the later work, however, it seems possible that some changes could be due to Lyndsay's encounters furth of Scotland. It is only after Denmark, for example, that Lyndsay speaks of the need for the 'bukis necessare / To commoun weill, and our Saluatioun,/ Iustlye translatit in our toung Uulgare'

---

59 See J. Hadley Williams, 'Shady Publishing in Sixteenth-Century Scotland: the case of David Lyndsay's Poems', *Bulletin of the Bibliographical Society of Australia and New Zealand*, XVI, No. 3 (1992), 97–105 (102–3).
60 B. Peterson, 'Dr Johannes Macchabæus', p. 218.
61 Ibid, p. 212; see also T. Riis, *Auld Acquaintance*, I, 116 and note 18, where Macalpine, with a medical colleague, Morsing, is described as 'in charge of the sale of the authorised Danish Bible'.
62 By this I am not suggesting that *Ane Dialog* was printed in Copenhagen; its printer was John Scot, who appears to have worked in St Andrews and Edinburgh; his device appears on the verso of N8.
63 See, for example, A.J. Mill, 'The Influence of Continental Drama on Lyndsay's *Satyre of the Thrie Estaitis*', *Modern Language Review*, XXV (1930), 425–42 (442).

(*Ane Dialog*, 678–80). Before that, Lyndsay satirises Church abuses and appeals to the prelates to preach and to explain the Scriptures, but his direct references to the importance of biblical translation into the vernacular come after the 1548 mission.[64] Similarly, Lyndsay's references to reformist thinkers by name do not appear in earlier works, whereas they are part of the fabric of the later, but this is perhaps as much a reflection of the changing Scotland as it is of Lyndsay's greater awareness of European reformers.[65]

Whether and how continental Europe was aware of Lyndsay is another matter. One printer (possibly Jean Petit or his heirs, possibly of Rouen) undoubtedly was. In 1558, the year that Franco-Scots ties were renewed in the marriage of Mary and the Dauphin Francis, a handsome edition of Lyndsay's works, printed in France, outraged the local printer John Scot on its arrival in Scotland.[66] Indeed the foreign compositors had had occasional difficulty with the Scottish tongue,[67] but from this it is clear that the French printer had aimed from the first at the Scottish, not the French market.[68] On the other hand, by the end of the century there was a local readership for Lyndsay's works in one continental country: in 1591, Lyndsay's works appeared in Denmark, this time translated into the native tongue.[69]

---

64 See the close examination of J.K. Cameron, 'Humanism and Religious Life', *Humanism in Renaissance Scotland*, ed. J. MacQueen (Edinburgh 1990), 161–77 (168–71), which, without setting out to do so, confirms this.
65 See *Ane Dialog*, 6252 (Erasmus); *Thrie Estaitis*, 2071–72 (Bullinger, Luther, Melanchthon).
66 See *The Works*, ed. Hamer, IV, 33–6.
67 For example, in the quarto text of the *Papyngo*, the French compositors replaced 'amang' (104) with 'amand', recalling a more familiar French word 'amande' or less possibly, 'amant'; and the Scottish word 'feid' (463) was replaced, with faintly comic effect, by 'feit'.
68 Hamer argues, on the flimsy evidence of a handwritten addition of 'a l'enseigne d'aegle' to the imprint of one copy, that copies were sold in France (*The Works*, IV, 30).
69 For bibliographic details, see *The Works*, ed. Hamer, IV, 60–2. Interestingly, one of the translators was Andrew Robertson, a Scot from Aberdeen.

M. NIEVES RODRÍGUEZ LEDESMA

31.   *Scots/English Interaction in* The Complaynt of Scotland?

1. Introduction

The sixteenth century can be considered a key period for the Scots language. While in the first half Scots is a national language with distinctive features, used for all kinds of purposes – literature (poetry as well as prose), public records, official documents, diaries, letters, etc.-, in the second, it begins to decline, mainly because of the growing prestige of English. 1549, the year when *The Complaynt of Scotland* was written, is particularly interesting in that it lies at the turning-point between these two opposite trends.

This paper analyses some aspects of the degree of anglicisation which exists in that work in order to establish whether Scots or English is the dominant variety. For this purpose, the three pairs of linguistic features studied by A.J. Devitt (1982 and 1989) which show the greatest degree of anglicisation have been chosen, that is, the spelling of the indefinite article, the spelling of the negative particles *no* and *not*, and the present participle inflection.

The Complaynt is a literary work in prose, written, according to A.M. Stewart (1979), by Robert Wedderburn and apparently printed in France, probably Paris, so that any anglicisation present in the text is not likely to be due to the printer but rather to the author. Modelled on Chartier's *Quadrilogue Invectif*, *The Complaynt* is full of axioms, exampla, sententiae, and proverbs taken from the Bible and from classical sources (Aristotle, Cicero, Pliny, among others), and it makes use of a lofty and rhetorical style, a prose parallel of the 'courtly verse in the grand manner' established by Aitken (1983) for the poetry of the period.

The analysis of the three linguistic features has not been carried out using the whole text. Instead, eleven out of the twenty chapters have been chosen, four from the beginning (epistle, prologue, chapters 1 and 2), three from the middle (chapters 6, 7 and 8), and four from the end (chapters 15, 16, 17 and 19), representing different subject matters (history, religion, science, pastoral), different types of discourse (epistle, prologue, description, narrative, monologue), and, although to a lesser extent, different styles, in order to establish whether these variables are significant in reflecting the degree of the process of anglicisation.[1] The

---

1   The following are the titles of the chapters chosen to carry out this analysis: 'epistil to the qvenis grace'; 'prolog to the redar'; 'the fyrst cheptour declaris the cause of the mutations of monarchis'; 'the sycond cheptor declaris the thretnyng of god contrar obstinat vicius pepil'; 'the sext cheptor rehersis ane monolog recreatyue of the actor'; 'the 7 cheptor is of the visione that aperit to the actor in his sleip'; 'the 8 cheptor declaris quhou the affligit lady dame Scotia reprochit hyr thre sounis callit the thre estatis of scotland'; 'quhou the thrid soune callit lauberaris ansuert vitht ane lamentabil complaynt' (ch. 15); 'quhou the affligit lady ansuert tyl hyr ʒongest soune' (ch. 16); 'quhou the affligit lady accusit hyr eldest soune callit nobilis and gentil men' (ch. 17); 'quhou the affligit lady accusit hyr sycond soune callit sperutualite' (ch. 19).

epistle is lofty, and so is the 'Monolog Recreatyue' (ch. 6), the longest chapter, which makes use of the aureate and alliterative diction of the courtly verse of grand manner. It includes most of the pieces of 'business' found in this genre according to Aitken's classification (1983:22): the zodiacal setting; the landscape and weather setting; the pastoral scene, and innumerable catalogues, in this case, of animals, birds, herbs, musical instruments, tales, songs, and dances. A naval scene, a list of nobles who preferred the village to the court, and a dissertation on astronomy are also included in this Monolog Recreatyue. These two chapters stand out from the rest, which are written in a simpler style.

2. Indefinite article

In early Scots the usual practice regarding the indefinite article is the same as that of Modern English usage: *a* before consonants, and *an*, *ane* before vowels and *h*. This is what we find, for instance, in Barbour, Wyntoun, Harry the Minstrel and Holland, as illustrated by Murray, who posits that 'instances of *ane* before a consonant are extremely rare before 1475; after this date it becomes more frequent, and the regular form after 1500' (1873: 55–6), so that, by the date of *The Complaynt*, the Scots *ane* before vowels and consonants contrasts with the English *an/a*, and, in spite of the mixed practice of some writers, the exclusive use of *ane* before vowels and *h* becomes marked as an anglicism, found for instance in the works of John Knox.

Concerning the origin of this tendency, Murray points out that 'it was introduced in literature and set speech in imitation of the French, so that the Sc. *ane kyng* answered to the French *un roi* -that is, both "one king", and "king" ' (p. 57), but he doubts that it was ever introduced into the language of common life, as this form does not survive in any living dialect.

Smith (1902) agrees with Murray on the date for the establishment of this form in 'literary' usage (the beginning of the sixteenth century), but denies a French origin: 'no hint of proof is forthcoming, and it is extremely difficult to imagine the intellectual or literary condition which imposed such an arbitrary rule so effectively throughout a clearly defined period. The proposition cannot be brought under any of the ordinary categories of linguistic imitation, for it implies more than the mere gallicising of native forms. It amounts to the admission of a *grammatical* interference in a quarter least liable to interference of any kind, and to an absolute recognition by every writer and scribe of the propriety of an affectation as ingenious as uncalled for. Whether *ane* be merely an orthographical mannerism, perhaps entirely scribal, or an illustration of the Northern craving for grammatical uniformity, it is best to class it . . . among the unexplained eccentricities of M.Sc.' (Smith 1902: lx).

Aitken (1971:209) points to an earlier date for the establishment of this practice, the second half of the fifteenth century, and *DOST* has 1462, 1472, and 1481 as the earliest examples illustrating the use of *ane* before consonants. There seems to be, thus, general agreement concerning the date of the introduction of this practice, and the fact that it is a mere spelling convention without correspondence at the phonetic level, since the practice is not applied to other compounds of *ane*, such as *na/nane*, and *the ta/the tane*, nor does it survive in any living dialect. There is no agreement, however, concerning the origin of this practice: it is as difficult to posit a native origin (it was not the practice in Early Scots), as a foreign (French) one. Devitt (1982:98) suggests that *ane* may have been marked as a spelling considered to be more formal or literary, but this does not explain how or why it was first introduced, although it may be a reason for its rapid establishment in the literature of the period.

The usage in *The Complaynt* is totally consistent with sixteenth-century Scots practice, and *ane* is found both before vowels and consonants regardless of differences in subject matter, type of discourse, or style. The following are the only apparent exceptions to this rule: 'mait keip ful and by, *a* luf' (p. 32),[2] 'bille, vil thou cum by *a* lute and belt the in Sanct Francis cord' (p. 51), 'thai began vitht tua bekkis and vitht *a* kysse' (p. 52), and 'schaik *a* trot' (p. 52), in the sixth chapter; 'the poiet francis petrarch *a* florentyne' (p. 118), in chapter 17, and 'this veil considrit, suld be *an* animaduertens' (p. 128), in chapter 19.

The first example of chapter 6 occurs in a technical naval context and it is not clear whether it is an instance of the indefinite article, or rather part of an adverb, *aluf*. The examples *a burde* 'aboard' and *a bak* 'aback' (p. 32), also found in the naval scene, seem to reinforce the second hypothesis, as well as the fact that the author tried to represent phonetically what he heard, as he himself explains: 'i herd mony vordis amang the marynalis bot i vist nocht quhat thai menit. ʒit i sal reherse and report ther crying and ther cals' (p. 31). That may be the reason, for instance, why he writes first *a burde* as two separate words, but as only one three lines later: 'hail doune the lufe close *aburde*' (p. 32). The second and fourth examples of chapter 6 correspond to the titles of a song and a dance tune respectively; since these are part of the common folklore of the two countries, it is not odd to find mixed spellings here, as the use of the preposition *by*, instead of the more usual *be*, which is used throughout the text, confirms. The other example in this chapter occurs when talking about the shepherds' dances, and is twice as odd, as it seems to be an instance of the numeral rather than the indefinite article. The examples of chapters 17 and 19 do not seem to have an explanation either.

The five examples which follow the English usage (four of which are cases of *a* before a consonant, and only one of *an* before a vowel) contrast with more than 500 instances of the Scots *ane*, both before vowels and consonants. The degree of anglicisation concerning the indefinite article is, thus, 1% in *The Complaynt*. These results do not coincide with those established by Devitt (1989:23), according to which already in 1520 16% of all instances of the indefinite article follow the English usage. This pattern remains basically unaltered until 1560, when a significant change in this trend may be observed.

---

2 All references to *The Complaynt* are to Stewart's edition.

3. Negative particles

In Early and Middle Scots, *na* is used both as a determiner and as an adverb. Originally, *na* as a determiner was followed by consonants; *nan, nane* by vowels, and this usage may appear sporadically in later texts: 'He hes nocht disponit *na* part of his gudis to *nan* vtheris', in 1538 *Breadalbane Collection of Documents and Letters*, No. 49 (*DOST*). But already by the end of the fourteenth century and throughout the fifteenth, examples of *na* before vowels are found: 'thinkand *na* ewil' (*Legends of the Saints*, iv, 339; in *DOST*), 'Na thare is *na* obligacioun worth that is oblist till impossible thing' (Haye's *The Buke of the Law of Armys* 193/19; in *DOST*), and in the sixteenth century they become the norm: 'Abrogat and of *na* effecte' (Dalrymple's *The Historie of Scotland*, I. 78/20; in *DOST*), 'ande that *na* ordinance of policye' (*The Complaynt*, p. 55), 'beystis that has *na* vndirstanding of raison' (*The Complaynt*, p. 57), 'as thou makis *na* acceptione of personis' (*The Complaynt*, p.100).

Na is also an adverb in *The Complaynt*, followed in all the cases by comparatives: 'ande *na* les prolixt to rehers . . .' (p. 3), 'this tracteit is *na* bettir nor as mekil vattir' (p. 6), 'ane gude man can be *na* bettir nor ane vthir man' (p. 8), 'vil be *na* mair gracius' (p. 128).

The form *no* is also found in *The Complaynt*, both as a determiner and as an adverb: 'hed *no* thyng' (p. 6), '*no* man suld' (p. 9), '*no* art nor mecanyc craft' (p. 8) are examples of the first; '*no* les prudent' (p. 35), '*no* les tideus' (p. 50) of the second. The difference in spelling between these two forms, parallel to that found in other couplets such as *mair/more, baith/both, fra/fro, sa/so*, reflects a different phonetic development of the O.E. long *a*, which is kept in the north and fronted to an /ɛ:/ in the fifteenth century, whereas in the south it is changed into an /ɔ:/. This anglicised variant is very common in all kinds of texts, appearing even in plain narrative verse, that is, 'those pieces which otherwise eschew anglicised forms' (Aitken 1983: 28), such as Barbour's *Bruce*: 'that [this] was *no* gabbing' (*DOST*), *Wallace*: 'with my gud will I wyll *no* lemman be to *no* man born' (*DOST*), or the Asloan Ms of *The Buke of the Sevyne Sagis*, where *no* as a determiner is found three times, the combination *no thing* twice, and *no* as an adverb five times (Van Buuren 1982: 71).

With regard to *The Complaynt*, *no* occurs thirty-eight times (once in the epistle, three times in the prologue, three times in the first chapter, once in the second, ten times in the sixth, once in the eighth, twice in the fifteenth, twice in the sixteenth, fifteen times in the seventeenth) as against the fifty-six occurrences of *na* (five times in the epistle, three times in the prologue, once in the first chapter, once in the second, eight times in the sixth, twice in the seventh, twice in the eighth, thirteen times in the fifteenth, twice in the sixteenth, twelve times in the seventeenth, and seven times in the nineteenth). *Na* is dominant in the adverbial position: it occurs nine times, followed by inflected and periphrastic forms of the comparative ('na les prolixt', 'na bettir', 'na mair gracius'); in contrast, *no* only occurs three times in that position, and it is followed by *les* in the three cases. On the other hand, *no* is used twice as often as *na* in the combination *no thing* (eight out of twelve times). In conclusion, it can be said that, although *na* is dominant overall (60%), the two forms are in free variation, occurring in all kinds of contexts, regardless of differences in subject matter, type of discourse or style (cf. the results of chapters 16, 17 and 19, all of them monologues spoken by the same character, Dame Scotia).

Nocht (O.E. *noht*), on the other hand, can be both a pronoun meaning 'nothing' and an adverb. The origin of the adverb *nocht*, according to Mustanoja (1960: 339–40), is found in O.E., in cases where the original negative adverb, *ne*, placed before the verb, is intensified by the negative pronoun *noht* (< *nawiht, nowiht*) after the verb. This double negative construction occurs down to the end of the M.E. period, but already in early M.E. the unstressed, weakened *ne* begins to be dropped, and by the middle of the fourteenth century, *noht*, placed after the verb (as it originally was), is seen as the new negative adverb.

There is only one example of the pronoun in *The Complaynt*: 'al verteous industrie sal be brocht to notht' (p. 62); elsewhere the combination *no/na thing* is found. By this time, then, *nocht* has almost lost its original pronominal character, and become the new negative adverb, with the total exclusion of earlier *ne*. The adverb, however, keeps the position of the original pronoun, and thus always follows the main verb, except in complex verb phrases, where it occurs between the auxiliary and the lexical verb, and in non-finite clauses, where it precedes the verb: 'i vait *nocht* quhat ansuere to mak' (p. 12), 'that accords *nocht* vitht the lateen' (p. 13); 'there can *nocht* be' (p. 3); 'i *nocht* heffand' (p. 5), 'the quhilkis humours *nocht* beand degeistit' (p. 7).

Not, a reduced variant of *nought*, is the counterpart of the adverb *nocht* in the South. There is only one example of this form in *The Complaynt*, which may be dismissed as an error, since the second negative in a correlation should be *nor*, never *not*, as, for instance, in 'thai hef nothir prudens *nor* knaulege' (p. 102), or 'be cause ve hef nothir knaulage reches *nor* subtilite' (p. 105). Thus 'trason is neuyr generit *not* inuentit in the hartis . . .' (p. 102) should read 'trason is neuyr generit *nor* inuentit . . .', and this, in fact, is the version Murray gives (p. 130).

That there is no anglicisation concerning this particle is not only apparent in that the adverb *not* does not occur at all in the text, but in the fact that spellings such as <nought, noucht>, which reflect the diphthongisation that O.E. *o* followed by *h* underwent in the South, are not found either, <nocht> being the only spelling of this variable.

These results do not agree with the ones obtained by Devitt. Although she points out that, contrary to the other variables studied, which remain relatively stable, the negative particle anglicises significantly from 1520 to 1560, she holds the variable *nocht* as the one responsible for this pattern, and states that 'by 1560, *not* has increased to nearly 60% while *no* remains less than 30%' (Devitt 1989:27). Her conclusion, that 'the spelling shift from *nocht* to *not* occurs before the shift from *na* to *no*, beginning before 1520' (p. 28) is not only against the evidence provided by *The Complaynt*, but also against that of the plain narrative verse, one of the genres most resistant to anglicisation, which has examples of *no*, but none of *not*.

4. The present participle

The ending of the present participle in Older Scots is *-and*, borrowed from Old Norse, corresponding to native *-inde* (Macafee, 1992/93:22). This is kept distinct from the ending of the gerund, or verbal noun, *-ing* up to the sixteenth century in Scots, although in Southern English the two inflections are syncretised as early as the fourteenth century. In the sixteenth century, however, the verbal noun and the verbal adjective are confused in literary Middle Scots, which is based on the dialect of Central Scotland, mainly due to the loss of the final consonant in both inflections, and the confusion of the vowels in unstressed syllables, so that both forms are written *-ing, -in'*. In the Southern Counties, the final consonants are also lost in these inflections, but the vowels are not confused, so that present participle and gerund are still kept distinct there as well as in Northern England (Murray 1873:210–11).

The dropping of post-nasal [g] and [d] is explained by Murray as being due to Celtic influence, and he supports this argument with the evidence of the present day Gaelic forms for the English words *London, window, candle*, and *island: Lunuinn, uinneag, coinneal, eilean*. This would have caused not only the mixing of the gerund and the present participle, but in many cases also the confusion of both with the past participle *-in* (1873: 53). That at least the final post-nasal [g] had been lost is shown in reverse spellings found in texts of the period, such as *basyng* 'basin', *courting* 'curtain', *garding* 'garden' (Van Buuren 1982: 86), or *lating* 'Latin' (*The Complaynt*, p. 13). But, as Macafee points out (p. 23), even though the confusion of gerund and present participle in sixteenth-century Scots may be explained on phonetic grounds, and consequently be considered a native development, it is reinforced by Southern usage, so that anglicisation underlies this shift.

The situation in *The Complaynt*, however, is that found in the earlier stages of the language, when the two forms were kept distinct. *-and*, represented by the spellings < -and, -ant, -end (*spekend*) > is the ending of the present participle, which may function both as a verb and as an adjective. Examples of both functions are found in *The Complaynt*: 'as plutois paleis hed been *birnand* in ane bald fyir' (p. 33), 'ther tua symmyrs ar vondir *birnand* heyt' (p. 41); 'to hald my spretis *valkand* fra dulnes' (p. 29), 'and quhen it slais ane *valkand* man' (p. 47); 'that *blaberand* eccho' (p. 30). On the other hand, *-ing*, represented by the spellings < -ing, -yng > , is the ending of the gerund, or verbal noun, which may occur with both noun-modifiers and verb-modifiers: 'for the *delyuering* of hyr heretage furtht of captiuite' (p. 2), 'in the *conuoyng* and in the *diuising* diuerse consaitis to bring' (p. 103).

The distinction between the two forms is clearly seen in these pairs of examples: 'ane man that castis vlye on ane heyt *birnand* fyir' (p. 127), 'na statutis, lauis, punitions, bannessing, *byrnyng*, hayrschip nor torment' (p. 126); 'quhilkis mouit ther bodeis as thai hed bene *dansand*' (p. 52), 'quhen this *dansing* vas dune' (p. 52); 'that blaberand eccho hed beene hid in ane houhole, *cryand* hyr half ansueir' (p. 30), 'i sal reherse and report ther *crying* and ther cals' (p. 31); 'quhen ve entrit in this mortal lyif ve var naikyt and *vepand*' (p. 122), 'for the *vepyng* of pure men' (p.

98). There are only two examples where the ending of the present participle is -*ing*: 'rycht soirly *musing* in my mynde', and 'al *musing* of meruellis amys hef i gone' (p. 51), but, as the two instances of the indefinite article *a* found above,[3] they occur in the titles of songs, and since these belong to the common folklore of the two countries, it is not odd to find mixed spellings here.

To sum up, the present participle in *The Complaynt* is carefully kept distinct from the gerund, and thus remains unaffected by Southern usage. This is consistent with the usage found in other sixteenth-century texts, such as those analysed by Van Buuren (1982) and Kuipers (1964), but not with the results obtained by Devitt, who concludes that this is the most highly anglicised feature, with the Anglo-English -*ing* already dominant 1520–1539 (occurring in more than 60% of instances of the present participle), and increasing considerably between 1540–59 and 1560–79 (Devitt 1982:131).

The analysis of these variables in *The Complaynt* reveals two -or rather, three-important facts: first, that some of Devitt's conclusions, especially those regarding the negative particle and the present participle, must be considered as general trends, and not be expected to hold true for every text. From this first conclusion we can draw a second, fairly obvious one, that we need to carry out studies of the kind done by Devitt on as many works of the period as possible. I hope that my work on *The Complaynt* will be a contribution to this effort. The third conclusion, and possibly the most important one, is that – at least as far as the three variables analysed here are concerned – by the middle of the sixteenth century it is still possible to find texts written exclusively in Scots, with little or no anglicisation. Such is the case of *The Complaynt*, which, in terms of these three variables, lies at the same level as the vernacular narrative verse, one of the genres most resistant to the process of anglicisation.[4]

Bibliography

AITKEN, A.J. (1971) 'Variation and variety in written Middle Scots', in A.J. Aitken, A. McIntosh and H. Pálsson eds. *Edinburgh Studies in English and Scots*. London: Longman, pp. 177–209.

AITKEN, A.J. (1983) 'The language of Older Scots poetry' in J.D. McClure ed. *Scotland and the Lowland Tongue*. Aberdeen University Press, pp. 18–49.

CRAIGIE, W. and AITKEN, A.J. eds. (1932–) *A Dictionary of the Older Scottish Tongue from the Twelfth Century to the End of the Seventeenth, Founded on the Collections of Sir William A. Craigie*. Chicago: University of Chicago Press, and London: Oxford University Press.

DEVITT, Amy J. (1982) 'Standardizing Written English: The influence of genre, audience, and medium, on Scots-English usage, 1520 to 1659'. Unpublished PhD thesis, University of Michigan.

---

3 'Bille, vil thou cum by a lute and belt the in Sanct Francis cord' (p. 51), and 'schaik a trot' (p. 52), in chapter 6.

4 The little anglicisation which exists in *The Complaynt* -at least as far as the three linguistic features analyzed here are concerned- may be due to the nationalist nature of this work, and the political ideology of its author. This hypothesis cannot be confirmed, however, until a thorough linguistic study of *The Complaynt* has been carried out.

DEVITT, Amy J. (1989) *Standardizing Written English. Diffusion in the case of Scotland 1520–1659*, Cambridge: Cambridge University Press.

GRANT, W. and DIXON, J.M. (1921) *Manual of Modern Scots*, Cambridge: Cambridge University Press.

KUIPERS, C.H. (1964) 'Kennedy's language', in *Quintin Kennedy (1520–1564): Two Eucharistic Tracts. A Critical Edition*. Nijmegen: Drukkerij Gebr., pp. 75–103.

MACAFEE, C.I. (1992/93) 'A short grammar of Older Scots', in *Scottish Language* 11/12, pp. 10–36.

MURRAY, James A.H. ed. (1872) *The Complaynt of Scotlande*. London: Early English Text Society, Extra Series, No. xvii. Reprinted 1973.

MURRAY, James A.H. (1873) *The Dialect of the Southern Counties of Scotland*. London: Philological Society.

MUSTANOJA, T. (1960) *A Middle English Syntax*. Helsinki: *Mémoires de la Société Néophilologique* 23. Part I. *Parts of Speech*.

SMITH, G. Gregory (1902) 'Introduction', in *Specimens of Middle Scots*. Edinburgh and London: William Blackwood and Sons, pp. xi–lxxv.

STEWART, A.M. ed. (1979) *The Complaynt of Scotland*. Edinburgh: The Scottish Text Society.

VAN BUUREN, C. (1982) 'Introduction', in C. Van Buuren ed. *The Buke of the Sevyne Sagis*. Leiden University Press, pp. 1–130.

EVELYN S. NEWLYN

32. Traditions of Myth and Fabliau in 'The Cupar Banns'

The 'Cupar Banns,'[1] a 'Proclamation' announcing the future performance of Lindsay's *Satyre of the Thrie Estaitis*, functioned like the 'coming attractions' in today's movie theatres, where clippings from future films, usually containing sex and violence, are shown to tempt prospective audiences.[2] The 'coming attractions' for today's movies are actual segments of films that will appear, making them closer in nature to the Middle English banns for the cycle dramas of Chester and N-Town, each of which summarises in a stanza the plays to come in the cycle.[3] In contrast, 'The Cupar Banns' offers autonomous material that is not directly connected to the play that it is announcing, but material that is nonetheless designed to draw an audience both to itself and to Lindsay's later play.[4] In this sense, Lindsay's Proclamation differs markedly from the banns for the cycle drama, since it not only announces the upcoming play, but actually advances its own themes.

The structure of the 'Cupar Banns' is composed of three separate dramatic entities which form a tightly-knit unit thematically as they interweave in the course of the performance. They are the vignette of Cotter and his wife, the interlude of Bessy and the Auld Man, and the linking strand focusing on Fyndlaw

---

1 The Bannatyne Manuscript is the only witness to the 'Cupar Banns'; see W. Tod Ritchie's diplomatic transcription, *The Bannatyne Manuscript Writtin in Tyme of Pest, 1568*, STS, 4 vols. (London, 1928–34); and the Scolar Press Facsimile Edition, *The Bannatyne Manuscript, National Library of Scotland Advocates' MS. 1.1.6* (London, 1980), with an introduction by Denton Fox and William A. Ringler. Bannatyne in his headnote refers to this work as a 'Proclamatioun,' while Douglas Hamer observes that 'In England down to 1609 such proclamations were called Banns'; see Hamer's edition of *The Works of Sir David Lindsay of the Mount*, STS, 4 vols. (Edinburgh and London, 1931–6), vol. 4, p. 163. A more recent edition is Roderick Lyall's *Ane Satyre of the Thrie Estaitis* (Edinburgh, 1989), which offers 'The Cupar Banns' in an appendix, but with little commentary. I assume that Lindsay wrote the Proclamation; Anna J. Mill observed that 'no really cogent arguments against his authorship' have been raised, in her 'Representations of Lindsay's *Satyre of the Thrie Estaitis*,' *PMLA* 47 (1933), p. 642. Moreover, both Proclamation and *Satyre* have themes and attitudes in common. Quotations here are from Hamer's edition of Lindsay's works.
2 Hamer notes the performance intends 'to attract an audience to listen to the proclamation' and 'to arouse a sense of anticipation for the more important play later' (vol. 4, p. 163). Making a thematic connection between the Proclamation and the *Satyre*, Joan Hughes and W.S. Ramson describe 'The Cupar Banns' as 'a foretaste of folly' that is demonstrated in part by 'the cuckolding of the old man'; see their partial edition of the Bannatyne Manuscript, *Poetry of the Stewart Court* (Canberra, 1982), p. 106.
3 See *The Chester Plays*, ed. Hermann Deimling, EETS., E.S. LXII, vol. 1 (1892; rpr. London, New York, Toronto, 1968); and for N-Town, see *Ludus Coventriae or The Plaie called Corpus Christi*, ed. K.S. Block, EETS., E.S. CXX (1922; rpr. Oxford, 1960).
4 For a discussion of Lindsay's tact and tactics in bringing ideas before King James, see Claude Graf's 'Theatre and Politics: Lindsay's *Satyre of the Thrie Estaitis*' in *Bards and Makars*, eds. Adam J. Aitken, *et al.* (Glasgow, 1977), pp. 143–55.

of the Foot-band, which are loosely framed by the opening and closing speeches of the announcer, Nuntius. Although Lindsay's *Satyre* is about social, political, and ecclesiastical reform,[5] the Proclamation lures the populace to that play by bawdy themes, plebeian characters, and *topoi* familiar from myth and fabliau.[6]

Further to engage the Proclamation's audience,[7] Lindsay employs techniques that blur, or breach, the usual boundaries between actors and audience, and between drama and life.[8] Since all the characters in the Proclamation, except for Nuntius, are purportedly 'in and of' the audience, the Proclamation in that sense is *about* the audience. This blurring of the real and the unreal is reinforced and symbolised by the Fool, a transcendent character with a long and complex history who balances 'between good and evil, order and chaos, reality and illusion, existence and nothingness'.[9] While the Fool in part serves in the Proclamation as a connecting device, linking and unifying the vignette and the interlude, his principal role is to be an instrument of resolution and retaliation in the stories of Bessy and the Auld Man, and that of Fyndlaw. In both stories the Fool operates as an instrument of common justice; even if the Fool's justice may, by some standards, be morally questionable, his resolutions[10] nonetheless have popular appeal because they accord with communal notions of justice.

With his opening speech announcing the future performance in Fife,[11] Nuntius

5 Janet Smith has linked Lindsay to Pierre Gringore for loving satire for 'political purposes,' for using 'dramatic form to embody political themes,' and for having a 'love of sermonizing,' in *The French Background of Middle Scots Literature* (Edinburgh and London, 1969), p. 128. See also J.A. Lester's earlier analysis of Gringore's influence in 'Some Franco-Scottish Influences on the Early English Drama,' *Haverford Essays: Studies in Modern Literature* (1909; rpr. Freeport, NY, 1967). Additionally, see John MacQueen's 'Ane Satyre of the Thrie Estaitis,' *Studies in Scottish Literature* 3 (1966): 129–43; and Anna J. Mill's response to MacQueen, 'The Original Version of Lindsay's *Satyre of the Thrie Estaitis,*' *Studies in Scottish Literature* 6 (1968): 67–75.
6 Both the vignette and the interlude fit Mary Jane Schenck's description of a fabliau as 'a short verse narrative about deception and misdeeds which teaches the value of cunning and aggression'; Bessy, of course, is 'cunning,' and Cotter's wife is certainly aggressive. See Schenck's *The Fabliaux: Tales of Wit and Deception* (Philadelphia, 1987), p. 120). Keith Busby offers an explanation for the paucity of fabliaux in Middle English, explaining that Old French fabliaux 'parody or ironically evoke certain aspects of chivalric or courteous behaviour found in the Old French romances'; since Middle English romances 'play down these very elements,' they 'do not provide conditions conducive to the creation or development' of Middle English fabliaux. See Busby's 'Conspicuous by Its Absence: The English Fabliau,' *Dutch Quarterly Review of Anglo-American Letters* 12 (1982), p. 41. See also R. Howard Bloch's *The Scandal of the Fabliaux* (Chicago and London, 1986).
7 Claude Graf has a valuable and interesting study of Lindsay's efforts to involve the audience in the *Satyre*, but mentions 'The Cupar Banns' only briefly in his 'Audience Involvement in Lindsay's *Satyre of the Thrie Estaitis,*' *Scottish Studies*, eds. Dietrich Strauss and Horst W. Drescher (New York, 1986), pp. 423–35.
8 As a result of this blurring of boundaries the Proclamation 'denies its own nature as drama' as it 'pretends to share the reality of its audience'; Anne Righter discusses the *Satyre*'s use of this technique in *Shakespeare and the Idea of the Play* (1961; rpr. Baltimore, 1967), p. 183.
9 Enid Welsford's preface to William Willeford, *The Fool and His Scepter: A Study in Clowns and Jesters and Their Audience* (Evanston, IL, 1969), p. x; see also Welsford's earlier study, *The Fool: His Social and Literary History* (Gloucester, MA, 1966).
10 The terms 'resolution' and 'retaliation' are part of Schenck's 'nine functions' of a fabliau: 'arrival, departure, interrogation, communication, deception, misdeed, recognition, retaliation, and resolution' (p. xi).
11 On the date of the performance in Cupar, and on the larger question of dating the play, see J.S. Kantrowitz, *Dramatic Allegory: Lindsay's Ane Satyre of the Thrie Estaitis* (Lincoln, NE, 1975), pp. 11–23.

conventionally establishes a frame for the three interior dramas. Typifying the fluid interaction between the performer and the audience, this frame is immediately breached by an actor playing the part of Cotter, a local farmer, who bustles up from the audience and promises to attend the future play.[12] The conversation between Nuntius and Cotter moves the audience into the Proclamation's first segment, the vignette, as Nuntius leads the farmer to pronounce on marriage, his wife, and the clergy. Speaking in a tradition common in the fabliau, Cotter extrapolates from his own wife and his unhappy marriage to condemn all wives and all marriages, thereby reifying a number of familiar stereotypes. Blending misogamy and anticlericism, Cotter confides to Nuntius that if his wife should die he would never marry again, but would instead live 'chest as abbottis, monkis, and freiris' and like priests, who 'swyve & nevir mary' (11.56–8). Certainly Cotter reflects the Reformist attitude in his anticlerical comments,[13] but in linking sexuality, anticlericism, and misogamy his attitude especially reflects the fabliau.[14]

When Cotter's wife also appears from the audience Nuntius fades into the background, allowing the vignette to focus on the interaction between Cotter and his wife and on their stereotypical characterisations and behaviours. Confirming her husband's description of her as a loud-mouthed, dominating shrew, the wife shows her stupidity as well, chastising her husband for being in town when she had herself given him permission to be there. Although the husband appears on the surface as meek and mealy-mouthed, he is nevertheless sly, and possessed of a sharp tongue. Presenting himself as the voice of calm patience and sweet reason, Cotter explains why the wife should remain at home and he should attend the play:

> Byid 3e at hame, for cum 3e heir
> 3e will mak all the toun a steir.
> Quhen 3e are fow of barmy drink
> Besyd 3ow nane may stand for stink (11. 72–76)

While they argue ostensibly over which of them shall attend the play, the fundamental issue, of course, is the locus of control in the marriage.

In accord with the custom of popular humour, and as one would expect from

---

12 Claude Graf observes that Lindsay's strategy is to make 'the two worlds of audience and play meet, or at least, interpenetrate very closely'; see Graf's 'Audience Involvement in Lindsay's *Satyre of the Thrie Estaitis*,' p. 426. This strategy, used also in the *Satyre*, is further explained by Anne Righter, who states that 'Throughout the performance, the actors pretend to share the reality of their audience, to be caught up in events which are quite unrehearsed, which the spectators overhear by chance'; Righter then concludes that 'Instead of drawing the spectators into the world of the play,' Lindsay has 'constructed the drama around them' (pp. 34–5).
13 Hamer declares Lindsay 'one of the greatest of Scottish reformers, and a man of whom it is truly said that he sowed the seed the fruits of which were reaped by Knox,' in 'The Bibliography of Sir David Lindsay,' *The Library* 10.1 (1929): 1–41.
14 'The Freiris of Berwik,' for example, which is also located in the Bannatyne Manuscript, satirises both women and the clergy; see Melissa Farrow's edition in *Ten Fifteenth-Century Comic Poems* (New York, 1985).

their character types, the wife wins the argument by physically beating her husband. Shown to be mean as well as violent, the wife forbids her husband to attend Lindsay's play and denies him a drink to sustain him on his way home.[15] Yet, the husband has the last word, as his negative statements about the wife end the vignette. Misogyny and misogamy demonstrate their popular appeal as the vignette captures the audience with its reiteration of such familiar themes as the wickedness of wives, the weakness of husbands against wifely domination, and the inherent conflict in marriage over authority.

Following a brief transition introducing Fyndlaw and the Fool, these same themes are recast, with different characters and within a different context, in the Proclamation's second drama, the interlude of Bessy and the Auld Man. Although the term 'interlude' was applied to a wide variety of plays, the genre can be defined fundamentally as 'a dramatic form, the action of which was restricted to two or three stages of a single episode, and which was comic in spirit and intention.'[16] The plot of this interlude centers upon Bessy's ability to deceive her husband and have sex with another man even though her husband sleeps with the key to her chastity belt under his head.[17] Appearing simple, the plot is typical of a fabliau[18] in relying on cleverness and trickery to achieve a sexual goal, and in employing stock characters: the lustful and deceitful young wife, the amorous suitor, and the naive but jealous old husband.[19] Nonetheless, this seemingly simple story of Bessy and her aged husband embodies ancient mythic elements connected to seasonal pagan rituals.[20] By the time of the late Middle Ages, however, those ancient elements have been greatly mediated by the Judeo-Christian tradition and patriarchal politics, and their presentation in the Proclamation reveals the transformation of these ancient rituals and *topoi*.

The interlude begins as Bessy and the Auld Man enter, seemingly from the audience, the husband 'leidand / his wyfe in ane dance' (stage direction following 1.141). Since the husband is described as 'Auld' and Bessy is referred to as a

---

15 E. Jane Burns points out that such conflicts are 'staged typically in terms of an either/or proposition. If men give up their subjective stronghold, they will fall into the dreaded category of object: object of the cajoler's unpredictable desire, of the nag's threatening speech, an object without power or purchase on the world.' See Burns's *Bodytalk: When Women Speak in Old French Literature* (Philadelphia, 1993), p. 59.

16 See J.A.W. Bennett and G.V. Smithers, eds., *Early Middle English Verse and Prose*, 2nd edn. (Oxford, 1968), p. 196.

17 My analysis of Bessy and the Auld Man has evolved and expanded from an earlier brief discussion oriented in another direction; see 'The Function of the Female Monster in Middle Scots Poetry: Misogyny, Patriarchy, and the Satiric Myth,' in *Misogyny in Literature: An Essay Collection*, ed. Katherine Ackley (London and New York, 1992), pp. 33–66.

18 For a discussion of some common plots in fabliaux see John Hines, *The Fabliau in English* (London and New York, 1993), chapter 1.

19 Anna J. Mill refers to the story of Bessy and the Auld Man as one of the play's 'farcical episodes' in her *Mediaeval Plays in Scotland* (1924; rpr. New York and London, 1969), p. 102.

20 C.R. Baskerville, 'Mummers' Wooing Plays in England,' *Modern Philology* 21 (1924), p. 231. Writers from Apollodorus and Ovid through Chaucer and the authors of the wooing plays are part of a tradition that assumes such rituals; see also the work of contemporary scholars such as historian Gerda Lerner, archaeologist Marija Gimbutas, and literary critic John Hines.

damsel, they undoubtedly present a ludicrous picture,[21] their dancing entrance magnifying their January-May contrast. The husband's first words further emphasise their age difference, his need to rest suggesting their dancing has exhausted him. In order to rest easily, however, he must first secure his wife's sexual parts:[22]

> Bessy my hairt, I mon ly doun and sleip,
> And in myne arme se quyetly thow creip.
> Bessy my hairt, first lat me lok thy cunt,
> Syne lat me keip the key, as I was wount (ll. 142–5)

Having, in preparation for his short nap, locked his wife's genitalia into a chastity belt, he places the key under his head as, we are told, is his custom. In addition to being old, the husband thus reveals himself to be both feeble and domineering, and above all suspicious; Bessy, acquiescing to all his wishes, is portrayed as meek, pliant, and subservient.

While her husband then sleeps with the key under his head, Bessy obediently sits beside him, where passes a procession of male suitors. First to appear is a 'courteour' who asks permission to be in her company, who observes that he is 'cumly,' and who assures her he is a man who never dishonored women (ll. 148–51). Evidently not favourably received, he is succeeded by a second petitioning suitor describing himself as the richest merchant in town; offering to clothe Bessy in silk garments, he asks, more suggestively, to 'luge' in her 'chalmer' (ll. 152–5). Apparently as unmoved by silk as by courtliness, Bessy is next visited by a third admirer, a Clerk who addresses her as 'lady bricht' but who then, abruptly altering his level of discourse, asks to lie with her all night and be allowed to 'schut the lokkis' of her 'quomam' in exchange for a box of 'fyne gold' (ll. 156–9). As the parade of suitors progresses, the requests become more sexually explicit and the promised gifts grander. In spite of the richness of his offer, however, the Clerk is as unsuccessful as his predecessors.

Last in the procession is the Fool; contrasting the Courteour, the Merchant, and the Clerk, the Fool states forthrightly that he offers only himself, but he demonstrates the nature and quality of the goods at her disposal, perhaps using a prop one editor describes as a 'gross phallus'.[23] As significant as what

---

21 Such images surely elicit the audience's sympathy for the character-type of Bessy, and also reveal what Alcuin Blamires refers to as authorial 'admiration for the ingenuity shown by women in circumventing sexually unattractive, possessive husbands'; see his edition, *Woman Defamed and Woman Defended: An Anthology of Medieval Texts* (Oxford, 1992), p. 130.

22 Hamer delicately notes in his list of required properties that the old man 'Produces a *ceinture de chastete*, with lock and key' (vol. 4, p. 152).

23 Hamer so describes this 'exhibition of the Fool's penis,' noting that this sexual display, which is repeated in the *Satyre* when Folie addresses a lady in the audience, indicates 'an extra liberty of utterance and personal exhibition allowed to the Food' (vol. 4. p. 165). Willeford discusses the traditional association of the phallus with the Fool, and quotes Niklaus's comment that such characters were descendants of the satyrs of Greek comedy, who were in turn connected to the worship of Dionysus and its phallic rituals (p. 11). If so, one observes with regret the transmogrification of the maenad into the Bessy figure.

he shows, however, is what he says, as the Fool makes to Bessy the following pledge:

> Swa lang as this may steir or stand
> It sall be ay at your command.
> Na it is the best that evir 3e saw (ll. 162–4).

The Fool wins Bessy's favours not by offering her an elevated abstraction like courtesy, nor gifts of silk or gold which might or might not materialise, but that which he can display to her, and demonstrate the excellence of which, on the spot. Moreover, whereas the Courteour, the Merchant, and the Clerk are largely self-focused, speaking of who they are and what they want, the Fool, in contrast, places power in Bessy's hands, positioning her as the controlling agent in their future sexual activity. Understanding this, perhaps it is not surprising that Bessy chooses the Fool, clearly indicating her estimation of him in comparison to those suitors who were socially superior: 'Now welcome to me aboif tham aw' (1.165).

The story of Bessy and the Auld Man obviously encompasses a number of themes common in both myth and fabliau, including the theme of mismatched age. This theme reflects a myth at least as old as the 'Hymn to Demeter' from the seventh century B.C.E., which tells the story of Hades (Pluto) and Persephone.[24] Retold throughout literary history, this myth is represented symbolically in the seasonally inappropriate wedding of May and January, and may be most familiar to us in the form of Chaucer's 'Merchant's Tale'.[25]

Among the interlude's less familiar aspects is the procession of would-be sexual partners, and Bessy's choice from among them, elements with antecedents in the tradition of wooing plays which in turn echo myths and traditional customs thought to date from ancient culture.[26] Brody explains that in the wooing plays, 'a Lady is wooed by a series of suitors,' but 'She rejects all of them until the Fool finally wins her.'[27] The Fool in those wooing plays is 'the phallus-bearer,' representing the 'male fertility figure'.[28] In his role as the unusually endowed and especially potent younger male who takes sexual place from the aging incumbent, and who also triumphs sexually over those considered his superiors,

---

24 See 'The Hymn to Demeter' in *The Homeric Hymns*, ed. Thelma Sargent (New York, 1973), pp. 2–14. The myth more briefly treated is found in another seventh-century B.C.E. account in Hesiod's *Theogony*, ed. Norman O. Brown (Indianapolis and New York, 1953), p. 78. See also the first century B.C.E. account in Apollodorus, *The Library*, trans. Sir James G. Frazer, Loeb Classical Library no. 121 (London and Cambridge, 1967), vol. 1, pp. 35–41; and the first century C.E. account in Ovid, *Metamorphoses*, trans. Rolfe Humphries (Bloomington and London, 1955), pp. 119–25.
25 For 'The Merchant's Tale' see Chaucer's *Canterbury Tales*, ed. F.N. Robinson, 2nd edn. (Boston, 1957); for other sources of Chaucer's tale see *The Literary Context of Chaucer's Fabliaux*, eds. Larry D. Benson and Theodore M. Andersson (Indianapolis and New York, 1971), pp. 206–73.
26 See 'Veiling the Woman,' the sixth chapter in Gerda Lerner's *The Creation of Patriarchy* (Oxford, 1986).
27 Alan Brody, *The English Mummers and Their Plays: Traces of Ancient Mystery* (Philadelphia, 1969), p. 103.
28 Brody, p. 106. *Contra*, E.C. Cawte, 'It's an Ancient Custom – But How Ancient?' in *Aspects of British Calender Customs*, eds. Theresa Buckland and Juliette Wood (Sheffield, 1993), pp. 39–41.

the Fool in the Cupar Banns partakes of this figuring, a figuring linked in turn to the ancient tradition of the *hieros gamos*, or Sacred Marriage.[29] Plays in English employing this tradition customarily depict an old man who woos a younger woman, only to have the young woman reject him for a younger man; this tradition has been thought to replicate action once part of an ancient ritual that symbolised a union with the new season and displacement of the old.[30] Chaucer's 'Merchant's Tale' clearly echoes this tradition as May, uninspired by her aged husband, Januarie, engages in mutual seduction with the young squire Damyan.

In this late medieval Proclamation, however, the procession of suitors, the sexually-endowed Fool, and the notion of renewal as youth supplants age, exist within a context starkly altered from that surrounding the ancient myths and the seasonal rituals believed to be their genesis. In the context of 'The Cupar Banns,' as in medieval culture and society, women's sexuality cannot be freely expressed as in a pagan celebration of fertility and autonomous female sexual choice; instead, female sexuality must be situated under male authority where it can be controlled through such means as a chastity belt, a device reflecting the monastic belief that women's sexuality is dangerous unless strictly governed.

The manner in which Bessy's choice is construed and presented further reveals the cultural distortion of those ancient elements. Having a selection of men from various rungs on the social ladder who offer her courtesy, material goods, and even gold, Bessy chooses as partner the man who not only offers sex for its own sake, but who also assumes that she will have sexual power; in this regard the story thus preserves the component of free female sexual choice. As presented in the Proclamation and in the medieval Christian context, however, Bessy's choice does not, and cannot, reflect the positive exercise of female sexuality; instead, Bessy, her choice, and her choosing, would inevitably be understood as sinful, even though comic. For most members of the medieval audience, and most critics, Bessy's rejection of other men for the Fool, who appears on the surface to offer only his sexual apparatus,[31] serves merely to signify her lustful nature and to cast her as the stereotypical 'bad' wife with an insatiable sexual appetite.[32]

Having accepted the Fool, Bessy acquaints him with the obstacle of the locked chastity belt, lamenting 'Was nevir wyf sa straitly rokkit' (1. 166). Moved by both sympathy and outrage, the Fool asks if her husband, 'that brybor blunt' (1.168), does not think it a shame to put a lock upon her sexual parts. The Fool's multivalent question invites a number of interpretations that deepen his characterisation. His question is, of course, in keeping with the sexual tradition

---

29 For discussions of the *hieros gamos*, see Lerner (pp. 148–50) and Marija Gimbutas's *The Goddesses and Gods of Old Europe*, updated edn. (Berkeley, 1982), pp. 227–30. Agnes Mackenzie observes that the Proclamation contains 'a sequence going back at least to Athens,' but does not elaborate, in her introduction to James Kinsley's edition, *Ane Satyre of the Thrie Estaitis* (London, 1954), p. 21.
30 Baskerville, p. 227.
31 Hamer pronounces the Fool 'a simpleton of pronounced sexual fervour' (vol. 4, p. 163, n. 101–269); my reading of the Fool obviously finds him to be anything but simple, and instead a complex character who partakes of a long historical tradition and who serves several important functions in the Proclamation.
32 Chaucer's Wife of Bath is, of course, a prime example of this stereotype.

surrounding the Fool, 'that he wants sexuality to flourish in everyone'.[33] The Fool may also mean, however, that 'it is a shame your husband is so suspicious and paranoid,' thus indicating insight into the conditions of Bessy's life. Or he may mean 'it is a shame that someone else exerts control over your sexuality,' thereby articulating a belief in individual personal freedom for Bessy.

In any case, at Bessy's suggestion the Fool proceeds with ease to steal the key from beneath the sleeping husband's head, readily overcoming the obstacle and indicating he is a person of special skill. The Fool's action after obtaining the key reinforces the assumption that Bessy chooses the Fool as lover because he offers her not just sex, but sexual power; the Fool immediately gives Bessy the key, remarking, 'Lo, heir the key, do quhat 3e will' (1.174). In sharp contrast to Bessy's husband, who rigorously controls the key, the Fool unequivocally accepts Bessy's sexual autonomy, assuming that she will control the lock and decide if they will have a sexual experience. Showing no hesitation, Bessy promptly unlocks the belt, responding 'Na then, lat ws ga play our fill' (1.175), and they go off together to 'sum quyet place' (stage direction following 1.175). While Bessy and the Fool are off for their tryst, the story of the braggart soldier Fyndlaw winds into the interlude, occupying the necessary gap in stage time with a conversation between Fyndlaw and the rejected Clerk.

Unfortunately, Bessy's husband wakes before she returns and commences to fret and cry at his wife's absence. Wondering aloud where she is, he naively suggests that she may have gone to the mass, a comment surely meant to evoke from the audience loud guffaws. The husband's question, however, has more than a comic purpose, as with that comment Lindsay sharply delineates the difference between the reality that is Bessy and the vision of Bessy that her husband wishes to hold. The Auld Man's wonderings cease, however, when he cannot find the key, and his attitude quickly changes to horror as he realises he will no longer have sexual access to his wife:

> Allace for evir now am I fey,
> For of hir cunt I tynt the key . . .
> Or I swyve I mon brek the lok (11. 215–19).

Although the husband here acknowledges to himself and seems to believe that he is responsible for the lost key, his deep-seated ambivalence toward his wife is reflected in the dissidence between his acknowledgement at this point and his later questioning of Bessy about the key's whereabouts.

When Bessy returns, the husband disingenuously says nothing at first of the lost key, asking instead if she has been doing 'sum bissy wark'. This *double entendre* must have caused the audience again to erupt in raucous laughter. While the question certainly serves a comedic function, it also offers insights into the couple's characterisations and their marital relationship, as did the husband's earlier suggestion that Bessy had gone to the mass. Both questions embed their

---

33 Willeford, p. 183.

inapplicability to Bessy as she really is, as they simultaneously reveal how deceived and self-deceived the Auld Man is. Nonetheless, his remark about her 'bissy wark' surely delighted Bessy, providing her the opportunity to explain that she has been sewing him a shirt that he must at once try on for size.[34] While the husband struggles with the shirt over his head the Fool, unknown and unseen, deftly replaces the key. When the husband then suspiciously asks Bessy where the key is, she innocently reminds him that he placed it under his head, where he looks and of course finds it.

Only at this point, when his unspoken fears have been alleviated, does the husband overtly admit to having suspected his wife (1.233). Apologising to her for his suspicions, he suggests that he and Bessy go off to 'rest,' thereby ending their story and the interlude. Like Januarie in 'The Merchant's Tale,'[35] only too eager to believe in his wife's innocence, the Auld Man carefully chooses the facts he will accept.[36] Unlike Januarie, however, the Auld Man never sees the man with whom his wife has made him a cuckold. Invisible to the Auld Man, the Fool functions as a mythic figure replicating an ancient form of renewal,[37] and as a fabliau-type character enacting justice upon a suspicious old man inappropriately wed to a vibrant young woman. Partaking of both existence and nothingness, and thus functioning transcendently, the Fool can work anonymously, unseen and undiscovered, to accomplish necessary resolutions.[38]

The Fool, this character of inherent instability who stands on the border between chaos and order, is not, of course, solely responsible for the interlude's sexual resolution, which is also accomplished by Bessy's agile wit, what Muscatine has called 'the weapon of the servant, of the woman, and . . . of the poor scholar'.[39] Bessy's wit, this 'weapon,' enables her to exercise some control over her life. Fabliaux celebrate this ability, Muscatine explains, and in doing so 'are to an extent subversive of Christian teaching, of the class basis of feudal society, of the conventional notion of sex roles, and of conventional ideas of stability, economy, security, and justice.'[40] Living in a patriarchal society

---

34 Mill contextualizes Bessy's use of a shirt temporarily to blind her husband within a motif Mill traces through European farces back to the Sanskrit ('The Influence of the Continental Drama,' *Modern Language Review* 25 (1930): 433–34.
35 Chaucer, ed. Robinson, pp. 115–27.
36 Gregory Kratzmann draws a similar conclusion about the Auld Man, remarking that 'even this hilariously farcical episode carries a moral which is highly relevant to both parts of the play: in the words of the Clerk, "Thay ar not sonsy that so dois ruse [deceive] thame sell" '; see Kratzmann's *Anglo-Scottish Literary Relations 1430–1550* (Cambridge, 1980), p. 222.
37 Willeford points out that the audience may or may not have been consciously aware of the ancient rituals which Bessy and the Fool reenact, and whether or not they are aware does not matter; in such a play, Willeford explains, 'what were once matters of ritual importance may inspire a momentary thrill. This does not necessarily mean that either the fool actors or the audience have felt that ritual importance, but it may mean that the fool actors have touched the same fundamental human concern that was expressed in ritual' (p. 98).
38 In this regard the interlude is more akin to myth than fabliau, since in fabliaux 'in no case does a heroic figure emerge to establish harmony or a just conclusion to the conflict' (Schenck, p. xi). Here the Fool, whether or not perceived as an heroic figure, does accomplish some temporary justice.
39 Charles Muscatine, *The Old French Fabliaux* (New Haven, 1986), p. 91.
40 Muscatine, p. 92.

with a jealous and controlling husband, Bessy's wit enables her to achieve sexual autonomy and a freedom which does, in fact, subvert Christian teaching, traditional sex roles, class hierarchy, and 'conventional ideas of stability.' Her actions also help to effect the popular justice that occurs in the interlude: she is able to act as a free agent, and the Auld Man is punished for his arrogance and selfishness in marrying so young a woman. Like the marriage of Chaucer's Januarie and May, and that of their mythic models, Pluto and Persephone, the marriage of the Auld Man and Bessy is exposed as an antitype, in fact, of the *hieros gamos*.[41]

In thus using her wit to achieve subjectivity, and to subvert conventional social and moral codes, Bessy uses one of the few tools she has. As Joan Ferrante explains, women who have 'limited opportunities to exercise real power over their own or others' lives . . . in medieval literature and sometimes in real life find subtle or hidden ways to exercise such power, to manipulate people and situations.'[42] Such an action can cause in the audience, as Muscatine puts it, 'a developed awareness of the instability of life,'[43] an awareness intensified by the presence of the Fool. Thus, even though her husband may choose not to know of Bessy's actions, the audience recognises that Bessy's wit has enabled her to destabilise the traditional hierarchy in patriarchal marriage. Her triumph is, however, both small and momentary; the audience also recognises that she may have 'gained a temporary advantage, but the underlying conflict is not resolved'.[44] Although there has been for Bessy a sexual resolution that on some levels is entirely 'just,' the end of the interlude restores conventional patriarchal stability. Just as May goes off with Januarie, Bessy goes off with her husband. Bessy may have had some moments of self-determination, but she is still controlled by the chastity belt, and the Auld Man holds the key.

Although the interlude itself is concluded at this point, a number of lines prior to the Proclamation's end, Bessy's significance does not end with the interlude's completion. In the Proclamation's final framing stanza, after reminding the audience again of Lindsay's coming play, Nuntius singles out the women in the audience for special attention. After addressing the women present with scatological references to their 'leddir' (pudendum) and their 'bleddir,' Nuntius suggests that most women are Bessies who use their skills to similar ends; he ends the Proclamation, in fact, by charging that before the players will be half done in Fife that many of the women there will, like Bessy, 'mak ane richt wait sark' (ll. 274–7). Although one might puzzle over this gratuitous slandering of totally unknown women, such slander functions importantly in patriarchal society to control, by attempting to prevent, female agency; in such a society, women must be discouraged from following Bessy's example and pursuing sexual independence.

The Proclamation's third dramatic strand concerning Fyndlaw of the Foot-

---

41 Hines also calls this sort of relationship a 'winter-prison' (p. 192).
42 Ferrante, *Woman as Image in Medieval Literature* (New York, 1975), p. 213.
43 Muscatine, p. 104.
44 Schenck, p. 107.

band,[45] is interwoven with the other two stories; Fyndlaw's story begins as a transition linking the vignette and the interlude, appears as a brief interpolation in the interlude to fill a gap in dramatic time, and concludes just prior to the final stanza. Although this dramatic strand helps in these ways to unify the Proclamation, its principle function is thematic: the resolution of Fyndlaw's story, and the Fool's role in that resolution, emphasise and reconfirm a central theme in the Proclamation, the imposition of a communal justice.

Fyndlaw is first introduced as he thrusts through the crowd that just witnessed the Proclamation's first dramatic component, the vignette of Cotter and his wife. Even before Fyndlaw speaks the audience would undoubtedly recognize his type, since hanging about him is an excess of military impedimenta, including a sword and belt, a knapsack, plate gloves, a metal helmet, a purse, and a knife. Acting as the *miles gloriosus*, Fyndlaw brags that he has slain more than two thousand, that no man can stand against him, that had he been at 'pynky craiggis' he would have triumphed, and that he never has his fill of fighting. The audience's enjoyment of Fyndlaw's character is undoubtedly attested by the length of his opening speech, at thirty-three lines the longest in the Proclamation.

After his speech of braggadocio Fyndlaw lies down to rest. Then, probably at some distance from Fyndlaw, or perhaps in a lowered voice, the Fool speaks directly to the audience of Fyndlaw's falsity, denies Fyndlaw's claims to bravery and prowess, and discloses that Fyndlaw was in fact present at Pyncky Clewch, where he was the first to flee. Promising the audience he will retaliate for Fyndlaw's lies and pomposity, the Fool vows to frighten this braggart with a sheep's head and thus teach him a lesson. Interestingly, just as the Auld Man never sees or knows of the person who cuckolds him, neither is Fyndlaw aware of the person who unmasks him. In fact, Fyndlaw and the Fool have no direct interaction at all until the penultimate scene, and even then Fyndlaw remains ignorant of the Fool himself and the Fool's motivation. Despite the Fool's central role in these two dramas, he speaks only to Bessy, and to the audience.

Fyndlaw appears again during Bessy's tryst with the Fool when the Clerk, one of Bessy's rejected suitors, questions Fyndlaw's claims and condemns him and his brawling, boasting brothers for their love of war. Responding with insolence and cynicism to the Clerk's advocacy of peace, Fyndlaw asserts war's inevitability. The Clerk's comments, however, situate Fyndlaw within a wider social and moral context as practitioner of a dangerous philosophy:

> Sen sic as thow began to brawll & boist,
> The commoun weill of scotland hes bene loist . . .
> I pray to god till send ws peice & rest,

---

45 Anna J. Mill discusses sources in France and the Netherlands for Lindsay's '*miles gloriosus*' in 'The Influence of the Continental Drama on Lyndsay's *Satyre of the Thrie Estaitis.*' The *miles gloriosus* is a pretentious, boastful soldier; Hamer notes that to expose this figure has been 'a favourite theme of farce and comedy from classical times,' and has also been part of the *commedia del arte* (vol. 4, p. 163).

> On that conditioun that thow, and all thy fallowis,
> War be the craiggis heich hangit on the gallowis,
> Quha of this weir hes bene the foundament (11. 184–90)

Some critics have considered the Clerk to be a priest, perhaps because Fyndlaw asks the Clerk, 'Domine doctor, quhair will 3e preiche to morne?' (1.194). Given the 'preachy' nature of the Clerk's speech, however, Fyndlaw could simply be addressing satirically a man who, in Fyndlaw's opinion, pontificates. On the other hand, to cast a priest as one of Bessy's suitors, especially a priest willing to pay gold for her favours, would be an anticlerical statement entirely in keeping with the *Satyre*'s content. Whatever his presumed role in life, the Clerk's speech establishes that men like Fyndlaw are not just repugnant as lovers of violence, but are a detrimental component of society, thus expanding Fyndlaw's significance and justifying the retaliation that comes to him. Fyndlaw is thus solidly positioned as a character deserving a lesson, not just because he is a liar, a braggart, and a coward, but because the values he holds are dangerous to society.

The final scene in Fyndlaw's story occurs just before the Proclamation ends. Again boasting, Fyndlaw claims that he surpasses Hector and Gawain, that he would not fear Goliath, and that he killed Sir Bevis of Southhampton. At this point the Fool enters with a sheep's head on a staff,[46] utterly terrifying Fyndlaw, who believes he is seeing a ghost, or a spirit. Alternately shrieking and praying for a hole to hide in, Fyndlaw offers the ghost all his gear, even his sword. His cowardice nakedly exposed, he flees.

The justice accorded Fyndlaw reiterates and underscores the Fool's role in the Proclamation as a force creating resolutions that accord with communal notions of justice. Just as the jealousy, dominance, and pretensions of the Auld Man cause him in the Proclamation, as elsewhere in literature, virtually to deserve cuckolding, so do the lies, boasting, and pretensions of Fyndlaw cause him to deserve his deflation. Moreover, in both instances justice is achieved with great irony, highlighting, as it pierces, the pretensions of each: although the Auld Man ultimately decides not to know, he is wounded through his wife's chastity, which he most jealously guards; Fyndlaw is similarly wounded through the bravery he claimed to hold and manifest. A rough justice is thus visited on each man as he loses that which he most values, in resolutions accomplished by the Fool. The story of Cotter and his wife, while not involving the Fool, functions similarly in the Proclamation, since Cotter's wife, the dominant figure in the relationship, is undercut by what is revealed of her in the course of the vignette.

Clearly aware of his audience, Lindsay knew the themes, characters, and plots that would please. Members of his audience would identify with or find comical the traditional misogynistic story of the meek husband and the bullying wife, would take pleasure in seeing the false braggart revealed and brought low, and would undoubtedly experience a perverse satisfaction, and perhaps respond as

---

46 Hamer speculates that the staff also had white cloth attached, causing Fyndlaw to believe the apparition a ghost or spirit (vol. 4, p. 166, n. 247).

well to mythic echoes, in the interlude of Bessy and the Auld Man. Creating fluid boundaries between actors and viewers, and drawing elements from the traditions of myth and fabliau, Lindsay engaged his audience in the bawdy but popular morality of the Proclamation so as to entice them, and with his theme of justice perhaps prepare them, for the later performance of the *Satyre*.

RODERICK J. LYALL

33. *Alexander Allan (Alesius) and the Development of a Protestant Aesthetics*

The importance of the Biblical Psalms for the development in the sixteenth century of a distinctively Protestant poetics is now fairly well understood, due in no small measure to the recent work of such scholars as Barbara Lewalski and John N. King.[1] The rhetoric of self-abnegation and divine praise, punctuated with frequent allusions to political oppression, corresponded so well with the devotional priorities and secular circumstances of early Protestants that it was natural that they should not only translate them into their own vernaculars, but also take them as models for 'original' spiritual verse. In taking the Psalms as the sum of the devotional experience offered by the Bible, Reforming writers were, of course, doing no more than echo the views of many of the Church Fathers; but the argument acquired greater point in the sixteenth-century context. It is taken up by both Luther and Calvin, and was reflected in the many vernacular versions of the Psalms which were published all over Protestant Europe. Again, this was essentially a continuation of a late medieval practice; but again it acquired new ideological significance within the framework of the Reformation debate. In some ways, the re-emergence of the psalms as a source of rhetorical inspiration encouraged the growing importance of the 'plain style' in Protestant poetry; but the lessons offered by these texts were not as univocal as we might suppose, as we shall see in a moment.

Among the many texts articulating this emerging Protestant aesthetics, one early and generally neglected instance is the *De Autore et Vtilitate Psalmorum Oratio* given by the Scottish Lutheran Alexander Allan, or Alesius, in Frankfurt-an-der-Oder in 1541, and published there by Johann Hanaw in November of that year. Alesius had been professor of theology at the newly-established university of Frankfurt-an-der-Oder since the beginning of 1540, having been recommended for the post by Melanchthon himself.[2] By June 1540 he had given what appears to have been an inaugural lecture, a work on educational reform entitled *De restituendis scholis*.[3] His first regular lectures appear to have been on the Epistle

1 Barbara Kiefer Lewalski, *Protestant Poetics and the Seventeenth-Century Religious Lyric* (Princeton 1979), esp. pp. 39–53; John N. King, *English Reformation Literature: The Tudor Origins of the Protestant Tradition* (Princeton 1982), pp. 209–25. For an earlier, and influential, discussion of the subject, see Hallett Smith, 'English Metrical Psalms in the Sixteenth Century and their Literary Significance', *HLQ* 9 (1946), 268–70.
2 Melanchthon's letter of recommendation, dated 1 December 1539, is printed in *Corpus Reformatorum*, III, 842–44.
3 This work was published in Frankfurt/Oder in 1540, again by Johannes Hanaw; the only known surviving copy is in Edinburgh University Library (RE.5.31). A copy formerly in the Saxon State Library has been missing since 1945. The *De restituendis scholis* was reprinted among Melanchthon's

to the Romans, five of them being published by Hanaw in a series of fascicles between September 1540 and some date in 1541.[4] In the autumn of 1541, however, he began lecturing on the Psalms as well, and it would seem that his *De auctore et utilitate Psalmorum* was a kind of introduction to a more detailed discussion of particular psalms. Alesius' intentions are revealed in a remarkable note printed along with one of the two surviving copies of the text, headed '*Intimatio lectionis Theologicae*':

Quod olim promisi praelecturum me Dauidis hymnos Nunc, volente Deo, prestabo. Nec tamen Paulum mancum manere permittam, sed alternis diebus in dauide, alternis in Paulo praelegam. Cum autem epistola ad Romanos absolutam totius scripturae methodum, & grauissimarum controuersiarum, quae hoc tempore in ecclesia agitantur, explicationem contineat, debet ipsa per se vtilitas, quam vere maxima est, inuitare studiosos, vt hanc lectionem libenter audiant. Et iam accedunt psalmi qui sunt ceu practica theologia, & Christi meditatationes, ac orationes de tota lege domini, & omnibus sacris libris. Nam Christus est ille vir beatus, de quo in prima pagina libri scriptum est, quod omnis ipsius meditatio, ac voluntas sit in lege domini. Sed encomium psalmorum vsque ad meam praefationem differam. Iam polliceor me optima fide, & quanta possum diligentia vtrumgue Authorem expositurum. Praefabor autem ad D[ie]m Lunae proximum. Interim in his vacationibus Vindemialibus pergam in Paulo.
Alexander Alesius

[*Announcement of Theology Lectures*
Because I previously promised to lecture on the hymns of David, I shall now, God willing, do it. I shall not, however, leave Paul neglected; rather, I shall lecture on David and Paul on alternate days. Although the Epistle to the Romans, on the one hand, holds the complete key to all Scripture and the explication of the gravest controversies which are disturbing the Church at present, that usefulness, which is truly great, ought in itself to bring in the diligent, that they willingly hear this lecture. And now are added the Psalms, which are like practical theology and the meditations of Christ, and declarations of the whole law of God, and all the sacred books. For Christ is that blessed man who is mentioned in the first page of that book, whose meditation and will is in the law of God. But I defer my praise of the Psalms until my introduction, and I promise to interpret both authors with the greatest fidelity and as much diligence as I can. I shall begin next Monday. Meanwhile, during these grape-harvesting holidays, I sh all go on with Paul.
Alexander Alesius.][5]

orations in the edition published at Zerbst in 1587. Its authorship remains controversial; for the view that it, like the *Oratio de gratitudine* which Alesius gave at a Wittenberg graduation ceremony in 1534 and which also occurs in the 1587 collection, was actually written by Melanchthon see Gotthelf Wiedermann, *Der Reformator Alexander Alesius als Ausleger der Psalmen* (doctoral diss., Friedrich-Alexander-Universitat, Erlangen-Nurnberg, 1988), pp. 56–7.
4 Dresden, Sächsische Landesbibliothek (SLB), 25 8° 2079, angeb. 2.

From the reference to the grape harvest, we can conclude that this announcement relates to the autumn of 1541, shortly before Hanaw published his volume, and that the lectures on Psalms were to run through the winter term. Alesius may have begun them; but by January 1542 he had, in spite of contrary advice from his patron Melanchthon, fallen out with Christoph von der Strassen, one of his Frankfurt colleagues, on the issue of whether the civil authorities had jurisdiction over cases of fornication, and had quit his post in disgust. With the active support of Melanchthon, however, he was able to obtain a chair in theology at the University of Leipzig, where he began teaching in the autumn of 1542, remaining there until his death in 1565.

Alesius had come to Frankfurt by a circuitous route.[6] Born in Edinburgh in 1500, he studied in the newly-founded College of St Leonard at St Andrews, taking the bachelor's degree in 1515, before becoming an Augustinian canon (and presumably studying theology) in the same city. There is no room here for a full account of the traumatic events of 1528–32, in the course of which Alesius was involved in the trial and execution of Patrick Hamilton, was persuaded by his conduct of the errors of the contemporary Church, fell foul of Patrick Hepburn, prior of the Augustinian house, and suffered a period of imprisonment before fleeing to the Continent. It is enough to say that his wanderings brought him, by the end of October 1532, to Wittenberg, where he acquired – from Melanchthon – his Greek-derived nickname and a more systematic training in Lutheran theology. Here he also began teaching in the Arts Faculty, quickly becoming its Dean, and, responding to the decision of the Scottish bishops to reinforce the ban on the vernacular New Testament, commenced his prolific publishing career with a vigorous defence, in the form of an open letter to James V, of wider access to Scripture. This led to a series of exchanges with the Catholic propagandist Johannes Cochlaeus, who was paid £50 by the Scottish king for his defence of the bishops' position.[7]

After three years in Wittenberg, Alesius was given the politically sensitive task of building links between the Wittenberg theologians and Henry VIII of England. In September 1535 he travelled to London, bearing a presentation copy of Melanchthon's new edition of his *Loci communes*, dedicated to Henry, and letters of introduction to the king and to Thomas Cranmer. The mission was well

---

5 Dresden, SLB, 25 8° 2079, angeb. 1, sig. D vii^v–viii^r. I am grateful to Dr John Durkan for his assistance with the translation of this and other passages from Alesius.

6 For a comprehensive survey of Alesius' career, see John T. McNeill, 'Alexander Alesius, Scottish Lutheran (1500–1565)', *Archiv fur Reformationsgeschichte* 55 (1964), 161–91, which should be supplemented by the article of Ernst Siegmund-Schultze, *TRE* i, 231–5, and by Wiedermann, *op. cit.*, pp. 12–75.

7 Alesius' *Epistola contra Decretum quoddam Episcoporum in Scotia, quod prohibet legere Novi Testamenti libros lingue vernacula* (?Wittenberg 1533) was answered in the same year by Cochlaeus' *An expediat laicis, legere Novi Testamenti libros lingue vernacula?* ([Augsburg: Alexander Weissendorn]). Alesius replied with his *Responsio ad Cochlei Calumnias*, two editions of which seem to have been published in 1534, drawing forth a *Pro Scotiae regno apologia* from Cochlaeus (Leipzig: Michael Blum 1534). For the payment to Cochlaeus, see *Treas. Accts.*, vi, 236; that this payment (made to the messenger who delivered the presentation copy) was intended for Cochlaeus is evident from James' letter of 1 July 1534 (*Letters of James V*, ed. R.K. Hannay [Edinburgh 1954], p. 271).

received, and Alesius was quickly appointed to a post at Queen's College, Cambridge, under the patronage of Thomas Cromwell.⁸ He was certainly lecturing there in early April 1536, but by the end of the month he was again in London, having abandoned Cambridge because of an ideological dispute. Alesius' subsequent account of this crisis makes it clear that he objected to an edict of the bishops and the royal Council; and that he gave up his lectureship because he could neither speak out against the new law nor reconcile it with his conscience. Gotthelf Wiedermann has recently demonstrated that Alesius' difficulty must be associated with the fall of Anne Boleyn and the reversal to the Lutheran cause that it represented; nearly a quarter of a century later, Alesius would write to Elizabeth I that 'true religion in England had its beginning and its end with your mother'.⁹ He returned to London, trying to obtain from Cromwell payment for the lectures he had given, and remained there until his abrupt return to Germany, a refugee from the English government's prohibition of clerical marriage, in 1539.

Since he taught in the Arts Faculty at Wittenberg, Alesius would not have lectured on the Psalms there, but he certainly did so during his brief spell in Cambridge. As Wiedermann has shown, these lectures form the basis of the commentary on the first twenty-five Psalms preserved in Hatfield MS. 50, which is dedicated to Henry VIII of England and which may well be in Alesius' own hand.¹⁰ We find here the first articulation of the principles which would underlie the argument of the *De autore*, and indeed of Alesius' later, much more extended, commentary on Psalms 1–50, published in Leipzig in 1554. In his dedicatory letter to Henry VIII, Alesius adopts Melanchthonian humanist values by demanding that scriptural exegesis must pay proper attention to the '*contextum, dispositio et artificium orationis*'; while Wiedermann is doubtless correct in emphasising that the contexts and structures intended are essentially theological ones, it is nevertheless true that in both principle and practice Alesius' hermeneutic system depends upon careful attention to the rhetorical expression of the Biblical text. Theology may teach us what questions to ask, but philology is an indispensable tool in answering them. And nowhere is this more true, of course, than in the essentially poetic book of Psalms. This awareness is clearly evident in Alesius' Frankfurt lecture.

The *De autore et utilitate Psalmorum* survives in at least two copies, in the Saxon State Library in Dresden and the Austrian National Library in Vienna: a third copy was formerly in the University Library in Konigsberg, among a rich collection of Lutheran works, but I have not so far been able to establish whether they survived the destruction of the city in 1945 and subsequent obliteration of its Prussian past. The text was, in addition, incorporated, with some revisions, into the *Primus liber Psalmorum* printed by Georg Hantzsch in Leipzig in 1554, of which

---

8 The most complete account of Alesius' stay in England is still that by A.F. Scott Pearson, 'Alesius and the English reformation', *RSCHS* 10 (1948–50), 57–87.
9 *CSPFor. 1558–59*, no. 1303, pp. 524–34, at 532.
10 This text is fully edited by Wiedermann, *op. cit.*, pp. 141–246; and cf. his 'Alexander Alesius' Lectures on the Psalms at Cambridge, 1536', *JEH* 37 (1986), 15–41.

a dozen or so copies are extant; here it fulfills what was presumably its original function, as an introduction to a commentary on the psalms themselves.

As its title suggests, the focus of the *De autore et utilitate Psalmorum Oratio* is twofold. In the earlier section, Alesius ventures into biographical criticism, relating the nature of the psalms to David's career as shepherd and as king. This provides, among other things, an opportunity for the traditional association to be made between the inspiration David received as a shepherd '*ex consuetudine angelorum et singulari dono Spiritus Sancti*' (sig. A vi^v) and the singing of the angels to the shepherds at Christ's birth. But some of Alesius' criticism in this section is, in a rudimentary way, also generic: Vulgate Psalm 79, *Qui pastor es Israelis*, he declares, '*plane Georgicon est*', and he proceeds to enumerate the range of agricultural activities attributed to the Lord in that text, implying that they have an allegorical significance without actually spelling out what that is.

It is in the latter section of his lecture, however, that devoted to the value of the psalms, that Alesius develops arguments which are directly relevant to the emergence of a Protestant poetics. This is not to suggest that he deals explicitly with stylistic questions; but aesthetic considerations *are* implied in the functional purpose he attaches to the publication of the psalms in vernacular translation. Much of the thrust of his argument contrasts the ways in which Protestants employ these texts with Catholic practice:

> Experientia ipsa testatur abundantius in Germania habitasse verbum Christi per psalmorum cantiones, populari lingua, quam vlla alia ratione, & Euangelium adhuc apud eos qui psalmos sine mente canunt, aut latine canentes quasi barbares audiunt, veluti nouum hospitem tantum ex nomine notum habitare sine fr[u] ctu.

> [Experience shows that the Word of Christ is more generally available in Germany through the singing of psalms in the language of the people than through any other cause, and that the Gospel has until now lived without profit among those who mindlessly sing the psalms or hear them sung in Latin like barbarians, just like a newly-arrived foreigner known only by name.]

Invoking the authority of Augustine and Jerome, Alesius goes on to claim that the psalms are the most suitable of all Biblical books for doctrinal instruction, particularly of the young, provided they are put into an accessible form. It has long been the practice, however, to prevent such understanding, and Alesius' polemical rhetoric leaves no doubt about whose interest the Church has been serving:

> Sed Diabolus, vt omnes alias ordinationes Dei peruertere, & ad abusum transferre nos docuit, sic effecit, vt putaremus boatum & murmur psalmorum sine mente esse cultum Dei, & ex opere operato, vt loquuntur, mereri remissionem peccatorum, hinc nati sunt exequiae pro defunctis, & alij abusus psalmorum in collegijs & monasterijs.

[But the Devil, to pervert all God's other ordinances, taught us to go over to sin, so bringing it about that we believed the mindless bellowing and muttering of psalms to be worship of God, and *ex opere operato*, as they say, to obtain the remission of sins; and so are born Masses for the dead, and other abuses of the psalms in collegiate churches and monasteries.[11]

It is significant that Alesius here uses the second person plural, implicating himself, as it were, in the former abuses: like other early converts to Lutheranism, his repeated attacks on monastic conduct have something of a confessional quality. But his central point is that the many other non-canonical features of Catholic custom and theology stem from ignorance of Biblical truth, symbolised by what he regards as the mindless chanting of the psalms.

Nor, it would seem, is mere availability enough: while it is true that translation of the psalms into the vernacular has enabled laypeople to understand the truth they contain, there is evidently a regrettable tendency (attributable, of course, to the wiles of Satan) to adopt the *forms* of Reformed worship without paying heed to their substance:

Et iam cum videt Diabolus hanc suam fraudem detectam esse, & psalmos sic lingua populari redditos, vt posset quisquis ex Germanica versione melius psalmos intelligere, quam olim ex patrum commentarijs, alia arte conatur nobis eripere, ingens hoc dei beneficium, scilicet per ingratitudinem, & nescio per quos, imperitis persuasum est, satis esse audire contiones, & psalmos istic in templo pro vsu magis quam ex animi affectu cantare, & a priuata oratione non aliter quam ab hypocrisi abhorrendum esse . . .

[And now, when the Devil sees his deceits to be discovered and the psalms thus translated into the vernacular, so that anyone can understand them better in the German version than formerly through the commentaries of the Fathers, he strives by other arts to snatch from us this great benefit of God, namely through ingratitude, and the ignorant are persuaded, I know not by whom, that it is enough to hear sermons and to sing psalms there in the church out of habit rather than through the motions of the spirit, and private prayer to be, through hypocrisy, nothing but abhorrent . . .][12]

There is certainly no complacency in Alesius' position here: there is a keen sense of a struggle against an enemy that is within the Reformed Church as well as outside it, more than a little reminiscent of the strictures against insincere Protestants in Alexander Scott's *New Yeir Gift to the Quene Mary*:

---

11 *De autore*, sig. B vii^v–viii^r.
12 *ibid.*, sig. D v^{r-v}.

> For sum ar sene at sermonis seme sa halye,
> Singand Sanct Dauidis psalter on thair bukis,
> And ar bot biblistis fairsing full thair bellie,
> Bakbytand nychtbouris, noyand thame in nwikis . . .[13]

But what is it about the psalms that gives them such a central place in Alesius' – and his fellow-Lutherans' – scheme for religious renewal? Not least, of course, it is their musical quality, and Alesius deals at some length with the value of music as a means of transforming the human spirit, citing Galen, Cicero and other Classical authorities to reinforce his point. Alesius' classicism is a topic worth a paper to itself, as we might expect of one of Melanchthon's proteges, and there is insufficient space to do it justice here. Throughout his *Oratio* he displays his awareness of a wide range of pagan literature, comparing the pastoral element in the psalms to the pastoral poetry of Hesiod, Aratus, Theocritus and Virgil, for example (sig. C iii^v); but there is always a proper qualification to the praise – these authors are admirable, but they wrote without the understanding of higher truth which is only available through revelation. How much more admirable, then, are such divine texts as the psalms, which combine the rhetorical skill of the ancients with the certainty of divine truth?

> Scripserunt eleganter Comoedias & Tragoedias, Aristophanes, Sophocles, Terentius & Seneca, sed noster non turpes amores nec parrecidia, sed amorem filij Dei erga genus humanum, qui eum tam crudelem & ignominiosam mortem subire fecit, concinit.
>
> Sed superant psalmi poaemata omnia quibus tamen ab humano ingenio nihil potuit artificiosius excogitari, nihil sapientius aut suaui[us] dici, non solum, verum etiam alios sacras libros, propria quadam vtilitate, propterea quod ea quae sunt late dispersa, per vasta volumina bibliorum & vulgari oratione proposita, hic in locos communes, & piarum praecationum formulas, ac suauissimos hymnos composita, & poaeticis ornamentis omnis generis sunt ornata.

> [Aristophanes, Sophocles, Terence and Seneca wrote comedies and tragedies elegantly, but our [poet] did not celebrate disgraceful love or parricide, but the love of the Son of God for humanity, who put him to death so cruelly and ignominiously.
>
> But not only are the psalms superior to all poems, than which nothing could be conceived by the human genius that is more elegant, nothing be said that is wiser or sweeter, but they are also superior to the other sacred books with their own particular value; because of which they are widely distributed through the vast volumes of the Bible and published in common speech, composed here in commonplaces, formulae for pious prayers, and in the sweetest hymns, and are decorated with poetic ornaments of all kinds.][14]

---

13 Alexander Scott, *Poems*, ed. James Cranstoun (STS, Edinburgh 1898), p. 5.
14 *De autore*, sig. D i^{r-v}.

Revising this passage in 1554, Alesius adds Euripides and Plautus to his list, but the point remains the same: great as the achievements of Classical authors may have been, their work is flawed by its moral and theological framework, while the psalms are superior, not only in themselves, but also as a basis for imitation.

The value of 'poetic ornaments', clearly and unsurprisingly, is determined by the purpose to which they are put: Alesius does not, it should be noted, condemn rhetoric in itself, but rather seems to praise it as a tool in the service of divine writers. This rhetorical relativism becomes fully explicit when he turns, in the peroration of his lecture, to the contemporary rivals of the spiritual music of the psalms. For there are, of course, dangers in the power of music upon the human soul, dangers which are evident even in the life of David himself:

Habet enim Diabolus suam musicam, suam poaeticam & organa, ac decachordo decem capitalium vitiorum, nos a studio psalterij decem mandatorum auocat ... Mirabilem fuisse musicam oportet, & timothei modis quibus Alexander magnus ad bellum accendebatur multo excellentiorem, quae primis hominibus persuasit illud dulce bellum inexpertis. Et quanta sit vis Chordae Venereae in Dauidae videmus, qui decachordum decalogi pro huius dulcedine abiecit. Sed insitum nobis a serpente venenum, suauius sonare facit, Cithaerae Citharam, & Martis mauortia bella, quam psalterium decem mandatorum. Videmusque omnes poaetas foelissimos esse, cum res Martis, ac Veneris tractant & Musicam atque poaeticam quam olim sacrae erant, & ad diuinas res celebrandas institutae, ad canendos amores, bella, ac furores prostitutas esse, & nullum poaema esse dulce mortalibus, quod sales Veneris & Martis caedes inspersas non habeat, Et ad hanc ingenij deprauationem accedunt aliae artes Diaboli, ac primum vt dixi, eripuit nobis diuini Poaematis intellectum, ex quo petenda erant remedia contra ipsius incantationes.

[For the Devil has his music, his poetry and harmony, and by the ten-stringed instrument of the ten deadly sins, calls us away from the study of the Ten Commandments of the psalter ... It is fitting that the music should be wonderful, and much more excellent than the God-fearing modes by which Alexander the Great was fired to war, which persuaded the first men, inexperienced in that gentle war. And we see how great the force of the music of love is in David, who throws away the decachord of the Decalogue for this sweetness. But the serpent makes this poison he plants in us, the Cithaeronian harp and the martial wars of Mars, sound sweeter than the Ten Commandments of the psalter. We see the poets to be most happy when they deal with the things of Mars and Venus, and music and poetry, which formerly were sacred, and instituted to celebrate divine things, prostituted by singing about love, war and passion, and no poem to be sweet to mortals which does not have interspersed in it the salt of Venus and the slaughters of Mars. And to this clever depravity are added other arts of the Devil, and first, as I said, he snatched from us the understanding of divine poetry, through which were offered remedies against such singing.]¹⁵[15]

This is, we may think, the authentic voice of Puritanism, and its message is unequivocal: rhetoric in the service of sin is a powerful threat to Christian truth. But the test remains what is sung, not the manner of its singing; the objection is not to 'poetic ornaments' in themselves, but the purpose to which they are put. The emphasis on popular instruction which runs through the *Oratio* may imply that the functional purpose of vernacular praise is best served by comparative plainness, but Alesius does not take the view that stylistic elegance is in itself a thing to be avoided. There is an important point here, of central relevance to the development of vernacular rhetorical practice: it is easy to see the 'plain style' as one devoid of rhetorical figures, but that is, I believe, a misconception. It is rather the case that certain kinds of figure are appropriate because they are consistent with the communicative priorities of Protestant verse; we should not take Alesius' '*omnis generis*' too literally, then, for it is only a limited range of rhetorical devices which are in practice consistent with the functional purposes to which Protestant lyricists direct themselves. It is certainly true, as John King puts it, that 'because they identified poetry with truth, the gospellers subordinated poetic form and diction to biblical content';[16] this should not, however, be taken to imply that they paid no attention to poetic form and diction at all.

There is no evidence that the *De auctore et vtilitate psalmorum*, published by a relatively obscure press in the further reaches of Brandenburg, received much, or indeed any, attention in Alesius' native Scotland. But its spirit, if not its influence, is undoubtedly reflected in one of the most significant manifestations of early Scottish Protestant activity, *The Gude and Godlie Ballatis*. Nor is it improbable, indeed, that John Wedderburn, who is generally regarded as the principal author of the *Ballatis*, was aware of Alesius' work, for he was apparently in Wittenberg at the time of its publication. If Calderwood's circumstantial account is given any weight, Wedderburn 'departed to Almaine' when he was prosecuted for heresy in Scotland, was taught by Luther and Melanchthon, and only returned – and then only briefly – after the death of James V in 1542.[17] The timing suggested by this is confirmed, as has long been known, by references in the Treasurer's Accounts, to a search of Wedderburn's goods in March 1539 and to his brother's payment at about the same time of John's fine for conviction '*de certis criminibus heresieos*'.[18] It seems quite likely that he was the 'Joannes Scotus' who matriculated in Wittenberg later in 1539.[19] A student in St Andrews from 1525 to 1528, Wedderburn no doubt already knew

---

15 *ibid.*, sig. D v^v–vi^r.
16 King, *op. cit.*, p. 212.
17 David Calderwood, *The History of the Kirk of Scotland*, ed. T. Thomson (8 vols, Wodrow Soc., Edinburgh 1842–49), i, 142–3.
18 *Treas. Accts*, vii, 153; 79.
19 *Album Academiae Vitebergensis 1502–1602*, ed. C.E. Förstemann (Leipzig/Halle 1841–1905), i, nn.

Alesius, and he *may* have been involved in his flight through Dundee in the early 1530s; the two Scots may also have met again in Wittenberg in 1539, for Alesius arrived there on 9 July and apparently stayed for some months before taking up his new post in Frankfurt.[20]

Whatever the extent of their acquaintance, it is clear that the *Gude and Godlie Ballatis* are infused with the spirit of Alesius' treatise. He may refer approvingly to the use of 'poetic figures of all kinds' in the service of divine music, but we have seen that the emphasis of his argument is more upon the effective communication of spiritual truth than upon rhetorical display for its own sake. In the same way, the Protestant aesthetics exemplified in the *Ballatis* evidently places a much higher premium on straightforwardness of communication than on ornamentation. In the Scots versions as in their (largely) German sources, there is a predominance of familiar verse-forms, the most elaborate of which is the rhyme-royal stanza, with a sprinkling of quatrains and couplets. Even where something a little more demanding is adopted, as in Psalm 137 where the Scots text imitates the unusually intricate *ababccdeed* of Dachstein's German version, neither the syntax nor the lexis suggests that the stylistic possibilities of the form are at the forefront of the poet's concerns:

> An Wasserflussen Babilon
> da sassen wir mit schmertzen
> Als wir gedachten an Sion
> da weynten wir von hertzen
>   Wir hingen vff mit schweren můt
>   die orgeln vnd die harpffen gůt
>   an nere boum der weyden
>   Die drinnen sind in irem land
>   da musten wir vil schmach vnd schand,
>   teglich von jenen leyden.[21]
> At the revers of Babilone,
> Quhair we dwelt in captiuitie,
> Quhen we remembered on Syone
> We weipit all full sorrowfullie.
> On the sauch treis our harpis we hang,
> Quhen thay requyrit vs ane sang,
> That held vs in sic thirldome . . .[22]

The *hymne/in* rhyme of ll. 8–9, for example – parallelled by *game/Jerusalem* (ll. 18–19) and *Jerusalem/ouerquhelm* (ll. 22, 24) – indicates that quite approximate

---

20 Alesius wrote to Cromwell from Wittenberg on 9 July 1539; see *LP* xiv (1), no. 1353. Another letter, dated 16 November, reveals that he stayed there for some months; see Wiedermann, *Der Reformator*, p. 247. For Melanchthon's recommendation of him to the University of Frankfurt/ Oder, see *CR* iii, 842–4.
21 *Das deutsche Kirchenlied*, ed. Phillip Wackernagel (5 vols, Leipzig 1864–84), iii, 98.
22 *The Gude and Godlie Ballatis*, ed. A.F. Mitchell (STS, Edinburgh 1897), p. 114.

rhymes were acceptable provided the doctrinal content of the psalm was effectively communicated. The structure of the German, and the adaptation of that structure into Scots, stay close to the sequence of ideas in the Biblical text, and it is only when the demands of syntax, metrical pattern and rhyme require it – as, for instance, in the positioning of '*salices/weyden/*sauch tries', that the translators depart from the strict order of the Latin.

Some of the same formal characteristics are generally apparent in the *Ballatis* even where the Biblical authority of the psalms is not constraining the poets' choices. Consider, for example, 'The Greit Louing and Blyithnes of Goddis Word', translated from 'Ein geistlich lied von der krafft Gottlichs wort', first published in a *Gesangbuch* produced in Erfurt in 1527, where despite the adoption in both German and Scots of the comparatively demanding internal rhymes of the 'roundel' or triolet form, recently discussed by Mrs Bawcutt in a different context,[23] the emphasis is upon plain declaration. But at the same time the absence of a Biblical text acting as a canonical control is apparent in the much greater freedom with which the Scots translator deals with the ideas and the wording of his original:

> Hilff, Herre Gott, nun dieser not,
> das sich die thun bekeren,
> Die nichts betrachten, dein wort verachten,
> und wollens auch nicht leren.
> Sie sprechen schlecht, es sey nicht recht,
> vnd habens nie gelesen.
> Auch nicht gehort das edel wordt,
> ists nicht eyn teuffelisch wesen?[24]

> Lord lat thy hand help in all land,
> That thy elect conuertit be,
> Thy word to leir, quhilk now dar sweir
> That thy word is bot heresie.
> They geue thy word ane fals record,
> Quhilk neuer hard the veritie:
> Nor neuer it red, bot blindlingis led,
> With doctouris of idolatrie.[25]

The reference to the Elect in the *Ballatis* version might at first glance be taken to imply a later, Calvinist influence here, but no such inference is necessary: the concept of the conversion of the elect, requiring the direct *vocatio* of God, is in fact thoroughly Augustinian, and was taken up by such neo-Augustinian theologians as Johann von Staupitz, whose influence on the Lutheran Reformation has been shown by Heiko Oberman to have been

---

23 Priscilla Bawcutt, 'The Commonplace Book of John Maxwell', in *A Day Estivall*, ed. Alisoun Gardner-Medwin and Janet Hadley Williams (Aberdeen 1990), pp. 59–68, at 65–6.
24 Wackernagel, iii, 123–4.
25 *Gude and Godlie Ballatis, ed. cit.*, p. 56.

considerable.[26] But there is no hint of this motif in the German, and it is noteworthy that the language of the Scots version is general more doctrinally explicit than that of its source – the ideas are parallel, the expression is to a greater degree independent. That said, in its comparatively simple syntax and strict literalism, the *Ballatis* text remains true to the spirit of its original, and to the functional approach to rhetoric which we have taken to be characteristic of the Protestant style.

In one other important respect, we can relate Alesius' views to the nature of the *Gude and Godlie Ballatis*. Alesius, you will recall, laments the prevalence of the 'clever depravity' of secular song, that perversion of divine music and poetry by which the Devil calls us away from 'the decachord of the Decalogue'. And one of the most striking features of the *Ballatis* is the way in which its authors have sought to recover this lost ground by stealing back from the Devil, as it were, his own perverted music, converting secular songs to a spiritual purpose. The role of the *contrafactum*, the sacred parody, is an important one in the sixteenth and seventeenth centuries (one, of course, with medieval precedents), and later exponents of the genre include St John of the Cross, Alexander Montgomerie and George Herbert;[27] but it also represents one of the most significant aspects of the *Ballatis*. The conversions may often be comparatively crude, but there is no mistaking their purpose: they seek to snatch back the power of music, to apply it once again to those sacred uses to which it was so effectively put by the author of the Psalms. In this sense, *The Gude and Godlie Ballatis* might legitimately be seen as a direct response to the closing lament of Alesius' *Oratio*.

Alexander Alesius has manifestly been a victim of those processes of canonical exclusion which I discussed in more general terms at the previous conference.[28] He falls foul of at least four criteria which have implicitly been used to define the Scottish canon: the geographical; the linguistic; the generic; and the doctrinal. He left Scotland soon after turning thirty and, so far as we can tell, never returned; and his writings were all produced, published, and largely circulated, in Central Europe and in England. Aiming at such audience, he wrote almost exclusively in Latin. His works, moreover, are almost wholly theological, and in a number of genres – Biblical commentary, doctrinal controversy, and the public lecture or sermon – which have long been regarded as extra-literary. And finally, he was a Lutheran, whose writings were disregarded by Knox and his Calvinist contemporaries and successors. Yet Alesius is a skilled commentator and controversialist, and like many writers of considerable technical competence but limited originality, he captures with unusual clarity the spirit of his age. I do not

---

26 Heiko A. Oberman, *Masters of the Reformation*, trans. Dennis Martin (Cambridge 1981), pp. 64–110.
27 See Bruce W. Wardroper, 'The Religious Conversion of Profane Poetry', in *Studies in the Continental Background of Renaissance English Literature*, ed. Dale B.J. Randall and George Walton Williams (Durham NC 1977), pp. 203–21.
28 ' "A new maid channoun"? Redefining the Canonical in Older Scots Literature', *SSL* 26 (1992), 1–18.

claim that the *De Autore et Utilitate Psalmorum* is one of the lost masterpieces of the sixteenth century, but *its* author deserves more serious scholarly consideration than he has so far received; and it is even more true now than it was nearly fifty years ago that

> a biography of the Scottish exile, who played . . . 'a not altogether insignificant part in the English Reformation', as well as in the history of the Church in Germany and in his native land, is long overdue.[29]

Indeed, it is as valid to say, as Robert Wodrow did in 1729, that Alesius

> is as much now notticed by our Neighbours & Forraigners, as well as Better knouen to them, than to us.[30]

Perhaps it is time for him to be given proper recognition in Scotland as a key Scottish contributor to the *European* Reformation.

---

29 Pearson, *op. cit.*, 87.
30 GUL, MS. 1211, no. 79, f. 1ʳ.

CLAUSDIRK POLLNER

34. *Scots Words and their Glosses in the Kailyard Novels*

The Kailyard novels[1] still fascinate their readers and they still cause some controversy; but they seem to have made it permanently into literary histories of Scotland: precisely because their authors are seen as backward-looking sentimentalists by the majority of critics. Hugh MacDiarmid saw the mere existence of the Kailyard writers as one of the reasons why there ought to be a new vernacular movement: '[. . .] the old Kailyaird guff which has no correspondence to Scottish realities and against which the new movement is a long-overdue protest.'[2] In MacDiarmid's eyes these writers were 'preservationists' rather than 'innovators' and in this respect they stood for everything he was against.

In a letter to Duncan Glen written in 1970 MacDiarmid had this to say about some of Glen's contributors to *Akros*, the literary magazine:

> While I agree with you about the number of young poets now writing in Scots you have gathered round you, I wish they were setting their sights higher and using a lot more Scots vocabulary. Their work for the most part is simply the kind of Scots still in conversational use – and that is not the kind of Scots in which high poetry can be written, and what can be done in it, and is being done by these poets, is qualitatively little, if at all, above Kailyaird level, viz. emotion without intellect, and fancy without imagination.[3]

This may all be very true; but to say: 'I wish they were using a lot more Scots vocabulary' and then to compare these poets with the Kailyard authors is unfair to the latter – their pages are positively bristling with Scots vocabulary, a fact, indeed, which makes them such interesting reading matter even today. But then MacDiarmid disliked the way they appear to merely preserve Scots items rather

---

1 For the purpose of this paper, the following novels were consulted: J.M. Barrie, *Auld Licht Idylls* (1888; repr. London, 1913) [abbr. ALI]
—, *Margaret Ogilvy* (1896; repr. London, 1913) [abbr. MO]
—, *A Window in Thrums* (1889; repr. London, 1913) [abbr. WT] [All repr. in the Kirriemuir Edition.]
S.R. Crockett, *The Lilac Sunbonnet* (1894; repr. London, 1897) [abbr. LS]
—, *The Stickit Minister* (London, 1893) [abbr. SM]
I. Maclaren [=John Watson], *Beside the Bonnie Brier Bush* (1894; repr. Leipzig, 1895) [abbr. BBB]
—, *The Days of Auld Lang Syne* (1895; repr. Leipzig, 1895) [abbr. DALS].
2 L.G. Gibbon and H. MacDiarmid, *Scottish Scene, or the Intelligent Man's Guide to Albyn* (London, 1934 [?], p. 52.
3 A. Bold, ed., *The Letters of Hugh MacDiarmid* (London, 1984), p. 687.

than use them in a more innovative manner, or use them for less nostalgic subject matters and in less nostalgic contexts.

Apart from two articles by McClure[4] and a book by Letley[5] I have not come across any extended studies of the language of the Kailyard novels and their use of Scots words in particular. (The first of McClure's articles is actually not about the Kailyard at all, but about George Douglas Brown's *The House with the Green Shutters*, seen by most critics as an anti-Kailyard novel – but a novel that shares a number of characteristics with the proper Kailyarders.)

The majority of critics just mention the role of Scots in passing. Knowles is a good example; he remarks about the Scots dialect that it was '[. . .] a medium which potentially expressed national and local identity, but which eventually became an established and marketable literary convention.'[6] And he points out that the Kailyard authors had some awareness of a readership compromise – the novels had to sound and look Scottish and yet they had to be comprehensible to non-Scottish readers.[7]

Watson, for example, does not mention the role of Broad Scots in the Kailyard novels at all.[8]

Shepherd[9] only has a brief paragraph on the use of Scots; she points out quite correctly that there is a great deal of linguistic inconsistency in these books, criticising for example the fact that a character in Maclaren's *Beside the Bonnie Brier Bush* composes a letter in Broad Scots. This is indeed highly improbable or even nonsensical: a person – even a country person – in the nineteenth century who was able to write would have written in (Standard) English, of course. (Incidentally, Letley points out that John Galt and Sir Walter Scott can be accused of exactly the same mistake.[10]) Shepherd then goes on to complain about 'unwieldy phonetic transcriptions of dialect speech'.[11] There are, indeed, in all these novels some attempts to render common-core words, shared by English and Scots, in their specific Scottish pronunciation: cf. e.g. *verra obleeged* (Barrie, ALI), *spleet new* (Barrie, WT), *sojer* (Barrie, WT), *poalismen* (Crockett, SM), *langidge* (Maclaren, BBB). But these are usually quite straightforward rather than unwieldy, and Shepherd does not really mean 'transcriptions' in the technical sense at all: what she refers to is the rendering of Scots speech into writing. The 'unwieldiness' of the result is explained by the fact that there is no standard

---

4 J.D. McClure, 'Dialect in *The House with the Green Shutters*', *Studies in Scottish Literature* 9, 1971/72, pp. 148–63; —, 'Scots in Dialogue: Some Uses and Implications', in J.D. McClure and A.J. Aitken, eds., *Scotland and the Lowland Tongue* (Aberdeen, 1983), pp. 129–48
5 E. Letley, *From Galt to Douglas Brown. Nineteenth-Century Fiction and Scots Language* (Edinburgh, 1988).
6 T.D. Knowles, *Ideology, Art and Commerce. Aspects of Literary Sociology in the Late Victorian Scottish Kailyard* (Goteborg, 1983), p. 27.
7 Knowles, p. 34.
8 R. Watson, *The Literature of Scotland* (London, 1984).
9 G. Shepherd, 'The Kailyard', in D. Gifford, ed., *The History of Scottish Literature*, vol. III: *Nineteenth Century* (Aberdeen, 1988), pp. 309–20.
10 Letley, p. 221.
11 Shepherd, pp. 311–12.

orthography/written standard; the Kailyard writers can hardly be blamed for this.

The question of the comprehensibilitiy of the Kailyard novels has been raised again and again – particularly in view of their large non-Scottish readership at the end of the nineteenth/beginning of the twentieth century. As early as 1895 Millar said about Barrie's novels that they 'are eagerly devoured in England by people who, on the most charitable hypothesis, may possibly understand one word in three.'[12] And Blake, commenting on Crockett's *Lilac Sunbonnet*, talks about this writer's 'absurd excess' in the use of Broad Scots, giving the following excerpt as an example: ' "Deed, I'm no sae unbonny yet, for a' yer helicat flichtmafleaters, spriggit goons, an' laylac bonnets."' Blake comments: 'The bewildered Englishman may be assured that even the Scottish reader with an interest in the old tongue finds these passages just a little bit too deliberately elaborate.'[13] Blake's example is taken from the speech of an elderly lady, who uses Broad Scots consistently, and apart from *helicat* (CSD has *hellicat* 'noisy, crazy') and the rather fancy *flichtmafleat(h)ers* (glossed by Warrack as 'frippery, trifles') – which sounds as though MacDiarmid had lifted it straight from Jamieson – there does not seem to me to be anything particularly excessive about such passages.

And when Blake informs his readers that even 'the simplest dialect word must be within quotation marks, so that one is driven to believe that [Barrie] was ashamed of his own Scottishness'[14] he misses the point completely by exaggerating in this way. The inconsistency in Barrie's, Crockett's and Maclaren's treatment of Broad Scots words lies exactly in the fact some Scots items (both in the dialogue and, mainly, in the narrative) are indeed marked by inverted commas: but by no means all and 'even the simplest one'. Why this practice should indicate a sense of shame on Barrie's part is left unexplained. The use and marking of Scots items in the narrative simply underlines the fact that it is not only the novels' characters who use Broad Scots but the narrator as well. Here are some examples from Barrie's *Margaret Ogilvy*; the narrative text has the following items in inverted commas: *a 'hoast', a great 'stoop', her bonnet 'sets' her, she was 'cried' in the church, she is 'on the mend', she may 'thole thro'', very 'forward' to help her.*

The following items, again from the narrative, are without inverted commas: *to run ben, ettling to be ben, look doited, down these wynds, forenoon, the haver of a thing, she ettled, redding up the drawers*. The problem here is not that 'the simplest dialect word must be within quotation marks', but rather why some items are marked while others are not. Similar lists can be drawn up for other Kailyard novels. In addition to the typographical marking of some Scots words and expressions, the Kailyard authors use another device that seems to me to be worth analysing and that critics so far have only mentioned in passing: they gloss certain Scotticisms, but obviously by no means all of them, and again in rather an inconsistent way. Maclaren's *The Days of Auld Lang Syne*, for example, has two occurrences of the

---

12 J.H. Millar, 'The Literature of the Kailyard', *New Review* XII, 1895, p. 384.
13 G. Blake, *Barrie and the Kailyard School* (London, 1951), p. 49.
14 Blake, p. 66.

word *collieshangie*, which is glossed at the first instance ('disturbance'), unglossed at the second. The much simpler term *sober* occurs five times in the dialogue of this novel – and is glossed every time, either as 'ill' or as 'weak(ly)'. This certainly looks inconsistent; a possible explanation, however, may be that the author wants to make quite sure that his non-Scottish readers do not mis-read the adjective for English *sober* 'not drunk'.

In what follows I would like to look at these linguistic glosses in some detail, concentrating again on the narrative text, even though dialogue words and expressions are sometimes glossed as well. By looking at these glosses we shall come back to typographical markings as well.

Having read seven Kailyard novels, one knows what Crosland meant when he remarked after an intake of only five of them: 'I have read enough to know all that I want to know about Thrums.'[15]

McClure's remark about the distribution of English and Scots in *The House with the Green Shutters* applies exactly to the Kailyard novels:

> A cursory glance at the novel would suggest that the narrative is predominantly in English and the dialogue predominantly in Scots. More careful examination shows that the number and variety of Scots words in the narrative is in fact very considerable.[16]

The distinction between narrative text and dialogue in the Kailyard books is not always straightforward, because the three authors considered here like to quote, in the narrative text, short phrases as used (or potentially used) by their fictional characters. 'He was looked on as "byordnar' clever", "a dungeon o' learnin" ' is one example of many, in this case from Crockett's *The Stickit Minister*. These quotes in the narrative are not glossed and they repeat verbatim what someone in the village thinks/says about the person in question.

As far as typographical markings and glosses are concerned, the following taxonomy of seven categories can be suggested:

(I)   Scots words/expressions in quotation marks, but without a gloss.
(II) Scots items that do not have any typographical marking and no gloss either; here I refer to items that a non-Scottish reader might expect to be marked and/or glossed.
(III) Scots words in quotation marks plus a gloss.
(IV) Scots items without typographical marking but with a gloss.

Barrie's *Auld Licht Idylls* is a novel that has examples of all four categories:

(ex. I)   'girning', 'dam-brod', 'ben the hoose', 'divet', 'orra man', 'hairst', 'shaws', 'cruizey', 'pecks', 'droukin', 'tow', 'pirns', 'poorshouse', 'kebec', 'joukin'', 'divets', 'pend', 'lippy', 'brew'.

15 T.W.H. Crosland, *The Unspeakable Scot* (London, 1902), p. 74.
16 McClure, 'Dialect', p. 149.

(ex. II) manse, kirk, kirk-wynd, brae, buckie-man, douce, dander, roup(-ing), forenoon, clachan, bothies, quoits, canty stock, whins, stickit, dandered, wob, redd-up, but and ben, mutch, doited, guid-wife, tattie-roup, pirns, wincey gown, callant, cruizey, bailie, lum.

At least two items occur in both (I) and (II) – the unmarked forms of *pirns* and *cruizey* occur later in the text than the forms in inverted commas.

(ex. III) 'press' or cupboard, 'laft' or gallery, 'brot' or apron, 'lum hat' (chimney pot), 'bole' or little window.
(ex. IV) the commonty (or common), Mistress (which is Miss), saut-backet or salt-bucket, cleek or hook, toad (fox), doulie yates (ghost gates), mous (canny).

Why does *girn*, for example, have inverted commas, whereas *roup* does not? Why is *press* explained and in inverted commas, while *cleek* is only glossed? An easy but unsatisfactory way out of this would be to say that Barrie and his colleagues sprinkled their pages with typographical markings and glosses quite randomly. I would like to suggest another answer. A few years ago, A.J. Aitken introduced the terms 'covert (or "unmarked") Scotticisms' and 'cultural and overt (or "marked") Scotticisms.'[17] My suggestion is that the Kailyard writers tried to indicate – in an admittedly haphazard and inconsistent way – a distinction of this kind: by visual markings and/or explanations. Categories (III) and (IV) above could then be considered 'overt' Scotticisms from the point of view of our authors: 'that special diction of Scottish-tagged locutions used self-consciously by many Scottish speakers as a kind of stylistic grace and as a way of claiming membership of the in-group of Scotsmen.'[18] Moreover, items like *press, laft/loft, bole, toad* were possibly seen as deserving a gloss because they exist in English as well, albeit with a different meaning.

Category (II) may be considered to consist of 'covert' items: 'employed by many Scottish speakers without their being very much or at all aware that in so doing they are revealing their Scottish origins.'[19] Items such as *manse, kirk, brae, stickit, guidewife, forenoon, but and ben, bailie* are quite obvious candidates for membership in this group.

Finally, category (I) would then be a collection of items in regard to which the author/narrator seems to be sitting on the fence: they are marked as 'non-English' but remain unglossed.

It has to be pointed out again that this distinction between overt and covert items was only followed by our writers in the vaguest possible way; there are, for example, some cases where an item is both marked and unmarked. In *Auld Licht Idylls* we find *lum* in category (II) and, as '*lum hat*', in category (III).

17 A.J. Aitken, 'Scottish Speech: A Historical View with Special Reference to the Standard English of Scotland', in A.J. Aitken and T. McArthur, eds., *Languages of Scotland* (Edinburgh, 1979), pp. 106–7.
18 Aitken, p. 107.
19 Aitken, p. 106.

In addition to categories (I) to (IV), there are two further kinds of glosses in the Kailyard novels:

(V) In some cases, English items are given their Scots equivalent rather than the other way round (as in (III) and (IV)).

(VI) Some explanations/definitions are given as part of the syntactic structure.

Again, examples can be found in *Auld Licht Idylls*:

(ex. V) waterhen (whit-rit and beltie they are called in these parts);
a big kettle ('boiler' they called it); playing draughts, or, as they called it, the 'dam-brod';
resin, called 'rozet';
a little hole, known as the 'bole'.
Bole, incidentally, is glossed twice in this novel: in category (III) – the Scots word followed by its English equivalent – and in category (V).

(ex. VI) '[. . .] some distant part where the people speak of snecking the door, meaning shut it. In Thrums the word is steck [. . .]'
A rather extreme example of this kind of gloss occurs in Barrie's *Margaret Ogilvy*:
'My sister is but and I am ben – I mean she is in the east – tuts, tuts! Let us get at the English of this by striving: she is in the kitchen and I am at my desk in the parlour.'

In this last instance of category (VI) the reader witnesses a Scottish narrator trying hard ('striving') to find a 'proper' English equivalent of *but and ben*.

Finally, there is a mixed-bag category of miscellaneous types of glosses:

(VII) (a) Some of Crockett's novels were published with glossaries at the end of the books. These word-lists were later published separately.[20]

(b) Some of Crockett's glosses are given in square rather than round brackets, making them even more obtrusive.

(c) Some items in Crockett's books are underlined rather than in inverted commas, others have index numbers plus an explanatory footnote on the same page: still an increase in obtrusiveness.

Category (VII) no doubt adds to the general impression of inconsistency; it is the books' publishers who ought to take some of the blame here.

---

20 P. Dudgeon, *Glossaries to S.R. Crockett's The Stickit Minister, The Raiders, The Lilac Sunbonnet* (London, 1895).

The Kailyard writers may have been inconsistent in their use and treatment of Broad Scots and they certainly portrayed the speech of what by the nineteenth century had become a tiny minority of Scottish speakers. But within such limitations and from a language point of view they are still worth reading. Murison mentions Barrie, Crockett and Maclaren together with Stevenson, George Douglas Brown, Neil Munro and John Buchan as having 'good passages [in Scots]'.[21] This then is a more positive reason for including the Kailyarders in literary histories of Scotland – plus the fact that the modern reader may glean some information about the covertness/overtness of certain Broad Scots items at the end of the 19th century, at least as perceived in their admittedly haphazard way by these writers.

---

21 D. Murison, *The Guid Scots Tongue* (Edinburgh, 1977), p. 23.

ALAN MacGILLIVRAY

35. *Memoirs of a European Scotland*

When Sir David Lindsay creates his dream of the state of Scotland addressed to King James V in 1528,[1] he interestingly sets himself as dreamer in a sheltered crevice on a rocky shore early on New Year's Day morning. The normal conventions of a soft spring season and a pleasing landscape are overturned in favour of realistic Scottish temperatures and location, probably based on Lindsay's own experience of wild winter days on the Firth of Forth, observed from his home estates in East Lothian and Fife. There is more of a parallel with Robert Henryson describing a piercingly cold Spring night on the east coast at the beginning of 'The Testament of Cresseid' than with William Dunbar in 'The Goldyn Targe' and 'The Thrissill and the Rois'. It is interesting to see Lindsay in 'The Dreme' both following the established poetic dream convention and departing from it to impart a sterner and more austere atmospheric context for his strictures on Scotland's political and social condition.

For us here at the end of the twentieth century faced with a condition of Scotland that, for all the inevitable changes in political institutions and labels, seems in a number of essentials to be quite unchanged from Lindsay's day, a major interest may be in the way that successive poets have used the dream to express the continuing disquiet and anger felt by thoughtful and observant Scots writers at how their country is consistently misgoverned and held back from its true potential. So there is Allan Ramsay's imitation of the medieval in 'The Vision', Robert Burns' poem of the same name, 'The Vision', which in fact is more eulogistic than satirical, and primarily for our twentieth-century consciousness, Hugh MacDiarmid's 'A Drunk Man Looks at the Thistle'. This drunk man's rambling dream-like vision of Scotland and its ills is probably the highpoint of this convention in Scottish poetry. For our purposes today I want to pick out two topics from within its near-2700 lines. First, there is the theme of what Scotland has turned its back on, the tradition of the Makars and their immediate successors, whom we are celebrating at this conference:

> . . . The Gairdens o' the Muses may be braw,
> But nane like oors can breenge and eat ana'!
>
> And owre the kailyaird wa' Dunbar they've flung,
> And a' their countrymen that e'er ha'e sung
> For ither than ploomen's lugs or to enrichen
> Plots on Parnassus set apairt for kitchen.

1 'The Dreme of Schir David Lyndesay', ed. D. Hamer, *The Works of Sir David Lindsay*, STS (1931).

> Ploomen and ploomen's wives – shades o' the Manse
> May weel be at the heid o' sic a dance,
> As through the polish't ha's o' Europe leads
> The rout o' bagpipes, haggis, and sheep's heids!
>
> The vandal Scot! Frae Brankstone's deidly barrow
> I struggle yet to free a'e winsome marrow,
> To show what Scotland micht ha'e hed instead
> O' this preposterous Presbyterian breed.'[2]

MacDiarmid is crying out primarily against the Kailyard in Scottish writing, the excessively parochial and sentimental rural view of Scottish life that blighted the later nineteenth- and early twentieth-century literary scene, something that, thanks to MacDiarmid and his successors, has largely been superseded by a more honest and critical approach to Scotland in writing. Yet the main point of MacDiarmid's outburst still holds, since the most polished and cosmopolitan era of Scottish writing, symbolised for MacDiarmid by Dunbar, is still largely ignored by a wider readership than scholars.

Secondly from 'A Drunk Man Looks at the Thistle', we can take another theme, related to that of our conference:

> Whatever Scotland is to me,
> Be it aye pairt o' a' men see
> O' Earth and o' Eternity
>
> Wha winna hide their heids in't till
> It seems the haill o' Space to fill
> As 'twere an unsurmounted hill.
>
> He canna Scotland see wha yet
> Canna see the Infinite,
> And Scotland in true scale to it.[3]

Here MacDiarmid is trying to set Scotland in its proper context in a cosmic sense, suggesting also that it is not a fitting habitation or refuge if one cannot see anything else. Scotland has its place in the scheme of things and one must be aware of this place if Scotland is to be properly understood. Although MacDiarmid does not say so here, Europe is part of Scotland's context, and we must look at Scotland within it.

Putting Scotland very clearly in its context is part of the business of Sir David Lindsay's 'Dreme'. Dame Remembrance leads the Dreamer through the cosmos:

---

2 *A Drunk Man Looks at the Thistle*, Hugh MacDiarmid: ed. Kenneth Buthlay, Scottish Academic Press, 1987, pp. 58 and 60, 11. 725–38.
3 *A Drunk Man Looks at the Thistle*, p. 182, 11. 2521–9.

through Hell and Purgatory, then up through the elements of Earth, Water, Air and Fire, past the planetary spheres with their deities and on to Heaven; back to Earth with its main divisions of Asia, Europe and Africa (thirty years after Columbus, it is still too soon to have America included as a major continent); a visit to the Garden of Eden and finally an overview of Scotland as one of the two parts of the Isle of Britain.

> Quhen this lufesum lady Remembrance
> All this foresaid had gart me understand,
> I prayit hir, of hir benevolence,
> To schaw to me the countre of Scotland.
> Weill, Sonne, scho said, that sall I tak on hand.
> So, suddanlie scho brocht me, in certane,
> Evin juste abone the braid Yle of Bertane,
>
> Quhilk standis northwest, in the Occiane see,
> And devydit in famous regionis two,
> The south part, Ingland, ane full ryche countre,
> Scotland, be north, with mony Ylis mo.
> Be west Ingland, Yreland doith stand, also,
> Quhose properteis I wyll nocht tak on hand
> To schaw at lenth, bot only of Scotland.[4]

For Lindsay, of course, Scotland and England are two quite separate entities. England is identified as being 'full ryche', but is not his present concern any more than Ireland is. His concern is with the poverty and unhappiness of Scotland, all the more surprising given that Scotland has so many natural advantages and blessings. In his dream he asks Dame Remembrance the reasons:

> Quharefor, I pray yow that ye wald defyne
> The principall cause quharefor we ar so pure;
> For I marvell gretlie, I yow assure,
> Considderand the peple, and the ground,
> That ryches suld nocht in this realme redound.[5]

And he receives Dame Remembrance's answer that it is all to do with the lack of justice, good government and a settled peace in the kingdom, themselves caused by defects in the princes of the realm, the governors. To this is added the Complaynt of the Commonweill of Scotland, personified in the ragged figure of John the Commounweill, the common good of the Scottish people portrayed as the ordinary man, your average punter as the Glasgow term has it. What John the Commounweill has to complain about is of course detailed at greater length and with greater force in the later *Satire of the Thrie Estaitis*. However, in 'The

---

4 'The Dreme of Schir David Lyndesay', ll. 785–98.
5 'The Dreme', ll.836–40.

Dreme' Lindsay is concerned to inform and remind the young King James V of pressing matters in his kingdom. I think that for us the message is rather different in orientation and in the moral to be drawn.

Just as Dame Remembrance comes to the Scottish Dreamer to remind him of Scotland's valid and respectable place in the great scheme of things and give him some standard of comparison for the evaluation of the state of Scottish society, so Memory must be used by us today to help us estimate what is due to Scotland in its contemporary context and what its status as a commonwealth or community should be. 'Memory' should be interpreted here, not merely as our own individual memories of the past or even the reminiscences of an earlier generation (although comparisons of the present with the immediate past can be quite revealing in social criticism and evaluation: already Scotland of the comparatively recent Seventies is taking on a kind of golden glow as of a lost Arcadia, the blue remembered hills of a land where you could get a bus to where you wanted to go and whisky was only five pounds a bottle.) Rather Memory is to be seen as the collective social memory of Scotland's past and traditions expressed through continuing historical and cultural scholarship, education at all levels, and dissemination by the media.

Unfortunately, when we speak of these things in Scotland, we are for the most part speaking of areas of deprivation and neglect. Much has been done to recover the Scottish Memory in historical and literary scholarship, as this conference amply testifies. A group of dedicated historians, of whom the late Gordon Donaldson was only one distinguished member, has done magnificent work in rediscovering and re-evaluating the long sweep of Scottish history that has hitherto been only partly known and generally misunderstood; in literature, many distinguished researchers, including the scholars of this conference, have consolidated the work, begun long ago by Bannatyne and Maitland and continued in the eighteenth century by Watson and Ramsay, in preserving the achievements of earlier Scottish literature. In very recent years, the rich Scottish traditions in art and music have been restored to popular appreciation, and the names of Duncan MacMillan and John Purser should be specially honoured in this context. Yet it is not in denigration of scholarship and research to say that the processes of investigation, interpretation and academic publication are not enough; the wider processes of dissemination, communication, presentation to the people of society at large are the vital extension of your work without which it remains the preserve of a tiny minority. The crying need is to make Scottish culture, including literature, part of the collective memory of the Scottish people through the large-scale communication of what it has to offer to individual minds. Dame Remembrance has to come to John and Jean the Commounweill and remind them of what they have largely forgotten over the centuries of the British Interlude in Scottish history.

In Lindsay's 'Dreme' Dame Remembrance does her work of informing the Dreamer by carrying him 'in twinkling of ane ee'[6] to every part of the cosmos

---

6 'The Dreme', 1.161.

so that he can see at first hand and by answering his inevitable questions so that he 'gart cleirly understand'.[7] Today the corresponding instruments of Dame Remembrance in this work are the mass media of communication, particularly broadcasting and the press, and the institutions of education at all levels from primary school to university. The first of these, the mass media, cannot be our concern here today; the topic is too vast and complex. For us here in Scotland, the problems of transmitting a meaningful and coherent Scottish culture through the media are familiar causes of anger and frustration. Currently they have come back into prominence because of the debate and controversy over the future of the BBC in Scotland. The problem basically is of a Southern-orientated anglicising tendency which has operated in all areas of Scottish life for fully three hundred years and which has been given added power by the forces of commercialism and modern technology. What we need to consider, briefly because of the time restriction, is the attitude of educational institutions to the older Scottish tradition and what is failing to be imparted as a result.

It is not actually my intention to say much about the universities and the state of Scottish studies within them; many of you will be more familiar at first hand with the difficulties than I am. I only wish to remind you of the words of George Davie in his brilliant and crucially important study, *The Democratic Intellect*, where he shows how during the nineteenth century the Scottish universities shed most of their traditional Scottish characteristics and traditions:

> With the passing and implementation of the Act of 1889, these educational struggles apparently came to a definitive close. Henceforward, the Scots, despite certain grave misgivings, abandoned the attempt to regulate the higher education of their country according to their own ideals. Hitherto they had been striving to introduce into their Universities the specialisms required by modern life in a form suited to their hereditary ideas of education – namely as courses to be taken only after the student had gone through a general education, distinguished from other countries by the prominence given to the teaching of philosophy. From now on, however, the Scots became gradually reconciled to an arrangement of a rather peculiar sort, whereby the abler and more ambitious students went in for specialisations on the English model from the very start of their University career, without having to study any philosophy, and the tradition of compulsory philosophy and a broad all-round degree was kept going only for those students who on the whole were weaker. In short, they broke away from an educational system, at once unified and flexible, which had directly developed out of the medieval heritage, which had a close historical relationship to Continental educational norms and which, indeed, had long been world-famous, in favour of a piece-meal, opportunist policy, destined to conciliate the English rather than impress the world, according to which the principal departments of the system were to

---

7 'The Dreme', 1.661.

become increasingly anglicised and only in subordinate sectors and at lower levels were vestiges of independence to be retained.[8]

It is tempting to linger on the university situation. However, I must turn to my main area of concern, the secondary schools of Scotland. The secondary sector of education inevitably takes some of its attitudes and preoccupations from the tertiary. The schools of Scotland, over many generations and until comparatively recently, have looked, wrongly as we now realise, to the universities for some guidance in curriculum content, even though only a minority of their students exposed to such a curriculum would ever reach higher education. Until quite recently, the implicit guidance given or the example set by universities would not have encouraged any significant Scottish cultural elements. Partly because of this and partly because of the other strong social tendencies towards anglicisation, the place of both Scottish history and Scottish literature, especially relating to the earlier independent European Scotland, has always been insecure, indeed at times non-existent. Currently, there is controversy about the declining requirement to teach Scottish history for the Scottish Certificate of Education. And in the field of Scottish literature, although on the one hand there has been a strengthening of the position of modern Scottish literature, mostly in Standard English, there has on the other hand been a continuing readiness to ignore earlier Scots writing completely. If this readiness rests on the assumption that earlier Scottish literature has little to offer young minds and sensibilities, I can rebut that from my own experience in this university. Students taking the Scottish Literary Tradition course and meeting the power of Older Scots literature for the first time frequently express surprise and excitement at its vigour and force, and wonder why as Scottish pupils in Scottish schools they had not heard of its existence before.

It is now almost twenty-five years since, along with other enthusiasts, I first started trying to encourage the greater use of Scottish literature in schools, first in my own school department, then through a college of education, and most recently through the university and the Association for Scottish Literary Studies. Some progress has been made but it has been patchy and too dependent on individuals being fortunately placed in particular positions in the education system. However, within the last two years something quite significant has happened which could alter the way in which Scottish literature and culture are regarded in the schools. Up till now, Scottish education has existed within an Anglocentric model, whereby the aims and methods of Scottish educational institutions have been directed to fulfilling the expectations of a solely English language social system (i.e., within the UK and other English-speaking countries, including the USA); in this system, which is basically an English imperial and post-imperial construct, Scots language and Scottish culture are very peripheral. Now, however, the British Isles with their different linguistic and cultural communities inhabit a European context – multi-lingual, multi-cultural, multi-

---

8 *The Democratic Intellect*, George Davie, Edinburgh University Press, 1961, p. 7.

national. More and more, education both at university and pre-university levels is having to take account of other European education systems with their different structures, standards and syllabuses. Most of us are familiar with ERASMUS and ECTS exchanges; these are only a beginning. Harmonisation of education qualifications is a real goal being worked towards, slowly as yet but with increasing urgency.

For schools in Scotland, the most relevant development in this area so far has been in a set of proposals for a revision of the upper level of Certification in secondary schools, known to Scottish teachers, after the chairman of the working group, as the Howie Report.[9] The Howie proposals are a contentious issue in Scottish education; they have aroused both support and bitter opposition, and it would only be realistic to recognise that they are unlikely to be implemented as they stand. There are too many difficulties about getting a proper level of funding, about overcoming fears that the proposals will create a divided system after years of trying to create a unified one, about the implications for teachers' work-loads in a period of already intolerable stresses. The significance of the Howie recommendations resides not in the way they in themselves will change Scottish educational organisation, but in the fact that they were based upon a new way of looking at Scottish education. Nobody will be able to go back to the old viewpoint.

The first main thing that Howie did was to look at Scottish education in the upper secondary levels within a European context, comparing the structures of curriculum and examination in Scotland with other European countries. For example, the document makes specific reference to the systems in France, Germany, Denmark, and The Netherlands, as well as general reference to Continental practices and European Community memoranda on higher education. The most obvious debt to the European context is the controversial recommendation for a Scottish Baccalaureate (SCOTBAC) as the upper level of a two-tier examination system. Whatever the fate of this suggestion, the principle is well established of looking at Scottish education as a European system rather than as a sub-division of an Anglocentric UK system.

The second significant thing done by Howie was to take some account of Scottish culture, language and literature within the organisation of the curriculum. To those from beyond the British Isles, it may be astonishing that this is not already the case. I can assure you that in some quarters within Scottish politics and administration, teaching Scottish culture, history and literature is regarded as a dangerous novelty. What Howie has done, going further than earlier Government-inspired documents, is to confirm the validity of Scottish language and literature within the traditionally termed 'English' curriculum. The same line has been taken in a parallel set of proposals for education in the age-range 5–14.

So where do Medieval and Renaissance Scottish literature stand in this educational context? I think that for the first time in centuries they are at a

---

9 *Upper Secondary Education in Scotland*, Scottish Office Education Department, HMSO, 1992.

window of major opportunity, which should be boldly opened. In a European sense, the older Scottish literature and the language in which it was written are memorials of Scotland's European Age, memoirs of a European Scotland coexisting with its neighbours to the east and south, the least parochial and most international corpus of Scottish writing, needing to be interpreted and taught as such. In the Scottish sense, this language and literature is the most native and indigenous, coming from a time of Scottish independence and self-validated confidence. These are the messages of Dame Remembrance to the Dreamer and John the Commounweill, that his country and its culture are individual plants with roots in the soil of Europe and that beautiful blossoms and rich fruits have grown on them. John the Commounweill sorely needs these messages. For nearly three hundred years he has taken a terrible battering at the hands of Scottish education. His land, both literally and metaphorically, has been taken out of his ownership; his history has been separated from him and either misrepresented or left untaught; his language, the authentic language of the Scottish kingdom, has been devalued, depreciated, betrayed by the aristocracy, the middle classes and the professions, split into increasingly divergent dialects, excluded from the high-status activities of society and demeaned in the media and in art.

Yet to say that an opportunity for expansion and encouragement exists to be exploited, that something can be done now is not the same as saying it is possible to do it. For many teachers, the task is frankly impossible, at least in the short term. Whatever the will to perform may be, the means to perform are largely lacking. Four years ago, I wrote a document for the Glasgow University M. Phil. distance-learning degree in Scottish Literature on the Classroom Applications of Medieval and Renaiisance Literature.[10] Looking back at it, I am struck again by how much it is concerned with creating the conditions and materials for teaching rather than with the specific teaching itself. Nothing has changed. The problems are the same; the deficiencies of provision still exist.

To illustrate these matters, let me take as a conclusion to this paper a teaching example from the literature. And since I have been referring to it throughout, let that example be 'The Dreme of Schir David Lyndesay'.

Immediately, the question arises, is this example a suitable one for consideration? Will this poem in fact be one that can be used in the classroom? This is not something to be judged hastily on very superficial criteria: too long, language too obscure, antiquated references – these are possible immediate reactions. Yet if these were our determining criteria, then no major poem from before the twentieth century would ever be taught. Well, you may say, that is virtually the position in schools as it is. So what's new? We have to overcome the tendency towards too simplistic judgements about what can or cannot be taught in the present school situation. Matters of length or language difficulty or social/historical context of a text are the most typical problems to which solutions need to be found in planning the teaching of a new text. The question of length is

---

10 *M. Phil. in Scottish Literature: Paper 1 (Medieval and Renaissance Literature, 1375–1625) Classroom Applications*, University of Glasgow, Department of Scottish Literature.

always a subjective matter: in the case of 'The Dreme' with a total length of 1036 lines, I would look for sections to concentrate on in detail, sections to skim over quickly, and sections to cut completely in favour of a brief prose summary. A variable pace and depth of treatment is usually the answer to the length problem. In the cases of both language and contextual references, I would be trying to make the poem text more user-friendly by presenting it in a format that both allows the provision of helpful teacher's notes and the insertion of pupils' notes close to relevant sections of text.

The real criteria for selection of an Older Scots text for secondary classroom teaching are based on the desirability of setting up an imaginative and intellectual meeting between the pupils and the text with resulting benefit to both. Taking the latter first, the benefit to the text is a real one: a text that does not merely exist within the covers of a scholarly collection but lies within the memories of people within society, having been encountered by them through an active reading and thinking process so that it is a part of their experience of life – such a text can be said to be living and fulfilling its author's purposes. The benefit to the pupil must always be indefinable. Who can say what anything that we have taught to others ultimately means to them? All that we can do as teachers is to maximise the chances of any text's survival within the chancy environment of another person's consciousness. And so we play up its *positive characteristics*, whether they be capacities for enjoyment like a good story, humour, excitement, escapism and romance, links with the pupils' own locality, interesting ideas and inventive language; we tap and encourage the pupils' *motivation* to read the text, perhaps by arousing curiosity about the text and its world, stimulating the desire to find out the answers to questions both explicit and implicit within the text, and establishing the relevance of the text to the pupils' lives today in a very different world; and we create *contexts* for the teaching of the text that will support and facilitate the pupils' experiencing of it.

In this task of presenting the text in the most positive and active way, with the maximum amount going for it in terms of possible pupil interest and motivation, it is no use relying on the conventional teacher-dominated and authority-orientated methods of teaching. It is a false assumption that traditional material is best taught by traditional methods. The exploration of a poem like 'The Dreme' is best undertaken as a co-operative venture between teacher and student, between student and student, and the methods that place emphasis on group discussion, the exchange of opinions and information, the agreed allocation of tasks, and an accepted responsibility for reporting on findings, are the methods that will involve the student most fully. Whether or not the findings fully accord with the teacher's views is not the most important result. Equally the aids to teaching and learning cannot be merely those of a past age. Just as modern technology has found a welcome place within university research and increasingly within university teaching, so it is appropriate to give it its place within the school situation. The audio-cassette recorder and the video-recorder and camera, along with the micro-computer and the word-processor, have as much to do with the study of Medieval and

Renaissance Scottish literature as they have with the newest science kids on the academic block.

In conclusion, it seems to me that, although the study within secondary schools of medieval and Renaissance Scottish literature has been largely neglected within the matrix of educational attitudes and expectations created in Scotland during the British Interlude, the developing European dimension in education is creating a new opportunity for it. Nobody who knows anything about this older literature of Scotland can doubt that it says much to us today both explicitly and implicitly about Scotland as one of the constituent elements in Christendom, the European Community of the past. We need to acknowledge publicly as teachers that, as part of the collective cultural memory of Scotland, it has an important part to play in current education. It can enable the Scots of the New European Community of the present and the future to see their potential place within that community and it can validate their aspirations to that place. After his dream of Dame Remembrance and John the Commounweill and what they have shown him, the Dreamer is startled awake by a ship arriving at anchor with the noises of cannon salutes and shouts of sailors and the taking in of sail; reality has arrived, and the Dreamer has to exchange his vision for action, translating it into a programme for the king to consider. In the same way, teachers in Scotland have to devise the programme that will transmit the Scottish and European vision in literature to their students.

The Dreme of Schir David Lyndsay

Division of text into sections for variable levels of study.
Sections marked with * are for detailed reading and study.

1. *The Epistil (11. 1–56): reading and discussion to establish Lindsay's relationship with the king.
2. *The Prolog (11. 57–147): close reading and discussion to establish situation of poem and mixture of realism and allegory.
3. *Dame Remembrance (11. 148–163): close reading to identify Remembrance as guide.
4. Hell (11. 164–336): very rapid reading to establish the types of sinners in damnation, with particular attacks on church corruption, tyrannical government, sexual immorality and dishonest dealing.
5. Purgatory and Limbo (11. 337–364): very rapid reading to complete picture of unredeemed afterlife.
6. Elements and Planetary Spheres (11. 365–511): rapid reading to give picture of medieval cosmos.
7. Heaven (11. 512–616): very rapid reading to establish the hierarchy of heaven.
8. Earth (11. 617–756): rapid survey to establish the nature of the earth and its continents, especially Europe.
9. *Paradise (Eden) (11. 757–784): close reading to confirm conventional nature of the description.
10. *Scotland and its problems (11. 785–917): close reading and discussion of the picture presented of Scotland and its condition.

11. *Complaynt (ll. 918–1014): close reading and discussion to analyse the information.
12. *Conclusion (ll. 1015–1036): Close reading to round off work on poem.

Note: Since this paper was delivered, the Howie Report recommendations have been rejected by the teaching profession and the Government. They have been replaced by Higher Still developments, which give an increased place in the curriculum to Scottish Language & Literature but have nothing to say about a 'European Scotland'.

A.MacG.

JOHN CORBETT

36.   *Teaching Older Scots . . . as a Foreign Language?*

What is 'TOSFL'?

Over the past decade, I have spent much of my time as a teacher of English as a Foreign Language (EFL) to overseas students, both here in Scotland and elsewhere. My intention today is to combine two interests by considering the teaching of Older Scots from the point of view of EFL methodology – the time alloted is brief and I am aware that I can hardly do justice to both subjects. I should also state here that the activities described in this paper are largely speculative – I have introduced some Older (and Modern) Scots poetry in some classes, but not systematically. However, the activities I shall focus on are well-established in EFL, and I believe they could be adapted profitably to the teaching of Older Scots, both to natives of Scotland, and others, if the spirit were willing.

Why should the spirit be willing? In his introduction to Glasgow University's excellent M. Phil Unit on Classroom Applications of Medieval and Renaissance Literature, MacGillivray writes that:

> Undoubtedly, in dealing with older Scottish texts, the major stumbling block, both for teachers and pupils, will be the nature of the language in which texts were written. Middle Scots and, to a lesser extent, Renaissance Scots are forms of the language that are bound to present initially severe difficulties to readers who, all too often, claim to have problems with the varieties of Modern Scots that they encounter.[1]

The Unit goes on to advise teachers on a variety of ways to reduce these difficulties for Scottish teachers and pupils (eg using local associations, annotating and illustrating texts, etc.). The activities I shall suggest might be seen as complementary to those in the M. Phil Unit; that is, they are intended to increase familiarity with and fluency in the target variety, they are not primarily intended to increase knowledge *about* Older Scots.

Which aspects of EFL methodology, then, might be most usefully adapted to Teaching Older Scots as a Foreign Language (hereafter TOSFL)? First of all, EFL focuses on needs. What does the learner need to do in the target variety? In the case of Older Scots, the primary purpose in learning the language is presumably to gain access to the written literature. I shall therefore concentrate

---

1 A. MacGillivray, *M. Phil in Scottish Literature Paper 1: Medieval and Renaissance Literature 1375–1625: Unit 1F: Classroom Applications* Dept of Scottish Literature, University of Glasgow, c 1988 p. 13.

on the acquisition of second language reading skills. I should also note here that research into reading in a second language is largely limited to comprehension – my own feeling is that literary analysis and the formulation of a literary response are quite separate skills, and I do not wish to go into them here. I would simply claim that reasonably fluent reading is a prerequisite to further analysis, and that if learners can read fluently then the stumbling block to appreciation that MacGillivray notes will be greatly reduced. But what do we do when we read in a second language?

Second language reading

There is no perfect and universally-agreed model of reading in a first or second language. However, research over the past thirty years has evolved a useful if rough model which, in second language reading research, is particularly associated with Patricia Carrell. I shall summarise her views, and suggest activities in line with her suggestions for classroom practice, using the poetry of William Dunbar as a source of illustrative material. Carrell's model of reading is that of an interactive activity which involves two simultaneous processes: top-down and bottom-up.[2]

Top-down processing

Meaning is not something which resides in a text to be decoded by a reader. Rather, a fluent reader comes to a text with a set of expectations and a reserve of background knowledge. In technical terms the mental structures of background knowledge are *schemata*, and these schemata are used by readers to *create* meaning in interaction with a text. Reading, according to this model, is a 'psycholinguistic guessing game':[3] the reader creates meaning in conjunction with the text by making hypotheses and inferences, which are confirmed or denied by checking with the text. If the reader is thrown a decontextualised text which is perfectly coherent but written in such a way as to frustrate the reader's access to schemata, then it can be very difficult even for a native speaker to comprehend, as a famous experiment, investigating the contextual prerequisites for understanding, has shown.[4] Try reading one of the experimental texts and see how long it takes for you to understand what it is about:

> A newspaper is better than a magazine. A seashore is a better place than the street. At first it is better to run than to walk. You may have to try several times. It takes some skill, but it's easy to learn. Even young children can enjoy

---

2 See, for example, P. Carrell, 'The Effects of Rhetorical Organization on ESL Readers' *TESOL Quarterly* 18:3 (1984).
3 K.S. Goodman, 'Reading: A Psycholinguistic Guessing Game' in H. Singer and R. B. Ruddell, eds. *Theoretical Models and Processes in Reading* (Newark: International Reading Association, 1970).
4 J.D. Bransford and M.K. Johnson, 'Contextual Prerequisites for Understanding: some investigations of Comprehension and Recall' *Journal of Verbal Learning and Verbal Behaviour* 11 (1972) pp. 717–26.

it. Once successful, complications are minimal. Birds seldom get too close. Rain, however, soaks in very fast. Too many people doing the same thing can also cause problems. One needs lots of room. If there are no complications, it can be very peaceful. A rock will serve as an anchor. If things break loose, however, you will not get a second chance.[5]

The answer is at the end of this paper. If you found this modern English text difficult to understand, then you will appreciate how a lack of background information – or schemata – makes the comprehension of an older text more difficult. One of the tasks facing teachers of Older Scots texts, then is to supply learners with enough background information to facilitate reading comprehension. But what exactly do we mean by background information and how best can it be 'supplied'?

Various types of schemata have been suggested. One important type are *formal schemata* or knowledge of the generic structure of texts, from sports reports to scientific journal articles to medieval fables or the legends of saints' lives. Research suggests that ignorance of formal schemata or the disruption of formal schemata affects the recall of texts – texts which conform to known forms are easier to remember.[6] Similar findings hold for *content schemata*, or the reader's knowledge about the topic – whether microcomputers, the sexual failings of Scottish husbands, or the status and perception of widows in sixteenth-century society and literature. Again, the more you know about the topic of a text before you read it, the more you are able to remember about that text at a later date. Or in the words of Carrell:

> ... the implicit cultural content knowledge presupposed by a text interacts with the reader's own cultural background knowledge of content to make texts whose content is based on one's own culture easier to read and understand than syntactically and rhetorically equivalent texts based on a less familiar, more distant culture.[7]

The relevance of these points should be clear to those teachers among us who are faced with the problem of increasing the accessibility of texts whose form and content is distanced, if not geographically, then temporally. To increase the learner's fluency, then, one of the teacher's jobs is to extend the student's formal and content schemata to embrace the conventions and topics of older Scots poetry.

Classroom implications

The point I wish to make is that it might not be enough to fill in the gaps in students' knowledge by *explanation*. No doubt it helps, but there may be other

---

5 This text is also discussed in B. Mikulecky *A Short Course in Teaching Reading Skills* (Reading, Mass: Addison-Wesley, 1990) pp 1–2.
6 eg Carrell, *op.cit*.
7 P. Carrell *Interactive Approaches to Second Language Reading* (Cambridge: CUP, 1988) p. 80.

strategies available to help students *experience* formal and content schemata, and so store and access them more efficiently.

TEFL has long made the distinction between *knowledge* about language and language *skills*. The former is learned by explanation, the latter are acquired through language use. At the heart of current EFL methodology is the concept of *tasks*, that is, goal-directed activities designed to promote language acquisition through the *use* of target structures, functions, lexis and so on. Task-based learning is not, of course, exclusive to EFL: similar tasks are evident in some of the materials being produced for teaching literature in schools.[8] So what kind of *tasks* might promote the acquisition of the kind of formal and content schemata required by TOSFL?

Below I have listed some suggestions to encourage top-down processing. None is particularly original; all are presently used in EFL. It has to be said that the learning environment I envisage for these activities is the school or continuing education classroom, where time is perhaps in greater supply than in the university lecture or seminar. And I stress that I am not saying that such activities should replace academic work into the nature of Older Scots – I am simply proposing some supplementary activities directed at those readers whose interest may be more of a general than a specialist nature, at least initially.

Classroom activities: top-down processing

1. Present texts in groups related by topic and/or form. Topic-related texts may bridge the time-gap between present and past. For example I have slipped Dunbar into an advanced EFL lesson on religious poetry by comparing different poets' treatment of Easter. Assuming students are aware of the crucifixion story (not always a valid assumption), we can set the task of comparing the presentation of Christ and the positioning of the speaker/reader in a range of poems. (Many anthologies, of course, already do this to a certain extent; as teachers we can point up areas of comparison and contrast.)
2. Alan MacGillivray, as I have noted, suggests the illustration of certain poems. This task (known in EFL jargon as information transfer) might be adapted for top-down processing. A general discussion of the seven deadly sins might be followed by a drawing of their dance *before* the poem is read. Learners' visual portrayal can then be matched up with Dunbar's verbal version.
3. A related task might be adapted from Zamel.[9] She recommends that students be encouraged to *write* their own generic texts as part of a strategy to equip them to be better *readers*. The idea again is that by requiring students to come to grips with the production of a generic text, they will better acquire schemata with which to process further examples. If we apply this logic to the conclusion of 'The Tretis of the Tua Mariit Wemen and the Wedo', we

---

8 E.g. R. Little, P. Redsell and E. Wilcock, *GCSE Contexts* (Oxford: Heinemann, 1989).
9 V. Zamel 'Writing One's Way into Reading' *TESOL Quarterly* 26:3 (1992) pp 463–86.

may ask students to compose a sermon, or a mock sermon, presenting the life of a public figure (eg Madonna) as if it were the life of a saint. This task would be complicated by the requirement of producing it according to a certain format (see Appendix 1; cf Ross[10]). Students could then compare their own handling of a generic form with Dunbar's.

4. As readers become familiarised with texts written in novel forms about culturally distanced topics, we can explicitly encourage the relation of new texts to old by asking students to *preview* key concepts and *predict* form and content accordingly. So, for example, having introduced Dunbar's poem on the resurrection by comparing it with Tom Leonard's poem on the crucifixion and George Herbert's poem, 'Easter wings', we could ask students to predict the form and content of (a) Dunbar's poem on the nativity and (b) his hymn to the Virgin. We could then ask why the nativity poem is a closer match to the resurrection poem than to the invocation to Mary.

5. Finally, MacGillivray suggests that teachers reading texts aloud can help convey content and tone to students. A complementary activity, favoured at the moment in second language reading and writing research, is the use of *think-aloud protocols*. Very briefly, training in think-aloud protocols involves readers verbalising *everything that comes to mind* while reading or writing a text. Think aloud activities were initially devised to give access (however indirect) to the cognitive strategies involved in reading. However, teachers quickly became aware that continued use of such strategies, and class discussion of the records (protocols) they produce, both help to improve learners' reading skills. A detailed guide to setting up a small-scale think-aloud project is given by Rankin.[11]

Bottom-up processing

I have already noted that reading is currently viewed as an interactive process. It is interactive in two senses: first, the reader interacts with the text to create meaning. Secondly, two simultaneous types of processing interact: top-down (the accessing of schemata) and bottom-up (the sampling of input from the text to confirm or reject one's hypotheses and expectations).

It is important to stress that these two types of processing are both interactive *and* simultaneous. Language is very difficult to process without a familiar context, as we have seen; equally, it is well nigh impossible to confirm or deny one's textual expectations if the words on the page are incomprehensible. Fluent reading for comprehension requires understanding of enough of the text to confirm or deny and modify the expectations we have of it.

Several points need to be made here. First, to the horror, perhaps, of the literary critic and stylistician, we do not need to understand every word in the

---

10 I.S. Ross, *William Dunbar* (Leiden: Brill, 1981) p. 227.
11 J.M. Rankin, 'Designing Think-Aloud Studies in ESL Reading' *Reading in a Foreign Language* 4:2 (1988) pp 119–32.

text. Everyday fast, fluent reading for comprehension involves *sampling* from texts. Readers slow down and read every word only when their hypotheses need to be revised, and perhaps not even then. Those branches of analysis and criticism that lay stress on textual patterning will of course dissect the smallest detail of a poem, and legitimately, but I am not here concerned with these extended skills. I am only here concerned with reading for comprehension.

Secondly, I am making the assumption that most readers who come to Older Scots for the first time are nevertheless proficient in a cognate tongue, Modern English. I think this will also be true of those whose knowledge of English is as a foreign language — in my limited experience of EFL students taking on Older Scots, the students are intermediate level and higher in terms of English language proficiency.

In other words, I am assuming that those who are learning Older Scots 'as a foreign language' will already have an excellent grasp of the principles guiding the syntax. Activities could be designed to further their awareness of the peculiarities of this particular variety, but I shall confine myself here to a consideration of probably a much greater source of difficulty: Older Scots vocabulary.

Given a high degree of competence in English syntax, the learner's bottom-up processing abilities will hinge largely on their facility in recognising words and phrases. This recognition should be as near to automatic as possible. What does TOSFL have to tell us about the acquisition of vocabulary?

Vocabulary

Traditionally vocabulary has been presented in second language textbooks as lists of items to be memorised. In literature anthologies, obscure words are glossed, either on the same page or at the well-thumbed end of the book. The learning strategy in each case is implicit and identical: translate and memorise.

Recent research into vocabulary acquisition in a second language has questioned the traditional approach, and supplemented it with a range of tasks which, it must be said, owe a lot to new technology and new approaches to lexicography. With the increasing accessibility of machine-readable text, and computer concordancing programmes, and such excellent reference books as the *Concise Scots Dictionary* and *The Scots Thesaurus*, there is little reason why such tasks should not also be applied to Older Scots in the classroom.

What is the pedagogical purpose of vocabulary tasks? They should promote knowledge of a lexical item on a variety of levels; for example:

— the frequency of the item in the target language
— the register of the item
— semantic collocation and syntactic colligation
— morphology
— semantic denotation and connotation
— how sound relates to spelling

— how the target item maps onto items available in the 'mother tongue' (eg. when Dunbar uses 'lusti' in the phrase 'moste lusti branche of our linnage', how does it compare with most modern English or Modern Scots uses of 'lusty'?)[12]

Knowledge about all these aspects of the vocabulary of the target language (here, Older Scots) may not always be recoverable (we may not know the exact denotation of 'wallie gowdye' in 'In secreit place' although we can have little doubt about the function of the phrase). But for many items, simple tasks can be devised to encourage lexical processing at a deeper level than rote memorisation, and, incidentally, to show some of the major concerns in a corpus of texts.

Classroom Activities: Bottom-up processing

The activities listed below suggest ways of improving bottom-up processing, here mainly by increasing familiarisation with vocabulary.

1. If available, computers and machine-readable texts can be used in a variety of ways. Zettersten suggests the use of available software for the kind of gap-filling vocabulary exercise that computers seem somehow to charge with an eroticism denied traditional book formats.[13] The Glasgow University STELLA programme also uses hypertext to give students ready access to glossaries and textual commentary. Computer concordances can be employed (1) to gain easy access to the most frequent items in a corpus of texts, (2) to show patterns of occurrence of lexical and grammatical items. Such displays can be made the basis of comparative tasks, eg:

    — take a certain number of the most frequent lexical items in a corpus of Dunbar's poems and look for patterns of meaning (eg recurring associations with light and purity may occur in celebrations of religious and/or secular love).
    — compare the most frequent lexical items of two different poets: do they reveal recurring concerns?
    — use a concordancer to compare the function of grammatical items in a corpus of Dunbar's poems with the function of a cognate item in a corpus of Modern English or Modern Scots texts. (Does, for example, the relative pronoun in Older Scots function the same way as it does in modern varieties?

2. Teachers who do not have access to such high-tech facilities can still create equally useful vocabulary tasks. A class project might involve turning a

---

12 See, for example, J. Richards, 'The Role of Vocabulary Teaching' *TESOL Quarterly* 10:1 (1976) pp. 77–90, and L. Taylor *Teaching and Learning Vocabulary* (NY: Prentice-Hall, 1990).
13 A. Zettersten, 'Teaching Middle Scots by Computer' in C. Macafee and I. Macleod, eds. *The Nuttis Schell* (Aberdeen: AUP, 1987) pp 124–30.

textbook glossary into a thesaurus. Groups could take several pages each and work on superordinate categories which then could be compared and combined with other groups' efforts. At some point in the process (preferably not the beginning) the *Scots Thesaurus* could be introduced for comparison. Vocabulary research suggests that items are better learned when 'chunked' into semantic groups. This kind of task allows the learners to determine the nature of the semantic field into which items are grouped.
3. Pre-reading vocabulary tasks can be used to familiarise learners with items and also to act as a stimulus for top-down processing. Learners might be presented with lists of items which they would be required to sort according to different criteria, eg:

   — semantic field (eg descriptions of weather/people)
   — parts of speech (using morphology as a clue)
   — illocutionary force (praise versus insult)
   — register (high, plain or low style)

   Various tasks along these lines are given in Appendix 2. Once the items have been sorted, learners might be asked to predict further characteristics of the texts in which they will be found.
4. Among a variety of stimulating tasks in their resource book,[14] Morgan and Rinvolucri suggest the use of a 'word rose'. This is simply the random listing of various items on the chalkboard. Using these items the learners (in groups) try to predict what kind of text would employ them. This type of activity would be better performed once a fair amount of vocabulary has been presented in other ways. By judicious choice of word many of the connotations of poetic texts can be previewed before the text is actually read.
5. An adaptation of the game 'Call My Bluff' (again in Morgan and Rinvolucri[15] for those who are unaware of the BBC version) is a very learner-friendly way of introducing new vocabulary.

Again, these tasks are offered as possible models for a variety of types of vocabulary exploitation. I make no claims for their originality or for the efficacy of any one task in isolation. The point that I am perhaps labouring is that there is more to vocabulary acquisition than rote memorisation and that a variety of activities are probably more effective in promoting learning. And such activities are readily accessible, already staples of foreign language teaching.

Is Older Scots a foreign language?

Which returns me to my title, where those fluent readers who sampled it to the end will have noticed a question mark. Is Older Scots a foreign language? The answer to this question is, I think, 'yes and no'.

14 M. Rinvolucri and J. Morgan, *Vocabulary* (Oxford: OUP, 1986).
15 Op.cit.

Older Scots is of course a foreign language for a learner who does not speak *any* variety of World English. Presumably one could devise a programme of instruction which would teach such a learner Older Scots without reference to Modern English. This would be difficult, for reasons I shall come to shortly, but up to a point it could be done. The learner's performance probably would not bear close resemblance to the chatter on the streets of Edinburgh from the fourteenth to the seventeenth century, but it would be such that it could cope with the literature. Still, I think most of us would regard such an exercise as eccentric: it would demand a lot of effort for a quite limited objective. However, using Scots in the EFL classroom, as I and many others have done, at least occasionally, is less eccentric than may at first seem. I have encountered few learners with no curiosity about different varieties of English, and, varieties can be temporal as well as geographical. Many teachers indeed use nonsense poems like 'Jabberwocky' sometimes to focus learners' attention on morphological features of texts, sometimes simply as a stimulus to the students' own creative narratives. Some Scots texts can be used in similar ways (indeed Macafee suggests similarities between the attractions that the modern reader finds in both Scots literature and in nonsense poetry.[16] Scots poems have an added payoff in that they actually mean something).

But is Older Scots a foreign language to contemporary Scots learners? As I have suggested, yes and no. Many of the syntactical features are shared by the two varieties. The problems are largely cultural and lexical and up to a point these can be overcome by activities such as those suggested here. However one obvious limitation is that Older Scots is no longer a *spoken* language. Full competence in a foreign language requires interaction with speakers of that language – that option is no longer open to today's learners. Interaction is restricted to the reading of literature. For this reason if for no other I would not like to be misinterpreted as advocating the revival of Older Scots as a fully-fledged language of everyday discourse. But there is absolutely no reason that I can see for students' competence in their mother tongue not to be extended to include fluent comprehension of the literary texts of a past age.

Note

The Bransford and Johnson text is about flying a kite.

Appendix 1: Further top-down activities

Writing into Reading
In the Middle Ages, a popular genre was the 'legend' or 'saint's life'. This could be presented as a sermon, following a certain structure, apparently spoken by the saint him/herself. In the concluding section of *The Tretis of the Tua Mariit Wemen and the Wedo* by William Dunbar, the poet parodies this genre by having a scandalous widow present herself to two friends as a saint-like example to be

---

16 C. Macafee, 'Dialect Vocabulary as a Source of Stylistic Effects in Scottish Literature' *Language and Style* 19:4 (1986) pp 325–37.

followed. Before reading the poem, familiarise yourself with the legend structure by doing the following activity. (This activity can be completed individually or in pairs/small groups.)

1. Think of a character (real or fictional, saintly or notorious) who might be the suitable subject of a 'legend'. For example, you might wish to write a saint's life of the actress and singer, Madonna.
2. In the words of your character, write the legend, using the following structure:

   a) invocation: ask God to inspire your legend
   b) theme: explain your most remarkable characteristic
   c) protheme: give examples of how your most remarkable characteristic determines your behaviour.
   d) division: talk about the two most important events in your life.
   e) declaration: state the reason why you should be considered a 'saint'.
   f) confirmation: give examples of your 'saintly' actions

Once you have finished, compare your 'saint's life' with that of other groups. Then read the widow's 'legend' in Dunbar's *Tretis*. Can you find the above sections in the poem?

Appendix 2: Further vocabulary activities

A. Weather or People?
Look at the word-list below. Individually or with a partner, sort the words into those describing weather and those describing people. (Use the CSD if you get stuck.) Then try to fit the words into the gaps in the stanzas below.

renownit	dirk
worthie	wight
drublie	lusti
mystie	of high parage
cluddis	haill
schouris	valyeand

a) In to thir ____ and ____ dayis
    Quhone sabill all the hevin arrayis
    With____vapouris, ____ and skyis.
    Nature all curage me denyis
    Of sangis, ballattis, and of playis.

   Quhone that the nycht dois lenthin houris
   With wind, with ____, and havy ____
   My dule spreit dois lurk for schoir
   My hart for langour dois forloir
   For laik of symmer with his flouris.

b)   ____, ryall, right reverend, and serene
       Lord, hie tryumphing in wirschip and valoure,
       Fro kyngis downe, most Cristin knight and kene,
       Most wyse, most ____, most laureat hie victour,
       Onto the sterris upheyt is thyne honour;
       In Scotland welcum be thyne Excellence
       To King, Queyne, lord, clerk, knight and servatour,
       With glorie and honour, lawde and reverence.
       Welcum, in stour most strong, incomparable knight,
       The fame of armys, and flour of vassalage;
       Welcum, in were moste ____, wyse and ____;
       Welcum, the soun of Mars of most curage;
       Welcum, most ____ branche of our linnage,
       In every realme oure scheild and our defence;
       Welcum, our tendir blude ____,
       With glorie and honour, lawde and reverence.

B. *Praise or Insult?*
Look at the word-list below. Individually or with a partner, sort the items into those which praise people, and those which insult people. (Use the CSD if you get stuck.) Then try to fit the words and phrases correctly into the stanzas below.

empryce of prys	vyle beggar	crawdoun
precious stane	victrice of vyce	coward of kynd
salvatrice	evill farit	sterne meridiane
flour delice of	rebald	mismaid monstour
paradys		

a)   Iersch brybour baird, with thy brattis,
       Cuntbittin ____ Kennedy, ____,
       ____ and dryit, as Densmen on the rattis,
       Lyk as the gleddis had on they gule snowt dynd;
       ____, ilk mone owt of thy mynd;
       Renunce, ____, thy rymyng, thow bot royis,
       Thy trechour tung hes tane ane heland strynd;
       Ane lawland ers wald mak a bettir noyis.

       b)   ____, imperatrice,
              Brycht polist ____
              ____, hiegenetrice
              Of Jhesu, lord soverayne:
              Our wys pavys fra enemys,
              Agane the feyndis trayne;
              Oratrice, mediatrice, ____,
              To God gret suffragane!

> Ave Maria, gracia plena!
> Haile, ____!
> Spyce, ____,
> That baire the gloryus grayne.

C: Levels of style

The word-list below contains items praising women. Some words and phrases are used to praise the virgin Mary; others are used by a country lover to praise his mistress. Can you distinguish the two sets of words? When you are finished, try to fit the items into the appropriate gaps in the stanzas below.

empryce of prys	kyd
bony baib	precious stane
wallie gowdye	victrice of vyce
tyrilie myrlie	crowdie mowdie
salvatrice	sterne meridiane
bony ane	flour delice of paradys

a)
> ____, imperatrice,
> Brycht polist ____
> ____, hie genetrice
> Of Jhesu, lord soverayne:
> Our wys pavys fra enemys,
> Agane the feyndis trayne;
> Oratrice, mediatrice, ____,
> To God gret suffragane!
> Ave Maria, gracia plena!
> Haile, ____!
> Spyce, ____,
> That baire the gloryus grayne.

b)
> Quod he, 'My ____, my capirculyoun
> My ____ with the ruch brylyoun,
> My tendir gyrle, my ____,
> My ____, my ____;
> Quhone that oure mouthis dois meit at ane,
> My stang dois storkyn with your towdie;
> Ye brek my hert, my————!'

D: Parts of Speech

Identify the following words as noun, adjective or verb. Then check your answers by fitting the words into the stanzas below.

matutyne   foulis   menstrale   war   purpur   begouth   bemes   stern

Ryght as the ___ of day ___ to schyne
Quhen gone to bed ___ Vesper and Lucyne,
I raise and by a rosare did me rest;
Up sprang the golden candill ___,
With clere depurit ___ cristallyne
Glading the mery ___ in thair nest;
Or Phebus was in ___ cape revest
Up raise the lark, the hevyns ___ fyne,
In May, in till a morow myrthfullest.

E. Word rose

Look at the 'word rose' given below. All of the words in the rose appear in a poem by Dunbar. In groups, discuss together the possible content of the poem.

                  almous
   discretioun   frustrat
   grugeing   threit
               huidpyk

MORNA R. FLEMING

37.   Teaching Henryson in Senior School

The Scottish secondary school takes pupils aged around 12 years who have already completed seven years of primary schooling, and provides four more years of compulsory schooling to the leaving age at 16. My concern in this paper is with those students who opt to stay on for a further one or two years, studying towards Higher Still qualifications, Higher at the end of fifth year, and Advanced Higher (roughly equivalent to the A Level in England) at the end of the sixth year. This paper takes the form of a plea to teachers of English to expand the provision of Scottish literature, with detailed suggestions on how *The Fables* and *The Testament of Cresseid* might be presented to these senior students. It has to be admitted that there is a certain resistance to studying medieval texts among students and teachers, and its introduction has to be handled with care, to prevent passive resistance becoming active rebellion.

Why study medieval texts?

I find this question surprisingly easy to answer. The inclusion of older Scottish texts in the syllabus for the certificate of Sixth Year Studies (CSYS) – the course will be replaced by Advanced Higher from 2002 – attests their importance in informing an understanding of how Scottish culture has developed over the centuries and shows the essential difference from *English* literature. Interestingly, Henryson has appeared for several years as one of the writers whose works may be studied in the Poetry section of the CSYS Literature paper, which sets him in company with Chaucer, Donne, Coleridge, Clare, Morgan, Heaney and Dylan Thomas, and is not one of the specifically Scottish writers set in a further section of the paper.

Study of Henryson's *Fables* and *The Testament of Cresseid* also shows the reader that the characters therein described are essentially unchanged through time; the same preoccupations exercise their minds; the same divisions exist between the haves and have-nots; the same injustices and oppressions bear down on the most powerless in society; there is the same need for a champion. What tends to surprise students coming to Henryson for the first time is his modernity in outlook, his concern for the poor and the downtrodden, man's essential compassion for his fellow man. There is nothing old-fashioned about a fabulist pointing out the failings of his fellows and attempting to right wrongs – is not this only a difference in form from what political cartoonists and satirists do in our times? Henryson's role can be seen as similar to that adopted in our days by political and environmental activists, all devoted to the cause of improving the lot of humanity in general. Where Henryson differs from present-day polemicists, of course, is that his activism is theologically rather than politically grounded, although it is not difficult to find what today would be seen as politically radical thought in some of the *Fables*. Although in our essentially non-religious society, the idea of looking towards a reward in the afterlife for sufferings undergone in the present is unsatisfactory, this is a difference of outlook rather than of essence. Criticism of injustice and wrong-doing on the part of the politically and economically powerful is a perennial activity among right-thinking people of whatever political or religious persuasion, and it is not difficult to situate Henryson within this continuing tradition.

Another important reason for studying the works of Henryson in particular is that he lived and worked for at least part of his life in Dunfermline, the area where I teach. As the 'local' poet, he can be seen as having something to say about Dunfermline in the days when it was a centre of culture as well as of religion. If 'The Ballad of Sir Patrick Spens' is considered particularly appropriate for pupils in this area, as its hero was a local man, how much more so is Henryson's poetry, which is firmly grounded in the Dunfermline of the last years of the fifteenth century and gives us a picture of what the town and the surrounding country were like at that time. In fact, study of old maps and records shows that the plan of the centre of Dunfermline is essentially unchanged since Henryson walked its streets, and it is fairly easy to establish a town map of the period where only the names of the streets may have changed. It may even be possible to identify the leper hospital where Henryson imagined Cresseid being taken after her terrible judgement. A walk through the centre of Dunfermline, noting the remains of the Abbey Wall on the way to the well-preserved Abbey itself with the ruins of the Palace alongside, can situate Henryson's writings in a tangible space. It does no harm to bring in allusions from other media, such as the film of Umberto Eco's *The Name of the Rose*, or music of the period, now available in John Purser's excellent *The Music of Scotland*, to enable students to recreate in their minds the world of a medieval monastery town.

Students who have studied Henryson in past years have said that they found some kind of general background very useful in enabling them to situate the writing in context, and to make them think about the essential differences between medieval life and the present. The lives of ordinary people whether in town or country can be illustrated by reference to 'The Two Mice' and 'The Preaching of the Swallow', both of which recreate a vivid picture of the absolute dependence of all people on the vagaries of the weather and the produce of the fields for their sustenance. It can be pointed out that this kind of urban dependence on the rural economy has emerged in the former Soviet Union with the collapse of the communist system and the collective farm economy. The medieval world is not so far away after all.

How can students be given the capability to deal with a language and a belief system which are essentially foreign?

This question is rather more difficult, and requires a good deal more forward planning if the work studied is to give enjoyment and a wider outlook. The language is difficult, much more so in my own students' experience than is the language of Chaucer, which they tend to study at the same time. For this reason, anything which can alleviate the problems is to be welcomed, which includes editions in which editors have lightly modernised and regularised the spelling and orthography without interfering with the texts themselves. My past practice has been to use Denton Fox's 1987 edition of Henryson, as that was the edition I had been taught from, but students have found it rather too scholarly for their needs, and, as glossary and notes are all appended at the end of the book, it is necessary to flick back and forward continually to understand the text. As students are concentrating on the narratives themselves, glosses of the language and explanation of difficult points must be as immediate, accessible and straightforward as possible. For this reason, I have decided that future lessons will be based on Priscilla Bawcutt and Felicity Riddy's *Selected Poems of Henryson & Dunbar* (Scottish Academic Press, 1992) which, as the editors state in their introductory note, provides 'a selection of poems that will show the range, variety and characteristic strength of both poets' and makes the poems 'intelligible to the non-specialist'. This edition's extensive glossary on each page makes it much easier for the apprentice medievalist to read straight through the poems, and, although the existence of notes could be more clearly signalled within the text, it is for the teacher to ensure that students are directed not only to the notes at the back of this edition, but also to the fuller notes in Fox.

A further possible advantage of this edition is that, by including only six of the *Fables* plus the Prologue, it solves the problem of which fables to miss out. The CSYS requirement is for study of *The Testament of Cresseid* and *five* of the *Fables*, and the choice of fables is fraught with difficulty. Bawcutt and Riddy's selection of 'The Prologue', 'The Cock and the Jasp', 'The Two Mice', 'The Cock and the Fox', 'The Lion and the Mouse', 'The Preaching of the Swallow' and 'The Fox, the Wolf and the Cadger' gives a reasonable selection from the purely Aesopian tradition, the Chaucerian beast-epic, and the beast-fable in the Roman de Renart tradition, allowing students to appreciate the range and intention of Henryson in his moral writings. Ideally, one would hope that students would be interested enough to read all thirteen fables eventually, but realistically it has to be acknowledged that pressure of time makes this rather unlikely. There is nothing to prevent the teacher presenting additional fables in the form of practical criticism exercises, which I have done with reasonable success with 'The Sheip and the Dog' and 'The Wolf and the Lamb', as I thought that they were particularly illustrative of one of Henryson's main preoccupations: the unjust oppression of the poor and powerless by the avaricious, or by trickster lawyers, or by powerful landlords to whom they are beholden.

While previous generations might have been familiar with the Fables of Aesop in English, and some might have studied the French versions of La Fontaine, and the lucky few might have managed to obtain a copy of the Fables in Modern Scots before the publisher went out of business, it cannot be taken as read that the storylines will be known to present-day students. All my students have said that they found it useful to have the original version of the fable to hand before reading Henryson's version, so that the basic storyline was known, and Henryson's development and particular application could then be better appreciated. There are numerous editions of Aesop available, and what will strike students comparing Aesop and Henryson is the wealth of additional detail and cunning characterisation which can be found in the Scots versions, as well as the subtly different moral values in places.

Students unanimously agreed that hearing the fables read aloud greatly enhanced their understanding, and made them more willing to attempt readings and interpretations for themselves, and in any case, Henryson intended them to be 'plesand . . . unto the *eir* of man' (Prologue, 4) (emphasis mine). Whether the readings are authentic in terms of pronunciation I do not consider of vital moment, as understanding and appreciation are paramount, but it is useful for students to have access to different voices reading, and the Scotsoun cassette of Henryson's poems provides an alternative voice to that of the teacher. I should like at some stage to investigate the possibility of a dramatised reading of some of the *Fables*, preferably exploiting the considerable talents of Scottish actors, as yet another way of bringing the *Fables* to dramatic life.

As far as work on the *Fables* is concerned, the Scottish Qualifications Authority demands a high level of *personal* response from students, which means that they will have to explore their own reactions to the chosen tales rather than simply relying on the teacher's or editor's views. However, as this type of text is so different from anything that has been tackled before, most students feel happier with a couple of introductory lectures which show them how to approach the *Fables*, and Bawcutt and Riddy's selection allows this to be achieved in a logical fashion.

Close study of the 'Prologue', makes clear Henryson's didactic purpose: to instruct through pleasure: 'with sad materis sum merines to ming' (26) by showing men in their true state 'like to beistis in conditioun' (49). It also brings into play the medieval notion of authority in the references to Aesop and Gualterus Anglicus, and it introduces the *excusatio topos*, knowledge of both of which students will need for further study of the texts.

The first fable, 'The Cock and the Jasp', is a beautiful example of Henryson's method, mingling the Cok's desire for food, a natural animal characteristic, with his very human recognition of his place in the scheme of things, and his lowly status, unworthy of the jewel he finds. Students misread, as I did on first reading, the Cock's arguments, and are made more appreciative of Henryson's method of reaching readers of all levels of education and apprehension, as they have had to have the true meaning explained to them. The jasp of understanding and wisdom is laid there for them to pick up as they read on in the *Fables*.

Confidence is restored in reading 'The Two Mice', partly because the narrative itself is so familiar to them, but also because the *Moralitas* is more 'conventional', in terms of being what was expected. However, the note of caution is reinforced in the description of both mice as 'pykeris' who live 'in uther mennis skaith' (167). The rural mouse has a difficult life, finding her food 'quhyle under busk and breir,/Quhilis in the corne' (166–7) and '. . . into the wynter tyde/Had hunger, cauld and tholit grit distres' (169–70) to such an extent that a visit by her burgess sister to the seat of such privation is seen as a pilgrimage. Country-dwellers reading Henryson would picture vividly the realities of such a precarious existence.

What is also shown in this fable is the description of animals in very human terms, which is illustrated beautifully in the rather comical but touching scene when the two mice greet each other:

> The hartlie joy God geve ye had sene
> Beis kithit quhen that thir sisteris met.
> And grit kyndnes wes schawin thame betwene,
> For quhylis thay leuch, and quhylis for joy thay gret,
> Quhylis kissit sweit, quhylis in armis plet; (190–4)

The humour continues in the disparagement of the wholesome food offered and the courtly air of superiority adopted by the burgess mouse towards her lowlier sister, who, however, maintains her down-to-earth common sense in a series of proverbial sayings until unable to resist her sister's offer of an exchange visit to see how the other half lives.

But this kindly humour of the narrator has a darker edge as seen in the cat's torture of the mouse discovered in the pantry cat-and-mouse game, which in its realism presents a terrifying picture:

> Fra fute to fute he kest hir to and fra,
> Quhylis up, quhylis doun, als cant as ony kid.
> Quhylis wald he lat hir rin under the stra,
> Quhylis wald he wink, and play with hir buk heid. (330–3)

The *moralitas* in this tale points to one of Henryson's main preoccupations: that security even in poverty is preferable to the twists of fate that can overcome the aspiring. The *Moralitas* here uses a different stanza form, eight lines against the usual seven, and rhyming *ababbcbc* with refrain 'with small possessioun', both form and refrain recalling 'The Abbey Walk', which similarly counsels satisfaction with one's lot in life, whatever it be.

Students are now seeing the humour in the *Fables* and, perhaps, are taking in Henryson's teachings exactly as he intended, thinking about his moral values as they read on. The very dramatic narrative will help them to picture the events depicted and carefully structured worksheets will enable them to home in on the important points of the moral questions.

Since students will usually be studying Chaucer at the same time, the next fable, 'The Cock and the Fox', could be a useful point of comparison. The very different forms used by the two writers, and the very different purposes in their writing could prove illuminating and useful not only for a reading of this fable but also for *The Testament of Cresseid*.

We have now read the Prologue and the first three fables, but Bawcutt and Riddy's selection, clearly through a desire to include as wide a range as possible, omits the following two fables centred on the fox and his son, and, unfortunately, 'The Sheep and the Dog', which latter fable I consider essential for a full understanding of Henryson's feeling for the underdog (or in this case undersheep) in society. Perhaps because the *moralitas* in this fable departs from the convention, by including the sheep's complaint, it should be left until later when its unconventionality can be better appreciated, but I certainly feel it should be included at some stage.

We now move to the central fable, 'The Lion and the Mouse', in which the authority for the *Fables* is brought to life in a dream vision, shown to be living in heaven freed of his earthly disabilities and presented in a *locus amoenus* setting, which gives two more elements for the students to add to their notes on medieval rhetoric. In two further ways the fable signals its difference from the rest: it has its own prologue and is not told by the narrator of the rest of the poem, being Aesop's own unwilling telling of the tale, for as he says, 'My sone, lat be;/For quhat is it worth to tell ane fenyeit taill,/Quhen haly preiching may na thing availl?' (1388–90). Students should by this time be familiar enough with the conventional form to be alert to the differences here and to wonder what Henryson is doing in this fable. That he seems to be undermining his own *oeuvre* should not escape them, and they should now be questioning Henryson's attitude to his subject. It is probably necessary at this point to give some account of the political events which probably prompted the *moralitas*, if not the fable itself, in order to show the versatility of the fable-form in criticising all ranks of society up to and including the king. There could perhaps be some comparison between this surprisingly overt critique and the criticism of government which is found in contemporary newspapers – students would find some striking similarities in the precise criticisms levelled.

What students will find useful here for future study is an examination of the mouse's several arguments presented to the lion in her attempt to prove to him that she should not be killed, and they should remember the success of these arguments later, when reading 'The Wolf and the Lamb', where a similarly powerless creature finds powerful and theologically-backed arguments are futile against merciless jaws and teeth. Henryson's inveighing against crooked and biased courts and lawyers, seen also in the appalling 'The Sheep and the Dog', is another theme which students will remember when they come to *The Testament of Cresseid*.

'The Preaching of the Swallow' must come immediately after 'The Lion and the Mouse' as it exemplifies Aesop's complaint, that people do not listen to good advice. This fable in addition gives a beautiful introduction to the medieval world picture in terms of the divinely ordained order. Although 'The Preaching' is often seen as a very difficult fable, for students going on to study *The Testament* it is essential for full understanding. We are given an account of divine wisdom compared with 'mannis jugement' (1625) which is blinded 'lyke ane bakkis ee' (1637) with sensuality in the 'presoun corporall' (1630). That faith in divine providence is the only means of living is then exemplified in the examination of the surrounding world, from 'The firmament payntit with sternis cleir' (1657) to the basic elements 'The fyre, the air, the watter, and the ground' (1661) by way of the flowers, fish, beasts of the land, birds of the air, culminating in the last-made: man. A very Scottish account of the seasons shows the dependence on the natural world – summer and autumn are given one stanza each, with winter in a heavily-alliterated two stanzas, reflecting the extended period of cold and hardship, which, in this fable, helps to explain the susceptibility of the small birds to the fowler's snares. A clear picture of the agricultural world year round adds to students' knowledge of the times before the fable proper begins with the swallow's lesson, opening with the preacher's 'Ye sall weill knaw and wyislie understand' (1737).

Students will examine the swallow's prudence and compare it with the other birds' unconsidered replies. They will be reminded of 'The Cock and the Jasp' which similarly disparages present fulfilment of animal needs in favour of future gratification, but will see that here the danger is made manifest and birds die a horrible death despite all the swallow's attempts to save them. Coming immediately after 'The Lion and the Mouse', the darker note is inescapable – while the Cock was merely ignorant but could possibly have learnt with teaching, the small birds *have* been taught and have rejected the voice of wisdom. Henryson's attitude to his subject could be thought to be becoming more despairing, but the *Moralitas* makes clear that for *man* there is still hope. As a rational animal he can be expected to listen to reason.

This darker note continues through the remaining fables, and is exemplified in the final fable in Bawcutt and Riddy's selection, 'The Fox, the Wolf and the Cadger', a salutary warning to those whose greedy desires put them in danger of hell. Students appreciate the black comedy of the tale, where the fox easily outwits both the brutal and stupid wolf and the cadger. The fox's flattering of Chantecleir in the earlier fable will be remembered here, and students will be able to see the characteristic qualities of the fox reiterated. That the wolf's stupidity and brutality do not always cause him to lose his prize will be seen in 'The Wolf and the Wether' and 'The Wolf and the Lamb' following, which is why I consider that the latter fable at least is indispensable for a full appreciation of Henryson's moral teachings in the *Fables*.

Once the main work on the *Fables* has been completed, the themes of *The Testament* can be introduced by reviewing 'The Cock and the Jasp' and 'The Preaching of the Swallow' and adding a brief look at 'The Puddock and the Mouse'. Study of the *Fables* will have given students an idea of Henryson's world view, but before beginning detailed study of *The Testament*, it is probably a good idea to review what has been learnt about medieval morality, and add the necessary information on the doctrine of authority, the belief in planetary influence and the doctrine of the humours, and the essentially moral and didactic purpose of fiction: to praise the good and condemn the bad, and to narrate with dramatic power the stages of the spiritual ascent, supremely evident here.

Before studying *The Testament*, I had a video made of the relevant scenes from

Shakespeare's *Troilus and Cressida*, edited from the BBC production, which would give students the story up to the point where Henryson starts his narrative and the opportunity to visualise the characters and their passionate love for each other. I had also prepared Study Notes which would divide the poem into several shorter sections, setting written or discussion tasks at the end of each section. This was adapted from the Study Guide on Henryson and Dunbar that I had used while studying for the M. Phil. in Scottish Literature at Glasgow University. The idea of these Study Notes was to give students the opportunity of preparing sections of the poem before class study, and would therefore mean that we could spend class time on discussion of difficult points and on sharing opinions on interpretation rather than on reading and explanation. The suggested written assignments also required students to build up their own notes on the poem, which would be useful both as preparation for extended essays to be written at the end of the course, and for revision for the examination.

I divided *The Testament* into ten sections, according to the dramatic movement of the poem, to allow students to get to grips with what could otherwise have been rather an unwieldy text. Where appropriate, I was able to refer them to the work we had done on the *Fables*, to ensure that they could see the texts as forming part of a unified *oeuvre*.

The first section, lines 1 to 42, introduces the narrator and the setting, pointing out the pathetic fallacy of the opening, 'Ane doolie sessoun to ane cairfull dyte/ Suld correspond and be equivalent' (1–2). Students are asked to examine the character of the narrator from his own description of himself and from his actions, and note all the references to heat and cold which will be so significant for the rest of the poem.

The introduction in lines 43 to 70 of Chaucer's poem, and the putative 'uther quhair' (61) will develop the medieval notion of authority, which I presented to students in the form of an appendix to the Study Notes. From that point, the depiction of Cresseid and her wretched fate introduces notions of the role of Fortune in the lives of men, and students are required to take careful note of the numerous references to fate in this section, to line 91, and to attempt to judge the narrator's attitude to her. A preliminary comparison of the narrator and his heroine, in terms of temperament and situation will be built on as the rest of the poem is read.

As Cresseid comes to dramatic life, from line 92, her own words and actions can be examined. The multiplying references to worship of Venus, in literal and metaphorical terms, must here be examined. The narrator 'sum tyme . . . hecht obedience' (23) to Venus as 'luifis quene' (22), while Cresseid 'maid . . . sacrifice' (126) to Venus and Cupid in response to their 'devine responsaill/That [she] suld be the flour of luif in Troy' (127–8), and her father, Calchas, is a fully-fledged priest of Venus the goddess. This issue will be returned to later.

The longest and most complicated section of the poem is the dream vision from lines 141 to 344, which must be subdivided to make it more manageable. There is a need for some kind of input on the medieval notions of dreams and their import, which I have tried to simplify as much as possible, while still giving students a working vocabulary with which to discuss this part of the poem. Fortunately, the dream breaks down quite readily into three sub-sections: the catalogue of the gods, Cupid's accusation and the judgment of Saturne and Cynthia.

What will be learnt by studying the catalogue of the gods in detail is the medieval belief in the planetary influences, the powers of each of the gods, and how the balance of the universe is achieved. Students are familiar with the idea of sublunary lives being ruled by planetary influences, as most take some interest in astrology, and therefore the basic premise is not alien to them. If detailed notes are taken of these points, understanding of the whole poem, and of the narrator's interest, will be facilitated.

In addition to the content of the catalogue, the form is vitally important. Differences in diction should be noted, which will show that the most vigorous language is reserved for the gods most opposed to humanity, with heightened aureation for those more well-disposed. It is vigour rather than aureation that will win the day in this instance, which could be a pointer to the otherwise very problematic *moralitas*.

Cupid's accusation (lines 267 to 301) is clearly related to Cresseid's earlier outburst against the two gods, and should be examined in those terms, in which case the accusation of blasphemy should not come as too great a surprise. The oracular nature of the 'devine responsaill' can also be looked at in terms of the multiple references to the 'blasted spring' of the opening stanzas. What is problematic, however, is Mercurius' decision that Saturne and Cynthia, as greatest and least planets should pass judgment on Cresseid. Students will have to examine the description of Mercurius in more detail, will have to be reminded that both eloquence and medicine can be equated with duplicity and trickery (as Henryson has shown in 'Sum Practysis of Medecyne'), and come to some conclusion about why he makes such an arbitrary (but loaded) decision. Having discussed the nature and personalities of the gods concerned, students will appreciate the inevitability of the judgment.

When reading the section on the judgment (lines 302 to 343), students should be reminded of the variability of Venus as she is pictured here, like Fortune herself, and should look at the *form* of Saturn's judgment before pronouncing on its appropriateness. They will also analyse the narrator's interjection (lines 323 to 329) in terms of its content and its placing. Why is there no further outburst after Cynthia's unnecessarily cruel addition, for instance, and what relevance does a request for the Christian attributes of mercy and grace have to a pagan god? There are difficult issues here which students have to be guided through carefully, as most of them do not have a firm grounding in the basic tenets of religious teaching of *our* days, never mind of medieval times.

Once Cresseid has awoken from the dream and realised what has happened to her (line 344 onwards), the very human scenes create a determined contrast with what has just been read. Cresseid's relationship with her father is close and loving, and helps to relieve the feeling of excessive cruelty of the previous scene, before plunging us into the despair of the following.

The removal to the leper hospital can be illustrated by reference to the reconstructed map of the Dunfermline of the time, where the hospital of St Leonards could be the source for 'yone hospitall at the tounis end' (382). The association of leprosy with a lascivious life (as all venereal diseases are associated with excessive indulgence in venery) brings us back to the central role of Venus in this tragedy. We have to note that Cresseid does not see this connection yet, and has some distance to go before she reaches true self-knowledge.

The next easily-identifiable section is the Complaint (lines 407 to 469) which gives students a number of *topoi* to add to their notes on medieval rhetoric. They can clearly see the different stanza form and rhyme-scheme and may perhaps be able to hypothesise Henryson's reasons for giving her this highly aureate and stylised speech at this point in the narrative. They will note the use of the *ubi sunt topos* to heighten the sense of loss, and the true *locus amoenus* which she remembers in distinct contrast both to the setting of the whole poem and to her immediate surroundings. Her specific complaints will be examined to see what her state of mind is, and her warning to 'ladyis fair of Troy and Grece' (452) analysed in terms of its application to *all* women as opposed to women like herself.

The contrast between the heightened language and feeling of the complaint and the following section (from line 470) where Cresseid is forced to become one of the leper band is easy for students to sympathise with, and draws them deeper into the awful situation. They understand easily Cresseid's inability to follow the leper's advice to 'mak vertew of ane neid' (478). From this point, the tragedy deepens and worsens, with the long-expected introduction to Troylus in line 495 and his remembrance, provoked by the unseeing Cresseid's look, of his lost love. We are reminded once again of what has been lost, to two people now, but we are also reminded, in the memory of Cresseid's 'amorous blenking' (503) of the role of Venus in the affair, as that was one of the aspects of her description in the catalogue of the gods (226). That Troylus has also been guilty of venery is shown in his very physical reaction to the memory, but Henryson makes clear that this sensual feeling has been sublimated into generous alms-giving which is his character note, also picked up by the lepers.

Cresseid's second complaint from line 540, once she realises who has been so generous, has to be compared with the formal complaint studied earlier. The differences are striking in form and content, and the integration of the complaint with the rest of the poem, following the same stanza form, although with a refrain, shows that this complaint is part of her journey, part of the narrative movement of the poem, rather than a set-piece dramatic utterance. That the complaint deals with the present, and what has led to this present, rather than the past which is lost, is an important aspect. The sense of realism rather than stylised complaint may relate to the differences already noted in the catalogue of the gods. Her testament, which may be what gives the poem its title (a point for students to discuss at some stage) requires detailed study to see how far she has come since our first introduction to her, her self-knowledge and her ability to think of others besides herself. Her dedication of her spirit to Diana will have to be explained, as the identification of Diana with Cynthia is otherwise problematic. Remembrance here of 'The Puddock and the Mouse' will be useful in terms of the body/soul division.

We have now reached the end of Cresseid's story, but need to know how Troylus responds to the news of her death, brought to him by one of the lepers with the ruby ring. This section, from 596 to 609, presents a remarkable number of problems in its short scope, such as what Troylus means by 'Scho was untrew and wo is me thairfoir' (602) (here reference to the end of 'The Preaching of the Swallow' may help); why he erects the magnificent tomb but puts such a cold and unfeeling inscription on it; why he addresses the inscription to 'fair ladyis'. The numerous other warnings to ladies have to be seen as building into some kind of pattern, and students will have to establish what that pattern is.

The very last section of the poem, the final stanza, is generally read as the *moralitas*, as it comes out of the language of the poem, and gives an instruction again to ladies, although this time addressed as 'worthie wemen' (610) about love. This presents a great many problems for scholars as well as students, as it is not clear who is speaking, whether the original narrator or Henryson himself, and who these women would be in any case, given the predominantly male readership; the poem appears to be dismissed as a 'ballet' (610) although with a didactic aim; the syntax is problematic in lines 612 and 613; and the narrator abruptly dismisses Cresseid, almost as Troylus had in his inscription. Students should find a good deal to discuss in this single stanza, and it is hoped that they can arrive at some answers for themselves, to complete their personal response to the poem.

Students enjoy studying Henryson's works once they have gained confidence in the language, and respond sincerely to his dramatic narratives, even while finding some of the moral teaching rather alien. Although I should retain *The Testament* for my oldest students, I see no reason for not allowing younger pupils to read and enjoy some of the *Fables*, particularly if a lively, preferably illustrated version could be produced to entice them.

Bibliography

Bawcutt, Priscilla, and Felicity Riddy (eds), *Selected Poems of Henryson and Dunbar* (Edinburgh, Scottish Academic Press, 1992) from which all references are taken.

Fox, Denton (ed), *Robert Henryson: The Poems* (Oxford, University Press, 1987)

Papers from the Distance-taught M. Phil. in Scottish Literature – Medieval and Renaissance Literature 1375–1625 Unit 1C Henryson and Dunbar (© Glasgow University)

Robert Henryson. Selected and read by Matthew McDiarmid (Scotsoun cassettes SSC 018, 109)

BBC Television Shakespeare, *Troilus and Cressida* (© BBC Enterprises)

THEO VAN HEIJNSBERGEN

38. *The Bannatyne Manuscript Lyrics: Literary Convention and Authorial Voice*

When James V died in 1542, Scotland not only entered a phase of instability in the social and political spheres but, if we take into account the importance of royal patronage, literature, too, faced a period of unsettlement. However, waiting in the wings was a new source of patronage: already in the reign of James IV (1488–1513) the increasingly self-confident burghs had begun to take over the role of major cultural patron, as witnessed by local pageants, royal entries and the erection of burgh song schools, and this became even more prominent after 1542, when Crown, nobility and Church were increasingly occupied with more pressing affairs such as the 'Rough Wooing' by the English troops and the upheavals of the Reformation. The fact that in 1561 a Catholic sovereign came from France to rule over an Edinburgh elite that had newly been reformed but still retained many Catholic features complicated matters even further; nevertheless, the commencement of Mary Stewart's reign also contained the promise of renewed cultural vigour through royal patronage. The Bannatyne Manuscript (1568; henceforth BM), the anthology in which most of the extant vernacular poetry of this period has been preserved, reveals traces of these cultural and sociopolitical developments in its secular poetry, especially with respect to the emergence of a new authorial voice out of medieval conventions of courtly literature.[1] Although this is in itself a purely literary process, it is tied in with historical developments, and some historicising is in order here.

There is one other document that George Bannatyne, the collector of the manuscript, has left us, a 'memoriall buik', in which he records the births, marriages, deaths and godparents of his parents, brothers, sisters and children. This inventory of relatives and godparents, yielding some eighty-five names of people that the Bannatynes associated with, provides the best checklist available should we wish to reconstitute an audience for the BM. I have presented elsewhere a more detailed account of this list, but for the present purpose a short summary will suffice.[2] The names on the list can be divided into four groups: leading merchants and craftsmen from Edinburgh (with connections to

---

1 For a diplomatic transcription of the Bannatyne manuscript, see *The Bannatyne Manuscript Writtin in Tyme of Pest, 1568*, ed. W. Tod Ritchie (STS, 4 vols, 1928–34); for the facsimile edition, see *The Bannatyne Manuscript*, eds. Denton Fox and William A. Ringler (London, 1980). The only book-length study of the manuscript to date is Joan Hughes and W.S. Ramson, *Poetry of the Stewart Court* (Canberra, 1982).
2 Theo van Heijnsbergen, 'The Interaction between Literature and History in Queen Mary's Edinburgh: The Bannatyne Manuscript and its Prosopographical Context,' in *The Renaissance in Scotland. Studies in Literature, Religion, History and Culture*, eds. A.A. MacDonald, Michael Lynch and Ian B. Cowan (Leiden, 1994), pp. 183–225.

the world of printing); secular clergymen in collegiate churches or with benefices in royal patronage; crown servants or their wives, mostly crown officers working in government bodies such as the office of the Chancery or the Signet (the Bannatynes belong to this group themselves); and, finally, a large group of prominent local administrators. It is exactly this mix of people that executed the day-to-day government of the Stewart sovereigns, the major representatives of noble houses frequently being occupied with their own dynastic interests away from Edinburgh. Many of these men were university graduates whose links went back to intellectual circles at the court of James V; as such, they had been the recipients as well as promotors of the twin priorities of Scottish humanism, education and legal reform, and the 'memoriall buik' provides a string of names of public officers with a background of legal studies who had kept up the administration of the country when it was without personal royal rule in the 1540s and 1550s.

The 'memoriall buik', like the BM, is very much a family document, both manuscripts featuring a Bannatyne coat of arms (from two different branches of the family) as well as highlighting the Bannatyne connection with the families of John Bellenden and William Stewart, prominent poets at the court of James V. Poems by John Bellenden both open and close the BM (the latter in an earlier stage of its composition) while three close kinsmen of this poet head the list of names in the 'memoriall buik' almost as if they were family patrons. The 'memoriall buik' also lists William Stewart, the grandson of the poet William Stewart; he belonged to a branch of the Stewarts that also had close connections to the Bellendens. Another Bannatyne godparent was George Clapperton, almoner to James V from 1538 to 1542 and subdean of the Chapel Royal from 1535 to 1574; his poem *Wa worth maryage for evirmair* is included in the Maitland Folio Manuscript. Finally, the list of names in the 'memoriall buik' includes Henry Foulis, son and heir of James Foulis of Colintoun, the neo-Latin poet who, among other things, co-wrote the welcome to Mary of Guise when she came to Scotland in 1538.

The section of love lyrics in the BM is clearly dominated by Alexander Scott, a prebendary of the Chapel Royal who sang in the choir of St. Giles', and who, like George Clapperton, was a personal acquaintance of the Bannatynes. Furthermore, Clapperton and Scott were colleagues at the Chapel Royal, where we also find John Fethy, one of the few named poets in the section of love lyrics in the BM; he was precentor of the Chapel Royal, musician, and Master of the Aberdeen and Edinburgh song schools. Alexander Kyd was another poet who held a prebend of the Chapel Royal and whose work is featured in the BM. Moreover, the paths of Fethy and Scott also crossed at St Giles' in Edinburgh in the 1550s, where we also find James Lauder, to whom Alexander Montgomerie – by means of an anagram – dedicated one of his poems; the BM also contains verse from Alexander Montgomerie, but it should be noted that we are dealing here with later additions.[3]

---

3 For details, see Theo van Heijnsbergen, 'Interaction'. For Kyd, see A.A. MacDonald, 'William Stewart and the Court Poetry of the Reign of James V', in *Stewart Style, 1513–1542: Essays on the Court of James V*, ed. J. Hadley Williams (East Linton, 1996), pp. 179–200.

The above-mentioned links between manuscript, poets and audience indicate that the material contained in the BM presents an accurate reflection of the status, level and 'location' of contemporary vernacular literature, its poets continuing and re-defining, within an urban, semi-courtly setting, cultural tastes that earlier generations had originated. That we are here dealing with fairly close-knit *côteries* is also suggested by the side-by-side appearance of these same names in contemporary lists of poets; in his *The Testament and Complaynt of our Souerane Lordis Papyngo* (1530) David Lindsay mentions Bellenden, Stewart and Kyd as prominent poets at the court of James V, while in a slightly later work he also mentions Steill, another lyricist from the section of love lyrics in the BM. Whereas the existence of a literary elite at the courts of James IV, V and VI has for a long time been acknowledged – in the 1580s, Montgomerie in one of his poems groups together Scott, Robert Sempill and himself, while the Castalian band at James VI's court, with the King's own 'Reulis and Cautelis' at its programmatic centre, brought together many poets and musicians – the BM provides evidence for the fact that there was a literary culture in mid sixteenth-century Scotland as well, with the town of Edinburgh as its setting.[4]

The identity of both poets and audience as established above indicates that, in the period in which the BM was collected, interest in a national literary inheritance had widened down the social scale, especially among the merchant and professional classes. That there was indeed an urban market for the type of vernacular verse produced by poets such as the above is, for example, also suggested by George Bannatyne's contemporary, the poet-notary John Rolland. The latter's aunt, having read Rolland's *The Court of Venus*, asked him to write another book, but now one without inkhorn terms. She told the poet that 'fra clerklie termes [his] pen suld be suspendit'; Rolland promised her he would bend his bow 'with toun termes' (i.e. 'town words') and indeed wrote a more accessible piece, *The Seuin Seages*.[5] In the paragraphs below, a necessarily brief survey of a few erotic dialogues from the BM illustrates what these mid sixteenth-century poets did with their poetical heritage, tracing an emergent urban vantage-point in the adaptation of courtly as well as popular conventions to new social practices and norms. On account of these findings, a strategy will be suggested with which to approach other poems from this period, and as a test-case this strategy will be applied to the amorous lyrics of Alexander Scott, who seems

---

4 *The Works of Sir David Lindsay of the Mount, 1490–1555*, ed. Douglas Hamer (STS, 4 vols, 1930–6), i, 57 (*The Testament and Complaynt of our Souerane Lordis Papyngo*, ll. 43–4 and 51) and 92 (*The Complaint and Publict Confessioun of the Kingis Auld Hound. callit Bagsche*, l. 17). On Steill, see also Helena Mennie Shire, *Song, Dance and Poetry of the Court of Scotland under King James VI* (Cambridge, 1969), 39–41 and 64; *Ballattis of Luve*, ed. John MacQueen (Edinburgh, 1970), xxxiv–xxxv; and *Musica Brittanica. Vol XV: Music of Scotland. 1500–1700*, eds. Kenneth Elliott and Helena Mennie Shire (3rd, revised edn., London, 1975), items 39 and 45; note that Steill's authorship in the case of item 39 is assumed rather than proven. For Montgomerie's reference to Scott and Sempill, see *The Poems of Alexander Montgomerie*, ed. James Cranstoun, (STS, 1887), 101 (*My best beloiut brother of the band*, l, 12). The 'Reulis and Cautelis' was part of James VI's *The Essayes of a Prentise in the Divine Art Poesie* (1584), included in *The Poems of James VI of Scotland*, ed. James Craigie (STS, 2 vols, 1955 58), I, 65–83.

5 John Rolland, *The Seuin Seages*, ed. George F. Black (STS, 1932), 'Prologue', ll. 130–1.

to have commanded the widest range of erotic poetry in the era of Mary Stewart.

To start with, however, we have to move back in time. Compared with Middle Scots poems on love such as *The Kingis Quair* or Henryson's *Robene and Makyne* (which only survives in the BM), the satire in Dunbar's *In secreit place this hindir nycht* (henceforth *In secreit place*; included in the BM) provides a departure from these earlier poems which much more self-evidently embraced medieval or pastoral conceptions of sexual love. Even though Dunbar's treatment of the 'backstairs fornicator' and the 'giggling kitchen girl' in their attempt at emulating courtly lovers[6] still suggests a self-confident courtly identity on the poet's part, the fact that this court poet actually selected such upstarts as butts for his satire signals the very existence of an increasingly prominent 'upwardly mobile' movement of those not initiated in the arts of courtly love.

Half a century later, these same butts of satire had become the producers, audience and procurors of such literature (as well as its patrons?), and it is not surprising that these mid sixteenth-century writers and readers were rather ambivalent in their reception of a body of literature that, one or two generations earlier, had depicted their social kin with such poignant irony. They had to develop literary strategies of their own to come to terms with a complex court poet such as Dunbar, who could parody in one poem what he sublimated in another. For example, when Dunbar's *My hartis tresure and sweet assured fo* was copied into the Maitland Folio Manuscript (1570–85), the scribe added a colophon to this plea for love, 'quod Dumbar [*sic*] quhone he list to feyne'.[7] The present-day debate about, first of all, what exactly this implies, and, secondly, whether this then constitutes a correct interpretation of Dunbar's original intention by the writer of the colophon, proves that Bannatyne's contemporaries already shared our problems with regard to the interpretation of Dunbar's poetry or that of late medieval poetry generally.[8]

Another, though more hidden indication of how earlier court poetry was re-inscribed by these later generations of readers and writers may be gleaned from the way in which *In secreit place* was copied into the BM. Whereas in the text of this poem as it appears in the Maitland Folio Manuscript we read that the lover 'wes townysche, peirt and gukit' (1. 10, the version generally accepted by modern editors), the corresponding line in the BM version of this poem neutralises the mocking anti-urban element: here, the lover is 'to mich, fulich and gukkit', i.e.: 'too much' instead of 'townish'.[9] The question whether this is an unconscious or deliberate re-writing is less relevant than the conclusion that it indicates a shifting cultural perspective, especially since there are reasons to believe that this slip by Bannatyne was indeed less than accidental. First of all, much of Bannatyne's

---

6 These labels come from *The Poems of William Dunbar*, ed. James Kinsley (Oxford, 1979), 257; all quotations of Dunbar's poetry have been taken from this edition.
7 Kinsley, *Dunbar*, 39.
8 See, for example, Priscilla Bawcutt, *Dunbar the Makar* (Oxford, 1992), 300–1, where she disagrees with Kinsley's interpretation of this poem as a parody.
9 *Maitland Folio Manuscript*, ed. W.A. Craigie (STS, 2 vols, 1919–27), i, 368; Ritchie, *Bannatyne Manuscript*, ii, 275.

editing was purposive; he generally adapted his copy-texts with little reverence for textual authority, and, although claiming that the BM is a better witness than the Maitland Folio Manuscript, Kinsley in this instance prefers the Maitland version (in only one other instance out of a total of more than thirty other differences between the two texts does he accept the Maitland variant).[10] Secondly, Bannatyne has changed another part of the line as well – he has 'fulich' instead of 'peirt' – which is the only discrepancy between the Maitland and the Bannatyne versions of this poem in which neither aural nor orthographic similarity nor formulaic interchangeability offers a satisfactory explanation. In accounting for the line's awkward metre in the Bannatyne version, Kinsley's argument that Bannatyne may have been trying to read a difficult manuscript sounds plausible with respect to 'tounich' and 'to mich' but this does not apply to 'peirt' v. 'fulich'.[11] Moreover, as indicated by the appeal to Rolland to use 'toun termes' rather than 'clerklie' ones, there was an acute awareness of the distinctions between various literary registers in this period, with that of the town as an increasingly authoritative standard. The latter is also documented by the *Oxford English Dictionary*: for the period 1500 to 1520 it sets apart the Scottish use of the adjective 'townish' in the sense of 'pertaining to or characteristic of the town or town life, esp. as distinguished from the *court*' from the more common use of the word, 'pertaining to or characteristic of the town or town life, esp. as distinguished from the *country*' (my italics). To exemplify this special use it quotes the above line from Dunbar's *In secreit place* as well as line 39 from his *Bewty and the Presoneir* – a poem for which the BM is the earliest source – in which the persona is considered unfit to be his lady's lover or 'presoneir' because he is 'to townage' (i.e. 'too townish').[12]

This brings us to another erotic dialogue from the BM, the anonymous *Commonyng betuix the mester and the heure* (henceforth *Commonyng*; see Appendix A), a poem which can be dated 'post-Dunbar': the first examples of the use of the phrase 'play the counter pane' (l. 30) meaning 'to imitate' are in the *Dictionary of the Older Scottish Tongue* given to Rolland (two instances) and to Montgomerie (in the *Oxford English Dictionary* the first occurrence dates from 1549), while the figurative use of the verb 'plaster up' (l. 62) is only recorded for the late sixteenth and early seventeenth century.[13] The *Commonyng* is related to both of Dunbar's

---

10 Kinsley writes that 'Maitland is textually weak' where Bannatyne has a 'tendency to regulate, simplify, and improve his texts – obvious from a collation of his draft and main manuscripts' (Kinsley, *Dunbar*, xv–xvi). For Bannatyne's religious self-censorship, see A.A. MacDonald, 'Poetry, politics and Reformation censorship in sixteenth-century Scotland,' *English Studies*, 64 (1983), 410–21; idem, 'The Bannatyne Manuscript – A Marian Anthology,' *The Innes Review*, 37 (1986), 36–47; idem, 'The printed book that never was: George Bannatyne's poetic anthology,' in *Boeken in de late middeleeuwen*, eds. Jos M.M. Hermans and Klass van der Hoek (Groningen, 1993), 101–10. For his 'secular' editing, see Hughes and Ramson, *Poetry of the Stewart Court*, passim., esp. 104–8; and Gregory Kratzmann, 'Sixteenth-century Secular Poetry,' in *The History of Scottish Literature. Vol. I: Origins to 1660*, ed. R.D.S. Jack (Aberdeen, 1988), 105–23 (esp. 111).
11 Kinsley, *Dunbar*, 257.
12 *Oxford English Dictionary*, 2nd edn (henceforth *OED*), vol XVIII, prep. by J.A. Simpson and E.S.C. Weiner (Oxford, 1989), 323; Kinsley, *Dunbar*, 26.
13 Ritchie, *Bannatyne Manuscript*, iv, 38–40; for 'counter pane', see *Dictionary of the Older Scottish Tongue* (henceforth *DOST*), ed. W.A. Craigie *et al* (London and Chicago, 1931-), i, 709, and *OED*, iii, 1033; for 'plaster up', see *DOST*, v, 555, and *OED*, xi, 986–7 (1^b and 1^c).

above-mentioned poems in various ways: line 34 is an exact parallel to the refrain of *In secreit place* ('Ye brek my hairt my bony one'), while line 3, in which the 'mester' claims to be a 'presoneir' of love, picks up the theme and the refrain of Dunbar's *Bewty and the Presoneir*. Thirdly, the *Commonyng*, in its own variations on the phrase 'quhill the court be of the toun', raises to refrain status the very 'town v. court' motif that we have just found to be central to both of Dunbar's poems.

In the *Commonyng*, the male persona tries to persuade a lady to give in to his physical desires, but she tells him to 'byd quhill the court be of the toun' (l. 16), and the insistent identification of 'court' with 'lechery' in this poem completely subverts the courtly lover-as-prisoner motif of Dunbar's *Bewty and the Presoneir*. The wooer adopts courtly diction in ll. 1–3, performs stereotype courtly actions such as walking up and down like a caged animal in line 4, and succumbs to the obligatory recurrent swoon in line 7:

> Lord God my hairt is in distres
> And wrappit full of havines,
> And I as wofull presoneir
> Gois walking vp and doun in weir.
> My lady will not on me blent
> That movis me maist in myne entent;
> Daly in point to fall in swoun
> Ay sen the court come to þe toun. (ll. 1–8)

This offers opportunities for the idealisation of a courtly type of love (as in *Bewty and the Presoneir*) or its subversion, but also for its opposite, an ironical treatment of would-be courtly lovers (as in Dunbar's *In secreit place*), and the text indeed seems to mock its own protagonists and theme. However, in the final stanza of the *Commonyng*, rather than remaining detached from the text, the poet, in a relentless drive towards straightforward misogynist catharsis, merges with the narrator-persona who takes revenge for being rejected by his 'lady'. Disregarding his own questionable moves and motives, the 'I' brands the woman's conduct as that of a prostitute who will serve him for a crown (l. 55). In the end, he ditches the by now pox-ridden 'heure' for a 'bonyar' lover (l. 60), making for a self-congratulatory finale:

> Syne met hir I spak with befoir
> Weill plestert vp in the glengoir
> Quha had bene flamet and new laid doun
> Lang or the court yeid of the toun. (ll. 61–4)

The 'matter' of Dunbar's poems is still present in this type of verse, most of this poem reading like an imitation of a poem such as *In secreit place*. However, if we look at its final lines, the earlier court poet's transcendence of a one-dimensional, physical reality has been lost, together with the distancing perspective of the third-person pronoun within the well-known medieval genre of the *chanson d'aventure* or, alternatively, 'overheard dialogue'. As a result, the turn towards the use of the first-person pronoun in the *Commonyng* is ultimately a change for the worse, robbing the poem of most of its creative appeal. The crudeness in content is in fact underlined by a primitive rhyme scheme (*aabbccdd*) and by occasional metrical inconsistencies, and in the end the mechanical nature of content as well as form backfires on both narrator, persona and poet, there being little to distinguish between these potential sources of signification.

Evelyn Newlyn has drawn attention to other poems in the BM that display the same type of crudity in sexual politics combined with a similar lack of literary detachment as found in the final lines of the *Commonyng*. Thus, the first poem she deals with (*All to lufe and nocht to fenyie*) is a poem which for its effect relies exclusively on the audience's identification with the narrator-persona's sexual self-indulgence.[14] However, there are erotic dialogues of finer tissue in the BM, such as *In somer quhen flouris will smell* (henceforth *In somer*; see Appendix B), a poem containing words that roughly date it 'mid sixteenth-century'.[15] This poem shares features of traditional medieval misogyny and of male sexual fantasy with the *Commonyng*: the woman is portrayed on a bestial level, answering her wooer's first kisses by grunting like a pig (1. 32), and her sexual voracity, stimulated and enjoyed by the male wooer, is used to portray her as morally inferior. However, there are elements in the text that suggest the poem is not solely an act of male sexual wish-fulfilment, elements that draw the poem in the direction of comedy instead, with part of the ridicule being also directed at the male speaker. The fact that the satire aimed at the woman is more insidious and damaging than that directed at the man is not contested here, on the contrary; but a reading that would focus exclusively on the misogynyst potential of this poem lays bare only part of the channels of production that lie behind it, and would moreover suggest that its audience as a whole did not rise above the level of voyeurists, something which seems belied by other poems in the manuscript and by the formal, art-song characteristics of *In somer* itself. The present paper intends to suggest a complementary interpretation by drawing attention to elements of formal control that provide the reader or listener with an opportunity to take up a position within this open-ended text, in great contrast to verse such as provided by the *dénouement* of the *Commonyng* which ultimately subjects a defenceless audience to a one-dimensional authorial perspective.

The diversification of satire in *In somer* is underlined by the margins of this poem that warn us not to locate its inception entirely or even primarily in wishful thinking. These margins not only exercise formal control but also highlight a discontinuity between poet and persona, between author and text. The formal

---

14 Evelyn S. Newlyn, 'The Political Dimensions of Desire and Sexuality in Poems of the Bannatyne Manuscript,' in *Selected Essays on Scottish Language and Literature. A Festschrift in Honor of Allan H. Maclaine*, ed. Steve R. McKenna (Lewiston, 1992), 75–96 (77–80); for the text of *All to lufe and nocht to fenyie*, see Ritchie, *Bannatyne Manuscript*, iii, 6–8.
15 Ritchie, *Bannatyne Manuscript*, iii, 26–7. This poem is discussed by Newlyn on pp. 80–2. Line 57 of this poem provides the first instance of the verbal noun 'fukking': see *DOST*, ii, 578, and cf. *OED*, vi, 237.

set-up of the poem is that of the *pastourelle*, a traditional courtly genre in which an innocent maiden is wooed during a chance meeting. Although *In somer* features the above-mentioned elements of sexual self-indulgence and a misogynous depiction of the woman, in open rebellion against more conventional *pastourelles* such as Robert Henryson's *Robene and Makyne* or *Robeyns lok come to wow our lynny* (both in the BM), and although *In somer* has a first-person narrator who participates as a 'character' (the wooer) in the poem rather than a third-person narrator-persona who overhears two lovers (as used in Dunbar's *In secreit place*), it nevertheless preserves the generically-determined distance between poet and persona throughout. As a result, *In somer* does not run into extremes of straightforward catharsis like the *Commonyng* but, instead, communicates subjective elements through an impersonal play of style, form and generic expectations, and thus capitalises on the successful use of irony in lines such as 'I luve you leill and nocht to le' (1. 21), where the context to this line as provided by the poem as a whole clearly intimates that sexual pleasure is by far the more potent motive behind the male persona's declarations of 'leill lufe'; consequently, his courtly semblance of loyalty is evidently presented as preposterous. An audience sophisticated enough to appreciate the varied literary modes of poets such as Chaucer, Henryson, Dunbar and Lindsay (all prominently represented in the BM) must be credited with a reading expertise that would read a line such as 'Scho said scho comptit me nocht a peir' (1.50) in a detached way, decoding it as comedy rather than mechanically appreciating its sexual boastfulness. In this way, the use of figures of speech such as irony together with the preservation of an awareness of generic and formal conventions – for example with regard to the role and status of a persona – points away from a one-dimensional reading. Through the text's participation in a genre, *In somer* salvages sufficient creative control to preserve a potential ambiguity which could be aimed at both male and female 'lover'.

Within such a formally and generically intact framework the very fact that the narrator of *In somer* – speaking in the first person – is also the persona and the main protagonist paradoxically enables the creation of distance between the poem and its events and 'characters' (the latter including both narrator and persona) on the one hand and the author and his audience on the other. This involves a distinction between the separate identities of author, persona and narrator, the author splitting the narrator from the persona within the first-person pronoun by making the narrator unwittingly (through the author's text) transmit elements that channel the audience's perception of the persona in ways that the 'I' in the poem does not envisage. Thus, the author controls the persona from outside the text proper, rather than – as happens in the *Commonyng* – identifying with him which yields a sophisticated narrative perspective in which the reader has to create meaning without the explicit guidance of an authorial voice in the shape of a poet-narrator. By withdrawing the author from the text in such a way while at the same time using a first-person narrative perspective, the author of *In somer* creates the illusion of overhearing an erotic dialogue without any authorial intervention, which greatly enhances the immediacy of the poem and thus its illusion of truthfulness, while at the same time, from outside the text proper, conveying the notion of the text's essence as 'game' and fiction. The reader is thus persuaded to identify with the persona, but through its formal characteristics the text at the same time delays and complicates identification, creating a dual framework of reference. In the transition of lyric poetry from public and performed to private and mimetic text, a blending of medieval, popular and courtly genres such as the *chanson d'aventure* and the *pastourelle*, as instanced by *In somer*, illustrates one of several channels through which the notion of a text's impersonality and that of a literary text as a formal work of art was handed down to later generations of readers and writers in an era in which the concept of individual, autonomous authorship and the notion of a literary text as mimetic act became increasingly central concerns with regard to what was seen as the source of literary creativity, the individual self. In this way, these poems bring into focus what has become one of the main areas of attention in modern literary theory, the relations between reader, author and text. Scottish literature of this period attempts to transform popular notions and courtly ideals into terms of contemporary social practice according to a standard which is increasingly determined by an urban, literate layer of society. Middle Scots literature lacked literary importers such as Wyatt and Surrey, and instead continued to draw on native, medieval types of lyric; consequently, it is within such manipulations of genre and form (be they conscious or unconscious) as instanced above that an organic development of Scottish literature from late medieval to early modern has to be found.

There is another significant difference between *In somer* and Dunbar's *In secreit place*, a difference that brings us back to the issue of the tension between town and court. If we consider *In somer* in the tradition of the *pastourelle*, this poem follows the inclination towards democratic levelling that characterises adaptations of this and other courtly genres in both Scotland and England generally in that it does not represent the male lover as socially superior to the lady, thus neutralising the inherent potential of the genre to highlight social distinctions.[16] Moreover, the anonymous poet of *In somer* not only changed the nature of the satire but also its *direction*: whereas the irony of *In secreit place* was exclusively aimed at the 'townysche, peirt and gukit' lover, in *In somer* the epithet 'courtly' in the lady's enthusiastic review of her lover's exertions ('your courtly fukking garis me fling, ye wirk so weill', ll. 57–8) shows that, even if these lovers are here still seen as social upstarts, the ridicule is in this poem aimed at the courtly art of love itself as much as at the protagonists' clumsy, 'townish' imitation of it.

It would be fascinating to know to what extent the author of *In somer* was aware of such processes. However, it is more important to realise that the contemporary reader apparently did recognise such distinctions and developments. The best evidence for this is the fact that *In somer* appears in the section of 'ballettis mirry and vther solatius consaittis' in the BM, whereas the *Commonyng* is entered in the

---

16 On this 'democratic levelling', see *The Poems of Robert Henryson*, ed. Denton Fox (Oxford, 1981), 469, where Fox quotes the claim made by H.E. Sandison, *The 'Chanson d'Aventure' in Middle English* (Bryn Mawr, 1913), 65–6, that English poets 'delivered the *pastourelle* from much of its aristocratic bias' and brought it instead closer to the popular ballad.

section of 'ballatis aganis evill wemen'; in other words, the compiler of the anthology must have sensed the distance between author and narrator in the former poem and consequently read it in an ironical light, as opposed to his reading of the *Commonyng*.

Poems such as *In somer* and the *Commonyng* make explicit the implication of many earlier literary expositions of courtly love which show that underneath courtly moves and motives lie very basic sexual instincts. Pushing this to its logical conclusion, these poems yield quite graphic poetry in which outdated (or rather: out-discoursed) courtly models of sexual relations are parodied by means of a discursive contestation which is both subversive as well as appropriative. In such a shift from earlier, courtly satire of 'upwardly mobile' imitations of courtly love to an increasingly dominant urban perception of courtly love, the distance preserved between poet and persona, between author and text, enables a poem – and, thus, its audience – to merge literary differences that had previously separated radically different traditions and vocabularies, such as the courtly and non-courtly. Rechannelling social energy by these literary means, poems such as *In somer* help shape the identity of the social class of which they themselves are part, the best of these poems having by no means merely a passive role of reflection or imitation but also an active, formative one, redefining social boundaries as well as creating a modern literary persona. In order to measure the former we may need a much more fully documented insight into the period than we have now, but in literary terms at least the BM might be considered a sufficiently substantial corpus for a further investigation into the existence of such a transitional coalescence of courtly, urban and native.

By far the most prominent contemporary love-poet in the BM is Alexander Scott. His extant poetry (preserved in the BM) is similar in kind to that of Thomas Wyatt in its decoding of the courtly lover and the transubstantiation of that 'type' into an autonomous persona.[17] However, whereas in many poems by Wyatt we begin to find a rather full-bodied private universe projected onto the surface of the text, in Scott's lyrics we have to seek the poet outside or beneath rather than *in* or *on the surface of* the text. To a larger extent than Wyatt's, Scott's poems and projections – rather like those of *In somer* – are still those of a community, and in his poems the conflict is still between a convention and its own expectations rather than between a convention and an individual poet. Consequently, we should not look for the author Scott in the contents as a transcendent ego, but rather in what he does with his lyrics in terms of genre, style and form, an approach also required by *In somer*. Scott, as has been said of Dunbar, dissipated identity in generic difference: lacking new diction and imagery, he deliberately juxtaposed conflicting registers such as 'courtly' and 'popular'. This confused later critics who were looking for what was not there and what moreover had never been intended, a 'coherent and consistent authorial

---

17 For Scott's poems, see *The Poems of Alexander Scott*, ed. James Cranstoun (STS, 1896); *The Poems of Alexander Scott*, ed. Alexander Karley Donald (EETS, 1902); and, for a modernised edition, *The Poems of Alexander Scott*, ed. Alexander Scott (Edinburgh, 1952).

project', or, on the other hand, an entirely culturally constructed court poet.[18] Consider a passage like the following:

> Sum thinkis na schame to clap
> And kiss in opin wyiss;
> Sum can nocht keip hir gap
> Fra lansing as scho lyiss.

These are lines from Scott's *Ane ballat maid to þe derisioun and scorne of wantoun wemen* (ll. 73–6), lines which have made critics condemn the poem as 'so prurient an exercise in defining sexual mechanics under guise of pretended moral purpose that the "scorne" gets turned back upon the writer', a comment that puts Scott's verse on a level with a poem such as the *Commonyng*.[19] But in Scott's poem there *is* no writer in the sense of an individual who expresses his private feelings in transparent texture; nor is there, on the other hand, an author who exclusively and mechanically writes towards the affirmation of a set of collective social assumptions, be it a courtly, moral or even misogynous one. From the final stanza as well as from the body of the text it appears that this poem should be read as provocative play, that was meant to elicit a reply rather than to make a statement, and in the final lines of the poem (ll. 101–4) the author withdraws from the body of the text in a manner that is anything but unprecedented in medieval poetry:

> Lo ladeis, gif this bie,
> Ane gud counsale I geif yow,
> To saive your honestie
> Fra sklander to releif yow.
> Bot ballatis ma to breif yow
> I will nocht brek my brane,
> Suppois ye sowld mischeif yow
> I sall not said agane. (ll. 96–104)

This combination of a debate on women with a 'destroying refrain', an instance of literary play with social and sexual reverberations, was something of a vogue at the English court in the mid-sixteenth-century.[20] This text, too, is participating in a genre rather than reflecting personal experience, and in Scott's other lyrics a persona in the modern sense is likewise conspicuously absent. In this particular poem, Scott is all the time 'not saying it', the refrain – 'I sall not said [i.e. say it]

---

18 Antony J. Hasler, 'William Dunbar: the Elusive Subject,' in *Bryght Lanternis. Essays on the Language and the Literature of Medieval and Renaissance Scotland*, eds. J. Derrick McClure and Michael R.G. Spiller (Aberdeen, 1989), 194.
19 Maurice Lindsay, *History of Scottish Literature* (revised edn., London, 1992), 91.
20 See Francis Lee Utley, *The Crooked Rib. An Analytical Index to the Argument about Women in English and Scots Literature to the End of the Year 1568* (reprint, New York, 1970), items 134 and 304 (pp. 164 and 262; the latter text was set to music). The refrains are: 'But I wyll say nothinge' and 'But I will nott say so'.

agane' – presenting in thirteen consecutive stanzas an absence which the audience has to trace in what the 'I' has just 'not said'. This is a sophisticated piece of deconstruction, in which 'meaning' (i.e. the authority behind the words) is deliberately deferred from stanza to stanza, which effectively lures the audience deeper and deeper into the text but away from the author.

In Scott's *May is the moreth maist amene*, the pronoun 'I' is again strategically used, or rather: avoided. A whole catalogue of pronouns ('thay', l. 59; 'ye', l. 63; and 'sum', ll. 49, 53–5, 59–60, etc.) as well as phrases like 'men of amouris' (l. 46) and 'dammosalis and dammis' (l. 51) parade as the agents of the actions described, engaged in activities traditionally associated with the May season. The 'I' finally enters the poem in the last stanza, counselling 'yow' to 'delyt nocht lang in luvaris lesure' (l. 67). At first sight, this poem thus seems to present a traditional piece of moral instruction. However, if we investigate individual stanzas we find that, although they begin innocently, they end in highly ambiguous lines in ways that significantly qualify the final moral advice, a procedure that indicates that the author and audience shared a literary consciousness that was comprehensive enough to incorporate traditional forms and meanings while at the same time producing as well as containing subversive expectations raised by genre and register.

For example, an archery contest is described in the following terms:

> In May frank archeris will affix
> In place to meit, syne marrowis mix
> To schute at buttis, at bankis and brais,
> Sum at the reveris, sum at the prikkis,
> Sum laich and to beneth the clais. (ll. 40–5)

The archers meet as 'marrowis', i.e. 'friends' or 'equals', but the word also echoes the meaning of 'sexual mates', as in bird poetry, and these amorous overtones are confirmed by the last line of the stanza in which the archers shoot low beneath the clothes. A stanza that reveals a similar 'disintegration' is the following:

> In May gois madynis till Lareit,
> And hes thair mynyonis on the streit
> To horss thame quhair the gait is ruch;
> Sum at Inchebukling Bray thay meit,
> Sum in the middis of Mussilburch. (ll. 56–60)

In the geographical context of the poem, Musselburgh (l. 60), a town near Edinburgh, is indeed a plausible location. However, considering the bestial imagery of the maidens horsing their minions (l. 57) and the well-documented reputation of the chapel of Lareit near Edinburgh (l. 56) as a gathering place for amorous rather than devout pilgrimages, the fact that mussels were also a widely-known euphemism for the female genitals makes the phrase 'to meet in the middle of Musselburgh' rather less innocent. Such a reading is confirmed by the fact that a similar pun may also be intended by 'Inchbuckling Brae' (occasionally also known as 'Edgebuckling Brae'), a hill near Musselburgh, a topographical reference that may likewise carry sexual overtones judging from the common medieval allusion to buckles as emblems of sexual intercourse.[21]

In these poems by Scott, an authorial voice can only be instantiated in the frame of the poem and its tongue-in-cheek counsel, not in the poem that it frames. Instead of searching for coherence, recent literary theory foregrounds such margins of a text as the place where one can trace discontinuities or *aporias*, 'the places or topoi which lead nowhere but further into textuality, revealing not monadic totality but a perpetual play of hidden relations and fragmentariness'.[22] These disruptions in the transmission of a text's meaning from author to reader may provide information about the process of negotiation between author, text, reader, 'meaning' and 'reality'. This is an approach that is particularly promising for the sixteenth century, which shows so many traces of processes of negotiation – usually hidden underneath a deceptively polished verbal surface – that accompany the emancipation of the individual as the dominant ideological concept in literary as well as in social and political spheres. It is in these places that the tension between rhetoric and logic comes to the surface, and they are peepholes through which we can get behind texts and obtain a clearer view of the creative dynamics that structures them.

In this context, a fascinating pictorial parallel to Scott's subversive imagery of archery can be found in the margins of an illuminated manuscript of *Lancelot du Lac*, on a page that describes courtly pastimes such as courting and jousting. At the bottom of this page, an archer is aiming at the exposed buttocks of a crouching figure, in itself a common enough topos in these marginal illuminations, and one that parallels Scott's May poem as quoted above, 'To schute . . . laich and to beneth the clais'. The interest of this particular illustration lies in the erasure of the crouching figure's arm. It originally rested on his own behind – traces of this are still clearly visible – probably in anticipation of the archer's missile; however, this arm has been erased, and the arm that replaces it points upwards rather insinuatingly, its stretched finger clearly making a link between the scene it is itself part of and the text that it points to. The marginal drawing is thus linked to the text proper in a manner that explicitly undermines the notions expressed in the courtly text and illustrations (jousting and courting) that it accompanies, and this topos of the 'arrow in the hindquarters', found in other manuscript illuminations as

---

21 Elements of both of Scott's stanzas quoted here (namely 'Lareit' and 'marrowis meit') come together in a passage from David Lindsay's *Ane dialogue betuix Experience and ane Courteour*: 'For tyll adore one image in Loreit / Mony came with thare marrowis for to meit / Committand thare fowll fornication' (Hamer, *Lindsay*, i, 278, ll. 2664–6; see also l. 2675: 'Sic pylgramage heth maid mony one hure'). On the reputation of the chapel of Loretto, see Hamer, *Lindsay*, iii, 347–9, and Cranstoun, *Scott*, 135–6. The fact that shells were both a distinctive part of the outfit of pilgrims to the shrine of St James of Compostela as well as a symbol of the vulva is here also exploited; for this shell imagery, see Ad de Vries, *Dictionary of Symbols and Imagery* (Amsterdam, 1974), 419.
22 Gary F. Waller, 'Deconstruction and Renaissance Literature,' in *Assays* 2 (1982), 80; see also 71 and 85.

well, has been interpreted as 'an inverted metaphor of the look of love'.[23]

Scott functioned as a cultural intermediary in a similar vein: while his work as a whole illustrates the movement from courtly to popular, from court to town and from monastic to secular community,[24] a study of his poetic techniques shows how he preserves and passes on the formal craftsmanship of earlier makars in the margins of his poetry; the meaning of a poem such as Scott's May poem is communicated through its style, its selection of images and its manipulation of conflicting generic expectations, rather than through the use of an empirical 'I'. And, significantly, Bannatyne did not put this poem among the 'ballatis full of wisdome and moralitie' which told young lovers to restrain themselves, but among the 'mirry ballettis'; in other words, he was aware of the 'discontinuity', of the incongruity between this poem and the ostensibly Christian tradition from which it was breaking away.

Another poem by Scott is *The slicht remeid of luve*; as indicated by the title, it is based on the genre of 'remedies of love', a tradition going back to Ovid, so here, too, Scott is writing in and preserving a residual genre. The interest of these poems for us today, however, lies not in their conformance to prescribed amorous conventions but rather in the way in which they decode and then redefine such conventions. For example, neither moralist nor wanton lover can object to Scott's advice to the lover to offer his ladies 'daly observance', but such conventional admonitions are in this poem either directly or indirectly undermined, a process repeated so frequently that one eventually can no longer deny the encroachment of this de(con)structive subtext upon a more conventional surface text. In this particular case, the immediately following line rather qualifies the advice offered and exposes the recommended *Frauendienst* as mere lip-service: 'offir thame your daly observance / Be tung, thocht naþir hairt nor mynd consentis' (ll. 22–3). The poem provides a catalogue of such paradoxically-phrased pieces of advice in which the code of courtly love is played off against an earthier practice, as in: 'hecht thame [i.e. ladies] giftis howbeid ye gif thame nocht' (l. 34), and: 'hald yow koy in quiet quhill ye get hir' (l. 54). These two sets of behaviour, courtly servitude and courtly dissimulation, are mutually exclusive when carried to their logical extremes, but in Scott's poems they are often rather mischievously presented as complementary. The fact that we are here dealing with attitudes that rationally and morally are irreconcilable is covered up by the rhetoric of a seemingly smooth textual surface: Scott was well aware of the fact that if a text satirically or even cynically inverts the meaning of any signifying system (here the code of courtly love), the threat of this text to that system is covered up if the actual words it employs are those that are used to define the signifying system itself.

In this way, through manipulations of poetic traditions and of their conventional words and images rather than through speaking directly to us in the first person,

---

23 Michael Camille, *Images on the Edge. The Margins of Medieval Art* (London, 1992), 101 (illustration). The topos of the 'arrow in the hindquarters' is discussed on pp. 43–7 and 106–8.
24 Such a movement is also suggested by the locations specified in Scott's poetry (in addition to the ones mentioned above: the Potter Row in Edinburgh; the Drum near Dalkeith) and by the biographical details of his life, for which see MacQueen, *Ballattis*, xxxv–xliv, and the present writer's forthcoming thesis.

Scott, like the author of *In somer*, communicates 'meaning' from underneath the verbal surface of the poem, a surface that thus covers a text which only at a superficial glance is written exclusively in either a courtly, moral, misogynist or any other single one tradition. His texts frequently deny the successful application of monological models of coherence and instead, as indicated above, indeed 'lead nowhere but further into textuality, revealing not monadic totality but a perpetual play of hidden relations and fragmentariness.' These poems do not voice superseded rhetoric but, on the contrary, make it the subject of analysis, and they generate a counter-rhetoric in the process by manipulating formal, generic and stylistic conventions. This enables the author to incorporate subjective reflections upon normative prescriptions that within formerly separate traditions had begun to assume the status of natural imperatives, the latter being partly attributable to the political and cultural dominance of its practitioners (notably church and court).

In such a way, some of the more intriguing poems of Scott and his contemporaries address an authorial audience (one that reads a text as an author's fictional communication) rather than a narrative one (which reads a text as a narrator's communication), and so are able to escape the one-dimensional, purely reflectionist readings that have occasionally been imposed upon them; these poems do not merely reflect, they actively project, evaluate and produce. Rather than belonging to the category of 'readerly' texts – texts that comply with accepted conventions and in which readers are merely passive recipients of structures of language and meaning – such poems fall into the category of 'writerly' text, texts that challenge the conventions that normally (i.e. 'normatively') isolate meaning and instead invite readers to create such meaning for themselves. In this way, such early modern poems force readers to enter the text and turn reading into a more autonomous, subjective activity. This combination of the contrastive theoretical notions of authorial *v.* narrative audience and writerly *v.* readerly texts yields a model of literary criticism that allows creative power to both author and reader, and one that can make use of combinations of essentialist, structuralist, historicist and other critiques.[25] Moreover,

---

25 Recognition of such processes is in itself not new, but the insights that resulted from this recognition have not yet been applied in conjunction to Scottish literature of the sixteenth century. The distinction between authorial and narrative audience is the subject of an article by Peter J. Rabinowitz, 'Truth in Fiction: A Re-examination of Audiences,' *Critical Inquiry* 4 (1977), 121–41. The terms 'readerly' and 'writerly' are derived from Roland Barthes, who labelled such texts *lisible* and *scriptible* respectively, in his S/Z (Paris, 1970), 10. Such an application of theoretical generalisations to specific texts provides a good example of how literary theory and literary criticism (as well as appreciation) might meet in the near future in an area of criticism which has been tentatively labelled 'descriptive poetics' or 'middle-range theory', where critical readers, safeguarding the literary element in critical debates, try to grasp the conditions and multiplicity of meanings in a text rather than select 'a single plane of abstraction' in advance and read texts mechanically as direct expressions of such an abstraction: Brian McHale, 'Whatever happened to descriptive poetics?', in *The Point of Theory. Practices of Cultural Analysis*, eds. Mieke Bal and Inge E. Boer (Amsterdam, 1994), 56–65 (esp. 56). This stress on the multiplicity of texts fits well with the nature of popular verse, a body of literature that responds to many different traditions and as result continually thwarts the imposition of retrospective models of coherence. The late medieval mix of popular and courtly literature in the BM therefore requires a suspension of identification, a reading strategy that was practised by its contemporary contemporary audience as well and which gives shape to a medieval rather than modern appreciation of literature as an enhanced feeling for life.

for the sixteenth-century text, this is a productive reading strategy, since its text-based bias delays the imposition of any interpretational superstructure that tries to gain control over the 'meaning' of a text by turning writerly texts back into readerly ones that comply with the conventions and aims of interpretation as set out by that same superstructure. In contrast, the above matrix allows the text to pass on to us a more resilient, supra-individual reading strategy, and it also shows that, while latently medieval, these texts are potentially modern. It is in the new, predominantly secular meeting-place of the urban community that such interplay of cultural and poetic traditions takes place.

In the light of the above suggestions regarding sixteenth-century reading and writing practices, it is interesting to look briefly at the colophon of Scott's *To luve vnluvit it is ane pane*, the Scott poem that arguably comes closest to subjective reflection on experience. The distinction between poet and persona seems almost negligible here, and, significantly, it is at the end of this poem that we find the colophon: 'quod Scott quhen his wyfe left him'.[26] Past criticism has extracted only biographical information from this colophon, but surely from a literary point of view it is much more interesting that here, in an extratextual comment of which there are only a few in the manuscript, the copyist, George Bannatyne, gave voice to a reading of the poem as no longer play but as a text bearing a direct link with lived experience, notably the poet's own. Once again (as with the colophon at the end of Dunbar's *In secreit place*, discussed above), Bannatyne's editing and his selection of Scott as the major poet of his day suggests that the contemporary milieu which produced a manuscript such as the BM was highly sensitive to the 'discontinuities' between residual and emergent modes of writing as well as to the shift of emphasis in poetry from 'conventional' to 'individual' experience. In its exploitation of genre and form, such poetry pointed towards a more modern notion of poetry as an individual author's manipulation of language and meaning *outside* given fields of reference. In this way, these texts questioned the absolute nature of language and reality and their mutual correspondence as well as the social and moral values that went with them – such as those of town *v.* court. Thus, in Scott's poetry we do not find an absolute framework of reference in which meaning is unequivocally grounded, but rather a fluid intertextuality which eventually gives birth to the modern universe of endlessly deferred meaning as analysed in post-structuralist criticism.

In some of his best lyrics, in their blend of conventional form with personal tone, Scott emerges as the Scottish poet who in this transitional period comes closest to developing a modern lyric identity. His achievement may pale somewhat in comparison with more prolific writers of similar lyrics from other European literatures, but that does not alter this conclusion. Moreover, apart from the quite likely irretrievable loss of much of his work, this 'paleness' is also caused by undiscriminating critical attention; for one thing, Middle Scots literary scholarship has only recently begun to develop insights that can sufficiently appreciate the values of such intermediatory poetry by schematically discrimi-

26 Fox and Ringler, *Bannatyne Manuscript*, f.256r.

nating between author, narrator and persona, in order to 'perceive of the "I" as above all a rhetorical figure, a troping pronoun mediating text to audience but retaining in the process an essential multiplicity and openness' which enables it to 'preserve freedom of access to a text which becomes a site of debate for audiences or readers'.[27]

Unfortunately, in late sixteenth-century Scotland the rudiments of a modern literary awareness stood little chance of being further developed. The compilation of the BM (1565–8) coincided with the outbreak of open hostility between Catholics and Protestants, a rupture that ended the precarious balance that had been maintained in the earlier sixties. This historical development had important cultural consequences. While in this period other national literatures profited from their appropriation of (and opposition to) royal and aristocratic discourse in their development towards a secular poetic identity, Scotland had to rely on a very fragile and intermittent court culture from 1568 until well into the 1580s. Moreover, the vacuum caused by the absence of a stable royal court was filled by the Calvinist kirk, which recognised the political nature of autonomous, open-ended texts and was therefore increasingly concerned to make all fictional texts once more subject to a godly superstructure, turning 'writerly' into 'readerly' texts again.[28] Consequently, the nature of the poetry produced in this period is almost exclusively polemical. The revival of court culture after James VI had established his personal authority in the 1580s was too fragile and short-lived – the royal court moved to London in 1603 when James VI succeeded Elizabeth I – to bring Scottish literature securely back to the 'European' level it had enjoyed under earlier Stewart monarchs. Nevertheless, it is interesting to speculate on the impact that a printed BM would have had on Scottish literature. Literary consciousness can be measured by the extent to which text 'draws awareness to its own processes of meaning production and makes of these processes its own subject matter, its own "content" ',[29] and, as the above analysis suggests, the fact that Scottish literature of this period did not blossom into an indigenous Renaissance in subsequent decades is not a result of the absence of such a literary awareness but rather because that of the very *presence* of a potential for developing autonomous structures to generate meaning made it suspect.

The BM emerges as a testimonial to the presence of a literary consciousness in mid-sixteenth-century Scotland. Many poems in the BM bring together native and foreign lyrical traditions in their different ways of transforming literary conventions and social rituals into moral rules of life. They illustrate how contemporary Scottish literature followed general European trends and con-

---

27 Hasler, 'Dunbar,' 195.
28 The development of church music in Scotland provides one of several interesting parallels to this renewed call for a 'monadic totality' in literature, the Calvinist church attempting to curb polyphony, the most distinctive feature of modern Western music; the comparison is particularly apt here since Scott was a musician specialised in part song. For the most recent discussion of this subject, see D. James Ross, *Musick Fyne. Robert Carver and the Art of Music in Sixteenth Century Scotland* (Edinburgh, 1993).
29 Hayden White, *The Content of the Form. Narrative Discourse and Historical Representation* (Baltimore and London, 1987), 211.

tributed to the debate on the 'feinyit' nature of fiction by working out solutions as to how late medieval ethics could be converted into early modern aesthetics. Unfortunately, this has remained largely unnoticed partly because our awareness of the *absence* of such a literary self-consciousness in the post-Marian period has tended to discourage any quest for its *presence* in the years that immediately preceded it. Moreover, the poets of this era were writing in a historical vacuum, a period in which the paradigms of the past had become obsolete but new ones had not yet crystallised. These contexts force us to look for rudimentary 'impulses towards' a modern (as distinct from a medieval) literary awareness rather than for a fully-developed poetics. Closer analysis of the poetry of these mid- sixteenth-century makars, who functioned as cultural intermediaries between court and town as well as between medieval and early modern modes of lyric, shows that these texts cannot be studied without an awareness of such a literary potential as well as of such extra-literary developments. If we look closely, we see that, in terms of content, courtly conventions and other traditions of self-representation were in this period, in Scotland as well as in late medieval Europe generally, confronted with a demand on literature to function as mimetic representation, and that, consequently, attempts were made to convert such literary traditions into social practice.[30] In this process, the discontinuity between rhetoric and logic was not covered up but rather exposed and exploited, and the transposition of the code of courtly love from a courtly to a semi-urban environment is one of the gauges by which this process may be measured. At the same time, an awareness of the literary text as being both fiction as well as formal art was preserved, a feat which later criticism more often than not has failed to take into account.

Postscript

W.T.H. Jackson, 'The Medieval Pastourelle as a Satirical Genre', *The Challenge of the Medieval Text. Studies in Genre and Interpretation*, eds. Joan M. Ferrante and Robert W. Hanning (New York, 1985), 66–80, confirms several of the above hypotheses. Such 'erotic dialogue' verse is usually inherently satirical, and its satire works in two directions, in terms of gender ('often, though not always, this scorn is extended by implication to the male participant', 72) as well as socially: the peasant girl is naive in her assessment of the situation, while the courtier is both *vilain* and oppressor. Courtly culture is targeted because its unsophisticated love-making and crude enforcement of social hierarchy in sexual pursuits are both in flagrant contradiction of courtly culture. Such satire comes from 'the clerics and those professional or amateur singers who were educated under their influence' (69). If we insert 'town' into this triangle of courtly, peasant and cleric, we see how urban elites used such 'erotic dialogues' to satirise both courtly pretence and a peasant lack of refinement. It turns both into *vilainie*, identifying with the clerical perspective of the worldly-wise observer, while

---

30 For this pressure of 'Konkretisierung' on late medieval literature, see R. Schnell, 'Grenzen literarischer Freiheit im Mittelater,' *Archiv für das Studium der neueren Sprachen und Literaturen*, 133 (1981), 241–70.

adding a topical, domestic anti-feminism to the traditionally misogynous clerical viewpoint. However, the BM reveals how the urban also *distances* itself from the clerical perspective. Dunbar's *In secreit place* indeed lampoons court, town, the ignorant and the female, but, as we saw, the BM scribe is at pains to exempt 'townysh' paradigms from such criticism in *his* transcript of the poem: the urban perspective here emerges from behind and within the clerical. All this exactly matches the BM audience as well as poets outlined above, and also helps explain the appearance of these poems in the manuscript.

Appendices

(In both appendices, yogh has been printed as 'y', and initial 'i' as 'j')
App. A *Commonyng betuix the mester and the heure* (BM f.264r)

	Lord god my hairt is in distres	
	And wrappit full of havines	
	And I as wofull presoneir	
	Gois walking vp and doun in weir	
5	My lady will not on me blent*	look, glance
	That movis me maist in myne entent	
	Daly in point to fall in swoun	
	Ay sen the court come to þe toun	
	I said to hir my darling deir	
10	My luve my hairt and all my cheir	
	The conforting of all my cair	
	Quhen pleisis yow I mak repair	
	Tell me your mynd and nothing lane*	conceal
	My hairt with yow sall ay remane	
15	In to myne eir than cowld scho roun*	whisper
	Byd quhill the court be of þ toun	
	I said to hir my speciall luve	
	My mind fra yow sall nevir remve*	'remuve'
	Scho anserit me be not displesit	
20	At this tyme ye ma not be eisit	
	I sichet than and said allace	
	Can ye not fynd na tyme or place	
	Quhair I may quitly lay yow doun	
	Na not quhill court be of the toun	
25	Quhy say ye so my awin sweit thing	
	Knaw ye not weill and I war king	
	That I wald evir yow plesour do	
	And daly reddy þairvnto	
	Evir with yow for to remane	

30 Sowld ye not play the counter pane*   do the like
    Scho said to me ga glaik yow loun
    The court is new cum to the toun

    Than said I with ane dolerus mone
    Ye brek my hairt my bony one
35 My travell I may think ill sett
    Gif I no mair kyndnes yit gett
    Ye gart me trow or thay war gane
    Ye lovit me best of any ane
    Quhat ailis yow now for to luik doun
40 Becauss the court is in the toun

    I said my hairt not yow to greve
    Sa sone I will not taik my leve
    To me ye sowld not be vnkynd
    My hony my joy remord your mynd
45 I hald me speciall for your man
    With all the serwice that I can
    Now grant me this my birdy broun
    Na byd quhill court be of the toun

    Ga hyne quod scho methink ye vary
50 Ourlang with tratlingis me ye tary
    Now yit my langour for to less
    My gentill jo gif me a kiss
    It is ourlait to schute* me owte   shut
    Thane byd and tak your sait abowt
55 Ye salbe servit for a croun
    Howbeit the court be in the toun

    Thus I ouirdraif fra day to day
    To spy quhen court sowld gone away
    Quhill of hir luve my langour was gane
60 I had provydit ane bonyar ane
    Syne met hir I spak with befoir
    Weill plestert vp in the glengoir*   venereal disease
    Quha had bene flamet and new laid doun
    Lang or the court yeid of the toun

App. B *In somer quhen flouris will smell* (BM f.141r)

    In somer quhen flouris will smell
    As I fure our fair feildis and fell
    Allone I wanderit by ane well

On weddinsday
5   I met a[ne] cleir[est] vndir kell*   women's cap
        A weilfaird may

    Scho had ane hatt vpoun hir heid
    Off claver cleir bayth quhyt and reid
    With catclukis* strynklit in that steid   trefoil
10   And fynkill* grene   fennel (an aphrodisiac)
    Wit ye weill to weir þat weid
        Wald weill hir seme

    Ane pair of beidis abowt hir thrott
    Ane Agnus Day with nobill nott
15 Jyngland weill with mony joitt
        War hingand doun
    It wes full ill to fynd ane moit
        Vpoun hir goun

    Alss sone as I þat schene cowth se
20 I halsit hir with hairt maist fre
    I luve yow leill and nocht to le
        Wald ye me lane*   ? adv alone; v. conceal
    Out hay quod scho my joy latt be
        Ye speik in vane

25 Quhat is the thing þat ye wald haif
    Na thing bot a kiss I craif
    As I þat luvis yow our the laif
        Wald ye me trow
    Gif þatt yow may of sorrow saif
30   Cum tak it now

    Than kissit I hir anis or twyiss
    And scho to gruntill as a gryiss
    Allace quod scho I am vnwyiss
        That is so meik
35 Itss lyk þat ye had eitin pyiss
        Ye are so sweit

    My hatt is youris of proper dett
    And on my heid scho cowth it sett
    Than in my armes I cowth hir plett
40   And scho to thraw*   twist, writhe
    Allace quod scho ye gar me swett
        Ye wirk so slaw

　　　　Than doun we fell bayth in feir
　　　　Allace quod scho þat I come heir
45　I trow this labour I may yow leir
　　　　　　Thocht I be ying
　　　　Yit I feir I sall by full deir
　　　　　　Your sweit kissing

　　　　Quhen I was grathit in hir gcir
50　Scho said scho comptit me nocht a peir*　　　　something of small value
　　　　Sen ye haif wonnyn me on weir
　　　　　　Do furth at anis
　　　　Thairwith I schot be neth hir scheir*
　　　　　　　　　　　　the part of the body where the legs fork
　　　　　　Deip to þe stanis*　　　　　　　　　testicles

55　Than to ly still scho wald nocht blin*　　　　cease
　　　　Allace said scho my awin sweit thing
　　　　Your courtly fukking garis me fling*　　　dance, kick
　　　　　　Ye wirk so weill
　　　　I sall yow cuver quhen þat ye clyng
60　　　So haif I seill

　　　　Sen ye stummer* nocht for my skippis　　stumble, stagger
　　　　Bot hald your taikill by my hippis
　　　　I byd a quasill* of your quhippis　　perh. 'quhissil', i.e. exchange;
　　　　　　　　　　　　　　　　　　or 'quheiss', a lash or blow with
　　　　　　Thocht it be mirk
65　Bot and ye will I schrew þe lippis
　　　　　　þat first sall irk

　　　　Als sone as we our deid had done
　　　　Scho reiss sone vp and askit hir schone
　　　　Als tyrd as scho had weschin a spone
70　　　To yow I say
　　　　This aventur anis to me come
　　　　　　On weddinsday

CHARLES CALDER

39.   *Enargeia in* The Cherrie and the Slae

'The speech of man is a magnificent and impressive thing when it surges along like a golden river, with thoughts and words pouring out in rich abundance.' So writes Erasmus in the arresting opening of *De Copia*.[1] The twin preoccupations evident here – with the art of discourse in general and with the quality of *copia* in particular – find expression not only in this work but in others: letters, prefaces, handbooks. *Copia* has two aspects: richness of expression and richness of subject-matter. The first is attained by the evolving of synonyms, metaphor, *enallage* (substitution of one part of speech for another), *hyperbole, periphrasis* and other methods of diversifying diction. The second involves the use of *exempla*, comparisons, similarities, opposites. This is a familiar theme in Erasmus, who exerts himself tirelessly to demonstrate the rhetorical applications of *similia, exempla*, and *sententiae*.

In his general reflections on copiousness in *De Copia*, Book I (1–10), Erasmus asserts that the orator who knows how to compress his speech will also be skilled in enriching it with ornament of every kind. Attaining such skill is in accord with the precepts of Nature; for Nature delights in variety, and the craftsman in words rightly follows her example. Book II describes the eleven methods of enriching material. Method 1 is the unwrapping of the constituent parts of a statement. Method 2 records in detail the events which preceded an action. Method 3 enumerates the causes underlying the bare fact. Of course there is overlapping between the Books; the seventh method of enriching material is in fact the same as Erasmus' third method of diversifying expression (*antonomasia*).

Our concern is with *enargeia* or *evidentia*, the fifth method of achieving abundance of subject-matter. Erasmus writes that we employ this when, instead of setting out our subject in bare simplicity, we

> fill in the colours and set it up like a picture to look at, so that we seem to have painted the scene rather than described it, and the reader seems to have seen rather than read. We shall be able to do this satisfactorily if we first mentally review the whole nature of the subject and everything connected with it, its very appearance in fact. Then we should give it substance with appropriate words and figures of speech, to make it as vivid and clear to the reader as possible.[2]

---

1   Translated by Betty I. Knott as volume 24 of *The Collected Works of Erasmus* (Toronto: 1978). The quotation appears on p. 296.
2   *Ibid.*, p. 579.

This definition is close to that offered by Henry Peacham in his 1577 version of *The Garden of Eloquence*. He declares that *hypotyposis* (Puttenham's generic figure of 'counterfeit representation') occurs when

> by a diligent gathering of circumstaunces, we expresse & set forth a thing so plainely, that it seemeth rather paynted in tables, then expressed with wordes, and the hearer shall rather thincke he see it, then heare it.[3]

Peacham's *hypotyposis* serves the same office as Erasmian *enargeia*.[4] Mastery of this figure is an essential part of the poet's activity. The specific figures are *prosopographia, prosopopoeia, topographia, chronographia,* and *pragmatographia*. *Prosopographia,* Puttenham informs us, is the figure which depicts the 'visage, speach and countenance of any person absent or dead ... as our poet Chaucer doth in his Canterbury tales set foorth the Sumner, Pardoner, Manciple, and the rest of the pilgrims, most naturally and pleasantly'.[5] *Prosopopoeia* is the attribution of human qualities to dumb or insensible creatures or to abstractions. *Chronographia* is the description of time – 'winter, summer, harvest, day, midnight, noone, evening, or such like'. *Topographia* is description of place, whether real or imagined. *Pragmatographia* is the depiction of action – battles, feasts, marriages, or 'any other matter that lieth in feat and activitie'.

Montgomerie, like his compatriots Henryson and Lyndsay, is adept at the deployment of the specific figures of representation. For example, here is the opening of *The Cherrie and the Slae*:[6]

> About ane bank, quhair birdis on bewes
> ten thousand tymis thair notes renewes
>   Ilk houre into the day,
> The Merle, the Maveis, [micht] be seine,
> the Progney and the Phelomeine,
>   Quhilk caussit me to stay.
> I lay and leind me to ane busse,
>   to heir thir birdis beir;
> Thair [mirth was] so melodiousse,
>   throwe natour of the yeir:
>   Some singing, some springing
>   with wingis into the skye;
>   So nymlie and trimlie,
>   thir birds thay flew me by.

---

3 *The Garden of Eloquence* (1577). Oii^r.
4 Erasmus comments that vivid description is particularly apposite in poetry, since this is a medium which exists principally to give pleasure.
5 *The Arte of English Poesie*, ed. Edward Arber (London: 1895), p. 245.
6 I quote from the first Waldegrave print (1597), as edited by George Stevenson (STS, 1910). Where necessary, I have introduced emendations from the second Waldegrave edition (also 1597), using Stevenson's apparatus.

The *topographia* continues for the next seven stanzas. The third stanza enriches the depiction:

> The ayr was so attemperat,
> but ony mist Immaculat,
>   baith puryfeit and cleir:
> The flouris fair ware flurischit,
> as natour had thame nurischit,
>   baith delicate and deir:
> And every blome on branche and bewche
>   so prettillie was spred:
> Syne hang thair heids out over ane hewche,
>   in Mayis cullour cled.

To depict all the pleasures of this place is not within the narrator's ability; he will leave the task to poets employing 'staitlie verse and ornat style' (75). The enterprise 'passis my Ingyne' – an avowal of poetic incapacity which is familiar to us from medieval and late medieval verse. Lyndsay, for example, excuses himself (in *The Dreme*) from describing all the marvels of the empyrean because 'myne Ingyne is nocht sufficient' (540); by contrast, to specify all the miseries of hell 'were ane cummer'. The figure by which the author indicates those things which he will not narrate is called *paralapsis* (Latin, *occupatio*).

Nevertheless, in spite of this modest disclaimer, the 'diligent gathering of circumstances' permits us to see the scene that is being 'paynted' for us – and indeed to hear the music of the waters and of the birds (stanzas 7 and 8). We notice that Montgomerie energises his *topographia* by the use of localised figures such as *erotema* and *anaphora*. *Erotema* is the figure which substitutes the interrogative form for the affirmative: 'this figure I call the Questioner or inquisitiue' (Puttenham). One can recognise the efficacy of *erotema* as used here:

> Quha wald haue tyrit to heir that tune,
> quhilk birds corroborate abune,
>   throw schouting of the Larkis?

The texture is enriched by *anaphora* (initial repetition):

> Quha flewe sa hie into the skyis,
> quhil Cupid walknit throw the cryis,
>   of natures chappell clarkis;
> Quha leueing all the heuins aboue,
>   syne lichtit on the eird.

(A pleasing touch is the *antonomasia* – substitution of a descriptive phrase for a proper name – of 'natures chappell clarkis').

The depiction of Cupid is an example of *prosopographia*. As Erasmus notes, one can use this term for the presentation of personifications (Opportunity, Fame, Justice) and of such mythological characters as the Muses, the Graces, and the Furies. An ingredient which contributes to the vitality of *prosopographia* is *dialogismus*, the provision of appropriate speech – that is, speech which is fitting in terms of character and circumstances. In the case of Cupid (see stanza 10) the persuasive utterance of the God of Desire is enhanced by *anaphora*: we register his seductive delivery:

> 'Quhat wald thow giue, my freind,' quod he,
> 'till haue thir prettie wings to flie,
>   to sport thee for ane quhile?
> Or quhat, gif I suld lend thee heir
> my bowe and all my schuitting geir,
>   some bodie to begyle?'
> 'That geir,' quod I, 'cannot be bocht,
>   yit wald I haue it faine.'
> 'Quhat gif,' quod he, 'it cost thee nocht,
>   Bot rander it againe?'

The stanza is so organised that the progression is irresistible. The series of questions can be distinguished as *pysma* (the figure by which the speaker asks not one but several insistent questions).

Topographia and *prosopographia* are the prevailing specific figures of *enargeia* in the first ten stanzas. In 11 we embark on *pragmatographia*. Erasmus observes that epithets contribute markedly to the distinctiveness with which an action is rendered ('airy' cliffs, 'sky-blue' sea, 'turret-crowned' cities). Metaphors and similes are also serviceable. One can see these devices in operation in stanzas 11–13. Erasmus, one imagines, would have approved of the use of *icon* (a figure of *homoeosis* or resemblance):

> I sprang so heich on Cupid's wings . . .
> As Icarus with borrowit flicht,
>   qua mountit heicher nor he micht.
> As fulisch Phaetone, be suite,
>   his fathers cairte obteind,
> I langit in luiffis bowe to schuite,
>   and wist not quhat it meind.

The powerful effect of stanza 13 is largely obtained by the combination of insistent *anaphora* ('To lait . . . to lait . . . to lait . . . To lait . . . To lait . . . To lait') and *parison* (a succession of clauses of corresponding structure). Thus we find 'To lait I knaw' / 'to lait I hard' / 'To lait I find' / 'To lait . . . I steik'.

The splendidly vital *pragmatographia* of stanzas 22–5 displays Montgomerie's richest vein. Stanza 22 presents the first view of the cherry-tree and the sloebush. The pattern accommodates *ploche* (swift repetition) on 'ore' ('ore craig, ore clewch, ore schoir') and *epitheton* (the provision of the expected or standard qualifying word) in the phrase 'bitter Slais'. Puttenham says of *epitheton*, the 'figure of attribution', that 'he must be apt and proper for the thing he is added vnto, and not disagreable or repugnant'. The figure is in evidence again in 23:

> The chirries hang abune my heid,
> like twinkling rewbeis round and reid,
> so hich vp in the hewch;
> Quhais scaddowes in the River schew,
> Als graithlie glansing, as thay grewe,
> on trimbling twistis tewch.

The effectiveness lies in the provision of the expected adjective. If I quote stanza 24 the prevailing techniques which are employed at this cardinal point in the poem will become clear:

> With ernest eye, I can espye
> the fruit betwix me and the skye,
> half gaite almaist to hevin:
> The craige so cumbersome to clime,
> the trie so hich of growth and trime,
> as ony arrow evin;
> I call to minde how Daphne did
> within the Laurell schrink,
> Quhan from Appollo scho hir hid.

Epitheton recurs in the attribution 'cumbersome' to the crag. *Homoeosis* plays a significant part in the design:

> like twinkling rewbies
> as ony arrow evin.

An operation of *homoeosis* occurs in the allusion to Apollo and Daphne; this is an example of the poet's dipping into that 'ocean of parallels' (*similium pelagus*) which Erasmus delights in celebrating in his educational writings. Grammatically, we note the working of *parison* at 326–7:

> The craige so cumbersome to clime,
> the trie so hich of growth and trime.

Erasmus tells us that that the poet / orator should have seen – or clearly envisaged – the action or location he is to present. The supreme practitioner is Homer. Is there anything, asks Erasmus, that Homer cannot display vividly 'by putting in the appropriate circumstantial detail, which, even if it sometimes seems insignificant, yet somehow or other presents the thing marvellously to our eyes'?[7] To my mind, Montgomerie fulfils the requirement of Erasmus in the conclusion to stanza 23:

> Reflexe of Phoebus in the firth
> [Newe colourit] all the knoppis,
>   With dansing, and glansing,
>   in tirles dornik champ
> Quhilk streimet, and gleimet,
>   throw lichtnes of that lamp.

Helena Shire glosses lines 317–20 as follows: 'Light reflected up on [the clusters of cherries] from the waters of change lent them a new colour, their radiant and changeful motion suggesting the lively patterns of [Tournay] weave'.[8] How alluring those cherries are; how radiant those beams of light!

The debate which ensues offers us varieties of *dialogismus*. Danger, fittingly, makes use of proverbial lore (cf. stanza 37, for example) to dissuade the narrator from pursuing his quest. George Stevenson suggested that much of the poem's enduring popularity could be traced to its 'neatly rhymed expression of . . . old saws and sayings'.[9] Courage robustly argues the opposing case (463):

> 'Quhat is the way to heal thy hurt?
> Quhat way is thair to stay thy sturt?
>   quhat meanes my mak thee merrie?
> Quhat is the comfort that thou craues?
> suppois the Sophists thee dessaues,
>   thou knawis it is the Cherrie.

One hardly needs to labour the combined effect of *anaphora, parison,* and *pysma*. There is an interesting operation at 468. This is *anthypophora* (also called *hypophora*), by which the speaker answers his own questions. As Puttenham indicates, the figure is one of argument and also of amplification. So on this occasion; the speaker advances his case and also 'enlarges [the] tale'. The poem would collapse unless the debate retained vigour and urgency. In sustaining the debate, Montgomerie shows his command of 'fitting' utterance; indeed, this part of the poem is a compendium or treasury of *dialogismus*.

In the completed version of the poem, which occupies 114 quatorziems, the cherry falls for very ripeness (stanza 113) and brings refreshment to the seeker. The concluding stanza celebrates the eternal glory of God, who has provided spiritual succour to Montgomerie. In this paper I have taken my quotations from

---

7 Knott, p. 580.
8 *Song, Dance and Poetry of the Court of Scotland under King James VI* (Cambridge: 1969), p. 129. [Should we emend 'tirles dornik champ' to 'tirlis lik dornik champ' – the Laing MS reading?] The classic exposition of the poem is contained in Chapter V of Shire.
9 Stevenson, p. xix.

the first Waldegrave print, which ends in the midst of the contention, half-way through stanza 67. Even so, I have not been able to do more than suggest *some* of the operations which are of rhetorical interest. Montgomerie's verse is not – by Elizabethan standards – thickly studded with schemes; he is fairly abstemious in this respect. But this comparative austerity means, I think, that figures of interrogation and repetition (for example) play an effective part in the design when Montgomerie decides to enlist them. We can appreciate the usefulness of these localised devices in enhancing *topographia, pragmatographia, prosopographia*. And these specific figures themselves contribute to *enargeia*, which is an important constituent in the poet's command of *copia*.

DANIEL FISCHLIN

40.   *'Counterfeiting God': James VI (I) and the Politics of* Dæmonologie

In introductory comments to his edition of the *Malleus Maleficarum* Montague Summers argues that 'Witchcraft was inextricably mixed with politics' (v). The *Malleus*, published in 1484 by Heinrich Kramer and James Sprenger, two of the inquisition's foremost prosecutors and both Dominican monks, pieces together a patchwork of the many political, religious, and personal anxieties associated with the construction of the witch in the late fifteenth century. In this document, formulated out of obscure legalistic and Scriptural arguments, perhaps the most revealing historical material lies in the anecdotal evidence of witches' activities collected by Kramer and Sprenger and unevenly disseminated through the length of the document. A form of narrative derived from oral popular culture founds many of the key evidential moments in the *Malleus*, moments in which its legal and Scriptural arguments are given their basis in material reality by virtue of fictional anecdotes passed off as legitimate testimony. The legal and juridical structures at the centre of the *Malleus* are intricately related to those marginal anecdotes that validate the larger discursive structures of the document.

One such anecdote, intertextually linked with humorous fabliau narratives, evokes many of the issues that circulate through the historical and literary discourses associated with witchcraft:

> And what, then, is to be thought of those witches who . . . sometimes collect male organs in great numbers, as many as twenty or thirty members together, and put them in a bird's nest, or shut them up in a box, where they move themselves like living members, and eat oats and corn, as has been seen by many and is a matter of common report? It is to be said that it is all done by devil's work and illusion, for the senses of those who see them are deluded in the way we have said. For a certain man tells that, when he had lost his member, he approached a known witch to ask her to restore it to him. She told the afflicted man to climb a certain tree, and that he might take which he liked out of a nest in which there were several members. And when he tried to take a big one, the witch said: You must not take that one; adding, because it belonged to a parish priest. (121)

It is revealing that Kramer and Sprenger saw fit to include this passage as evidence, however preposterous, of witches' activities in the dry legal context usually associated with canonical lawmaking. Perhaps the most noticeable anxiety in the passage relates to possession – in this case of the phallus, symbol both literal and figurative of male sexuality and empowerment. The threat of witches emanates from their power to dismember male sexuality, their control over the symbolic potency of man and their restorative powers with regard to the loss of that potency. Such a threat is not merely localised in the episteme of sexuality but has further extensions into the realm of power and its manipulation. The negative of male empowerment is gendered as threateningly female, even though this threat is somewhat undermined by the humorous narrative context. If a witch can control the male member by separating it from the body, nesting it elsewhere – suggesting a further related anxiety associated with the vulnerability and permeability of the male body – is it not also possible that the witch poses an incipient threat to other forms of male empowerment embodied symbolically, for example, in the monarch's sceptre?[1]

The answer is a qualified yes. The history of witchcraft is the history, in part, of male anxieties about their own empowerment, sexual or otherwise. But it is also the history of women's oppression as gendered political subjects constructed by the patriarchy and as subjects who posed in their demonised collectivity particular threats to male empowerment.[2] There is a substantial, though often unrecognised connection, between sexual empowerment and political empowerment and, as Deborah Willis has noted, 'To varying degrees and with varying emphases, elite discourse about the witch was . . . concerned with promoting a new religious orthodoxy and maintaining political order and social hierarchy' (115). In the incident just cited, the witch gains subversive power not only through her ability to dismember but also through her control over the choice of the male member. She also has the power of critique, her comment regarding the parish priest being an obvious anti-clerical dig at the widespread corruption of the clergy and thus an attack on a form of religious hierarchy. And in her nurturing of the nested male members with oats and corn the witch has the power of sustenance over the very symbol of male empowerment, the phallus, the marker of sexual difference that must anxiously be recuperated by the 'dismembered' man in Kramer's and Sprenger's narrative.

1 See Fig. 1, the frontispiece from James's *The Workes* (1616). The sceptre and the globe, along with other symbols of political and religious order – the Order of the Garter, the *Verbum Dei*, and the Crown – iconographically depict the ideological coherence of absolutism.
2 For a useful account of witchcraft as a gendered form of persecution see Anderson and Zinsser: 'The historian E. William Monter has called it a time of "lethal misogyny". Men fell victim, but at least two-thirds of those who died were women. In the waves of panic and fear, sometimes all were women, sometimes 80 percent or more, always the vast majority. The most conservative estimate of the numbers of European women strangled, drowned, burned, and beheaded is 100,000. Most historians believe there were many more' (167). Of England and Scotland, Anderson and Zinsser report that 'Persecution came in two waves in England, in the 1580s and 1590s, then again from 1645 to 1647 when 490 were executed in Essex, one third of those accused. Women suffered in clusters of persecution in Scotland: 200 and 300 identified at a time from the 1590s to the 1660s – over 3,000 trials, and 1,000 executed' (167). The connection between these persecutory waves and the dates of James's rise to power poses an interesting historical coincidence. For more information on these questions in specific relation to Scotland, see Christina Larner, 'Who Were the Witches?' in *Enemies of God*, 89–102. Larner observes that 'The witches of Scotland were typical of the witches of rural Europe. They were predominantly poor, middle-aged or elderly women' (89). See also Larner's comments in 'Witchcraft Past and Present' (*Witchcraft and Religion*), especially 84–8. It is not my intention to go over the complicated questions related to the number of people who were persecuted and died during the European witchcraze, there being considerable difficulty in establishing the accuracy of such numbers. In this latter regard, see Cohn (1975), especially 253–5.

Crounes haue their compasse, length of dayes their date,
Triumphes their tombes, felicitie her fate:
Off more then earth, can earth make none partakers,
But knowledge makes the KING most like his maker.

Simon Pasæus sculp: Lond.   Ioh: Bill excudit.

Fig.1: frontispiece from James VI (I)'s *The Workes* (1616).

Dismemberment, choice, critique, sustenance. All are crucial motifs, both literal and figural, in the ontological construction of the absolute sovereign's relations to the political subject. The first part of the *Malleus* clearly affirms, despite its often paradoxical attempts to deny the power of witches ('no operation of witchcraft has a permanent effect among us'[1]), that 'Witchcraft is high treason against God's Majesty' (6), a phrase that James VI (I) echoes in the third book of *Dæmonologies* (78). The conflation of 'God' and 'Majesty' is not accidental. It frames the symbiotic relationship necessary to create structures of political empowerment, and more specifically, structures related to the enactment of absolute power so crucial to the history of early modern Europe. Power must be seen as originating from an unspeakable dimension that gives it its privileges, its validity. In the early modern period that dimension is inevitably constructed out of the unspeakability of god as a fictive principle out of which material power gains its credibility and exercisability. '[T]he reality of the divine,' as René Girard argues, 'rests in its transcendental absence' (143). The power to create the mental image of a god who gives meaning to the operations of the material world's hierarchies is the basis out of which the consensual hallucination of sovereignty comes to exist. As a consequence, any form of contradictory or alternative power with regard to the making of images is potentially threatening, as it was in the case of the witch's putative power to conjure images of glamours, incubi, succubi, demons, devils, and familiars.

After relating the incident with which I began, Kramer and Sprenger continue:

> All these things are caused by devils through an illusion or glamour, in the manner we have said, *by confusing the organ of vision by transmuting the mental images in the imaginative faculty*. And it must not be said that these members which are shown are devils in assumed members, just as they sometimes appear to witches and men in assumed aerial bodies, and converse with them. *And the reason is that they effect this thing by an easier method, namely, by drawing out an inner mental image from the repository of the memory, and impressing it on the imagination*. (121; my emphasis)

This passage reflects an equal if not surpassing anxiety over the confusion caused by the power to transmute 'the mental images in the imaginative faculty.' The power to draw 'out an inner mental image from the repository of memory' and to impress that mental image 'on the imagination' was crucial in justifying the hierarchical relationship of the monarch over his subjects, just as it was crucial in allowing the sovereign to exercise his political will. Witches were constructed as having effectively usurped this shaping power to themselves. And that imaginative power is a significant source of at least some of the structures of absolute political power operative in early modern Europe. Ultimately, then, the full passage from Kramer and Sprenger reflects a sexual anxiety masking for the even more full-blown anxiety over the possession of the mind of the subject. Witchcraft, the demonisation of people who were thought capable of producing this effect of bodily and imaginative possession, is thus the site of a complex struggle over the mind and body of the political subject, the sometimes unwilling participant in the consensual hallucination that, at least partially, founds the absolute power embodied in the figure of the Renaissance monarch.[3]

The fact that this struggle for the body and mind of the subject was localised, more often than not, in the bodies and minds of women – that it was thus a gendered struggle – is highly suggestive. The question needs to be asked: Why were the vast majority of accused witches women? Why were women so frequently seen as the locus for male anxieties about power? What associations did men make between the imaginative faculties of women and male constructions of power? The answers to these questions are not simple but provide useful insights into the literary and historical phenomena associated with witchcraft. When Anne Boleyn, mother to Elizabeth I, was imprisoned in the King's House within the Tower of London for failure to produce a male heir, it is perhaps noteworthy that Henry VIII putatively demonised her for possessing what was construed to be a sixth finger, not to mention a witch's mole. Whether true or not – there is no solid, contemporary evidence to support the claim – the connections between political expediency and demonisation are evident in the somewhat prurient narratives constructed in the aftermath of Boleyn's execution.[4] Despite its potentially destructive, material effects, demonisation is very much a function of potent narrative fictions. It is no accident that the third witch in *The Tragedy of Macbeth* (first performed in 1611, probably composed in 1605–6) makes the fateful prediction 'All hail, Macbeth, that shalt be king hereafter!' (I.3.48), after the first and second witches have accurately described his positioning in the

---

3 I do not wish to dismiss the construction of witchcraft from the position of the witch, that is, the person who had a personal investment in participating in the activities associated with witchcraft, whether that be the ritual Witches' Sabbath, the use of herbal lore to produce potions, the use of charms and incantations to produce material effects in the real world, or the search for ecstatic experience outside the parameters of state control. This essay, however, seeks to move away from the trend of attempting to understand the 'ecstatic' experiences instantiated in witchcraft practices – a trend to be found in the work of Carlo Ginzburg, for instance – while focusing on the state constructions of and investments in those same practices.

4 The same may be said (in a more accurate, historical context) of how useful charges of witchcraft were to James in disposing of his treasonous cousin, Francis Stewart, Earl of Bothwell (known as Bothwell), a prominent member of the extreme Protestants opposed to James. Stuart Clark notes, in discussing the events of 1590–91 at North Berwick in which a large number of witches were 'discovered,' that 'Each of the witches at Newhaven had apparently "blessed" [a] wax effigy with the words, "This is King James the Sext, ordonit to be consumed at the instance of a noble man Francis Erle Bodowell." Bothwell protested his innocence but was committed to custody in May 1591' (158–9). See also, in this same regard, James Craigie's comments in *The Basilicon Doron* (2.236), Christina Larner's comments in 'James VI and I and Witchcraft' (82), and Edward J. Cowan's comments in 'The Darker Version of the Scottish Renaissance: the Devil and Francis Stewart'. Similar instances involving the demonisation of political opposition can be noted during Elizabeth's reign. One such instance is the demonic diction used in Elizabeth's letter to the Lord Mayor of London (1586) after conspirators planning her assassination were apprehended: 'Being given to understand how greatly our good and most loving subjects of that city did rejoice at the apprehension *of certain devilish and wicked minded subjects of ours*, that through the great and singular goodness of God have been detected, to have most wickedly and unnaturally conspired, not only the taking away of our own life, but also to have stirred up (as much as in them lay) a general rebellion throughout our whole realm' (modernised; my emphasis; n.p.).

Scottish hierarchy, 'Thane of Glamis,' 'Thane of Cawdor.' The prophesy, made just after Macbeth's first appearance in the play, effectively locates the source of Macbeth's drive to power in the witch's craft. Nor is it accidental that the very first words spoken by Macbeth – 'So foul and fair a day I have not seen' (I.3.36) – are but echoes of the witches' incantation that ends the very first scene of the play 'Fair is foul, and foul is fair, / Hover through the fog and filthy air' (I.1.10–11). Macbeth literally enters the play speaking in the words of the witches' incantation, a not-so-subtle reminder, perhaps, of the latent connections among tragic narrative structure, witchcraft, and the will-to-power to which Macbeth will soon succumb.

The power of the witches' incantation in *Macbeth* is all the more potent in that it frames the paradox, 'Fair is foul, and foul is fair': a discursive construct that renders improbable opposites into the illusion of an homologous, imaginative whole. Which is to say that the witches' power as it is constructed literarily is the power over words and their effects, their power to bend reality, to shape the imagination through incantation. And it is a power to which Macbeth succumbs both in his appropriation of their incantation as well as in living out the power of their prophesy. Women speak imaginatively. Men act accordingly, albeit tragically. The wierd sisters represent precisely the imaginative and discursive power feared by Kramer and Sprenger. It is in their power to impress on Macbeth's imagination the notion of the absolute power he will pursue, just as it is in the wierd sisters' power to transmute 'the mental images in the imaginative faculty' of the audience which they entertain with their heady combination of charm, dance, music, image and incantation.

But this is only one example of the associative power embodies in women as practitioners of witchcraft. A more modern example occurs with Sigmund Freud, who is reported to have read the *Malleus* 'with ardour' and who 'customarily went so far as saying, in his correspondence with Wilhelm Flies and others, that between the inquisitor (the exorcist) and the possessed woman (or the sorcerer) there existed something analogous to the relation between the analyst and the client' (cited in de Certeau 244).[5] Again, as in *Macbeth*, we see a similar structural model at work: the analysand (witch) gives meaning to the analyst (male) by virtue of her presence in his office. The witch provides the imaginative material that allows the inquisitor to formulate his own relationship to power, just as the analyst produces his own place in the structures of psychoanalysis out of, for example, the dream material provided by the analysand.[6] The parallels are

---

5   For further comments on Freud's ambiguous relations with the demonic, see 'Sorceress and Hysteric,' in Cixous and Clément, 3–39.
6   James's private as opposed to his publically stated beliefs about dreams are of relevance here. George Nicholson, the English agent at the Scottish court, wrote that 'I have hard but in great secret and so I beseche your honour [Sir William Cecil] to kepe it. That .126 [a cypher for James] was troubled in his chamber in his slepe. and [sic] hathe taken conceipt that .200 [a cypher for Elizabeth] shall out live him. and [sic] thereon hath he written an appollogy and rule howe his soun shalbe brought to succede .200. to that place, and how all shalbe governed for the attayninge thereunto (*The Basilicon Doron* 1.4). In the *Basilikon Doron* proper James has this to say about dreaming, in distinction from what Nicolson had reported about him: 'Take no heede to any of

uncanny: the imagination – construed as feminine – empowers the hierarchical structures in which men operate.

A final historical example of the associative and imaginative powers embodied in women or their representation taken from the mid-seventeenth century should make my point. In 1649 Gerrard Winstanely led the Diggers, a small group of politico-religious subversives who were seen as extraordinarily threatening to the goals of the anti-monarchical forces precisely because they felt that these forces had not gone far enough in the revolution. Winstanley wrote an account of the persecution suffered by himself and other Diggers in which the following marginal incident is mentioned: '*Divers of the Diggers were beaten upon the* Hill *by* William Star *and* John Taylor, *and by men in womens apparel, and so sore wounded, that some of them were fetched home in a cart*' (Winstanley 96). The incident, which involves demonisation of the Diggers because of the subversive political forces they embodied, also marks an interesting case of transvestitism. Why did men feel it necessary to dress in women's clothes in order to attack the Diggers? The obvious answer is that women represent the ultimate form of disempowerment, so what could be more humiliating and disempowering than being beaten by these false representations of femininity?

A less obvious answer is that the men in women's clothing were literally empowering themselves with the imaginative and subversive powers associated with women in any number of historical, political, or literary contexts.[7] In other words, how else to undermine the potentially dangerous political subversions which the Diggers represented than by employing the mask of what was seen as the ultimate source of imaginative and subversive power, women? Accounts of the incident do not indicate whether or not these men dressed the part of witches, but if we recall the Kramer and Sprenger anecdote, it is not too much of a leap to suggest that men could easily be transformed into things other than themselves (such as demons or witches) by the subversive imaginative powers associated, however indirectly, with women. A man in woman's clothing is no longer necessarily a man, just as a man

---

your dreams: for all Prophecies, visions, and prophetick dreames are accomplished and ceased in Christ. And therefore take no heede to freets [superstitions] either in dreames, or any other things: for that errour proceedeth of ignorance, & is vnworthy of a Christian' (1. 171). In *Dæmonologie* James, oddly enough using a prophet as his authority, says the following about prophesy: 'in the Prophet *Ieremie* it is plainelie forbidden, to beleeue or hearken vnto them that Prophecies & forespeakes by the course of the Planets & Starres' (1.14). The obvious tensions between his public and (putatively) private views on dreaming and prophesy indicate the extent to which the realm of the imaginative is the site of contestation, particularly in regard to how the work of the imagination locates, if Nicolson's report is reliable, the sources of anxiety and threat to the stability of the monarch's power.

7 Stephen Greenblatt suggests that 'The cross-dressing was perhaps a disguise – though the magistrates were far more interested in prosecuting than in protecting the Diggers – but it was also a familiar and traditional emblem of the carnivalesque. The festive gesture seems calculated to deride the Diggers, to avoid the impression of an official military or judicial repression, to deprive them of the possibility of dignity in defeat, and to pit one conception of the common people against another' (76). This reading sidesteps the obvious inflections, political and otherwise, that the incident has in terms of gender.

who deludedly believes his penis to be missing is no longer necessarily a man. An imaginative transformation is effected through the way in which subjects are constructed, be it through the clothing they wear, as in the Winstanley incident, the words they speak, as in *Macbeth*, or the dismembering powers they embody, as in the Kramer and Sprenger anecdote. My argument is that the power to effect such an imaginative transformation is a form of political power that is threatening to the established order and, ultimately, necessary to the way in which that order shapes itself.

The witch, then, is the locus of a particular kind of gendered and imaginary power seen as threatening. I now wish to propose, however paradoxically, that this imaginary subversive power was a necessary construction of the very political hierarchies that sought to eradicate it. Georges Bataille has stated that '[m]yth is born in ritual acts concealed from the static vulgarity of a disintegrated society, but the violent dynamic belonging to it has no other object than the return to a lost totality' (23). Consensual myths, what I have called earlier consensual hallucinations, are necessary to construct the 'lost totalit[ies]' of kingship and absolute power as deployed in Europe during the fifteenth and sixteenth centuries.[8] These consensual myths are 'born,' in Bataille's sense, in the ritual act of constructing the witch as an inverted emblem of that absolute power.[9]

If one reads the European witchcraft phenomena as an expression of collective anxieties about the imaginary status of the absolute, especially from the vantage point of those most invested in absolutism, then it becomes possible to argue that witches incarnate the lost dimensions of absolutism. The witch is a material reminder of those lost dimensions restored to visibility by the operations of the absolute as a representation of a political collectivity: '[o]nly the social utility of . . . collective violence can account for a politico-ritualistic scheme that consists not only of constantly repeating the process but also of making the surrogate victim [in this case, the witch] . . . a veritable incarnation of absolute sovereignty' (Girard 109). The anxieties circulating around the construction of the illusion of absolutism originate, at least partially, in the tenuous relations extant between the monarch and the commonwealth, the individual and the collectivity: '[t]hat State desire moves

---

8 For more on absolutism and the the myths upon which it was founded, see Henshall, especially 80–147.
9 See Stuart Clark, especially 173–6, for more on the argument by inversion or contrary in direct relation to James. Of particular relevance is Clark's assertion that 'the Devil's style of government was universally acknowledged to be tyranny, the antithesis of true kingship: "the prince is a kind of likeness of divinity; and the tyrant, on the contrary, a likeness of the boldness of the Adversary" ' (175). Also see Jonathan L. Pearl's comments on Jean Bodin's *De La Démonomanie des Sorciers* (1580): 'For Bodin, the worst thing that witches did was to renounce God and make a pact with the devil (196, v ff.). The crimes committed against mankind, such as murder or causing impotence, paled before the enormity of the crime of divine treason (191, v ff.) . . . Bodin explicitly stated: 'There is no penalty so cruel that can suffice to punish the evil deeds of witches, *since all their evil deeds, blasphemies and designs are directed against the Majesty of God in order to offend him by a thousand means*' (196, v)' (543; emphasis mine). For a useful discussion of the Biblical passage (Exodus 22:18) on which this extreme punishment was based, see H.C. Erik Midelfort.

in the direction of a transcendental concentration in the body of a more or less divinised leader does not belie the immanence of its functioning, which is always collective' (Dean and Massumi 80). In the particular historical case of James VI (I) the troublesome recognition of the immanent power of the collective required extraordinary measures to reduce apprehensions about the exercise of absolute power. Absolute power I define, ultimately, as the ability of the state to inscribe, literally and figuratively, its presence on the body through the intervention of ideologies and technologies associated with torture and punishment.

II

To make this point I now turn to James's treatise on witchcraft *Dæmonologie* (1597) as well as a related earlier text, *Newes from Scotland* (1591) in terms of how the ritual acts associated with constructing the witch are associated with the ritual acts of constructing the king. The witch is a fetish object – the locus of unauthorised activities – around which are gathered, paradoxically, the constitutive myths associated with kingship. When James argues in *Dæmonologie* that 'who denyeth the power of the Deuill, would likewise denie the power of God' (54–5), he is instantiating God's ontological presence and therefore his own through a negative proof. Such a proof is dependent upon the construction of the devil as a mythic confirmation of divine presence, a negative construction whose material manifestation is the witch and her unauthorised activities – *Contra negantem principia non est disputandum (Dæmonologie* 2). James's argument is based on the old saw that 'there can be no better way to know God, then by the contrarie' (*Dæmonologie* 55), an argument that insured, in the political logic of the time, that if witches did not exist they would be created in order to affirm God's presence and, by extension, the divine right of the monarch, that troubled material and transcendent embodiment of the imagined midpoint between the commonwealth and the divinity.[10]

10 Hints at similar sorts of arguments have been made by a number of scholars in the field, though none, to my knowledge, has produced a close reading of the mechanics of the argument as evinced in *Dæmonologie*. See, for example, Maurice Lee Jr.'s assertion that 'Witchcraft was a necessary aspect of his theory of kingship: not to believe in witches was not to believe in the power of the Devil, their master, which disbelief in turn raised the possibility of disbelief in God' (72). Larner observes that 'It was not the witch theory which James had been incubating during his fearful and clergy-ridden youth; it was the doctrine of the divine right of kings' ('James VI and I and Witchcraft' 83). See also Larner's seminal work in *Enemies of God* and *Witchcraft and Religion*. Another recent book to deal with politics and demonology (from a politico-sociological perspective) is Jon Oplinger's *The Politics of Demonology*. Oplinger asserts that 'The witchcraze and the modern nation state emerged together and are a product of the same strategy of social control' (48; see also 110–16). Finally, it is my position that the political context underlies the religious context of James's *Dæmonologie*, my argument opposing Sheldon Hanft's rather one-sided notion that 'James wrote Daemonologie . . . because he felt there was a rational theological explanation for both the existence and the exercise of evil in the real world' (52). As is so often the case in James, the rationale behind theological positioning is a function of the political uses to which such a positioning could be put.

Fig. 2: Satan's (Pluto's) court, from Gerard d'Euphrates' *Livre de l'histoire & ancienne cronique* (Paris, 1549).

James argues that 'by the falsehood of the one [the Devil] . . . consider the truth of the other [God], by the injustice of the one . . . consider the Iustice of the other: And by the cruelty of the one . . . consider the mercifulnesse of the other: And so foorth in all the rest of the essence of God, and qualities of the Deuill' (55). The monarch, of course, is implicated in this inversion, for the inversion allows James to argue covertly toward a monarchic theodicy. Monarchic power not only creates the threat of witchcraft by convincing the 'manie [that] can scarcely beleeue that there is such a thing as Witch-craft' (28), but also exposes 'the limites of his [the Devil's] power [which] were set down before the foundations of the world were laid, which he hath not power in the least jote to transgresse' (30–1). The monarch constructs the devil's power as a lesser inversion of his own power to punish transgression. Epistemon, one half of the dialoguic entity that gives shape to James's argument in *Dæmonologie*,[11] formulates the monarch's power to punish transgression most clearly toward the end of the third book:

> The Prince or Magistrate for further tryals cause, may continue the punishing of them [convicted witches] such a certaine space as he thinkes conuenient: But in the end to spare the life, and not to strike when God bids strike, and so seuerelie punish in so odious a fault & treason against God, it is not only vnlawful, but doubtlesse no lesse sinne in that Magistrate, nor it was in SAULES sparing of AGAG. And so comparable to the sin of Witch-craft it selfe, as SAMVELL alleaged at that time. (78)

The passage explicates the inverted relation between the monarch and the witch, for if the monarch does not punish the witch severely, he is committing 'treason' against God and committing a sin 'comparable' to witchcraft itself. The language of statecraft, then, is inexorably intertwined with that of witchcraft in the perverse logic of *Dæmonologie* – a fact borne out in visual representations of Satan from the period, which often depict him enthroned before a court composed of witches.[12] The treasonous activities of witches are comparable to the treasonous monarch who fails to punish their transgressions with appropriate severity. The religious and theological dimensions of witchcraft are thus profoundly implicated in the material politics of absolutism.

In this regard, it is possible to argue, as does Norman Cohn, that witches were

---

11 Larner notes that '*Daemonologie* is written as a dialogue between one Philomathes, who asks sceptical and sometimes highly pertinent questions, and Epistemon, who gives learned but often unsatisfactory answers, which Philemon invariably accepts gratefully' ('James VI and I and Witchcraft' 85).

12 See Fig. 2 from Gerard d'Euphrates' *Livre de l'histoire & ancienne cronique* (Paris, 1549). See also Clark's assertion that 'Both in genesis and in content the *Daemonologie* may be read as a statement about ideal monarchy . . . demonism was, logically speaking, one of the presuppositions of the metaphysics of order on which James's political ideas ultimately rested' (156–7). Clark affirms that James 'thought of the *Daemonologie* as one of his most important works' (157) and notes that after its initial publication in Edinburgh in 1597, *Dæmonologie* 'went through two London editions in 1603 and was later translated into Latin, French and Dutch' (156).

'a collective inversion of Christianity' (*Witchcraft and Sorcery* 143), the witches' Sabbath which usually culminated in the witches kissing the Devil's anus, being an inversion of the Mass culminating in the symbolic union of the worshipper with Christ's body in commmunion. The wonderful paradox in this symbolic inversion, as James notes in his prefatory comments 'TO THE READER' in *Dæmonologie*, is that

> *God by the contrarie, drawes euer out of that euill glorie [the Devil] to himself, either by the wracke of the wicked in his justice, or/by the tryall of the patient, and amendment of the faithfull, being wakened up with that rod of correction.*(xiv)

God literally feeds upon the evil which he produces just as he feeds upon the prohibitions he places on that evil. The analogies to the absolute monarch should not go unnoted here for the absolute monarch has a vested interest in producing the very threats which his power prohibits: 'the absolute state' as Kenneth Dean and Brian Massumi argue, literally '*requires* the existence of an enemy' (176). The threat, as in the case of witchcraft, becomes an artificial construct, a political ruse, that empowers. James's construction of the demonic in *Dæmonologie* thus serves the covert political purpose of confirming his own absolute power – or its material basis in illusion.

James's awareness of the illusions on which his own power rested, though a matter of conjecture, seem to be quite carefully coded into the discursive structures in *Dæmonologie*. Twice James devotes extended attention to counterfeiting, suggesting that it is a trope around which particular anxieties circulate.[13] The first such passages occurs just after James describes Satan's supposed ability to make 'schollers to creepe in credite with Princes, by fore-telling them manie greate things; parte true, parte false': (22)

> And yet are all these things ['juglarie trickes at Cardes, dice . . . and such innumerable practices'] but deluding of the senses, and no waies true in substance, as were the false miracles wrought by King *Pharaoes* Magicians, for counterfeiting *Moyses*: For that is the difference betuixt Gods myracles and the Deuils, God is a creator, what he makes appeare in miracle, it is so in effect. As *Moyses* rod being casten downe, was no doubt turned in a natural Serpent: where as the Deuill (as Gods Ape) counterfetting that by his *Magicians*, maid their wandes to appeare so, onelie to mennes outward senses . . . (22–3)

It is an ironic twist in the logic of the passage that James begins by introducing, in the Egyptian Pharaoh, a failed, or perhaps inferior, example of the absolute ruler's capacity to counterfeit. The Pharoah uses 'false miracles' in his attempt to

---

13 James Craigie, in his edition of *Dæmonologie (Minor Prose Works)*, glosses 'counterfeit' as 'imitation' but also, in its adjectival form, as 'false.' Its double sense of 'imitation' and 'feigning' seems to be active in the text, thus lending considerably to the ambiguity of the passages in which it is used.

'[counterfeit] Moyses,' who serves as an emblem of divine right. The passage, in its use of the Pharoah as a figure for failed power, makes explicit the contestatory anxiety implicit in the relations between absolute power and divinity. What matters here is who has the superior power to counterfeit, who has the control over the crucial illusions and imitations that underpin absolutism.

A further related irony is that the passage asserts the 'effect[s]' of God as 'a creator' using, as an example of these effects, the transformation of Moses's rod into a 'natural Serpent.' The transformation of the staff into a serpent that goes on to devour the serpents created by the Pharoah's magicians – as described in Exodus 7: 8–13 – is an ambiguous trope for the evil embodied in the Pharoah, or possibly for Moses's superior resistance to the will of that sovereign. Whatever the trope's significance, it is clear that James expects his readers to believe the material phenomenon authorised by divine will – the 'natural Serpent' – while relegating the Devil to status of unnatural counterfeit whose effects are evident 'onelie to mennes outward senses.'[14] The battle, in other words, is over the unmentioned inner senses, that is, the imaginative faculties that produce faith and credence in God, the Devil, or the sovereign.

The anxieties sublimated in the passage arise out of the knowledge that the operations of 'counterfeiting' are evident, ultimately, in relation to *both* the construction of the Devil and God. This would be one reason why the symbolic logic of the passage is so skewed, James mixing symbols of absolute power with the power's capacity to counterfeit the devil's operations on the sensual faculties of his subjects. In the same way that the Devil is 'Gods Ape,' so is the sovereign, who counterfeits both God and the Devil in order to produce the figural and material illusions of power on which his unnatural capacity to govern depends. The struggle is over authenticity, or as Epistemon says shortly after this passage, 'authenticque histories' (23), which is to say an epistemological struggle over the act of knowing. To write such 'authenticque histories' is to produce the necessary narrative illusions, the artificial kinds of knowledge, that gather the will of the

---

14 The use of 'natural' in relation to the serpent marks an attempt by James to naturalise or legitimate God's power over the devil's artificial power. The taxonomies associated with magic enact a similar hierarchy: 'Magic is of two kinds, natural and artificial. Natural or legitimate magic was, together with all other knowledge, a gift from God to Adam . . . [and] is no more than a more exact knowledge of the secrets of Nature . . . The other kind is artificial magic, which effects marvels by means of human skill,' skills involving prestidigitation and mathematics and skills associated with the devil who 'is able to make one thing seem as if it were another' (Guazzo 3–5). Such an attempted naturalisation is in line with the ideology of absolutism as described by Jonathan Goldberg in his discussion of Robert Filmer's treatise on the theory of absolutism, *Patriarcha*, in relation to James. For Filmer, 'the king is quite literally the father of his country, for parents are "natural magistrates" and children "natural subjects," and kings simply act within the "natural law of a Father" in making their absolute claims to obedience' (85). Goldberg continues on to suggest, I think accurately, that 'ideology is never more apparent than when it is treated as a transparency, when the political system is allowed to be an extension of natural laws and processes' (85). Such 'an extension of natural laws and processes' coupled with Slavoj Žižek's observation that 'the Law is always illuminated by the charismatic power of fascination' (80) creates a political subject pinned down by the twin Goliaths of a fictive naturalism and a potent fascination with the workings of that fiction. *Dæmonologie* represents James's attempt to confirm the operations of both structures in the anxious construction of his own notions of absolute power.

collectivity into the figural body of the absolute ruler.[15] Little wonder, then, given the basis of that ruler's power in the mimetic knowledge of the unspeakable dimensions of either God or the devil, that the witch came to represent such a tangible, not to mention necessary, expression of the material workings of absolute power.

The second passage from *Dæmonologie* in which counterfeiting appears begins by suggesting a reason for the Satanic appropriation of churches as locales for the performance of Witches' Sabbaths: 'Yea, that he [Satan] may the more viuelie counterfeit and scorne God, he oft times makes his slaues to conveene in these verrie places, which are destinat and ordeined for the conveening of the servantes of God (I mean by Churches)' (36). The passage localises at least two sources of concern for James. The first relates to a mimetic anxiety about the representations of images of God, images that in James's context would have had significance if only for the fact that his own power was founded on the same act of mimesis, the same counterfeiting. The second relates to the notorious lack of separation between Church power and state power in England subsequent to Henry VIII's establishment of the Church of England through the Statute of Supremacy, passed by Parliament on November 11, 1534. The possibility of Satanic influence in the locale of the Church represents a direct threat to the state's capacity to '[conveene] . . . the servantes of God,' that is, to exercise political control over the subjects of the King. It is no accident, in such a context, that James had advised his son Henry in the *Basilikon Doron* (1599), to 'suffer no conventions nor meetings among Churche-men, but by your knowledge and permission' (I. 145–7) and that a 1584 act of the Scottish Parliament had forbidden such meetings without the king's explicit permission.

Moreover, James, in his political writings, explicitly recognised that 'there is not a thing so necessarie to be knowne by the people of any land, next the knowledge of their God, as the right knowledge of their alleageance, according to the forme of gouernement established among them, especially in a *Monarchie* (which forme of gouernment, as resembling the Diuinitie, approcheth nearest to perfection, as all the learned and wise men from the beginning haue agreed vpon)' (*The Trew Law of Free Monarchies* 193). Monarchic rule metonymically 'resemble[s]' that of the divinity, but, as James describes in the following passage from *Dæmonologie*, there are also metonymic parallels between the operations of Satan and God. The passage is extraordinary because James, at great length (almost two pages), takes special pains to explicate the parallel that suggests, ultimately, an uncomfortable relation among God, Satan, and the Monarch:

> For the forme that he [Satan] used in counterfeiting God amongst the *Gentiles*, makes me so to thinke: As God spake by his Oracles, spake he not so by his? As GOD had aswell bloudie sacrifices, had not he the like? As God had Churches sanctified to his seruice, with Altars, Priests, Sacrifices, Ceremonies and

---

15 The quatrain used as an epigraph to the portrait of James that appears as the frontispiece to his *The Workes* (1616), concludes with the line '*But knowledge makes the KING most like his maker.*' See Fig. 1.

Prayers; had he not the like polluted to his seruice . . . As God by visiones, dreames, and extases reueiled what was to come, and what was his will vnto his seruantes; vsed he not the like meanes to forwarne his slaues of things to come? (*Dæmonologie* 36–7)

In addressing Satan's counterfeit of God, James is inevitably led, logically and rhetorically, to consider the many parallels between the two: one can use the metonymies of the oracle, church, or vision as meaningful substitutes for *either* God or Satan. What is left unspoken here is the parallel between the operations of the absolute ruler and the operations of both Satan and God. Just as Satan is God's monstrous double, so is the absolute monarch a monstrous double to Satan, if only for the fact that both use forms of counterfeit to produce the illusory nature of their power. This anxious formulation is at the core of the rhetorical and ideological structures evident in *Dæmonologie*, however sublimated such structures may be. The consistent emphasis evident in these passages on counterfeiting – and on the mimetic relationship implicit among God, Satan and James – betrays an intense anxiety about any form of power founded on such a counterfeit.[16]

'[C]ounterfeiting God' as a Satanic strategy becomes akin to the Divine counterfeit that the absolute monarch perpetrates in order to legitimate his or her own volatile sense of power. James's writing of *Dæmonologie* thus coincides with a powerful self-interest, for the Satanic mirrors the monarchic power to counterfeit. And *Dæmonologie* explores the very ruses that lie at the core of the illusions about absolute power, the very ruses necessary to its sustenance. The witch, in such a context, provides the material locus, the point of transition, in which the movement from abstract embodiment to physical reality is situated and, as Lucia Folena argues, the 'evil practices of the witch [serve] the fundamental purpose of offering a displaced reaffirmation of legitimate power' (226).[17] The witch is therefore the point at which the counterfeit is made real: 'real' people, most often women, suffered extreme tortures and painful deaths in order to produce the illusion of absolutism; for them absolutism was no illusion.

The power to inscribe the State – the will of the absolute monarch – on the bodies of its members produces yet another strange symmetry analogous to the

---

16 See Simon Wortham for a similar argument in relation to James's extraordinary attendance in May of 1611 at the trial of the pyx at the Royal Mint in London. According to Wortham, the trial demonstrated that 'conspicuously 'true' images . . . were held most likely to be counterfeit' (351), further arguing that James was confronting 'a problem of representation that struck at the grounds of knowledge and power' (353). Wortham concludes that 'James's attendance at the 1611 trial of the pyx . . . happened because the coins held in the coffers below were suspected as counterfeits. But this suspicion arose partly because of – and not just despite – the fact that they bore the stamp of sovereignty' (357).
17 Folena affirms that 'If the politics of self-representation in a restricted-code culture is always and necessarily displaced into the ethics of self-legitimation, and if the language of ethics in Jacobean culture is one and the same with the language of Christian religion, the constitution of any form of alterity other than one directly associated with the negative side religious postulates would there require a double displacement . . . The witch in Jacobean culture is, by virtue of her demonic alliance: she is thus its ideal figure of otherness, its perfect *antitheton*' (223).

devil's putative power to leave his mark on the body of the witch in the form of blemishes, supernumerary nipples, or other bodily deformations. Such strange symmetries encapsulate one of the fundamental anxieties associated with kingship: namely, how can the material body of the king sustain the illusion that it represents the body of the commonwealth, let alone the presence of the Divine right which authorises its powers? In the preface to *Dæmonologie* James articulates this anxiety by displacing it. Instead of attempting to prove that sovereignty exists through a divine right transmitted by God, itself a highly debatable political assertion as the history of monarchic succession has proven time and time again, James anxiously argues that it is '*My intention in this labour . . . only to proue two things, as I have alreadie said: the one, that such diuelish artes have bene and are. The other, what exact trial and seuere punishment they merite*' (xii). The need to prove that the demonic exists – that '*divelish artes have bene and are*' – displaces the need to prove that God exists. A politically expedient reason for this displacement is, of course, that individuals can be co-opted into this evidentiary process through impressive ritual acts of punishment and prohibition that enhance the monarch's anxious sense of his own absolute power. Instead of the rather limited human representations of Divine Right which could be used to bolster anxieties about absolute power – these representations requiring costly structures of state ritual, such as processions, and theatrical spectacles, such as the masque – the construction of the threat around demonised and marginal elements of the political spectrum affords multiple and instantly renewable opportunities for the State to regenerate the phantasmic images of the necessary threats by which it defines itself.

III

An example of James's involvement in constructing and giving credence to the activities and powers of witches is to be found in *Newes from Scotland*, an anonymous but possibly authorised account of James's attendance and participation in trials resulting from an outbreak of witchcraft at North Berwick.[18] James attended the sessions in which the witches were 'put to the question,' that is, tortured and made to confess. The document gives a precise account of the methods used for torture as well as of James's involvement in the process. Towards the end of the *Newes*, for example, is a description of Dr. Fian's (a

---

18 I argue that the *Newes* seems to be authorized on the basis of its final paragraph, which goes to unusual rhetorical lengths to justify James's participation in the trials. A reading of this paragraph is given below. Further study of the dictive patterns in the chronicle may provide more evidence regarding its authorship. Latham, in her discussion of *Newes from Scotland* and *Dæmonologie* attributes the former to James. Larner gives a short description of why the tract was probably 'written directly for an English reading public' ' "according to the Scottish copie" ' (1973 84). For accounts of other European monarchs and elements of the hegemony that took an active interest in the conduct of witch trials compare Jules Michelet's accounts of Gauffridi, the Nuns of Loudun, the Nuns of Louvier and Charlotte Cadière. The list of those from the upper echelons of the French political and religious hierarchies involved in the various witchcraft trials demonstrates the degree to which the hegemony saw its self-interest at stake in those proceedings.

schoolmaster in Saltpans [Prestonpans] named John Cunningham) final torture session authorised by James:

> Wherevpon the kinges maiestie perceiuing his [Fian's] stubbourne wilfulnesse, conceiued and imagined that in the time of his [unclear with possible reference either to Fian or James] absence hee had entered into newe conference and league with the deuill his master, and that hee had beene agayne newly marked, for the which hee was narrowly searched, but it could not in any wise bee founde, yet for more tryall of him to make him confesse, hee was commaunded to haue a most straunge torment which was done in the manner following.
>
> His nailes vpon all his fingers were riuen and pulled off with an instrument called in Scottish a *Turkas*, which in England wee call a payre of pincers, and vnder euerie nayle there was thrust in two needles ouer euen up to the heads. At all which tormentes notwithstanding the Doctor never shronke anie whit, neither woulde he then confesse it the sooner for all the tortures inflicted vpon him.
>
> Then was hee with all conuenient speed, by commandement, conuaied to the torment of the bootes, wherein hee continued a long time, and did abide so many blowes in them, that his legges were crushte and beaten togeather as small as might bee, and the bones and flesh so brused, that the bloud and marrowe spouted forth in great abundance, whereby they were made unseruiceable for euer. And notwithstanding al these grieuous paines and cruell torments hee would not confesse anie thing, so deeply had the deuill entered into his heart, that hee vtterly denied all that which he had before auouched, and would saie nothing thereunto but this, that what hee had done and sayde before, was onely done and sayde for feare of paynes which he had endured.

The description shows the monarch's figural power being made materially evident on the body of Dr. Fian, who was later burned in a 'great fire . . . [at] Castle hill of Edenbrough on a saterdaie in the ende of Ianuarie last past. 1591' (28–9). Power is figured in the body of the witch as victim – before being figured, quite literally, in the smoke rising from the pyre on which the victim is consumed. The mark of absolute power is its ability to inflict such extreme punishment through the inscriptive processes of torture that rewrite the body of the subject. Torture literally refigures the subversive power embodied in the victim as an example of the monarch's apparent capacity to contain that subversive power.[19]

---

19 See Elizabeth Hanson's comments to the effect that 'In torture, the object of discovery and the site of its failure was the subject – in both the political and ontological senses of the word. The epistemological anxiety that attached to the subject in Renaissance England is suggested in the privy councilors' use of "truth" and "treason" as interchangeable terms in the torture warrants to designate what the torturer was to discover . . . But the ability of discovery to reveal only treason also bespeaks the fact that every project of discovery, "successful" or not, revealed that impenetrable sanctum it had created' (76–7). We may note that anxiety is produced in the case

The passage exemplifies why this subversive power is always so dangerous. Its unsettling logic seems to suggest that the more painful the torture inflicted on Fian, the more resistant he is to confessing, the more insistent he is 'that what hee had done and sayde before, was onely done and sayde for feare of paynes which he had endured.' The narrative of Fian's torture twice iterates that the 'Doctor neuer shronke anie whit' despite the extreme physical pain he must have been suffering. Fian's resistance under such circumstances may indicate the truth of his innocence, a truth that is irrelevant to the business of exercising absolute power, which only asks that state violence produce the image of the compliant and fearful political subject that does and says what it is asked to do and say. Violence and fear are written into the body of the subject, both materially and in the narrative reconstruction of that subject, regardless of the subject's apparent courage in withstanding their assault.[20]

Despite Fian's bravery in the face of his torments it is the image of the king's successful exercise of his power that is crucial to the narrative at this point. The buried moral in the incident is that such courage is futile when faced with the inexorable execution of the monarch's will, which affords a visible simulacrum of an absent divinity. James's violence against Fian is a reminder that 'violence is the signifier of the cherished being, the signifier of divinity' (Girard 151). If anything, Fian's courage, as it is constructed in this narrative, exemplifies and reinforces the power of the king to overcome extraordinary acts of resistance. The notion of 'convenien[ce]' is strangely apparent again, as it was in the passage cited earlier in which Epistemon speaks of the right of the 'Prince or Magistrate' to punish the witch 'as he thinkes conuenient'. Fian's utter denial of the accusations against him under extreme torment are of no consequence when placed in the context of the need to demonstrate the 'conuenient speed' at which the monarch's power can be exercised. The witch, then, to echo Paul Virilio, is a speed vector along which the material dimensions of absolutism travel.[21]

---

of Fian because this capacity for containment or discovery is always potentially failed. Fian's steadfast resistance marks the limit at which absolute power over material and spirit leaves off and, once the subject has been executed, the power of narrative takes over. For words, ultimately, become the means by which James – or the anonymous chronicler – both instantiates his anxieties over resistant political subjects as well as asserts the inexorable quality of his absolute power to control those same subjects. For a further reading of torture, and the relationship between physical pain and discursivity, see Elaine Scarry's 'The Structure of Torture: The Conversion of Real Pain into the Fiction of Power,' 27–59, Michel Foucault's 'The Body of the Condemned,' 3–31, and Kate Millett's, *The Politics of Cruelty: An Essay on the Literature of Political Imprisonment*.

20 Folena, in discussing this same passage, suggests that 'Torture is . . . not primarily meant to produce a confession, but to reproduce a truth which has already been uttered as pertaining to the accused's body and does not even demand the echo of "his" avowal in order to manifest itself fully. Torture is still necessary as a self-validating strategy of the inquisitor: for it provides this further evidence of guilt that consists in the absence of the confessing voice of the Other. Thus the material body is excluded from language and deprived of its voice . . . The body thus becomes the sounding board of a word that is already there, since it belongs to its speaker, the inquisitor, but needs a material obstacle to manifest itself. The Other has been reduced to the pure function of providing a definition, an outer margin for the self-voicing of the culture' (228–9).

21 See Virilio, especially, 'The State of Emergency,' 33–51.

Again, it must be asked why James was there? Why was he so actively interested – to the point of noting and reacting to Fian's 'stubbourne wilfulnesse'? Why at the end of the *Newes* does the anonymous chronicler feel it necessary to state:

> *This strange discourse before recited, may perhaps give some occasion of doubt to such as shall happen to reade the same, and thereby coniecture that the Kings maiestie woulde not hazarde himselfe in the presence of such notorious witches, least therby might have insued great danger to his person and the generall state of the land, which thing in truth might wel have bene feared. But to answer generally to such, let this suffice: that first it is well knowen that the King is the child & servant of god, and they but servants to the devil, hee is the Lords anointed, and they but vesselles of Gods wrath: he is a true Christian, and trusteth in God, they worse than infidels, for they onely trust in the devill, who daily serve them, till he have brought them to utter destruction*[?] (29)

The passage marks precisely why James had so much invested in his own presence and association with these witch trials: they literally offered proof, by contrary, of his place in a necessary political and religious hierarchy, one which provided the very source and sustenance of the absolute power on which his identity as sovereign depended. The rhetorical strategy, in its antithetical comparison of the witches' evil with the king's godliness, is notable for its affirmation of the king's power at the expense of the witches' '*utter destruction.*' This '*utter destruction*' of the witches is attributed to the Devil in the fictive narrative of the *Newes*, but is, in the material reality of the account, *directly attributable to the Scottish legal system embodied in the King's presence at the trials*. The King, again through a process of covert inversion, literally and materially embodies the Devil's power to destroy utterly.

A notable problem with the narrative structure of the *Newes*, especially given the emphasis on the genderedness of witchcraft as female in relation to absolutist and partriarchal ontologies, is that the fullest anecdote in the document concerns itself with a male witch, Fian. Is Fian an honorary female? Is his male status importantly different, the exception which proves the rule? Is Fian the male invert who corroborates the terrifying power of female witches to alter some essential masculinity that is permanently threatened by female witches' powers? Does Fian represent, in the logic of absolutism, the exemplary form of male enforcement and absolutist regulation, the extended narrative of his torture depicting the monarch's ineluctable capacity to destroy *any* form of threatening difference? Is Fian in effect the ultimate signifier of that threatening difference, a man in the social place of a woman? Answers to these questions must necessarily remain inconclusive given the lack of clearer contextual evidence for understanding how to read Fian's role in the passage. It is clear, however, that Fian's torture, especially in the care with which its narrative details are rendered, plays a crucial role in exemplifying the regulatory effects of the absolute ruler on the *socius*. The sovereign effectively effaces any form of difference, whether male or female, and perhaps Fian's torture is given such prominence precisely because his form of difference, by way of its perversion of gender norms associated with witchcraft, is symbolically most menacing. The narrative logic of the passage demonstrates simultaneously that male abjection plays a role in confirming the assumptions of absolutist discourse, even as that male abjection displaces focus from those women deemed witches who suffered most the historical consequences of this insidious logic. The narrative clearly alerts readers to the fact that assumptions about the way in which witchcraft is gendered are not unproblematic, especially when understood in terms of anomalous texts like the *Newes*, which offer significant exceptions to the rule.

Other details in the construction of the narrative that the *Newes* tells are also notable. In one instance after having listened with 'great delight' (14) to one of the accused witches, Geilles Duncane dance and play a reel upon a 'small Trump, called a Iewes Trump' (14), another witch, Agnis Tompson informs James that

> the Diuell being then at North Barrick Kerke attending their comming in the habit or likenes of a man, and seeing that they tarried ouer long, he at their comming enioyned them all to a penance, which was, that they should kisse his Buttockes, in signe of duetye to him: which being put over the Pulpit barre, euerye one did as he enioyned them: and having made his ungodly exhortations, wherein he did greatly inveighe against the King of Scotland, he received their oathes for their good and true service towards him, and departed . . . (14)

The narrative, as it is told by the anonymous chronicler, insures that the reader's attention is directed toward the subversive political power the Devil represents in his forcing the witches to take an oath to him – symbolised quite theatrically in the buttock-kissing on the pulpit – as well as in the Devil's 'inveighe[ing]' against the King. The incident reminds us of how necessary it is in the exercise of absolute power to construct a threat to the political *status quo* in order for that threat to be eradicated, thus confirming the stability and the inescapability of that power.

A last incident recorded in the *Newes* demonstrates the degree to which even the minor details of the textual representations and manipulations associated with witchcraft were critical to James's deployment of an illusion of absolute power. Agnis Sampson is said to have 'confessed before the Kings Maiestie sundrye thinges which were so miraculous and strange, as that his Maiestie saide they were all extreme lyars, wherat she answered, she woulde not wishe his Maiestie to suppose her woordes to be false, but rather to beleeue them, in that she would discouer such matter unto him as his maiestie should not any way doubt off' (15). Agnis then goes on to tell James of the 'verye woordes' spoken between James and his wife at 'Vpslo in Norway' on the first night of their marriage.

The narrative never reveals what was said but the assumption is that the King's interpretation of what Agnis tells him, if in fact she ever told him anything at all, is correct.[22] His version of the narrative truth supplants hers;

---

22 It is surprising that James was able to remember such a conversation given the goings-on at the Danish court in 1590. For one account of these goings-on, see David Harris Willson, 92–3.

her voice is displaced by his, thus insuring that her 'subjectivity' is wholly determined and made contingent upon James as 'author.' And this small act of narrative coercion, in which Agnis's words are co-opted by the king as well as by the anonymous chronicler of the incident, indicates what was at stake in attributing true powers to witches. Without their magical abilities to prophesy, to encounter the Devil, or even to overhear nuptial conversations, James's own magical ability to assert his absolute power, a form of power always under the anxious threat of contestation because of its totalising tendencies, would have been diminished. Thus, the links between the control of the imaginary, discussed at the beginning of this essay, and the machinations required to maintain the illusions of absolute power are made explicit in the anecdote. The construction of absolute power in textual form requires a carefully manipulated opacity of language, one in which the narrative displacement of Agnis's voice by James's is hardly noticeable. Such an opacity of narrative technique contributes to the mythification, mystification, and ultimately, the 'authority' on which the politics of absolutism is founded – an authority that led to the execution of Agnis Sampson on the 27th of January 1590/91 on the Castlehill at Edinburgh.[23]

A final question: why did James take such an interest in witchcraft, not only attending trials and tortures,[24] but also writing a learned treatise on the subject? One response would be to suggest, as I have throughout this essay, that James played and understood himself to be playing a central role, through both his political and literary interventions on the issue of witchcraft, in the construction of a myth of absolute power. Such a myth was necessary to his political survival, especially in the perilous and anxiety-producing political context prior to his ascension to the throne of England in 1603. The unauthorised activities located in the marginal discourses of the witch's craft were exploited to sustain the mythic construction of absolute power, a dynamic that reveals the potency of the unauthorized as a means to achieve political agency.

References

Anderson, Bonnie S. and Judith P. Zinsser. 'The Extraordinary.' *A History of Their Own: Women in Europe*. Vol. 1. New York. Harper & Row. 1988: 151–73.

Bataille, Georges. 'The Sorcerer's Apprentice.' *The College of Sociology 1937–39*. Ed. Denis Hollier. Tr. Betsy Wing. Minneapolis: U of Minnesota P, 1988: 12–23.

Cixous, Hélène and Catherine Clément. *The Newly Born Woman*. Tr. Betsy Wing. Minneapolis: U of Minnesota P, 1986.

Cohn, Norman. *Europe's Inner Demons: An Enquiry Inspired by the Great Witch-Hunt*. New York: Basic Books, 1975.

—, 'The Non-Existent Society of Witches.' *Witchcraft and Sorcery: Selected Readings*. Ed. Max Marwick. London: Penguin Books, 1990: 140–57.

---

23 See Craigie, *The Minor Prose* 152.

24 *Newes from Scotland* is not the only evidence of James's interest in witches. In 1589 'James had indulged some special curiosity about witchcraft . . . when at Aberdeen he insisted on seeing the 'notorious and rank' witch Marioune McIngaruch' (Dunlap 41).

Cowan, Edward J.. 'The Darker Version of the Scottish Renaissance: the Devil and Francis Stewart.' *The Renaissance and Reformation in Scotland*. Eds. Ian B. Cowan and Duncan Shaw. Edinburgh: Scottish Academic Press, 1983: 125–40.

Clark, Stuart. 'King James's *Dæmonologie*: Witchcraft and Kingship.' *The Damned Art: Essays in the Literature of Witchcraft*. Ed. Sydney Anglo. London: Routledge, 1977: 156–81.

Craigie, James. Ed. *The Basilicon Doron of King James VI*. 2 vols. Edinburgh: William Blackwood & Sons, 1944.

—, Ed. *Minor Prose Works of King James VI and I*. Edinburgh: Scottish Text Society, 1982.

Dean, Kenneth and Brian Massumi. *First & Last Emperors: The Absolute State and the Body of the Despot*. Brooklyn: Autonomedia, 1992.

de Certeau, Michel. *The Writing of History*. Tr. Tom Conley. New York: Columbia UP, 1988.

Dunlap, Rhodes. 'King James and Some Witches: The Date and Text of the *Dæmonologie*.' *Philological Quarterly* 54 (1975): 40–46.

Elizabeth I. 'Letter from the Queens Maiestie to the Lord Maior of London (1586).' Amsterdam: Da Capo Press, 1969.

Folena, Lucia. 'Figures of Violence: Philologists, Witches, and Stalinistas.' *The Violence of Representation: Literature and the History of Violence*. Eds. Nancy Armstrong and Leonard Tennenhouse. London: Routledge, 1989: 219–38.

Foucault, Michel. *Discipline and Punish*. Tr. Alan Sheridan. New York: Vintage Books, 1979.

Ginzburg, Carlo. *Ecstasies: Deciphering the Witches' Sabbath*. Tr. Raymond Rosenthal. New York: Penguin Books, 1991.

Girard, René. *Violence and the Sacred*. Tr. Patrick Gregory. Baltimore: Johns Hopkins UP, 1977.

Goldberg, Jonathan. *James I and the Politics of Literature*. Stanford: Stanford UP, 1989.

Greenblatt, Stephen. 'Filthy Rites.' *Learning to Curse: Essays in Early Modern Culture*. New York: Routledge, 1992: 59–79.

Guazzo, Francesco Maria. *Compendium Maleficarum*. Tr. E.A. Ashwin. New York: Dover Publications, 1988.

Hanft, Sheldon. 'The True King James Version: His Bible or His Daemonologie?' *Selected Papers from the West Virginia Shakespeare and Renaissance Association* 6 (Spring 1981): 50–57.

Hanson, Elizabeth. 'Torture and Truth in Renaissance England.' *Representations* 34 (Spring 1991): 53–84.

Harrison, G.B. Ed. *King James the First Dæmonologie (1597) and Newes from Scotland declaring the Damnable Life and death of Doctor Fian, a notable Sorcerer who was burned at Edenbrough in Ianuary last (1591)*. New York: Barnes & Noble, 1966.

Henshall, Nicholas. *The Myth of Absolutism: Change and Continuity in Early Modern European Monarchy*. London: Longman, 1992.

The Holy Bible. Authorized King James Version. Grand Rapids, Michigan, Zondervan Bible Publishers, 1983.

James I. *The Workes* (1616). Hildesheim: Georg Olms Verlag, 1971.

Kramer, Heinrich and James Sprenger. *The Malleus Maleficarum*. Tr. Montague Summers. New York: Dover, 1971.

Larner, Christina. *Enemies of God: The Witch-hunt in Scotland*. Baltimore: Johns Hopkins UP, 1981.

—, 'James VI and I and Witchcraft.' *The Reign of James VI and I*. Ed. Alan G. R. Smith. London: Macmillan, 1973: 74–90.

Larner, Christina. *Witchcraft and Religion: The Politics of Popular Belief*. Oxford: Basil Blackwell, 1984.

Latham, Jacqueline E. M. '*The Tempest and King James' Dæmonologie*.' *Shakespeare Studies* 28 (1975): 117–23.

Lee, Maurice Jr. *Great Britain's Solomon: James VI and I in His Three Kingdoms*. Urbana: U of Illinois P, 1990.

Lehner, Ernst and Johanna. *Picture Book of Devils, Demons and Witchcraft*. New York: Dover Publications, 1971.

Michelet, Jules. *Satanism and Witchcraft*. Tr. A. R. Allinson. New York: Citadel Press, 1992.

Midelfort, H.C. Erik. 'Social History and Biblical Exegesis: Community, Family, and Witchcraft in Sixteenth-Century Germany.' *The Bible in the Sixteenth Century*. Ed. David C. Steinmetz. Durham: Duke UP, 1990: 7–20.

Millett, Kate. *The Politics of Cruelty: An Essay on the Literature of Political Imprisonment*. New York: Norton, 1994.

Oplinger, Jon. *The Politics of Demonology: The European Witchcraze and the Mass Production of Deviance*. London: Associated University Presses, 1990.

Pearl, Jonathan L. 'Humanism and Satanism: Jean Bodin's Contribution to the Witchcraft Crisis.' *The Canadian Review of Sociology and Anthropology* 19: 4 (November 1982): 541–48.

Scarry, Elaine. *The Body in Pain*. New York: Oxford UP, 1987.

Shakespeare, William. *The Tragedy of Macbeth. The Complete Works*. Compact Edition. Eds. Stanley Wells and Gary Taylor. Oxford: Clarendon Press, 1991: 975–1000.

Virilio, Paul. *Speed and Politics*. Tr. Mark Polizzotti. New York: Semiotext(e), 1986.

Willis, Deborah. 'Shakespeare and the English Witch-Hunts: Enclosing the Maternal Body.' *Enclosure Acts: Sexuality, Property, and Culture in Early Modern England*. Eds. Richard Burt and John Michael Archer. Ithaca: Cornell UP, 1994: 96–120.

Willson, David Harris. *King James VI and I*. London: Jonathan Cape, 1959.

Winstanley, Gerrard. *Selected Writings*. Ed. Andrew Hopton. London: Aporia Press, 1989.

Wortham, Simon. 'Sovereign Counterfeits: The Trial of the Pyx.' *Renaissance Quarterly* 49.2 (1996): 334–59.

Žižek, Slavoj. *The Sublime Object of Ideology*. London: Verso, 1989.

T. HOWARD-HILL

41. Sir William Alexander: The Failure of Tragedy and the Tragedy of Failure

William Alexander of Menstry is known to literary history mainly for his sonnet sequence, *Aurora* (1604), his four *Monarchic Tragedies* (1616), and his *Supplement to a Defect in the Third Book of Arcadia* (1621). The course of his life tellingly illustrates the the prevailing theme of his four tragedies, the insecurity of worldly success. Having, during his service to two kings of Scotland and England, held such offices as Master of Requests for Scotland, member of the Scottish Privy Council, hereditary lieutenant of Nova Scotia, Keeper of the Signet and Principal Secretary of State for Scotland, he died in 1640 as Sir William Alexander, Earl of Stirling, Viscount Canada and Lord Alexander of Tullibody, hated and reviled in the country of his birth. Amongst the poetic squibs that expressed the popular reaction to his death, this conveys the moral of his life:

> Hier layes a fermer and a millar,
> A poet and a psalme book spillar,
> A purchassour by hook and crooke,
> A forger of the service book,
> A coppersmith quho did much evill,
> A friend to bischopes and ye devill,
> A waine ambitious flattering thing,
> Late secretary for a kinge;
> Soum tragedies in verse he pen'd,
> At last he made a tragicke end.[1]

To anyone interested in Jacobean history, Alexander's life invites explication of this verse, an invitation which must be refused here. The anonymous versifier dealt justly with Alexander. His hopes for wealth from royal patents, his colonial speculations, and, indeed, his dynastic ambitions, came to nothing: both his heir and his second son pre-deceased him. His memory is invoked now almost exclusively by the four tragic poems he wrote as a young man before he joined James's court in Whitehall.[2]

The earliest of the *Monarchic Tragedies* to be printed, in 1603, *Darius* is the first

---

[1] Denmiln MSS. Quoted from McGrail; see next note.
[2] Alexander has attracted little modern interest. The standard (because only) modern life is Thomas H. McGrail's *Sir William Alexander, First Earl of Stirling; a Biographical Study* (Edinburgh: Oliver and Boyd, 1940) on which, for Alexander's biography, this essay is completely dependent.

work to appear under his name.³ Attempts to situate Alexander's early compositions within his history are substantially impeded by the paucity of reliable information about his early years. Even his birthdate is undocumented and contested. It was first taken to be 1580 from the evidence of the inscription on Marshall's portrait prefixed to copies of Alexander's *Recreations of the Muses*, published in 1637: it depicts Alexander in the fifty-seventh year of his life.⁴ However, the engraving was not made for the 1637 publication.⁵ Further, the witness of the engraving is inconsistent with the birthdate usually cited by modern authorities, 1567.⁶ McGrail points out that given his birth in 1567, Alexander would have been 'sixty-six years of age in 1633, the earliest year in which the engraving [that represents him as 57] could have been made'.⁷ Noting a reference to the coincidence of Alexander's horoscope and William Vaughan's (b. 1577), he settled on 1577 as the most likely year of Alexander's birth. The later date seems to fit the subsequent course of his career more comfortably than the earlier date, but that may be a partial judgement. In any event, on this assumption Alexander was about twenty-six years old when his first tragedy was published.

Another biographical lacuna is not so important for a consideration of his early literary career. No details of his university education survive, though, as his sons studied at Glasgow University, there is a good presumption that that was Alexander's own university. Were Alexander an English author (as some might well claim him to be), we would search the circumstances of his formal education for the genesis of his early interest in dramatic composition and seek signs of the influence of university plays in his works. However, unlike English and continental universities, Scottish universities did not employ plays for the training of their students in the classic tongues and deportment.⁸ To this extent Alexander's university education is irrelevant here, save that it probably provided his first acquaintance with the works of the Roman playwright, Seneca, whose closet dramas, it is usually asserted, were the original models for Alexander's tragedies.

Nor is it known exactly when he first met his future patron and the dedicatee of the successive editions of his tragedies. In *Traits and Stories of the Scottish People*, Charles Rogers imagines how, when hunting falcons in the Ochils, 'James VI met

---

3   Bibliographical details are drawn from L. E. Kastner and H. B. Charlton, eds. *The Poetical Works of Sir William Alexander, Earl of Stirling*. 2 vols. Scottish Text Society Pulbications, new series, nos. 11 and 24 (Edinburgh: Printed for the Society by W. Blackwood, 1921) which remains the standard edition of Alexander's works, and *STC*. Both Kastner (vol. 2, p. xxv) and McGrail (pp. 21–2) attribute to Alexander the prose pamphlet on James's escape from the Gowry conspiracy, *A Short Discourse of the Good Ends of the Higher Providence*, published anonymously in 1600.
4   This date was favoured as recently as Maurice Lindsay's *History of Scottish Literature* (London: R. Hale, 1977).
5   McGrail, p. 4.
6   Charles Rogers, ed., *The Earl of Stirling's Register of Royal Letters Relative to the Affairs of Scotland and Nova Scotia from 1615 to 1635* (Edinburgh: 1885) originated this date, McGrail says (p. 4), 'for no particular reason'. It was followed by *DNB* and works like *CBEL* dependent on it for such details.
7   McGrail, p. 4.
8   See Sarah Carpenter, 'Early Scottish Drama', in *The History of Scottish Literature*. Volume 1: *Origins to 1660*, ed. R. D. S. Jack (Aberdeen U.P., 1988), pp. 199–212.

William Alexander, the young laird of Menstry, who had already made the tour of Europe, and acquired reputation both as a scholar and poet. He was a sprightly youth, and possessed elegant manners. The King invited him to Stirling Castle . . .'[9] It is true that Alexander travelled on the continent for three or four years with his contemporary and kinsman, Archibald Campbell, the seventh earl of Argyle, some time in 1597–1600; McGrail conjectures plausibly that Argyle introduced him at the Scottish court. But there is no documentary evidence that James knew Alexander in Scotland and even less likelihood that Alexander was commended to him by a literary reputation. It is possible, even likely, that his novice works circulated amongst his friends, particularly his sequence of sonnets, *Aurora*, but the facts remain that he published no poetical works before James's accession to the English throne, to borrow a phrase from Greg,[10] and no public record of his literary prowess survives from before he started to publish his works after James's accession on March 24th, 1603. It is tempting to think that Alexander formed part of 'the advance guard of an army of optimistic Caledonians who flocked' after James during his progress to London during the Spring of 1603 but, McGrail says, he 'seems not to have been in the royal retinue, nor is there any evidence as to just when he joined the migration to the new Court.'[11] It is true that his *Aurora*, *A Paranaesis to Prince Henry*, and *Monarchic Tragedies* were published in London in 1604, but McGrail doubted that this gave grounds for assuming Alexander's 'permanent establishment at Court'.[12] However, permanency is not really the issue. Effectively, the Scots court was now in London where clients seeking patronage must direct their addresses.

This brief survey of the uncertainties of Alexander's early life is intended to provide a basis for the assessment of his intentions in writing his four tragedies in the style and language that he did. Fully to understand the peculiar quality of his achievement in dramatic writing we need to know whether he was writing for the sake of attracting patronage and employment in worldly affairs or for the sake of literary renown, or both. In the light of the substantially antagonistic criticism of the *Monarchic Tragedies* embodied in McGrail's study, and in the earlier Kastner-Charlton edition where several errors about Alexander's relationship to his literary contemporaries first took root, it is as important to understand the significance of the tragedies for Alexander's career as it is to understand their connections with different schools of Senecan dramatic composition. Therefore the critic must establish a biographical narrative within which Alexander's earliest works may be comfortably situated. In this task, it must be admitted, the very lack of information already mentioned makes it possible to adopt an explicatory strategy that may rehabilitate the *Monarchic Tragedies* to the extent that their intrinsic qualities allow. These few biographical details enable us to see

---

9 Charles Rogers, *Traits and Stories of the Scottish People* (London: Houlston and Wright, 1877), quoted from McGrail, p. 13.
10 W. W. Greg, *A Bibliography of the English Printed Drama to the Restoration*, Vol. 1 (London: Bibliographical Society, 1939), p. 308.
11 McGrail, p. 61.
12 McGrail, p. 61.

Alexander as a well-educated, well-connected Scotsman, young (twenty-six years old in 1603) and, no doubt, ambitious.

That he recognised the court as the source of his advancement is shown by his dedication of his first avowed publication to James; that he was ambitious is revealed by the terms of the address 'To the Reader' prefixed to *Darius* (1603). There he presents the reader with 'the first essay of my rude and unskilfull Muse in a Tragical Poeme. Wherein I thought my time and paines better employed, than in those idle & vaine toyes, which by their sweet allurements infect the mindes both of the writer and reader with the contagion of vice and brutish sensualitie.'[13] Perhaps here he is thinking of his own sonnet sequence which he later excluded from his collected works. In any event, he has announced his intention to have written a work of high seriousness and stern morality. Significantly, 'The language of this Poeme is . . . mixt of the English and Scottish Dialects; which perhaps may be unpleasant and irksome to some readers of both nations. But I hope the gentle and Judicious English reader will beare with me, if I retain some badge of mine owne countrie, by using sometimes words that are peculiar thereunto, especiallie when I find them propre, and significant. And as for my owne country-men, they may not justly finde fault with me, if for the most parte I vse the English phrase, as worthie to be preferred before our owne for the elegance and perfection thereof. Yea I am perswaded that both country-men will take in good part the mixture of their Dialects, the rather for that the bountifull providence of God doth invite them both to a straiter union and conjunction as well in language, as in other respects'. The last phrase is a transparent reference to James's double hegemony.

Thus Alexander attempted to navigate the shoals of each nation's preference for its own language. Charlton comments rather unfairly that '*Darius* is, then, written in an Anglo-Scottish language by a Scot who declares himself more enamoured of English than of his native speech'.[14] In fact, the significant drift of the address to the reader is its appeal to both nations for linguistic tolerance. In subsequent years Alexander was to work assiduously to remove traces of their Scottish origin from his tragedies but in 1603 he was concerned only to employ that kind of language that he felt was appropriate to the new relationship between the two nations. (There is more to be said about Alexander's linguistic revisions, later). Everything about the first edition of *Darius* signals its intention to attract the interest of the Scots king in his English court: implicit in the address to the reader was the message that Alexander was such another man as James who could thrive in both the nations. Within four years Alexander published the other three tragedies that complete the *Monarchic Tragedies: Croesus* (1604), *The Alexandrean* (1607), and *Julius Caesar* (1607). Over the same period, his dedicatory poem 'To his Sacred Majestie' swelled from three to fourteen stanzas, a visible index to Alexander's hopes, stabilising around the time when he was referred to as Gentleman of the Privy Chamber Extraordinary to Prince Henry.[15] Sweet are the uses of poesy. The

---

13 Quoted from Kastner and Charlton, vol. 1, p. cxcvi.
14 Kastner and Charlton, vol. 1, p. cxcvi.
15 McGrail, p. 61.

following year, 'sometime between 1608 and 1609', Alexander was knighted, an event that McGrail reads as probably marking Alexander's permanent attachment to the court in London.[16] While we cannot be absolutely certain that Alexander adopted literary means to seek preferment at court, the likelihood increases when we consider the particular form of his approach.

We need not regard McGrail, whose study originated as a dissertation at the University of New Hampshire, as the arbiter of the value of Alexander's tragedies. Nevertheless, some of his comments bear quotation, for two reasons. In certain measure he elaborates and exaggerates features of Charlton's extensive history of Senecan drama which formed a good part of the first volume of Kastner and Charlton's edition.[17] Second, the two standard authorities together established a climate of critical opinion about Alexander's tragedies that has impeded their appropriate consideration. This outcome is particularly unfortunate in that none of the few recent writers on Alexander's tragedies gives any evidence of having read them. Charlton wrote of them generally:

> ... as a poet the precision of phrase and the sense of the perfect word he lacks entirely. His notion of style is a moderately exalted level of expression in which outstanding features of his sources are lost. As with verbal qualities of style, so too with the sentiments in his dramas and the characters who express them: the particular is lost in the general, sentiment becomes platitude, opinion nothing but moral commonplace.[18]

The fullest expression of these qualities occurs in *The Alexandrean*, of which McGrail writes:

> This lengthiest of Alexander's tragedies is by far the very worst. Even considering its models, the literary tastes of the group for which it was written [a reference to the Pembroke circle?], and the didactic impulse behind it, *The Alexandrean Tragedy* must still remain one of the dreariest, dullest, most tedious, involved, and prosy attempts at the dramatic ever written in the English language. Not one of its nearly 3500 lines ever rises above the most commonplace moralising prose, and the general theme is reiterated with the dull and monotonous insistence of a throbbing tooth:
> > O blinde ambition! Great minds viprous brood,
> > The scourge of mankinde, and the foe to rest.[19]

(I hope he had as much enjoyment in penning those words as I have in quoting them.) In order to attempt to rehabilitate Alexander's tragedies, we need to

---

16 McGrail, p. 63.
17 Charlton's essay occupies 200 pages in the first volume of Kastner and Charlton's edition. Subsequently, lamenting that his essay had been overlooked as part of the edition, Charlton republished it separately as *The Senecan Tradition in Renaissance Tragedy* (Manchester: Manchester U.P., 1946). It remains the standard scholarly treatment of its subject.
18 Kastner and Charlton, vol. 1, p. clxxxvi.
19 McGrail, p. 37.

consider his purpose in writing them and the characteristics of the form he chose to imitate.

Anyone who approaches these works of Alexander with expectations formed by knowledge of Senecan tragedies presented on the public stages of London will be disappointed. Those plays – such works as Thomas Kyd's *The Spanish Tragedy*, Marston's *Antonio's Revenge*, and Middleton's *The Revenger's Tragedy* – were in their way as aberrant representations of their model as the French Senecan plays that influenced Alexander. It somewhat exaggerates the characteristics of Seneca's plays to describe them as amalgams of lurid accounts of bloody acts and reflective passages of detached moralising. However, it is scarcely possible to exaggerate the avidity with which the writers for the public theatres seized upon them as models for their compositions. They authorised the existing licences of the English stage by classical precedent, while the dramatists adopted stylistic features, such as stichomythia and soliloquies to express extreme states of emotion, that in a short time became naturalised: *Hamlet* is a leading example. It was possible to emphasise the reflective, moralising, and philosophical elements of Seneca's dramas, so to produce a kind of drama that owed little to the theatre but rather, like Seneca's own closet plays, was intended to be heard by discriminating audiences: Sackville and Norton's *Gorboduc* (1561) is the prototypical English Senecan play of this kind. How lurid horrors and detached reflections on political life intermingle may be illustrated by Seneca's *Thyestes*, a play well-known to Elizabethan playwrights and drawn on by Shakespeare for his early *Titus Andronicus*.[20] Atreus resolves to revenge himself on his brother, Thyestes. The vengeance is the murder, dismemberment, and baking of Thyestes' sons to be consumed by their drunken father at a feast:

> With a savage blow
> The king drove in the sword, and pressed it home
> Until his hand was at the throat; the body
> Stood, with the sword plucked out, as if deciding
> Which way to fall, then fell against the king.
> Immediately the brutal murderer
> Seized Plisthenes and dragged him to the altar
> To add his body to his brother's, struck
> And hacked his head off; the truncated corpse
> Fell forward to the ground, and from the head
> That rolled away a last faint sob was heard . . .
> The entrails torn from the warm bodies lay
> Quivering, veins still throbbing, shocked hearts beating . . .
> Finding no blemish in the sacrifice,
> He was content, and ready to prepare

---

20 *Thyestes, Phaedra, The Trojan Women, Oedipus with Octavia*. Trans. with an introduction by E. F. Watling (Harmondsworth, Middlesex: Penguin Books, 1966, rpr. 1970).

> The banquet for his brother; hacked the bodies
> Limb from limb – detached the outstretched arms
> Close to the shoulders – severed the ligaments
> That tie the elbow joints – stripped every part
> And roughly wrenched each separate bone away –
> All this he did himself; only the faces,
> And trusting suppliant hands he left intact.
> And soon the meat is on the spits, the fat
> Drips over a slow fire . . . (747–78)

and so on.

Yet such horrors were not all that the philosopher-dramatist offered the Renaissance reader. Appropriately to his function as Nero's tutor, Seneca's plays are larded – if I might say so – with reflections on the nature of kingship and government. It is readily conceived that no would-be courtier such as Alexander was would win promotion by retailing the barbarities of Graeco-Roman tragedy, and one can readily detect the possibilities of a radically different kind of drama in a passage like this, spoken by the Chorus:

> It is not worldly wealth that makes a king,
> Nor the rich diadem encompassing
> His royal head, nor the proud gaudiness
> Of gilded halls and Tyrian purple dress.
> A king is he who has no ill to fear,
> Whose hand is innocent, whose conscience clear;
> Who scorns licentious greed, who has not bowed
> To the false favour of the fickle crowd . . .
> He is the man who faces unafraid
> The lightning's glancing stroke; is not dismayed
> By storm-tossed seas; whose ship securely braves
> The windy rage of Adriatic waves;
> Who has escaped alive the soldier's arm,
> The brandished steel; who, far removed from harm,
> Looks down upon the world, faces his end
> With confidence, and greets death as a friend. (348–67)

Seneca's plays provided a possible model for Alexander's tragedies; he must have read them at university.[21] Nevertheless, Charlton detected no direct influence. Rather, Alexander chose to model his plays on the denatured Senecan imitations of Robert Garnier and other sixteenth-century French tragedians. In some measure this choice justifies McGrail's negative assessment

---

21 Twenty-one editions of Seneca's plays in Latin were published in Europe by 1589. They were translated into English individually from 1559; Seneca's *Tenne Tragedies* (1581; *STC* 22221) was particularly influential on the burgeoning appearance of formal tragedies in the public theatres.

of Alexander's artistic achievement. In fact, however, it was Alexander's very success in emulating the French school of Senecan playwrights that is responsible for his low standing as a dramatist of the period amongst modern critics. Garnier and the others advanced into a cul-de-sac; Alexander bricked it up after them.

Senecan drama had developed in France on the austere classicist foundations laid by Buchanan, in contempt of the traditions of popular drama, as a consciously-reformist movement. The earliest French tragedians were further influenced by the sixteenth-century French court's lack of interest in the new tragedy and the small likelihood that their plays would be staged to discard every element of theatricality that could be discerned in Seneca's tragedies. (These had in any case been written for recitation rather than performance). Without an interest in performance the early French Senecan plays failed to give any sense of the theatrical scene but rather were set in a featureless, indeterminate everywhere or nowhere. They rejected not only the 'traditional instruments of theatrical effect'[22] such as ghosts, but also the presentation of violent actions and deaths on stage. 'Often', Charlton remarks, 'there is hardly an action at all.'[23] The *dramatis personae* was restricted as far as possible and no more than three characters were allowed to speak in the same scene. As the fable or narrative was attentuated and any touch of theatricality avoided on principle, the tragedies became sequences of reflections, soliloquies and monologues united mainly by their common rhetorical qualities and, in the plays drawn from Roman history, their preoccupation with 'political disquisition'.[24] The plays ceased to be dynamic and became static, divorced from the possibility of performance: for the French the tragedies were compositions intended to be read. They became, in short, not tragedies but instead, didactic poems on political themes, owning only the exterior formalities of drama. Alexander himself rightly termed his first published tragedy a 'Tragicall Poeme',[25] indicating how his works should be assessed.

It is now perhaps easier to understand the attraction of the French Senecans for a classically-educated gentleman who sought to employ his literary skills to seek advancement in the court. There can be no doubt that that was Alexander's purpose. The content of the *Monarchic Tragedies* reveals his intention to offer advice to his monarch and his *Paraenesis to the Prince*, which McGrail described as 'an epitome of the observations on the behaviour of kings contained in the four tragedies', confirms it.[26] Further, as his models, Alexander rejected the Biblical line of formal tragedy established by George Buchanan's *Baptistes* and *Jephthes*. He chose instead the French Senecan dramas that drew on the matter of Rome,

---

22 Kastner and Charlton, vol. 1, p. cxxi.
23 Kastner and Charlton, vol. 1, p. cxxii.
24 Kastner and Charlton, vol. 1, p. cxxxvii.
25 In 'To the Reader' in *Darius*, quoted in Kastner and Charlton, vol, 1, p. cxcvi. 'Tragicall' here refers principally to the content of the work rather than its form and should not establish expectations. In the middle ages 'tragedy' did not imply drama. See *O.E.D.* Tragedy. 1.
26 McGrail, p. 31.

capable of bearing a heavy freight of political moralising, in order to render Caesar his due.[27]

Turning to English influences on the ambitious dramatist, Charlton places Alexander amongst 'a narrow coterie of poets bound together by personal ties' who were responsible for a group of English plays 'made on the model of French Seneca'.[28] The coterie was headed by Mary Sidney, the Countess of Pembroke, who, according to reputable authorities and T.S. Eliot, 'tried to assemble a body of wits to compose drama in the proper Senecan style, to make head against the popular melodrama of that time',[29] on the lines of the neo-classical principles set out by her brother in his *Apology for Poetry*. Her translation of Garnier's *Marc Antoine* was published in 1592. A playwright for the commercial theatres, Thomas Kyd, translated Garnier's *Cornélie*: it was published as *Cornelia* in 1594. Samuel Daniel dedicated his *Tragedy of Cleopatra* (1594) to the Countess, and Samuel Brandon's *The Virtuous Octavia* (1598) continues Anthony's story from a perspective designed to interest the noble patron. Finally, but too late to have influenced Alexander at the first, Sir Philip Sidney's friend and literary executor, Fulke Greville, Lord Brooke, published formal tragedies of *Alaham* (1633) and *Mustapha* (1609) of a Senecan kind. According to Charlton, 'nearly all the members of the group incorporated material from the French tragedians in their own plays'. Charlton is somewhat apologetic at including Alexander in this dramatic miscellany: he notes that his 'personal relations to the coterie are not so obvious' as those of the others, 'but Daniel knew of him and praised him as a tragedian in 1605'.[30] This, of course, is only evidence of a personal association on the basis of a prior assumption.

The whole construction of a coterie of reformist dramatists centered on the Countess of Pembroke was convincingly exploded by Mary-Ellen Lamb in 1981: 'There was no dramatic circle surrounding the Countess of Pembroke, and the idea of reforming the English stage probably never entered her head'.[31] Finding that there was no evidence to link her with Kyd or Alexander, she observed specifically that Alexander lived in Scotland before James's accession and 'wrote his plays long after the Countess's own period of literary activity and patronage'.[32] It should be

---

27 Lamb has suggested that 'The influence of French drama . . . probably came to him through his fellow Scotsman George Buchanan, whose brother was Alexander's tutor' (p. 200), citing McGrail. What McGrail wrote was that James Alexander, William's grand-uncle '*possibly* [my emphasis] sent the youthful William to the grammar school' (p. 6) in Stirling, where Dr. Thomas Buchanan, a *nephew* [my emphasis] of George Buchanan, was the teacher.
28 Kastner and Charlton, vol. 1, p. clxxvi. Witherspoon (see note 33) states that 'It is well-nigh certain that he was not a member of the coterie, but there is little doubt that he was familiar with the works of its members, and *he may have been* [my emphasis] on more or less intimate terms of friendship with some of the members of the group'. He goes on to fantasise that when Alexander reached England 'he paid his respects to Sidney's sister, and was in general touch with her ideas' (pp. 128–9).
29 T. S. Eliot, 'Seneca in Elizabeth Translation', *Selected Essays* (London: Faber, 1932), p. 92.
30 Kastner and Charlton, vol. 1, p. clxxvii. McGrail endorsed Charlton's notion of an English reformist coterie, but thought that Alexander was probably not a member of the Pembroke group because John Davies, who was, in 1611 speaks of not having known him (p. 18).
31 Mary-Ellen Lamb. 'The Myth of the Countess of Pembroke: The Dramatic Circle', *Yearbook of English Studies* 11 (1981): 194–202.
32 Lamb, p. 200. She also points out that there are only small resemblances between Garnier and Greville's surviving plays, which contain un-Garnier-like Senecan violence.

mentioned, also, that the dedications and commendatory poems of the *Monarchic Tragedies* show no connections with the Sidney circle, and the tragic poems reveal no direct connection with any of the plays mentioned here beyond their common indebtedness to French Senecan tragedy. The notion that the aspirant Scottish dramatist associated himself at the beginning of his career with a flourishing school of English Senecans has no substance. One cannot deny – or prove – that Alexander had read any of the English plays when he came to write *Darius* in the first years of the seventeenth century, but it is equally possible – but unprovable – that he learned of the French Senecan plays while he was on tour on the continent with Argyle. Or he could have read some of the plays in French while still in Scotland.[33] The channels of literary influence are not always deeply engraved in the sands of literary history.

His model chosen and his purpose decided, Alexander was governed principally by considerations of decorum. Tragedy, especially when separated from the vulgarities of the public stage, was a high form, challenging the epic in seriousness of theme and loftiness of diction. No-one undertook the public advice of princes lightly or couched the advice in specific terms. The French Senecan dramas embodied sententious reflections on the properties and responsibilities of kingship, shrowded in decorous fictions and a diction deliberately purged of individuality. Their model suited Alexander exactly, and he adopted its conventions with such thoroughness and remarkable success that he forfeited any claim he might have made to a distinguished place in the history of British drama. One cannot believe that he did not recognise the quality of his achievement. All his tragedies employ speech marks to mark the conspicuously sententious passages, the 'beauties' as it were of the *Monarchic Tragedies*. Associating Alexander with Greville, Charlton concludes that their plays were 'the final crystallisation of all the tendencies of Seneca of the French school. They are, indeed, much more characteristic than Greville's; for the latter's speculative genius gives his dramas an individuality denied to Alexander's more commonplace moralisings'.[34] Such muted praise could scarcely be more condemnatory. There can be little doubt that Alexander intended to distil his deep reading of classical historical and philosophical sources into the poetic statements of his tragedies, with no purpose of originality. Carpenter is correct to describe his dramas as 'meditative moral poems . . . extended reflective monologues on the issues of mortality and decay, betrayal and trust, and "the great uncertainty of worldly things" '.[35] However,

33 Garnier's works were collected in 1585 and 'more than forty editions are recorded within the thirty years from 1586 to 1616' (Alexander Maclaren Witherspoon, *The Influence of Robert Garnier on Elizabethan Drama*, New Haven, Conn.: Yale University Press, 1924, p. 11). Witherspoon further comments on 'The great popularity of French literature among educated men in Scotland' (pp. 133–4).
34 Kastner and Charlton, vol. 1, p. cxci. Charlton seems to regard the suggestion of individuality as a paramount critical criterion, as indeed it may be for a modern reader. Hence, '. . . if this contemplative trend had added weight to the content of his Choruses, it has robbed them of every mark of originality. After his earlier work, it is impossible to find a personality behind his writings; in its stead, a very solemn person with a rigorously commonplace mind impresses himself heavily on the very face of all of them' (vol. 2, p. xviii). He appears to takes little account of neo-classical principles of composition and the requirements of genre.
35 Carpenter, 'Early Scottish drama', p. 209.

modern critics have made no attempt to read them as examples of that kind but rather, they treat them as failed Senecan tragedies, denying to Alexander even the credit of accomplishing well exactly what he had intended. Alexander's works merit a fresh critical assessment.

In this light, it may be possible even for Scotsmen to regard more sympathetically the progressive anglicisation of the language of the tragedies. Carpenter suggests this as a 'reason for the almost negligible impact of Alexander's tragedies on Scottish drama as a whole',[36] no doubt imagining the possibility that had Alexander not purged the Scotticisms he admitted in the first edition of *Darius*, he would have been responsible for a large-scale revival of the exiguous Scottish drama in the form of unactable sententious plays. However, the adaptation of the language to the Court standard was only part of the scope of Alexander's revisions. These again show the significance of linguistic decorum for him, and perhaps, his concept of literary propriety. Once he had secured the attention of the Scottish king of England with plays couched in a diplomatic blend of Scots and English dialects, his obligation to his patron commended more far-reaching alterations. According to Charlton, 'The most considerable modification of his taste occurred after he had written *Darius* and *Croesus . . . i.e.* between 1604 and 1607'.[37] This was the period in which he published his *Paraenesis to the Prince* (1604) and received his appointment in Prince Henry's household. Thereafter, successive prints of the *Monarchic Tragedies* were revised in a multitude of details. Besides Scottish words and phrases, Alexander removed archaic words and words that may be considered pedantic or affected; besides revising 'Scotticisms of every description – in spelling, pronunciation, vocabulary, grammar, or syntax',[38] he purged the text of provincialisms and thoroughly reformed its English grammar. Charlton distinguished such alterations from 'many other[s] . . . which seek a more purely artistic object', notably the removal of contractions, expletives, and terms judged inappropriate in a dignified style of writing. Much attention was given to metrical matters, and he removed particularising words in order to give wide significance to his moral observations. It seems fair to claim that *all* Alexander's revisions were motivated by artistic considerations. He could not perfect his compositions for the readership to which they were directed while retaining the evidences of their provincial origin.

Finally, there is the ironic possibility that the naturalisation of his tragedies – justifiable on grounds of linguistic decorum – was instigated by the Scots king himself. James's *Short Treatise containing some Rules and Cautels to be observed in Scots Poetry* (1584) had condemned the employment of contractions, but Alexander did not purge those until he was closer to the court. Later, James wrote a sonnet, 'The Complaint of the Muses to Alexander upon himselfe, for his ingratitude towards them, by hurting them with his hard hammered words, fitter to be used upon his

---

36 Carpenter, 'Early Scottish drama', p. 209.
37 Kastner and Charlton, vol. 1. p. cxcv.
38 Kastner and Charlton, vol. 1, p. cxcviii. The discussion of Alexander's revisions generally occurs on pp. cxciv–cc, and vol. 2, pp. xi–xvi.

mineralles'.[39] This, or some other words conveying James's opinion of Alexander's diction, may very well have brought about the reformation of his tragedies. In any event, considerations of national linguistic pride seem inappropriate when the compositions are so firmly imbedded within the European literary tradition as Alexander's are. They should not deter literary historians from a balanced assessment of his contribution to literature.

---

39 See Allen F. Westcott, ed., *New Poems by James I of England* (New York: Columbia University Press, 1911), pp. 37–8. The title cited is that given in the Balfour MS in the Advocates Library, Edinburgh. Alexander and his heirs had been granted 'rights of the mines, minerals, and metals of every kind within the barony of Menstry, a tenth of the proceeds to go to the King' (McGrail, p. 62) on 24 September, 1607, and other grants were made in 1611 and 1613. Charlton comments that Alexander's opinions about the language of his tragedies 'became firmer and progressed still further' (vol. 1, p. cxcv) during the period 1607–16, and Westcott suggests 'somewhere between 1616 and 1625' (p. xiii) for the compilation of BM MS Add. 24195. However, it must be said that, apart from the title which varies and may not be James's, it is not clear whether the king objected to the original or the reformed language of Alexander's tragedies.

D. ANGUS

42. *Who was Laurence Fletcher?*

It is, as they say, a good question. Until the other day all that was known of Laurence – and it was known only to students of Elizabethan and Jacobean theatre – might have fitted comfortably on to Churchill's famous half-sheet of paper.

Laurence Fletcher: actor-manager. His company of 'English comedians' played before the Scottish Court at Holyrood (in the old Tennis Court theatre, round the corner from the Abbey Strand); and toured those Scottish burghs which would permit their performances, in the 1590s and up until 1603.

From Autumn 1599 the company of 'comedians' (i.e. actors) performed publicly in Edinburgh at a house fitted up as a theatre in Blackfriars' Wynd. (It is good to know there is still provision for drama at the new Italian Institute in the same thoroughfare.) These public performances were done with King James's strong financial backing, and his overbearing support against the Kirk, who hated the performances, and tried to ban their congregations from seeing them. James won that battle with the Kirk.

In 1601, when the company played Aberdeen at Woolmanhill, Fletcher, described as 'comedian-serviture to His Majesty' was made a burgess of that city. In 1603 Fletcher went south with James, and in May his name appeared at the head of the list of the King's Men, the new theatrical company formed mainly from the old Lord Chamberlain's Men by the new King of Britain, and including Shakespeare and Richard Burbage. He became a shareholder of the Globe Theatre with Shakespeare, Burbage and others and the King's Men walked in the 1604 Coronation Procession in fine new clothes specially provided for the occasion.

The rest, curiously, is almost silence. From 1605 to 1607 Fletcher lived in actors' digs at Hunt's Rents in Maid Lane, Southwark, near the Globe, but no record exists of his having acted there. In 1605 a fellow-actor, Augustine Phillips, died and left him and other King's Men, including Shakespeare, money in his will. But in September 1608 it seems Fletcher himself died, for the records state that on the 12th of that month he was buried at St. Saviour's Church (now Southwark Cathedral) 'with an afternoon knell of the great bell.' The final couplet indeed.

All of which leaves Laurence a shadowy figure. Think of all we do not know. Where and when was he born? Was he Scots or English? Our only anecdote about Fletcher suggests he was a Scot. In the early 1590s we find King James discussing him with two English diplomats at the Scottish Court, one of them Sir Roger Aston. I should have said that the 'company of English comedians' operating in

Scotland was actually borrowed from Queen Elizabeth's own acting company, and this had been arranged by (or through) Sir Roger Aston.

At the time of this conversation Fletcher had recently returned to Edinburgh from a sojourn in England. While there, the rumour had spread in Scotland that he had been arrested, tried and executed by order of Elizabeth. King James now remarked jocularly that even had the rumour proved true, he could have got his own back by having Aston and his friend executed. A tit-for-tat. In other words he, the Scottish King, would have answered Elizabeth's having hanged a Scottish courtier in England by hanging two English courtiers in Scotland. To me that does suggest Fletcher was a Scot.

But other questions remain. What did he look like? What kind of parts did he play? What was his position in the distinguished company of The King's Men? What were his relations with them – especially Shakespeare?

In general theatre historians have tended to discount Fletcher as a Johnny-Come-Lately from Scotland (the provinces, you know!) who was pushed into the King's Men on James's kingly say-so, but who never really fitted in, never got to act at the Globe, and died a few years later, unhonoured and unsung.

The truth may be very different, as we shall see. After all, it's not every actor-manager who has a monarch set him up in a theatre, in his own capital, at his own expense, and in the teeth of outraged (and powerful) opposition. And we know the plays that Fletcher presented were often highly critical of James and his advisers. In England in 1603 Laurence was just as lucky. His name ended up above Shakespeare's and Burbage's. I shall adduce other evidence to suggest he was boss-man at the Globe – at the very least.

As to looks and parts, a few other possibilities emerge. The youthful actor who seems to have replaced Fletcher in the company in 1608 – William Ostler – specialised in playing kings, usually with some flaw of character. Probably Fletcher did before him. As for appearance – in a poem published in 'The Scourge of Folly' by John Davies of Hereford, we find a description of an uncomfortable interview Davies had had with an actor he called 'The English Aesop,' an actor who evidently acted the King off-stage as well as on. (It is unlikely 'the English Aesop' was Ostler, for the latter has another poem in 'The Scourge of Folly' dedicated to him by name.)

Aesop – the Greek Aesop – not only wrote fables; according to legend he was also an actor and a hunchback. So – did Fletcher play Richard III? The latter is nicknamed 'Aesop' in one of Shakespeare's History Plays. Curiously Richard is never referred to as hunchbacked in Shakespeare – indeed no-one is. Even the word 'Crookback' does not appear in 'King Richard III'.

At this point in my researches the printed sources seemed to peter out, so I turned to the Manuscript Room of the National Library of Scotland. And there, lo and behold, a breathtaking discovery – a great gold nugget lying on the surface, waiting to be picked up. There, in the index, under 'Laurence Fletcher,' I found reference to a copy of a personal letter of his, addressed to King James. Incredible! It is written out, with copies of other letters of the period 1586–1623, in a nondescript little volume now tied together with a ribbon because the front cover is loose. The letter-book in question is known simply and unromantically as Adv. 33.7.19.

The contents, all in the same neat, if slightly variable, scribe's hand – an English hand, not Scottish – amounts to 48 pieces of prose (generally in English, though one or two are in Latin). These are mainly letters to and from notable people of the period. The National Library has no doubts about the authenticity of the letter-book. Nor had the late Professor Gordon Donaldson, Historiographer-Royal for Scotland, when he examined the book one day in my presence.

Fletcher's letter to King James is remarkable. A half-hearted attempt has been made to cancel it – diagonal pen-strokes run through it – and when one reads it, one understands why.

On internal evidence Fletcher probably wrote the original in 1606. In London the plague has broken out again, and the King's Men are about to go on tour. King James is also about to leave the city. The actors have just bought new clothes (players acted in their own then) and Laurence's main purpose in writing is to make sure that the King pays the bill. That is the gist of the missive, but the gist is the least of it. The tone is at once witty, biting and profoundly insulting.

There is no salutation or greeting. The opening, like the rest, is blunt, abrupt, disdainful. The first sentence reads: 'First, before you read any further, we sue.'

That is to say, we have a request to make. Fletcher then pauses briefly to give a mock-explanation of his failure even to mention he is addressing his King:

> For, though holding no monopoly (i.e. of the title of King), go your ways, you are well commended, for that none ought to profane that title, which is something too sacred for my mouth.

There follows a swaggering, defiant list of his own pseudo-titles. He says:-

> Know by my Arms what I am. I Laurence, Lord Cobbler of Chester, Sir Mr. Knave Universal, Vice-gerent of all irregular foppery (foolery), Captain of merry honest beggars, thus salute you.

The chances are that these 'titles' referred to stages in Laurence's own peculiar career, the last referring to his present status as leader of the King's Men. Even they were only 'comedians,' counted as rogues and vagabonds by the respectable citizenry. 'Vice-gerent' may be an echo of James's claim in his speech at the opening of the 1605 Parliament to be 'God's vicegerent on earth.'

With ambiguous politeness Fletcher proceeds:

> I first commend me to your grace and your greatness. Fear not, I'll be brief. [In other words, that won't take long; you don't have much of either]. Now follows my petition.

But it doesn't. In fact what follows amounts to a royal command. It is not always clear if Fletcher, in his use of the first person plural, is referring to the company or to himself. The royal 'we' and 'us' come easily to him.

> See us before you go into the country. For though we be blest in thy protection, we are at this instant crossed (i.e. cursed) with the plague.

Then, recalling James's sensitivity to the Catholic threat, Fletcher adds sourly:

> Take heed you carp not. There is no papistry in this crossing and blessing.

There follows a sustained, elaborate and blatant series of allusions to James's popular nickname, 'The Wisest Fool in Christendom':

> You are troubled with wise men enough, and therefore, for the manuring of your spirit, hear a fool. You must not, upon my suit, admit another fool into our company (in other words, make a fool of yourself by ignoring it), unless you will put yourself to charge and exhibition to more fools (i.e. become one of our company of fools). Which, though you will not willingly do, yet Adam's children of that star (i.e. folly) will live under you. There (It) is one thing to profess, another thing to be condemned. For the profession we are settled. Otherwise we might sue for offices and perhaps neither have them upon suit nor discharge them well if we had them.

The essential point that emerges from all this is that he and the other actors are content to be professional fools, but James is another kind of fool, as are the people who let him rule. Fools who are truly foolish are to be condemned; in particular, James, with his pretensions to wisdom, consorting with so-called 'wise men' at Court but doing a foolish job of ruling, as they do a foolish job of helping him.

There follows (at last) the practical point of the letter, or what is explicitly so. The tone remains insouciant and insulting:

> We have put ourselves in new apparel, and we would fain have you look out at a window and laugh at us. Our feathers (i.e. new clothes) have cost crowns apiece. Our murrie (i.e. mulberry-coloured) cloaks and lace are Kentish cloth with gold trimming, and these things are to be answered (i.e. paid for). But that is all one. If we be arrested, it must be in your name, and in your name we wear them, but as we will pay no debt under your countenance; so we get nothing to pay withal but under countenance (i.e. with your approval). Therefore smile upon us.

The first sentence here must refer to some occasion when James was observed to laugh at the 'comedians' away from the theatre. I would guess it happened during the Coronation Procession through London, in 1604, where the King's

Men were seen in their unusually fine clothes. Clearly Laurence has not forgiven the King this.

In any case there is no question of the King's Men paying for their second lot of new clothes. They are His Majesty's Men, so – James must pay, or suffer discredit. And he must pay not only for the new apparel, but for his insulting laughter two years before.

There are echoes of Shakespeare throughout this letter. For example, you may remember the end of Act III of 'As you Like It' (1599?) where Phebe, recalling some fancied rudeness on Ganymede's (i.e. Rosalind's) part, says:

> I marvel why I answered not again:
> But that's all one; omittance is no quittance.
> I'll write to him a very taunting letter . . .
> The matter's in my head and in my heart:
> I will be bitter with him, and passing short.

Laurence turns now to another practical point:

> If you will command us any service ere we go [i.e. on tour], hold up your finger. If you will not, you are for the crown and we for the rest of the Kingdom.

'Hold up your finger' may simply mean 'You have but to ask,' and may refer to a last-minute Court performance before they all head for the country. But 'finger' has a sexual connotation, certainly in Shakespeare, and it is not clear why James should use a secret signal while giving a public audience – unless, perhaps, we have here an indication of a homosexual relationship, or some kind of sexual relationship between the two men. The implication of the second sentence is clear: James has the crown, with all its restrictions and responsibilities; but Fletcher (and his actors) have the freedom of the country.

Up to this point you could perhaps discount all this as privileged persiflage, the kind expected from a King's Fool (or comedian/serviture) to reduce his master's ego. But hear how Fletcher goes on:

> If you look for any flatteries at my hand, take it in your hand and throw it at my head. So only this will I speak: you are the best man in Kent.

Now the reference in the last phrase is to 'King Henry VI Part II' and to one of the characters, Jack Cade, leader of the Peasant's Revolt, who, when dying, describes himself as 'the best man in Kent'.

Remember that in those days – and since – rumour was rife that James was not the child of Mary, Queen of Scots and Lord Darnley. Some averred he *was* her son by David Rizzio her secretary. Others swore James was a changeling, substituted when her real child was stillborn. Certainly we know that the adult James, whatever his attributes, had no kingly presence or appearance of royalty. That fed the rumours.

492 *The European Sun*

So, in the Cade reference, Fletcher is equating the King with a mere commoner trying to replace a true sovereign. Not only that. You will note flatteries are due to himself, not to James.

In the peroration of this letter Laurence pretends to withdraw from this extreme position, but only makes matters worse by reverting to the 'Wisest Fool' sneer:

> If my enemy will say not (i.e. disagree), I will call Kent Christendom. Go to, here is enough for you. (That's as far as my flatteries go). I and my fellows will pray for you. And so fare you well.

Fletcher here virtually dismisses James. And his last few words are particularly grand:

> Dated at my manor, the world
> Thine, and no lecher,
> Sir
> Laurence Fletcher.

Now, 'the world' may mean simply the Globe theatre, or it may mean the world. There is no date on the letter. This man really sees himself, in short, as a 'King of infinite space' – and time.

But we're back to the theatre with the last rhyming couplet. Such couplets ended play scenes, and alerted the actors waiting off stage it was time to go on. But even this little couplet is (I think) heavily loaded. If Laurence Fletcher is no lecher, then perhaps he is saying or implying that James is. Does this refer back to a line in Act IV of 'Troilus and Cressida'? 'You like a lecher out of whorish loins are pleased to breed out your inheritors.'

It is not impossible, if James had no sexual interest in Anne, his queen, that Laurence – possibly bisexual, possibly an unacknowledged royal (as he seems to claim throughout the letter) – was Anne's lover as well as James's, and fathered the royal children. The phrase 'vicegerent of all irregular foppery' is suggestive of this, as is the word 'service' in this context. But if this be true, it was James who 'bred his inheritors' out of 'whorish loins' for Anne was *his* wife, not Laurence's, and the *children* were *his* inheritors. James bred, however, only in the sense that a man breeds dogs or horses.

Incidentally the last royal child was born (allegedly to James and Anne) in 1607. This was the Princess Sophia – was she the result of Laurence's last service? Shortly after her birth James and Anne took up separate establishments. As we have seen, Laurence Fletcher departed the London scene in 1608.

So – who *was* Laurence Fletcher? Rumours were rife at that time not only about James's true identity, but about his mother, Mary, Queen of Scots and the paternity of her children. Don't forget – in addition to James there were the twins alleged to have been born to her in Loch Leven Castle during her Scottish captivity.

Mary herself, dictating to her Secretary, Claude Nau, during her English captivity, claimed to have borne twin boys there, having miscarried. But Mary could lie like a trooper; she would certainly have lied to protect surviving twins, twins smuggled elsewhere and brought up by friends – I suspect in the Highlands.

Let's suppose she bore twins – one boy, one girl – and that they survived in the way I've suggested, with assumed identities. Fantastic though the hypothesis may seem, suppose Fletcher was correct in his assumptions about James's true identity, and his own. If he was, then a mere accident of history – or rather a chapter of such accidents – had robbed him of his crown, his kingdom (or kingdoms) and his regal destiny.

What could he – a man of striking looks, brilliant abilities and royal temper – do with his life? What else but become the substitute King's 'all-licensed fool', his 'comedian/serviture' able to comment freely on all his actions and words, to criticise, taunt, advise him – in short, to rule him and so rule through him, without fear of punishment?

Why no fear of punishment? Because Laurence was playing the Establishment's game. He was *not* laying claim to the throne – whatever he implied about his rights to it. He *didn't* wish to rule. He was another Edward VIII – a royal on holiday. But he *was* a royal, fit, able and willing to pass on the royal genes; to advise his commoner substitute.

But is there more to it? In this letter, was he merely echoing old playscripts by Shakespeare, or was he quoting from himself? Did *he* write the plays? Could he have written the plays? Surely he could.

Shakespeare is alleged to have dashed off the plays – to have never blotted a line. Yes, but was Shakespeare blessed with what we today call a photographic memory. Having read (and destroyed) Fletcher's originals, did he simply dash them off to his memory's dictation? Accepting the credit?

Why all this? I suspect because plays written by Fletcher and publicly performed would be suspect by that same Establishment. How many deadly double entendres could have been read or imagined into them? He needed an innocent front man, a stalking-horse.

And if you don't believe a Scot wrote 'Shakespeare's plays', I suggest you consult my 'The Scotching of Shakespeare' in *Bryght Lanternis*, or Arthur Melville Clark's book *Murder Under Trust*.

J. D. McCLURE

43. *Drummond of Hawthornden and Poetic Translation*

If there is a critical axiom concerning Drummond of Hawthornden, it is that he is an imitative and derivative poet. L.E. Kastner, after listing several examples of poems in Drummond's oeuvre which are close imitations or translations of European models, concludes 'All claim to originality he must forego';[1] R.H. MacDonald calls him 'an exceptionally derivative poet';[2] Michael Spiller uses a tactful neologism to say the same thing in describing him as 'one of the most intertextual of our poets.'[3] His indebtedness to Latin, French, Italian, Spanish and English sources was demonstrated in fascinating detail in Kastner's 1913 edition; more recently R.D.S. Jack has shown that he was not above borrowing from compatriot poets as well;[4] and the task of identifying his models and discussing the use he made of them has been the topic of much equally interesting work to the present day.

Drummond, as is quite clear from his actual practice, regarded himself as being at full liberty to use his sources precisely as he saw fit, reworking them as anything and everything from translations of almost literal verbal accuracy to poems linked to their originals only by the common presence of some words, ideas or elements in the rhetorical structure. His well-stocked library, as the illuminating study by MacDonald makes clear,[5] was a quarry on which he could draw for the raw – or the partly cooked – material of his poetic work: across the gulf of centuries and enormous changes in the perceived role and accepted practice of a poet one can see a resemblance to MacDiarmid, the scale of whose derivations, borrowings and barefaced thefts has probably not even yet been exposed in its entirety. Drummond, as every reader knows, could even praise his *confrère* Patrick Gordon for his originality with an almost verbatim quotation from Sidney: 'Thy Syre no pyick-purse is of others witt'[6] – a borrowing which, at first blush, might be thought to show a degree of either naivety or temerity bordering on the incredible.

---

1 *The Poetical Works of William Drummond of Hawthornden*, Scottish Text Society New Series nos. 3 and 4, Blackwoods, Edinburgh, 1913, Vol. I p. xliii. All references are to this edition.
2 *Poems and Prose of William Drummond of Hawthornden*, Scottish Academic Press, Edinburgh 1976, p. xiii.
3 'Poetry after the Union,' in *The History of Scottish Literature vol. 1, origins to 1660*, ed. R.D.S. Jack, Aberdeen University Press 1988, p. 150.
4 'Drummond: the major Scottish sources,' *Studies in Scottish Literature* 6, 1968, pp. 36–46.
5 Robert H. MacDonald, *The Library of Drummond of Hawthornden*, Edinburgh University Press and Aldine, Chicago, 1971.
6 In his commendatory Sonnet to Gordon's *The Famous Historye of Penardo and Laissa*. Kastner vol. 2, p. 162.

To the extent that this should be seen as evidence of a relatively limited poetic talent in Drummond (and that is, of course, highly debatable), the counter-balancing argument which is presented to save his status as a major figure in the Scottish literary roll-call is that he is almost invariably successful in transmuting the works of Ronsard, Marino, Sidney and the rest into poetry which is both attractive and individual: his poetic achievement is by no means a mere *mélange* of other men's lines, tropes, thoughts or whole passages but a cohesive set of poems in a distinctive and consistent literary idiolect. Drummond has been, and still is, predominantly seen as an extreme, but also an extremely skilful, example of a poet for whom the Renaissance doctrine of 'imitation' was a dominant principle. However, the relationship between those two aspects of his work remains curiously indeterminate. Drummond is a very derivative poet, and he is a very good poet; but what precisely have those two unchallenged facts to do with each other? Many years ago Ruth C. Wallerstein, in a landmark article in Drummond criticism,[7] presented a detailed examination of his treatment of some of his most important sources, and more recently R.D.S. Jack addressed the same issue in his *The Italian Influence on Scottish Literature*.[8] But though both those scholars provide expert analyses of Drummond's poems in comparison with their models, the general issue of how we should accommodate his practice of wholesale borrowing in an assessment of his place in literary history remains undecided. My intention in this paper will be to discuss his poetry in the light of late-Renaissance attitudes to poetic translation, and to see whether this provides a way towards a more comprehensive judgement of his work.

The principles and practice of translation occupied the minds of many of Europe's scholars and poets in the Renaissance period, and Drummond could scarcely be unaware of or uninterested in the controversy. An intriguing piece of evidence regarding his own attitude is provided by his three translations, representing different degrees of freedom in his treatment of the originals, of two Italian sonnets.[9] That these exercises were juvenilia, never printed in Drummond's lifetime probably because he did not think them worth preserving, is shown not only by the presence of some of the Scotticisms of which his published work is almost completely purged, but more impressionistically by the inferiority of some of the writing, and of the transference of the poetic statements of his models, to what we expect of Drummond: would the mature poet, for example, have been reduced to making *is* rhyme with itself in the sestet of a sonnet? Nonetheless, something of Drummond's practice, in his formative years as later, is revealed by a comparison of the poems. As Kastner once again has pointed out, Drummond found his idea for this exercise in *Les Recherches de la France* of Étienne Pasquier, published in 1594, an erudite series of essays on the history, literature, language and culture of France. The use of multiple versions of the same original work to illustrate different approaches to translation,

---

7 'The style of Drummond of Hawthornden in its relation to his translations,' PMLA 48 (1933), pp. 1090–1107.
8 Edinburgh U.P. 1972, pp. 113–43.
9 Originals and translations in Kastner vol. 2, 231–4.

however, is his own inspiration. Pasquier's aim in this whole chapter of his book is to argue the full parity of French to Italian as a literary language, which he does by demonstrating that French can be used to translate Italian poems with no sacrifice of poetic merit. For the sonnet by Cardinal Bembo of which Drummond offers three translations, Pasquier quotes renderings by Desportes, Baïf and himself, but makes no suggestion that they differ in degree of fidelity to the original: nor do they to any extent, as far as I can judge, all showing close correspondence to their model. The second sonnet is cited by Pasquier along with only two French renderings, by Desportes and himself: this time not close translations but very free adaptations; but again not differing significantly in degree of freedom.

The readings 'in the same sort of rime' and 'in frier sort of rime' in fact show little difference in the exercise of what may be called translator's licence. In both versions the most conspicuous departure from the original occurs at lines 7–8: the 'frier' version abandons entirely Teobaldi's contrast between mortals and angels, bringing in instead of the first a rhetorical catalogue intended, perhaps, to complement the catalogue two lines earlier; the other retains the comparison but seriously weakens the poetic effect by losing the symmetrical balance between the two lines and the litotes in *Ne lascia senza inuidia*, and substituting a vague and singularly unevocative circumlocution for Teobaldi's *divin choro*. The second version makes another change, again undeniably for the worse, by rejecting Teobaldi's *aspra fortuna e gli empi dei* to apostrophise *absence* as a 'foul traitour'. If neither poem can be considered an impressive foretaste of what Drummond was later to achieve, however, the intentions behind them are clear. In the first he has allowed himself very little freedom to depart from the words of the original, except when constrained to do so by the requirements of metre or rhyme. In the second, though again he has followed the words and the lines of the Italian poem quite closely, he has taken the liberty of departing from its verse form, writing in couplets instead of quatrains and tercets. This is a somewhat puzzling proceeding, since a sequence of seven couplets is a less elaborately structured verse than a sonnet and therefore necessarily less challenging; and there is no sign that he has attempted to compensate for this diminution of the poetic force of his model by heightening the effect at any other level. The implication of his word 'frier' may simply be that in this version he has set his poetic sights rather lower than in the first.

The 'paraphrasticalie translated' version obviously bears far less resemblance to its model than do the other two; but it is of interest to note what, specifically, Drummond has assumed the licence to do. The 'argument' or paraphrasable thought-sequence of the poem is unaltered; so is the sonnet form, though not with exactly the same rhyme scheme. The tropes of the original, however, are replaced by a new set: the 'bird' simile is gone, and so is the notion of the beloved's beauty surpassing all on earth and making even Heaven jealous; and in their place is a varied and attractive use of metaphors of flowers: a device not even suggested in Teobaldi's poem (nor in either of the French versions, incidentally). The 'juel' image in line 10 likewise corresponds to nothing in the original. Teobaldi's already well-worn metaphor of hair as gold is re-invigorated by Drummond's novel treatment: the word 'golden' is applied not to the hair when spoken of literally – here gold is suggested by a witty reference to Midas – but to the metaphorical *chain* which it has become in the last line. On a different level, Teobaldi's catalogue in line 5 is not imitated: Drummond, however, introduces other decorative devices, the wordplay on 'knots' and 'nets', the oxymoron '*Deare fatall* present', and the paradox 'when ye loosest hang me fastest band . . .'. (The phrase *présent fatal* appears in Desportes's version; but Drummond's addition of 'deare' is a considerable augmentation of its poetic force.) The idea of the lover as prisoner till death, stated overtly in the original, is reduced in Drummond's version to the implications of the words 'fatall' and 'mortall'. Finally, the ending is notably strengthened, by comparison both with Drummond's other versions and with the original, by 'I *take delyt* to veare his goldin chaines' – a much more imaginative qualifier than 'I *foolish* beare about his nets and chains' in the second version.

In this example at least, the best poem, as a poem, is certainly the one in which Drummond has allowed himself the most freedom to exercise his own poetic imagination. The same is true of his other set of three translations from a common original, in this case a sonnet by Bembo in which the poet as lover compares himself to a wounded fawn, where Drummond's 'paraphrastical' translation includes figures such as the sun 'turning old vinters snowie haire in streames' (Bembo simply has it that winter *parte e da loco a le stagion migliori*), or balancing phrases, no such device being present in the Italian, such as

>   Vanton he cares not ocht that dolour brings,
>   Hungry he spares not flowres vith names of kings.

The notion that closely literal translation was unlikely to result in poetry of merit had been a well-established literary credo since long before Drummond's time. One of the summative works in this phase of intellectual history is Dryden's Preface to *Ovid's Epistles, Translated by Several Hands*. Published in 1680 this of course post-dates Drummond's work; but the approach to translation which Dryden here encapsulates, and even the terminology which he uses, had been common currency for well over a century and had their origins in classical antiquity. Dryden quotes Horace's injunction

>   *Nec verbum verbo curabis reddere, fidus*
>   *Interpres –*

and goes on to argue '"Tis almost impossible to translate verbally and well, at the same time . . .' Excessive concern to adhere to the actual words of the original, he says, is 'much like dancing on Ropes with fetter'd Leggs: a man may shun a fall by using Caution, but the gracefulness of Motion is not to be expected: and when we have said the best of it, 'tis but a foolish Task; for no sober man would put himself into a danger for the Applause of scaping without breaking his Neck.' Dryden's careful summary of what was then a generally accepted stance on translation is as follows:

> All Translation I suppose may be reduced to these three heads: First, that of Metaphrase, or turning an Authour word by word, and Line by Line, from one language into another . . . The second way is that of Paraphrase, or Translation with Latitude, where the Authour is kept in view by the Translator, so as never to be lost, but his words are not so strictly follow'd as his sense, and that too is admitted to be amplyfied, but not alter'd . . . The third way is that of Imitation, where the Translator (if now he has not lost that Name) assumes the liberty not only to vary from the words and sence, but to forsake them both as he sees occasion: and taking only some general hints from the Original, to run division on the ground-work, as he pleases.

Of these three modes of translation, Dryden upholds *paraphrase* as the most acceptable. As *metaphrase* is a betrayal of the translator's native language, *imitation* is a betrayal of the original author: the result may be an excellent poem, but 'He who is inquisitive to know an Authours thoughts will be disappointed in his expectation. And 'tis not always that a man will be content to have a Present made him, when he expects the payment of a Debt.' (It should be noted that his use of the word *imitation* to indicate something to be avoided is a departure from the customary usage; but the procedure which he so designates was of course well known and regularly criticised. For convenience I will use the word in Dryden's sense throughout this paper.)

Accepting this schema for the moment, though the distinctions between the three categories are on any showing far less clear-cut than Dryden's account suggests, it is readily possible to find in Drummond's work poems which could be taken as exemplifying each of the three methods. The first Madrigal in his 1616 *Poems* is very close to being a 'word by word, and line by line' rendition of its original, a madrigal by Marino:

>   *A dedale of my Death,*
>   *Now I resemble that subtile Worme on Earth*
>   *Which prone to its owne euill can take no rest.*
>   *For with strange Thoughts possest,*
>   *I feede on fading Leaues*
>   *Of Hope, which me deceaues,*
>   *And thousand Webs doth warpe within my Brest.*
>   *And thus in end vnto my selfe I weaue*
>   *A fast-shut Prison, no, but euen a Graue.*[10]

>   *Fabro dela mia morte*
>   *Sembr' io verme ingegnoso,*

---

10 Kastner vol. 1, p. 17.

> *Che 'ntento al proprio mal mai non riposo.*
> *De le caduche foglie*
> *D'una vana speranza mi nodrisco:*
> *E uarie fila ordisco*
> *Di pensier, di desiri insieme attorte.*
> *Così, lasso, a me stesso*
> *Prigion non sol, ma sepoltura intesso.*[11]

In the first three lines, except for Drummond's 'on Earth' (which I cannot believe to be a mere otiose line-filler, though its exact significance escapes me), the word-for-word equivalence is almost complete. Drummond's fifth and sixth lines directly translate Marino's fourth and fifth: 'I feede on . . .' and *mi nodrisco de . . .* are translation equivalents, notwithstanding the syntactic rearrangement; and the very slight expansion of *una vana speranza* to 'Hope, which me deceaues' scarcely affects the referential meaning. Drummond's final lines likewise are made up almost entirely of literal equivalents for Marino's words: the Italian *lasso*, to which 'in end' corresponds only in position, is the exception. Only Marino's lines 6–7 are not translated closely; and even here, *fila* gives 'webs', *ordisco* gives 'I warpe', *varie*, since it suggests multiplicity as well as diversity, is not totally misrepresented by 'thousand', and *pensier* gives, though at a different point in the poem, 'thoughts'. Certainly Drummond's poem differs from Marino's in ways more subtle than simple diversity of reference. Edwin Morgan, six conferences ago, expounded on the far-reaching change made by Drummond's replacement of the general word *fabro* by the name, used like a common noun, of Daedalus – not just any *fabro* but the builder of the Labyrinth.[12] The various meanings of *subtile* certainly incorporate those of *ingegnoso*, but the English word could convey not only skill but cunning and treachery (as for example in Coverdale's Bible: 'The serpent was sotyller than all the beasts of the felde'). The sense of 'can take no rest' is not implied by the Italian, and is strongly reinforced by the word *possest*. These and other seemingly minor, or minimal, alterations result in delicate contrasts between the sense of the original and that of even a very close translation. However, in this poem Drummond's literal adherence to his source is at least comparable in degree to that of Dryden's example of metaphrase, Ben Jonson's translation of Horace's *Ars Poetica* – and, it may be added, very much less strained and awkward.

> *Let* Fortune *triumph now, and Iö sing,*
> *Sith I must fall beneath this Load of Care,*
> *Let Her what most I prize of eu'rie Thing*
> *Now wicked Trophees in her Temple reare.*
>   *Shee who high Palmie Empires doth not spare,*
>   *And tramples in the Dust the prowdest King,*

---

11 *Rime*, 1602, pt.ii, p. 81; quoted in full in Kastner vol. 1, p. 178.
12 'Gavin Douglas and William Drummond as translators,' in *Bards and Makars*, eds. A.J. Aitken, M.P. McDiarmid and D.S. Thomson, Glasgow U.P. 1977, p. 199.

> Let Her vaunt how my Blisse shee did impaire,
> To what low Ebbe Shee now my Flow doth bring.
>   Let Her count how (a new Ixion) Mee
> Shee in her Wheele did turne, how high nor low
> I neuer stood, but more to tortur'd bee:
> Weepe Soule, weepe plaintfull Soule, thy Sorrows know,
>   Weepe, of thy Teares till a blacke Riuer swell,
>   Which may Cocytus be to this thy Hell.[13]

> Vinca fortuna homai, se sotto il peso
> Di tante cure al fin cader conviene,
> Vinca, e del mio riposo, e del mio bene
> L'empio trofeo sia nel suo tempio appeso
>   Colei, che mille eccelsi imperi ha reso
> Vili, et eguali a le più basse arene,
> Del mio male hor si vanta, e le mie pene
> Conta, e mi chiama da' suoi strali offese.
>   Dunque natura, e stil cangia, perch'io
> Cangio il mio riso in pianto? Hor qual più chiaro
> Presagio attende del mio danno eterno?
>   Piangi, alma trista, piangi, e del tuo amaro
> Pianto si formi un tenebroso rio,
> Ch'il Cocito sia poi del nostro Inferno.[14]

The sonnet 'Let Fortune triumph now', which is still recognisably a translation from an identifiable original but this time not, or not so consistently, rendered with word-for-word or line-for-line fidelity, may suggest the approach which Dryden terms *paraphrase*. Very probably for the simple practical reason that English words are shorter than Italian words, Drummond reduces Tasso's *se sotto il peso Di tante cure al fin cader conviene* to a single line, filling up his first line by a metonymic re-expression of the idea of the first clause and thus intensifying its ironic force. His use of an indefinite clause as a direct object, 'what most I prize of eu'rie Thing', where Tasso uses noun phrases *mio riposo e [. . .] mio bene*, does not really make his language less specific or less concrete than the Italian, since the abstract nouns *riposo* and (still more) *bene* are about as empty of exact referential content as they could be. Drummond's lines 5–6 first make a statement in literal terms and then re-state its sense figuratively: Tasso's lines, which state exactly the same idea, contain the same device at the level of smaller grammatical units (*vili – et eguali a le più basse arene*): the word *arene* clearly suggests Drummond's 'dust'. Tasso's *strale* is gone, replaced by a wholly different metaphor; Drummond's reference to Ixion, however, far from being an arbitrary decoration, is clearly suggested by Tasso's mentioning *danno eterno*

---

13 Kastner vol. 1, p. 30.
14 *Scielte delle Rime*, 1582, pt. ii p. 26., quoted in full in Kastner vol. 1, pp. 192–3.

here in the context of a poem of Fortune – whose inseparable attribute is the *wheel*. Finally, in the last three lines of the translation Drummond virtually adopts metaphrase rather than paraphrase to render Tasso's thought in a very close translation of Tasso's words.

> *O than the fairest Day, thrice fairer Night!*
> *Night to best Dayes in which a Sunne doth rise,*
> *Of which that golden Eye, which cleares the Skies,*
> *Is but a sparkling Ray, a Shadow light:*
>   *And blessed yee (in sillie Pastors sight)*
> *Milde Creatures, in whose warme Cribe now lyes*
> *That Heauen-sent Yongling, holie-Maide-borne Wight,*
> *Midst, end, beginning of our Prophesies:*
>   *Blest Cotage that hath Flowers in Winter spred,*
> *Though withered blessed Grasse, that hath the grace*
> *To decke, and bee a Carpet to that Place.*
>   *Thus sang, vnto the Soundes of oaten Reed,*
> *Before the Babe, the Sheepheards bow'd on knees,*
> *And Springs ranne Nectar, Honey dropt from Trees.*[15]

> *Felice notte, ond' a noi nasce il giorno,*
> *Di cui mai più sereno altro non fue,*
> *Che fra gli horrori, e sotto l'ombre tue*
> *Copri quel Sol, ch' al' altro Sol fa scorno.*
>   *Felici uoi, che 'n pouero soggiorno,*
> *Pigro asinello, e mansuetuo bue,*
> *Al pargoletto Dio le membra sue*
> *State a scaldar co' dolci fiati intorno.*
>   *Felici uoi, degnate a tanti honori,*
> *Aride herbette, e rustica capanna,*
> *Ch' aprir vedete a mezzo 'l Verno i fiori.*
>   *Così diceano a suon di rozza canna*
> *Innanzi al gran bambin chini i pastori,*
> *E sudò l' elce, e 'l pin nettare, e manna.*[16]

In the sonnet on the Nativity, for the most part, the resemblance of Drummond's poem to Marino's original is on the level of ideas and images rather than actual words. The opening quatrains of the two poems express the same conceit, and Drummond's third and fourth lines could be seen as stating more figuratively and with greater elaboration the sense of Marino's *fa scorno*. Except for such obvious and inescapable coincidences of vocabulary as *notte* 'night', *giorno* 'day' and *sole* 'sun', however, there is no verbal correspondence. The affectionate tone of

15 Kastner vol. 2, p. 11.
16 *Rime*, pt. i p. 190; quoted in full in Kastner vol. 2, p. 332.

Marino's *pigro asinello e mansuete bue* is perhaps implied by Drummond's choice of adjective in his much briefer reference to '*milde* creatures': conversely, Marino's concise *pargoletto Dio* is expanded to two lines consisting of three epithets (is Drummond's altering of the proportions of Marino's references to the animals and to Christ perhaps somewhat pointed?). The ideas of warmth and of poverty are are also present in the second quatrains of both poems, though with no correspondence in phrasing. In the first tercet the verbal relationship becomes closer, but Drummond's ordering of the ideas is different from Marino's; and he fills the space left by his omission of his model's somewhat vacuous *degnate a tanti honori* by developing the implication of *aride herbette*. The changes which Drummond makes in the last three lines are of a different kind, being alterations at the level of individual words: *rozza canna* becomes 'oaten Reed' and the specific items mentioned in the last line are different, though the poetic force of the images remains essentially unchanged and, perhaps, a tightening up can be seen in the literary logic: why, in Marino's poem, *elce* and *pino* rather than any other trees, especially since oaks are not noted for exuding anything at all?[17] On the whole, this is a clear example of a poem written by 'taking only some general hints from the Original'; and though it is impossible to locate a definite point beyond which a poem derived by interlingual transfer from another poem loses the claim to be regarded as a translation, it is hard to see that a poem standing in a more tenuous relationship to its original than this one could be so described without allowing the word a range of meaning so wide as to call its usefulness into question.

Accepting, as every critic since Kastner has done, that Drummond's poetry includes examples of every degree of closeness to an orginal, it is *a priori* likely that specimens could be found of each of Dryden's three categories; and the poems just examined certainly seem to fit the bill. Yet if the question is raised whether their actual quality is in any sense whatever a function of their fidelity as translations, the answer must surely be that there are no grounds for such a conclusion. The rendering of Marino's madrigal is not inferior to that of his sonnet because it is verbally closer to the original: there is no obvious case for saying that it is inferior at all.

The truth is that the statements by Dryden, and all his predecessors, on literal translation cannot be taken at their face value. The concept of metaphrase, or *verbum verbo* translation, attacked by every writer on the subject since Roman times, is a straw man.[18] It is perfectly obvious that even in utilitarian prose word-for-word translation is simply out of the question, since the differences between the grammatical patterns of any two languages would necessarily give unacceptable results; and if equivalence in verse form is sought, it has never required to be argued that if a certain sequence of Italian words rhymes and scans, the sequence of their translation equivalents in English will not do so. The danger of producing work which is false to the idiom of the target language as a result of

---

17 David Reid kindly pointed out to me at the conference that oaks in Mediterranean countries *do* exude honeydew.
18 This point is argued on the first page of a recent interesting book, *The Translator's Turn* by Douglas Robinson, Baltimore and London 1991.

excessive fidelity to the words of the original is so obvious, and the need to avoid it so elementary, that even the most minimal degree of competence in a poet-translator would make caution against it unnecessary. The *real* risk entailed by over-literalism is not this but that a poet-translator will be prevented from giving full scope to his own particular poetic skills, and will thus produce work which displays neither the peculiar genius of the original poet nor the translator's literary gifts in his own language. This is the reason for the inferiority of Drummond's close translation of the Teobaldi sonnet to his 'paraphrastical' version: he has not allowed himself the licence to exercise his own poetic imagination and technical skill, and therefore has not written as well either as Teobaldi or as he himself can do when not working under those restrictions.

It is perhaps not so immediately obvious that what Dryden calls 'imitation' is equally a straw man. 'The liberty not only to vary from the words and sence, but to forsake them both as he sees occasion: and taking only some general hints from the Original, to run division on the ground-work, as he pleases' is a concept which by its nature is not susceptible of precise or even approximate de-limitation. If a poet-translator may act *as he sees occasion*, then clearly the concept of 'imitation' can cover any treatment whatever of an original. Drummond's Nativity sonnet may be an example of it; so may his Sonnet XVII,[19] beginning 'With flaming Hornes the *Bull* now brings the Yeare,' which resembles the poem Kastner identifies as its source to the extent that both are spring poems, both refer to melting snow, flowing rivers, bird song, animal cries, etc., and both conclude with a contrast between the happiness of the natural world and the sadness of the rejected lover, but correspondence between the actual words is minimal; so may his Sonnet XLIV,[20] according to Kastner 'probably suggested by' a poem by Claude de Buttet but having nothing more in common with it than that they both are love poems in which a window is apostrophised.

From this it follows that the notion of metaphrase, paraphrase and imitation as points on a line, with paraphrase as the desirable *via media* between the two dangerous extremes, is wholly factitious and without theoretical foundation. What is the status of a line drawn between a procedure which is in practice never applied and would be deserving of no serious consideration if it were, and a procedure which turns out to be virtually co-terminous with writing poetry? (For it has always been true, and is of course strongly emphasised in contemporary literary theory, that all poetry is more or less, and more or less overtly, derivative of previous work.) And since, as is at once noticeable, the arguments against metaphrase and imitation are of different kinds (the first being condemned on literary and the second on ethical grounds), from what point of view is paraphrase to be judged preferable? This by no means warrants the conclusion that the schema summarised by Dryden is without validity: it is, after all, a statement of principles which have been applied throughout the history of poetic translation up to and including the present day. But it is simply an impressionistically-

19 Kastner vol. 1, p. 21.
20 ibid. p. 40.

determined set of pragmatic guidelines, with no claim to theoretical status. Nor are the principles necessarily of any help whatever in assessing a poet such as Drummond, whose work runs the full gamut from metaphrase to imitation and beyond. Anything offered as poetic translation can be judged to be close, paraphrastic or free, given that genuinely literal translation is a *reductio ad absurdum* which never occurs as a credible literary endeavour. A pronouncement on this aspect of the work, however, is certainly not a judgement of its literary merit as a poem in the translator's language. It is not necessarily a judgement of its adequacy as a representation of the original: the differences between the two languages, between the canons of literary merit in the two poetic cultures, and between the original poet's and the translator's respective historical backgrounds, form a set of factors so variable that it is perfectly possible to find instances in which the original poet's intention is more accurately conveyed for a foreign readership by a less than by a more literally faithful translation (this, admittedly, is not a consideration which applies in Drummond's case, since he and all his models belong to a common cultural tradition). Even the issue of adequacy of representation of the original – the moral issue with reference to which imitation is condemned – may not be a relevant one to raise: Drummond was not attempting to represent (or 're-present') Bembo or Desportes by giving them an English voice, for the readership he anticipated was one which would have been familiar with the originals, but to draw on Bembo or Desportes for poetic material to be expressed in the voice of Drummond.

From another point of view, George Steiner, in the course of what is surely one of the most wide-ranging, most profound and most stimulating books on translation published this century,[21] argues that 'The perennial distinction between literalism, paraphrase and free imitation turns out to be wholly contingent. It has no precision or philosophic basis.' (First ed. p.303, new ed. p. 319.) This is the conclusion to his exposition of what he calls the hermeneutic motion: a four-stage operation involving 'trust, penetration, embodiment and restitution.' The argument is too elaborate to summarise here, but what I take to be a crucial point is that a translation is not only a demonstration but an enhancement of the richness of its original: since the new artifact stands in some definite relationship to the old (but one which will differ in every individual case), it allows its model to appear through the comparison in new and possibly illuminating perspectives. And since this can be accomplished as well by a free as by a literal translation, the issue of verbal correspondence is fundamentally irrelevant: what does matter is that the translator should repay his debt by returning, through his enrichment of the meaning of the original poem, the gift which his own poetic culture has received through his translation.

It will at once be evident that this view of translation is particularly appropriate in the case of Drummond, since the poems on which his are based could be expected to be readily recognisable to his readers. In the reign of James VI, no literary Scot (or Englishman) would have needed a Kastner to point out the

---

21 *After Babel*, New York and London (OUP), first edition 1975, new edition 1992.

indebtedness of this or that poem by Drummond to Guarini or Garcilaso; and the counterpointing of the new against the old poem would have formed a major part of their pleasure in reading Drummond's works. (The notorious line referred to earlier, 'Thy Syre no pyick-purse is of others witt,' would have been thought neither naive nor temerarious but would have been recognised at once as meaning 'The author of this poem is another Philip Sidney.')

If we wish to consider Drummond's relationship to his originals in assessing his poetic achievement, then the appropriate question to ask is not 'How radically has he departed on any given occasion from the words of his model?' Answering this question may be an interesting and agreeable exercise – I hope it has been – but it does not help us to determine how *well*, in a moral as well as a literary sense, Drummond has treated the poets who provided him with his material. The question is, rather, 'How and to what extent is the original poem illuminated by Drummond's version: would readers familiar with, say, Marino find their interest in and appreciation of his work enhanced after reading Drummond?' This is the only sense I can find in which MacDonald's statement 'The difficulty is to decide whether Drummond's borrowings are legitimate'[22] can be seen as raising a real issue – since we surely cannot suspect Drummond (unlike MacDiarmid, to return to that comparison) of simply trying fraudulently to claim credit for work which is not his own. MacDonald does not make it clear in what sense he intends 'legitimate' to be understood; and given that Drummond's 'intertextuality' is nothing but a more extensive than usual, and in some cases more obvious than usual, application of an established and accepted poetic technique, the basis for a distinction between legitimate and illegitimate borrowing is not at all evident. But if a legitimate borrowing is one of which the result fully repays the literary debt to the original and an illegitimate borrowing one which fails to do so, then the question at once becomes a relevant and vital one. Unfortunately, it indeed presents a practical difficulty, in that it can be credibly answered only by readers with an intimate knowledge of the language, the individual poetic achievements, and the general literary-historical backgrounds of the writers who served Drummond for models. I would judge that in the Nativity sonnet, for example, he gives more than he receives, bestowing on Marino the reflected glory from a statement finer than his of the poetic idea which he first expressed;[23] but my knowledge of the Italian language is amateurish and of the literature sketchy: it may well be that Marino's poem has subtleties which I cannot recognise.

However, it is by this approach to the poems – by an examination of what Drummond has done not only *with* his models but *to* and *for* them – that the hitherto missing dimension in Drummond criticism can be supplied. Excellent studies of his work considered simply as poetry have been made: an entirely licit procedure, of course, since a poetic translation being by definition a poem in the translator's language must be capable, and deserving, of being read, appreciated

---

22 *Library*, op. cit., p. 23.
23 See Morgan, 'Douglas and Drummond,' op. cit., p. 199, for discussion of a case where he fails to do this.

and judged simply as such: and the task of identifying his sources continues to exercise researchers. Those two aspects of Drummond scholarship require to be integrated into a single critical approach directed specifically towards his highly idiosyncratic achievement. For Drummond is, after all, a very peculiar literary figure: he is not a translator in the rigid sense of a poet whose entire reputation is founded on his success in purveying versions of foreign originals for his co-linguists like, say, Edward FitzGerald; yet he owes so much more to specific foreign models than most of his compatriots and contemporaries that it seems less than adequate to criticise him on precisely the same basis as they are criticised. The aim of literary criticism – that is, serious literary criticism and not the assorted mixtures of fantasy and polemic that pass under that name in our time – is to assess, or to provide the means of assessing, how well a writer has succeeded in what he may be assumed to have been attempting to do; which in Drummond's case was not merely to write good poetry but to write good poetry owing a massive and obvious debt to a range of European models. To ascertain how honourably his debt has been repaid, it is necessary to consult his creditors.

DAVID W. ATKINSON

44. *The Poetic Voices of Robert Ayton*

Perhaps because it is difficult to characterise Ayton as Scottish after his departure from Scotland to the court of James I, he remains, like a number of others who moved south from Scotland, relatively unappreciated and most certainly unstudied. As Rod Lyall has observed, Ayton was one of those Scottish poets who 'plunged into the larger pool of the English court and vanished almost without trace.'[1] At the same time, though, Ayton, unhindered by Scottish parochialism, or any particular nationalistic sentiment, may be viewed as one caught up in the larger movements of English poetry, who constitutes an important, even if a secondary, figure in early seventeenth-century poetry. While one must be cautioned about 'discovering' poets who are perhaps best left in obscurity, Ayton is a poet, who, never really accepted as Scottish, and overshadowed by the major English poets of the seventeenth century, ought to be given some new consideration.

Much of Ayton's English poetry is of a 'type,' very often addressed to an ungrateful mistress, and expressing many of the conventions of Petrarchan fashion: the beauty of his mistress, her coldness, the exaggerated torments of the lover, his submissiveness. Most certainly Ayton shared Petrarch's desire to provide a 'minute analysis of the sentiments of the heart'.[2] At the same time, however, Ayton, while never setting aside his Petrarchan roots, did not always write poetry that could be easily dismissed as imitative. Ayton may never have reached the heights of Donne, or indeed any other of the major English metaphysicals, but his poetry nonetheless goes well beyond the tired Petrarchan norms of the last half of the sixteenth century, and is quite clearly a Stuart poetry that 'has its voice and quality and something of its own to say'.[3] As Mary Jane Scott remarks, Ayton 'demonstrates the shift from the Elizabethan manner of lyric poetry to the Metaphysical mode, characterized – alongside of its dependence on irony and paradox and its fondness for intellectual conceits – by plain words and strong lines.'[4] While one must assume that Ayton, like all poets, writes from experience, it is also the case that his poetry does not so much present a man in love as it does a man writing about love,[5] who in his poetry speaks with a voice ranging from the Petrarchan lover with all its excesses to that of a sceptic

1 R. J. Lyall, '"A New Maid Channoun"? Redefining the Canonical in Medical and Renaissance Scottish Literature ' *Studies in Scottish Literature* XXVI (1991), 15.
2 Lu Emily Pearson, *Elizabethan Love Conventions* (Berkley: University of California Press, 1933), p. 2.
3 A.J. Smith, *The Metaphysics of Love* (Cambridge: Cambridge University Press, 1985), p. 41.
4 Mary Jane Wittstock Scott, 'Robert Ayton: Scottish Metaphysical,' *Scottish Literary Journal*, 2 (1975), 5.
5 Jerome Mazzaro, *Transformations in the Renaissance English Lyric* (Ithaca and London: Cornell University Press, 1970), p. 16.

exhibiting an ironic detachment towards love that suggests a much more worldly attitude towards the vicissitudes of the human heart.

Regrettably, what meagre reputation Ayton currently enjoys is based on some of his least successful poetry, of which his longest poem, 'Diophantus and Charidora,' is an example. The poem's hero, Diophantus, is dying, and so he takes the opportunity to recount his many pledges of attachment to his mistress, Charidora. The images are commonplace, and the almost doggeral-like quality of the verse hardly exudes the pathos and loss one expects, and even demands, of such a poem. Take, for example, the opening stanzas:

> When Diophantus knew
> The destinies Discreete,
> How he was forced to forgoe
> His deare and lovely sweete,
> Ou'r volted with the vaile
> Of Beame rebeating trees
> And Ghostly gazeing on the ground
> Even death struck in his eyes,
> Oft pressed he to speake,
> But when he did Essay
> The Agonizeing dreads of death
> His wrastling voice did stay.[6]

One would be hard pressed to defend this maudlin sentimentality, which is only made worse by the exaggerated praise the speaker heaps upon his lady, and by his own expressions of grief and loss. She is 'the starr that sav'd my shipp, / From tempest of Dispaire' (1.17), 'the Soveraigne balme, / That sweete Cathalicon / Which cured mee of all my cares / When I did grieve and grone' (1.19). Ayton refers to Diophantus' 'due-disstilling Eyes' that 'Have shedd such streames of teares' (1.28). In typical Petrarchan fashion, she is the ideal, and he in 'lyfe and death' is her 'best affected slave' (1.56).

Many of Ayton's poems, like 'Diophantus and Charidora,' dwell in a predictable and repetitive way on the vagaries of love, and provide little in the way of the sustained argument and wit expected of the metaphysicals. In a number of poems, however, Ayton is able to exhibit a distinctive style even while repeating Petrarchan commonplaces. Ayton's poem on inconstancy in love,[7] for example, possesses an energy and sharpness, as it draws on the pattern, well established since Horace,[8] of heaping disdain on one's unfaithful mistress. The first stanza suggests that for the most part the poet is resolved to his loss:

---

6 Robert Ayton, *The English and Latin Poems of Sir Robert Ayton*, ed. Charles B. Gullans (Edinburgh and London: William Blackwood & Sons, 1963), 2a, 11. 1–7. All other references to Ayton's poems are from this edition and are inserted parenthetically into the text.
7 Gullans is uncertain that Ayton wrote this poem, and classifies it as 'doubtful' in his edition.
8 H.M. Richmond, *The School of Love: The Evolution of the Stuart Love Lyric* (Princeton: Princeton University Press, 1964), pp. 81–6.

> I doe confess th'art smooth, and faire,
> & I might ha' gone neer to loue thee
> . . . .
> but I can let [th]ee now a lone
> as worthy to be loued by none. (57, ll.1–6)

Consistent with tradition, however, his condemnation of his lady further argues that he is seeking to convince himself far more than his mistress, as her lack of discrimination in bestowing her 'favours' suggests that she is herself not worthy of any herself.

> I doe confess thart sweet, yet finde
> thee such an vnthrift of thy Sweetes,
> thy favors are but like the winde
> w[hich] kisseth eurythinge it meetes,
> and since thou canst w[ith] more then one
> th'arty worthy to be kist by none. (ll.7–12)

It is the third stanza of the poem that transforms it from just being ordinary, as it stands apart as a meditation on the rigours of mutability, and captures, not only the inevitability of change, but also the pathos of lost youth and beauty. Beauty's decay is evoked with the detail that produces both immediacy and regret:

> The morninge rose [that] vntoucht standes,
> Armd w[ith] her briers how sweet she smels,
> but pluckd, & straind through ruder Hands,
> her sweets noe longer w[ith] her dwels,
> but sent and beautye soone are gone
> And leaues fall from her one, by one. (ll. 13–18)

This stanza, in turn, heightens the effect of the opening line of the last stanza, 'Such fate ere longe will thee betide' (1.19), and reinforces the rather frank line, 'when thou hast handled bin a whyle' (1.20), now directed towards the lady, as it is she who becomes the 'morning rose.' Thus roles are reversed, as, her beauty gone, like leaves that are cast aside, the lady

> . . . shall syghe, when som will smile,
> to see thy loue to evry one.
> hath brought thee to be loude by none (57, ll.22–4)

A poem expressing similar sentiments is Ayton's sonnet based on Guarini's *Il Pastor Fido*.[9] An attack on the folly and fickleness of women, the poem's intent is obvious in its opening invocation to 'Faire cruell Silvia' (20, 1.1), who 'scornes

---

9 R. D. S. Jack, *The Italian Influence on Scottish Literature* (Edinburgh: University Press, 1972), pp. 98–100.

my teares/And over lookes my cares with careless Eye' (1.2). More than this, the poem is an expression of self-pity, as the poet indignantly complains, 'Since my request in love offends thy eares,/Hence forth I vow to hold my peace and dye' (1.4). Silence becomes an expression of contempt, a *quid pro quo* to her disdain. Finally, the poem is an exercise in 'one upmanship,' as nature first takes up his lament, thus confirming the lasting and deep-seated nature of his love, and then, too, elects to fall into silence:

> The brookes shall murmur and the winds complaine,
>   The hills, the Dales, the Deserts where I lye
> With Echhoes of my sighes shall preach my paine.
> . . . .
>   Imagine Brookes and windes should hold ther peace,
>   Say that hills, vailes and deserts would disdaine
>   T'acquaint thy deafe disdaines with my disgrace . . . (ll.6–12)

Should nature refuse to speak for him, so that 'thou deafe to me shall prove' (1.13), then only death will know and be able to tell of his suffering. Without being obtrusive, the *carpe diem* theme is nonetheless omnipresent, the message being that the lady's scorn results in nothing but lost opportunity.

Also deserving mention is another of Ayton's sonnets, this time modelled on a French original,[10] which, despite its fairly conventional topic, is also more distinctly metaphysical than any other of his poems. Its highly controlled syntax provides a sharpness and focus consistent with the general sense of light and sight that also characterise the poem. Ayton's use of astronomical imagery enhances in a strikingly effective way his appreciation of the lady's beauty. His initial question, 'Were those thine Eyes or Lightings from above/Whose glorious glimpses dazled soe my sight? (21, ll.1–2), and the subsequent response, 'I tooke them to be lightnings sent from love' (1.3), establish the context for the extended metaphor developed in the remainder of the poem:

>   Yet Lightnings could not be soe long, soe bright,
>   They rather seem'd to be some sunns, whose rayes,
>   Promoved to the Meridian of there hight,
>   Did change my noisome nights in Ioyfull dayes.
>   Yet even in that there Number them betrayes,
>   Sunns were they not, the world indures but one,
>   There force, their figure, and their Coulor sayes
> That they were heavens, yet heavens on Earth are none . . . (ll.5–12)

Noteworthy is how Ayton first affirms the metaphor, and then negates it, the implication being that there is no earthly thing that matches his mistress' beauty. The final couplet, in drawing together the macrocosm of the universe

---

10 See Gullans' commentary, p. 282.

and the microcosm of his lady, suggests that her eyes transcend description yet possess all the glories the universe can display: 'What ere they were, my sight noe odds espyes/Twix't heavens, Twix't sunns, twixt lightnings and thine eyes' (1.14).

Another poem effective in dealing with the commonplace is Ayton's sonnet on the purported death of his mistress, which dwells on the connection of love and death often repeated in seventeenth-century poetry. The poem begins with no indication of this intention:

> Loe how the Sailer in a stormy night
> Wailes and complaines, till he the starrs perceive
> Whose situation and assured hight
> Should guide him through the strong and watrie wave. (23, ll.1–4)

The stars provide the sailor with a fixed point in an environment over which he has little control, and constitute a point around which all else revolves and which gives direction to everything else. In the second quatrain, however, Ayton personalises the metaphor, as he craves sight of his mistress, the 'Loadstare' (1.8) of his life. The pathos and sense of loss in the poem are especially intense because, while the clouds will eventually clear for the sailor, the clouds, for the poet, are permanently in place. The pain of loss becomes yet more unbearable because hope itself is lost:

> Amidds my paines which passes all compare,
> No helpe, noe hope, noe comfort, noe repose,
> Noe sunn appeares to cleare those clouds of care. (ll.10–12)

The only remaining consolation is that nothing could further increase his sufferings; as he says, no sun appears 'Save this, that fortune neither may nor dare / Make my misshapes more hapless then they are' (ll.13–14).

Such poems, effective though they are, nonetheless express an attitude towards love and loss that is unexceptional, and that is typical of a large number of his poems. A second group of poems, however, possess an additional stylistic distinctiveness that reflects a subtle shift in Ayton's attitude. For example, in a 'valediction' on the departure of his mistress, there is a conviction and a level of expression absent in other of Ayton's more conventional poems. The poem begins with the question, 'Then wilt thou goe and leave me here?' (37, 1.1), which is answered predictably enough by the poet, 'Ah doe not soe my dearest deare' (1.2). From this point, however, the poem moves in unexpected directions. In the second stanza, for example, Ayton observes, 'Thou canst not goe but with my heart, / Even that which is my cheifest part' (ll.5–6), and then exaggerates the loss with 'Then with two hearts thou shall be gone / And I shall rest behinde with none' (ll. 7–8). Along similar lines, the 'heart' metaphor, initially used to convince the lady not to leave, is carried forward to the fourth stanza, changing the focus to one of fatalistic acceptance that his mistress is indeed leaving. He asks that she not take both hearts with her, and then, in a surprising redirection of what was said in stanza one, that she

> . . . leave one heart with mee to stay,
> Take myne, Let thine in pawne remaine,
> That thou will quickly come againe. (ll. 14–16)

Ayton's 'valediction' suggests that he is capable of a wide, if a still reasonably predictable, range of emotion and sentiment. This is similarly confirmed in Ayton's lengthy poetic protestation concerning the cruelties of love. There is no questioning how the poet feels at the beginning of this poem, as Ayton dwells on the Petrarchan commonplace that to live without love is not to live, yet to 'foster love' is itself to die:

> My heart Exhale they greife
> With an Eternall grone
> And never sease to sigh and mourne
> Till life or love begone.
>
> Thy life is crost with love,
> Thy love is loathed breath,
> Thou heats thyselfe to live such lyffe,
> A life even such is death. (11, ll. 1–8)

The poem builds on this initial stanza as the poet struggles with the irresolvable paradox,

> Soe thou must live and love,
> Live wretched, love disgrac'd,
> Disgrac'd by her in whome thy life,
> In whome thy love was plac'd . . . (ll.17–20)

As he discovers no resolution, he can only presume that he is the victim of an unkind destiny: 'In what strange postures was the starrs/The houre that thou was borne' (ll. 23–4). Whatever one might say about the fates, however, the poet accepts that, without love, he is without worth: 'Thy love bringes life to mee,/ And I esteeme him as starke dead/That lives vnloving thee' (ll.54–6). But such acceptance does not mean he completely forgives her, even while he recognises and more or less accepts her contempt: 'Thou takes as greate delight/To murder with dissdaine' (ll. 73–74). In an interesting reversal of how physical beauty expresses spiritual beauty, Ayton refers to his 'saint,' and to how her 'shaddow . . . infect[s]/A world of hearts with love' (ll. 31–2).

Nothing in the poem is thus far unusual. It is, however, put into an interesting context when Ayton purposefully indicates delight in his own suffering, and allows that, despite his lady's disdain, 'My soule shall still abide / Content to saile the seas of love/Against both winde and tyde' (ll.78–80). While one might take what Ayton says at face value, one might also view these rather 'tired' lines as an ironic commentary on what he feels about the supposed excesses of love. Nothing in these lines engages the reader, leaving the impression that the poet himself is not committed to what he writes.

This possibility is confirmed by the internal conflict of the forelorn lover, who ought to know better than to give away his heart, but who is incapable of helping himself.

> O that thou hadest not beene
> But either had bin voyde of sense
> Or else depriv'd of eene.
> And yet I would not soe,
> Noe, noe, I wish that thou
> Had lov'd her many yeares agoe
> And seene her long ere now. (ll. 34–40)

The internal dialogue exhibited here, with its truncated style and conflated syntax, not only conveys the speaker's distraction, but also suggests how the ways of love are often needlessly complex. The initial response is to flee love; the poet neither wishes to be a martyr to love, nor to be 'Canoniz'd/In Kallendars of love' (ll. 127–8), although the early association of 'infection' with love in the poem might be interpreted as a telling signal of the poet's real attitude. Despite what common sense might dictate, however, he holds on to the fading hope that there is some mercy remaining in his mistress' breast, that 'in thyne Eyes/There shynd some beames of grace' (ll. 157–8), which allows him to conclude:

> I will believe the best
> And thinke that thou art myne,
> As well as thou may safely say
> That I am only thyne. (ll. 161–4)

One might object to this ending on the grounds that it runs counter to what one expects: that out of all this misery should come a happy ending. Such wishful thinking may seem gratuitous after what has come before in the poem. A more intriguing interpretation is that Ayton provides an additional context for the poem, suggesting that no matter how much one debates the subtle metaphysics of love, the issues are really very simple. Moreover, one might go a step further, and suggest that there is a definite scepticism about love encoded in Ayton's rather 'too pat' ending.

This scepticism is expressed in a much stronger voice in some of Ayton's other poems. In a lengthy poem addressing love's neglect, he recognises the futility of unrequited love, and clearly says so:

> I lov'd thee once, I'le love noe more,
> Thyne be the griefe, as is the blame
> Thou art not what thou was before
> What reason I should be the same? (50, ll.1–4)

There is a refreshing awareness of the frailty of love, as self-serving lament is replaced by a mocking frankness and lucidity that reduces love to simple mindedness: 'Hee that can love vnlov'd againe / Hath better store of love then braine' (ll. 5–6). The expected response to unrequited love would be either to look for revenge, or to continue to love, albeit futilely, from a distance; here, however, there is an almost casual recognition of the silliness of not accepting the inevitable: 'It had been Lethargie in mee, / Noe constancy to love the still' (ll. 19–20).

But Ayton is not without ambiguity, as it becomes obvious towards the end of the poem that it is as much an attempt to rationalise and to justify human feelings as it is to offer practical insight into them. Towards the one who has replaced him in the affections of his now former lady, he expresses complete indifference; he writes, 'I'le neither greive nor yet rejoice / To see him gaine what I have lost' (ll.27–8). But it is obvious that he is saying one thing while meaning another, and that while his brain tells him the common sense thing to do, his heart is a long way from being healed:

> The hight of my disdaine shall bee
> To laugh at him, to blush for thee,
> To love the still, but goe noe more
> A begging at a beggers dore. (ll.29–33)

One finds much the same sort of conflicting message in two short poems, critical of the lady's scorn and carelessness. In the first of these, Ayton accuses his lady of being a sham, although he remains puzzled why such cruelty lies in her heart:

> Lovely eyes and Loveless heart,
> Why doe you soe disagree?
> How can sweetness cause such smart
> Or smarting soe delightful be? (36, ll.13–14)

The contraries of his lady are revealed in the juxtaposition of her 'lovely eyes' and 'loveless' heart, while the paradoxes of love are syntactically conflated when Ayton turns 'How can sweetness cause such smart' back onto itself with the phrase, 'And smarting soe delightful be' (ll. 15–16). Despite the metaphysics of the heart, however, the poet recognises and accepts her irresistibility, 'Hee whose heart is not your prey/Must either be a foole or blinde' (ll. 23–4). While his only hope is to throw himself on the mercy of his mistress – 'I cannot chuse but dye, / Or els begg Physick from my foe' (ll.3–4) – he already knows, 'You are only sweete in show' (l.19). Absent in the poem, however, is the accusatory attitude one might expect from a poem addressed to a 'scornful' mistress. A distinctive feature of the poem is that, while the poet might bemoan the loss of his love, the poem itself is decidedly understated, and suggests a guarded awareness about love.

This distancing from both Petrarchan effusiveness and metaphysical wit is exhibited, as well, in a second poem, in this case distinctive for its quiet conversational style. The simple introduction, 'Deare, why doe you say you love' (45,1.1), generates the intimacy of an overheard conversation. The poem is never more than gently critical, as Ayton chides his lady for telling 'sweete lyes' (1. 6), and for her changeability: 'be not deceiv'd, my faire,/Love will not be fedd on Ayre' (ll. 11–12). And for the twentieth-century reader, perhaps even more than the reader of the seventeenth century, there is a humorous resonance when the lady is told, 'Leave to Statesman tricks of State, / Love doth Politicians heate' (ll.7–8). The poem's intent is one of convincing his mistress not to deceive herself, and thereby not to deceive others; his only instruction therefore is not to be careless, or as he says in the poem itself, 'Prove true, say you cannot love' (1.20). His exhortation to his lady is one we often hear: honesty is the best policy.

Understatement is also a critical feature of Ayton's 'Song' on love and grief, suggesting that, whereas glory comes from wearing one's heart on one's sleeve, it is also the cause of further grief:

> I rather chuse to want releife
> Than venter the revealing;
> Where glory recommends the greefe,
> Dispayre distrusts the healing. (56, ll.13–16)

Our 'desires,' what we want from love, are, quite simply, 'too high' (1.17), and thus Ayton insists that, 'When reason cannot make them dye, / Discretion doth them cover' (ll.19–20). Ayton's scepticism is indicated when he again draws on the Renaissance love poetry commonplace of the lover being reduced in his anguish to silence, which, with his juxtaposition of the lover and the beggar, adds an element of trivialising humour to his supposed expression of grief:

> Silence in love bewrayes more woe,
> Then words though never soe witty,
> A beggar that is dumbe, you knowe,
> May challenge double pitty. (ll.25–8)

This ambiguous attitude towards love is especially noticeable in a long meditation on love that might be simply called 'On Love.' The poem begins innocently enough, expressing the commonplace that love, while the greatest form of folly, is nonetheless the 'sweetest folly' (43,1.4). But Ayton abruptly changes direction in the second stanza, insisting that the love of which he speaks is not amorous passion, which only 'with fooles consent' (1.5) holds sway over reason. Such passion, which ought to engender joy, becomes a thing of 'perpetuall Lent,/As if a man were borne to fast and pray' (ll.7–8). It is never satisfied, and it therefore becomes a source of frustration and anxiety. Decidedly careful, Ayton looks for 'a milde and Lukewarm zeale in love' (1.11), and draws on the double meaning of 'die' so popular among seventeenth-century poets to mock gently those who invoke the extravagances of Petrarchan love making:

> To thinke that Lovers dye as they pretend,
> If all that say they dye, had dyed indeed,
> Sure long ere now the world had had an end. (ll.14–16)

In direct opposition to the accepted convention that the lover, paradoxically, enjoys, and indeed invokes, the torments of love, Ayton condemns both too little love and too much as 'Extreames, and all Extreames are vice' (1.32). His scepticism is most pronounced, however, when he purposefully deflates the self importance of the Petrarchan lover. While he admits that, although he has 'dyed for love as others doe' (1.34), it is a death from which he revives 'within an houre or two' (1.36). Rather than being slandered by the 'true apostates' of love, or becoming a false martyr to love, Ayton matter-of-factly asserts that he is neither Iphis nor Leander, and that under no circumstances would he 'drown' or 'hang' himself for love, two of the more popular alternatives contemplated but rarely pursued by the abandoned lover.

Such poems provide an interesting context by which to evaluate Ayton's Petrarchanism; if nothing else, they suggest that Ayton assumes a poetic voice which contemporary tastes expected but with which he had little sympathy, and which leaves us conjecturing whether such exaggeration is cultivated with a definite ironic intention in mind. This possibility is especially interesting to consider in light of a poem which is clearly among Ayton's best. In this 'declaration' on the nature of love, Ayton observes how his muse greets the prospect of writing such a poem with 'Comick grones' (10,1.2). There is a humorous edge to the poem when he describes how

> Now tragick trumpetts blowes,
> And sorrowing sounds out sought
> Vnto my Muses mourning mouth
> A wailing vayne hath wrought. (ll.5–8)

The repeating alliteration ('tragick triumpetts,' 'sorrowing sounds out sought,' 'Muses mourning mouth') of the first stanza, not only trivialises what is being said, and is incongruent with the pretences that follow, but confirms that the initial response of 'comic groans' was the correct one. So, even though the stanzas that follow are 'poetically' more satisfying, they may well be seen as stylised exaggeration designed more to generate smiles than tears.

One might legitimately take the poem as a sincere statement concerning the pain of separation, all the while realising that Ayton is himself writing within a stylised tradition that does not presume that the poet's voice is necessarily that of the poet. Most certainly, this long poem of nineteen eight-line stanzas is in its own a way a 'tour de force' as an analysis of love. Its sometimes terse and colloquial speech, along with its dramatic realism, and carefully orchestrated disjointedness, effectively captures the surface complexities of the lover, which belie the more fundamental recognition that love is not something about which we need to talk at length.

> Before alternant Ioyes
> Did promise some releife,
> Now care and love conspired in one
> Have sworne my Endless greife,
> Soe that I see noe soule
> Companion of my paines,
> Vnless it be those wretched ones
> Which Plutos raing retaynes. (10, ll.9–16)

Although the poem begins predictably enough, as the poet bemoans how the 'care and love' (l.11) he has extended to his lady mitigate the possibility even of 'alternate Ioyes,' this is not a poem directed to a cruel mistress, even if, at one point, he does talk of 'faire cruele she/Whose lookes set mee on fyre' (ll.125–6); rather, it is a poem about the death or failure of love, or, perhaps, the impossibility of love, and it is unclear whether the motivating circumstances of the poem are love that has gone wrong, or unrequited love, or even love that is one sided and perhaps completely unknown to the lady. All one knows is Ayton's admission:

> ... I since first I did
> This luckless love imbrace,
> I never felt, no, not by dreame,
> The smallest glance of grace (ll. 29–32)

It is true that Ayton exhibits all the characteristics of the suffering lover, trapped as he is in the "no win" situation of one who loves but is not loved, and there is an effective plaintiveness when he admits:

> I dyed and liv'd againe,
> I lived againe to dye,
> I dyed I knew not what a death,
> A life it could not be. (ll. 37–40)

The poet's dilemma, it seems, is a desire to share his grief with others, but with the understanding that to do so will only worsen an already impossible situation. Admitting, then, that he is better to say nothing, or, as he says, to 'to disclose my greefe / Vnto my fatall foe' would be 'the ready way / For to aggredge my woe' (ll. 73–76), his 'wonted Secretaryes' (l.139) remain

> The high and stately trees
> The valleyes low, and Mountains high,
> Whose topps escapes our eyes. (ll. 142–4)

The element of the pastoral is obvious, the impression being that only nature can listen to and appreciate his sorrow, and then offer solace; to speak of one's love in the exaggerated manner of the Petrarchans is to somehow cheapen its significance. In this poem, there is again an element of understatedness; there is no attempt to be needlessly clever. Interesting about the poem is that the poet's comments are directed, not so much towards his mistress as at love itself, and the impossible situation in which it leaves him. On the one hand, he feels he is not alive 'Since that I had noe heart' (l.42), yet, on the other, he knows he is not dead because he still suffers; indeed, love is cruel because it incorporates the pain of both life and death, and is worse than both:

> It was then such a mids
> As takes part of the two,
> Or rather such, as both Extreames
> Do vtterly missknowe. (ll. 45–8)

Thus love is at best an enigma, for which there is no adequate explanation; of his own experience with love, he can only conclude:

> Noe neither this nor that,
> For anything that I can see,
> It was I knowe not what. (ll. 50–2)

With the impossibility of there ever being an adequate explanation of love, the best he knows is how he feels; with decided understatement, therefore, he says, 'I was the vnhappyest hee, / That ever lov'd or liv'd' (ll. 55–6).

Paul Siegel has drawn a distinction between Petrarchan love, which was exaggerated and decidedly sensual, and 'heroical love,' which was marked by gentility and was intended as courtly compliment. As such, it was, he says, 'bound up with the entire aristocratic fashion of melancholy,'[11] which was rooted as much in the recognition of human mutability, of which the desolation of lost love was a poignant reminder. Or, as A.J. Smith remarks, 'the lover's intuition of time's wastes puts in question a love and beauty which may be just the functions of a process that "feeds on the rareties of nature's truth."' [12] It is clear that Ayton works within the same tradition. The final stanza is really about his poem and its ultimate significance; following on from his invocation to nature, he writes:

---

11 Paul N. Siegel, 'The Petrarchan Sonneteers and Neo-Platonic Love,' *Studies in Philology*, XLII (1945), 168.
12 Smith, pp. 181–2.

> And while I show't to them,
> The nearest Ayre shall hear't,
> The Ayre shall carry't to the fyre,
> The fyre to th'heavens shall bear't.
> The heavens shall lay't abroad
> Before the Gods above,
> And if they will not send releife,
> Farewell both life and love. (ll. 145–52)

Despite Ayton's general reticence in revealing his heart, and despite the possibility that the memory of his love relies on the good will of the gods, there is throughout the poem the implied understanding that everything in time passes away, and that nothing earthly possesses lasting significance. In his farewell to 'both life and love,' Ayton suggests, not only a repudiation of his mistress, but also of the sentiments of love which, in Louis Martz's words, exist under 'the shadow of time and death.'[13]

While it would be wrong to classify Ayton as a poet of the first rank, or even as a consistently good poet, it is the case that he represents in his poetry a broad range of responses which at once incorporate the commonplaces of Petrarch and the new wit of the seventeenth century. Sometimes Ayton's efforts are strained, and there is no question that his verse is repetitious. But it is also the case that he deserves better than he has received, and that, had he been English rather than Scottish, he might have enjoyed some modest reputation. Ayton in his poetry can be slavishly imitative, but he is also able, with deft irony, to distance himself from the experience of love that he describes to provide a gently critical reflection on how one too often takes far too seriously those matters of the heart that are so much subject to the rigours of time and mutability.

---

13 Louis L. Martz, *The Wit of Love* (Notre Dame: University of Notre Dame Press, 1969), p. 54.

DAVID REID

45. *What William Lithgow was Doing Abroad: The Rare Adventures and Painfull Peregrinations*

In 1609 William Lithgow set out on foot on the first of his peregrinations. This took him through France to Italy, and from there to the Turkish Empire, Greece, Constantinople, Cyprus, the Holy Land, Egypt, and so back to Britain, where he presented King James, Queen Anne and Prince Charles with curios from his travels. His account of this journey came out in 1614, *A Discourse of a Peregrination in Europe, Asia and Afrike*. Within a year of his return, he left court and was off again through Italy, this time to Malta, Tunis, Algiers and Fez, where with a Frenchman he was tempted to walk to Ethiopia through the Sahara. The Frenchman fell ill and had to turn back, the guide deserted, and after wandering through sands full of serpents and 'interlarded with Rockey-heights, faced with Caues and Dens, the verie habitacle of Wilde beasts . . . especiallie Iackals, Beares and Boares and sometimes Cymbers, Tygers and Leopards,' he and his dragoman ran out of food and water and were 'forced to relye vpon Tobacco, and to drinke our own wayning piss' for seven days (p.375).[1] Finally his dragoman had enough and forced Lithgow to retire in a northeasterly direction, steering by his compass, to Tunis. From there, Lithgow set out through Sicily and Italy on a tour of Eastern Europe, returning again from this excursion to King James with gifts and tales. After that he set out again for Ethiopia, this time taking in Ireland and Spain first. In Malaga, however, he was arrested as a spy. The governor feared that the English fleet intended to sack the town (not surprisingly in view of Spanish experience of English fleets) and had Lithgow tortured in secret by water, the rack and vermin. Lithgow did not confess to any designs and the danger from the fleet was discovered to be imaginary, but he was handed over to the Inquisition anyway as a heretic, from whose attentions he was delivered by chance. This time Lithgow returned to King James on a litter. For six years he tried to obtain redress from the Spaniards, was promised much, but obtained nothing, except imprisonment in the Marshalsea for getting into a fight with the Spanish Ambassador, Gondomar. James 'of matchlesse memory; who sometimes (besides my soueregin), in some respect, . . . was a father to me' (p. 489), died in 1625. Charles's Parliament of 1626 broke up without a hearing of his suit. And Lithgow returned to Scotland, where he continued his travels. He wrote, but never published, *Lithgow's Survey of Scotland*. Of his Scottish travels we have only the short, but eulogistic, sketch added to the much expanded 1632 edition of his book,

---

1 All citations to the *Peregrinations* are to William Lithgow *The Totall Discourse of the Rare Adventures and Painefull Peregrinations of Long Nineteene Yeares Travayles from Scotland to the Most Famous Kingdomes in Europe, Asia and Africa* (London, 1632).

now entitled *The Totall Discourse of the Rare Adventures and Painefull Peregrinations of Long Nineteene Yeares Travayles from Scotland to the Most famous Kingdomes in Europe, Asia and Africa.*

The Peregrinations went through perhaps as many as ten editions in the seventeenth century (at least the 1692 edition claims to be the tenth) and was translated into Dutch. Further editions came out in the eighteenth and nineteenth centuries. In the twentieth, there have been two editions, and a volume of the Travellers' Library is made up of selections.

Apart from the projected but aborted trip to Ethiopia, Lithgow had not made an extraordinary journey. Readers of Hakluyt will know of many English trips to the Levant. There was an English Ambasador at Constantinople, and wherever he went, there were Venetians and Frenchmen. Englishmen were not infrequent, nor Scotsmen, at least in Italy and Poland. His walks through Crete and Cyprus were sometimes off the beaten track, but in outline the course he took was mostly not at all unknown to Western Europeans. George Sandys took much the same route in the Middle East on his travels that began in 1611. Thomas Coryat, 'the Odcombian Legge-stretcher', had walked to Venice and back in three months by way of self-advertisement.[2] The frequent publication of Lithgow's book shows that it was a success, but novelty can hardly explain that.

Neither can informativeness. Anyone who wanted a guidebook to prices, customs to be observed, how to manage the Inquisition in Italy or Janizaries under the Turk would go to Fynes Moryson. Anyone who wanted to find out about the antiquities or history of the lands Lithgow visited would go to Sandys. Lithgow reads Latin but he is no scholar and his accounts of classical sites are mere compilations of what those with an average classical education knew or could make good from easily available dictionaries. His historical accounts of Byzantium are again desultory compilations of facts, from which his mind picks out curious coincidences such as that Constantinople was 'built by a *Constantine*, the Sonne of *Helena*, a *Gregory* being Patriarch; and was lost by a *Constantine*, the Sonne of *Helena*, a *Gregory* being also Patriarch' (p. 135). Sandys is incomparably more exact and inquiring, and anyone who wanted to understand the political organisation of the Turkish Empire would at least get from him a thorough and consequential survey. Again, as far as the civilisation of the Renaissance in Italy is concerned, Lithgow was simply too uncultivated to notice: by contrast, Moryson at least took in the Titians in St Mark's and Coryat was a remarkable observer of architecture.[3]

Sandys, Moryson and Coryat were all English gentlemen. Lithgow claimed a connection with Montrose, but was distinctly a rude Scotchman. It would be nice to show that because he was less polished, he was more receptive to other cultures and other modes of existence.

2 George Sandys, *A Relation of a Iorney Begun An: Dom: 1610*, 6th ed. (London, 1670); Thomas Coryate, 'To the Reader', *Coryats Crudities* (London, 1611; rept. London: Scolar Press, 1978), n.p. Fynes Moryson, *An Itinerary, Containing His Ten Yeeres Travell*, 3 vols. (Glasgow: MacLehouse, 1907), took much the same route as Lithgow in the Levant, including Crete (II, 72–84), though he did not visit Egypt.
3 Moryson, I, 182.

A rough indication of a traveller's receptivity to other cultures might be his reactions to women, assuming with Levi-Strauss that women are a medium of cultural communication.[4] Here is a selection of Lithgow's observations. In Crete 'the women . . . are insatiably inclined to Venery; such is the nature of the soyle and the climate' (p.90). In Chios 'the women are the most beautiful Dames (or rather Angelicall creatures) of all Greekes vpon the face of the earth and greatly given to Venery' (p. 102). In Malta the women 'are much inclined to licentiousnesse; their beauties being borrowed from helpe more than nature' (p. 332). In Fez the women 'are damnable Libidinous, beeing prepared both wayes to satisfie the lust of their Luxurious Villaines' (p. 366). One might be inclined to ask how he knows all this. But of course he doesn't. His views do not tell us about his experience but about the attitudes he brought along with him. Their salacious puritanism shows only that he went through lands of unlikeness with a closed mind. He filled them with attractions he could condemn. In this he confirms British views that Abroad is a wicked place and also seventeenth-century British (and not only seventeenth-century or British) ideas about women. Here Lithgow is full of bitter outbursts. Mycenae and Helen provoke a tirade about whoredom (p. 70). Arabian women who give birth naked in the caves of the desert and within three days of giving birth rejoin their men in brigandage arouse sarcastic reflections on the delicacy of European women (p. 294). On at least two occasions Lithgow owed his life to the kindness of women. At Pikehorno in Crete, a woman warned him that the villagers meant to kill him (p.81). In Malaga 'an Indian Negro woman' at considerable risk brought him food and drink while the Inquisition was starving him (p.477). But these incidents count for little. Lithgow allows the 'Indian Negro woman' a little paradoxical praise (pp. 478–9) but nothing to call into question his Jacobean misogyny. In the same way, he met with kindness and equity from Jews in the Turkish Empire. That does not in the least modify his considered opinion that 'the *Iewes* and the *Iesuites* are brethren in blasphemies; for the *Iewes* are naturally subtill, hatefull, avaritious and aboue all, the greatest calumniators of Christs name; and the ambitious *Iesuites* are flatterers, bloudy-gospellers, treasonable tale tellers, the onely railers vpon the sincere life of good Christians. Wherefore I end with this verdict, the *Iewe* and the *Iesute* is a Pultrone and a Parasite' (p.43). In his world, significant gratitude is all directed to men in power, mead-lords, particularly British ones, above all 'Royal James' (p.380).

It is not only with women that Lithgow faced the foreign with the breastplate of righteousness. He applies a scheme of prejudices with remarkable consistency. He divides the world into Protestant, Catholic, Islamic and savage.

Protestant countries are good. The Netherlands, still at war with Spain when he passed through, are for him the admired land, though he says little about them because they are well known; 'onely this, for policies, industries, strong Townes, and fortifications, it is the mirrour of vertue, and garden of *Mars*; yea, and the light of all *Europe*, that he who hath exactly trade it, may say he hath seene the

---

4 Claude Levi-Strauss, *Elementary Structures of Kinship*, tr. James Harte Bell *et al.* (Boston: Beacon Press, 1969), p. 496.

mappe of the whole Vniuerse' (p.344). Geneva next, though not drawn up in order of war, is still a pattern, 'that *Light shining Syon*' (p.349). Catholic countries are generally bad. France is bad, though he has little to say about it and his disparagement brings in other traditions of anti-French feeling than anti-Catholicism. It is really in Italy that he finds how true what he had always believed about Catholicism is. There he finds a land corrupted by superstition, priestly imposture and unnatural vice.

Throughout his book Lithgow comes forward as the traveller who reports what he sees, not what all have heard, the man for instance who can explode false traditions about the buoyancy of the Dead Sea (p.256) or the flooding of the Nile 'in spight of the lyeing world, and all doting varieties of auncient Relations' (pp.317–18), the bold spirit who risked entering the Grotto di Cane near Naples, which was reputed to kill with poisonous fumes (he was poisoned but not killed) (p.403). This natural desire to show up what others believe takes the form with the miraculous traditions of the Church of coarse but lively ridicule. The chapel of Loretto particularly excites his scorn. After setting down its fabulous history for our derision, he records 'a pretty jest.' He and a Scotsman he has latched onto in Italy,

> going in to see the inravled image [of Mary] with sparrets of iron, and musing on the blacknesse of her face, and the richnesse of her gowne, all set with precious Stones and Diamonds; and because she is sightlesse, four lampes of oyle they keepe always burning before her face, that the people may see her, because she cannot see them. There was, I say, a young lusty woman hard by my elbow, busie at her Beades, who, with the heate of the throng, and for lack of ayre, fell straight in a swound: the women about her gaue a shoute, and cryd that our blessed Lady had appeared to her; whereupon she was carried forth, and layd vpon the steppes that discend from the Chappell to the Churche-floore, fiue hundreth more came to visite her with salutations of Saint, Saint, O euer blessed Saint; Now it was Friday in the forenoone, and the woman hauing trauelled all night, and to saue charges of fish, had eaten a cold bit of her owne meat priuately in the Tauerne, with halfe a *Bukale* of red Wine. The people admiring more the imaginary heauenly trance, than the reliefe of the woman, at last sayd I, brother *Arthur*, I will goe open yonder womans breast; and I did so: and holding vp her head before all the people, there sprung a flood of *vin garbo* down the Alabaster stayres, intermingled with lumpes of ill-chewd flesh: Whereat the people being amazed, from a Saint, swore she was a Diuell: And if my friend and I, had not made hast to carry the sicke woman from the Churche to a Tauerne, doubtlesse, they had stoned her to death; and here was one of their miracles. (p.32)

Another of his favourite themes about Catholic Italy is the unnatural vices of the clergy. On his first landing in Venice he had sprung through the crowd to see a friar burned for getting fifteen noble young nuns pregnant 'and my friend followed me, and came just to the pillar [of St Mark], as the halfe body and right arme fell flatlings in the fire ... I cannot forget, how after all this, we being inhungered, and also overioyed, tumbled in by chance, *Alla capello Ruosso*, the greatest ordinary in all *Venice*, near to which the friar's bones were yet aburning: And calling for a Chamber, we were nobly and richly serued' (pp.37–8). It is only in the morning when the bill comes that the scruffy hikers notice their mistake and 'wish the diuell in the Friars bollocks', 'for we had paid soundly for his lechery' (p.38). This merriment seems not quite sane, but if one recalls how Knox wrote merrily of the assassination of Cardinal Beaton it seems possible that Lithgow's idea of fun was one to which many Protestant bosoms returned an echo.[5]

About Spain he has little to say until his crowning experience of Catholic Europe, his tortures in Malaga, where there was proved upon his body all that the British feared of the arbitrariness, inhuman cruelty and clerical direness of what was still seen as the leading Catholic power. To emphasise the point, the only people who take pity on him are the 'Indian Negro woman' and a Moorish slave, who not only brings him food and drink secretly but sweeps away and burns the lice that his captors are using as a special torment. The implication is that Catholicism has made the Spanish Christian more devilish than the infidel or the savage. Lithgow would not consider that his own horrible pleasure in the execution of lecherous priests had any bearing on the sort of judgements he was making here.

Finally among countries corrupted by Catholicism, he really has something to say about Ireland. The native Irish are savages. They cannot, because they will not, learn the use of harness and so they draw the plough by the horse's tail (p.433). He has seen a woman give suck to the child on her back by throwing a breast over her shoulder (p.433). This was the subject of an engraving in an account in Purchas of the Cape, so if Lithgow was fabricating, or even telling the truth, he was probably saying the Irish are a sort of Hottentot.[6] But in spite of his exceptional natural crassness, Lithgow does feel sorry for the Irish and see that they have been reduced to savagery by bad government. They are rackrented by absentee landlords, overtithed by ignorant and lazy Protestant churchmen and taxed again by a malicious Catholic priesthood, with whom the Protestant clergy live on good terms, partly out of fear.

The gleam of sympathy here for a Catholic people is made possible by political views that are the Renaissance commonplaces of the *Basilikon Doron* and that Kevin Sharpe has recently shown to be operative in the personal rule of Charles I.[7] Civilisation is brought about by good government. A good king will

---

5 *The Works of John Knox* ed. David Laing, 4 vols. (Edinburgh: Calderwood Society, 1846–55), I, 180. Lithgow enjoyed the spectacle of Catholic churchmen being executed for lechery so much that, on his second peregrination, he made a special jaunt from Geneva to Lyons to see an an 'incestuous Buggerono' of a priest hanged (p. 348).
6 Or as Lithgow put it, 'The *Irish* I protest, liue more miserably in their brutish fashion, than the vndaunted or vntamed *Arabian*, the Diuelish-idolatrous *Turcoman*, or the Moone-worshipping *Caramines*' (p. 433).
7 Kevin Sharpe, *The Personal Rule of Charles I* (New Haven: Yale University Press, 1922), pp. 179–208. The sympathy Lithgow shows here would be quite compatible with an Irish policy such as Wentworth pursued in the 1630s, which, in strengthening and improving Protestant rule, oppressed Catholics more firmly than the previous slackness.

govern according to the laws and moderate the unruly members of his kingdom.[8] He will foster general civility and learning by seeing to the good order and true religion of the church of which he is head and an ideal of service to the laws by promoting the dignity of his peers.[9] Bad government, or misrule, means, as in the case of Ireland, reversion to barbarity, or devilish perversion as in the monstrous regiment of the Church in Italy or the tyranny of the Spaniards.

The same scheme that lies behind his condemnation of Catholic countries applies to the Turkish Empire. The Turks are the infidel, the enemies of the true religion. Lithgow's account of Mahomet as an impostor is even coarser than his scoffing at Catholic fraud (pp. 145–9). He sees the Turks always in adversarial terms: 'the appearance of their further increasing, is very euident, except God of his mercy toward vs, preuent their bloodsucking threatnings, with the vengeance of his iust iudgements' (pp. 160–1). All the same he is sure that the Christian powers could topple the Turkish Empire in a year, if they united (p.162), and he remarks that it would be easy to recapture Cyprus from them (pp. 186–7) or to take Algiers from the landward (p.360). Being the enemies of true religion, the Turks are subject to misrule. This comes out in small things: 'The Turkes have no Bels in their Churches, neither the vse of a Clocke, nor numbring of houres; but they haue high round Steeples, for they contrafact and contradict all formes of Christians' (p.141). Nor does he fail to point out that under Islam 'the Women ... pisse standing, and the men ... coure low on their knees, doing the like' (p.308). Misrule equally governs the greater concerns of the Turkish polity. Lithgow was not inquiring enough to find out, like Sandys, the extraordinary achievement of political organisation required to unite the Turkish Empire, and he equally lacked the sceptical intelligence of Sir Henry Blunt who wondered 'whether to an impartiall conceit, the Turkish way appears absolutely barbarous, as we are given to understand, or rather another kind of civility, different from ours, but no less pretending'.[10] He simply knew, as every Christian knew, that the Sultan was a type of arbitrary tyrant, ruling without any hereditary peers through bashaws, whom he created and who depended on his will.[11] Tyranny and false religion extirpate the arts, and learning fled to the west with the fall of Constantinople. Everywhere civilisation is in decay or devastated. The Holy Land, once flowing with milk and honey, is now mostly desert, this to punish the

---

8 *The Basilikon Doron of James VI*, ed. James Craigie, vol. 1 (Edinburgh: Scottish Text Society, 1944), pp. 55–65, 69, 71ff.
9 *Basilikon Doron*, p. 73f.
10 Sir Henry Blount, *A Voyage to the Levant*, 4th ed. (London, 1650), p. 5. Acording to C.E. Bosworth, 'William Lithgow's Travels in Greece and Turkey, 1609–11', *Bulletin of the John Rylands Library of the University of Manchester*, 65 (1983), 16, Lithgow probably drew largely on Richard Knolles, *The Generall Historie of the Turkes* (London, 1603).
11 See, for instance, Knolles, *A Briefe Discourse of the Greatness of the Turkish Empire*, appended to his *Generall Historie*, for an account of the master-slave relation of the Sultan to his subjects (pp. 2–3 of the unpaginated text; cited Bosworth, p. 33); for other less instructed references to the despotism of the Turk, see *Basilikon Doron*, p. 119, where James advises his son to treat his courtiers as the Turk his Jannisaries; Robert Baillie, 'Letter to William Spang, Sept. 28, 1639', *Letters and Journals*, (Edinburgh: Bannatyne Club, 1841–2), vol. 1, p. 184; Milton, *Paradise Lost*, II, 347, calls Satan the 'great Sultan' of the fallen angels, to suggest their subjection and his arbitrary power over them.

sins of the Jews (p.214). Lithgow does not say what the sins of the Greeks were, but they have been devastated too. Learning has vanished, even the monuments of antiquity – this from a man who was feasted for four days within sight of the Acropolis of Athens(p.72).[12]

Tyranny means government by arbitrary will rather than reason.[13] Appetite rules. Lithgow actually invokes this platonic scheme to explain barbarous treatment from a Moorish prince, whose people had barely been touched by Islam (p. 373). Islam, however false, instils some rudimentary civility in its believers; at least that is what Lithgow thinks when he is confronted by savage Moors. But on the whole his picture of Islam itself is pretty unmodulated: it is misrule and with it go voluptuousness and depravity. I've already mentioned the libidinous women of Fez; there are also twelve thousand brothels and in summer 'three thousand common stews of sodomitical boys' there (p. 367).[14] Christians under Turkish misrule are themselves corrupted. The Emir of Nazareth sends a party of six women slaves with his compliments to entertain an Armenian prince in the caravan in which Lithgow is travelling to Jerusalem. Lithgow is invited but refuses to join the fun, 'little regarding such a friuolous commodity' (p.219). He leaves the Armenians to commit 'with these Infidelish harlots a twofold kind of voluptuous abhomination, which my conscience commands me to conceale, least I frequent this Northern world, with that which their nature neuer knew, nor their knowledge haue heard, hearing of the like' (pp. 219–20). He is led to reflect on how slavery to the slaves of passion reduces men to a condition worse than that of brutes.

Beyond the Turkish empire of misrule are the true savages, represented for Lithgow by a naked tribe of nine hundred Sabunks, who rescued him in the Sahara. Their prince talked to him for an hour, giving him his bow which Lithgow in turn gave to Prince Charles (pp. 373–80). If Lithgow's story is even a little bit true, it must have been an extraordinary experience. But judgement comes easily to him: the prince's 'religion is damnable, so is his life, for he and all the foure tribes of Lybia worship onely garlic for their God' (p. 377). Outside the rule of true religion or even Islam, the Sabunks represent the depraved natural state of humanity.[15]

---

12 Samuel C. Chew, *The Crescent and the Rose: Islam and England during the Renaissance* (New York: Oxford University Press, 1937), p. 245, suspects that Lithgow has plagiarised from Sir Anthony Sherley, *Sir Anthony Sherly His Relation of His Travels into Persia* (London, 1636), p. 6, on the defacing of all ancient monuments in Greece, but notes (p. 64) that Lithgow is the only traveller of the time to mention the 'Castle [in Athens] which formerly was the Temple of Minerva'.
13 A point insisted on even by so strong a contender for royal prerogative as James in *Basilikon Doron*, pp. 55–9.
14 C. E. Bosworth, 'Wiliam Lithgow of Lanark's Travels in North Africa, 1615–16', *Journal of Semitic Studies*, 23 (1978), thinks the account of Moorish libidinousness unlikely of so austere a city as Fez (p. 210), considers this and other tales of Islamic voluptuousness instances of a tradition of Christian slander (p. 211) and thinks indeed the whole account of the Fez mostly a concoction out of Leo Africanus (p. 213).
15 Although Bosworth (p. 211) notes that there was trade between Fez and Abyssinia, he is sceptical about Lithgow's expedition. It is indeed most unlikely that anyone would set out on foot through the Sahara with only a mule to carry baggage, and impossible that he should encounter tigers,

In a few places, however, Lithgow does go beyond confirming by experience the limited and limiting scheme of ideas he set out with. He gives, for instance, a fair amount of curious information, which sticks in his mind without adding up to a significant idea about the places he visits. He describes coffee drinking (p.136)[16] and the pigeon post between Aleppo and Babylon (p.203). He describes a Turkish pipe in detail (p.205), the irrigation of the Nile (pp. 316–17), hatching chickens in ovens in Tunis (p.380) and Moorish wedding customs (pp. 362–3).[17] It is a pity there is not more of this observation: Lithgow's eyes are sharper than his understanding, and the detail suggests fragmentarily alien textures of life.

These details are not personal impressions, the sort of thing we might find in modern travel books, but just odd, hard facts. In this, Lithgow is representative of seventeenth-century travelers. What is missing is the sort of subjective writing that one can find everywhere in English since at least Gray's letters. As an illustration, take this small but typical detail from Robert Byron's *The Road to Oxiana*: 'The beach was crowded with people; a blazing heat rose from the shimmering sand; and against the lucid pink-blue sky, a line of camels and a line of willows disarranged each other's silhouettes'.[18] That is not the sort of impression Lithgow would form. He has in any case very little feeling for landscape and for the landforms that make up the surface of the earth. Although he dismisses three claims for the location of Paradise as superstition, he still tends to celebrate places he specially enjoyed, Mount Lebanon and Damascus (two of the supposed situations of Paradise), the Vale of Suda and, as we have noted, Holland as paradisal microcosms. In between such happy epitomes of creation, he notices where good wines and fruits grow and where strong fortresses stand. And he also takes in the Dead Sea and Sodom, which in his account become a type of purgatory and, by a weird conceit, of Rome (p.257). His world is a world

---

boars and bears there or survive for seven days on urine and tobacco. Lithgow's collecting certificates from Ward the pirate in Tunis testifying to his expedition suggests a guilty mind (p. 380). He may nevertheless have made some expedition into the Sahara and encountered a savage tribe. His account, however, is too bare to support the sort of analysis of an encounter between European and savage (as other) to be found in Mary B. Campbell, *The Witness and the Other World: Exotic European Travel Writing, 400–1600* (Ithaca: Cornell University Press, 1988), esp. ' "The End of the East", Columbus Discovers Paradise', pp. 165–209, and Stephen Greenblatt, *Marvellous Possessions: The Wonder of the New World* (Oxford: Clarendon, 1991), esp. the chapters 'Marvellous Possessions,' pp. 52–85, and 'Kidnapping Language,' pp. 86–118.

16 Chew, p. 183, notes that contrary to *DNB*, Lithgow was not the first European to describe coffee-drinking, nor even the first writer in English, citing, for example, *A New and Large Discourse of the Travels of Sir Anthony Sherley* (London, 1601), p. 10.
17 Bosworth (1978), p. 214, thinks the account of Moorish marriage customs is drawn mainly from Leo Africanus.
18 Robert Byron, *The Road to Oxiana* (London: Pan, 1981), p. 256. What Jonathan Haynes, *The Humanist as Traveller: George Sandys' 'Relation of a Journey Begun'*, (Rutherford, N.J.: Fairleigh Dickinson University Press), remarks about the attenuation of personal narrative and of the recording of personal impressions applies in an obvious but not really exceptional way to Lithgow: 'There is a level of generalization hovering above descriptive passages, or an ulterior descriptive intention running through them, pulling them away from involvement. These ulterior motives are exactly what the literature of educated travellers sought to inculcate. The modern reader may have the depressing feeling that this means that Renaissance travellers will always be bound to the stereotypes they brought with them' (p. 55).

of types and figures rather than of exactly observed particularities, or at least there are strong traces of such a world-view. Moreover his inner life, such as it is, seems to have a way of detaching him from the world he travels through. I should not wish to exaggerate the personal mark on him of what was after all a highly conventional form of spirituality. Still one feels his experience of faith when he was tortured by the Inquisition brings to a head a sort of religious feeling that turned inwards away from the world around him to God, who is always the same everywhere, annihilating the accidents of geography that travel is concerned with. Equally his occasional stoical meditations draw him away from taking in the circumstantiality of the world. The mind is its own place.[19] This cast of thought made him tough and resolute but also impercipient.

In any case, Lithgow is not the sort of person who knows how to talk about his personal impressions, or indeed about his own experiences except in stereotyped form. Two cases bear this out in a striking way. In each he seems to have been moved out of his ordinary ways of feeling by what he went through. The first case is the meeting with the Sabunk chief, which I have already brought up to show how limited Lithgow's ideas are. Yet, if we are to believe him, Lithgow has been delivered from a seven days diet of smoke and urine in the Sahara by this tribe. The experience would have raised the dourest spirit. What tells us perhaps that it did so is the royal seal on the experience. Lithgow spoke with the prince for an hour and passed on his gifts to another prince. He also learned 'a merry secret' about the women, which he passed on to James, but does not pass on to us. He puts a similar royal seal on his experience of the cedars of Lebanon. These he goes out of his way to see and expresses his delight in a royal conceit.

> When we arrived to the place where the Cedars grew, we saw but twenty foure of all, growing after the manner of Oake trees, but a great deal taler, straighter, and greater, and the braunches grow so straight and interlocking, as though they were kept by Arte. And yet from the Roote to the toppe they bear no boughes, but grow straight vpward, like to a Palme-tree; who, as may-poles invelope the ayre, so their circle spred toppes, do kisse or enhance the lower clouds; making their grandure ouerlooke the bodies of all other aspiring trees; and, like Monarchick Lyons to wild beasts, they become the chiefe Champions of Forests and Woods. (pp. 190–1)

The description starts circumstantially enough but quickly is transported into hyperbolical fancies, in particular the comparison to the royal lion. Royalty is one of the chief figures by which Lithgow's undeveloped sensibility could express a sense of specialness. Generally, by the way, he is open in biblical countries to impressions of place as he is nowhere else. The bible had seized on his imagination as the classics had not and he went about eager to confirm or revise the pictures of his mind, or at least to place himself where he believed miraculous events had

---

19 For example pp. 48, 60–1 on the resolved mind; p. 187 on God's stability as against the accidents of fortune; pp. 229, 423 for quotations from Seneca's *De re fortunae*.

occurred. A sign of his unusual state of mind is that he weeps at the sight of Jerusalem as he sings the hundred and third psalm (p. 234).[20]

Still such signs of receptiveness do not amount over a course of five hundred pages to much in the way of openness to the foreign, and that can never have counted as one of the charms of the book. On the contrary, at least one thing that would have recommended it to the British Protestant reader would have been its impossibly morose unreceptivity to the foreign: it would have told him that his prejudices about Abroad were justified, that, as Mr Podsnap held, 'other countries were a mistake'.

But there is another reason for the success of Lithgow's book. Appalling person as he is, he is rather a card. Like other seventeenth-century travel books, Lithgow's *Peregrinations* is not a journal. It is a purported eye-witness account of places he passed through, with occasional excursions into his adventures and experiences. It is the personal element, however, that makes his book. This personal element is partly a matter of the adventures he tumbles into, such as shipwreck, falling among thieves and above all his sufferings at the hands of the Inquisition; it is also a matter of the contradictory and slightly improbable character he bears toward his readers. I'll focus on the character; the appeal of the adventures needs no explanation.

The high colour of Lithgow's character comes out clearly if one places him alongside those other travellers to Italy and Jerusalem, Sandys and Moryson. They share the same views of Catholicism, the same suspicion of holy fraud in holy places, the same general ideas about the Turks. But Sandys and Moryson are cultivated English gentlemen. They do not express their views about Abroad in outlandish ways such as leaping through crowds to see lecherous friars burn. They are always decently in charge of themselves and, while probably not really more open to foreign ways than Lithgow, nevertheless draw the line between our ways and their ways with more sophistication. Lithgow by contrast is not in charge of his character. It runs to an extravagance, which he can exploit, though at the same time it seems to run away with him. To illustrate. In Turkish lands Moryson tells us he always went about in a doublet lined with green taffetta,

> wherein lice cannot breed or harbour: so as howsoever I wore one and the same doublet till my returne into England, yet I found not the least uncleanlinesse therein. And give me leave to joy in my good fortune, (as the common sort speake). Namely that the taffety lining of my doublet, being of greene colour, which colour none may weare upon greate danger, but onely they who are of the line and stock of Mahomet, (of whom I could challenge no kindred), yet it happened that by sleeping in my doublet aswell by land as by sea, no Turke ever perceived this my errour. Neither did I understand by any Christian . . . in what danger I was . . . till I came to Constantinople, where our English

---

20 For the attitude of travellers to the Holy Land, see Campbell. Lithgow's Protestant attitude to holy places is remarkably like Sandys's, though strongly coloured by his personality. See Haynes, p. 104.

Ambassadour told mee of the strict Law forbidding the use of this colour; and that a poore Christian some few dayes before had been beaten with cudgels at Constantinople, and was hardly kept from being killed, because ignorantly he wore a paire of greene shoo-strings. (I, 451)

Here is a man who has reason to be pleased with the discreetness of his clothing, which he wore in such a way that he went free from any foreign invasion of his body, whether of Turkish lice or Turkish blows. And he has a nice way of telling us about the matter and passing on a useful tip about green dress. He might have been laughed at for mentioning what he wears under his doublet, but two little jokes, one about not being of the common sort and the other about not being of the race of Mahomet, bring him out comfortably on top of that social hazard. Contrast this agreeable and cool self-presentation with Lithgow's in his vastly more amusing account of an incident when, after bathing in the Jordan, he climbs a turpentine tree and cuts a branch three yards long. While he is up there, the Arabs attack:

I hearing the harquebuse go off, was straight in admiration, and looking downe to the place where I left my associates, they were gone; so bending my eyes a little further in the Plaine, I saw them at a martial combate: which sight gaue me suddenly the threatning of despaire: not knowing whether to stay intrenched, within the circumdating leaues, to approue the euents of my auspicious fortunes: Or in prosecuting a reliefe to be the participant of their doubtfull deliuerance. In the end pondering, I could hardly or neuer escape their hands, either there, or by the way going vp to *Ierusalem*, leapt downe from the tree, leauing my Turkish cloathes lying vpon the ground, tooke onely in my hand the rod, and *Shasse* which I wore on my head, and ranne stark naked aboue a quarter of a mile, among thistles and sharpe pointed grasse, which pittifully bepricked the soles of my feete, but the great fear of death for the present, expel'd the griefe of that vnlooked for paine. Approaching on the safe side of my company, one of our souldiers broke forth on horsebacke, being determined to kill mee for my staying behinde: Yea, and three times stroke at me with his half-pike; but his horse being at his speed, I prevented his cruelty, first by falling downe, next by running in among the thickest of the Pilgrimes, recouering the *Guardians* face, which when the *Guardian* espied, and saw my naked body, he presently pulled off his gray gowne, and threw it to me, whereby I might hide the secrets of nature: By which meanes, (in the space of an hour) I was cloathed three manner of wayes: First like a Turke: Secondly, like a wild *Arabian*: and thirdly, like a *grey friar*, which was a barbarous, a sauage, and a religious habit. (pp. 258–9)

The success of this story depends, not on Lithgow's carrying it off with a pleasantly light dignity, but on his being caught as eccentrically as possible, not just stark naked, but with a turban on his head and a nine foot turpentine rod in his hand and later covered in a friar's gown. In the middle Lithgow makes a little ceremony of rational deliberation. Rational deliberation was a serious undertaking in the Renaissance, the activity for most in which above all human dignity was lodged. Lithgow frequently puts words of rational counsel into his own mouth in desperate circumstances, and his advice and resolution save the situation. But here the ceremony seems mildly preposterous, especially because the orotund balance of 'to wait the events of my auspicious fortunes' with 'to be participant in their doubtful deliverance' is ponderous and logically not very neat. If Moryson had been in charge of the mock heroic effect, it would have been a self-deprecating joke that would have brought the whole performance within the scope of a modest, self-contained relation about life abroad. In Lithgow's hands, the mock-heroic effect is not quite intentional. He is not sure what effect he makes. His exuberance is always getting out of hand. But he seems to have a shrewd inkling that where he cannot come over as a hero he can succeed as a clown. And after all, in real life this incident did turn out a success since he presented the nine foot pole to James.[21]

Lithgow comes over as a rogue as well as a clown, and that too is part of the interest and the appeal of his character. He teases his readers with questions about where he gets the money for his travels. But we begin to suspect that he gets it by travelling itself. Lithgow is a character who, even as a rogue, cannot contain himself and he is not discreet. He cannot conceal that he is a scrounger. Any fellow Briton is good for a drink. He celebrates this as friendship and the freedom of the bottle. In Malta for example he made merry for three days with the company of an English ship, especially with their purser, 'who striung to plant in my braines a *Maltezan* Vineyard, had almost perished his owne life' (p. 355). *The Peregrinations* are full of meetings like that. It was carousing with the English fleet at Malaga that brought him under suspicion of the Spanish authorities. He had clearly learned how to sing for his supper, how to turn himself and his travels into entertainment. He even managed to stay for three months with the English Ambassador in Constantinople, Sir Thomas Glover, whose virtues he praises so that they begin to reflect on so intimate an acquaintance as himself (pp. 131, 139–41). He also has a knack of fastening on rich fellow travellers. He makes himself agreeable to six jolly Lutherans travelling through the Holy Land and Egypt, until in Cairo, 'the season being cruel hot, and their stomacks surfeited with burning wine, vpon the fourth day, long or noone, the three [remaining] *Dutch* men were all dead; and yet me thought they had no sicknesse, the red of their faces staying pleasant, their eyes staring always on mine, and their tongues perfit, euen to the last of their breath' (p. 302). They leave him their goods and money, which amount to a very tidy sum, even when he has to disgorge a third to the Venetian consul. Nor does it end there. On the second of his peregrinations, he travels with the news of their deaths to Nuremberg, where he is feasted for ten days and is 'greatly regarded and rewarded' by their relatives (pp. 346–7). After Cairo, on the boat to Malta four French pilgrims die, but he feels unable to claim their effects, because 'they were Papists and they and I always aduerse to other' (p. 326).

21 Moryson, II, 19, remarks how wood of the terebinth was taken home by pilgrims as a curio.

With the six Lutherans, Lithgow probably believes he deserves 'regard and reward' and feasting, and it may be unduly suspicious to think a man so prompt to help and encourage and drink with fellow pilgrims a parasite. But his comment on the Frenchmen so soon after his success with the Lutherans does suggest a sort of wink, a sort of doubtful consciousness that his behaviour might be read as disreputable. On other occasions Lithgow is quite shameless. In Sicily, he finds two young noblemen lying in the fields where they have killed each other in a duel. He strips them of their purses and rings and reflects comfortably, 'Well, in the mutability of time there is aye some fortune falleth by accident, whether lawfull or not, I will not question' (p. 355).

In his *Peregrinations*, Lithgow, as I have said, is not entirely open about how he maintains himself abroad. But in a poem published in 1618 between his second and third peregrinations, 'A Conflict between the Pilgrim and his Muse', he makes it clear that he has pretended to be a Catholic, pretended to adore the host and even kissed the Pope's toe, all this to sponge on the charity of the church.[22] Protestants in Italy had to pretend if they wished to avoid the attentions of the Inquisition, and Moryson has a chapter of precepts of dissimulation, showing how far a Protestant might pretend with honour.[23] But Lithgow has observed no limits, whatever he claims to have been doing in his mind. In this poem, as in the *Peregrinations*, the contradictions in Lithgow's character refuse to settle down. On the one hand, the voice of the Muse does express something like conscience; on the other hand, the voice of the Pilgrim delights in the tricks he has played on churchmen. In the *Peregrinations*, though he leaves out his shifty treatment of the church, he presents a similarly inconsistent character. There is, on the one hand, the sanctimonious Protestant, himself already an extravagant figure. Then there is, on the other, the rogue: the toper, sponger, parasite and thief. Lithgow makes no attempt to pull himself together into a consistent character. Perhaps out of naivety (but it is quite a cunning naivety) he gives us both versions of himself, at once self-righteous and conscious of being a scamp.

Lithgow's book must always have been read as much for the traveller as for the travels. As if that was his intention, the frontispiece of the book shows him at Troy in Turkish dress, Troy reduced to emblems round the edges. In Sandys's self-effacing *Relation of a Journey*, by contrast, the engraving of Troy is a carefully drawn map (p.19). For Lithgow, travel is a means of self-promotion. Most of Abroad he found deplorable. A year after he returned from his first peregrination he had evidently exhausted his welcome at court and went abroad again in a huff, cheering himself up with thoughts from Seneca that one's homeland is where it is well with one (p.339). But he did not find anything to equal home in other countries. Frequently his thoughts return to Scotland. The Orkneys and the Shetlands are superior to the Aegean Isles (pp. 105–6). The rock at Dumbarton may at least stand comparison with the rock at Carabusa in Crete (p. 79). In spite of the vile misrepresentation of Peter Heylin, 'for true valour, courage and

---

22 *The Poetical Remains of William Lithgow, 1618–60* (Edinburgh: Stevenson, 1863), n.p.
23 Moryson, III, 409–20.

magnanimity; there is no Kingdome, or Nation, within the compasse of the whole vniuerse, can excel, or compare with [Scotland]' (p. 108). And as we have seen he keeps making connections with King James. Why then did he not stay at home? The answer seems to be that he travelled to dine out for the rest of his life as Lithgow, the traveller, preferably at court, but gentlemen's boards, especially in the Orkneys and Shetlands do quite well too.

In 'A Conflict between the Pilgrim and his Muse', Lithgow makes it clear that he travelled to escape narrow circumstances at home.

> To liue below my minde, I cannot bow,
> To loue a priuate life, O there I smart;
> To mount beyonde my meanes, I know not how,
> To stay at home still cross'd I breake mine heart;
>   And Muse take heede, I finde such loue in Strangers,
>   Makes mee affect all Heathnike tortring dangers.
>
> The Worlde is wide, GODS Prouidence is more,
> And Cloysters are but Foote-stooles to my Bellie;
> Great Dukes and Princes oint my Palme with Ore,
> And *Romane* Clergic Golde, with griede I swellie.

In *The Peregrinations* Lithgow is much less frank. He gives commonplace Renaissance reasons for travelling: it makes a man and his country wise (pp. 1–2). And he hints obscurely in bombastic verse and prose at personal motives, some monstrous injury he had suffered in love (pp. 4–7). He does not clearly connect this injury with his travelling, but we may suppose he felt humiliated and travelled to come home famous and respected for travelling. In places he seems to be angling for a patron (p. 341), but above all he has James and the court as the true end of his travels.

For Lithgow, then, travelling and travel-writing are a social performance. He is not interested in Abroad for its own sake, but rather as a means of enlarging himself. As a traveller, his extravagant and protean character, his unresolved mixture of pretension and baseness, of Protestant censor, man of sorrows, clown and rogue, is not only allowable, as it would not have been to someone who had known his place and stayed at home; it makes him the focus of entertaining, if limited wondering. It is part of his stock in trade as traveller that his character should not settle down to something respectable and easily placed. So while, as I have said, his travels show little talent for Abroad but merely confirm boundaries and home grown prejudices, still as mediator between home and abroad he has at least gained a licence to be himself with a diversity he would not have been allowed if he had stayed at home.

EDWARD J. COWAN

46. *Mistress and Mother as Political Abstraction: The Apostrophic Poetry of James Graham, Marquis of Montrose, and William Lithgow*

The 1630s and 1640s represent two of the most tempestuous decades in all of Scottish history. The period produced two poems by very different men whose lives briefly touched, both effusions providing admirable summations of their respective author's political philosophies while directly reflecting the calamitous events with which they were confronted. Both, more widely, articulate the views of the social strata to which the poets belonged and the social tensions which were among the main dynamos of the Scottish Revolution. Furthermore, deconstruction of the political metaphor in each case – Montrose's 'Address to his Mistress' and Lithgow's 'Scotlands Welcome to Her Native Sonne' – may tell us something about gender relationships in Scotland in the first half of the seventeenth century, a subject which has so far received precious little attention.

To judge from their surviving compositions both Montrose and Lithgow would appear to be assured of distinguished positions in the Scottish branch of the Bad Poets Society, but both could, on the odd occasion, hit the poetic mark. Montrose penned what is surely one of the best known stanzas in Scottish literature:

> He either fears his Fate too much,
> Or his Deserts are small,
> That puts it not unto the Touch,
> To win or lose it all.[1]

On the other hand it was remarkably prescient of William Lithgow, to anticipate one of the luminaries of the twentieth-century Scottish sporting galaxy by asking,

> Why should Strangers
> Enjoy the profit from fantastick Rangers?[2]

though he failed to mention their great rivals as befitted one who had once attracted the attention of the Inquisition.

John Buchan's suggestion, that Montrose wrote 'To His Mistress' during the summer of 1642 at a particularly confused and difficult period in his life, is quite

---

[1] J.L. Weir (ed.) *Poems of James Graham, Marquis of Montrose* (London 1938) 19.
[2] *The Poetical Remains of William Lithgow* (ed.) James Maidment (Edinburgh 1863) (facsimile reprint) 'Scotlands Welcome' B2v.

acceptable.³ Lithgow's 'Scotlands Welcome to Her Native Sonne, and Soveraigne Lord King Charles' is always dated to 1633 since Charles visited Scotland that year for his coronation but the title page, as reproduced by Maidment in the only available edition of Lithgow's poetical works, in fact bears no date. An internal reference indicates that the poem was written in 1629. Scotland recalls that 'just, threescore two yeare presently expire' (B1v) since she had crowned king James VI whose coronation took place exactly sixty two years earlier on 29 July 1567. Maidment also notes an edition of 1632 in Charles I's personal library (p.xliv).

James Graham, fifth earl and later first marquis of Montrose was born in 1612. He enjoyed the privileged upbringing which his status demanded, spent mostly in the comfortable confines of the Graham kindred. It was during his last months at St Andrews University, in 1629, that his chamberlain paid £5. 16s. 'to Mr Lithgow delyvering his book to my Lord'. If the dating of 'Scotland's Welcome' suggested above be accepted, and given that the poem contains an effusive eulogy to the young Montrose, it may well be that this was the very book delivered on that occasion:

> that hopefull Youth, the young Lord Grahame,
> James Earle of Montrose; whose war-lyke Name,
> Sprung from redoubted worth, made Manhood try,
> Their matchles deeds, in unmatched Chivalry:
> I do bequeath him, to thy gracious Love,
> Whose Noble Stocke, did ever faithful prove:
> To thyne old-agd Auncestors; and my bounds,
> Were often freed, from thraldome, by their wounds:
> Leaving their roote, the stamp of fidele trueth,
> To be inherent, in this noble Youth:
> Whose Hearts, whose Hands, whose Swords,
>   whose Deeds, whose Fame,
> Made Mars for valour, cannonize the Grahame. (F3v)

Since the object of such praise was only seventeen years old he had so far enjoyed little opportunity to acquire the accolade of Mars or any of the other deities; hence Lithgow could only appeal to the glorious martial reputation of his ancestors. It could be objected that Montrose was the third Scottish noblemen to receive this flattering treatment, after Hamilton and Mar, but it is quite possible that the impecunious Lithgow made a point of visiting all three – as well as others of their peers similarly commended – in search of the patronage which was to him a lifelong necessity. There were additional links since Lithgow claimed that his mother was a Graham and he had dedicated an earlier publication to Montrose's father.

---

3 John Buchan *Montrose* (London 1928) 128–9. Buchan's biography remains the most popular on the subject although he lifted much of his material from Montrose's nineteenth-century apologist Mark Napier.

Montrose went off on a European grand tour of three years' duration in 1632, travelling to France and Italy. On his return he eagerly joined in the agitation against the prayer book since, as a jealous aristocrat, and one whose pride and 'stately affectation' were noted at the time, he was bitterly opposed to Charles I's attempts to curb the power of the nobility through the Act of Revocation and his plans for the abolition of heritable jurisdictions. The young earl was among the first to subscribe the National Covenant in Greyfriars churchyard, Edinburgh, on 28 February 1638. In the name of the Covenant he led three military expeditions against Aberdeen and the hostile forces of the conservative north, the third time distinguishing himself by winning the Battle o'the Brig o'Dee in June 1639.

Soon thereafter Montrose was to experience some doubts about the schemes and ambitions of Archibald Campbell eighth earl of Argyll who was not yet the Graham's obvious foil and rival who would emerge during the later campaigns. By 1642 Montrose was truly wracked by doubts though absolutely convinced that Argyll's kirk party was intent upon usurping the power of the Crown.[4]

A major problem confronting the reader of Montrose's 'To His Mistress' is that it does not make sense. Even the marquis's great apologist, Mark Napier, described the piece as a 'long and wild ballad, somewhat incoherently designed'.[5] So far as is known not one word of Montrose's verse survives in his own handwriting. 'Mistress' is incoherent because, incredibly, it has never been edited, not even in Robin Bell's 'edition' published so recently as 1990.[6] Since 1850 one anthologist after another has quite uncritically followed Napier who wrongly attributed eighteen stanzas to Montrose, utilising a broadside of 1711 which, incidently, is not attributed. In 1859 William Chappell demonstrated that a ballad 'My dear and only love, take heed' was in existence in the reign of James VI, printed at London by John Trundle who was mentioned as a ballad printer by Ben Jonson in *Every Man in His Humour* (1598), and who was dead by 1628 when Montrose was still a student at St Andrews.[7] The tune was very well known since several other ballads were set to it.

There is, of course, nothing unusual about Montrose attaching his ballad to a popular tune but what seems to have happened in his case is that the stanzas of the older ballad have also been attributed to Montrose's composition. With diligent research and the encyclopaedic knowledge of a Chappell the matter might admit of resolution but this enquirer can make claims in neither department. If Montrose did write the whole thing it is longer by far than any of his other efforts some of which are quite puerile. In Weir's version every single stanza, except one, ends negatively – 'I'll never love thee more', 'I could love thee no more' etc. The exception is stanza 5, 'And love thee evermore', which seems

---

4 Edward J. Cowan *Montrose: For Covenant and King* (London 1977) 1–129.
5 Mark Napier *Memorials of Montrose and His Times* 2 vols (Edinburgh 1850) vol. 2, 464.
6 *The Collected Poems of James Graham, First Marquis of Montrose* (ed.) Robin Graham Bell (Hitchin 1990).
7 William Chappell *Popular Music of the Olden Time* 2 vols (London 1859) vol. 1 378–81. See also note by Edward Rimbaud, 'The Great Marquis of Montrose's Song' *Notes and Queries* 4th Series XII (1873) 522.

upbeat and climactic. Also the verbal parallels with his letters occur in the first five stanzas which seem much more coherent and better organised than the rest; two missives from the poet to Prince Rupert in December 1648 and January 1649 contain the lines 'and either win it or be sure to lose it fairly' and 'either gain or lose the whole'.[8] The other parallels suggested by Mark Napier do not convince any more than does his assessment that 'those wild but noble verses, which, for their own sake as poetry, and from the fire and originality of the expressions, will adhere to the mind while language lasts'. It thus seems likely that Montrose composed the first five stanzas as published by Weir or 'The First Part' in Napier (2 470–5). What, then, is the poem about?

Obviously it belongs to the 'intangible mistress' genre.[9] There was a craze amongst Montrose's contemporaries for such poems. Almost every poet worthy of the name who wrote in his lifetime addressed at least one poem to his mistress. Examples were penned by such writers as Ayton, Donne, Edward Lord Herbert, Crashaw, Herrick, Carew, Lovelace, Waller and Andrew Marvell whose 'coy mistress' is probably the best known example of the genre. Many of these poems (unlike Montrose's) were explicitly erotic but others were addressed to females who were fictitious, imaginary, unknown or unknowable and who were used as vehicles for the introspection of the poets. For example John Gwynne produced a piece entitled 'Upon my inseparable devotion to Loyalty I called Mistress' and Richard Crashaw composed 'Wishes to his (Supposed) Mistress'. Such effusions were associated, in particular, with the 'cavalier poets' of which Montrose was Scotland's most prominent example, though if Robin Skelton is correct in distinguishing such poets as being 'cavalier' in the sense that they 'distrust the over-earnest, the too intense',[10] the Graham does not quite fit the mould, nor, generally speaking, does he display the wit and raciness of some of the English practioners. There is a little wit in 'Some Lynes on the Killing of Ye Earle of Newcastell's Sonne's Dogge' (Weir 18) but none whatsoever in the appalling,

> There's nothing in the World can prove
> So true and real Pleasure,
> As perfect sympathy in Love,
> Which is a real Treasure. (Weir 28).

Such productions as 'Mistress', 'On the Faithlessness and Venality of the Times', 'Speechless Grief', 'His Metrical Vow' and his 'Metrical Prayer' he shows himself to be the very antithesis of the cavalier genre, earnest and intense to a fault, and a Calvinist cavalier if ever there was one.

Most commentators seem to assume that it is Montrose himself who is addressing his mistress, thus furthering the unintelligibility of the poem. For Dame C. V. Wedgwood's suggestion that the piece was inspired by Montrose's

8 Napier *Memorials* 2, 465–6.
9 H.M. Richmond 'The Intangible Mistress' *Modern Philology* LVI (1959) 217–23.
10 Robin Skelton *Cavalier Poets* British Council (Harlow 1960) 7. Skelton *The Cavalier Poets* (Oxford 1970) prints the first five stanzas of 'Mistress' but does not say why.

political and domestic estrangement from his wife, Magdalen Carnegie, there is no evidence whatsoever.[11] Rather it is Sovereignty which apostrophises the kingdom of Scotland, his 'dear and only love'. What Sovereignty seeks is 'purest Monarchie', which turns out to be absolutism – no rivals, no committees, no mixed constitution, no representation, no democracy:

> But I must rule and govern still,
> And always give the Law,
> And have each Subject at my will,
> And all to stand in awe. (Weir 20)

The lines echo the sentiment of Montrose's letter on supreme power – 'When a King is restrained from the lawful use of his power, and subjects can make no use of it, as under a King they cannot, what can follow but a subversion of government, anarchy and confusion?'[12] Yet the poetry steps far beyond the pragmatism of the epistle. As I have suggested elsewhere the poetic reflections on 'purest monarchie' are the words of a man temporarily unhinged;[13] indeed, to judge from the rest of his output poetry appears to have come readily to James Graham in a state of unhingement. In 'Mistress', as in his other poems, he shows himself to be an unrepentant egotistical aristocrat who sees everything in black and white and who exactly shares the reactionary views of his monarch, Charles I, whose personality did so much to bring the executioner's axe of the British Civil Wars down on his own his neck. Montrose was, in short, a rather terrifying anachronism which the forces of History were intent upon extinguishing. It is something of a relief to turn to William Lithgow.

Lithgow, son of a burgess of Lanark, was a magnificent original, perhaps the first Scot who was truly a citizen of the world but one who was also a fierce Scottish chauvinist; he claimed to have travelled thirty six thousand miles in the course of his life. His first journey, described in his *Most Delectable and True Discourse of an admired and painefull peregrination from Scotland to the most famous Kingdoms in Europe, Asia and Affricke* (London 1614), took him from Paris to the Holy Land and on to Cairo, Malta and Sicily. 'William of the Wilderness' as he was dubbed by a fellow poet, described his critics as mere 'vomiters of venom'. While at Jerusalem he had a device tattooed on his right arm with on one side the lettering 'the never conquered Crowne of Scotland' and on the other 'the now inconquerable Crowne of England', lines echoed in 'Scotland's Welcome'. He had many incredible and often hilarious adventures during which he was sustained by an intense courage and a remarkable single-mindedness. Subsequent expeditions took him to Algiers and Ethiopia and he was tortured by the Spanish Inquisition in 1620, though some of course questioned the reality of his bold claims.

---

11 C.V. Wedgwood *Montrose* (London 1966 rep.) 57–8.
12 Napier *Memorials* 2 51.
13 Cowan *Montrose* 135.

In 1640 he dedicated to Montrose 'The Gushing Teares of Godly Sorrow', pronounced by William Maidment 'a most unreadable and unsatisfactory production' which he was tempted to exclude from his anthology. It is painful to peregrinate through its lines but it is not all bad. Who could resist an effusion which contains the following gem?

> How precious were these tears of Magdalen?
> who washt Christs feet, with eye-repenting drops;
> Yea with her haire, did dry these feet agen,
> And kiss'd them, with her lip-bepearled chops.
> ('Gushing Teares' I.4)

In places he is almost a blend of Zachary Boyd and Sir Thomas Urquhart of Cromarty, a strange conflation of neological ingenuity and couthy mundanity, assuring his reader that his own name is an anagram of 'I Love Almighty Wel' ('Gushing Teares' Cv) and coming away with lines like 'the more we strive to know, the less we ken' ('Gushing Teares' C3v). Throughout 'Gushing Teares' Lithgow's humanity is obvious, mirroring the sentiments of 'Scotlands Welcome' and displaying in both an exhilarating sense of native pessimism, while stunning sycophancy is demonstrated in the dedication to Montrose:

> Your Noble and Heroicke Vertues light this
> Kingdome, and who can give them light: for as the
> Aurore of your honoured reputation is become that
> Constantinopolitan Hyppodrome to this our
> Northerne and virgine Albion; so lykwise, the
> same singularitie of worth, hath raised your
> auspicious selfe, to be the monumentall glorie of
> your famous, and valiant Predecessours, justly
> termed 'The Sword of Scotland': Your morning of
> their Summers day hath fullie enlarged, the sacred
> Trophees of their matchlesse memorie; best
> befitting the generositie of your magnanimous
> minde . . . My prayse and prayers, the two sisters
> of myne Oblation, rest solidlie ingenochiated at
> the feete of your conspicuous clemencie (A3).

'Scotlands Welcome' belongs to the wheenging tradition in Scottish literature which follows a familiar current from Dunbar and *The Complaynt of Scotland* to far beyond. It is the kind of poem beloved by historians because it so beautifully captures the contemporary mood of disenchantment with the absentee monarch and so pointedly illustrates popular attitudes conditioned not so much by the great debates over constitution and religion but rather by the disappointments and discomforts of daily life. The poem deserves its own fully annotated edition in order to bring out its full richness; space permits only a flavour of its content.

At his succession in 1625 Charles had expressed his intention of visiting Scotland for his coronation. Because his policies were so unpopular his advisors feared for his safety and so he did not arrive until 1633 thus compounding a bitterness and frustration which the Scots had experienced ever since the Union of the Crowns in 1603. As the title page states the 'Welcome' details 'the whole Grievances and abuses of the Common-wealth of this kingdome . . . worthy to be by all the Nobles and Gentry perused; and to be layd up in the hearts and chests of the whole Commouns', while Lithgow's preface reflects uncertainty about whether Charles will ever visit his native kingdom, the king having been born in Dunfermline:

> Say if he come this yeare, say he come not,
> Yet tyme shall praise mee for a loving Scot.
> Then read, misconster not, but wysely looke,
> If reason be, the Mistrisse of my Booke,
> And if I finger, what thou fayne wouldst touch,
> O!, thank mee, and be pleasd; whylst I avouch,
> The commoun sorrowes of this groaning Land,
> Which I lay open, to thyne open hand:
> Then ponder, and peruse it, thou shalst fynd,
> The *Sole Idea* of thy Countreyes Mynd.

As the poem opens Scotland is depicted as a widow in mourning since James VI's death in 1625. She now prepares to meet Charles as her Son, Husband and Father. Nature herself displays transports of delight at the advent of the new king; rivers bellow their welcome; mountains (specifically 'piramized Tinto' and Goat Fell in Arran) rejoice. Edinburgh has prepared great pageants and 'rarest dainties'. Charles comes not as a conqueror but 'of right indubitable', to be conferred with Scotland's 'never-conquered Crowne', preserved by the great heroes and families of Scottish history:

> How many hundreth thousand lyves were lost?
> Which from my bowells sprung; nay; I dare boast,
> Of Millions which to save, this Crowne for Thee,
> And purchase freedome, car'd not for to dye (A5).

They would die again for the Crown, those brave soldiers, envied by every country in Europe.

Charles' coronation will be a 'sacred work and happy union,/Twixt Prince and People; O! thryse blessed communion!' As soon as the anticipated coronation is over Charles' real problems commence as Lithgow begins to list the abuses of the Commonwealth. Justice is lacking. True religion must be settled. The king must give ear to parliament. Merchants and trades are suffering. Nobles and gentry squander their wealth at court, in London, at the expense of their tenants. The land market is unstable, rents rise, tenants are oppressed. Everybody posts up to London at the slightest excuse; they should be banned from so doing,

> Els they will vexe Thee, and such custome bring,
> That Woemen, too, will post up to the King.

One result of this activity is the decay of good housekeeping. Stately homes are in ruin, their one time occupants drawn to brothels and flesh-pots. Curiously, deadly feud is no more,

> that's gone of late
> But they're at deadly feud with their owne state,
> And care not for Allyes, blood, wives, nor friends,
> Kinred nor bairnes, save their owne wasting ends:
> Whose Riggs speake English, and their falted furres,
> Forgetting Scots, can speek with gilded Spurres (Cv).

By now the theme of the poem is obvious. It is a lengthy composition and the catalogue of woes grows more extensive with each line. There is an absence of agricultural improvement. The tithing system is abused so adversely impacting upon the provision of hospitals, schools and bridges. Bankruptcies are common, fugitive marriages frequent. Youth is corrupted through card-playing, drunkenness and lust. There is a deplorable fashion for long hair; men are

> growne effeminat, weare Woemens loks,
> Freize-hanging combd, o're Shoulders, Necks, and Cloks;
> That many doubt, if they bee Mayds, or Men,
> Till that their Beards sprout foorth, and then they ken. (Dv)

A lengthy passage condemning tobacco sycophantically reflects king James VI's views on that obnoxious weed in the use of which even women indulge. The latter are criticised for wearing plaids which allegedly look like winding sheets so transforming those they adorn into ghosts, night visitors or whores. What this curious passage seems to be attacking is the plaids' tendency to obscure the relative status of women so that matrons cannot be distinguished from drudges. The solution lies in the gallows or the burgh loch.

Swearing is universal. Witch burnings are creating a coal shortage. Brokers, usurers and con men abound. Tavern owners enchant with stories of Robin Hood and Wallace, 'make their Ale/Flee out of Pynts in Quarts', and then cheat their customers. And so the list of woes continues. War is the fault of monarchs whose employment of minions interferes with good government. Scotland is kind enough to put in a good word for Lithgow and his sufferings overseas. She then alludes to the kirk and wronged ministers before commending a list of loyal (and protestant) noblemen to her native son – an undisguised pitch for patronage which has already been mentioned above. Sir William Alexander's colonial schemes in Canada are highly commended, the nobility urged to support them. In the concluding flourish Scotland hopes that Charlie is 'no awa to bide awa', and she is left 'wrapt up, within the gloomy shade/of sad oblivion' and is 'a Mourner made'.

Every single criticism that Lithgow made in 'Scotlands Welcome' can be corroborated from contemporary sources.[14] His poem neatly encapsulates the widespread views of a generation – 'the sole idea of (the) countrey's mind', as he put it. He did not condemn the king but rather he looked to the monarch for remedy and had Charles paid attention to Lithgow's chronicle of Scotland's grievances he might have avoided the Scottish revolution and his own tragic fate. The poem was essentially a long plea, or petition, which the poet expected the monarch to heed. Such pleading was as well grounded in Scottish literature as it was in Scottish history. Throughout Lithgow clearly assumed the notion of a contract between king and people which lay at the very heart of the covenanting movement.

On the wider issue of gender attitudes exemplified by the two poets the comparison may not be entirely sound since, hopefully, a man's reaction to his mistress is likely to be somewhat different than that to his mother, but the contrasting rhetoric of the two poems is instructive. So far as is known Montrose never actually had a mistress; if he did she was probably one and the same as his wife, Magdalen Carnegie. Montrose does not seem to have been particularly interested in romantic love. Later a raid on his home at Auld Montrose turned up 'some letters from ladies to Montrose in his younger years, flowered with Arcadian compliments',[15] but who wrote them is not recorded. For his supposed later attachment to Princess Louise, daughter of Elizabeth of Bohemia, there is very little convincing evidence.

As an aristocrat Montrose's approach to his women was probably as pragmatic and single-minded as his approach to battle. His close contemporary and rival, Archibald Campbell earl, and later marquis, of Argyll, commended virtue and plainness in a wife while admitting that 'money is the sinew of love, as well as war; you can do nothing happily in wedlock without it'.[16] James Graham would have shared that view but what is remarkable is that, to judge from his poems, his absolutist political views were matched by a wholly egocentric attitude towards love. The idea is obvious in 'To His Mistress' as it is in 'In Praise of Women' which perfectly sums up the view under discussion:

> But yet, fair Ladies, you must know
> Howbeit I do adore you so:
> Reciprocal your Flames must prove,
> Or my Ambition scorns to love:
> A Noble Soul doth still abhore
> To strike, but where its Conqueror. (Weir 32)

14 Edward J. Cowan 'The Union of the Crowns and the Crisis of the Constitution in Seventeenth Century Scotland' *supra*.
15 Henry Guthry *Memoirs* (2nd edn. Glasgow 1747) 112.
16 Archibald Marquis of Argyle *Instructions To A Son* (Glasgow 1743) 33.

Montrose thus deals with affective relationships as he does with constitutional crisis.

Lithgow, on the other hand, demonstrates that love is entirely possible, even when the object of one's affection disappoints. It could be objected that a mother always loves her offspring even in the most extreme situation,[17] yet if Lithgow's mother figure is compared to Dame Scotia in *The Complaynt of Scotland* the former is depicted as much the more sympathetic and less cantankerous persona. In both 'Scotlands Welcome' and 'Godly Teares' Lithgow shows himself to be as obsessed as Sir Richard Maitland had been in the previous century with the decline of family values and kinship ties.[18] In another poem he penned the lines,

> No woman yet so fiercely set,
> But she'll forgive, but not forget,[19]

which sentiment is also present, if not explicitly stated, in 'Scotlands Welcome'. An even more significant couplet is expressed in 'Godly Teares' – 'Mother behold thy Sonne,/And Sonne, Behold there, thy consolation' (N2). Although Lithgow adopts the metaphor of husband and sire (as had James VI in his writings and speeches on the monarch 'married' to his kingdoms, urging the integral union of Scotland and England in 1603 on the grounds that otherwise as the husband of both kingdoms he would stand accused of bigamy)[20] the ascendant figure of Scotland as Mother provides the son, Charles, with consolation, but she also demands respect. By extension Lithgow expects Charles to respect his maternal kingdom who is expressing the grievances of Scotland and thus, again, articulating the ancient Scottish contract between king and people.

Both poems are understandably andro-centric despite the female metaphor which each employs. Inhabitants of the seventeenth century could no more escape the strictures of their language than can their successors of the twentieth. The author of *The Complaynt* struck a chord which continues to sound when he noted that the Latin term *homo* 'signifeis baytht man ande woman, bot ther is nocht ane Scottis terme that signifeis baytht man ande woman'.[21] Many historical problems are problems of language and lexis; that high-lighted by *The Complaynt* is still with us.

Lithgow's Mother pleads for the restoration of the well being of the Commonwealth. Montrose, detecting corruption in his Mistress, advocates the

---

17 The contemporary Duke of Hamilton's mother allegedly threatened to shoot him if he landed in Lothian with a royalist force in 1639, Hilary L. Rubenstein *Captain Luckless. James First Duke of Hamilton 1606–1649* (Edinburgh 1975) 99.
18 On Maitland and his views see *The Maitland Folio Manuscript* (ed.) W.A. Craigie vol.1. Scottish Text Society (Edinburgh and London 1919) Nos. xiv–xxviii; *The Maitland Quarto Manuscript* (ed.) W.A. Craigie Scottish Text Society (Edinburgh and London 1920) Nos. i–xxxiv, 1-lix.
19 Maidment *Poetical Remains* 'Dunglass' p. xxviii. 'Godly Teares' also laments the corruption of kinship at considerable length, see p. L2, M2.
20 *The Political Works of James I Reprinted From the Edition of 1616* (ed.) Charles Howard McIlwain (New York 1965) 272; King James VI and I *Political Writings* (ed.) Johann P. Sommerville (Cambridge 1994) 136.
21 *The Complaynt of Scotland* A.M. Stewart (ed.) STS (Edinburgh and London 1979) 13.

furtherance of his own political corruption – tyranny. For Lithgow decay in the values of kinship and family reflects the predicament of a kingdom without a king. Montrose offers a solution that would ensure that the king was parted from his kingdom forever. Ultimately both poems illustrate the incontrovertible truth that male attitudes to gender are closely associated with male attitudes to politics. The events of the 1640s were to demonstrate, however, that the Scots would heed the wisdom of their Mother rather than the uncompromising sentiments which Montrose proffered to his Mistress.